INTERNATIONAL LAW AND POLITICS

INTERNATIONAL LAW AND POLITICS

Key Documents

edited by
Shirley V. Scott

LYNNE
RIENNER
PUBLISHERS

BOULDER
LONDON

Published in the United States of America in 2006 by
Lynne Rienner Publishers, Inc.
1800 30th Street, Boulder, Colorado 80301
www.rienner.com

and in the United Kingdom by
Lynne Rienner Publishers, Inc.
3 Henrietta Street, Covent Garden, London WC2E 8LU

Library of Congress Cataloging-in-Publication Data
International law and politics : key documents / edited by Shirley V. Scott.
    p. cm.
  Includes index.
    ISBN-13: 978-1-58826-417-6 (hardcover : alk. paper)
    ISBN-10: 1-58826-417-3 (hardcover : alk. paper)
    ISBN-13: 978-1-58826-442-8 (pbk. : alk. paper)
    ISBN-10: 1-58826-442-4 (pbk. : alk. paper)
    1. International law—Sources. I. Scott, Shirley V. II. Title.
KZ64.I576 2006
341—dc22

                                                        2006002389

British Cataloguing in Publication Data
A Cataloguing in Publication record for this book
is available from the British Library.

Printed and bound in the United States of America

   The paper used in this publication meets the requirements
       of the American National Standard for Permanence of
       Paper for Printed Library Materials Z39.48-1992.

    5   4   3   2   1

Contents

Preface

This collection has been compiled in the hope of encouraging those interested in any aspect of international law or global governance to read carefully the original texts of key documents. There is a tendency among many students to rely on paraphrased accounts of international law documents in preference to studying the documents themselves. This is understandable insofar as many people, particularly those without legal training, set out on their explorations of international law with some trepidation. But, as with poetry or painting, no secondary account of an international law document can replace the original. A line of legal argument may, for example, turn on the precise language used in a particular treaty, and a reader familiar only with the language of a paraphrased version of that treaty might easily miss the point.

International law has grown enormously in the years since 1945, and choosing what to omit or include in a selection of international law documents is a difficult task. Emphasis in this collection has been placed on those documents essential to a student of contemporary world politics. Arms control treaties and documents of international humanitarian law are often not included in general collections of international law documents, but are essential reading for those interested in the political operation of international law. The emphasis here is on documents, especially treaties, at a global rather than regional level. Documents other than treaties, including resolutions of the UN Security Council, are included where they are germane to contemporary debates.

The collection is made up primarily of post-1945 documents. Readers should be aware that in a number of instances the documents have antecedents that are not reproduced here. Perhaps most fundamentally, the UN Charter was preceded by the Covenant of the League of Nations. The Biological Weapons Convention was, similarly, foreshadowed by the 1925 Protocol for the Prohibition of the Use in War of Asphyxiating, Poisonous or Other Gases, and of Bacteriological Methods of Warfare; and the 1996 Comprehensive Nuclear Test-Ban Treaty was preceded by the 1963 Treaty Banning Nuclear Weapons Tests in the Atmosphere, in Outer Space and Under Water (Partial Test Ban Treaty). Even where there is no specific precursor to a treaty, it is important to remember that international law did not begin in 1945. Even in a field of international law that is predominantly post-1945 such as human rights, earlier treaties can be found—in this case, for example, the 1926 Slavery Convention.

The documents are arranged chronologically within subject headings, although where a later protocol to a treaty is included it appears immediately after the treaty. A short introduction to each document provides context and also points to supplementary readings. A chronological list of all treaties in the volume, together with their status, is included, as is a glossary of terms. While the aim of the collection is to encourage reading of original documents, understanding will be enhanced if these documents are read in conjunction with a textbook. I envisioned this collection as a companion to my own text, *International Law in World Politics* (Lynne Rienner Publishers, 2004), which is intended especially for students of political science and those seeking to understand international law who have no prior legal training.

Acknowledgments

I would like to thank the United Nations for permission to reproduce the UN documents, and extracts thereof, contained in this book. I acknowledge the United Nations as the author of the UN material.

The extract of the letter from Mr Webster (US) to Mr Fox of 24 April 1841 is taken from *British and Foreign State Papers* XXIX (1840–1841), pages 1137–1138. The extract of the letter from Mr Webster to Lord Ashburton of 6 August 1842 is taken from *British and Foreign State Papers* XXX (1841–1842), page 201.

I would like to thank Michelle Barisic, Radhika Withana, and Orli Zahava for their wonderful research assistance in the preparation of this book.

—*Shirley V. Scott*

1
The Foundations of International Law

1.1
Charter of the
United Nations (1945)
(as amended)

The Charter is the closest we have to a world constitution. Early drafts were prepared in the US Department of State. The US then entered into "conversations" with representatives of the United Kingdom, the USSR, and China at the Dumbarton Oaks Estate, Washington, D.C., in August–October 1944. The text of the Charter was finalized at the United Nations Conference on International Organization, held in San Francisco from 25 April to 26 June 1945, and the United Nations officially came into existence on 24 October 1945.

On the relationship of the Charter to the Covenant of the League of Nations, see J. L. Brierly, "The Covenant and the Charter," British Yearbook of International Law *23 (1946): 83–94. For an authoritative article-by-article analysis of the Charter, see Bruno Simma, ed.,* The Charter of the United Nations: A Commentary, *2nd ed. (New York: Oxford University Press, 2002). On the question of its constitutionality, see Bardo Fassbender, "The United Nations Charter as Constitution of the International Community,"* Columbia Journal of Transnational Law *36 (1998): 529–619.*

WE THE PEOPLES OF THE UNITED NATIONS DETERMINED

to save succeeding generations from the scourge of war, which twice in our lifetime has brought untold sorrow to mankind, and

to reaffirm faith in fundamental human rights, in the dignity and worth of the human person, in the equal rights of men and women and of nations large and small, and

to establish conditions under which justice and respect for the obligations arising from treaties and other sources of international law can be maintained, and

to promote social progress and better standards of life in larger freedom, AND FOR THESE ENDS

to practice tolerance and live together in peace with one another as good neighbours, and to unite our strength to maintain international peace and security, and

to ensure, by the acceptance of principles and the institution of methods, that armed force shall not be used, save in the common interest, and

to employ international machinery for the promotion of the economic and social advancement of all peoples,

HAVE RESOLVED TO COMBINE OUR EFFORTS TO ACCOMPLISH THESE AIMS

Accordingly, our respective Governments, through representatives assembled in the city of San Francisco, who have exhibited their full powers found to be in good and due form, have agreed to the present Charter of the United Nations and do hereby establish an international organization to be known as the United Nations.

Chapter 1: Purposes and Principles

Article 1

The Purposes of the United Nations are:

1. To maintain international peace and security, and to that end: to take effective collective measures for the prevention and removal of threats to the peace, and for the suppression of acts of aggression or other breaches of the peace, and to bring about by peaceful means, and in conformity with the principles of justice and international law, adjustment or settlement of international disputes or situations which might lead to a breach of the peace;

2. To develop friendly relations among nations based on respect for the principle of equal rights and self-determination of peoples, and to take other appropriate measures to strengthen universal peace;

3. To achieve international co-operation in solving international problems of an economic, social, cultural, or humanitarian character, and in promoting and encouraging respect for human rights and for fundamental freedoms for all without distinction as to race, sex, language, or religion; and

4. To be a centre for harmonizing the actions of nations in the attainment of these common ends.

Article 2

The Organization and its Members, in pursuit of the Purposes stated in Article 1, shall act in accordance with the following Principles.

1. The Organization is based on the principle of the sovereign equality of all its Members.

2. All Members, in order to ensure to all of them the rights and benefits resulting from membership, shall fulfil in good faith the obligations assumed by them in accordance with the present Charter.

3. All Members shall settle their international disputes by peaceful means in such a manner that international peace and security, and justice, are not endangered.

4. All Members shall refrain in their international relations from the threat or use of force against the territorial integrity or political independence of any State, or in any other manner inconsistent with the Purposes of the United Nations.

5. All Members shall give the United Nations every assistance in any action it takes in accordance with the present Charter, and shall refrain from giving assistance to any State against which the United Nations is taking preventive or enforcement action.

6. The Organization shall ensure that States which are not Members of the United Nations act in accordance with these Principles so far as may be necessary for the maintenance of international peace and security.

7. Nothing contained in the present Charter shall authorize the United Nations to intervene in matters which are essentially within the domestic jurisdiction of any State or shall require the Members to submit such matters to settlement under the present Charter; but this principle shall not prejudice the application of enforcement measures under Chapter Vll.

Chapter II: Membership

Article 3
The original Members of the United Nations shall be the States which, having participated in the United Nations Conference on International Organization at San Francisco, or having previously signed the Declaration by United Nations of 1 January 1942, sign the present Charter and ratify it in accordance with Article 110.

Article 4
1. Membership in the United Nations is open to all other peace-loving States which accept the obligations contained in the present Charter and, in the judgment of the Organization, are able and willing to carry out these obligations.

2. The admission of any such State to membership in the United Nations will be effected by a decision of the General Assembly upon the recommendation of the Security Council.

Article 5
A Member of the United Nations against which preventive or enforcement action has been taken by the Security Council may be suspended from the exercise of the rights and privileges of membership by the General Assembly upon the recommendation of the Security Council. The exercise of these rights and privileges may be restored by the Security Council.

Article 6
A Member of the United Nations which has persistently violated the Principles

contained in the present Charter may be expelled from the Organization by the General Assembly upon the recommendation of the Security Council.

Chapter III: Organs

Article 7

1. There are established as the principal organs of the United Nations: a General Assembly, a Security Council, an Economic and Social Council, a Trusteeship Council, an International Court of Justice, and a Secretariat.

2. Such subsidiary organs as may be found necessary may be established in accordance with the present Charter.

Article 8

The United Nations shall place no restrictions on the eligibility of men and women to participate in any capacity and under conditions of equality in its principal and subsidiary organs.

Chapter IV: The General Assembly

Composition

Article 9

1. The General Assembly shall consist of all the Members of the United Nations.

2. Each Member shall have not more than five representatives in the General Assembly.

Functions And Powers

Article 10

The General Assembly may discuss any questions or any matters within the scope of the present Charter or relating to the powers and functions of any organs provided for in the present Charter, and, except as provided in Article 12, may make recommendations to the Members of the United Nations or to the Security Council or to both on any such questions or matters.

Article 11

1. The General Assembly may consider the general principles of co-operation in the maintenance of international peace and security, including the principles governing disarmament and the regulation of armaments, and may make recommendations with regard to such principles to the Members or to the Security Council or to both.

2. The General Assembly may discuss any questions relating to the maintenance of international peace and security brought before it by any Member of the United Nations, or by the Security Council, or by a State which is not a Member of the United Nations in accordance with Article 35, paragraph 2, and, except as provided in Article 12, may make recommendations with regard to any such questions to the State or States concerned or to the Security Council or to both. Any such question on which action is necessary shall be referred to the Security Council by the General Assembly either before or after discussion.

3. The General Assembly may call the attention of the Security Council to situations which are likely to endanger international peace and security.

4. The powers of the General Assembly set forth in this Article shall not limit the general scope of Article 10.

Article 12

1. While the Security Council is exercising in respect of any dispute or situation the functions assigned to it in the present Charter, the General Assembly shall not make any recommendation with regard to that dispute or situation unless the Security Council so requests.

2. The Secretary-General, with the consent of the Security Council, shall notify the General Assembly at each session of any matters relative to the maintenance of international peace and security which are being dealt with by the Security Council and shall similarly notify the General Assembly, or the Members of the United Nations if the General Assembly is not in session, immediately the Security Council ceases to deal with such matters.

Article 13

1. The General Assembly shall initiate studies and make recommendations for the purpose of:

(a) promoting international co-operation in the political field and encouraging the progressive development of international law and its codification;

(b) promoting international co-operation in the economic, social, cultural, educational, and health fields, and assisting in the realization of human rights and fundamental freedoms for all without distinction as to race, sex, language, or religion.

2. The further responsibilities, functions and powers of the General Assembly with respect to matters mentioned in paragraph 1(b) above are set forth in Chapters IX and X.

Article 14

Subject to the provisions of Article 12, the General Assembly may recommend measures for the peaceful adjustment of any situation, regardless of origin, which it deems likely to impair the general welfare or friendly relations among nations, including situations resulting from a violation of the provisions of the present Charter setting forth the Purposes and Principles of the United Nations.

Article 15

1. The General Assembly shall receive and consider annual and special reports from the Security Council; these reports shall include an account of the measures that the Security Council has decided upon or taken to maintain international peace and security.

2. The General Assembly shall receive and consider reports from the other organs of the United Nations.

Article 16

The General Assembly shall perform such functions with respect to the international trusteeship system as are assigned to it under Chapters XII and XIII, including the approval of the trusteeship agreements for areas not designated as strategic.

Article 17

1. The General Assembly shall consider and approve the budget of the Organization.

2. The expenses of the Organization shall be borne by the Members as apportioned by the General Assembly.

3. The General Assembly shall consider and approve any financial and budgetary arrangements with specialized agencies referred to in Article 57 and shall examine the administrative budgets of such specialized agencies with a view to making recommendations to the agencies concerned.

Voting

Article 18

1. Each member of the General Assembly shall have one vote.

2. Decisions of the General Assembly on important questions shall be made by a two-thirds majority of the members present and voting. These questions shall include: recommendations with respect to the maintenance of international peace and security, the election of the non-permanent members of the Security Council, the election of the members of the Economic and Social Council, the election of members of the Trusteeship Council in accordance with paragraph 1(c) of Article 86, the admission of new Members to the United Nations, the suspension of the rights and privileges of membership, the expulsion of Members, questions relating to the operation of the trusteeship system, and budgetary questions.

3. Decisions on other questions, including the determination of additional categories of questions to be decided by a two-thirds majority, shall be made by a majority of the members present and voting.

Article 19

A Member of the United Nations which is in arrears in the payment of its financial contributions to the Organization shall have no vote in the General Assembly if the amount of its arrears equals or exceeds the amount of the contributions due from it for the preceding two full years.

The General Assembly may, nevertheless, permit such a Member to vote if it is satisfied that the failure to pay is due to conditions beyond the control of the Member.

Procedure

Article 20

The General Assembly shall meet in regular annual sessions and in such special sessions as occasion may require. Special sessions shall be convoked by the Secretary-General at the request of the Security Council or of a majority of the Members of the United Nations.

Article 21

The General Assembly shall adopt its own rules of procedure. It shall elect its President for each session.

Article 22

The General Assembly may establish such subsidiary organs as it deems necessary for the performance of its functions.

Chapter V: The Security Council

Composition

Article 23

1. The Security Council shall consist of fifteen[i] Members of the United Nations. The Republic of China, France, the Union of Soviet Socialist Republics, the United Kingdom of Great Britain and Northern Ireland, and the United States of America shall be permanent members of the Security Council. The General Assembly shall elect ten other Members of the United Nations to be non-permanent members of the Security Council, due regard being specially paid, in the first instance to the contribution of Members of the United Nations to the maintenance of international peace and security and to the other purposes of the Organization, and also to equitable geographical distribution.

2. The non-permanent members of the Security Council shall be elected for

---

i. Originally eleven. Amendment came into force 31 August 1965.

a term of two years. In the first election of the non-permanent members after the increase of the membership of the Security Council from eleven to fifteen, two of the four additional members shall be chosen for a term of one year. A retiring member shall not be eligible for immediate re-election.

3. Each member of the Security Council shall have one representative.

Functions and Powers

Article 24

1. In order to ensure prompt and effective action by the United Nations, its Members confer on the Security Council primary responsibility for the maintenance of international peace and security, and agree that in carrying out its duties under this responsibility the Security Council acts on their behalf.

2. In discharging these duties the Security Council shall act in accordance with the Purposes and Principles of the United Nations. The specific powers granted to the Security Council for the discharge of these duties are laid down in Chapters VI, VII, VIII, and XII.

3. The Security Council shall submit annual and, when necessary, special reports to the General Assembly for its consideration.

Article 25

The Members of the United Nations agree to accept and carry out the decisions of the Security Council in accordance with the present Charter.

Article 26

In order to promote the establishment and maintenance of international peace and security with the least diversion for armaments of the world's human and economic resources, the Security Council shall be responsible for formulating, with the assistance of the Military Staff Committee referred to in Article 47, plans to be submitted to the Members of the United Nations for the establishment of a system for the regulation of armaments.

Voting

Article 27

1. Each member of the Security Council shall have one vote.

2. Decisions of the Security Council on procedural matters shall be made by an affirmative vote of nine[ii] members.

3. Decisions of the Security Council on all other matters shall be made by an affirmative vote of nine members including the concurring votes of the permanent members; provided that, in decisions under Chapter VI, and under paragraph 3 of Article 52, a party to a dispute shall abstain from voting.

---

ii. Originally seven. Amendment came into force 31 August 1965.

Procedure

Article 28

1. The Security Council shall be so organized as to be able to function continuously. Each member of the Security Council shall for this purpose be represented at all times at the seat of the Organization.

2. The Security Council shall hold periodic meetings at which each of its members may, if it so desires, be represented by a member of the government or by some other specially designated representative.

3. The Security Council may hold meetings at such places other than the seat of the Organization as in its judgment will best facilitate its work.

Article 29

The Security Council may establish such subsidiary organs as it deems necessary for the performance of its functions.

Article 30

The Security Council shall adopt its own rules of procedure, including the method of selecting its President.

Article 31

Any Member of the United Nations which is not a member of the Security Council may participate, without vote, in the discussion of any question brought before the Security Council whenever the latter considers that the interests of that Member are specially affected.

Article 32

Any Member of the United Nations which is not a member of the Security Council or any State which is not a Member of the United Nations, if it is a party to a dispute under consideration by the Security Council, shall be invited to participate, without vote, in the discussion relating to the dispute. The Security Council shall lay down such conditions as it deems just for the participation of a State which is not a Member of the United Nations.

Chapter VI: Pacific Settlement of Disputes

Article 33

1. The parties to any dispute, the continuance of which is likely to endanger the maintenance of international peace and security, shall, first of all, seek a solution by negotiation, enquiry, mediation, conciliation, arbitration, judicial settlement, resort to regional agencies or arrangements, or other peaceful means of their own choice.

2. The Security Council shall, when it deems necessary, call upon the parties to settle their dispute by such means.

Article 34

The Security Council may investigate any dispute, or any situation which might lead to international friction or give rise to a dispute, in order to determine whether the continuance of the dispute or situation is likely to endanger the maintenance of international peace and security.

Article 35

1. Any Member of the United Nations may bring any dispute, or any situation of the nature referred to in Article 34, to the attention of the Security Council or of the General Assembly.

2. A State which is not a Member of the United Nations may bring to the attention of the Security Council or of the General Assembly any dispute to which it is a party if it accepts in advance, for the purposes of the dispute, the obligations of pacific settlement provided in the present Charter.

3. The proceedings of the General Assembly in respect of matters brought to its attention under this Article will be subject to the provisions of Articles 11 and 12.

Article 36

1. The Security Council may, at any stage of a dispute of the nature referred to in Article 33 or of a situation of like nature, recommend appropriate procedures or methods of adjustment.

2. The Security Council should take into consideration any procedures for the settlement of the dispute which have already been adopted by the parties.

3. In making recommendations under this Article the Security Council should also take into consideration that legal disputes should as a general rule be referred by the parties to the International Court of Justice in accordance with the provisions of the Statute of the Court.

Article 37

1. Should the parties to a dispute of the nature referred to in Article 33 fail to settle it by the means indicated in that Article, they shall refer it to the Security Council.

2. If the Security Council deems that the continuance of the dispute is in fact likely to endanger the maintenance of international peace and security, it shall decide whether to take action under Article 36 or to recommend such terms of settlement as it may consider appropriate.

Article 38

Without prejudice to the provisions of Articles 33 to 37, the Security Council may, if all the parties to any dispute so request, make recommendations to the parties with a view to a pacific settlement of the dispute.

Chapter VII: Action with Respect to Threats to the Peace, Breaches of the Peace, and Acts of Aggression

Article 39

The Security Council shall determine the existence of any threat to the peace, breach of the peace, or act of aggression and shall make recommendations, or decide what measures shall be taken in accordance with Articles 41 and 42, to maintain or restore international peace and security.

Article 40

In order to prevent an aggravation of the situation, the Security Council may, before making the recommendations or deciding upon the measures provided for in Article 39, call upon the parties concerned to comply with such provisional measures as it deems necessary or desirable. Such provisional measures shall be without prejudice to the rights, claims, or position of the parties concerned. The Security Council shall duly take account of failure to comply with such provisional measures.

Article 41

The Security Council may decide what measures not involving the use of armed force are to be employed to give effect to its decisions, and it may call upon the Members of the United Nations to apply such measures. These may include complete or partial interruption of economic relations and of rail, sea, air, postal, telegraphic, radio, and other means of communication, and the severance of diplomatic relations.

Article 42

Should the Security Council consider that measures provided for in Article 41 would be inadequate or have proved to be inadequate, it may take such action by air, sea, or land forces as may be necessary to maintain or restore international peace and security. Such action may include demonstrations, blockade, and other operations by air, sea, or land forces of Members of the United Nations.

Article 43

1. All Members of the United Nations, in order to contribute to the maintenance of international peace and security, undertake to make available to the Security Council, on its call and in accordance with a special agreement or agreements, armed forces, assistance, and facilities, including rights of passage, necessary for the purpose of maintaining international peace and security.

2. Such agreement or agreements shall govern the numbers and types of forces, their degree of readiness and general location, and the nature of the facilities and assistance to be provided.

3. The agreement or agreements shall be negotiated as soon as possible on

the initiative of the Security Council. They shall be concluded between the Security Council and Members or between the Security Council and groups of Members and shall be subject to ratification by the signatory States in accordance with their respective constitutional processes.

Article 44

When the Security Council has decided to use force it shall, before calling upon a Member not represented on it to provide armed forces in fulfilment of the obligations assumed under Article 43, invite that Member, if the Member so desires, to participate in the decisions of the Security Council concerning the employment of contingents of that Member's armed forces.

Article 45

In order to enable the United Nations to take urgent military measures, Members shall hold immediately available national air-force contingents for combined international enforcement action. The strength and degree of readiness of these contingents and plans for their combined action shall be determined within the limits laid down in the special agreement or agreements referred to in Article 43, by the Security Council with the assistance of the Military Staff Committee.

Article 46

Plans for the application of armed force shall be made by the Security Council with the assistance of the Military Staff Committee.

Article 47

1. There shall be established a Military Staff Committee to advise and assist the Security Council on all questions relating to the Security Council's military requirements for the maintenance of international peace and security, the employment and command of forces placed at its disposal, the regulation of armaments, and possible disarmament.

2. The Military Staff Committee shall consist of the Chiefs of Staff of the permanent members of the Security Council or their representatives. Any Member of the United Nations not permanently represented on the Committee shall be invited by the Committee to be associated with it when the efficient discharge of the Committee's responsibilities requires the participation of that Member in its work.

3. The Military Staff Committee shall be responsible under the Security Council for the strategic direction of any armed forces placed at the disposal of the Security Council. Questions relating to the command of such forces shall be worked out subsequently.

4. The Military Staff Committee, with the authorization of the Security Council and after consultation with appropriate regional agencies, may establish regional subcommittees.

Article 48

1. The action required to carry out the decisions of the Security Council for the maintenance of international peace and security shall be taken by all the Members of the United Nations or by some of them, as the Security Council may determine.

2. Such decisions shall be carried out by the Members of the United Nations directly and through their action in the appropriate international agencies of which they remembers.

Article 49

The Members of the United Nations shall join in affording mutual assistance in carrying out the measures decided upon by the Security Council.

Article 50

If preventive or enforcement measures against any State are taken by the Security Council, any other State, whether a Member of the United Nations or not, which finds itself confronted with special economic problems arising from the carrying out of those measures shall have the right to consult the Security Council with regard to a solution of those problems.

Article 51

Nothing in the present Charter shall impair the inherent right of individual or collective self-defence if an armed attack occurs against a Member of the United Nations, until the Security Council has taken measures necessary to maintain international peace and security. Measures taken by Members in the exercise of this right of self-defence shall be immediately reported to the Security Council and shall not in any way affect the authority and responsibility of the Security Council under the present Charter to take at any time such action as it deems necessary in order to maintain or restore international peace and security.

Chapter VIII: Regional Arrangements

Article 52

1. Nothing in the present Charter precludes the existence of regional arrangements or agencies for dealing with such matters relating to the maintenance of international peace and security as are appropriate for regional action provided that such arrangements or agencies and their activities are consistent with the Purposes and Principles of the United Nations.

2. The Members of the United Nations entering into such arrangements or constituting such agencies shall make every effort to achieve pacific settlement of local disputes through such regional arrangements or by such regional agencies before referring them to the Security Council.

3. The Security Council shall encourage the development of pacific settle-

ment of local disputes through such regional arrangements or by such regional agencies either on the initiative of the States concerned or by reference from the Security Council.

4. This Article in no way impairs the application of Articles 34 and 35.

Article 53

1. The Security Council shall, where appropriate, utilize such regional arrangements or agencies for enforcement action under its authority. But no enforcement action shall be taken under regional arrangements or by regional agencies without the authorization of the Security Council, with the exception of measures against any enemy State, as defined in paragraph 2 of this Article, provided for pursuant to Article 107 or in regional arrangements directed against renewal of aggressive policy on the part of any such State, until such time as the Organization may, on request of the Governments concerned, be charged with the responsibility for preventing further aggression by such a State.

2. The term enemy State as used in paragraph 1 of this Article applies to any State which during the Second World War has been an enemy of any signatory of the present Charter.

Article 54

The Security Council shall at all times be kept fully informed of activities undertaken or in contemplation under regional arrangements or by regional agencies for the maintenance of international peace and security.

Chapter IX:
International Economic and Social Co-operation

Article 55

With a view to the creation of conditions of stability and well-being which are necessary for peaceful and friendly relations among nations based on respect for the principle of equal rights and self-determination of peoples, the United Nations shall promote:

a. higher standards of living, full employment, and conditions of economic and social progress and development;

b. solutions of international economic, social, health, and related problems; and international cultural and educational cooperation; and

c. universal respect for, and observance of, human rights and fundamental freedoms for all without distinction as to race, sex, language, or religion.

Article 56

All Members pledge themselves to take joint and separate action in co-operation with the Organization for the achievement of the purposes set forth in Article 55.

Article 57

1. The various specialized agencies, established by intergovernmental agreement and having wide international responsibilities, as defined in their basic instruments, in economic, social, cultural, educational, health, and related fields, shall be brought into relationship with the United Nations in accordance with the provisions of Article 63.

2. Such agencies thus brought into relationship with the United Nations are hereinafter referred to as specialized agencies.

Article 58

The Organization shall make recommendations for the co-ordination of the policies and activities of the specialized agencies.

Article 59

The Organization shall, where appropriate, initiate negotiations among the States concerned for the creation of any new specialized agencies required for the accomplishment of the purposes set forth in Article 55.

Article 60

Responsibility for the discharge of the functions of the Organization set forth in this Chapter shall be vested in the General Assembly and, under the authority of the General Assembly, in the Economic and Social Council, which shall have for this purpose the powers set forth in Chapter X.

Chapter X:
The Economic and Social Council

Composition

Article 61

1. The Economic and Social Council shall consist of fifty-four[iii] Members of the United Nations elected by the General Assembly.

2. Subject to the provisions of paragraph 3, eighteen members of the Economic and Social Council shall be elected each year for a term of three years. A retiring member shall be eligible for immediate re-election.

3. At the first election after the increase in the membership of the Economic and Social Council from twenty-seven to fifty-four members, in addition to the members elected in place of the nine members whose term of office expires at the end of that year, twenty-seven additional members shall be elected. Of these twenty-seven additional members, the term of office of nine members so elect-

---

iii. Originally eighteen. Amendment increasing number to twenty-seven came into force 31 August 1965. Amendment increasing it to fifty-four came into force 24 September 1973.

ed shall expire at the end of one year, and of nine other members at the end of two years, in accordance with arrangements made by the General Assembly.

4. Each member of the Economic and Social Council shall have one representative.

Functions and Powers

Article 62

1. The Economic and Social Council may make or initiate studies and reports with respect to international economic, social, cultural, educational, health, and related matters and may make recommendations with respect to any such matters to the General Assembly to the Members of the United Nations, and to the specialized agencies concerned.

2. It may make recommendations for the purpose of promoting respect for, and observance of, human rights and fundamental freedoms for all.

3. It may prepare draft conventions for submission to the General Assembly, with respect to matters falling within its competence.

4. It may call, in accordance with the rules prescribed by the United Nations, international conferences on matters falling within its competence.

Article 63

1. The Economic and Social Council may enter into agreements with any of the agencies referred to in Article 57, defining the terms on which the agency concerned shall be brought into relationship with the United Nations. Such agreements shall be subject to approval by the General Assembly.

2. It may co-ordinate the activities of the specialized agencies through consultation with and recommendations to such agencies and through recommendations to the General Assembly and to the Members of the United Nations.

Article 64

1. The Economic and Social Council may take appropriate steps to obtain regular reports from the specialized agencies. It may make arrangements with the Members of the United Nations and with the specialized agencies to obtain reports on the steps taken to give effect to its own recommendations and to recommendations on matters falling within its competence made by the General Assembly.

2. It may communicate its observations on these reports to the General Assembly.

Article 65

The Economic and Social Council may furnish information to the Security Council and shall assist the Security Council upon its request.

Article 66

1. The Economic and Social Council shall perform such functions as fall

within its competence in connexion with the carrying out of the recommendations of the General Assembly.

2. It may, with the approval of the General Assembly, perform services at the request of Members of the United Nations and at the request of specialized agencies.

3. It shall perform such other functions as are specified elsewhere in the present Charter or as may be assigned to it by the General Assembly.

Voting

Article 67
1. Each member of the Economic and Social Council shall have one vote.

2. Decisions of the Economic and Social Council shall be made by a majority of the members present and voting.

Procedure

Article 68
The Economic and Social Council shall set up commissions in economic and social fields and for the promotion of human rights, and such other commissions as may be required for the performance of its functions.

Article 69
The Economic and Social Council shall invite any Member of the United Nations to participate, without vote, in its deliberations on any matter of particular concern to that Member.

Article 70
The Economic and Social Council may make arrangements for representatives of the specialized agencies to participate, without vote, in its deliberations and in those of the commissions established by it, and for its representatives to participate in the deliberations of the specialized agencies.

Article 71
The Economic and Social Council may make suitable arrangements for consultation with nongovernmental organizations which are concerned with matters within its competence. Such arrangements may be made with international organizations and, where appropriate, with national organizations after consultation with the Members of the United Nations concerned.

Article 72
1. The Economic and Social Council shall adopt its own rules of procedure, including the method of selecting its President.

2. The Economic and Social Council shall meet as required in accordance

with its rules, which shall include provision for the convening of meetings on the request of a majority of its members.

Chapter XI:
Declaration Regarding Non–Self-Governing Territories

Article 73
Members of the United Nations which have or assume responsibilities for the administration of territories whose peoples have not yet attained a full measure of self-government recognize the principle that the interests of the inhabitants of these territories are paramount, and accept as a sacred trust the obligation to promote to the utmost, within the system of international peace and security established by the present Charter, the well-being of the inhabitants of these territories, and, to this end:

(a) to ensure, with due respect for the culture of the peoples concerned, their political, economic, social, and educational advancement, their just treatment, and their protection against abuses;

(b) to develop self-government, to take due account of the political aspirations of the peoples, and to assist them in the progressive development of their free political institutions, according to the particular circumstances of each territory and its peoples and their varying stages of advancement;

(c) to further international peace and security;

(d) to promote constructive measures of development, to encourage research, and to cooperate with one another and, when and where appropriate, with specialized international bodies with a view to the practical achievement of the social, economic, and scientific purposes set forth in this Article; and

(e) to transmit regularly to the Secretary-General for information purposes, subject to such limitation as security and constitutional considerations may require, statistical and other information of a technical nature relating to economic, social, and educational conditions in the territories for which they are respectively responsible other than those territories to which Chapters XII and XIII apply.

Article 74
Members of the United Nations also agree that their policy in respect of the territories to which this Chapter applies, no less than in respect of their metropolitan areas, must be based on the general principle of good-neighbourliness, due account being taken of the interests and well-being of the rest of the world, in social, economic, and commercial matters.

Chapter XII: International Trusteeship System

Article 75
The United Nations shall establish under its authority an international trustee-

ship system for the administration and supervision of such territories as may be placed thereunder by subsequent individual agreements. These territories are hereinafter referred to as trust territories.

Article 76

The basic objectives of the trusteeship system, in accordance with the Purposes of the United Nations laid down in Article 1 of the present Charter, shall be:

(a) to further international peace and security;

(b) to promote the political, economic, social, and educational advancement of the inhabitants of the trust territories, and their progressive development towards self-government or independence as may be appropriate to the particular circumstances of each territory and its peoples and the freely expressed wishes of the peoples concerned, and as may be provided by the terms of each trusteeship agreement;

(c) to encourage respect for human rights and for fundamental freedoms for all without distinction as to race, sex, language, or religion, and to encourage recognition of the interdependence of the peoples of the world; and

(d) to ensure equal treatment in social, economic, and commercial matters for all Members of the United Nations and their nationals, and also equal treatment for the latter in the administration of justice, without prejudice to the attainment of the foregoing objectives and subject to the provisions of Article 80.

Article 77

1. The trusteeship system shall apply to such territories in the following categories as may be placed thereunder by means of trusteeship agreements:

(a) territories now held under mandate;

(b) territories which may be detached from enemy States as a result of the Second World War; and

(c) territories voluntarily placed under the system by States responsible for their administration.

2. It will be a matter for subsequent agreement as to which territories in the foregoing categories will be brought under the trusteeship system and upon what terms.

Article 78

The trusteeship system shall not apply to territories which have become Members of the United Nations, relationship among which shall be based on respect for the principle of sovereign equality.

Article 79

The terms of trusteeship for each territory to be placed under the trusteeship system, including any alteration or amendment, shall be agreed upon by the States directly concerned, including the mandatory power in the case of territories held under mandate by a Member of the United Nations, and shall be approved as provided for in Articles 83 and 85.

Article 80

1. Except as may be agreed upon in individual trusteeship agreements, made under Articles 77, 79, and 81, placing each territory under the trusteeship system, and until such agreements have been concluded, nothing in this Chapter shall be construed in or of itself to alter in any manner the rights whatsoever of any States or any peoples or the terms of existing international instruments to which Members of the United Nations may respectively be parties.

2. Paragraph 1 of this Article shall not be interpreted as giving grounds for delay or postponement of the negotiation and conclusion of agreements for placing mandated and other territories under the trusteeship system as provided for in Article 77.

Article 81

The trusteeship agreement shall in each case include the terms under which the trust territory will be administered and designate the authority which will exercise the administration of the trust territory. Such authority, hereinafter called the administering authority, may be one or more States or the Organization itself.

Article 82

There may be designated, in any trusteeship agreement, a strategic area or areas which may include part or all of the trust territory to which the agreement applies, without prejudice to any special agreement or agreements made under Article 43.

Article 83

1. All functions of the United Nations relating to strategic areas, including the approval of the terms of the trusteeship agreements and of their alteration or amendment shall be exercised by the Security Council.

2. The basic objectives set forth in Article 76 shall be applicable to the people of each strategic area.

3. The Security Council shall, subject to the provisions of the trusteeship agreements and without prejudice to security considerations, avail itself of the assistance of the Trusteeship Council to perform those functions of the United Nations under the trusteeship system relating to political, economic, social, and educational matters in the strategic areas.

Article 84

It shall be the duty of the administering authority to ensure that the trust territory shall play its part in the maintenance of international peace and security. To this end the administering authority may make use of volunteer forces, facilities, and assistance from the trust territory in carrying out the obligations towards the Security Council undertaken in this regard by the administering authority, as well as for local defence and the maintenance of law and order within the trust territory.

Article 85

1. The functions of the United Nations with regard to trusteeship agreements for all areas not designated as strategic, including the approval of the terms of the trusteeship agreements and of their alteration or amendment, shall be exercised by the General Assembly.

2. The Trusteeship Council, operating under the authority of the General Assembly shall assist the General Assembly in carrying out these functions.

Chapter XIII:
The Trusteeship Council

Composition

Article 86

1. The Trusteeship Council shall consist of the following Members of the United Nations:

(a) those Members administering trust territories;

(b) such of those Members mentioned by name in Article 23 as are not administering trust territories; and

(c) as many other Members elected for three-year terms by the General Assembly as may be necessary to ensure that the total number of members of the Trusteeship Council is equally divided between those Members of the United Nations which administer trust territories and those which do not.

2. Each member of the Trusteeship Council shall designate one specially qualified person to represent it therein.

Functions and Powers

Article 87

The General Assembly and, under its authority, the Trusteeship Council, in carrying out their functions, may:

(a) consider reports submitted by the administering authority;

(b) accept petitions and examine them in consultation with the administering authority;

(c) provide for periodic visits to the respective trust territories at times agreed upon with the administering authority; and

(d) take these and other actions in conformity with the terms of the trusteeship agreements.

Article 88

The Trusteeship Council shall formulate a questionnaire on the political, economic, social, and educational advancement of the inhabitants of each trust territory, and the administering authority for each trust territory within the competence of the General Assembly shall make an annual report to the General Assembly upon the basis of such questionnaire.

Voting

Article 89

1. Each member of the Trusteeship Council shall have one vote.

2. Decisions of the Trusteeship Council shall be made by a majority of the members present and voting.

Procedure

Article 90

1. The Trusteeship Council shall adopt its own rules of procedure, including the method of selecting its President.

2. The Trusteeship Council shall meet as required in accordance with its rules, which shall include provision for the convening of meetings on the request of a majority of its members.

Article 91

The Trusteeship Council shall, when appropriate, avail itself of the assistance of the Economic and Social Council and of the specialized agencies in regard to matters with which they are respectively concerned.

Chapter XIV:
The International Court of Justice

Article 92

The International Court of Justice shall be the principal judicial organ of the United Nations. It shall function in accordance with the annexed Statute, which is based upon the Statute of the Permanent Court of International Justice and forms an integral part of the present Charter.

Article 93

1. All Members of the United Nations are ipso facto parties to the Statute of the International Court of Justice.

2. A State which is not a Member of the United Nations may become a party to the Statute of the International Court of Justice on conditions to be deter-

mined in each case by the General Assembly upon the recommendation of the Security Council.

Article 94

1. Each Member of the United Nations undertakes to comply with the decision of the International Court of Justice in any case to which it is a party.

2. If any party to a case fails to perform the obligations incumbent upon it under a judgment rendered by the Court, the other party may have recourse to the Security Council, which may, if it deems necessary, make recommendations or decide upon measures to be taken to give effect to the judgment.

Article 95

Nothing in the present Charter shall prevent Members of the United Nations from entrusting the solution of their differences to other tribunals by virtue of agreements already in existence or which may be concluded in the future.

Article 96

1. The General Assembly or the Security Council may request the International Court of Justice to give an advisory opinion on any legal question.

2. Other organs of the United Nations and specialized agencies, which may at any time be so authorized by the General Assembly, may also request advisory opinions of the Court on legal questions arising within the scope of their activities.

Chapter XV: The Secretariat

Article 97

The Secretariat shall comprise a Secretary-General and such staff as the Organization may require. The Secretary-General shall be appointed by the General Assembly upon the recommendation of the Security Council. He shall be the chief administrative officer of the Organization.

Article 98

The Secretary-General shall act in that capacity in all meetings of the General Assembly, of the Security Council, of the Economic and Social Council, and of the Trusteeship Council, and shall perform such other functions as are entrusted to him by these organs. The Secretary-General shall make an annual report to the General Assembly on the work of the Organization.

Article 99

The Secretary-General may bring to the attention of the Security Council any matter which in his opinion may threaten the maintenance of international peace and security.

Article 100

1. In the performance of their duties the Secretary-General and the staff shall not seek or receive instructions from any government or from any other authority external to the Organization. They shall refrain from any action which might reflect on their position as international officials responsible only to the Organization.

2. Each Member of the United Nations undertakes to respect the exclusively international character of the responsibilities of the Secretary-General and the staff and not to seek to influence them in the discharge of their responsibilities.

Article 101

1. The staff shall be appointed by the Secretary-General under regulations established by the General Assembly.

2. Appropriate staffs shall be permanently assigned to the Economic and Social Council, the Trusteeship Council, and, as required, to other organs of the United Nations. These staffs shall form a part of the Secretariat.

3. The paramount consideration in the employment of the staff and in the determination of the conditions of service shall be the necessity of securing the highest standards of efficiency, competence, and integrity. Due regard shall be paid to the importance of recruiting the staff on as wide a geographical basis as possible.

Chapter XVI:
Miscellaneous Provisions

Article 102

1. Every treaty and every international agreement entered into by any Member of the United Nations after the present Charter comes into force shall as soon as possible be registered with the Secretariat and published by it.

2. No party to any such treaty or international agreement which has not been registered in accordance with the provisions of paragraph 1 of this Article may invoke that treaty or agreement before any organ of the United Nations.

Article 103

In the event of a conflict between the obligations of the Members of the United Nations under the present Charter and their obligations under any other international agreement, their obligations under the present Charter shall prevail.

Article 104

The Organization shall enjoy in the territory of each of its Members such legal capacity as may be necessary for the exercise of its functions and the fulfilment of its purposes.

Article 105

1. The Organization shall enjoy in the territory of each of its Members such privileges and immunities as are necessary for the fulfilment of its purposes.

2. Representatives of the Members of the United Nations and officials of the Organization shall similarly enjoy such privileges and immunities as are necessary for the independent exercise of their functions in connexion with the Organization.

3. The General Assembly may make recommendations with a view to determining the details of the application of paragraphs 1 and 2 of this Article or may propose conventions to the Members of the United Nations for this purpose.

Chapter XVII:
Transitional Security Arrangements

Article 106

Pending the coming into force of such special agreements referred to in Article 43 as in the opinion of the Security Council enable it to begin the exercise of its responsibilities under Article 42, the parties to the Four-Nation Declaration, signed at Moscow, 30 October 1943, and France, shall, in accordance with the provisions of paragraph 5 of that Declaration, consult with one another and as occasion requires with other Members of the United Nations with a view to such joint action on behalf of the Organization as may be necessary for the purpose of maintaining international peace and security.

Article 107

Nothing in the present Charter shall invalidate or preclude action, in relation to any State which during the Second World War has been an enemy of any signatory to the present Charter, taken or authorized as a result of that war by the Governments having responsibility for such action.

Chapter XVIII: Amendments

Article 108

Amendments to the present Charter shall come into force for all Members of the United Nations when they have been adopted by a vote of two thirds of the members of the General Assembly and ratified in accordance with their respective constitutional processes by two thirds of the Members of the United Nations, including all the permanent members of the Security Council.

Article 109

1. A General Conference of the Members of the United Nations for the purpose of reviewing the present Charter may be held at a date and place to be

fixed by a two-thirds vote of the members of the General Assembly and by a vote of any nine[iv] members of the Security Council. Each Member of the United Nations shall have one vote in the conference.

2. Any alteration of the present Charter recommended by a two-thirds vote of the conference shall take effect when ratified in accordance with their respective constitutional processes by two-thirds of the Members of the United Nations including all the permanent members of the Security Council.

3. If such a conference has not been held before the tenth annual session of the General Assembly following the coming into force of the present Charter, the proposal to call such a conference shall be placed on the agenda of that session of the General Assembly, and the conference shall be held if so decided by a majority vote of the members of the General Assembly and by a vote of any seven members of the Security Council.

Chapter XIX:
Ratification and Signature

Article 110

1. The present Charter shall be ratified by the signatory States in accordance with their respective constitutional processes.

2. The ratifications shall be deposited with the Government of the United States of America, which shall notify all the signatory States of each deposit as well as the Secretary-General of the Organization when he has been appointed.

3. The present Charter shall come into force upon the deposit of ratifications by the Republic of China, France, the Union of Soviet Socialist Republics, the United Kingdom of Great Britain and Northern Ireland, and the United States of America, and by a majority of the other signatory States. A protocol of the ratifications deposited shall thereupon be drawn up by the Government of the United States of America which shall communicate copies thereof to all the signatory States.

4. The States signatory to the present Charter which ratify it after it has come into force will become original Members of the United Nations on the date of the deposit of their respective ratifications.

Article 111

The present Charter, of which the Chinese, French, Russian, English, and Spanish texts are equally authentic, shall remain deposited in the archives of the Government of the United States of America. Duly certified copies thereof shall be transmitted by that Government to the Governments of the other signatory States.

---

iv. Originally seven. Amendment came into force 12 June 1968.

IN FAITH WHEREOF the representatives of the Governments of the United Nations have signed the present Charter.

DONE at the city of San Francisco the twenty-sixth day of June, one thousand nine hundred and forty-five.

1.2
Statute of the International Court of Justice (1945)

In 1946 the International Court of Justice (ICJ), located at the Peace Palace in The Hague, replaced the Permanent Court of International Justice (PCIJ). The crux of the political task of establishing an international court is coming to an agreement on whether recourse to it will be compulsory. The compromise found in article 36(2) echoes the one that had been included in the 1920 Statute of the PCIJ. Another key issue, which had been the stumbling block in an attempt in 1907 to establish a court of arbitral justice, is that of the composition of the court and the election of the judges. Here, too, the structure as set out in Chapter 1 of the Statute of the ICJ mirrors that of the PCIJ. The strong element of continuity between the PCIJ and the ICJ means that the term world court *can comfortably accommodate both institutions.*

The ICJ Yearbook *provides an annual account of the work of the Court. Decisions of the ICJ can be found at www.icj-cij.org. See also* Shabtai Rosenne, The World Court: What It Is and How It Works, 5th ed. *(Dordrecht: M. Nijhoff, 1995); Constanze Schulte,* Compliance with Decisions of the International Court of Justice *(Oxford: Oxford University Press, 2004); and Stephen M. Schwebel, "National Judges and Judges Ad Hoc of the International Court of Justice,"* International and Comparative Law Quarterly *48 (1999): 889–900.*

Article 1
The International Court of Justice established by the Charter of the United Nations as the principal judicial organ of the United Nations shall be constituted and shall function in accordance with the provisions of the present Statute.

Chapter I: Organization of the Court

Article 2
The Court shall be composed of a body of independent judges, elected regardless of their nationality from among persons of high moral character, who pos-

sess the qualifications required in their respective countries for appointment to the highest judicial offices, or are jurisconsults of recognized competence in international law.

Article 3

1. The Court shall consist of fifteen members, no two of whom may be nationals of the same State.

2. A person who for the purposes of membership in the Court could be regarded as a national of more than one State shall be deemed to be a national of the one in which he ordinarily exercises civil and political rights.

Article 4

1. The members of the Court shall be elected by the General Assembly and by the Security Council from a list of persons nominated by the national groups in the Permanent Court of Arbitration, in accordance with the following provisions.

2. In the case of Members of the United Nations not represented in the Permanent Court of Arbitration, candidates shall be nominated by national groups appointed for this purpose by their governments under the same conditions as those prescribed for members of the Permanent Court of Arbitration by Article 44 of the Convention of The Hague of 1907 for the pacific settlement of international disputes.

3. The conditions under which a State which is a party to the present Statute but is not a Member of the United Nations may participate in electing the members of the Court shall, in the absence of a special agreement, be laid down by the General Assembly upon recommendation of the Security Council.

Article 5

1. At least three months before the date of the election, the Secretary-General of the United Nations shall address a written request to the members of the Permanent Court of Arbitration belonging to the States which are parties to the present Statute, and to the members of the national groups appointed under Article 4, paragraph 2, inviting them to undertake, within a given time, by national groups, the nomination of persons in a position to accept the duties of a member of the Court.

2. No group may nominate more than four persons, not more than two of whom shall be of their own nationality. In no case may the number of candidates nominated by a group be more than double the number of seats to be filled.

Article 6

Before making these nominations, each national group is recommended to consult its highest court of justice, its legal faculties and schools of law, and its national academies and national sections of international academies devoted to the study of law.

Article 7

1. The Secretary-General shall prepare a list in alphabetical order of all the persons thus nominated. Save as provided in Article 12, paragraph 2, these shall be the only persons eligible.

2. The Secretary-General shall submit this list to the General Assembly and to the Security Council.

Article 8

The General Assembly and the Security Council shall proceed independently of one another to elect the members of the Court.

Article 9

At every election, the electors shall bear in mind not only that the persons to be elected should individually possess the qualifications required, but also that in the body as a whole the representation of the main forms of civilization and of the principal legal systems of the world should be assured.

Article 10

1. Those candidates who obtain an absolute majority of votes in the General Assembly and in the Security Council shall be considered as elected.

2. Any vote of the Security Council, whether for the election of judges or for the appointment of members of the conference envisaged in Article 12, shall be taken without any distinction between permanent and non-permanent members of the Security Council.

3. In the event of more than one national of the same State obtaining an absolute majority of the votes both of the General Assembly and of the Security Council, the eldest of these only shall be considered as elected.

Article 11

If, after the first meeting held for the purpose of the election, one or more seats remain to be filled, a second and, if necessary, a third meeting shall take place.

Article 12

1. If, after the third meeting, one or more seats still remain unfilled, a joint conference consisting of six members, three appointed by the General Assembly and three by the Security Council, may be formed at any time at the request of either the General Assembly or the Security Council, for the purpose of choosing by the vote of an absolute majority one name for each seat still vacant, to submit to the General Assembly and the Security Council for their respective acceptance.

2. If the joint conference is unanimously agreed upon any person who fulfills the required conditions, he may be included in its list, even though he was not included in the list of nominations referred to in Article 7.

3. If the joint conference is satisfied that it will not be successful in procuring an election, those members of the Court who have already been elected

shall, within a period to be fixed by the Security Council, proceed to fill the vacant seats by selection from among those candidates who have obtained votes either in the General Assembly or in the Security Council.

4. In the event of an equality of votes among the judges, the eldest judge shall have a casting vote.

Article 13

1. The members of the Court shall be elected for nine years and may be re-elected; provided, however, that of the judges elected at the first election, the terms of five judges shall expire at the end of three years and the terms of five more judges shall expire at the end of six years.

2. The judges whose terms are to expire at the end of the above-mentioned initial periods of three and six years shall be chosen by lot to be drawn by the Secretary-General immediately after the first election has been completed.

3. The members of the Court shall continue to discharge their duties until their places have been filled. Though replaced, they shall finish any cases which they may have begun.

4. In the case of the resignation of a member of the Court, the resignation shall be addressed to the President of the Court for transmission to the Secretary-General. This last notification makes the place vacant.

Article 14

Vacancies shall be filled by the same method as that laid down for the first election subject to the following provision: the Secretary-General shall, within one month of the occurrence of the vacancy, proceed to issue the invitations provided for in Article 5, and the date of the election shall be fixed by the Security Council.

Article 15

A member of the Court elected to replace a member whose term of office has not expired shall hold office for the remainder of his predecessor's term.

Article 16

1. No member of the Court may exercise any political or administrative function, or engage in any other occupation of a professional nature.

2. Any doubt on this point shall be settled by the decision of the Court.

Article 17

1. No member of the Court may act as agent, counsel, or advocate in any case.

2. No member may participate in the decision of any case in which he has previously taken part as agent, counsel, or advocate for one of the parties, or as a member of a national or international court, or of a commission of enquiry, or in any other capacity.

3. Any doubt on this point shall be settled by the decision of the Court.

Article 18

1. No member of the Court can be dismissed unless, in the unanimous opinion of the other members, he has ceased to fulfill the required conditions.

2. Formal notification thereof shall be made to the Secretary-General by the Registrar.

3. This notification makes the place vacant.

Article 19

The members of the Court, when engaged on the business of the Court, shall enjoy diplomatic privileges and immunities.

Article 20

Every member of the Court shall, before taking up his duties, make a solemn declaration in open court that he will exercise his powers impartially and conscientiously.

Article 21

1. The Court shall elect its President and Vice-President for three years; they may be re-elected.

2. The Court shall appoint its Registrar and may provide for the appointment of such other officers as may be necessary.

Article 22

1. The seat of the Court shall be established at The Hague. This, however, shall not prevent the Court from sitting and exercising its functions elsewhere whenever the Court considers it desirable.

2. The President and the Registrar shall reside at the seat of the Court.

Article 23

1. The Court shall remain permanently in session, except during the judicial vacations, the dates and duration of which shall be fixed by the Court.

2. Members of the Court are entitled to periodic leave, the dates and duration of which shall be fixed by the Court, having in mind the distance between The Hague and the home of each judge.

3. Members of the Court shall be bound, unless they are on leave or prevented from attending by illness or other serious reasons duly explained to the President, to hold themselves permanently at the disposal of the Court.

Article 24

1. If, for some special reason, a member of the Court considers that he should not take part in the decision of a particular case, he shall so inform the President.

2. If the President considers that for some special reason one of the mem-

bers of the Court should not sit in a particular case, he shall give him notice accordingly.

3. If in any such case the member Court and the President disagree, the matter shall be settled by the decision of the Court.

Article 25

1. The full Court shall sit except when it is expressly provided otherwise in the present Statute.

2. Subject to the condition that the number of judges available to constitute the Court is not thereby reduced below eleven, the Rules of the Court may provide for allowing one or more judges, according to circumstances and in rotation, to be dispensed from sitting.

3. A quorum of nine judges shall suffice to constitute the Court.

Article 26

1. The Court may from time to time form one or more chambers, composed of three or more judges as the Court may determine, for dealing with particular categories of cases; for example, labour cases and cases relating to transit and communications.

2. The Court may at any time form a chamber for dealing with a particular case. The number of judges to constitute such a chamber shall be determined by the Court with the approval of the parties.

3. Cases shall be heard and determined by the chambers provided for in this Article if the parties so request.

Article 27

A judgment given by any of the chambers provided for in Articles 26 and 29 shall be considered as rendered by the Court.

Article 28

The chambers provided for in Articles 26 and 29 may, with the consent of the parties, sit and exercise their functions elsewhere than at The Hague.

Article 29

With a view to the speedy dispatch of business, the Court shall form annually a chamber composed of five judges which, at the request of the parties, may hear and determine cases by summary procedure. In addition, two judges shall be selected for the purpose of replacing judges who find it impossible to sit.

Article 30

1. The Court shall frame rules for carrying out its functions. In particular, it shall lay down rules of procedure.

2. The Rules of the Court may provide for assessors to sit with the Court or with any of its chambers, without the right to vote.

Article 31

1. Judges of the nationality of each of the parties shall retain their right to sit in the case before the Court.

2. If the Court includes upon the Bench a judge of the nationality of one of the parties, any other party may choose a person to sit as judge. Such person shall be chosen preferably from among those persons who have been nominated as candidates as provided in Articles 4 and 5.

3. If the Court includes upon the Bench no judge of the nationality of the parties, each of these parties may proceed to choose a judge as provided in paragraph 2 of this Article.

4. The provisions of this Article shall apply to the case of Articles 26 and 29. In such cases, the President shall request one or, if necessary, two of the members of the Court forming the chamber to give place to the members of the Court of the nationality of the parties concerned, and, failing such, or if they are unable to be present, to the judges specially chosen by the parties.

5. Should there be several parties in the same interest, they shall, for the purpose of the preceding provisions, be reckoned as one party only. Any doubt upon this point shall be settled by the decision of the Court.

6. Judges chosen as laid down in paragraphs 2, 3, and 4 of this Article shall fulfill the conditions required by Articles 2, 17 (paragraph 2), 20, and 24 of the present Statute. They shall take part in the decision on terms of complete equality with their colleagues.

Article 32

1. Each member of the Court shall receive an annual salary.

2. The President shall receive a special annual allowance.

3. The Vice-President shall receive a special allowance for every day on which he acts as President.

4. The judges chosen under Article 31, other than members of the Court, shall receive compensation for each day on which they exercise their functions.

5. These salaries, allowances, and compensation shall be fixed by the General Assembly. They may not be decreased during the term of office.

6. The salary of the Registrar shall be fixed by the General Assembly on the proposal of the Court.

7. Regulations made by the General Assembly shall fix the conditions under which retirement pensions may be given to members of the Court and to the Registrar, and the conditions under which members of the Court and the Registrar shall have their travelling expenses refunded.

8. The above salaries, allowances, and compensation shall be free of all taxation.

Article 33

The expenses of the Court shall be borne by the United Nations in such a manner as shall be decided by the General Assembly.

Chapter II: Competence of the Court

Article 34

1. Only States may be parties in cases before the Court.

2. The Court, subject to and in conformity with its Rules, may request of public international organizations information relevant to cases before it, and shall receive such information presented by such organizations on their own initiative.

3. Whenever the construction of the constituent instrument of a public international organization or of an international convention adopted thereunder is in question in a case before the Court, the Registrar shall so notify the public international organization concerned and shall communicate to it copies of all the written proceedings.

Article 35

1. The Court shall be open to the States Parties to the present Statute.

2. The conditions under which the Court shall be open to other States shall, subject to the special provisions contained in treaties in force, be laid down by the Security Council, but in no case shall such conditions place the parties in a position of inequality before the Court.

3. When a State which is not a Member of the United Nations is a party to a case, the Court shall fix the amount which that party is to contribute towards the expenses of the Court. This provision shall not apply if such State is bearing a share of the expenses of the Court.

Article 36

1. The jurisdiction of the Court comprises all cases which the parties refer to it and all matters specially provided for in the Charter of the United Nations or in treaties and conventions in force.

2. The States Parties to the present Statute may at any time declare that they recognize as compulsory ipso facto and without special agreement, in relation to any other State accepting the same obligation, the jurisdiction of the Court in all legal disputes concerning:

(a) the interpretation of a treaty;

(b) any question of international law;

(c) the existence of any fact which, if established, would constitute a breach of an international obligation;

(d) the nature or extent of the reparation to be made for the breach of an international obligation.

3. The declarations referred to above may be made unconditionally or on condition of reciprocity on the part of several or certain States, or for a certain time.

4. Such declarations shall be deposited with the Secretary-General of the United Nations, who shall transmit copies thereof to the parties to the Statute and to the Registrar of the Court.

5. Declarations made under Article 36 of the Statute of the Permanent Court of International Justice and which are still in force shall be deemed, as between the parties to the present Statute, to be acceptances of the compulsory jurisdiction of the International Court of Justice for the period which they still have to run and in accordance with their terms.

6. In the event of a dispute as to whether the Court has jurisdiction, the matter shall be settled by the decision of the Court.

Article 37

Whenever a treaty or convention in force provides for reference of a matter to a tribunal to have been instituted by the League of Nations, or to the Permanent Court of International Justice, the matter shall, as between the parties to the present Statute, be referred to the International Court of Justice.

Article 38

1. The Court, whose function is to decide in accordance with international law such disputes as are submitted to it, shall apply:

(a) international conventions, whether general or particular, establishing rules expressly recognized by the contesting States;

(b) international custom, as evidence of a general practice accepted as law;

(c) the general principles of law recognized by civilized nations;

(d) subject to the provisions of Article 59, judicial decisions and the teachings of the most highly qualified publicists of the various nations, as subsidiary means for the determination of rules of law.

2. This provision shall not prejudice the power of the Court to decide a case ex aequo et bono, if the parties agree thereto.

Chapter III: Procedure

Article 39

1. The official languages of the Court shall be French and English. If the parties agree that the case shall be conducted in French, the judgment shall be delivered in French. If the parties agree that the case shall be conducted in English, the judgment shall be delivered in English.

2. In the absence of an agreement as to which language shall be employed, each party may, in the pleadings, use the language which it prefers; the decision of the Court shall be given in French and English. In this case the Court shall at the same time determine which of the two texts shall be considered as authoritative.

3. The Court shall, at the request of any party, authorize a language other than French or English to be used by that party.

Article 40

1. Cases are brought before the Court, as the case may be, either by the notification of the special agreement or by a written application addressed to the Registrar. In either case the subject of the dispute and the parties shall be indicated.

2. The Registrar shall forthwith communicate the application to all concerned.

3. He shall also notify the Members of the United Nations through the Secretary-General, and also any other States entitled to appear before the Court.

Article 41

1. The Court shall have the power to indicate, if it considers that circumstances so require, any provisional measures which ought to be taken to preserve the respective rights of either party.

2. Pending the final decision, notice of the measures suggested shall forthwith be given to the parties and to the Security Council.

Article 42

1. The parties shall be represented by agents.

2. They may have the assistance of counsel or advocates before the Court.

3. The agents, counsel, and advocates of parties before the Court shall enjoy the privileges and immunities necessary to the independent exercise of their duties.

Article 43

1. The procedure shall consist of two parts: written and oral.

2. The written proceedings shall consist of the communication to the Court and to the parties of memorials, counter-memorials and, if necessary, replies; also all papers and documents in support.

3. These communications shall be made through the Registrar, in the order and within the time fixed by the Court.

4. A certified copy of every document produced by one party shall be communicated to the other party.

5. The oral proceedings shall consist of the hearing by the Court of witnesses, experts, agents, counsel, and advocates.

Article 44

1. For the service of all notices upon persons other than the agents, counsel, and advocates, the Court shall apply direct to the government of the State upon whose territory the notice has to be served.

2. The same provision shall apply whenever steps are to be taken to procure evidence on the spot.

Article 45

The hearing shall be under the control of the President or, if he is unable to preside, of the Vice-President; if neither is able to preside, the senior judge present shall preside.

Article 46

The hearing in Court shall be public, unless the Court shall decide otherwise, or unless the parties demand that the public be not admitted.

Article 47

1. Minutes shall be made at each hearing and signed by the Registrar and the President.

2. These minutes alone shall be authentic.

Article 48

The Court shall make orders for the conduct of the case, shall decide the form and time in which each party must conclude its arguments, and make all arrangements connected with the taking of evidence.

Article 49

The Court may, even before the hearing begins, call upon the agents to produce any document or to supply any explanations. Formal note shall be taken of any refusal.

Article 50

The Court may, at any time, entrust any individual, body, bureau, commission, or other organization that it may select, with the task of carrying out an enquiry or giving an expert opinion.

Article 51

During the hearing any relevant questions are to be put to the witnesses and experts under the conditions laid down by the Court in the rules of procedure referred to in Article 30.

Article 52

After the Court has received the proofs and evidence within the time specified for the purpose, it may refuse to accept any further oral or written evidence that one party may desire to present unless the other side consents.

Article 53

1. Whenever one of the parties does not appear before the Court, or fails to defend its case, the other party may call upon the Court to decide in favour of its claim.

2. The Court must, before doing so, satisfy itself, not only that it has juris-

diction in accordance with Articles 36 and 37, but also that the claim is well founded in fact and law.

Article 54

1. When, subject to the control of the Court, the agents, counsel, and advocates have completed their presentation of the case, the President shall declare the hearing closed.

2. The Court shall withdraw to consider the judgment.

3. The deliberations of the Court shall take place in private and remain secret.

Article 55

1. All questions shall be decided by a majority of the judges present.

2. In the event of an equality of votes, the President or the judge who acts in his place shall have a casting vote.

Article 56

1. The judgment shall state the reasons on which it is based.

2. It shall contain the names of the judges who have taken part in the decision.

Article 57

If the judgment does not represent in whole or in part the unanimous opinion of the judges, any judge shall be entitled to deliver a separate opinion.

Article 58

The judgment shall be signed by the President and by the Registrar. It shall be read in open court, due notice having been given to the agents.

Article 59

The decision of the Court has no binding force except between the parties and in respect of that particular case.

Article 60

The judgment is final and without appeal. In the event of dispute as to the meaning or scope of the judgment, the Court shall construe it upon the request of any party.

Article 61

1. An application for revision of a judgment may be made only when it is based upon the discovery of some fact of such a nature as to be a decisive factor, which fact was, when the judgment was given, unknown to the Court and also to the party claiming revision, always provided that such ignorance was not due to negligence.

2. The proceedings for revision shall be opened by a judgment of the Court expressly recording the existence of the new fact, recognizing that it has such a character as to lay the case open to revision, and declaring the application admissible on this ground.

3. The Court may require previous compliance with the terms of the judgment before it admits proceedings in revision.

4. The application for revision must be made at latest within six months of the discovery of the new fact.

5. No application for revision may be made after the lapse of ten years from the date of the judgment.

Article 62

1. Should a State consider that it has an interest of a legal nature which may be affected by the decision in the case, it may submit a request to the Court to be permitted to intervene.

2. It shall be for the Court to decide upon this request.

Article 63

1. Whenever the construction of a convention to which States other than those concerned in the case are parties is in question, the Registrar shall notify all such States forthwith.

2. Every State so notified has the right to intervene in the proceedings; but if it uses this right, the construction given by the judgment will be equally binding upon it.

Article 64

Unless otherwise decided by the Court, each party shall bear its own costs.

Chapter IV: Advisory Opinions

Article 65

1. The Court may give an advisory opinion on any legal question at the request of whatever body may be authorized by or in accordance with the Charter of the United Nations to make such a request.

2. Questions upon which the advisory opinion of the Court is asked shall be laid before the Court by means of a written request containing an exact statement of the question upon which an opinion is required, and accompanied by all documents likely to throw light upon the question.

Article 66

1. The Registrar shall forthwith give notice of the request for an advisory opinion to all States entitled to appear before the Court.

2. The Registrar shall also, by means of a special and direct communication, notify any State entitled to appear before the Court or international organiza-

tion considered by the Court, or, should it not be sitting, by the President, as likely to be able to furnish information on the question, that the Court will be prepared to receive, within a time limit to be fixed by the President, written statements, or to hear, at a public sitting to be held for the purpose, oral statements relating to the question.

3. Should any such State entitled to appear before the Court have failed to receive the special communication referred to in paragraph 2 of this Article, such State may express a desire to submit a written statement or to be heard; and the Court will decide.

4. States and organizations having presented written or oral statements or both shall be permitted to comment on the statements made by other States or organizations in the form, to the extent, and within the time limits which the Court, or, should it not be sitting, the President, shall decide in each particular case. Accordingly, the Registrar shall in due time communicate any such written statements to States and organizations having submitted similar statements.

Article 67
The Court shall deliver its advisory opinions in open court, notice having been given to the Secretary-General and to the representatives of Members of the United Nations, of other States and of international organizations immediately concerned.

Article 68
In the exercise of its advisory functions the Court shall further be guided by the provisions of the present Statute which apply in contentious cases to the extent to which it recognizes them to be applicable.

Chapter V: Amendment

Article 69
Amendments to the present Statute shall be effected by the same procedure as is provided by the Charter of the United Nations for amendments to that Charter, subject however to any provisions which the General Assembly upon recommendation of the Security Council may adopt concerning the participation of States which are parties to the present Statute but are not Members of the United Nations.

Article 70
The Court shall have power to propose such amendments to the present Statute as it may deem necessary, through written communications to the Secretary-General, for consideration in conformity with the provisions of Article 69.

1.3
Vienna Convention on Diplomatic Relations (1961)

The text of the convention was drafted by the International Law Commission, and in its final form adopted by the United Nations Conference on Diplomatic Intercourse and Immunities, held in Vienna, Austria, from 2 March to 14 April 1961. The convention has two optional protocols: the Acquisition of Nationality (by members of a consular post) and the Compulsory Settlement of Disputes (arising out of the interpretation or application of the Convention). The texts of the convention and its optional protocols can be found at www.un.org/law/ilc/texts/consul.htm. The classic authority on the convention is Eileen Denza, Diplomatic Law: A Commentary on the Vienna Convention on Diplomatic Relations, *2nd ed. (Oxford: Clarendon, 1998). See also chapter 6 of "Diplomatic Privileges and Immunities," in Anthony Aust,* Handbook of International Law *(Cambridge: Cambridge University Press, 2005).*

The 1963 Vienna Convention on Consular Relations is closely related to the Vienna Convention on Diplomatic Relations, several of its articles having been modeled on the 1961 Convention. The 1963 Convention came into prominence with the Breard, LaGrand, *and* Avena *cases before the ICJ, which concerned US breaches of the convention. On these cases, see Sandy Ghandhi, "Avena and Other Mexican Nationals (Mexico v. United States of America),"* International and Comparative Law Quarterly *54 (2005): 779–787; and Nancy Serano Smartt, "What* Breard *and Its Progeny Mean for* Avena *and Other Mexican Nationals,"* Temple International and Comparative Law Journal *19 (2005): 163–188.*

The States Parties to the present Convention,

Recalling that peoples of all nations from ancient times have recognized the status of diplomatic agents,

Having in mind the purposes and principles of the Charter of the United Nations concerning the sovereign equality of States, the maintenance of international peace and security, and the promotion of friendly relations among nations,

Believing that an international convention on diplomatic intercourse, privileges and immunities would contribute to the development of friendly relations among nations, irrespective of their differing constitutional and social systems,

Realizing that the purpose of such privileges and immunities is not to benefit individuals but to ensure the efficient performance of the functions of diplomatic missions as representing States,

Affirming that the rules of customary international law should continue to govern questions not expressly regulated by the provisions of the present Convention,

Have agreed as follows:

Article 1

For the purpose of the present Convention, the following expressions shall have the meanings hereunder assigned to them:

(a) the "head of the mission" is the person charged by the sending State with the duty of acting in that capacity;

(b) the "members of the mission" are the head of the mission and the members of the staff of the mission;

(c) the "members of the staff of the mission" are the members of the diplomatic staff, of the administrative and technical staff and of the service staff of the mission;

(d) the "members of the diplomatic staff" are the members of the staff of the mission having diplomatic rank;

(e) a "diplomatic agent" is the head of the mission or a member of the diplomatic staff of the mission;

(f) the "members of the administrative and technical staff" are the members of the staff of the mission employed in the administrative and technical service of the mission;

(g) the "members of the service staff" are the members of the staff of the mission in the domestic service of the mission;

(h) a "private servant" is a person who is in the domestic service of a member of the mission and who is not an employee of the sending State;

(i) the "premises of the mission" are the buildings or parts of buildings and the land ancillary thereto, irrespective of ownership, used for the purposes of the mission including the residence of the head of the mission.

Article 2

The establishment of diplomatic relations between States, and of permanent diplomatic missions, takes place by mutual consent.

Article 3

1. The functions of a diplomatic mission consist, inter alia, in:

(a) representing the sending State in the receiving State;

(b) protecting in the receiving State the interests of the sending State and of its nationals, within the limits permitted by international law;

(c) negotiating with the Government of the receiving State;

(d) ascertaining by all lawful means conditions and developments in the receiving State, and reporting thereon to the Government of the sending State;

(e) promoting friendly relations between the sending State and the receiving State, and developing their economic, cultural and scientific relations.

2. Nothing in the present Convention shall be construed as preventing the performance of consular functions by a diplomatic mission.

Article 4

1. The sending State must make certain that the agrément of the receiving State has been given for the person it proposes to accredit as head of the mission to that State.

2. The receiving State is not obliged to give reasons to the sending State for a refusal of agrément.

Article 5

1. The sending State may, after it has given due notification to the receiving States concerned, accredit a head of mission or assign any member of the diplomatic staff, as the case may be, to more than one State, unless there is express objection by any of the receiving States.

2. If the sending State accredits a head of mission to one or more other States it may establish a diplomatic mission headed by a chargé d'affaires ad interim in each State where the head of mission has not his permanent seat.

3. A head of mission or any member of the diplomatic staff of the mission may act as representative of the sending State to any international organization.

Article 6

Two or more States may accredit the same person as head of mission to another State, unless objection is offered by the receiving State.

Article 7

Subject to the provisions of Articles 5, 8, 9 and 11, the sending State may freely appoint the members of the staff of the mission. In the case of military, naval or air attachés, the receiving State may require their names to be submitted beforehand, for its approval.

Article 8

1. Members of the diplomatic staff of the mission should in principle be of the nationality of the sending State.

2. Members of the diplomatic staff of the mission may not be appointed from among persons having the nationality of the receiving State, except with the consent of that State which may be withdrawn at any time.

3. The receiving State may reserve the same right with regard to nationals of a third State who are not also nationals of the sending State.

Article 9

1. The receiving State may at any time and without having to explain its decision, notify the sending State that the head of the mission or any member of the diplomatic staff of the mission is persona non grata or that any other member of the staff of the mission is not acceptable. In any such case, the sending State shall, as appropriate, either recall the person concerned or terminate his functions with the mission. A person may be declared non grata or not acceptable before arriving in the territory of the receiving State.

2. If the sending State refuses or fails within a reasonable period to carry out its obligations under paragraph 1 of this Article, the receiving State may refuse to recognize the person concerned as a member of the mission.

Article 10

1. The Ministry for Foreign Affairs of the receiving State, or such other ministry as may be agreed, shall be notified of:

(a) the appointment of members of the mission, their arrival and their final departure or the termination of their functions with the mission;

(b) the arrival and final departure of a person belonging to the family of a member of the mission and, where appropriate, the fact that a person becomes or ceases to be a member of the family of a member of the mission;

(c) the arrival and final departure of private servants in the employ of persons referred to in sub-paragraph (a) of this paragraph and, where appropriate, the fact that they are leaving the employ of such persons;

(d) the engagement and discharge of persons resident in the receiving State as members of the mission or private servants entitled to privileges and immunities.

2. Where possible, prior notification of arrival and final departure shall also be given.

Article 11

1. In the absence of specific agreement as to the size of the mission, the receiving State may require that the size of a mission be kept within limits considered by it to be reasonable and normal, having regard to circumstances and conditions in the receiving State and to the needs of the particular mission.

2. The receiving State may equally, within similar bounds and on a non-discriminatory basis, refuse to accept officials of a particular category.

Article 12

The sending State may not, without the prior express consent of the receiving State, establish offices forming part of the mission in localities other than those in which the mission itself is established.

Article 13

1. The head of the mission is considered as having taken up his functions in the receiving State either when he has presented his credentials or when he has notified his arrival and a true copy of his credentials has been presented to the Ministry for Foreign Affairs of the receiving State, or such other ministry as may be agreed, in accordance with the practice prevailing in the receiving State which shall be applied in a uniform manner.

2. The order of presentation of credentials or of a true copy thereof will be determined by the date and time of the arrival of the head of the mission.

Article 14

1. Heads of mission are divided into three classes, namely:

(a) that of ambassadors or nuncios accredited to Heads of State, and other heads of mission of equivalent rank;

(b) that of envoys, ministers and internuncios accredited to Heads of State;

(c) that of chargés d'affaires accredited to Ministers for Foreign Affairs.

2. Except as concerns precedence and etiquette, there shall be no differentiation between heads of mission by reason of their class.

Article 15

The class to which the heads of their missions are to be assigned shall be agreed between States.

Article 16

1. Heads of mission shall take precedence in their respective classes in the order of the date and time of taking up their functions in accordance with Article 13.

2. Alterations in the credentials of a head of mission not involving any change of class shall not affect his precedence.

3. This article is without prejudice to any practice accepted by the receiving State regarding the precedence of the representative of the Holy See.

Article 17

The precedence of the members of the diplomatic staff of the mission shall be notified by the head of the mission to the Ministry for Foreign Affairs or such other ministry as may be agreed.

Article 18

The procedure to be observed in each State for the reception of heads of mission shall be uniform in respect of each class.

Article 19

1. If the post of head of the mission is vacant, or if the head of the mission

is unable to perform his functions, a chargé d'affaires ad interim shall act provisionally as head of the mission. The name of the chargé d'affaires ad interim shall be notified, either by the head of the mission or, in case he is unable to do so, by the Ministry for Foreign Affairs of the sending State to the Ministry for Foreign Affairs of the receiving State or such other ministry as may be agreed.

2. In cases where no member of the diplomatic staff of the mission is present in the receiving State, a member of the administrative and technical staff may, with the consent of the receiving State, be designated by the sending State to be in charge of the current administrative affairs of the mission.

Article 20
The mission and its head shall have the right to use the flag and emblem of the sending State on the premises of the mission, including the residence of the head of the mission, and on his means of transport.

Article 21
1. The receiving State shall either facilitate the acquisition on its territory, in accordance with its laws, by the sending State of premises necessary for its mission or assist the latter in obtaining accommodation in some other way.

2. It shall also, where necessary, assist missions in obtaining suitable accommodation for their members.

Article 22
1. The premises of the mission shall be inviolable. The agents of the receiving State may not enter them, except with the consent of the head of the mission.

2. The receiving State is under a special duty to take all appropriate steps to protect the premises of the mission against any intrusion or damage and to prevent any disturbance of the peace of the mission or impairment of its dignity.

3. The premises of the mission, their furnishings and other property thereon and the means of transport of the mission shall be immune from search, requisition, attachment or execution.

Article 23
1. The sending State and the head of the mission shall be exempt from all national, regional or municipal dues and taxes in respect of the premises of the mission, whether owned or leased, other than such as represent payment for specific services rendered.

2. The exemption from taxation referred to in this Article shall not apply to such dues and taxes payable under the law of the receiving State by persons contracting with the sending State or the head of the mission.

Article 24
The archives and documents of the mission shall be inviolable at any time and wherever they may be.

Article 25

The receiving State shall accord full facilities for the performance of the functions of the mission.

Article 26

Subject to its laws and regulations concerning zones entry into which is prohibited or regulated for reasons of national security, the receiving State shall ensure to all members of the mission freedom of movement and travel in its territory.

Article 27

1. The receiving State shall permit and protect free communication on the part of the mission for all official purposes. In communicating with the Government and the other missions and consulates of the sending State, wherever situated, the mission may employ all appropriate means, including diplomatic couriers and messages in code or cipher. However, the mission may install and use a wireless transmitter only with the consent of the receiving State.

2. The official correspondence of the mission shall be inviolable. Official correspondence means all correspondence relating to the mission and its functions.

3. The diplomatic bag shall not be opened or detained.

4. The packages constituting the diplomatic bag must bear visible external marks of their character and may contain only diplomatic documents or articles intended for official use.

5. The diplomatic courier, who shall be provided with an official document indicating his status and the number of packages constituting the diplomatic bag, shall be protected by the receiving State in the performance of his functions. He shall enjoy personal inviolability and shall not be liable to any form of arrest or detention.

6. The sending State or the mission may designate diplomatic couriers ad hoc. In such cases the provisions of paragraph 5 of this Article shall also apply, except that the immunities therein mentioned shall cease to apply when such a courier has delivered to the consignee the diplomatic bag in his charge.

7. A diplomatic bag may be entrusted to the captain of a commercial aircraft scheduled to land at an authorized port of entry. He shall be provided with an official document indicating the number of packages constituting the bag but he shall not be considered to be a diplomatic courier. The mission may send one of its members to take possession of the diplomatic bag directly and freely from the captain of the aircraft.

Article 28

The fees and charges levied by the mission in the course of its official duties shall be exempt from all dues and taxes.

Article 29

The person of a diplomatic agent shall be inviolable. He shall not be liable to any form of arrest or detention. The receiving State shall treat him with due respect and shall take all appropriate steps to prevent any attack on his person, freedom or dignity.

Article 30

1. The private residence of a diplomatic agent shall enjoy the same inviolability and protection as the premises of the mission.

2. His papers, correspondence and, except as provided in paragraph 3 of Article 31, his property, shall likewise enjoy inviolability.

Article 31

1. A diplomatic agent shall enjoy immunity from the criminal jurisdiction of the receiving State. He shall also enjoy immunity from its civil and administrative jurisdiction, except in the case of:

(a) a real action relating to private immovable property situated in the territory of the receiving State, unless he holds it on behalf of the sending State for the purposes of the mission;

(b) an action relating to succession in which the diplomatic agent is involved as executor, administrator, heir or legatee as a private person and not on behalf of the sending State;

(c) an action relating to any professional or commercial activity exercised by the diplomatic agent in the receiving State outside his official functions.

2. A diplomatic agent is not obliged to give evidence as a witness.

3. No measures of execution may be taken in respect of a diplomatic agent except in the cases coming under sub-paragraphs (a), (b) and (c) of paragraph 1 of this Article, and provided that the measures concerned can be taken without infringing the inviolability of his person or of his residence.

4. The immunity of a diplomatic agent from the jurisdiction of the receiving State does not exempt him from the jurisdiction of the sending State.

Article 32

1. The immunity from jurisdiction of diplomatic agents and of persons enjoying immunity under Article 37 may be waived by the sending State.

2. Waiver must always be express.

3. The initiation of proceedings by a diplomatic agent or by a person enjoying immunity from jurisdiction under Article 37 shall preclude him from invoking immunity from jurisdiction in respect of any counter-claim directly connected with the principal claim.

4. Waiver of immunity from jurisdiction in respect of civil or administrative proceedings shall not be held to imply waiver of immunity in respect of the execution of the judgement, for which a separate waiver shall be necessary.

Article 33

1. Subject to the provisions of paragraph 3 of this Article, a diplomatic agent shall with respect to services rendered for the sending State be exempt from social security provisions which may be in force in the receiving State.

2. The exemption provided for in paragraph 1 of this Article shall also apply to private servants who are in the sole employ of a diplomatic agent, on condition:

(a) that they are not nationals of or permanently resident in the receiving State; and

(b) that they are covered by the social security provisions which may be in force in the sending State or a third State.

3. A diplomatic agent who employs persons to whom the exemption provided for in paragraph 2 of this Article does not apply shall observe the obligations which the social security provisions of the receiving State impose upon employers.

4. The exemption provided for in paragraphs 1 and 2 of this Article shall not preclude voluntary participation in the social security system of the receiving State provided that such participation is permitted by that State.

5. The provisions of this Article shall not affect bilateral or multilateral agreements concerning social security concluded previously and shall not prevent the conclusion of such agreements in the future.

Article 34

A diplomatic agent shall be exempt from all dues and taxes, personal or real, national, regional or municipal, except:

(a) indirect taxes of a kind which are normally incorporated in the price of goods or services;

(b) dues and taxes on private immovable property situated in the territory of the receiving State, unless he holds it on behalf of the sending State for the purposes of the mission;

(c) estate, succession or inheritance duties levied by the receiving State, subject to the provisions of paragraph 4 of Article 39;

(d) dues and taxes on private income having its source in the receiving State and capital taxes on investments made in commercial undertakings in the receiving State;

(e) charges levied for specific services rendered;

(f) registration, court or record fees, mortgage dues and stamp duty, with respect to immovable property, subject to the provisions of Article 23.

Article 35

The receiving State shall exempt diplomatic agents from all personal services, from all public service of any kind whatsoever, and from military obligations such as those connected with requisitioning, military contributions and billeting.

Article 36

1. The receiving State shall, in accordance with such laws and regulations as it may adopt, permit entry of and grant exemption from all customs duties, taxes, and related charges other than charges for storage, cartage and similar services, on:

(a) articles for the official use of the mission;

(b) articles for the personal use of a diplomatic agent or members of his family forming part of his household, including articles intended for his establishment.

2. The personal baggage of a diplomatic agent shall be exempt from inspection, unless there are serious grounds for presuming that it contains articles not covered by the exemptions mentioned in paragraph 1 of this Article, or articles the import or export of which is prohibited by the law or controlled by the quarantine regulations of the receiving State. Such inspection shall be conducted only in the presence of the diplomatic agent or of his authorized representative.

Article 37

1. The members of the family of a diplomatic agent forming part of his household shall, if they are not nationals of the receiving State, enjoy the privileges and immunities specified in Articles 29 to 36.

2. Members of the administrative and technical staff of the mission, together with members of their families forming part of their respective households, shall, if they are not nationals of or permanently resident in the receiving State, enjoy the privileges and immunities specified in Articles 29 to 35, except that the immunity from civil and administrative jurisdiction of the receiving State specified in paragraph 1 of Article 31 shall not extend to acts performed outside the course of their duties. They shall also enjoy the privileges specified in Article 36, paragraph 1, in respect of articles imported at the time of first installation.

3. Members of the service staff of the mission who are not nationals of or permanently resident in the receiving State shall enjoy immunity in respect of acts performed in the course of their duties, exemption from dues and taxes on the emoluments they receive by reason of their employment and the exemption contained in Article 33.

4. Private servants of members of the mission shall, if they are not nationals of or permanently resident in the receiving State, be exempt from dues and taxes on the emoluments they receive by reason of their employment. In other respects, they may enjoy privileges and immunities only to the extent admitted by the receiving State. However, the receiving State must exercise its jurisdiction over those persons in such a manner as not to interfere unduly with the performance of the functions of the mission.

Article 38

1. Except insofar as additional privileges and immunities may be granted by

the receiving State, a diplomatic agent who is a national of or permanently resident in that State shall enjoy only immunity from jurisdiction, and inviolability, in respect of official acts performed in the exercise of his functions.

2. Other members of the staff of the mission and private servants who are nationals of or permanently resident in the receiving State shall enjoy privileges and immunities only to the extent admitted by the receiving State. However, the receiving State must exercise its jurisdiction over those persons in such a manner as not to interfere unduly with the performance of the functions of the mission.

Article 39

1. Every person entitled to privileges and immunities shall enjoy them from the moment he enters the territory of the receiving State on proceeding to take up his post or, if already in its territory, from the moment when his appointment is notified to the Ministry for Foreign Affairs or such other ministry as may be agreed.

2. When the functions of a person enjoying privileges and immunities have come to an end, such privileges and immunities shall normally cease at the moment when he leaves the country, or on expiry of a reasonable period in which to do so, but shall subsist until that time, even in case of armed conflict. However, with respect to acts performed by such a person in the exercise of his functions as a member of the mission, immunity shall continue to subsist.

3. In case of the death of a member of the mission, the members of his family shall continue to enjoy the privileges and immunities to which they are entitled until the expiry of a reasonable period in which to leave the country.

4. In the event of the death of a member of the mission not a national of or permanently resident in the receiving State or a member of his family forming part of his household, the receiving State shall permit the withdrawal of the movable property of the deceased, with the exception of any property acquired in the country the export of which was prohibited at the time of his death. Estate, succession and inheritance duties shall not be levied on movable property the presence of which in the receiving State was due solely to the presence there of the deceased as a member of the mission or as a member of the family of a member of the mission.

Article 40

1. If a diplomatic agent passes through or is in the territory of a third State, which has granted him a passport visa if such visa was necessary, while proceeding to take up or to return to his post, or when returning to his own country, the third State shall accord him inviolability and such other immunities as may be required to ensure his transit or return. The same shall apply in the case of any members of his family enjoying privileges or immunities who are

accompanying the diplomatic agent, or travelling separately to join him or to return to their country.

2. In circumstances similar to those specified in paragraph 1 of this Article, third States shall not hinder the passage of members of the administrative and technical or service staff of a mission, and of members of their families, through their territories.

3. Third States shall accord to official correspondence and other official communications in transit, including messages in code or cipher, the same freedom and protection as is accorded by the receiving State. They shall accord to diplomatic couriers, who have been granted a passport visa if such visa was necessary, and diplomatic bags in transit the same inviolability and protection as the receiving State is bound to accord.

4. The obligations of third States under paragraphs 1, 2 and 3 of this Article shall also apply to the persons mentioned respectively in those paragraphs, and to official communications and diplomatic bags, whose presence in the territory of the third State is due to force majeure.

Article 41

1. Without prejudice to their privileges and immunities, it is the duty of all persons enjoying such privileges and immunities to respect the laws and regulations of the receiving State. They also have a duty not to interfere in the internal affairs of that State.

2. All official business with the receiving State entrusted to the mission by the sending State shall be conducted with or through the Ministry for Foreign Affairs of the receiving State or such other ministry as may be agreed.

3. The premises of the mission must not be used in any manner incompatible with the functions of the mission as laid down in the present Convention or by other rules of general international law or by any special agreements in force between the sending and the receiving State.

Article 42

A diplomatic agent shall not in the receiving State practise for personal profit any professional or commercial activity.

Article 43

The function of a diplomatic agent comes to an end, inter alia:

(a) on notification by the sending State to the receiving State that the function of the diplomatic agent has come to an end;

(b) on notification by the receiving State to the sending State that, in accordance with paragraph 2 of Article 9, it refuses to recognize the diplomatic agent as a member of the mission.

Article 44

The receiving State must, even in case of armed conflict, grant facilities in order to enable persons enjoying privileges and immunities, other than nationals of the receiving State, and members of the families of such persons irrespective of their nationality, to leave at the earliest possible moment. It must, in particular, in case of need, place at their disposal the necessary means of transport for themselves and their property.

Article 45
If diplomatic relations are broken off between two States, or if a mission is permanently or temporarily recalled:

(a) the receiving State must, even in case of armed conflict, respect and protect the premises of the mission, together with its property and archives;

(b) the sending State may entrust the custody of the premises of the mission, together with its property and archives, to a third State acceptable to the receiving State;

(c) the sending State may entrust the protection of its interests and those of its nationals to a third State acceptable to the receiving State.

Article 46
A sending State may with the prior consent of a receiving State, and at the request of a third State not represented in the receiving State, undertake the temporary protection of the interests of the third State and of its nationals.

Article 47
1. In the application of the provisions of the present Convention, the receiving State shall not discriminate as between States.

2. However, discrimination shall not be regarded as taking place:

(a) where the receiving State applies any of the provisions of the present Convention restrictively because of a restrictive application of that provision to its mission in the sending State;

(b) where by custom or agreement States extend to each other more favourable treatment than is required by the provisions of the present Convention.

Article 48
The present Convention shall be open for signature by all States Members of the United Nations or of any of the specialized agencies or Parties to the Statute of the International Court of Justice, and by any other State invited by the General Assembly of the United Nations to become a Party to the Convention, as follows: until 31 October 1961 at the Federal Ministry for Foreign Affairs of Austria and subsequently, until 31 March 1962, at the United Nations Headquarters in New York.

Article 49
The present Convention is subject to ratification. The instruments of ratification shall be deposited with the Secretary-General of the United Nations.

Article 50

The present Convention shall remain open for accession by any State belonging to any of the four categories mentioned in Article 48. The instruments of accession shall be deposited with the Secretary-General of the United Nations.

Article 51

1. The present Convention shall enter into force on the thirtieth day following the date of deposit of the twenty-second instrument of ratification or accession with the Secretary-General of the United Nations.

2. For each State ratifying or acceding to the Convention after the deposit of the twenty-second instrument of ratification or accession, the Convention shall enter into force on the thirtieth day after deposit by such State of its instrument of ratification or accession.

Article 52

The Secretary-General of the United Nations shall inform all States belonging to any of the four categories mentioned in Article 48:

(a) of signatures to the present Convention and of the deposit of instruments of ratification or accession, in accordance with Articles 48, 49 and 50;

(b) of the date on which the present Convention will enter into force, in accordance with Article 51.

Article 53

The original of the present Convention, of which the Chinese, English, French, Russian and Spanish texts are equally authentic, shall be deposited with the Secretary-General of the United Nations, who shall send certified copies thereof to all States belonging to any of the four categories mentioned in Article 48.

IN WITNESS WHEREOF the undersigned Plenipotentiaries, being duly authorized thereto by their respective Governments, have signed the present Convention.

DONE at Vienna, this eighteenth day of April one thousand nine hundred and sixty-one.

1.4
Vienna Convention on the Law of Treaties (1969)

The International Law Commission prepared the draft of this treaty, much of which codified existing customary international law. Given that treaties are the most important source of international law today, it is notable that close to 50 percent of states have not ratified the treaty. The United States did not ratify the convention promptly, in part because of the different meanings of "treaty" in US constitutional and international law. The convention was followed by the 1978 Vienna Convention on Succession of States in Respect of Treaties and the 1986 Vienna Convention on the Law of Treaties Between States and International Organizations or Between International Organizations.

A clear account of the law of treaties is found in Anthony Aust, Modern Treaty Law and Practice *(Cambridge: Cambridge University Press, 2000), presented as a practitioner's perspective on the law of treaties. On early UK ratification and US nonratification, see Richard W. Edwards Jr., Ian Sinclair, Robert E. Dalton, E. W. Verdag, Maria Frankowska, and Frederick S. Tipson, "The Vienna Convention on the Law of Treaties: The Consequences of Participation and Nonparticipation,"* Proceedings of the American Society of International Law at its Annual Meeting *78 (1984): 270–293. For a very brief introduction to the difference between a treaty in international law and in US constitutional law see the American Society of International Law Insight by Frederic Kirgis, "International Agreements and US Law" (May 1997) at www.asil.org/insights/insigh10.htm. A more detailed but still very readable explanation is found in Robert E. Dalton, "National Treaty Law and Practice: United States," in Monroe Leigh, Merritt R. Blakeslee, and L. Benjamin Ederington, eds.,* National Treaty Law and Practice *(Austria, Chile, Colombia, Japan, Netherlands, U.S.) (Washington, D.C.: American Society of International Law, 1999).*

The States Parties to the present Convention,

Considering the fundamental role of treaties in the history of international relations,

Recognizing the ever-increasing importance of treaties as a source of international law and as a means of developing peaceful co-operation among nations, whatever their constitutional and social systems,

Noting that the principles of free consent and of good faith and the pacta sunt servanda rule are universally recognized,

Affirming that disputes concerning treaties, like other international disputes, should be settled by peaceful means and in conformity with the principles of justice and international law,

Recalling the determination of the peoples of the United Nations to establish conditions under which justice and respect for the obligations arising from treaties can be maintained,

Having in mind the principles of international law embodied in the Charter of the United Nations, such as the principles of the equal rights and self-determination of peoples, of the sovereign equality and independence of all States, of non-interference in the domestic affairs of States, of the prohibition of the threat or use of force and of universal respect for, and observance of, human rights and fundamental freedoms for all,

Believing that the codification and progressive development of the law of treaties achieved in the present Convention will promote the purposes of the United Nations set forth in the Charter, namely, the maintenance of international peace and security, the development of friendly relations and the achievement of co-operation among nations,

Affirming that the rules of customary international law will continue to govern questions not regulated by the provisions of the present Convention,

Have agreed as follows:

Part I: Introduction

Article 1: Scope of the present Convention
The present Convention applies to treaties between States.

Article 2: Use of terms
1. For the purposes of the present Convention:

(a) "treaty" means an international agreement concluded between States in written form and governed by international law, whether embodied in a single instrument or in two or more related instruments and whatever its particular designation;

(b) "ratification," "acceptance," "approval" and "accession" mean in each case the international act so named whereby a State establishes on the international plane its consent to be bound by a treaty;

(c) "full powers" means a document emanating from the competent authority of a State designating a person or persons to represent the State for negotiating, adopting or authenticating the text of a treaty, for expressing the consent of the State to be bound by a treaty, or for accomplishing any other act with respect to a treaty;

(d) "reservation" means a unilateral statement, however phrased or named, made by a State, when signing, ratifying, accepting, approving or acceding to a treaty, whereby it purports to exclude or to modify the legal effect of certain provisions of the treaty in their application to that State;

(e) "negotiating State" means a State which took part in the drawing up and adoption of the text of the treaty;

(f) "contracting State" means a State which has consented to be bound by the treaty, whether or not the treaty has entered into force;

(g) "party" means a State which has consented to be bound by the treaty and for which the treaty is in force;

(h) "third State" means a State not a party to the treaty;

(i) "international organization" means an intergovernmental organization.

2. The provisions of paragraph 1 regarding the use of terms in the present Convention are without prejudice to the use of those terms or to the meanings which may be given to them in the internal law of any State.

Article 3: International agreements not within the scope of the present Convention

The fact that the present Convention does not apply to international agreements concluded between States and other subjects of international law or between such other subjects of international law, or to international agreements not in written form, shall not affect:

(a) the legal force of such agreements;

(b) the application to them of any of the rules set forth in the present Convention to which they would be subject under international law independently of the Convention;

(c) the application of the Convention to the relations of States as between themselves under international agreements to which other subjects of international law are also parties.

Article 4: Non-retroactivity of the present Convention

Without prejudice to the application of any rules set forth in the present Convention to which treaties would be subject under international law independently of the Convention, the Convention applies only to treaties which are concluded by States after the entry into force of the present Convention with regard to such States.

Article 5: Treaties constituting international organizations and treaties adopted within an international organization

The present Convention applies to any treaty which is the constituent instrument of an international organization and to any treaty adopted within an international organization without prejudice to any relevant rules of the organization.

Part II:
Conclusion and Entry Into Force of Treaties

Section 1: Conclusion of Treaties

Article 6: Capacity of States to conclude treaties
Every State possesses capacity to conclude treaties.

Article 7: Full powers
1. A person is considered as representing a State for the purpose of adopting or authenticating the text of a treaty or for the purpose of expressing the consent of the State to be bound by a treaty if:

(a) he produces appropriate full powers; or

(b) it appears from the practice of the States concerned or from other circumstances that their intention was to consider that person as representing the State for such purposes and to dispense with full powers.

2. In virtue of their functions and without having to produce full powers, the following are considered as representing their State:

(a) Heads of State, Heads of Government and Ministers for Foreign Affairs, for the purpose of performing all acts relating to the conclusion of a treaty;

(b) heads of diplomatic missions, for the purpose of adopting the text of a treaty between the accrediting State and the State to which they are accredited;

(c) representatives accredited by States to an international conference or to an international organization or one of its organs, for the purpose of adopting the text of a treaty in that conference, organization or organ.

Article 8: Subsequent confirmation of
an act performed without authorization
An act relating to the conclusion of a treaty performed by a person who cannot be considered under article 7 as authorized to represent a State for that purpose is without legal effect unless afterwards confirmed by that State.

Article 9: Adoption of the text
1. The adoption of the text of a treaty takes place by the consent of all the States participating in its drawing up except as provided in paragraph 2.

2. The adoption of the text of a treaty at an international conference takes place by the vote of two-thirds of the States present and voting, unless by the same majority they shall decide to apply a different rule.

Article 10: Authentication of the text
The text of a treaty is established as authentic and definitive:

(a) by such procedure as may be provided for in the text or agreed upon by the States participating in its drawing up; or

(b) failing such procedure, by the signature, signature ad referendum or initialling by the representatives of those States of the text of the treaty or of the Final Act of a conference incorporating the text.

Article 11: Means of expressing consent to be bound by a treaty

The consent of a State to be bound by a treaty may be expressed by signature, exchange of instruments constituting a treaty, ratification, acceptance, approval or accession, or by any other means if so agreed.

Article 12: Consent to be bound by a treaty expressed by signature

1. The consent of a State to be bound by a treaty is expressed by the signature of its representative when:

(a) the treaty provides that signature shall have that effect;

(b) it is otherwise established that the negotiating States were agreed that signature should have that effect; or

(c) the intention of the State to give that effect to the signature appears from the full powers of its representative or was expressed during the negotiation.

2. For the purposes of paragraph 1:

(a) the initialling of a text constitutes a signature of the treaty when it is established that the negotiating States so agreed;

(b) the signature ad referendum of a treaty by a representative, if confirmed by his State, constitutes a full signature of the treaty.

Article 13: Consent to be bound by a treaty expressed by an exchange of instruments constituting a treaty

The consent of States to be bound by a treaty constituted by instruments exchanged between them is expressed by that exchange when:

(a) the instruments provide that their exchange shall have that effect; or

(b) it is otherwise established that those States were agreed that the exchange of instruments should have that effect.

Article 14: Consent to be bound by a treaty expressed by ratification, acceptance or approval

1. The consent of a State to be bound by a treaty is expressed by ratification when:

(a) the treaty provides for such consent to be expressed by means of ratification;

(b) it is otherwise established that the negotiating States were agreed that ratification should be required;

(c) the representative of the State has signed the treaty subject to ratification; or

(d) the intention of the State to sign the treaty subject to ratification appears from the full powers of its representative or was expressed during the negotiation.

2. The consent of a State to be bound by a treaty is expressed by acceptance or approval under conditions similar to those which apply to ratification.

Article 15: Consent to be bound by a treaty expressed by accession
The consent of a State to be bound by a treaty is expressed by accession when:

(a) the treaty provides that such consent may be expressed by that State by means of accession;

(b) it is otherwise established that the negotiating States were agreed that such consent may be expressed by that State by means of accession; or

(c) all the parties have subsequently agreed that such consent may be expressed by that State by means of accession.

Article 16: Exchange or deposit of instruments
of ratification, acceptance, approval or accession
Unless the treaty otherwise provides, instruments of ratification, acceptance, approval or accession establish the consent of a State to be bound by a treaty upon:

(a) their exchange between the contracting States;

(b) their deposit with the depositary; or

(c) their notification to the contracting States or to the depositary, if so agreed.

Article 17: Consent to be bound by part
of a treaty and choice of differing provisions
1. Without prejudice to articles 19 to 23, the consent of a State to be bound by part of a treaty is effective only if the treaty so permits or the other contracting States so agree.

2. The consent of a State to be bound by a treaty which permits a choice between differing provisions is effective only if it is made clear to which of the provisions the consent relates.

Article 18: Obligation not to defeat the object
and purpose of a treaty prior to its entry into force
A State is obliged to refrain from acts which would defeat the object and purpose of a treaty when:

(a) it has signed the treaty or has exchanged instruments constituting the treaty subject to ratification, acceptance or approval, until it shall have made its intention clear not to become a party to the treaty; or

(b) it has expressed its consent to be bound by the treaty, pending the entry into force of the treaty and provided that such entry into force is not unduly delayed.

Section 2: Reservations

Article 19: Formulation of reservations

A State may, when signing, ratifying, accepting, approving or acceding to a treaty, formulate a reservation unless:

(a) the reservation is prohibited by the treaty;

(b) the treaty provides that only specified reservations, which do not include the reservation in question, may be made; or

(c) in cases not falling under sub-paragraphs (a) and (b), the reservation is incompatible with the object and purpose of the treaty.

Article 20: Acceptance of and objection to reservations

1. A reservation expressly authorized by a treaty does not require any subsequent acceptance by the other contracting States unless the treaty so provides.

2. When it appears from the limited number of the negotiating States and the object and purpose of a treaty that the application of the treaty in its entirety between all the parties is an essential condition of the consent of each one to be bound by the treaty, a reservation requires acceptance by all the parties.

3. When a treaty is a constituent instrument of an international organization and unless it otherwise provides, a reservation requires the acceptance of the competent organ of that organization.

4. In cases not falling under the preceding paragraphs and unless the treaty otherwise provides:

(a) acceptance by another contracting State of a reservation constitutes the reserving State a party to the treaty in relation to that other State if or when the treaty is in force for those States;

(b) an objection by another contracting State to a reservation does not preclude the entry into force of the treaty as between the objecting and reserving States unless a contrary intention is definitely expressed by the objecting State;

(c) an act expressing a State's consent to be bound by the treaty and containing a reservation is effective as soon as at least one other contracting State has accepted the reservation.

5. For the purposes of paragraphs 2 and 4 and unless the treaty otherwise provides, a reservation is considered to have been accepted by a State if it shall have raised no objection to the reservation by the end of a period of twelve months after it was notified of the reservation or by the date on which it expressed its consent to be bound by the treaty, whichever is later.

Article 21: Legal effects of reservations and of objections to reservations

1. A reservation established with regard to another party in accordance with articles 19, 20 and 23:

(a) modifies for the reserving State in its relations with that other party the provisions of the treaty to which the reservation relates to the extent of the reservation; and

(b) modifies those provisions to the same extent for that other party in its relations with the reserving State.

2. The reservation does not modify the provisions of the treaty for the other parties to the treaty inter se.

3. When a State objecting to a reservation has not opposed the entry into force of the treaty between itself and the reserving State, the provisions to which the reservation relates do not apply as between the two States to the extent of the reservation.

Article 22: Withdrawal of reservations and of objections to reservations

1. Unless the treaty otherwise provides, a reservation may be withdrawn at any time and the consent of a State which has accepted the reservation is not required for its withdrawal.

2. Unless the treaty otherwise provides, an objection to a reservation may be withdrawn at any time.

3. Unless the treaty otherwise provides, or it is otherwise agreed:

(a) the withdrawal of a reservation becomes operative in relation to another contracting State only when notice of it has been received by that State;

(b) the withdrawal of an objection to a reservation becomes operative only when notice of it has been received by the State which formulated the reservation.

Article 23: Procedure regarding reservations

1. A reservation, an express acceptance of a reservation and an objection to a reservation must be formulated in writing and communicated to the contracting States and other States entitled to become parties to the treaty.

2. If formulated when signing the treaty subject to ratification, acceptance or approval, a reservation must be formally confirmed by the reserving State when expressing its consent to be bound by the treaty. In such a case the reservation shall be considered as having been made on the date of its confirmation.

3. An express acceptance of, or an objection to, a reservation made previously to confirmation of the reservation does not itself require confirmation.

4. The withdrawal of a reservation or of an objection to a reservation must be formulated in writing.

Section 3: Entry into Force and Provisional Application of Treaties

Article 24: Entry into force

1. A treaty enters into force in such manner and upon such date as it may provide or as the negotiating States may agree.

2. Failing any such provision or agreement, a treaty enters into force as

soon as consent to be bound by the treaty has been established for all the negotiating States.

3. When the consent of a State to be bound by a treaty is established on a date after the treaty has come into force, the treaty enters into force for that State on that date, unless the treaty otherwise provides.

4. The provisions of a treaty regulating the authentication of its text, the establishment of the consent of States to be bound by the treaty, the manner or date of its entry into force, reservations, the functions of the depositary and other matters arising necessarily before the entry into force of the treaty apply from the time of the adoption of its text.

Article 25: Provisional application
1. A treaty or a part of a treaty is applied provisionally pending its entry into force if:
(a) the treaty itself so provides; or
(b) the negotiating States have in some other manner so agreed.

2. Unless the treaty otherwise provides or the negotiating States have otherwise agreed, the provisional application of a treaty or a part of a treaty with respect to a State shall be terminated if that State notifies the other States between which the treaty is being applied provisionally of its intention not to become a party to the treaty.

Part III: Observance, Application and Interpretation of Treaties

Section 1: Observance of Treaties

Article 26: Pacta sunt servanda
Every treaty in force is binding upon the parties to it and must be performed by them in good faith.

Article 27: Internal law and observance of treaties
A party may not invoke the provisions of its internal law as justification for its failure to perform a treaty. This rule is without prejudice to article 46.

Section 2: Application of Treaties

Article 28: Non-retroactivity of treaties
Unless a different intention appears from the treaty or is otherwise established, its provisions do not bind a party in relation to any act or fact which took place or any situation which ceased to exist before the date of the entry into force of the treaty with respect to that party.

Article 29: Territorial scope of treaties

Unless a different intention appears from the treaty or is otherwise established, a treaty is binding upon each party in respect of its entire territory.

Article 30: Application of successive treaties relating to the same subject-matter

1. Subject to Article 103 of the Charter of the United Nations, the rights and obligations of States parties to successive treaties relating to the same subject-matter shall be determined in accordance with the following paragraphs.

2. When a treaty specifies that it is subject to, or that it is not to be considered as incompatible with, an earlier or later treaty, the provisions of that other treaty prevail.

3. When all the parties to the earlier treaty are parties also to the later treaty but the earlier treaty is not terminated or suspended in operation under article 59, the earlier treaty applies only to the extent that its provisions are compatible with those of the latter treaty.

4. When the parties to the later treaty do not include all the parties to the earlier one:

(a) as between States parties to both treaties the same rule applies as in paragraph 3;

(b) as between a State party to both treaties and a State party to only one of the treaties, the treaty to which both States are parties governs their mutual rights and obligations.

5. Paragraph 4 is without prejudice to article 41, or to any question of the termination or suspension of the operation of a treaty under article 60 or to any question of responsibility which may arise for a State from the conclusion or application of a treaty the provisions of which are incompatible with its obligations towards another State under another treaty.

Section 3: Interpretation of Treaties

Article 31: General rule of interpretation

1. A treaty shall be interpreted in good faith in accordance with the ordinary meaning to be given to the terms of the treaty in their context and in the light of its object and purpose.

2. The context for the purpose of the interpretation of a treaty shall comprise, in addition to the text, including its preamble and annexes:

(a) any agreement relating to the treaty which was made between all the parties in connection with the conclusion of the treaty;

(b) any instrument which was made by one or more parties in connection with the conclusion of the treaty and accepted by the other parties as an instrument related to the treaty.

3. There shall be taken into account, together with the context:

(a) any subsequent agreement between the parties regarding the interpretation of the treaty or the application of its provisions;

(b) any subsequent practice in the application of the treaty which establishes the agreement of the parties regarding its interpretation;

(c) any relevant rules of international law applicable in the relations between the parties.

4. A special meaning shall be given to a term if it is established that the parties so intended.

Article 32: Supplementary means of interpretation

Recourse may be had to supplementary means of interpretation, including the preparatory work of the treaty and the circumstances of its conclusion, in order to confirm the meaning resulting from the application of article 31, or to determine the meaning when the interpretation according to article 31:

(a) leaves the meaning ambiguous or obscure; or

(b) leads to a result which is manifestly absurd or unreasonable.

Article 33: Interpretation of treaties
authenticated in two or more languages

1. When a treaty has been authenticated in two or more languages, the text is equally authoritative in each language, unless the treaty provides or the parties agree that, in case of divergence, a particular text shall prevail.

2. A version of the treaty in a language other than one of those in which the text was authenticated shall be considered an authentic text only if the treaty so provides or the parties so agree.

3. The terms of the treaty are presumed to have the same meaning in each authentic text.

4. Except where a particular text prevails in accordance with paragraph 1, when a comparison of the authentic texts discloses a difference of meaning which the application of articles 31 and 32 does not remove, the meaning which best reconciles the texts, having regard to the object and purpose of the treaty, shall be adopted.

Section 4: Treaties and Third States

Article 34: General rule regarding third States

A treaty does not create either obligations or rights for a third State without its consent.

Article 35: Treaties providing
for obligations for third States

An obligation arises for a third State from a provision of a treaty if the parties to the treaty intend the provision to be the means of establishing the obligation and the third State expressly accepts that obligation in writing.

Article 36: Treaties providing for rights for third States

1. A right arises for a third State from a provision of a treaty if the parties to the treaty intend the provision to accord that right either to the third State, or to a group of States to which it belongs, or to all States, and the third State assents thereto. Its assent shall be presumed so long as the contrary is not indicated, unless the treaty otherwise provides.

2. A State exercising a right in accordance with paragraph 1 shall comply with the conditions for its exercise provided for in the treaty or established in conformity with the treaty.

Article 37: Revocation or modification
of obligations or rights of third States

1. When an obligation has arisen for a third State in conformity with article 35, the obligation may be revoked or modified only with the consent of the parties to the treaty and of the third State, unless it is established that they had otherwise agreed.

2. When a right has arisen for a third State in conformity with article 36, the right may not be revoked or modified by the parties if it is established that the right was intended not to be revocable or subject to modification without the consent of the third State.

Article 38: Rules in a treaty becoming binding
on third States through international custom

Nothing in articles 34 to 37 precludes a rule set forth in a treaty from becoming binding upon a third State as a customary rule of international law, recognized as such.

Part IV:
Amendment and Modification of Treaties

Article 39: General rule regarding the amendment of treaties

A treaty may be amended by agreement between the parties. The rules laid down in Part II apply to such an agreement except in so far as the treaty may otherwise provide.

Article 40: Amendment of multilateral treaties

1. Unless the treaty otherwise provides, the amendment of multilateral treaties shall be governed by the following paragraphs.

2. Any proposal to amend a multilateral treaty as between all the parties must be notified to all the contracting States, each one of which shall have the right to take part in:

(a) the decision as to the action to be taken in regard to such proposal;

(b) the negotiation and conclusion of any agreement for the amendment of the treaty.

3. Every State entitled to become a party to the treaty shall also be entitled to become a party to the treaty as amended.

4. The amending agreement does not bind any State already a party to the treaty which does not become a party to the amending agreement; article 30, paragraph 4(b), applies in relation to such State.

5. Any State which becomes a party to the treaty after the entry into force of the amending agreement shall, failing an expression of a different intention by that State:

(a) be considered as a party to the treaty as amended; and

(b) be considered as a party to the unamended treaty in relation to any party to the treaty not bound by the amending agreement.

Article 41: Agreements to modify multilateral treaties between certain of the parties only

1. Two or more of the parties to a multilateral treaty may conclude an agreement to modify the treaty as between themselves alone if:

(a) the possibility of such a modification is provided for by the treaty; or

(b) the modification in question is not prohibited by the treaty and:

(i) does not affect the enjoyment by the other parties of their rights under the treaty or the performance of their obligations;

(ii) does not relate to a provision, derogation from which is incompatible with the effective execution of the object and purpose of the treaty as a whole.

2. Unless in a case falling under paragraph 1(a) the treaty otherwise provides, the parties in question shall notify the other parties of their intention to conclude the agreement and of the modification to the treaty for which it provides.

Part V: Invalidity, Termination and Suspension of the Operation of Treaties

Section 1: General Provisions

Article 42: Validity and continuance in force of treaties

1. The validity of a treaty or of the consent of a State to be bound by a treaty may be impeached only through the application of the present Convention.

2. The termination of a treaty, its denunciation or the withdrawal of a party, may take place only as a result of the application of the provisions of the treaty or of the present Convention. The same rule applies to suspension of the operation of a treaty.

Article 43: Obligations imposed by international law independently of a treaty

The invalidity, termination or denunciation of a treaty, the withdrawal of a party from it, or the suspension of its operation, as a result of the application of the present Convention or of the provisions of the treaty, shall not in any way impair the duty of any State to fulfil any obligation embodied in the treaty to which it would be subject under international law independently of the treaty.

Article 44: Separability of treaty provisions

1. A right of a party, provided for in a treaty or arising under article 56, to denounce, withdraw from or suspend the operation of the treaty may be exercised only with respect to the whole treaty unless the treaty otherwise provides or the parties otherwise agree.

2. A ground for invalidating, terminating, withdrawing from or suspending the operation of a treaty recognized in the present Convention may be invoked only with respect to the whole treaty except as provided in the following paragraphs or in article 60.

3. If the ground relates solely to particular clauses, it may be invoked only with respect to those clauses where:

(a) the said clauses are separable from the remainder of the treaty with regard to their application;

(b) it appears from the treaty or is otherwise established that acceptance of those clauses was not an essential basis of the consent of the other party or parties to be bound by the treaty as a whole; and

(c) continued performance of the remainder of the treaty would not be unjust.

4. In cases falling under articles 49 and 50 the State entitled to invoke the fraud or corruption may do so with respect either to the whole treaty or, subject to paragraph 3, to the particular clauses alone.

5. In cases falling under articles 51, 52 and 53, no separation of the provisions of the treaty is permitted.

Article 45: Loss of a right to invoke a ground for invalidating, terminating, withdrawing from or suspending the operation of a treaty

A State may no longer invoke a ground for invalidating, terminating, withdrawing from or suspending the operation of a treaty under articles 46 to 50 or articles 60 and 62 if, after becoming aware of the facts:

(a) it shall have expressly agreed that the treaty is valid or remains in force or continues in operation, as the case may be; or

(b) it must by reason of its conduct be considered as having acquiesced in the validity of the treaty or in its maintenance in force or in operation, as the case may be.

Section 2: Invalidity of Treaties

Article 46: Provisions of internal law regarding competence to conclude treaties

1. A State may not invoke the fact that its consent to be bound by a treaty has been expressed in violation of a provision of its internal law regarding

competence to conclude treaties as invalidating its consent unless that violation was manifest and concerned a rule of its internal law of fundamental importance.

2. A violation is manifest if it would be objectively evident to any State conducting itself in the matter in accordance with normal practice and in good faith.

Article 47: Specific restrictions on
authority to express the consent of a State

If the authority of a representative to express the consent of a State to be bound by a particular treaty has been made subject to a specific restriction, his omission to observe that restriction may not be invoked as invalidating the consent expressed by him unless the restriction was notified to the other negotiating States prior to his expressing such consent.

Article 48: Error

1. A State may invoke an error in a treaty as invalidating its consent to be bound by the treaty if the error relates to a fact or situation which was assumed by that State to exist at the time when the treaty was concluded and formed an essential basis of its consent to be bound by the treaty.

2. Paragraph 1 shall not apply if the State in question contributed by its own conduct to the error or if the circumstances were such as to put that State on notice of a possible error.

3. An error relating only to the wording of the text of a treaty does not affect its validity; article 79 then applies.

Article 49: Fraud

If a State has been induced to conclude a treaty by the fraudulent conduct of another negotiating State, the State may invoke the fraud as invalidating its consent to be bound by the treaty.

Article 50: Corruption of a representative of a State

If the expression of a State's consent to be bound by a treaty has been procured through the corruption of its representative directly or indirectly by another negotiating State, the State may invoke such corruption as invalidating its consent to be bound by the treaty.

Article 51: Coercion of a representative of a State

The expression of a State's consent to be bound by a treaty which has been procured by the coercion of its representative through acts or threats directed against him shall be without any legal effect.

Article 52: Coercion of a State by the threat or use of force

A treaty is void if its conclusion has been procured by the threat or use of force in violation of the principles of international law embodied in the Charter of the United Nations.

Article 53: Treaties conflicting with a peremptory norm of general international law (jus cogens)

A treaty is void if, at the time of its conclusion, it conflicts with a peremptory norm of general international law. For the purposes of the present Convention, a peremptory norm of general international law is a norm accepted and recognized by the international community of States as a whole as a norm from which no derogation is permitted and which can be modified only by a subsequent norm of general international law having the same character.

Section 3: Termination and Suspension of the Operation of Treaties

Article 54: Termination of or withdrawal from a treaty under its provisions or by consent of the parties

The termination of a treaty or the withdrawal of a party may take place:

(a) in conformity with the provisions of the treaty; or

(b) at any time by consent of all the parties after consultation with the other contracting States.

Article 55: Reduction of the parties to a multilateral treaty below the number necessary for its entry into force

Unless the treaty otherwise provides, a multilateral treaty does not terminate by reason only of the fact that the number of the parties falls below the number necessary for its entry into force.

Article 56: Denunciation of or withdrawal from a treaty containing no provision regarding termination, denunciation or withdrawal

1. A treaty which contains no provision regarding its termination and which does not provide for denunciation or withdrawal is not subject to denunciation or withdrawal unless:

(a) it is established that the parties intended to admit the possibility of denunciation or withdrawal; or

(b) a right of denunciation or withdrawal may be implied by the nature of the treaty.

2. A party shall give not less than twelve months' notice of its intention to denounce or withdraw from a treaty under paragraph 1.

Article 57: Suspension of the operation of a treaty under its provisions or by consent of the parties

The operation of a treaty in regard to all the parties or to a particular party may be suspended:

(a) in conformity with the provisions of the treaty; or

(b) at any time by consent of all the parties after consultation with the other contracting States.

Article 58: Suspension of the operation of a multilateral treaty by agreement between certain of the parties only

1. Two or more parties to a multilateral treaty may conclude an agreement to suspend the operation of provisions of the treaty, temporarily and as between themselves alone, if:

(a) the possibility of such a suspension is provided for by the treaty; or

(b) the suspension in question is not prohibited by the treaty and: (i) does not affect the enjoyment by the other parties of their rights under the treaty or the performance of their obligations; (ii) is not incompatible with the object and purpose of the treaty.

2. Unless in a case falling under paragraph 1(a) the treaty otherwise provides, the parties in question shall notify the other parties of their intention to conclude the agreement and of those provisions of the treaty the operation of which they intend to suspend.

Article 59: Termination or suspension of the operation of a treaty implied by conclusion of a later treaty

1. A treaty shall be considered as terminated if all the parties to it conclude a later treaty relating to the same subject-matter and:

(a) it appears from the later treaty or is otherwise established that the parties intended that the matter should be governed by that treaty; or

(b) the provisions of the later treaty are so far incompatible with those of the earlier one that the two treaties are not capable of being applied at the same time.

2. The earlier treaty shall be considered as only suspended in operation if it appears from the later treaty or is otherwise established that such was the intention of the parties.

Article 60: Termination or suspension of the operation of a treaty as a consequence of its breach

1. A material breach of a bilateral treaty by one of the parties entitles the other to invoke the breach as a ground for terminating the treaty or suspending its operation in whole or in part.

2. A material breach of a multilateral treaty by one of the parties entitles:

(a) the other parties by unanimous agreement to suspend the operation of the treaty in whole or in part or to terminate it either: (i) in the relations between themselves and the defaulting State, or (ii) as between all the parties;

(b) a party specially affected by the breach to invoke it as a ground for suspending the operation of the treaty in whole or in part in the relations between itself and the defaulting State;

(c) any party other than the defaulting State to invoke the breach as a ground for suspending the operation of the treaty in whole or in part with respect to itself if the treaty is of such a character that a material breach of its provisions by one party radically changes the position of every party with respect to the further performance of its obligations under the treaty.

3. A material breach of a treaty, for the purposes of this article, consists in:

(a) a repudiation of the treaty not sanctioned by the present Convention; or

(b) the violation of a provision essential to the accomplishment of the object or purpose of the treaty.

4. The foregoing paragraphs are without prejudice to any provision in the treaty applicable in the event of a breach.

5. Paragraphs 1 to 3 do not apply to provisions relating to the protection of the human person contained in treaties of a humanitarian character, in particular to provisions prohibiting any form of reprisals against persons protected by such treaties.

Article 61: Supervening impossibility of performance

1. A party may invoke the impossibility of performing a treaty as a ground for terminating or withdrawing from it if the impossibility results from the permanent disappearance or destruction of an object indispensable for the execution of the treaty. If the impossibility is temporary, it may be invoked only as a ground for suspending the operation of the treaty.

2. Impossibility of performance may not be invoked by a party as a ground for terminating, withdrawing from or suspending the operation of a treaty if the impossibility is the result of a breach by that party either of an obligation under the treaty or of any other international obligation owed to any other party to the treaty.

Article 62: Fundamental change of circumstances

1. A fundamental change of circumstances which has occurred with regard to those existing at the time of the conclusion of a treaty, and which was not foreseen by the parties, may not be invoked as a ground for terminating or withdrawing from the treaty unless:

(a) the existence of those circumstances constituted an essential basis of the consent of the parties to be bound by the treaty; and

(b) the effect of the change is radically to transform the extent of obligations still to be performed under the treaty.

2. A fundamental change of circumstances may not be invoked as a ground for terminating or withdrawing from a treaty:

(a) if the treaty establishes a boundary; or

(b) if the fundamental change is the result of a breach by the party invoking it either of an obligation under the treaty or of any other international obligation owed to any other party to the treaty.

3. If, under the foregoing paragraphs, a party may invoke a fundamental change of circumstances as a ground for terminating or withdrawing from a

treaty it may also invoke the change as a ground for suspending the operation of the treaty.

Article 63: Severance of diplomatic or consular relations

The severance of diplomatic or consular relations between parties to a treaty does not affect the legal relations established between them by the treaty except in so far as the existence of diplomatic or consular relations is indispensable for the application of the treaty.

Article 64: Emergence of a new peremptory norm of general international law (jus cogens)

If a new peremptory norm of general international law emerges, any existing treaty which is in conflict with that norm becomes void and terminates.

Section 4: Procedure

Article 65: Procedure to be followed with respect to invalidity, termination, withdrawal from or suspension of the operation of a treaty

1. A party which, under the provisions of the present Convention, invokes either a defect in its consent to be bound by a treaty or a ground for impeaching the validity of a treaty, terminating it, withdrawing from it or suspending its operation, must notify the other parties of its claim. The notification shall indicate the measure proposed to be taken with respect to the treaty and the reasons therefor.

2. If, after the expiry of a period which, except in cases of special urgency, shall not be less than three months after the receipt of the notification, no party has raised any objection, the party making the notification may carry out in the manner provided in article 67 the measure which it has proposed.

3. If, however, objection has been raised by any other party, the parties shall seek a solution through the means indicated in article 33 of the Charter of the United Nations.

4. Nothing in the foregoing paragraphs shall affect the rights or obligations of the parties under any provisions in force binding the parties with regard to the settlement of disputes.

5. Without prejudice to article 45, the fact that a State has not previously made the notification prescribed in paragraph 1 shall not prevent it from making such notification in answer to another party claiming performance of the treaty or alleging its violation.

Article 66: Procedures for judicial settlement, arbitration and conciliation

If, under paragraph 3 of article 65, no solution has been reached within a period of 12 months following the date on which the objection was raised, the following procedures shall be followed:

(a) any one of the parties to a dispute concerning the application or the interpretation of articles 53 or 64 may, by a written application, submit it to the International Court of Justice for a decision unless the parties by common consent agree to submit the dispute to arbitration;

(b) any one of the parties to a dispute concerning the application or the interpretation of any of the other articles in Part V of the present Convention may set in motion the procedure specified in the Annex to the Convention by submitting a request to that effect to the Secretary-General of the United Nations.

Article 67: Instruments for declaring invalid, terminating, withdrawing from or suspending the operation of a treaty

1. The notification provided for under article 65 paragraph 1 must be made in writing.

2. Any act declaring invalid, terminating, withdrawing from or suspending the operation of a treaty pursuant to the provisions of the treaty or of paragraphs 2 or 3 of article 65 shall be carried out through an instrument communicated to the other parties. If the instrument is not signed by the Head of State, Head of Government or Minister for Foreign Affairs, the representative of the State communicating it may be called upon to produce full powers.

Article 68: Revocation of notifications and instruments provided for in articles 65 and 67

A notification or instrument provided for in articles 65 or 67 may be revoked at any time before it takes effect.

Section 5: Consequences of the Invalidity, Termination or Suspension of the Operation of a Treaty

Article 69: Consequences of the invalidity of a treaty

1. A treaty the invalidity of which is established under the present Convention is void. The provisions of a void treaty have no legal force.

2. If acts have nevertheless been performed in reliance on such a treaty:

(a) each party may require any other party to establish as far as possible in their mutual relations the position that would have existed if the acts had not been performed;

(b) acts performed in good faith before the invalidity was invoked are not rendered unlawful by reason only of the invalidity of the treaty.

3. In cases falling under articles 49, 50, 51 or 52, paragraph 2 does not apply with respect to the party to which the fraud, the act of corruption or the coercion is imputable.

4. In the case of the invalidity of a particular State's consent to be bound by a multilateral treaty, the foregoing rules apply in the relations between that State and the parties to the treaty.

Article 70: Consequences of the termination of a treaty

1. Unless the treaty otherwise provides or the parties otherwise agree, the termination of a treaty under its provisions or in accordance with the present Convention:

(a) releases the parties from any obligation further to perform the treaty;

(b) does not affect any right, obligation or legal situation of the parties created through the execution of the treaty prior to its termination.

2. If a State denounces or withdraws from a multilateral treaty, paragraph 1 applies in the relations between that State and each of the other parties to the treaty from the date when such denunciation or withdrawal takes effect.

Article 71: Consequences of the invalidity of a treaty which conflicts with a peremptory norm of general international law

1. In the case of a treaty which is void under article 53 the parties shall:

(a) eliminate as far as possible the consequences of any act performed in reliance on any provision which conflicts with the peremptory norm of general international law; and

(b) bring their mutual relations into conformity with the peremptory norm of general international law.

2. In the case of a treaty which becomes void and terminates under article 64, the termination of the treaty:

(a) releases the parties from any obligation further to perform the treaty;

(b) does not affect any right, obligation or legal situation of the parties created through the execution of the treaty prior to its termination; provided that those rights, obligations or situations may thereafter be maintained only to the extent that their maintenance is not in itself in conflict with the new peremptory norm of general international law.

Article 72: Consequences of the suspension of the operation of a treaty

1. Unless the treaty otherwise provides or the parties otherwise agree, the suspension of the operation of a treaty under its provisions or in accordance with the present Convention:

(a) releases the parties between which the operation of the treaty is suspended from the obligation to perform the treaty in their mutual relations during the period of the suspension;

(b) does not otherwise affect the legal relations between the parties established by the treaty.

2. During the period of the suspension the parties shall refrain from acts tending to obstruct the resumption of the operation of the treaty.

Part VI: Miscellaneous Provisions

Article 73: Cases of State succession,
State responsibility and outbreak of hostilities
The provisions of the present Convention shall not prejudge any question that may arise in regard to a treaty from a succession of States or from the international responsibility of a State or from the outbreak of hostilities between States.

Article 74: Diplomatic and consular
relations and the conclusion of treaties
The severance or absence of diplomatic or consular relations between two or more States does not prevent the conclusion of treaties between those States. The conclusion of a treaty does not in itself affect the situation in regard to diplomatic or consular relations.

Article 75: Case of an aggressor State
The provisions of the present Convention are without prejudice to any obligation in relation to a treaty which may arise for an aggressor State in consequence of measures taken in conformity with the Charter of the United Nations with reference to that State's aggression.

Part VII: Depositaries,
Notifications, Corrections and Registration

Article 76: Depositaries of treaties
1. The designation of the depositary of a treaty may be made by the negotiating States, either in the treaty itself or in some other manner. The depositary may be one or more States, an international organization or the chief administrative officer of the organization.

2. The functions of the depositary of a treaty are international in character and the depositary is under an obligation to act impartially in their performance. In particular, the fact that a treaty has not entered into force between certain of the parties or that a difference has appeared between a State and a depositary with regard to the performance of the latter's functions shall not affect that obligation.

Article 77: Functions of depositaries
1. The functions of a depositary, unless otherwise provided in the treaty or agreed by the contracting States, comprise in particular:
(a) keeping custody of the original text of the treaty and of any full powers delivered to the depositary;
(b) preparing certified copies of the original text and preparing any fur-

ther text of the treaty in such additional languages as may be required by the treaty and transmitting them to the parties and to the States entitled to become parties to the treaty;

(c) receiving any signatures to the treaty and receiving and keeping custody of any instruments, notifications and communications relating to it;

(d) examining whether the signature or any instrument, notification or communication relating to the treaty is in due and proper form and, if need be, bringing the matter to the attention of the State in question;

(e) informing the parties and the States entitled to become parties to the treaty of acts, notifications and communications relating to the treaty;

(f) informing the States entitled to become parties to the treaty when the number of signatures or of instruments of ratification, acceptance, approval or accession required for the entry into force of the treaty has been received or deposited;

(g) registering the treaty with the Secretariat of the United Nations;

(h) performing the functions specified in other provisions of the present Convention.

2. In the event of any difference appearing between a State and the depositary as to the performance of the latter's functions, the depositary shall bring the question to the attention of the signatory States and the contracting States or, where appropriate, of the competent organ of the international organization concerned.

Article 78: Notifications and communications

Except as the treaty or the present Convention otherwise provide, any notification or communication to be made by any State under the present Convention shall:

(a) if there is no depositary, be transmitted direct to the States for which it is intended, or if there is a depositary, to the latter;

(b) be considered as having been made by the State in question only upon its receipt by the State to which it was transmitted or, as the case may be, upon its receipt by the depositary;

(c) if transmitted to a depositary, be considered as received by the State for which it was intended only when the latter State has been informed by the depositary in accordance with article 77, paragraph 1(e).

Article 79: Correction of errors in texts or in certified copies of treaties

1. Where, after the authentication of the text of a treaty, the signatory States and the contracting States are agreed that it contains an error, the error shall, unless they decide upon some other means of correction, be corrected:

(a) by having the appropriate correction made in the text and causing the correction to be initialled by duly authorized representatives;

(b) by executing or exchanging an instrument or instruments setting out the correction which it has been agreed to make; or

(c) by executing a corrected text of the whole treaty by the same procedure as in the case of the original text.

2. Where the treaty is one for which there is a depositary, the latter shall notify the signatory States and the contracting States of the error and of the proposal to correct it and shall specify an appropriate time-limit within which objection to the proposed correction may be raised. If, on the expiry of the time-limit:

(a) no objection has been raised, the depositary shall make and initial the correction in the text and shall execute a procés-verbal of the rectification of the text and communicate a copy of it to the parties and to the States entitled to become parties to the treaty;

(b) an objection has been raised, the depositary shall communicate the objection to the signatory States and to the contracting States.

3. The rules in paragraphs 1 and 2 apply also where the text has been authenticated in two or more languages and it appears that there is a lack of concordance which the signatory States and the contracting States agree should be corrected.

4. The corrected text replaces the defective text ab initio, unless the signatory States and the contracting States otherwise decide.

5. The correction of the text of a treaty that has been registered shall be notified to the Secretariat of the United Nations.

6. Where an error is discovered in a certified copy of a treaty, the depositary shall execute a procés-verbal specifying the rectification and communicate a copy of it to the signatory States and to the contracting States.

Article 80: Registration and publication of treaties

1. Treaties shall, after their entry into force, be transmitted to the Secretariat of the United Nations for registration or filing and recording, as the case may be, and for publication.

2. The designation of a depositary shall constitute authorization for it to perform the acts specified in the preceding paragraph.

Part VIII: Final Provisions

Article 81: Signature

The present Convention shall be open for signature by all States Members of the United Nations or of any of the specialized agencies or of the International Atomic Energy Agency or parties to the Statute of the International Court of Justice, and by any other State invited by the General Assembly of the United Nations to become a party to the Convention, as follows: until 30 November 1969, at the Federal Ministry for Foreign Affairs of the Republic of Austria, and subsequently, until 30 April 1970, at United Nations Headquarters, New York.

Article 82: Ratification
The present Convention is subject to ratification. The instruments of ratification shall be deposited with the Secretary-General of the United Nations.

Article 83: Accession
The present Convention shall remain open for accession by any State belonging to any of the categories mentioned in article 81. The instruments of accession shall be deposited with the Secretary-General of the United Nations.

Article 84: Entry into force
1. The present Convention shall enter into force on the thirtieth day following the date of deposit of the thirty-fifth instrument of ratification or accession.

2. For each State ratifying or acceding to the Convention after the deposit of the thirty-fifth instrument of ratification or accession, the Convention shall enter into force on the thirtieth day after deposit by such State of its instrument of ratification or accession.

Article 85: Authentic texts
The original of the present Convention, of which the Chinese, English, French, Russian and Spanish texts are equally authentic, shall be deposited with the Secretary-General of the United Nations.

IN WITNESS WHEREOF the undersigned Plenipotentiaries, being duly authorized thereto by their respective Governments, have signed the present Convention.

DONE at Vienna, this twenty-third day of May, one thousand nine hundred and sixty-nine.

Annex

1. A list of conciliators consisting of qualified jurists shall be drawn up and maintained by the Secretary-General of the United Nations. To this end, every State which is a Member of the United Nations or a party to the present Convention shall be invited to nominate two conciliators, and the names of the persons so nominated shall constitute the list. The term of a conciliator, including that of any conciliator nominated to fill a casual vacancy, shall be five years and may be renewed. A conciliator whose term expires shall continue to fulfil any function for which he shall have been chosen under the following paragraph.

2. When a request has been made to the Secretary-General under article 66, the Secretary-General shall bring the dispute before a conciliation commission constituted as follows:

The State or States constituting one of the parties to the dispute shall appoint:

(a) one conciliator of the nationality of that State or of one of those States, who may or may not be chosen from the list referred to in paragraph 1; and

(b) one conciliator not of the nationality of that State or of any of those States, who shall be chosen from the list.

The State or States constituting the other party to the dispute shall appoint two conciliators in the same way. The four conciliators chosen by the parties shall be appointed within sixty days following the date on which the Secretary-General receives the request.

The four conciliators shall, within sixty days following the date of the last of their own appointments, appoint a fifth conciliator chosen from the list, who shall be chairman.

If the appointment of the chairman or of any of the other conciliators has not been made within the period prescribed above for such appointment, it shall be made by the Secretary-General within sixty days following the expiry of that period. The appointment of the chairman may be made by the Secretary-General either from the list or from the membership of the International Law Commission. Any of the periods within which appointments must be made may be extended by agreement between the parties to the dispute.

Any vacancy shall be filled in the manner prescribed for the initial appointment.

3. The Conciliation Commission shall decide its own procedure. The Commission, with the consent of the parties to the dispute, may invite any party to the treaty to submit to it its views orally or in writing. Decisions and recommendations of the Commission shall be made by a majority vote of the five members.

4. The Commission may draw the attention of the parties to the dispute to any measures which might facilitate an amicable settlement.

5. The Commission shall hear the parties, examine the claims and objections, and make proposals to the parties with a view to reaching an amicable settlement of the dispute.

6. The Commission shall report within twelve months of its constitution. Its report shall be deposited with the Secretary-General and transmitted to the parties to the dispute. The report of the Commission, including any conclusions stated therein regarding the facts or questions of law, shall not be binding upon the parties and it shall have no other character than that of recommendations submitted for the consideration of the parties in order to facilitate an amicable settlement of the dispute.

7. The Secretary-General shall provide the Commission with such assistance and facilities as it may require. The expenses of the Commission shall be borne by the United Nations.

2

International Law
and the Use of Force

2.1
The *Caroline* Case

Correspondence between the governments of the United States and Great Britain in 1841–1842 addressed the question of the circumstances in which self-defense can be legally exercised. The impetus for the discussion was the British seizure of an American steamer, the Caroline, *which had been supplying rebels during the Canadian Rebellion of 1837. The British had sent the* Caroline *over the Niagara Falls, killing two US nationals. What ensured the long-term significance of the ensuing correspondence was that the two sides agreed on the conditions necessary for a valid act of self-defense. Even today, a state exercising the "inherent right" of self-defense recognized in article 51 of the UN Charter must ensure that its use of armed force is necessary (for the objective of defense) and proportional (to the injury threatened).*

On the Caroline *case, see Martin A. Rogoff and Edward Collins, Jr., "The* Caroline *Incident and the Development of International Law,"* Booklyn Journal of International Law *16 (1990): 493–527. On self-defense and the international law pertaining to the use of force more generally, see Stanimir A. Alexandrov,* Self-Defense Against the Use of Force in International Law *(The Hague: Kluwer, 1996); Yoram Dinstein,* War, Aggression, and Self-defense, *3rd ed. (Cambridge: Cambridge University Press, 2001); and Thomas M. Franck,* Recourse to Force: State Action Against Threats and Armed Attacks *(New York: Cambridge University Press, 2002).*

Letter from Mr Webster (US) to Mr Fox of 24 April 1841 (excerpt)

It will be for . . . [her Majesty's] Government to show a necessity of self-defence, instant, overwhelming, leaving no choice of means, and no moment for deliberation. It will be for it to show, also, that the local authorities of Canada, even supposing the necessity of the moment authorised them to enter the territories of The United States at all, did nothing unreasonable or excessive; since the act, justified by the necessity of self-defence, must be limited by that necessity, and kept clearly within it.

Letter from Mr Webster to
Lord Ashburton of 6 August 1842 (excerpt)

Your Lordship's note of the 28th of July, in answer to mine of the 27th of July, respecting the case of the *Caroline* has been received and laid before the President.

The President sees with pleasure that your Lordship fully admits those great principles of public law applicable to cases of this kind, which this Government has expressed; and that on your part, as on ours, respect for the inviolable character of the territory of independent States is deemed the most essential foundation of civilization. And, while it is admitted on both sides that there are exceptions to this rule, he is gratified to find that your Lordship admits that such exceptions must come within the limitations stated, and the terms used in a former communication from this department to the British Plenipotentiary here. Undoubtedly it is just, that while it is admitted that exceptions growing out of the great law of self-defence do exist, those exceptions should be confined to cases in which "the necessity of that self-defence is instant, overwhelming, and leaving no choice of means and no moment for deliberation."

Understanding these principles alike, the difference between the 2 Governments is only whether the facts in the case of the *Caroline* make out a case of such necessity for the purposes of self-defence. Seeing that the transaction is not recent, having happened in the time of one of his predecessors; seeing that your Lordship, in the name of your Government, solemnly declares that no slight or disrespect was intended to the sovereign authority of The United States; seeing that it is acknowledged that, whether justifiable or not, there was yet a violation of the territory of The United States, and that you are instructed to say that your Government consider that as a most serious occurrence; seeing, finally, that it is now admitted that an explanation and apology for this violation was due at the time; the President is content to receive these acknowledgments and assurances in the conciliatory spirit which marks your Lordship's letter, and will make this subject, as a complaint of violation of territory, the topic of no further discussion between the 2 Governments.

2.2
Resolution Authorizing the Gulf War: United Nations Security Council Resolution 678 (1990)

The UN Charter incorporates the principle of collective security by which the illegal use of force by one state is to be met by the use of force by a collectivity of states. The fact that the permanent members were given a veto over substantive decisions of the Security Council severely limited opportunities for the Council to practice collective security during the Cold War. Even the Council's authorization of the use of force against North Korea in response to its invasion of South Korea in 1950 was possible only because the Soviet member of the Security Council was not present when the vote was taken. Resolution 678 was adopted on 29 November 1990 by 12 votes to 2 (Cuba and Yemen), with 1 abstention (China). The prevailing view in the United States and elsewhere has been that resolution 678 symbolized a welcome post–Cold War opportunity for the Security Council to function as originally intended. A minority of commentators has challenged this interpretation of the resolution with the observation that both the use of force against Iraq and that against North Korea were essentially US efforts channeled through the UN so as to gain legitimacy.

See A. Pyrich, "United Nations: Authorizations to Use Force— Security Council Resolution 665, August 25, 1950, and Security Council Resolution 678, November 29, 1990," Harvard International Law Journal *32 (1991): 265–274; and Burns H. Weston, "Security Council Resolution 678 and Persian Gulf Decision–Making: Precarious Legitimacy,"* American Journal of International Law *85 (1991): 516–535.*

The Security Council,

Recalling, and reaffirming its resolutions 660 (1990) of 2 August (1990), 661 (1990) of 6 August 1990, 662 (1990) of 9 August 1990, 664 (1990) of 18 August 1990, 665 (1990) of 25 August 1990, 666 (1990) of 13 September 1990, 667 (1990) of 16 September 1990, 669 (1990) of 24 September 1990,

670 (1990) of 25 September 1990, 674 (1990) of 29 October 1990 and 677 (1990) of 28 November 1990.

Noting that, despite all efforts by the United Nations, Iraq refuses to comply with its obligation to implement resolution 660 (1990) and the above-mentioned subsequent relevant resolutions, in flagrant contempt of the Security Council,

Mindful of its duties and responsibilities under the Charter of the United Nations for the maintenance and preservation of international peace and security,

Determined to secure full compliance with its decisions,

Acting under Chapter VII of the Charter,

1. Demands that Iraq comply fully with resolution 660 (1990) and all subsequent relevant resolutions, and decides, while maintaining all its decisions, to allow Iraq one final opportunity, as a pause of goodwill, to do so;

2. Authorizes Member States co-operating with the Government of Kuwait, unless Iraq on or before 15 January 1991 fully implements, as set forth in paragraph 1 above, the above-mentioned resolutions, to use all necessary means to uphold and implement resolution 660 (1990) and all subsequent relevant resolutions and to restore international peace and security in the area;

3. Requests all States to provide appropriate support for the actions undertaken in pursuance of paragraph 2 of the present resolution;

4. Requests the States concerned to keep the Security Council regularly informed on the progress of actions undertaken pursuant to paragraphs 2 and 3 of the present resolution;

5. Decides to remain seized of the matter.

2.3

The "Cease-Fire Resolution": United Nations Security Council Resolution 687 (1991)

This resolution was adopted on 3 April 1991 by 12 votes to 1 (Cuba) with 2 abstentions (Ecuador, Yemen). The question as to whether resolution 687 suspended or terminated the authorization to use force in resolution 678 has been controversial. Those who would maintain that it merely suspended the authorization assert that the United States and the UK were entitled to use force again without further authorization from the Council should Iraq be in violation of resolution 687. In resolution 1441 (2002) the Security Council decided that Iraq "has been and remains in material breach of . . . resolution 687 (1991), in particular through Iraq's failure to cooperate with United Nations inspectors and the IAEA and to complete the actions required under paragraphs 8 to 13 of resolution 687 (1991)."

On the interpretation of this and other Security Council resolutions, see Michael Byers, "The Shifting Foundations of International Law: A Decade of Forceful Measures against Iraq," European Journal of International Law *13 (2002): 21–41. For an evaluation of the UN Special Commission created by resolution 687, see Charles Duelfer, "Arms Reduction: The Role of International Organizations, the UNSCOM Experience,"* Journal of Conflict and Security Law *5 (2000): 105–122. Resolution 1284 (1999) of 17 December 1999 replaced the Special Commission with the United Nations Monitoring, Verification and Inspection Commission (UNMOVIC). UNMOVIC documents, including Security Council Briefings and Reports, are available at www.unmovic.org.*

The Security Council,

Recalling its resolutions 660 (1990) of 2 August 1990, 661 (1990) of 6 August 1990, 662 (1990) of 9 August 1990, 664 (1990) of 18 August 1990, 665 (1990) of 25 August 1990, 666 (1990) of 13 September 1990, 667 (1990) of 16 September 1990, 669 (1990) of 24 September 1990, 670 (1990) of 25 September 1990, 674 (1990) of 29 October 1990, 677 (1990) of 28

November 1990, 678 (1990) of 29 November 1990 and 686 (1991) of 2 March 1991,

Welcoming the restoration to Kuwait of its sovereignty, independence and territorial integrity and the return of its legitimate Government,

Affirming the commitment of all Member States to the sovereignty, territorial integrity and political independence of Kuwait and Iraq, and noting the intention expressed by the Member States cooperating with Kuwait under paragraph 2 of resolution 678 (1990) to bring their military presence in Iraq to an end as soon as possible consistent with paragraph 8 of resolution 686 (1991),

Reaffirming the need to be assured of Iraq's peaceful intentions in the light of its unlawful invasion and occupation of Kuwait,

Taking note of the letter dated 27 February 1991 from the Deputy Prime Minister and Minister for Foreign Affairs of Iraq addressed to the President of the Security Council and of his letters of the same date addressed to the President of the Council and to the Secretary-General, and those letters dated 3 March and 5 March he addressed to them, pursuant to resolution 686 (1991),

Noting that Iraq and Kuwait, as independent sovereign States, signed at Baghdad on 4 October 1963 "Agreed Minutes Between the State of Kuwait and the Republic of Iraq regarding the restoration of friendly relations, recognition and related matters," thereby formally recognizing the boundary between Iraq and Kuwait and the allocation of islands, which Agreed Minutes were registered with the United Nations in accordance with Article 102 of the Charter of the United Nations and in which Iraq recognized the independence and complete sovereignty of the State of Kuwait with its boundaries as specified in the letter of the Prime Minister of Iraq dated 21 July 1932, and as accepted by the Ruler of Kuwait in his letter dated 10 August 1932,

Conscious of the need for demarcation of the said boundary,

Conscious also of the statements by Iraq threatening to use weapons in violation of its obligations under the Protocol for the Prohibition of the Use in War of Asphyxiating, Poisonous or Other Gases, and of Bacteriological Methods of Warfare, signed at Geneva on 17 June 1925, and of its prior use of chemical weapons, and affirming that grave consequences would follow any further use by Iraq of such weapons,

Recalling that Iraq has subscribed to the Final Declaration adopted by all States participating in the Conference of States Parties to the 1925 Geneva Protocol and Other Interested States, held in Paris from 7 to 11 January 1989, establishing the objective of universal elimination of chemical and biological weapons,

Recalling also that Iraq has signed the Convention on the Prohibition of the Development, Production and Stockpiling of Bacteriological (Biological) and Toxin Weapons and on Their Destruction, of 10 April 1972,

Noting the importance of Iraq ratifying the Convention,

Noting also the importance of all States adhering to this Convention and encouraging its forthcoming Review Conference to reinforce the authority, efficiency and universal scope of the Convention,

Stressing the importance of an early conclusion by the Conference on Disarmament of its work on a Convention on the Universal Prohibition of Chemical Weapons and of universal adherence thereto,

Aware of the use by Iraq of ballistic missiles in unprovoked attacks and therefore of the need to take specific measures in regard to such missiles located in Iraq,

Concerned by the reports in the hands of Member States that Iraq has attempted to acquire materials for a nuclear-weapons programme contrary to its obligations under the Treaty on the Non-Proliferation of Nuclear Weapons of 1 July 1968,

Recalling the objective of the establishment of a nuclear-weapon-free zone in the region of the Middle East,

Conscious of the threat that all weapons of mass destruction pose to peace and security in the area and of the need to work towards the establishment in the Middle East of a zone free of such weapons,

Conscious also of the objective of achieving balanced and comprehensive control of armaments in the region,

Conscious further of the importance of achieving the objectives noted above using all available means, including a dialogue among the States of the region,

Noting that resolution 686 (1991) marked the lifting of the measures imposed by resolution 661 (1990) in so far as they applied to Kuwait,

Noting also that despite the progress being made in fulfilling the obligations of resolution 686 (1991), many Kuwaiti and third State nationals are still not accounted for and property remains unreturned,

Recalling the International Convention against the Taking of Hostages, opened for signature in New York on 18 December 1979, which categorizes all acts of taking hostages as manifestations of international terrorism,

Deploring threats made by Iraq during the recent conflict to make use of terrorism against targets outside Iraq and the taking of hostages by Iraq,

Taking note with grave concern of the reports transmitted by the Secretary-General on 20 March 1991 and 28 March 1991, and conscious of the necessity to meet urgently the humanitarian needs in Kuwait and Iraq,

Bearing in mind its objective of restoring international peace and security in the area as set out in its recent resolutions,

Conscious of the need to take the following measures acting under Chapter VII of the Charter,

1. Affirms all thirteen resolutions noted above, except as expressly changed below to achieve the goals of the present resolution, including a formal cease-fire;

A

2. Demands that Iraq and Kuwait respect the inviolability of the international boundary and the allocation of islands set out in the "Agreed Minutes

Between the State of Kuwait and the Republic of Iraq Regarding the Restoration of Friendly Relations, Recognition and Related Matters," signed by them in the exercise of their sovereignty at Baghdad on 4 October 1963 and registered with the United Nations;

3. Calls upon the Secretary-General to lend his assistance to make arrangements with Iraq and Kuwait to demarcate the boundary between Iraq and Kuwait, drawing on appropriate material including the maps transmitted with the letter dated 28 March 1991 addressed to him by the Permanent Representative of the United Kingdom of Great Britain and Northern Ireland to the United Nations and to report back to the Council within one month;

4. Decides to guarantee the inviolability of the above-mentioned international boundary and to take, as appropriate, all necessary measures to that end in accordance with the Charter of the United Nations;

B

5. Requests the Secretary-General, after consulting with Iraq and Kuwait, to submit within three days to the Council for its approval a plan for the immediate deployment of a United Nations observer unit to monitor the Khawr 'Abd Allah and a demilitarized zone, which is hereby established, extending ten kilometres into Iraq and five kilometres into Kuwait from the boundary referred to in the "Agreed Minutes Between the State of Kuwait and the Republic of Iraq Regarding the Restoration of Friendly Relations, Recognition and Related Matters"; to deter violations of the boundary through its presence in and surveillance of the demilitarized zone and to observe any hostile or potentially hostile action mounted from the territory of one State to the other; and also requests the Secretary-General to report regularly to the Council on the operations of the unit, and to do so immediately if there are serious violations of the zone or potential threats to peace;

6. Notes that as soon as the Secretary-General notifies the Council of the completion of the deployment of the United Nations observer unit, the conditions will be established for the Member States cooperating with Kuwait in accordance with resolution 678 (1990) to bring their military presence in Iraq to an end consistent with resolution 686 (1991);

C

7. Invites Iraq to reaffirm unconditionally its obligations under the Protocol for the Prohibition of the Use in War of Asphyxiating, Poisonous or Other Gases, and of Bacteriological Methods of Warfare, signed at Geneva on 17 June 1925, and to ratify the Convention on the Prohibition of the Development, Production and Stockpiling of Bacteriological (Biological) and Toxin Weapons and on Their Destruction, of 10 April 1972;

8. Decides that Iraq shall unconditionally accept the destruction, removal, or rendering harmless, under international supervision, of:

(a) All chemical and biological weapons and all stocks of agents and all related subsystems and components and all research, development, support and manufacturing facilities related thereto;

(b) All ballistic missiles with a range greater than 150 kilometres, and related major parts and repair and production facilities;

9. Decides also, for the implementation of paragraph 8, the following:

(a) Iraq shall submit to the Secretary-General, within fifteen days of the adoption of the present resolution, a declaration on the locations, amounts and types of all items specified in paragraph 8 and agree to urgent, on-site inspection as specified below;

(b) The Secretary-General, in consultation with the appropriate Governments and, where appropriate, with the Director-General of the World Health Organization, within forty-five days of the adoption of the present resolution shall develop and submit to the Council for approval a plan calling for the completion of the following acts within forty-five days of such approval: (i) The forming of a Special Commission which shall carry out immediate on-site inspection of Iraq's biological, chemical and missile capabilities, based on Iraq's declarations and the designation of any additional locations by the Special Commission itself; (ii) The yielding by Iraq of possession to the Special Commission for destruction, removal or rendering harmless, taking into account the requirements of public safety, of all items specified under paragraph 8 (a), including items at the additional locations designated by the Special Commission under paragraph (i) and the destruction by Iraq, under the supervision of the Special Commission, of all its missile capabilities, including launchers, as specified under paragraph 8 (b); (iii) The provision by the Special Commission to the Director-General of the International Atomic Energy Agency of the assistance and cooperation required in paragraphs 12 and 13;

10. Decides further that Iraq shall unconditionally undertake not to use, develop, construct or acquire any of the items specified in paragraphs 8 and 9, and requests the Secretary-General, in consultation with the Special Commission, to develop a plan for the future ongoing monitoring and verification of Iraq's compliance with the present paragraph, to be submitted to the Council for approval within one hundred and twenty days of the passage of the present resolution;

11. Invites Iraq to reaffirm unconditionally its obligations under the Treaty on the Non-Proliferation of Nuclear Weapons, of 1 July 1968;

12. Decides that Iraq shall unconditionally agree not to acquire or develop nuclear weapons or nuclear-weapon-usable material or any subsystems or components or any research, development, support or manufacturing facilities related to the above; to submit to the Secretary-General and the Director-General of the International Atomic Energy Agency within fifteen days of the adoption of the present resolution a declaration of the locations, amounts and

types of all items specified above; to place all of its nuclear-weapon-usable materials under the exclusive control, for custody and removal, of the Agency, with the assistance and cooperation of the Special Commission as provided for in the plan of the Secretary-General discussed in paragraph 9 (b); to accept, in accordance with the arrangements provided for in paragraph 13, urgent on-site inspection and the destruction, removal or rendering harmless as appropriate of all items specified above; and to accept the plan discussed in paragraph 13 for the future ongoing monitoring and verification of its compliance with these undertakings;

13. Requests the Director-General of the International Atomic Energy Agency, through the Secretary-General, and with the assistance and coopera- tion of the Special Commission as provided for in the plan of the Secretary- General referred to in paragraph 9 (b), to carry out immediate on-site inspec- tion of Iraq's nuclear capabilities based on Iraq's declarations and the designation of any additional locations by the Special Commission; to develop a plan for submission to the Council within forty-five days calling for the destruction, removal or rendering harmless as appropriate of all items listed in paragraph 12; to carry out the plan within forty-five days following approval by the Council; and to develop a plan, taking into account the rights and obli- gations of Iraq under the Treaty on the Non-Proliferation of Nuclear Weapons, for the future ongoing monitoring and verification of Iraq's compliance with paragraph 12, including an inventory of all nuclear material in Iraq subject to the Agency's verification and inspections to confirm that Agency safeguards cover all relevant nuclear activities in Iraq, to be submitted to the Security Council for approval within one hundred and twenty days of the adoption of the present resolution;

14. Notes that the actions to be taken by Iraq in paragraphs 8 to 13 represent steps towards the goal of establishing in the Middle East a zone free from weapons of mass destruction and all missiles for their delivery and the objec- tive of a global ban on chemical weapons;

D

15. Requests the Secretary-General to report to the Council on the steps taken to facilitate the return of all Kuwaiti property seized by Iraq, including a list of any property that Kuwait claims has not been returned or which has not been returned intact;

E

16. Reaffirms that Iraq, without prejudice to its debts and obligations aris- ing prior to 2 August 1990, which will be addressed through the normal mech- anisms, is liable under international law for any direct loss, damage—includ- ing environmental damage and the depletion of natural resources—or injury to

foreign Governments, nationals and corporations as a result of its unlawful invasion and occupation of Kuwait;

17. Decides that all Iraqi statements made since 2 August 1990 repudiating its foreign debt are null and void, and demands that Iraq adhere scrupulously to all of its obligations concerning servicing and repayment of its foreign debt;

18. Decides also to create a fund to pay compensation for claims that fall within paragraph 16 and to establish a Commission that will administer the fund;

19. Directs the Secretary-General to develop and present to the Council for decision, no later than thirty days following the adoption of the present resolution, recommendations for the Fund to be established in accordance with paragraph 18 and for a programme to implement the decisions in paragraphs 16 to 18, including the following: administration of the Fund; mechanisms for determining the appropriate level of Iraq's contribution to the Fund, based on a percentage of the value of the exports of petroleum and petroleum products, not to exceed a figure to be suggested to the Council by the Secretary-General, taking into account the requirements of the people of Iraq, Iraq's payment capacity as assessed in conjunction with the international financial institutions taking into consideration external debt service, and the needs of the Iraqi economy; arrangements for ensuring that payments are made to the Fund; the process by which funds will be allocated and claims paid; appropriate procedures for evaluating losses, listing claims and verifying their validity, and resolving disputed claims in respect of Iraq's liability as specified in paragraph 16; and the composition of the Commission designated above;

F

20. Decides, effective immediately, that the prohibitions against the sale or supply to Iraq of commodities or products, other than medicine and health supplies, and prohibitions against financial transactions related thereto contained in resolution 661 (1990), shall not apply to foodstuffs notified to the Security Council Committee established by resolution 661 (1990) concerning the situation between Iraq and Kuwait or, with the approval of that Committee, under the simplified and accelerated "no-objection" procedure, to materials and supplies for essential civilian needs as identified in the report to the Secretary-General dated 20 March 1991, and in any further findings of humanitarian need by the Committee;

21. Decides to review the provisions of paragraph 20 every sixty days in the light of the policies and practices of the Government of Iraq, including the implementation of all relevant resolutions of the Council, for the purpose of determining whether to reduce or lift the prohibitions referred to therein;

22. Decides also that upon the approval by the Council of the programme called for in paragraph 19 above and upon Council agreement that Iraq has completed all actions contemplated in paragraphs 8 to 13, the prohibitions

against the import of commodities and products originating in Iraq and the prohibitions against financial transactions related thereto contained in resolution 661 (1990) shall have no further force or effect;

23. Decides further that, pending action by the Council under paragraph 22, the Security Council Committee established by resolution 661 (1990) concerning the situation between Iraq and Kuwait shall be empowered to approve, when required to assure adequate financial resources on the part of Iraq to carry out the activities under paragraph 20, exceptions to the prohibition against the import of commodities and products originating in Iraq;

24. Decides that, in accordance with resolution 661 (1990) and subsequent related resolutions and until it takes a further decision, all States shall continue to prevent the sale or supply to Iraq, or the promotion or facilitation of such sale or supply, by their nationals, or from their territories or using their flag vessels or aircraft, of:

(a) Arms and related materiél of all types, specifically including the sale or transfer through other means of all forms of conventional military equipment, including for paramilitary forces, and spare parts and components and their means of production for such equipment;

(b) Items specified and defined in paragraphs 8 and 12 not otherwise covered above;

(c) Technology under licensing or other transfer arrangements used in the production, utilization or stockpiling of items specified in paragraphs (a) and (b) above;

(d) Personnel or materials for training or technical support services relating to the design, development, manufacture, use, maintenance or support of items specified in paragraphs (a) and (b);

25. Calls upon all States and international organizations to act strictly in accordance with paragraph 24, notwithstanding the existence of any contracts, agreements, licences or any other arrangements;

26. Requests the Secretary-General, in consultation with appropriate Governments, to develop within sixty days, for the approval of the Council, guidelines to facilitate full international implementation of paragraphs 24, 25 and 27, to make them available to all States and to establish a procedure for updating these guidelines periodically;

27. Calls upon all States to maintain such national controls and procedures and to take such other actions consistent with the guidelines to be established by the Council under paragraph 26 as may be necessary to ensure compliance with the terms of paragraph 24, and calls upon international organizations to take all appropriate steps to assist in ensuring such full compliance;

28. Agrees to review its decisions in paragraphs 22 to 25, except for the items specified and defined in paragraphs 8 and 12, on a regular basis and in any case one hundred and twenty days following the adoption of the present resolution, taking into account Iraq's compliance with the resolution and general progress towards the control of armaments in the region;

29. Decides that all States, including Iraq, shall take the necessary measures

to ensure that no claim shall lie at the instance of the Government of Iraq, or of any person or body in Iraq, or of any person claiming through or for the benefit of any such person or body, in connection with any contract or other transaction where its performance was affected by reason of the measures taken by the Council in resolution 661 (1990) and related resolutions;

G

30. Decides that, in furtherance of its commitment to facilitate the repatriation of all Kuwaiti and third-State nationals, Iraq shall extend all necessary cooperation to the International Committee of the Red Cross by providing lists of such persons, facilitating the access of the International Committee to all such persons wherever located or detained and facilitating the search by the International Committee for those Kuwaiti and third country nationals still unaccounted for;

31. Invites the International Committee of the Red Cross to keep the Secretary-General apprised, as appropriate, of all activities undertaken in connection with facilitating the repatriation or return of all Kuwaiti and third-State nationals or their remains present in Iraq on or after 2 August 1990;

H

32. Requires Iraq to inform the Council that it will not commit or support any act of international terrorism or allow any organization directed towards commission of such acts to operate within its territory and to condemn unequivocally and renounce all acts, methods and practices of terrorism;

I

33. Declares that, upon official notification by Iraq to the Secretary-General and to the Security Council of its acceptance of the above provisions, a formal cease-fire is effective between Iraq and Kuwait and the Member States cooperating with Kuwait in accordance with resolution 678 (1990);

34. Decides to remain seized of the matter and to take such further steps as may be required for the implementation of the present resolution and to secure peace and security in the area.

2.4
ICJ Advisory Opinion on the Legality of Nuclear Weapons (1996)
(excerpt)

Lobbying by an umbrella grouping of NGOs called the World Court Project secured requests by both the World Health Organization (WHO) and the General Assembly for an advisory opinion on the legality of nuclear weapons. The court concluded that the WHO was not competent to make the request because, as a UN specialized agency, the WHO could only request advisory opinions "on legal questions arising within the scope of their activities." This excerpt is from the response of the court to the question asked of it by the UN General Assembly in Resolution 75 of 15 December 1994: Is the threat or use of nuclear weapons in any circumstances permitted under international law? The final paragraph of the excerpt should be read in conjunction with the 1968 Treaty on the Non-Proliferation of Nuclear Weapons, in particular article VI.

The origins of the process by which the ICJ came to address the question of the legality of nuclear weapons are traced in Kate Dewes and Commander Robert Green (retired), "The World Court Project: How a Citizen Network can Influence the United Nations," Pacifica Review 7, no. 2 (1995): 17–37. *See also Laurence Boisson de Chazournes and Philippe Sands, eds.,* International Law, the International Court of Justice, and Nuclear Weapons *(Cambridge: Cambridge University Press, 1999); and Ved Nanda,* Nuclear Weapons and the World Court *(Ardsley, N.Y.: Transnational, 1998). The full text of the advisory opinion, as with all decisions of the court, is printed in the series* Reports of Judgments, Advisory Opinions, and Orders. *It can be accessed in electronic form at www.icj-cij.org/icjwww/ipublications.htm.*

For these reasons,
  THE COURT,
  . . .

(2) Replies in the following manner to the question put by the General Assembly [Is the threat or use of nuclear weapons in any circumstances permitted under international law?]:

A. Unanimously,

There is in neither customary nor conventional international law any specific authorization of the threat or use of nuclear weapons;

B. By eleven votes to three,

There is in neither customary nor conventional international law any comprehensive and universal prohibition of the threat or use of nuclear weapons as such;

. . .

C. Unanimously,

A threat or use of force by means of nuclear weapons that is contrary to Article 2, paragraph 4, of the United Nations Charter and that fails to meet all the requirements of Article 51, is unlawful;

D. Unanimously,

A threat or use of nuclear weapons should also be compatible with the requirements of the international law applicable in armed conflict, particularly those of the principles and rules of international humanitarian law, as well as with specific obligations under treaties and other undertakings which expressly deal with nuclear weapons;

E. By seven votes to seven, by the President's casting vote,

It follows from the above-mentioned requirements that the threat or use of nuclear weapons would generally be contrary to the rules of international law applicable in armed conflict, and in particular the principles and rules of humanitarian law;

However, in view of the current state of international law, and of the elements of fact at its disposal, the Court cannot conclude definitively whether the threat or use of nuclear weapons would be lawful or unlawful in an extreme circumstance of self-defence, in which the very survival of a State would be at stake;

. . .

F. Unanimously,

There exists an obligation to pursue in good faith and bring to a conclusion negotiations leading to nuclear disarmament in all its aspects under strict and effective international control.

2.5
Self-Defence and Afghanistan: United Nations Security Council Resolution 1368 (2001)

Resolution 1368 was adopted unanimously on 12 September 2001, the day following the terrorist attacks in New York, Washington, D.C., and Pennsylvania. Resolution 1373 of 28 September 2001 again reaffirmed the inherent right of individual and collective self-defense. On 7 October 2001 the United States reported in a letter to the UN Security Council that it had "initiated actions in the exercise of its inherent right of individual and collective self-defense following the armed attacks that were carried out against the United States on 11 September 2001."

Antonio Cassese has referred to resolution 1368 as "ambiguous and contradictory" in his article "Terrorism is also Disrupting Some Crucial Legal Categories of International Law," European Journal of International Law *12 (2001): 993–1001. In support of the "propriety" of the US use of self-defense in response to September 11, see Jack M. Beard, "America's New War on Terror: The Case for Self-Defense Under International Law,"* Harvard Journal of Law and Public Policy *(2002): 559–590. Mary Ellen O'Connell has analyzed Operation Enduring Freedom in terms of the law of self-defense and concluded that it at first met the requirements for a lawful use of self-defense but may have later gone beyond the bounds of proportionality. See her "Lawful Self-Defense to Terrorism,"* University of Pittsburgh Law Review *63 (2002): 889–908. For a discussion as to why the US may have justified Operation Enduring Freedom solely in terms of self-defense, see Michael Byers, "Terrorism, the Use of Force, and International Law after 11 September,"* International and Comparative Law Quarterly *51 (2002): 401–414. For the text of the US letter of 7 October, see UN Doc. S/2001/946 (2001), available at www.un.int/usa/s-2001-946.htm.*

The Security Council,

Reaffirming the principles and purposes of the Charter of the United Nations,

Determined to combat by all means threats to international peace and security caused by terrorist acts,

Recognizing the inherent right of individual or collective self-defence in accordance with the Charter,

1. Unequivocally condemns in the strongest terms the horrifying terrorist attacks which took place on 11 September 2001 in New York, Washington, D.C., and Pennsylvania and regards such acts, like any act of international terrorism, as a threat to international peace and security;

2. Expresses its deepest sympathy and condolences to the victims and their families and to the people and Government of the United States of America;

3. Calls on all States to work together urgently to bring to justice the perpetrators, organizers and sponsors of these terrorist attacks and stresses that those responsible for aiding, supporting or harbouring the perpetrators, organizers and sponsors of these acts will be held accountable;

4. Calls also on the international community to redouble their efforts to prevent and suppress terrorist acts including by increased cooperation and full implementation of the relevant international anti-terrorist conventions and Security Council resolutions, in particular resolution 1269 (1999) of 19 October 1999;

5. Expresses its readiness to take all necessary steps to respond to the terrorist attacks of 11 September 2001, and to combat all forms of terrorism, in accordance with its responsibilities under the Charter of the United Nations;

6. Decides to remain seized of the matter.

2.6
The US National
Security Strategy (2002)
(excerpt)

This is a policy document, not a legal text. It is included here, however, because of its controversial promotion of preemption as a US security doctrine and the relevance of a policy of preemption to the US legal justification for its use of force against Iraq. The closest legal category to preemption is anticipatory self-defense, but this is a narrower concept than that of preemption. Whereas the 2003 invasion of Iraq may have appeared as the implementation of a policy of preemption, the Bush administration did not justify the attack in terms of self-defense, but as stemming from Iraq's failure to comply with resolutions of the Security Council. On the relationship of a policy of preemption to the international law of self-defense, see Mary Ellen O'Connell, "The Myth of Preemptive Self-Defense," American Society of International Law Taskforce on Terrorism Essay at www.asil.org/taskforce/oconnell.pdf.

Critics generally characterize the Bush doctrine of preemption as a radical departure from previous US strategic thinking, but not all writers agree. On preemption as a significant departure from Cold War policies of deterrence and containment, see Robert M. Lawrence, "The Preventive/Preemptive War Doctrine Cannot Justify the Iraq War," Denver Journal of International Law and Policy *33 (2004): 16–30. John Lewis Gaddis has traced preemption to the earliest days of the republic in* Surprise, Security, and the American Experience *(Cambridge, Mass.: Harvard University Press, 2004). The full text of the National Security Strategy can be found at www.whitehouse.gov/nsc/nss.html.*

Chapter V: Prevent Our Enemies From Threatening Us, Our Allies, and Our Friends with Weapons of Mass Destruction

. . .

For centuries, international law recognized that nations need not suffer an attack before they can lawfully take action to defend themselves against forces that present an imminent danger of attack. Legal scholars and international jurists often conditioned the legitimacy of preemption on the existence of an imminent threat—most often a visible mobilization of armies, navies, and air forces preparing to attack.

We must adapt the concept of imminent threat to the capabilities and objectives of today's adversaries. Rogue states and terrorists do not seek to attack us using conventional means. They know such attacks would fail. Instead, they rely on acts of terror and, potentially, the use of weapons of mass destruction—weapons that can be easily concealed, delivered covertly, and used without warning.

The targets of these attacks are our military forces and our civilian population, in direct violation of one of the principal norms of the law of warfare. As was demonstrated by the losses on September 11, 2001, mass civilian casualties is the specific objective of terrorists and these losses would be exponentially more severe if terrorists acquired and used weapons of mass destruction.

The United States has long maintained the option of preemptive actions to counter a sufficient threat to our national security. The greater the threat, the greater is the risk of inaction—and the more compelling the case for taking anticipatory action to defend ourselves, even if uncertainty remains as to the time and place of the enemy's attack. To forestall or prevent such hostile acts by our adversaries, the United States will, if necessary, act preemptively.

The United States will not use force in all cases to preempt emerging threats, nor should nations use preemption as a pretext for aggression. Yet in an age where the enemies of civilization openly and actively seek the world's most destructive technologies, the United States cannot remain idle while dangers gather.

We will always proceed deliberately, weighing the consequences of our actions. To support preemptive options, we will:

• build better, more integrated intelligence capabilities to provide timely, accurate information on threats, wherever they may emerge;

• coordinate closely with allies to form a common assessment of the most dangerous threats; and

• continue to transform our military forces to ensure our ability to conduct rapid and precise operations to achieve decisive results.

The purpose of our actions will always be to eliminate a specific threat to the United States or our allies and friends. The reasons for our actions will be clear, the force measured, and the cause just.

2.7
Resolution Preceding the 2003 Invasion of Iraq: United Nations Security Council Resolution 1441 (2002)

Resolution 1441 was sponsored jointly by the US and the UK and adopt-ed unanimously on 8 November 2002. It has been highly controversial as to whether this resolution, in combination with resolutions 678 and 687, provided sufficient legal authority for the 2003 invasion of Iraq.

International and Comparative Law Quarterly *has published the UK attorney general's "Answer to a Question in the House of Commons on the Question of Legality," in 52 (2003): 811–814; his advice on the Iraq War in 54 (2005) 767–778; and the "Legal Assessment of the Use of Force Against Iraq" prepared by the Legal Department of the Ministry of Foreign Affairs of the Russian Federation in 52 (2003): 1059–1063. On the US perspective, see the analysis by William H. Taft IV (then-legal adviser of the US Department of State) and Todd F. Bucchwald, "Preemption, Iraq, and International Law,"* American Journal of International Law *97 (2003): 557–563. For academic analysis, see Nigel White and Eric P. J. Myjer, "The Use of Force Against Iraq,"* Journal of Conflict and Security Law *8 (2003): 1–14; and Ben Saul "The Legality of the Use of Force Against Iraq in 2003: Did the Coalition Defend or Defy the United Nations?"* UCLA Journal of International Law and Foreign Affairs *8 (2003): 267–330. For a discussion intended for the general reader that is scathing of the British and US legal arguments, see chapter 8 of "Kicking Ass in Iraq," in Philippe Sands,* Lawless World: America and the Making and Breaking of Global Rules *(Camberwell, Victoria: Penguin, 2005).*

The Security Council,

Recalling all its previous relevant resolutions, in particular its resolutions 661 (1990) of 6 August 1990, 678 (1990) of 29 November 1990, 686 (1991) of 2 March 1991, 687 (1991) of 3 April 1991, 688 (1991) of 5 April 1991, 707 (1991) of 15 August 1991, 715 (1991) of 11 October 1991, 986 (1995) of 14

April 1995, and 1284 (1999) of 17 December 1999, and all the relevant statements of its President,

Recalling also its resolution 1382 (2001) of 29 November 2001 and its intention to implement it fully,

Recognizing the threat Iraq's non-compliance with Council resolutions and proliferation of weapons of mass destruction and long-range missiles poses to international peace and security,

Recalling that its resolution 678 (1990) authorized Member States to use all necessary means to uphold and implement its resolution 660 (1990) of 2 August 1990 and all relevant resolutions subsequent to resolution 660 (1990) and to restore international peace and security in the area,

Further recalling that its resolution 687 (1991) imposed obligations on Iraq as a necessary step for achievement of its stated objective of restoring international peace and security in the area,

Deploring the fact that Iraq has not provided an accurate, full, final, and complete disclosure, as required by resolution 687 (1991), of all aspects of its programmes to develop weapons of mass destruction and ballistic missiles with a range greater than one hundred and fifty kilometres, and of all holdings of such weapons, their components and production facilities and locations, as well as all other nuclear programmes, including any which it claims are for purposes not related to nuclear-weapons-usable material,

Deploring further that Iraq repeatedly obstructed immediate, unconditional, and unrestricted access to sites designated by the United Nations Special Commission (UNSCOM) and the International Atomic Energy Agency (IAEA), failed to cooperate fully and unconditionally with UNSCOM and IAEA weapons inspectors, as required by resolution 687 (1991), and ultimately ceased all cooperation with UNSCOM and the IAEA in 1998,

Deploring the absence, since December 1998, in Iraq of international monitoring, inspection, and verification, as required by relevant resolutions, of weapons of mass destruction and ballistic missiles, in spite of the Council's repeated demands that Iraq provide immediate, unconditional, and unrestricted access to the United Nations Monitoring, Verification and Inspection Commission (UNMOVIC), established in resolution 1284 (1999) as the successor organization to UNSCOM, and the IAEA, and regretting the consequent prolonging of the crisis in the region and the suffering of the Iraqi people,

Deploring also that the Government of Iraq has failed to comply with its commitments pursuant to resolution 687 (1991) with regard to terrorism, pursuant to resolution 688 (1991) to end repression of its civilian population and to provide access by international humanitarian organizations to all those in need of assistance in Iraq, and pursuant to resolutions 686 (1991), 687 (1991), and 1284 (1999) to return or cooperate in accounting for Kuwaiti and third country nationals wrongfully detained by Iraq, or to return Kuwaiti property wrongfully seized by Iraq,

Recalling that in its resolution 687 (1991) the Council declared that a cease-fire would be based on acceptance by Iraq of the provisions of that resolution, including the obligations on Iraq contained therein,

Determined to ensure full and immediate compliance by Iraq without conditions or restrictions with its obligations under resolution 687 (1991) and other relevant resolutions and recalling that the resolutions of the Council constitute the governing standard of Iraqi compliance,

Recalling that the effective operation of UNMOVIC, as the successor organization to the Special Commission, and the IAEA is essential for the implementation of resolution 687 (1991) and other relevant resolutions,

Noting that the letter dated 16 September 2002 from the Minister for Foreign Affairs of Iraq addressed to the Secretary-General is a necessary first step toward rectifying Iraq's continued failure to comply with relevant Council resolutions,

Noting further the letter dated 8 October 2002 from the Executive Chairman of UNMOVIC and the Director-General of the IAEA to General Al-Saadi of the Government of Iraq laying out the practical arrangements, as a follow-up to their meeting in Vienna, that are prerequisites for the resumption of inspections in Iraq by UNMOVIC and the IAEA, and expressing the gravest concern at the continued failure by the Government of Iraq to provide confirmation of the arrangements as laid out in that letter,

Reaffirming the commitment of all Member States to the sovereignty and territorial integrity of Iraq, Kuwait, and the neighbouring States,

Commending the Secretary-General and members of the League of Arab States and its Secretary-General for their efforts in this regard,

Determined to secure full compliance with its decisions,

Acting under Chapter VII of the Charter of the United Nations,

1. Decides that Iraq has been and remains in material breach of its obligations under relevant resolutions, including resolution 687 (1991), in particular through Iraq's failure to cooperate with United Nations inspectors and the IAEA, and to complete the actions required under paragraphs 8 to 13 of resolution 687 (1991);

2. Decides, while acknowledging paragraph 1 above, to afford Iraq, by this resolution, a final opportunity to comply with its disarmament obligations under relevant resolutions of the Council; and accordingly decides to set up an enhanced inspection regime with the aim of bringing to full and verified completion the disarmament process established by resolution 687 (1991) and subsequent resolutions of the Council;

3. Decides that, in order to begin to comply with its disarmament obligations, in addition to submitting the required biannual declarations, the Government of Iraq shall provide to UNMOVIC, the IAEA, and the Council, not later than 30 days from the date of this resolution, a currently accurate, full, and complete declaration of all aspects of its programmes to develop chemical, biological, and nuclear weapons, ballistic missiles, and other delivery systems such as unmanned aerial vehicles and dispersal systems designed for use on aircraft, including any holdings and precise locations of such

weapons, components, sub-components, stocks of agents, and related material and equipment, the locations and work of its research, development and production facilities, as well as all other chemical, biological, and nuclear programmes, including any which it claims are for purposes not related to weapon production or material;

4. Decides that false statements or omissions in the declarations submitted by Iraq pursuant to this resolution and failure by Iraq at any time to comply with, and cooperate fully in the implementation of, this resolution shall constitute a further material breach of Iraq's obligations and will be reported to the Council for assessment in accordance with paragraphs 11 and 12 below;

5. Decides that Iraq shall provide UNMOVIC and the IAEA immediate, unimpeded, unconditional, and unrestricted access to any and all, including underground areas, facilities, buildings, equipment, records, and means of transport which they wish to inspect, as well as immediate, unimpeded, unrestricted, and private access to all officials and other persons whom UNMOVIC or the IAEA wish to interview in the mode or location of UNMOVIC's or the IAEA's choice pursuant to any aspect of their mandates; further decides that UNMOVIC and the IAEA may at their discretion conduct interviews inside or outside of Iraq, may facilitate the travel of those interviewed and family members outside of Iraq, and that, at the sole discretion of UNMOVIC and the IAEA, such interviews may occur without the presence of observers from the Iraqi Government; and instructs UNMOVIC and requests the IAEA to resume inspections no later than 45 days following adoption of this resolution and to update the Council 60 days thereafter;

6. Endorses the 8 October 2002 letter from the Executive Chairman of UNMOVIC and the Director-General of the IAEA to General Al-Saadi of the Government of Iraq, which is annexed hereto, and decides that the contents of the letter shall be binding upon Iraq;

7. Decides further that, in view of the prolonged interruption by Iraq of the presence of UNMOVIC and the IAEA and in order for them to accomplish the tasks set forth in this resolution and all previous relevant resolutions and notwithstanding prior understandings, the Council hereby establishes the following revised or additional authorities, which shall be binding upon Iraq, to facilitate their work in Iraq:

• UNMOVIC and the IAEA shall determine the composition of their inspection teams and ensure that these teams are composed of the most qualified and experienced experts available;

• All UNMOVIC and IAEA personnel shall enjoy the privileges and immunities, corresponding to those of experts on mission, provided in the Convention on Privileges and Immunities of the United Nations and the Agreement on the Privileges and Immunities of the IAEA;

• UNMOVIC and the IAEA shall have unrestricted rights of entry into and out of Iraq, the right to free, unrestricted, and immediate movement to and from inspection sites, and the right to inspect any sites and buildings, including immediate, unimpeded, unconditional, and unrestricted access to Presidential

Sites equal to that at other sites, notwithstanding the provisions of resolution 1154 (1998) of 2 March 1998;

• UNMOVIC and the IAEA shall have the right to be provided by Iraq the names of all personnel currently and formerly associated with Iraq's chemical, biological, nuclear, and ballistic missile programmes and the associated research, development, and production facilities;

• Security of UNMOVIC and IAEA facilities shall be ensured by sufficient United Nations security guards;

• UNMOVIC and the IAEA shall have the right to declare, for the purposes of freezing a site to be inspected, exclusion zones, including surrounding areas and transit corridors, in which Iraq will suspend ground and aerial movement so that nothing is changed in or taken out of a site being inspected;

• UNMOVIC and the IAEA shall have the free and unrestricted use and landing of fixed- and rotary-winged aircraft, including manned and unmanned reconnaissance vehicles;

• UNMOVIC and the IAEA shall have the right at their sole discretion verifiably to remove, destroy, or render harmless all prohibited weapons, subsystems, components, records, materials, and other related items, and the right to impound or close any facilities or equipment for the production thereof; and

• UNMOVIC and the IAEA shall have the right to free import and use of equipment or materials for inspections and to seize and export any equipment, materials, or documents taken during inspections, without search of UNMOVIC or IAEA personnel or official or personal baggage;

8. Decides further that Iraq shall not take or threaten hostile acts directed against any representative or personnel of the United Nations or the IAEA or of any Member State taking action to uphold any Council resolution;

9. Requests the Secretary-General immediately to notify Iraq of this resolution, which is binding on Iraq; demands that Iraq confirm within seven days of that notification its intention to comply fully with this resolution; and demands further that Iraq cooperate immediately, unconditionally, and actively with UNMOVIC and the IAEA;

10. Requests all Member States to give full support to UNMOVIC and the IAEA in the discharge of their mandates, including by providing any information related to prohibited programmes or other aspects of their mandates, including on Iraqi attempts since 1998 to acquire prohibited items, and by recommending sites to be inspected, persons to be interviewed, conditions of such interviews, and data to be collected, the results of which shall be reported to the Council by UNMOVIC and the IAEA;

11. Directs the Executive Chairman of UNMOVIC and the Director-General of the IAEA to report immediately to the Council any interference by Iraq with inspection activities, as well as any failure by Iraq to comply with its disarmament obligations, including its obligations regarding inspections under this resolution;

12. Decides to convene immediately upon receipt of a report in accordance with paragraphs 4 or 11 above, in order to consider the situation and the need

for full compliance with all of the relevant Council resolutions in order to secure international peace and security;

13. Recalls, in that context, that the Council has repeatedly warned Iraq that it will face serious consequences as a result of its continued violations of its obligations;

14. Decides to remain seized of the matter.

. . . [Annex: Text of Blix/el-Baradei letter not included]

2.8
United Kingdom Explanation of Its Vote on UN Security Council Resolution 1441: Statement by Ambassador Greenstock to the Security Council (2002)

This is a statement of 8 November 2002 to the Security Council by UK ambassador Jeremy Greenstock. Ambassador John D. Negroponte, permanent representative of the United States to the UN, also made a statement to the Security Council on 8 November 2002, similarly denying that resolution 1441 (2002) contained "hidden triggers" or "automaticity."

I start by thanking the Secretary-General for his presence, his powerful statement and for his wisdom in advising the Council over these past weeks.

Mr President,

I said at the Council's open debate on Iraq on 17 October that no shadow of a doubt remained that Iraq has defied the United Nations—not any particular Member State, the United Nations—over the last eleven years. I itemised on that occasion the ways in which Iraq has sought to frustrate and hinder inspections since 1991.

With the adoption of this Resolution, the Security Council has clearly stated that the United Nations will no longer tolerate this defiance. As Operational Paragraph 2 makes crystal clear, Iraq is being given a final opportunity to comply with its disarmament obligations; a final opportunity to remedy its material breach of Security Council Resolution 687 set out in Operational Paragraph 1. The regime in Baghdad now faces an unequivocal choice: between complete disarmament and the serious consequences indicated in Operational Paragraph 13.

The fact, Mr President, that this Resolution has the unanimous support of Council members sends, as the Secretary-General has just said, the most powerful signal to Iraq that this is the only choice, that it can no longer evade its obligations under UN resolutions. Because of the strength of this signal, there is at last a chance that Iraq will finally comply with its obligations and that military action can be averted.

A key part of the Resolution we have adopted today is the provisions giving inspectors the penetrating strength needed to ensure the successful disarmament of Iraq. I am glad that the Council has recognised that we could not afford a return to the ambiguous modalities and Memoranda of Understanding of the past; that we could not afford exceptions to unconditional, unrestricted, and immediate access; that we could not afford to have inspectors again standing by helplessly while crucial documents are burnt or while convoys leave from the back doors as inspectors arrive in the front; and that we could not afford interviews compromised by intimidating minders. The provisions we have agreed, including making legally binding the practical arrangements set out by the inspectors themselves, will significantly strengthen the hand of the UN Monitoring, Verification and Inspection Commission and the International Atomic Energy Agency. This will reinforce international confidence in the inspectors. It will also, I hope, lead Iraq away from a fatal decision to conceal weapons of mass destruction (WMD). If Iraq is genuinely committed to full WMD disarmament, it can ensure inspections get off to a flying start by providing the complete and accurate declaration required under Operational Paragraph 3. The UK has full confidence in Dr Blix and Dr El-Baradei and their teams, and full respect for their integrity and independence, as they embark on a crucial and difficult task.

We heard loud and clear during the negotiations the concerns about "automaticity" and "hidden triggers"—the concern that on a decision so crucial we should not rush into military action; that on a decision so crucial any Iraqi violations should be discussed by the Council. Let me be equally clear in response, as a co-sponsor with the United States of the text we have adopted. There is no "automaticity" in this Resolution. If there is a further Iraqi breach of its disarmament obligations, the matter will return to the Council for discussion as required in Operational Paragraph 12. We would expect the Security Council then to meet its responsibilities.

Ultimately, Mr President, the choice lies with Iraq as to whether to take the peaceful route to disarmament. The UK hopes that Iraq will fully co-operate with the United Nations, meet its obligations, and take the path back to the lifting of sanctions laid out in Resolutions 1284 and 687. The disarmament of Iraq in the area of WMD by peaceful means remains the UK's firm preference. But if Iraq chooses defiance and concealment, rejecting the final opportunity it has been given by the Council in Operational Paragraph 2, the UK—together, we trust, with other Members of the Security Council—will ensure that the task of disarmament required by the Resolutions is completed.

3
Arms Control

3.1
Treaty on the Non-Proliferation of Nuclear Weapons (NPT) (1968)

This treaty has played a key role in minimizing the number of nuclear-weapon states and hence its importance is arguably close to that of the UN Charter. Although the terms of the treaty have always been controversial, the parties to the NPT agreed in 1995 to extend the treaty indefinitely. Opinions differ as to the future prospects for the NPT.

On negotiations leading to the NPT and the "profound lack of enthusiasm" with which the text was greeted by the General Assembly, see E. L. M. Burns, "The Nonproliferation Treaty: Its Negotiation and Prospects," International Organization *23, no. 4 (1969): 788–807. For contrasting views regarding prospects for the treaty, see Marianne Hanson, "The Future of the NPT,"* Australian Journal of International Affairs *59, no. 3 (2005): 301–316; and Michael Wesley, "It's Time to Scrap the NPT,"* Australian Journal of International Affairs *59, no. 3 (2005): 283–299. For updates on issues facing the nuclear non-proliferation regime, see the articles in* Arms Control Today, *published by the Arms Control Association and available at www.armscontrol.org. Archived issues are also available from this website.*

The States concluding this Treaty, hereinafter referred to as the "Parties to the Treaty,"

Considering the devastation that would be visited upon all mankind by a nuclear war and the consequent need to make every effort to avert the danger of such a war and to take measures to safeguard the security of peoples,

Believing that the proliferation of nuclear weapons would seriously enhance the danger of nuclear war,

In conformity with resolutions of the United Nations General Assembly calling for the conclusion of an agreement on the prevention of wider dissemination of nuclear weapons,

Undertaking to co-operate in facilitating the application of International Atomic Energy Agency safeguards on peaceful nuclear activities,

Expressing their support for research, development and other efforts to further the application, within the framework of the International Atomic Energy Agency safeguards system, of the principle of safeguarding effectively the flow of source and special fissionable materials by use of instruments and other techniques at certain strategic points,

Affirming the principle that the benefits of peaceful applications of nuclear technology, including any technological by-products which may be derived by nuclear-weapon States from the development of nuclear explosive devices, should be available for peaceful purposes to all Parties to the Treaty, whether nuclear-weapon or non-nuclear-weapon States,

Convinced that, in furtherance of this principle, all Parties to the Treaty are entitled to participate in the fullest possible exchange of scientific information for, and to contribute alone or in co-operation with other States to, the further development of the applications of atomic energy for peaceful purposes,

Declaring their intention to achieve at the earliest possible date the cessation of the nuclear arms race and to undertake effective measures in the direction of nuclear disarmament,

Urging the co-operation of all States in the attainment of this objective,

Recalling the determination expressed by the Parties to the 1963 Treaty banning nuclear weapons tests in the atmosphere, in outer space and under water in its Preamble to seek to achieve the discontinuance of all test explosions of nuclear weapons for all time and to continue negotiations to this end,

Desiring to further the easing of international tension and the strengthening of trust between States in order to facilitate the cessation of the manufacture of nuclear weapons, the liquidation of all their existing stockpiles, and the elimination from national arsenals of nuclear weapons and the means of their delivery pursuant to a Treaty on general and complete disarmament under strict and effective international control,

Recalling that, in accordance with the Charter of the United Nations, States must refrain in their international relations from the threat or use of force against the territorial integrity or political independence of any State, or in any other manner inconsistent with the Purposes of the United Nations, and that the establishment and maintenance of international peace and security are to be promoted with the least diversion for armaments of the world's human and economic resources,

Have agreed as follows:

Article I
Each nuclear-weapon State Party to the Treaty undertakes not to transfer to any recipient whatsoever nuclear weapons or other nuclear explosive devices or control over such weapons or explosive devices directly, or indirectly; and not in any way to assist, encourage, or induce any non-nuclear-weapon State to manufacture or otherwise acquire nuclear weapons or other nuclear explosive devices, or control over such weapons or explosive devices.

Article II
Each non-nuclear-weapon State Party to the Treaty undertakes not to receive

the transfer from any transferor whatsoever of nuclear weapons or other nuclear explosive devices or of control over such weapons or explosive devices directly, or indirectly; not to manufacture or otherwise acquire nuclear weapons or other nuclear explosive devices; and not to seek or receive any assistance in the manufacture of nuclear weapons or other nuclear explosive devices.

Article III

1. Each non-nuclear-weapon State Party to the Treaty undertakes to accept safeguards, as set forth in an agreement to be negotiated and concluded with the International Atomic Energy Agency in accordance with the Statute of the International Atomic Energy Agency and the Agency's safeguards system, for the exclusive purpose of verification of the fulfilment of its obligations assumed under this Treaty with a view to preventing diversion of nuclear energy from peaceful uses to nuclear weapons or other nuclear explosive devices. Procedures for the safeguards required by this Article shall be followed with respect to source or special fissionable material whether it is being produced, processed or used in any principal nuclear facility or is outside any such facility. The safeguards required by this Article shall be applied on all source or special fissionable material in all peaceful nuclear activities within the territory of such State, under its jurisdiction, or carried out under its control anywhere.

2. Each State Party to the Treaty undertakes not to provide: (a) source or special fissionable material, or (b) equipment or material especially designed or prepared for the processing, use or production of special fissionable material, to any non-nuclear-weapon State for peaceful purposes, unless the source or special fissionable material shall be subject to the safeguards required by this Article.

3. The safeguards required by this Article shall be implemented in a manner designed to comply with Article IV of this Treaty, and to avoid hampering the economic or technological development of the Parties or international co-operation in the field of peaceful nuclear activities, including the international exchange of nuclear material and equipment for the processing, use or production of nuclear material for peaceful purposes in accordance with the provisions of this Article and the principle of safeguarding set forth in the Preamble of the Treaty.

4. Non-nuclear-weapon States Party to the Treaty shall conclude agreements with the International Atomic Energy Agency to meet the requirements of this Article either individually or together with other States in accordance with the Statute of the International Atomic Energy Agency. Negotiation of such agreements shall commence within 180 days from the original entry into force of this Treaty. For States depositing their instruments of ratification or accession after the 180-day period, negotiation of such agreements shall commence not later than the date of such deposit. Such agreements shall enter into force not later than eighteen months after the date of initiation of negotiations.

Article IV

1. Nothing in this Treaty shall be interpreted as affecting the inalienable right of all the Parties to the Treaty to develop research, production and use of nuclear energy for peaceful purposes without discrimination and in conformity with Articles I and II of this Treaty.

2. All the Parties to the Treaty undertake to facilitate, and have the right to participate in, the fullest possible exchange of equipment, materials and scientific and technological information for the peaceful uses of nuclear energy. Parties to the Treaty in a position to do so shall also co-operate in contributing alone or together with other States or international organizations to the further development of the applications of nuclear energy for peaceful purposes, especially in the territories of non-nuclear-weapon States Party to the Treaty, with due consideration for the needs of the developing areas of the world.

Article V

Each Party to the Treaty undertakes to take appropriate measures to ensure that, in accordance with this Treaty, under appropriate international observation and through appropriate international procedures, potential benefits from any peaceful applications of nuclear explosions will be made available to non-nuclear-weapon States Party to the Treaty on a non-discriminatory basis and that the charge to such Parties for the explosive devices used will be as low as possible and exclude any charge for research and development. Non-nuclear-weapon States Party to the Treaty shall be able to obtain such benefits, pursuant to a special international agreement or agreements, through an appropriate international body with adequate representation of non-nuclear-weapon States. Negotiations on this subject shall commence as soon as possible after the Treaty enters into force. Non-nuclear-weapon States Party to the Treaty so desiring may also obtain such benefits pursuant to bilateral agreements.

Article VI

Each of the Parties to the Treaty undertakes to pursue negotiations in good faith on effective measures relating to cessation of the nuclear arms race at an early date and to nuclear disarmament, and on a treaty on general and complete disarmament under strict and effective international control.

Article VII

Nothing in this Treaty affects the right of any group of States to conclude regional treaties in order to assure the total absence of nuclear weapons in their respective territories.

Article VIII

1. Any Party to the Treaty may propose amendments to this Treaty. The text of any proposed amendment shall be submitted to the Depositary Governments which shall circulate it to all Parties to the Treaty. Thereupon, if requested to do so by one-third or more of the Parties to the Treaty, the Depositary

Governments shall convene a conference, to which they shall invite all the Parties to the Treaty, to consider such an amendment.

2. Any amendment to this Treaty must be approved by a majority of the votes of all the Parties to the Treaty, including the votes of all nuclear-weapon States Party to the Treaty and all other Parties which, on the date the amendment is circulated, are members of the Board of Governors of the International Atomic Energy Agency. The amendment shall enter into force for each Party that deposits its instrument of ratification of the amendment upon the deposit of such instruments of ratification by a majority of all the Parties, including the instruments of ratification of all nuclear-weapon States Party to the Treaty and all other Parties which, on the date the amendment is circulated, are members of the Board of Governors of the International Atomic Energy Agency. Thereafter, it shall enter into force for any other Party upon the deposit of its instrument of ratification of the amendment.

3. Five years after the entry into force of this Treaty, a conference of Parties to the Treaty shall be held in Geneva, Switzerland, in order to review the operation of this Treaty with a view to assuring that the purposes of the Preamble and the provisions of the Treaty are being realised. At intervals of five years thereafter, a majority of the Parties to the Treaty may obtain, by submitting a proposal to this effect to the Depositary Governments, the convening of further conferences with the same objective of reviewing the operation of the Treaty.

Article IX

1. This Treaty shall be open to all States for signature. Any State which does not sign the Treaty before its entry into force in accordance with paragraph 3 of this Article may accede to it at any time.

2. This Treaty shall be subject to ratification by signatory States. Instruments of ratification and instruments of accession shall be deposited with the Governments of the United Kingdom of Great Britain and Northern Ireland, the Union of Soviet Socialist Republics and the United States of America, which are hereby designated the Depositary Governments.

3. This Treaty shall enter into force after its ratification by the States, the Governments of which are designated Depositaries of the Treaty, and forty other States signatory to this Treaty and the deposit of their instruments of ratification. For the purposes of this Treaty, a nuclear-weapon State is one which has manufactured and exploded a nuclear weapon or other nuclear explosive device prior to 1 January, 1967.

4. For States whose instruments of ratification or accession are deposited subsequent to the entry into force of this Treaty, it shall enter into force on the date of the deposit of their instruments of ratification or accession.

5. The Depositary Governments shall promptly inform all signatory and acceding States of the date of each signature, the date of deposit of each instrument of ratification or of accession, the date of the entry into force of this Treaty, and the date of receipt of any requests for convening a conference or other notices.

6. This Treaty shall be registered by the Depositary Governments pursuant to Article 102 of the Charter of the United Nations.

Article X

1. Each Party shall in exercising its national sovereignty have the right to withdraw from the Treaty if it decides that extraordinary events, related to the subject matter of this Treaty, have jeopardized the supreme interests of its country. It shall give notice of such withdrawal to all other Parties to the Treaty and to the United Nations Security Council three months in advance. Such notice shall include a statement of the extraordinary events it regards as having jeopardized its supreme interests.

2. Twenty-five years after the entry into force of the Treaty, a conference shall be convened to decide whether the Treaty shall continue in force indefinitely, or shall be extended for an additional fixed period or periods. This decision shall be taken by a majority of the Parties to the Treaty.

Article XI

This Treaty, the English, Russian, French, Spanish and Chinese texts of which are equally authentic, shall be deposited in the archives of the Depositary Governments. Duly certified copies of this Treaty shall be transmitted by the Depositary Governments to the Governments of the signatory and acceding States.

IN WITNESS WHEREOF the undersigned, duly authorized, have signed this Treaty.

DONE in triplicate, at the cities of London, Moscow and Washington, the first day of July, one thousand nine hundred and sixty-eight.

3.2
Treaty Between the United States of America and the Union of Soviet Socialist Republics on the Limitation of Anti-Ballistic Missile Systems (Anti-Ballistic Missile Treaty or ABM Treaty) (1972)

This treaty was one of the most important arms control treaties of the Cold War. The rationale behind the limitations it placed on the development of systems to counter strategic ballistic missiles (or their elements) in flight trajectory was that, if both sides remained vulnerable, neither would be prepared to launch a first strike for fear of a larger retaliation. It thus brought some stability to the US-USSR relationship and provided a basis on which to negotiate reductions in the number of deployed strategic warheads. The Bush administration met with strong criticism when it announced in December 2001 that it was giving six months notice of its withdrawal from the ABM Treaty.

On the central place of deterrence in strategic thinking during the Cold War, see Daniel Gouré, "Nuclear Deterrence, Then and Now," Policy Review *116 (Dec. 2002–Jan. 2003): 43–55. For analysis pointing to the continued relevance of deterrence, see James H. Lebovic, "The Law of Small Numbers: Deterrence and National Missile Defense,"* The Journal of Conflict Resolution *46 (2002): 455–483. On the controversial withdrawal of the US from the treaty, see Rein Müllerson, "The ABM Treaty: Changed Circumstances, Extraordinary Events, Supreme Interests, and International Law,"* International and Comparative Law Quarterly *50 (2001): 509–539.*

The United States of America and the Union of Soviet Socialist Republics, hereinafter referred to as the Parties,

Proceeding from the premise that nuclear war would have devastating consequences for all mankind,

Considering that effective measures to limit anti-ballistic missile systems would be a substantial factor in curbing the race in strategic offensive arms and would lead to a decrease in the risk of outbreak of war involving nuclear weapons,

Proceeding from the premise that the limitation of anti-ballistic missile systems, as well as certain agreed measures with respect to the limitation of strategic offensive arms, would contribute to the creation of more favorable conditions for further negotiations on limiting strategic arms,

Mindful of their obligations under Article VI of the Treaty on the Non-Proliferation of Nuclear Weapons,

Declaring their intention to achieve at the earliest possible date the cessation of the nuclear arms race and to take effective measures toward reductions in strategic arms, nuclear disarmament, and general and complete disarmament,

Desiring to contribute to the relaxation of international tension and the strengthening of trust between States,

Have agreed as follows:

Article I

1. Each Party undertakes to limit anti-ballistic missile (ABM) systems and to adopt other measures in accordance with the provisions of this Treaty.

2. Each Party undertakes not to deploy ABM systems for a defense of the territory of its country and not to provide a base for such a defense, and not to deploy ABM systems for defense of an individual region except as provided for in Article III of this Treaty.

Article II

1. For the purpose of this Treaty an ABM system is a system to counter strategic ballistic missiles or their elements in flight trajectory, currently consisting of:

(a) ABM interceptor missiles, which are interceptor missiles constructed and deployed for an ABM role, or of a type tested in an ABM mode;

(b) ABM launchers, which are launchers constructed and deployed for launching ABM interceptor missiles; and

(c) ABM radars, which are radars constructed and deployed for an ABM role, or of a type tested in an ABM mode.

2. The ABM system components listed in paragraph 1 of this Article include those which are:

(a) operational;

(b) under construction;

(c) undergoing testing;

(d) undergoing overhaul, repair or conversion; or

(e) mothballed.

Article III*

Each Party undertakes not to deploy ABM systems or their components except that:

(a) within one ABM system deployment area having a radius of one hundred and fifty kilometers and centered on the Party's national capital, a Party may deploy:

(1) no more than one hundred ABM launchers and no more than one hundred ABM interceptor missiles at launch sites, and

(2) ABM radars within no more than six ABM radar complexes, the area of each complex being circular and having a diameter of no more than three kilometers; and

(b) within one ABM system deployment area having a radius of one hundred and fifty kilometers and containing ICBM silo launchers, a Party may deploy:

(1) no more than one hundred ABM launchers and no more than one hundred ABM interceptor missiles at launch sites,

(2) two large phased-array ABM radars comparable in potential to corresponding ABM radars operational or under construction on the date of signature of the Treaty in an ABM system deployment area containing ICBM silo launchers, and

(3) no more than eighteen ABM radars each having a potential less than the potential of the smaller of the above-mentioned two large phased-array ABM radars.

Article IV

The limitations provided for in Article III shall not apply to ABM systems or their components used for development or testing, and located within current or additionally agreed test ranges. Each Party may have no more than a total of fifteen ABM launchers at test ranges.

Article V

1. Each Party undertakes not to develop, test, or deploy ABM systems or components which are sea-based, air-based, space-based, or mobile land-based.

2. Each Party undertakes not to develop, test or deploy ABM launchers for launching more than one ABM interceptor missile at a time from each launcher, not to modify deployed launchers to provide them with such a capacity, not to develop, test, or deploy automatic or semi-automatic or other similar systems for rapid reload of ABM launchers.

Article VI

To enhance assurance of the effectiveness of the limitations on ABM

---

* Article I of the 1974 Protocol to the ABM Treaty limited Parties at any one time to a single area of the two provided for in Article III of the ABM Treaty.

systems and their components provided by the Treaty, each Party undertakes:

(a) not to give missiles, launchers, or radars, other than ABM interceptor missiles, ABM launchers, or ABM radars, capabilities to counter strategic ballistic missiles or their elements in flight trajectory, and not to test them in an ABM mode; and

(b) not to deploy in the future radars for early warning of strategic ballistic missile attack except at locations along the periphery of its national territory and oriented outward.

Article VII

Subject to the provisions of this Treaty, modernization and replacement of ABM systems or their components may be carried out.

Article VIII

ABM systems or their components in excess of the numbers or outside the areas specified in this Treaty, as well as ABM systems or their components prohibited by this Treaty, shall be destroyed or dismantled under agreed procedures within the shortest possible agreed period of time.

Article IX

To assure the viability and effectiveness of this Treaty, each Party undertakes not to transfer to other States, and not to deploy outside its national territory, ABM systems or their components limited by this Treaty.

Article X

Each Party undertakes not to assume any international obligations which would conflict with this Treaty.

Article XI

The Parties undertake to continue active negotiations for limitations on strategic offensive arms.

Article XII

1. For the purpose of providing assurance or compliance with the provisions of this Treaty, each Party shall use national technical means of verification at its disposal in a manner consistent with generally recognized principles of international law.

2. Each Party undertakes not to interfere with the national technical means of verification of the other Party operating in accordance with paragraph 1 of this Article.

3. Each Party undertakes not to use deliberate concealment measures which impede verification by national technical means of compliance with the provisions of this Treaty. This obligation shall not require changes in current construction, assembly, conversion, or overhaul practices.

Article XIII

1. To promote the objectives and implementation of the provisions of this Treaty, the Parties shall establish promptly a Standing Consultative Commission, within the framework of which they will:

(a) consider questions concerning compliance with the obligations assumed and related situations which may be considered ambiguous;

(b) provide on a voluntary basis such information as either Party considers necessary to assure confidence in compliance with the obligations assumed;

(c) consider questions involving unintended interference with national technical means of verification;

(d) consider possible changes in the strategic situation which have a bearing on the provisions of this Treaty;

(e) agree upon procedures and dates for destruction or dismantling of ABM systems or their components in cases provided for by the provisions of this Treaty;

(f) consider, as appropriate, possible proposals for further increasing the viability of this Treaty; including proposals for amendments in accordance with the provisions of this Treaty;

(g) consider, as appropriate, proposals for further measures aimed at limiting strategic arms.

2. The Parties through consultation shall establish, and may amend as appropriate, Regulations for the Standing Consultative Commission governing procedures, composition and other relevant matters.

Article XIV

1. Each Party may propose amendments to this Treaty. Agreed amendments shall enter into force in accordance with the procedures governing the entry into force of this Treaty.

2. Five years after entry into force of this Treaty, and at five-year intervals thereafter, the Parties shall together conduct a review of this Treaty.

Article XV

1. This Treaty shall be of unlimited duration.

2. Each Party shall, in exercising its national sovereignty, have the right to withdraw from this Treaty if it decides that extraordinary events related to the subject matter of this Treaty have jeopardized its supreme interests. It shall give notice of its decision to the other Party six months prior to withdrawal from the Treaty. Such notice shall include a statement of the extraordinary events the notifying Party regards as having jeopardized its supreme interests.

Article XVI

1. This Treaty shall be subject to ratification in accordance with the constitutional procedures of each Party. The Treaty shall enter into force on the day of the exchange of instruments of ratification.

2. This Treaty shall be registered pursuant to Article 102 of the Charter of the United Nations.

DONE at Moscow on May 26, 1972, in two copies, each in the English and Russian languages, both texts being equally authentic.

3.3
Convention on the Prohibition of the Development, Production and Stockpiling of Bacteriological (Biological) and Toxin Weapons and on Their Destruction (Biological Weapons Convention or BWC) (1972)

The 1925 Geneva Protocol for the Prohibition of the Use in War of Asphyxiating, Poisonous, or Other Gases, and of Bacteriological Methods of Warfare had banned the use of biological and chemical weapons in times of war, but did not ban their development, production, or possession. Many of the countries that ratified the protocol reserved the right to respond in kind if they were attacked with chemical or biological weapons. Hence, it came to be regarded as a no-first-use agreement. On 26 November 1969 the US president Richard Nixon declared that the United States unilaterally renounced the first use of lethal or incapacitating chemical agents and weapons and unconditionally renounced all methods of biological warfare. The 1972 convention is notable for its virtual lack of verification provisions. In 1992, the USSR acknowledged that despite ratifying the BWC in 1975 it had maintained a large biological weapons program.

On the origins of the convention see Jonathan B. Tucker, "A Farewell to Germs: The US Renunciation of Biological and Toxin Warfare, 1969–70," International Security *27 (2002): 107–149. On attempts to supplement the convention with a verification protocol, see Onno Kervers, "Strengthening Compliance with the Biological Weapons Convention: The Protocol Negotiations,"* Journal of Conflict and Security Law *7 (2002): 275–292.*

The States Parties to this Convention,

Determine to act with a view to achieving effective progress toward general and complete disarmament, including the prohibition and elimination of all types of weapons of mass destruction, and convinced that the prohibition of the development, production and stockpiling of chemical and bacteriological (biological) weapons and their elimination, through effective measures, will facilitate the achievement of general and complete disarmament under strict and effective control,

Recognizing the important significance of the Protocol for the Prohibition of the Use in War of Asphyxiating, Poisonous or Other Gases, and of Bacteriological Methods of Warfare, signed at Geneva on June 17, 1925, and conscious also of the contribution which the said Protocol has already made and continues to make, to mitigating the horrors of war,

Reaffirming their adherence to the principles and objectives of that Protocol and calling upon all States to comply strictly with them,

Recalling that the General Assembly of the United Nations has repeatedly condemned all actions contrary to the principles and objectives of the Geneva Protocol of June 17, 1925,

Desiring to contribute to the strengthening of confidence between peoples and the general improvement of the international atmosphere,

Desiring also to contribute to the realization of the purposes and principles of the Charter of the United Nations,

Convinced of the importance and urgency of eliminating from the arsenals of States, through effective measures, such dangerous weapons of mass destruction as those using chemical or bacteriological (biological) agents,

Recognizing that an agreement on the prohibition of bacteriological (biological) and toxin weapons represents a first possible step towards the achievement of agreement on effective measures also for the prohibition of the development, production and stockpiling of chemical weapons, and determined to continue negotiations to that end,

Determined, for the sake of all mankind, to exclude completely the possibility of bacteriological (biological) agents and toxins being used as weapons,

Convinced that such use would be repugnant to the conscience of mankind and that no effort should be spared to minimize this risk,

Have agreed as follows:

Article I
Each State Party to this Convention undertakes never in any circumstance to develop, produce, stockpile or otherwise acquire or retain:

Microbial or other biological agents, or toxins whatever their origin or method of production, of types and in quantities that have no justification for prophylactic, protective or other peaceful purposes;

Weapons, equipment or means of delivery designed to use such agents or toxins for hostile purposes or in armed conflict.

Article II
Each State Party to this Convention undertakes to destroy, or to divert to peaceful purposes, as soon as possible but not later than nine months after the

entry into force of the Convention, all agents, toxins, weapons, equipment and means of delivery specified in article 1 of the Convention, which are in its possession or under its jurisdiction or control. In implementing the provisions of this article all necessary safety precautions shall be observed to protect populations and the environment.

Article III
Each State Party to this Convention undertakes not to transfer to any recipient whatsoever, directly or indirectly, and not in any way to assist, encourage, or induce any State, group of States or international organizations to manufacture or otherwise acquire any of the agents, toxins, weapons, equipment or means of delivery specified in article 1 of the Convention.

Article IV
Each State Party to this Convention shall, in accordance with its constitutional processes, takes any necessary measures to prohibit and prevent the development, production, stockpiling, acquisition or retention of the agents, toxins, weapons, equipment and means of delivery specified in article 1 of the Convention, within the territory of such State, under its jurisdiction or under its control anywhere.

Article V
The States Parties to this Convention undertake to consult one another and to cooperate in solving any problems which may arise in relation to the objective of, or in the application of the provisions of, the Convention. Consultation and cooperation pursuant to this article may also be undertaken through appropriate international procedures within the framework of the United Nations and in accordance with its Charter.

Article VI
(1) Any State Party to this Convention which finds that any other State Party is acting in breach of obligations deriving from the provisions of the Convention may lodge a complaint with the Security Council of the United Nations. Such a complaint should include all possible evidence confirming its validity, as well as a request for its consideration by the Security Council.

(2) Each State Party to this Convention undertakes to cooperate in carrying out any investigation which the Security Council may initiate, in accordance with the provisions of the Charter of the United Nations, on the basis of the complaint received by the Council. The Security Council shall inform the States Parties to the Convention of the results of the investigation.

Article VII
Each State Party to this Convention undertakes to provide or support assistance, in accordance with the United Nations Charter, to any Party to the Convention which so requests, if the Security Council decides that such Party has been exposed to danger as a result of violation of the Convention.

Article VIII

Nothing in this Convention shall be interpreted as in any way limiting or detracting from the obligations assumed by any State under the Protocol for the Prohibition of the Use in War of Asphyxiating, Poisonous or Other Gases, and of Bacteriological Methods of Warfare, signed at Geneva on June 17, 1925.

Article IX

Each State Party to this Convention affirms the recognized objective of effective prohibition of chemical weapons and, to this end, undertakes to continue negotiations in good faith with a view to reaching early agreement on effective measures for the prohibition of their development, production and stockpiling and for their destruction, and on appropriate measures concerning equipment and means of delivery specifically designed for the production or use of chemical agents for weapons purposes.

Article X

(1) The States Parties to this Convention undertake to facilitate, and have the right to participate in, the fullest possible exchange of equipment, materials and scientific and technological information for the use of bacteriological (biological) agents and toxins for peaceful purposes. Parties to the Convention in a position to do so shall also cooperate in contributing individually or together with other States or international organizations to the further development and application of scientific discoveries in the field of bacteriology (biology) for prevention of disease, or for other peaceful purposes.

(2) This Convention shall be implemented in a manner designed to avoid hampering the economic or technological development of States Parties to the Convention or international cooperation in the field of peaceful bacteriological (biological) activities, including the international exchange of bacteriological (biological) agents and toxins and equipment for the processing, use or production of bacteriological (biological) agents and toxins for peaceful purposes in accordance with the provisions of the Convention.

Article XI

Any State Party may propose amendments to this Convention. Amendments shall enter into force for each State Party accepting the amendments upon their acceptance by a majority of the States Parties to the Convention and thereafter for each remaining State Party on the date of acceptance by it.

Article XII

Five years after the entry into force of this Convention, or earlier if it is requested by a majority of the Parties to the Convention by submitting a proposal to this effect to the Depositary Governments, a conference of States Parties to the Convention shall be held at Geneva, Switzerland, to review the operation of the Convention, with a view to assuring that the purposes of the preamble and the provisions of the Convention, including the provisions concerning negotiations on chemical weapons, are being realized. Such review shall take into account any new scientific and technological developments relevant to the Convention.

Article XIII

(1) This Convention shall be of unlimited duration.

(2) Each State Party to this Convention shall in exercising its natural sovereignty have the right to withdraw from the Convention if it decides that extraordinary events, related to the subject matter of the Convention, have jeopardized the supreme interests of its country. It shall give notice of such withdrawal to all other States Parties to the Convention and to the United Nations Security Council three months in advance. Such notice shall include a statement of the extraordinary events it regards as having jeopardized its supreme interests.

Article XIV

(1) This Convention shall be open to all States for signature. Any State which does not sign the Convention before its entry into force in accordance with paragraph (3) of this Article may accede to it at any time.

(2) This Convention shall be subject to ratification by signatory States. Instruments of ratification and instruments of accession shall be deposited with the Governments of the United States of America, the United Kingdom of Great Britain and Northern Ireland and the Union of Soviet Socialist Republics, which are hereby designated the Depositary Governments.

(3) This Convention shall enter into force after the deposit of instruments of ratification by twenty-two Governments, including the Governments designated as Depositaries of the Convention.

(4) For States whose instruments of ratification or accession are deposited subsequent to the entry into force of this Convention, it shall enter into force on the date of the deposit of their instrument of ratification or accession.

(5) The Depositary Governments shall promptly inform all signatory and acceding States of the date of each signature, the date of deposit of each instrument of ratification or of accession and the date of the entry into force of this Convention, and of the receipt of other notices.

(6) This Convention shall be registered by the Depositary Governments pursuant to Article 102 of the Charter of the United Nations.

Article XV

This Convention, the English, Russian, French, Spanish and Chinese texts of which are equally authentic, shall be deposited in the archives of the Depositary Governments. Duly certified copies of the Convention shall be transmitted by the Depositary Governments of the signatory and acceding States.

3.4
Convention on the Prohibition of the Development, Production, Stockpiling and Use of Chemical Weapons and on Their Destruction (Chemical Weapons Convention or CWC) (1993)

The 1925 Geneva Protocol for the Prohibition of the Use in War of Asphyxiating, Poisonous, or Other Gases, and of Bacteriological Methods of Warfare likely contributed to the stigmatization of chemical weapons, but when formal negotiations for a treaty on chemical weapons began in 1984 progress was at first slow. Impetus came from news of an attack on Kurdish civilians in Iraq in 1988 and from the Gulf War. The convention not only bans the development, production, stockpiling, transfer, and use of chemical weapons, but also requires their destruction. In contrast to the 1972 Biological Weapons Convention, the CWC is notable for its far-reaching verification provisions.

See M. Bothe, N. Ronzitti, and A. Rosas, eds., The New Chemical Weapons Convention—Implementation and Prospects *(The Hague: Kluwer, 1998). On recent US policy in relation to this and other arms control treaties, see Nichol Deller et al., eds.,* Rule of Power or Rule of Law? An Assessment of US Policies and Actions Regarding Security-Related Treaties *(New York: Apex, 2003). On the development of a chemical weapons stigma, see Richard Price, "A Genealogy of the Chemical Weapons Taboo,"* International Organization *49 (1995): 73–103. The Organisation for the Prohibition of Chemical Weapons, established in 1997, has a website at www.opcw.org.*

The States Parties to this Convention,

Determined to act with a view to achieving effective progress towards general and complete disarmament under strict and effective international control, including the prohibition and elimination of all types of weapons of mass destruction,

Desiring to contribute to the realization of the purposes and principles of the Charter of the United Nations,

Recalling that the General Assembly of the United Nations has repeatedly condemned all actions contrary to the principles and objectives of the Protocol for the Prohibition of the Use in War of Asphyxiating, Poisonous or Other Gases, and of Bacteriological Methods of Warfare, signed at Geneva on 17 June 1925 (the Geneva Protocol of 1925),

Recognizing that this Convention reaffirms principles and objectives of and obligations assumed under the Geneva Protocol of 1925, and the Convention on the Prohibition of the Development, Production and Stockpiling of Bacteriological (Biological) and Toxin Weapons and on their Destruction signed at London, Moscow and Washington on 10 April 1972,

Bearing in mind the objective contained in Article IX of the Convention on the Prohibition of the Development, Production and Stockpiling of Bacteriological (Biological) and Toxin Weapons and on their Destruction,

Determined for the sake of all mankind, to exclude completely the possibility of the use of chemical weapons, through the implementation of the provisions of this Convention, thereby complementing the obligations assumed under the Geneva Protocol of 1925,

Recognizing the prohibition, embodied in the pertinent agreements and relevant principles of international law, of the use of herbicides as a method of warfare,

Considering that achievements in the field of chemistry should be used exclusively for the benefit of mankind,

Desiring to promote free trade in chemicals as well as international cooperation and exchange of scientific and technical information in the field of chemical activities for purposes not prohibited under this Convention in order to enhance the economic and technological development of all States Parties,

Convinced that the complete and effective prohibition of the development, production, acquisition, stockpiling, retention, transfer and use of chemical weapons, and their destruction, represent a necessary step towards the achievement of these common objectives,

Have agreed as follows:

Article I: General obligations

1. Each State Party to this Convention undertakes never under any circumstances:

(a) To develop, produce, otherwise acquire, stockpile or retain chemical weapons, or transfer, directly or indirectly, chemical weapons to anyone;

(b) To use chemical weapons;

(c) To engage in any military preparations to use chemical weapons;

(d) To assist, encourage or induce, in any way, anyone to engage in any activity prohibited to a State Party under this Convention.

2. Each State Party undertakes to destroy chemical weapons it owns or possesses, or that are located in any place under its jurisdiction or control, in accordance with the provisions of this Convention.

3. Each State Party undertakes to destroy all chemical weapons it abandoned on the territory of another State Party, in accordance with the provisions of this Convention.

4. Each State Party undertakes to destroy any chemical weapons production facilities it owns or possesses, or that are located in any place under its jurisdiction or control, in accordance with the provisions of this Convention.

5. Each State Party undertakes not to use riot control agents as a method of warfare.

Article II: Definitions and criteria

For the purposes of this Convention:

1. "Chemical Weapons" means the following, together or separately:

(a) Toxic chemicals and their precursors, except where intended for purposes not prohibited under this Convention, as long as the types and quantities are consistent with such purposes;

(b) Munitions and devices, specifically designed to cause death or other harm through the toxic properties of those toxic chemicals specified in subparagraph (a), which would be released as a result of the employment of such munitions and devices;

(c) Any equipment specifically designed for use directly in connection with the employment of munitions and devices specified in subparagraph (b).

2. "Toxic Chemical" means:

Any chemical which through its chemical action on life processes can cause death, temporary incapacitation or permanent harm to humans or animals. This includes all such chemicals, regardless of their origin or of their method of production, and regardless of whether they are produced in facilities, in munitions or elsewhere.

(For the purpose of implementing this Convention, toxic chemicals which have been identified for the application of verification measures are listed in Schedules contained in the Annex on Chemicals.)

3. "Precursor" means:

Any chemical reactant which takes part at any stage in the production by whatever method of a toxic chemical. This includes any key component of a binary or multicomponent chemical system.

(For the purpose of implementing this Convention, precursors which have been identified for the application of verification measures are listed in Schedules contained in the Annex on Chemicals.)

4. "Key Component of Binary or Multicomponent Chemical Systems" (hereinafter referred to as "key component") means:

The precursor which plays the most important role in determining the toxic properties of the final product and reacts rapidly with other chemicals in the binary or multicomponent system.

5. "Old Chemical Weapons" means:

(a) Chemical weapons which were produced before 1925; or

(b) Chemical weapons produced in the period between 1925 and 1946 that have deteriorated to such extent that they can no longer be used as chemical weapons.

6. "Abandoned Chemical Weapons" means:

Chemical weapons, including old chemical weapons, abandoned by a State after 1 January 1925 on the territory of another State without the consent of the latter.

7. "Riot Control Agent" means:

Any chemical not listed in a Schedule, which can produce rapidly in humans sensory irritation or disabling physical effects which disappear within a short time following termination of exposure.

8. "Chemical Weapons Production Facility":

(a) Means any equipment, as well as any building housing such equipment, that was designed, constructed or used at any time since 1 January 1946: (i) As part of the stage in the production of chemicals ("final technological stage") where the material flows would contain, when the equipment is in operation: (1) Any chemical listed in Schedule 1 in the Annex on Chemicals; or (2) Any other chemical that has no use, above 1 tonne per year on the territory of a State Party or in any other place under the jurisdiction or control of a State Party, for purposes not prohibited under this Convention, but can be used for chemical weapons purposes; or (ii) For filling chemical weapons, including, inter alia, the filling of chemicals listed in Schedule 1 into munitions, devices or bulk storage containers; the filling of chemicals into containers that form part of assembled binary munitions and devices or into chemical submunitions that form part of assembled unitary munitions and devices, and the loading of the containers and chemical submunitions into the respective munitions and devices;

(b) Does not mean: (i) Any facility having a production capacity for synthesis of chemicals specified in subparagraph (a) (i) that is less than 1 tonne; (ii) Any facility in which a chemical specified in subparagraph (a) (i) is or was produced as an unavoidable by-product of activities for purposes not prohibited under this Convention, provided that the chemical does not exceed 3 per cent of the total product and that the facility is subject to declaration and inspection under the Annex on Implementation and Verification (hereinafter referred to as "Verification Annex"); or (iii) The single small-scale facility for production of chemicals listed in Schedule 1 for purposes not prohibited under this Convention as referred to in Part VI of the Verification Annex.

9. "Purposes Not Prohibited Under this Convention" means:

(a) Industrial, agricultural, research, medical, pharmaceutical or other peaceful purposes;

(b) Protective purposes, namely those purposes directly related to protection against toxic chemicals and to protection against chemical weapons;

(c) Military purposes not connected with the use of chemical weapons and not dependent on the use of the toxic properties of chemicals as a method of warfare;

(d) Law enforcement including domestic riot control purposes.

10. "Production Capacity" means:

The annual quantitative potential for manufacturing a specific chemical based on the technological process actually used or, if the process is not yet operational, planned to be used at the relevant facility. It shall be deemed to be equal to the nameplate capacity or, if the nameplate capacity is not available, to the design capacity. The nameplate capacity is the product output under conditions optimized for maximum quantity for the production facility, as demonstrated by one or more test-runs. The design capacity is the corresponding theoretically calculated product output.

11. "Organization" means the Organization for the Prohibition of Chemical Weapons established pursuant to Article VIII of this Convention.

12. For the purposes of Article VI:

(a) "Production" of a chemical means its formation through chemical reaction;

(b) "Processing" of a chemical means a physical process, such as formulation, extraction and purification, in which a chemical is not converted into another chemical;

(c) "Consumption" of a chemical means its conversion into another chemical via a chemical reaction.

Article III: Declarations

1. Each State Party shall submit to the Organization, not later than 30 days after this Convention enters into force for it, the following declarations, in which it shall:

(a) With respect to chemical weapons: (i) Declare whether it owns or possesses any chemical weapons, or whether there are any chemical weapons located in any place under its jurisdiction or control; (ii) Specify the precise location, aggregate quantity and detailed inventory of chemical weapons it owns or possesses, or that are located in any place under its jurisdiction or control, in accordance with Part IV (A), paragraphs 1 to 3, of the Verification Annex, except for those chemical weapons referred to in sub-subparagraph (iii); (iii) Report any chemical weapons on its territory that are owned and possessed by another State and located in any place under the jurisdiction or control of another State, in accordance with Part IV (A), paragraph 4, of the Verification Annex; (iv) Declare whether it has transferred or received, directly or indirectly, any chemical weapons since 1 January 1946 and specify the transfer or receipt of such weapons, in accordance with Part IV (A), paragraph 5, of the Verification Annex; (v) Provide its general plan for destruction of chemical weapons that it owns or possesses, or that are located in any place under its jurisdiction or control, in accordance with Part IV (A), paragraph 6, of the Verification Annex;

(b) With respect to old chemical weapons and abandoned chemical weapons: (i) Declare whether it has on its territory old chemical weapons and provide all available information in accordance with Part IV (B), paragraph 3, of the Verification Annex; (ii) Declare whether there are abandoned chemical weapons on its territory and provide all available information in accordance with Part IV (B), paragraph 8, of the Verification Annex; (iii) Declare whether it has abandoned chemical weapons on the territory of other States and provide all available information in accordance with Part IV (B), paragraph 10, of the Verification Annex;

(c) With respect to chemical weapons production facilities: (i) Declare whether it has or has had any chemical weapons production facility under its ownership or possession, or that is or has been located in any place under its jurisdiction or control at any time since 1 January 1946; (ii) Specify any chemical weapons production facility it has or has had under its ownership or possession or that is or has been located in any place under its jurisdiction or control at any time since 1 January 1946, in accordance with Part V, paragraph 1, of the Verification Annex, except for those facilities referred to in sub-subparagraph (iii); (iii) Report any chemical weapons production facility on its territory that another State has or has had under its ownership and possession and that is or has been located in any place under the jurisdiction or control of another State at any time since 1 January 1946, in accordance with Part V, paragraph 2, of the Verification Annex; (iv) Declare whether it has transferred or received, directly or indirectly, any equipment for the production of chemical weapons since 1 January 1946 and specify the transfer or receipt of such equipment, in accordance with Part V, paragraphs 3 to 5, of the Verification Annex; (v) Provide its general plan for destruction of any chemical weapons production facility it owns or possesses, or that is located in any place under its jurisdiction or control, in accordance with Part V, paragraph 6, of the Verification Annex; (vi) Specify actions to be taken for closure of any chemical weapons production facility it owns or possesses, or that is located in any place under its jurisdiction or control, in accordance with Part V, paragraph 1 (i), of the Verification Annex; (vii) Provide its general plan for any temporary conversion of any chemical weapons production facility it owns or possesses, or that is located in any place under its jurisdiction or control, into a chemical weapons destruction facility, in accordance with Part V, paragraph 7, of the Verification Annex;

(d) With respect to other facilities:

Specify the precise location, nature and general scope of activities of any facility or establishment under its ownership or possession, or located in any place under its jurisdiction or control, and that has been designed, constructed or used since 1 January 1946 primarily for development of chemical weapons. Such declaration shall include, inter alia, laboratories and test and evaluation sites;

(e) With respect to riot control agents: Specify the chemical name, structural formula and Chemical Abstracts Service (CAS) registry number, if assigned, of each chemical it holds for riot control purposes. This declaration shall be updated not later than 30 days after any change becomes effective.

2. The provisions of this Article and the relevant provisions of Part IV of the Verification Annex shall not, at the discretion of a State Party, apply to chemical weapons buried on its territory before 1 January 1977 and which remain buried, or which had been dumped at sea before 1 January 1985.

Article IV: Chemical weapons

1. The provisions of this Article and the detailed procedures for its implementation shall apply to all chemical weapons owned or possessed by a State Party, or that are located in any place under its jurisdiction or control, except old chemical weapons and abandoned chemical weapons to which Part IV (B) of the Verification Annex applies.

2. Detailed procedures for the implementation of this Article are set forth in the Verification Annex.

3. All locations at which chemical weapons specified in paragraph 1 are stored or destroyed shall be subject to systematic verification through on-site inspection and monitoring with on-site instruments, in accordance with Part IV (A) of the Verification Annex.

4. Each State Party shall, immediately after the declaration under Article III, paragraph 1 (a), has been submitted, provide access to chemical weapons specified in paragraph 1 for the purpose of systematic verification of the declaration through on-site inspection. Thereafter, each State Party shall not remove any of these chemical weapons, except to a chemical weapons destruction facility. It shall provide access to such chemical weapons, for the purpose of systematic on-site verification.

5. Each State Party shall provide access to any chemical weapons destruction facilities and their storage areas, that it owns or possesses, or that are located in any place under its jurisdiction or control, for the purpose of systematic verification through on-site inspection and monitoring with on-site instruments.

6. Each State Party shall destroy all chemical weapons specified in paragraph 1 pursuant to the Verification Annex and in accordance with the agreed rate and sequence of destruction (hereinafter referred to as "order of destruction"). Such destruction shall begin not later than two years after this Convention enters into force for it and shall finish not later than 10 years after entry into force of this Convention. A State Party is not precluded from destroying such chemical weapons at a faster rate.

7. Each State Party shall:

(a) Submit detailed plans for the destruction of chemical weapons specified in paragraph 1 not later than 60 days before each annual destruction period begins, in accordance with Part IV (A), paragraph 29, of the Verification Annex; the detailed plans shall encompass all stocks to be destroyed during the next annual destruction period;

(b) Submit declarations annually regarding the implementation of its plans for destruction of chemical weapons specified in paragraph 1, not later than 60 days after the end of each annual destruction period; and

(c) Certify, not later than 30 days after the destruction process has been completed, that all chemical weapons specified in paragraph 1 have been destroyed.

8. If a State ratifies or accedes to this Convention after the 10-year period for destruction set forth in paragraph 6, it shall destroy chemical weapons specified in paragraph 1 as soon as possible. The order of destruction and procedures for stringent verification for such a State Party shall be determined by the Executive Council.

9. Any chemical weapons discovered by a State Party after the initial declaration of chemical weapons shall be reported, secured and destroyed in accordance with Part IV (A) of the Verification Annex.

10. Each State Party, during transportation, sampling, storage and destruction of chemical weapons, shall assign the highest priority to ensuring the safety of people and to protecting the environment. Each State Party shall transport, sample, store and destroy chemical weapons in accordance with its national standards for safety and emissions.

11. Any State Party which has on its territory chemical weapons that are owned or possessed by another State, or that are located in any place under the jurisdiction or control of another State, shall make the fullest efforts to ensure that these chemical weapons are removed from its territory not later than one year after this Convention enters into force for it. If they are not removed within one year, the State Party may request the Organization and other States Parties to provide assistance in the destruction of these chemical weapons.

12. Each State Party undertakes to cooperate with other States Parties that request information or assistance on a bilateral basis or through the Technical Secretariat regarding methods and technologies for the safe and efficient destruction of chemical weapons.

13. In carrying out verification activities pursuant to this Article and Part IV (A) of the Verification Annex, the Organization shall consider measures to avoid unnecessary duplication of bilateral or multilateral agreements on verification of chemical weapons storage and their destruction among States Parties.

To this end, the Executive Council shall decide to limit verification to measures complementary to those undertaken pursuant to such a bilateral or multilateral agreement, if it considers that:

(a) Verification provisions of such an agreement are consistent with the verification provisions of this Article and Part IV (A) of the Verification Annex;

(b) Implementation of such an agreement provides for sufficient assurance of compliance with the relevant provisions of this Convention; and

(c) Parties to the bilateral or multilateral agreement keep the Organization fully informed about their verification activities.

14. If the Executive Council takes a decision pursuant to paragraph 13, the Organization shall have the right to monitor the implementation of the bilateral or multilateral agreement.

15. Nothing in paragraphs 13 and 14 shall affect the obligation of a State

Party to provide declarations pursuant to Article III, this Article and Part IV (A) of the Verification Annex.

16. Each State Party shall meet the costs of destruction of chemical weapons it is obliged to destroy. It shall also meet the costs of verification of storage and destruction of these chemical weapons unless the Executive Council decides otherwise. If the Executive Council decides to limit verification measures of the Organization pursuant to paragraph 13, the costs of complementary verification and monitoring by the Organization shall be paid in accordance with the United Nations scale of assessment, as specified in Article VIII, paragraph 7.

17. The provisions of this Article and the relevant provisions of Part IV of the Verification Annex shall not, at the discretion of a State Party, apply to chemical weapons buried on its territory before 1 January 1977 and which remain buried, or which had been dumped at sea before 1 January 1985.

Article V: Chemical weapons production facilities

1. The provisions of this Article and the detailed procedures for its implementation shall apply to any and all chemical weapons production facilities owned or possessed by a State Party, or that are located in any place under its jurisdiction or control.

2. Detailed procedures for the implementation of this Article are set forth in the Verification Annex.

3. All chemical weapons production facilities specified in paragraph 1 shall be subject to systematic verification through on-site inspection and monitoring with on-site instruments in accordance with Part V of the Verification Annex.

4. Each State Party shall cease immediately all activity at chemical weapons production facilities specified in paragraph 1, except activity required for closure.

5. No State Party shall construct any new chemical weapons production facilities or modify any existing facilities for the purpose of chemical weapons production or for any other activity prohibited under this Convention.

6. Each State Party shall, immediately after the declaration under Article III, paragraph 1 (c), has been submitted, provide access to chemical weapons production facilities specified in paragraph 1, for the purpose of systematic verification of the declaration through on-site inspection.

7. Each State Party shall:

(a) Close, not later than 90 days after this Convention enters into force for it, all chemical weapons production facilities specified in paragraph 1, in accordance with Part V of the Verification Annex, and give notice thereof; and

(b) Provide access to chemical weapons production facilities specified in paragraph 1, subsequent to closure, for the purpose of systematic verification through on-site inspection and monitoring with on-site instruments in order to ensure that the facility remains closed and is subsequently destroyed.

8. Each State Party shall destroy all chemical weapons production facilities

specified in paragraph 1 and related facilities and equipment, pursuant to the Verification Annex and in accordance with an agreed rate and sequence of destruction (hereinafter referred to as "order of destruction"). Such destruction shall begin not later than one year after this Convention enters into force for it, and shall finish not later than 10 years after entry into force of this Convention. A State Party is not precluded from destroying such facilities at a faster rate.

9. Each State Party shall:

(a) Submit detailed plans for destruction of chemical weapons production facilities specified in paragraph 1, not later than 180 days before the destruction of each facility begins;

(b) Submit declarations annually regarding the implementation of its plans for the destruction of all chemical weapons production facilities specified in paragraph 1, not later than 90 days after the end of each annual destruction period; and

(c) Certify, not later than 30 days after the destruction process has been completed, that all chemical weapons production facilities specified in paragraph 1 have been destroyed.

10. If a State ratifies or accedes to this Convention after the 10-year period for destruction set forth in paragraph 8, it shall destroy chemical weapons production facilities specified in paragraph 1 as soon as possible. The order of destruction and procedures for stringent verification for such a State Party shall be determined by the Executive Council.

11. Each State Party, during the destruction of chemical weapons production facilities, shall assign the highest priority to ensuring the safety of people and to protecting the environment. Each State Party shall destroy chemical weapons production facilities in accordance with its national standards for safety and emissions.

12. Chemical weapons production facilities specified in paragraph 1 may be temporarily converted for destruction of chemical weapons in accordance with Part V, paragraphs 18 to 25, of the Verification Annex. Such a converted facility must be destroyed as soon as it is no longer in use for destruction of chemical weapons but, in any case, not later than 10 years after entry into force of this Convention.

13. A State Party may request, in exceptional cases of compelling need, permission to use a chemical weapons production facility specified in paragraph 1 for purposes not prohibited under this Convention. Upon the recommendation of the Executive Council, the Conference of the States Parties shall decide whether or not to approve the request and shall establish the conditions upon which approval is contingent in accordance with Part V, Section D, of the Verification Annex.

14. The chemical weapons production facility shall be converted in such a manner that the converted facility is not more capable of being reconverted into a chemical weapons production facility than any other facility used for industrial, agricultural, research, medical, pharmaceutical or other peaceful purposes not involving chemicals listed in Schedule 1.

15. All converted facilities shall be subject to systematic verification through on-site inspection and monitoring with on-site instruments in accordance with Part V, Section D, of the Verification Annex.

16. In carrying out verification activities pursuant to this Article and Part V of the Verification Annex, the Organization shall consider measures to avoid unnecessary duplication of bilateral or multilateral agreements on verification of chemical weapons production facilities and their destruction among States Parties.

To this end, the Executive Council shall decide to limit the verification to measures complementary to those undertaken pursuant to such a bilateral or multilateral agreement, if it considers that:

(a) Verification provisions of such an agreement are consistent with the verification provisions of this Article and Part V of the Verification Annex;

(b) Implementation of the agreement provides for sufficient assurance of compliance with the relevant provisions of this Convention; and

(c) Parties to the bilateral or multilateral agreement keep the Organization fully informed about their verification activities.

17. If the Executive Council takes a decision pursuant to paragraph 16, the Organization shall have the right to monitor the implementation of the bilateral or multilateral agreement.

18. Nothing in paragraphs 16 and 17 shall affect the obligation of a State Party to make declarations pursuant to Article III, this Article and Part V of the Verification Annex.

19. Each State Party shall meet the costs of destruction of chemical weapons production facilities it is obliged to destroy. It shall also meet the costs of verification under this Article unless the Executive Council decides otherwise. If the Executive Council decides to limit verification measures of the Organization pursuant to paragraph 16, the costs of complementary verification and monitoring by the Organization shall be paid in accordance with the United Nations scale of assessment, as specified in Article VIII, paragraph 7.

Article VI: Activities not prohibited under this Convention

1. Each State Party has the right, subject to the provisions of this Convention, to develop, produce, otherwise acquire, retain, transfer and use toxic chemicals and their precursors for purposes not prohibited under this Convention.

2. Each State Party shall adopt the necessary measures to ensure that toxic chemicals and their precursors are only developed, produced, otherwise acquired, retained, transferred, or used within its territory or in any other place under its jurisdiction or control for purposes not prohibited under this Convention. To this end, and in order to verify that activities are in accordance with obligations under this Convention, each State Party shall subject toxic

chemicals and their precursors listed in Schedules 1, 2 and 3 of the Annex on Chemicals, facilities related to such chemicals, and other facilities as specified in the Verification Annex, that are located on its territory or in any other place under its jurisdiction or control, to verification measures as provided in the Verification Annex.

3. Each State Party shall subject chemicals listed in Schedule 1 (hereinafter referred to as "Schedule 1 chemicals") to the prohibitions on production, acquisition, retention, transfer and use as specified in Part VI of the Verification Annex. It shall subject Schedule 1 chemicals and facilities specified in Part VI of the Verification Annex to systematic verification through on-site inspection and monitoring with on-site instruments in accordance with that Part of the Verification Annex.

4. Each State Party shall subject chemicals listed in Schedule 2 (hereinafter referred to as "Schedule 2 chemicals") and facilities specified in Part VII of the Verification Annex to data monitoring and on-site verification in accordance with that Part of the Verification Annex.

5. Each State Party shall subject chemicals listed in Schedule 3 (hereinafter referred to as "Schedule 3 chemicals") and facilities specified in Part VIII of the Verification Annex to data monitoring and on-site verification in accordance with that Part of the Verification Annex.

6. Each State Party shall subject facilities specified in Part IX of the Verification Annex to data monitoring and eventual on-site verification in accordance with that Part of the Verification Annex unless decided otherwise by the Conference of the States Parties pursuant to Part IX, paragraph 22, of the Verification Annex.

7. Not later than 30 days after this Convention enters into force for it, each State Party shall make an initial declaration on relevant chemicals and facilities in accordance with the Verification Annex.

8. Each State Party shall make annual declarations regarding the relevant chemicals and facilities in accordance with the Verification Annex.

9. For the purpose of on-site verification, each State Party shall grant to the inspectors access to facilities as required in the Verification Annex.

10. In conducting verification activities, the Technical Secretariat shall avoid undue intrusion into the State Party's chemical activities for purposes not prohibited under this Convention and, in particular, abide by the provisions set forth in the Annex on the Protection of Confidential Information (hereinafter referred to as "Confidentiality Annex").

11. The provisions of this Article shall be implemented in a manner which avoids hampering the economic or technological development of States Parties, and international cooperation in the field of chemical activities for purposes not prohibited under this Convention including the international exchange of scientific and technical information and chemicals and equipment for the production, processing or use of chemicals for purposes not prohibited under this Convention.

Article VII: National implementation measures

General Undertakings

1. Each State Party shall, in accordance with its constitutional processes, adopt the necessary measures to implement its obligations under this Convention. In particular, it shall:

(a) Prohibit natural and legal persons anywhere on its territory or in any other place under its jurisdiction as recognized by international law from undertaking any activity prohibited to a State Party under this Convention, including enacting penal legislation with respect to such activity;

(b) Not permit in any place under its control any activity prohibited to a State Party under this Convention; and

(c) Extend its penal legislation enacted under subparagraph (a) to any activity prohibited to a State Party under this Convention undertaken anywhere by natural persons, possessing its nationality, in conformity with international law.

2. Each State Party shall cooperate with other States Parties and afford the appropriate form of legal assistance to facilitate the implementation of the obligations under paragraph 1.

3. Each State Party, during the implementation of its obligations under this Convention, shall assign the highest priority to ensuring the safety of people and to protecting the environment, and shall cooperate as appropriate with other States Parties in this regard.

Relations Between the State Party and the Organization

4. In order to fulfil its obligations under this Convention, each State Party shall designate or establish a National Authority to serve as the national focal point for effective liaison with the Organization and other States Parties. Each State Party shall notify the Organization of its National Authority at the time that this Convention enters into force for it.

5. Each State Party shall inform the Organization of the legislative and administrative measures taken to implement this Convention.

6. Each State Party shall treat as confidential and afford special handling to information and data that it receives in confidence from the Organization in connection with the implementation of this Convention.

It shall treat such information and data exclusively in connection with its rights and obligations under this Convention and in accordance with the provisions set forth in the Confidentiality Annex.

7. Each State Party undertakes to cooperate with the Organization in the exercise of all its functions and in particular to provide assistance to the Technical Secretariat.

Article VIII: The Organization

A. General Provisions

1. The States Parties to this Convention hereby establish the Organization for the Prohibition of Chemical Weapons to achieve the object and purpose of this Convention, to ensure the implementation of its provisions, including those for international verification of compliance with it, and to provide a forum for consultation and cooperation among States Parties.

2. All States Parties to this Convention shall be members of the Organization. A State Party shall not be deprived of its membership in the Organization.

3. The seat of the Headquarters of the Organization shall be The Hague, Kingdom of the Netherlands.

4. There are hereby established as the organs of the Organization: the Conference of the States Parties, the Executive Council, and the Technical Secretariat.

5. The Organization shall conduct its verification activities provided for under this Convention in the least intrusive manner possible consistent with the timely and efficient accomplishment of their objectives. It shall request only the information and data necessary to fulfil its responsibilities under this Convention. It shall take every precaution to protect the confidentiality of information on civil and military activities and facilities coming to its knowledge in the implementation of this Convention and, in particular, shall abide by the provisions set forth in the Confidentiality Annex.

6. In undertaking its verification activities the Organization shall consider measures to make use of advances in science and technology.

7. The costs of the Organization's activities shall be paid by States Parties in accordance with the United Nations scale of assessment adjusted to take into account differences in membership between the United Nations and this Organization, and subject to the provisions of Articles IV and V. Financial contributions of States Parties to the Preparatory Commission shall be deducted in an appropriate way from their contributions to the regular budget. The budget of the Organization shall comprise two separate chapters, one relating to administrative and other costs, and one relating to verification costs.

8. A member of the Organization which is in arrears in the payment of its financial contribution to the Organization shall have no vote in the Organization if the amount of its arrears equals or exceeds the amount of the contribution due from it for the preceding two full years. The Conference of the States Parties may, nevertheless, permit such a member to vote if it is satisfied that the failure to pay is due to conditions beyond the control of the member.

B. The Conference of the States Parties

Composition, Procedures and Decision-making

9. The Conference of the States Parties (hereinafter referred to as "the Conference") shall be composed of all members of this Organization. Each member shall have one representative in the Conference, who may be accompanied by alternates and advisers.

10. The first session of the Conference shall be convened by the depositary not later than 30 days after the entry into force of this Convention.

11. The Conference shall meet in regular sessions which shall be held annually unless it decides otherwise.

12. Special sessions of the Conference shall be convened:

(a) When decided by the Conference;

(b) When requested by the Executive Council;

(c) When requested by any member and supported by one third of the members; or

(d) In accordance with paragraph 22 to undertake reviews of the operation of this Convention.

Except in the case of subparagraph (d), the special session shall be convened not later than 30 days after receipt of the request by the Director-General of the Technical Secretariat, unless specified otherwise in the request.

13. The Conference shall also be convened in the form of an Amendment Conference in accordance with Article XV, paragraph 2.

14. Sessions of the Conference shall take place at the seat of the Organization unless the Conference decides otherwise.

15. The Conference shall adopt its rules of procedure. At the beginning of each regular session, it shall elect its Chairman and such other officers as may be required. They shall hold office until a new Chairman and other officers are elected at the next regular session.

16. A majority of the members of the Organization shall constitute a quorum for the Conference.

17. Each member of the Organization shall have one vote in the Conference.

18. The Conference shall take decisions on questions of procedure by a simple majority of the members present and voting. Decisions on matters of substance should be taken as far as possible by consensus. If consensus is not attainable when an issue comes up for decision, the Chairman shall defer any vote for 24 hours and during this period of deferment shall make every effort to facilitate achievement of consensus, and shall report to the Conference before the end of this period. If consensus is not possible at the end of 24 hours, the Conference shall take the decision by a two-thirds majority of members present and voting unless specified otherwise in this Convention. When the issue arises as to whether the question is one of substance or not, that question shall be treated as a matter of substance unless otherwise decided by the Conference by the majority required for decisions on matters of substance.

Powers and Functions

19. The Conference shall be the principal organ of the Organization. It shall consider any questions, matters or issues within the scope of this Convention, including those relating to the powers and functions of the Executive Council and the Technical Secretariat. It may make recommendations and take decisions on any questions, matters or issues related to this Convention raised by a State Party or brought to its attention by the Executive Council.

20. The Conference shall oversee the implementation of this Convention, and act in order to promote its object and purpose. The Conference shall review compliance with this Convention. It shall also oversee the activities of the Executive Council and the Technical Secretariat and may issue guidelines in accordance with this Convention to either of them in the exercise of their functions.

21. The Conference shall:

(a) Consider and adopt at its regular sessions the report, programme and budget of the Organization, submitted by the Executive Council, as well as consider other reports;

(b) Decide on the scale of financial contributions to be paid by States Parties in accordance with paragraph 7;

(c) Elect the members of the Executive Council;

(d) Appoint the Director-General of the Technical Secretariat (hereinafter referred to as "the Director-General");

(e) Approve the rules of procedure of the Executive Council submitted by the latter;

(f) Establish such subsidiary organs as it finds necessary for the exercise of its functions in accordance with this Convention;

(g) Foster international cooperation for peaceful purposes in the field of chemical activities;

(h) Review scientific and technological developments that could affect the operation of this Convention and, in this context, direct the Director-General to establish a Scientific Advisory Board to enable him, in the performance of his functions, to render specialized advice in areas of science and technology relevant to this Convention, to the Conference, the Executive Council or States Parties. The Scientific Advisory Board shall be composed of independent experts appointed in accordance with terms of reference adopted by the Conference;

(i) Consider and approve at its first session any draft agreements, provisions and guidelines developed by the Preparatory Commission;

(j) Establish at its first session the voluntary fund for assistance in accordance with Article X;

(k) Take the necessary measures to ensure compliance with this Convention and to redress and remedy any situation which contravenes the provisions of this Convention, in accordance with Article XII.

22. The Conference shall not later than one year after the expiry of the fifth and the tenth year after the entry into force of this Convention, and at such other times within that time period as may be decided upon, convene in special sessions to undertake reviews of the operation of this Convention. Such reviews shall take into account any relevant scientific and technological developments. At intervals of five years thereafter, unless otherwise decided upon, further sessions of the Conference shall be convened with the same objective.

C. The Executive Council

Composition, Procedure and Decision-making

23. The Executive Council shall consist of 41 members. Each State Party shall have the right, in accordance with the principle of rotation, to serve on the Executive Council. The members of the Executive Council shall be elected by the Conference for a term of two years. In order to ensure the effective functioning of this Convention, due regard being specially paid to equitable geographical distribution, to the importance of chemical industry, as well as to political and security interests, the Executive Council shall be composed as follows:

(a) Nine States Parties from Africa to be designated by States Parties located in this region. As a basis for this designation it is understood that, out of these nine States Parties, three members shall, as a rule, be the States Parties with the most significant national chemical industry in the region as determined by internationally reported and published data; in addition, the regional group shall agree also to take into account other regional factors in designating these three members;

(b) Nine States Parties from Asia to be designated by States Parties located in this region. As a basis for this designation it is understood that, out of these nine States Parties, four members shall, as a rule, be the States Parties with the most significant national chemical industry in the region as determined by internationally reported and published data; in addition, the regional group shall agree also to take into account other regional factors in designating these four members;

(c) Five States Parties from Eastern Europe to be designated by States Parties located in this region. As a basis for this designation it is understood that, out of these five States Parties, one member shall, as a rule, be the State Party with the most significant national chemical industry in the region as determined by internationally reported and published data; in addition, the regional group shall agree also to take into account other regional factors in designating this one member;

(d) Seven States Parties from Latin America and the Caribbean to be designated by States Parties located in this region. As a basis for this designation it is understood that, out of these seven States Parties, three members shall, as a rule, be the States Parties with the most significant national chemical industry in the region as determined by internationally reported and published data; in addition, the regional group shall agree also to take into account other regional factors in designating these three members;

(e) Ten States Parties from among Western European and other States to be designated by States Parties located in this region. As a basis for this designation it is understood that, out of these 10 States Parties, 5 members shall, as a rule, be the States Parties with the most significant national chemical industry in the region as determined by internationally reported and published data; in addition, the regional group shall agree also to take into account other regional factors in designating these five members;

(f) One further State Party to be designated consecutively by States Parties located in the regions of Asia and Latin America and the Caribbean. As a basis for this designation it is understood that this State Party shall be a rotating member from these regions.

24. For the first election of the Executive Council 20 members shall be elected for a term of one year, due regard being paid to the established numerical proportions as described in paragraph 23.

25. After the full implementation of Articles IV and V the Conference may, upon the request of a majority of the members of the Executive Council, review the composition of the Executive Council taking into account developments related to the principles specified in paragraph 23 that are governing its composition.

26. The Executive Council shall elaborate its rules of procedure and submit them to the Conference for approval.

27. The Executive Council shall elect its Chairman from among its members.

28. The Executive Council shall meet for regular sessions. Between regular sessions it shall meet as often as may be required for the fulfilment of its powers and functions.

29. Each member of the Executive Council shall have one vote. Unless otherwise specified in this Convention, the Executive Council shall take decisions on matters of substance by a two-thirds majority of all its members. The Executive Council shall take decisions on questions of procedure by a simple majority of all its members. When the issue arises as to whether the question is one of substance or not, that question shall be treated as a matter of substance unless otherwise decided by the Executive Council by the majority required for decisions on matters of substance.

Powers and Functions

30. The Executive Council shall be the executive organ of the Organization.

It shall be responsible to the Conference. The Executive Council shall carry out the powers and functions entrusted to it under this Convention, as well as those functions delegated to it by the Conference. In so doing, it shall act in conformity with the recommendations, decisions and guidelines of the Conference and assure their proper and continuous implementation.

31. The Executive Council shall promote the effective implementation of, and compliance with, this Convention. It shall supervise the activities of the Technical Secretariat, cooperate with the National Authority of each State Party and facilitate consultations and cooperation among States Parties at their request.

32. The Executive Council shall:

(a) Consider and submit to the Conference the draft programme and budget of the Organization;

(b) Consider and submit to the Conference the draft report of the Organization on the implementation of this Convention, the report on the performance of its own activities and such special reports as it deems necessary or which the Conference may request;

(c) Make arrangements for the sessions of the Conference including the preparation of the draft agenda.

33. The Executive Council may request the convening of a special session of the Conference.

34. The Executive Council shall:

(a) Conclude agreements or arrangements with States and international organizations on behalf of the Organization, subject to prior approval by the Conference;

(b) Conclude agreements with States Parties on behalf of the Organization in connection with Article X and supervise the voluntary fund referred to in Article X;

(c) Approve agreements or arrangements relating to the implementation of verification activities, negotiated by the Technical Secretariat with States Parties.

35. The Executive Council shall consider any issue or matter within its competence affecting this Convention and its implementation, including concerns regarding compliance, and cases of non-compliance, and, as appropriate, inform States Parties and bring the issue or matter to the attention of the Conference.

36. In its consideration of doubts or concerns regarding compliance and cases of non-compliance, including, inter alia, abuse of the rights provided for under this Convention, the Executive Council shall consult with the States Parties involved and, as appropriate, request the State Party to take measures to redress the situation within a specified time. To the extent that the Executive Council considers further action to be necessary, it shall take, inter alia, one or more of the following measures:

(a) Inform all States Parties of the issue or matter;

(b) Bring the issue or matter to the attention of the Conference;

(c) Make recommendations to the Conference regarding measures to redress the situation and to ensure compliance.

The Executive Council shall, in cases of particular gravity and urgency, bring the issue or matter, including relevant information and conclusions, directly to the attention of the United Nations General Assembly and the United Nations Security Council. It shall at the same time inform all States Parties of this step.

D. The Technical Secretariat

37. The Technical Secretariat shall assist the Conference and the Executive Council in the performance of their functions. The Technical Secretariat shall carry out the verification measures provided for in this Convention. It shall carry out the other functions entrusted to it under this Convention as well as those functions delegated to it by the Conference and the Executive Council.

38. The Technical Secretariat shall:

(a) Prepare and submit to the Executive Council the draft programme and budget of the Organization;

(b) Prepare and submit to the Executive Council the draft report of the Organization on the implementation of this Convention and such other reports as the Conference or the Executive Council may request;

(c) Provide administrative and technical support to the Conference, the Executive Council and subsidiary organs;

(d) Address and receive communications on behalf of the Organization to and from States Parties on matters pertaining to the implementation of this Convention;

(e) Provide technical assistance and technical evaluation to States Parties in the implementation of the provisions of this Convention, including evaluation of scheduled and unscheduled chemicals.

39. The Technical Secretariat shall:

(a) Negotiate agreements or arrangements relating to the implementation of verification activities with States Parties, subject to approval by the Executive Council;

(b) Not later than 180 days after entry into force of this Convention, coordinate the establishment and maintenance of permanent stockpiles of emergency and humanitarian assistance by States Parties in accordance with Article X, paragraphs 7 (b) and (c). The Technical Secretariat may inspect the items maintained for serviceability. Lists of items to be stockpiled shall be considered and approved by the Conference pursuant to paragraph 21(i) above;

(c) Administer the voluntary fund referred to in Article X, compile declarations made by the States Parties and register, when requested, bilateral agreements concluded between States Parties or between a State Party and the Organization for the purposes of Article X.

40. The Technical Secretariat shall inform the Executive Council of any

problem that has arisen with regard to the discharge of its functions, including doubts, ambiguities or uncertainties about compliance with this Convention that have come to its notice in the performance of its verification activities and that it has been unable to resolve or clarify through its consultations with the State Party concerned.

41. The Technical Secretariat shall comprise a Director-General, who shall be its head and chief administrative officer, inspectors and such scientific, technical and other personnel as may be required.

42. The Inspectorate shall be a unit of the Technical Secretariat and shall act under the supervision of the Director-General.

43. The Director-General shall be appointed by the Conference upon the recommendation of the Executive Council for a term of four years, renewable for one further term, but not thereafter.

44. The Director-General shall be responsible to the Conference and the Executive Council for the appointment of the staff and the organization and functioning of the Technical Secretariat. The paramount consideration in the employment of the staff and in the determination of the conditions of service shall be the necessity of securing the highest standards of efficiency, competence and integrity. Only citizens of States Parties shall serve as the Director-General, as inspectors or as other members of the professional and clerical staff. Due regard shall be paid to the importance of recruiting the staff on as wide a geographical basis as possible. Recruitment shall be guided by the principle that the staff shall be kept to a minimum necessary for the proper discharge of the responsibilities of the Technical Secretariat.

45. The Director-General shall be responsible for the organization and functioning of the Scientific Advisory Board referred to in paragraph 21 (h). The Director-General shall, in consultation with States Parties, appoint members of the Scientific Advisory Board, who shall serve in their individual capacity. The members of the Board shall be appointed on the basis of their expertise in the particular scientific fields relevant to the implementation of this Convention. The Director-General may also, as appropriate, in consultation with members of the Board, establish temporary working groups of scientific experts to provide recommendations on specific issues. In regard to the above, States Parties may submit lists of experts to the Director-General.

46. In the performance of their duties, the Director-General, the inspectors and the other members of the staff shall not seek or receive instructions from any Government or from any other source external to the Organization. They shall refrain from any action that might reflect on their positions as international officers responsible only to the Conference and the Executive Council.

47. Each State Party shall respect the exclusively international character of the responsibilities of the Director-General, the inspectors and the other members of the staff and not seek to influence them in the discharge of their responsibilities.

E. Privileges and Immunities

48. The Organization shall enjoy on the territory and in any other place under the jurisdiction or control of a State Party such legal capacity and such privileges and immunities as are necessary for the exercise of its functions.

49. Delegates of States Parties, together with their alternates and advisers, representatives appointed to the Executive Council together with their alternates and advisers, the Director-General and the staff of the Organization shall enjoy such privileges and immunities as are necessary in the independent exercise of their functions in connection with the Organization.

50. The legal capacity, privileges, and immunities referred to in this Article shall be defined in agreements between the Organization and the States Parties as well as in an agreement between the Organization and the State in which the headquarters of the Organization is seated. These agreements shall be considered and approved by the Conference pursuant to paragraph 21(i).

51. Notwithstanding paragraphs 48 and 49, the privileges and immunities enjoyed by the Director-General and the staff of the Technical Secretariat during the conduct of verification activities shall be those set forth in Part II, Section B, of the Verification Annex.

Article IX: Consultations, cooperation and fact-finding

1. States Parties shall consult and cooperate, directly among themselves, or through the Organization or other appropriate international procedures, including procedures within the framework of the United Nations and in accordance with its Charter, on any matter which may be raised relating to the object and purpose, or the implementation of the provisions, of this Convention.

2. Without prejudice to the right of any State Party to request a challenge inspection, States Parties should, whenever possible, first make every effort to clarify and resolve, through exchange of information and consultations among themselves, any matter which may cause doubt about compliance with this Convention, or which gives rise to concerns about a related matter which may be considered ambiguous. A State Party which receives a request from another State Party for clarification of any matter which the requesting State Party believes causes such a doubt or concern shall provide the requesting State Party as soon as possible, but in any case not later than 10 days after the request, with information sufficient to answer the doubt or concern raised along with an explanation of how the information provided resolves the matter. Nothing in this Convention shall affect the right of any two or more States Parties to arrange by mutual consent for inspections or any other procedures among themselves to clarify and resolve any matter which may cause doubt about compliance or gives rise to a concern about a related matter which may be considered ambiguous. Such arrangements shall not affect the rights and obligations of any State Party under other provisions of this Convention.

Procedure for Requesting Clarification

3. A State Party shall have the right to request the Executive Council to assist in clarifying any situation which may be considered ambiguous or which gives rise to a concern about the possible non-compliance of another State Party with this Convention. The Executive Council shall provide appropriate information in its possession relevant to such a concern.

4. A State Party shall have the right to request the Executive Council to obtain clarification from another State Party on any situation which may be considered ambiguous or which gives rise to a concern about its possible non-compliance with this Convention. In such a case, the following shall apply:

(a) The Executive Council shall forward the request for clarification to the State Party concerned through the Director-General not later than 24 hours after its receipt;

(b) The requested State Party shall provide the clarification to the Executive Council as soon as possible, but in any case not later than 10 days after the receipt of the request;

(c) The Executive Council shall take note of the clarification and forward it to the requesting State Party not later than 24 hours after its receipt;

(d) If the requesting State Party deems the clarification to be inadequate, it shall have the right to request the Executive Council to obtain from the requested State Party further clarification;

(e) For the purpose of obtaining further clarification requested under subparagraph (d), the Executive Council may call on the Director-General to establish a group of experts from the Technical Secretariat, or if appropriate staff are not available in the Technical Secretariat, from elsewhere, to examine all available information and data relevant to the situation causing the concern. The group of experts shall submit a factual report to the Executive Council on its findings;

(f) If the requesting State Party considers the clarification obtained under subparagraphs (d) and (e) to be unsatisfactory, it shall have the right to request a special session of the Executive Council in which States Parties involved that are not members of the Executive Council shall be entitled to take part. In such a special session, the Executive Council shall consider the matter and may recommend any measure it deems appropriate to resolve the situation.

5. A State Party shall also have the right to request the Executive Council to clarify any situation which has been considered ambiguous or has given rise to a concern about its possible non-compliance with this Convention. The Executive Council shall respond by providing such assistance as appropriate.

6. The Executive Council shall inform the States Parties about any request for clarification provided in this Article.

7. If the doubt or concern of a State Party about a possible non-compliance has not been resolved within 60 days after the submission of the request for clarification to the Executive Council, or it believes its doubts warrant urgent consideration, notwithstanding its right to request a challenge inspection, it

may request a special session of the Conference in accordance with Article VIII, paragraph 12 (c). At such a special session, the Conference shall consider the matter and may recommend any measure it deems appropriate to resolve the situation.

Procedures for Challenge Inspections

8. Each State Party has the right to request an on-site challenge inspection of any facility or location in the territory or in any other place under the jurisdiction or control of any other State Party for the sole purpose of clarifying and resolving any questions concerning possible non-compliance with the provisions of this Convention, and to have this inspection conducted anywhere without delay by an inspection team designated by the Director-General and in accordance with the Verification Annex.

9. Each State Party is under the obligation to keep the inspection request within the scope of this Convention and to provide in the inspection request all appropriate information on the basis of which a concern has arisen regarding possible non-compliance with this Convention as specified in the Verification Annex. Each State Party shall refrain from unfounded inspection requests, care being taken to avoid abuse. The challenge inspection shall be carried out for the sole purpose of determining facts relating to the possible non-compliance.

10. For the purpose of verifying compliance with the provisions of this Convention, each State Party shall permit the Technical Secretariat to conduct the on-site challenge inspection pursuant to paragraph 8.

11. Pursuant to a request for a challenge inspection of a facility or location, and in accordance with the procedures provided for in the Verification Annex, the inspected State Party shall have:

(a) The right and the obligation to make every reasonable effort to demonstrate its compliance with this Convention and, to this end, to enable the inspection team to fulfil its mandate;

(b) The obligation to provide access within the requested site for the sole purpose of establishing facts relevant to the concern regarding possible non-compliance; and

(c) The right to take measures to protect sensitive installations, and to prevent disclosure of confidential information and data, not related to this Convention.

12. With regard to an observer, the following shall apply:

(a) The requesting State Party may, subject to the agreement of the inspected State Party, send a representative who may be a national either of the requesting State Party or of a third State Party, to observe the conduct of the challenge inspection.

(b) The inspected State Party shall then grant access to the observer in accordance with the Verification Annex.

(c) The inspected State Party shall, as a rule, accept the proposed observer, but if the inspected State Party exercises a refusal, that fact shall be recorded in the final report.

13. The requesting State Party shall present an inspection request for an on-site challenge inspection to the Executive Council and at the same time to the Director-General for immediate processing.

14. The Director-General shall immediately ascertain that the inspection request meets the requirements specified in Part X, paragraph 4, of the Verification Annex, and, if necessary, assist the requesting State Party in filing the inspection request accordingly. When the inspection request fulfils the requirements, preparations for the challenge inspection shall begin.

15. The Director-General shall transmit the inspection request to the inspected State Party not less than 12 hours before the planned arrival of the inspection team at the point of entry.

16. After having received the inspection request, the Executive Council shall take cognizance of the Director-General's actions on the request and shall keep the case under its consideration throughout the inspection procedure. However, its deliberations shall not delay the inspection process.

17. The Executive Council may, not later than 12 hours after having received the inspection request, decide by a three-quarter majority of all its members against carrying out the challenge inspection, if it considers the inspection request to be frivolous, abusive or clearly beyond the scope of this Convention as described in paragraph 8. Neither the requesting nor the inspected State Party shall participate in such a decision. If the Executive Council decides against the challenge inspection, preparations shall be stopped, no further action on the inspection request shall be taken, and the States Parties concerned shall be informed accordingly.

18. The Director-General shall issue an inspection mandate for the conduct of the challenge inspection. The inspection mandate shall be the inspection request referred to in paragraphs 8 and 9 put into operational terms, and shall conform with the inspection request.

19. The challenge inspection shall be conducted in accordance with Part X or, in the case of alleged use, in accordance with Part XI of the Verification Annex. The inspection team shall be guided by the principle of conducting the challenge inspection in the least intrusive manner possible, consistent with the effective and timely accomplishment of its mission.

20. The inspected State Party shall assist the inspection team throughout the challenge inspection and facilitate its task. If the inspected State Party proposes, pursuant to Part X, Section C, of the Verification Annex, arrangements to demonstrate compliance with this Convention, alternative to full and comprehensive access, it shall make every reasonable effort, through consultations with the inspection team, to reach agreement on the modalities for establishing the facts with the aim of demonstrating its compliance.

21. The final report shall contain the factual findings as well as an assessment by the inspection team of the degree and nature of access and cooperation granted for the satisfactory implementation of the challenge inspection. The

Director-General shall promptly transmit the final report of the inspection team to the requesting State Party, to the inspected State Party, to the Executive Council and to all other States Parties. The Director-General shall further transmit promptly to the Executive Council the assessments of the requesting and of the inspected States Parties, as well as the views of other States Parties which may be conveyed to the Director-General for that purpose, and then provide them to all States Parties.

22. The Executive Council shall, in accordance with its powers and functions, review the final report of the inspection team as soon as it is presented, and address any concerns as to:

(a) Whether any non-compliance has occurred;

(b) Whether the request had been within the scope of this Convention; and

(c) Whether the right to request a challenge inspection had been abused.

23. If the Executive Council reaches the conclusion, in keeping with its powers and functions, that further action may be necessary with regard to paragraph 22, it shall take the appropriate measures to redress the situation and to ensure compliance with this Convention, including specific recommendations to the Conference. In the case of abuse, the Executive Council shall examine whether the requesting State Party should bear any of the financial implications of the challenge inspection.

24. The requesting State Party and the inspected State Party shall have the right to participate in the review process. The Executive Council shall inform the States Parties and the next session of the Conference of the outcome of the process.

25. If the Executive Council has made specific recommendations to the Conference, the Conference shall consider action in accordance with Article XII.

Article X: Assistance and protection against chemical weapons

1. For the purposes of this Article, "Assistance" means the coordination and delivery to States Parties of protection against chemical weapons, including, inter alia, the following: detection equipment and alarm systems; protective equipment; decontamination equipment and decontaminants; medical antidotes and treatments; and advice on any of these protective measures.

2. Nothing in this Convention shall be interpreted as impeding the right of any State Party to conduct research into, develop, produce, acquire, transfer or use means of protection against chemical weapons, for purposes not prohibited under this Convention.

3. Each State Party undertakes to facilitate, and shall have the right to participate in, the fullest possible exchange of equipment, material and scientific and technological information concerning means of protection against chemical weapons.

4. For the purposes of increasing the transparency of national programmes related to protective purposes, each State Party shall provide annually to the

Technical Secretariat information on its programme, in accordance with procedures to be considered and approved by the Conference pursuant to Article VIII, paragraph 21 (i).

5. The Technical Secretariat shall establish, not later than 180 days after entry into force of this Convention and maintain, for the use of any requesting State Party, a data bank containing freely available information concerning various means of protection against chemical weapons as well as such information as may be provided by States Parties.

The Technical Secretariat shall also, within the resources available to it, and at the request of a State Party, provide expert advice and assist the State Party in identifying how its programmes for the development and improvement of a protective capacity against chemical weapons could be implemented.

6. Nothing in this Convention shall be interpreted as impeding the right of States Parties to request and provide assistance bilaterally and to conclude individual agreements with other States Parties concerning the emergency procurement of assistance.

7. Each State Party undertakes to provide assistance through the Organization and to this end to elect to take one or more of the following measures:

(a) To contribute to the voluntary fund for assistance to be established by the Conference at its first session;

(b) To conclude, if possible not later than 180 days after this Convention enters into force for it, agreements with the Organization concerning the procurement, upon demand, of assistance;

(c) To declare, not later than 180 days after this Convention enters into force for it, the kind of assistance it might provide in response to an appeal by the Organization. If, however, a State Party subsequently is unable to provide the assistance envisaged in its declaration, it is still under the obligation to provide assistance in accordance with this paragraph.

8. Each State Party has the right to request and, subject to the procedures set forth in paragraphs 9, 10 and 11, to receive assistance and protection against the use or threat of use of chemical weapons if it considers that:

(a) Chemical weapons have been used against it;

(b) Riot control agents have been used against it as a method of warfare; or

(c) It is threatened by actions or activities of any State that are prohibited for States Parties by Article 1.

9. The request, substantiated by relevant information, shall be submitted to the Director-General, who shall transmit it immediately to the Executive Council and to all States Parties. The Director-General shall immediately forward the request to States Parties which have volunteered, in accordance with paragraphs 7 (b) and (c), to dispatch emergency assistance in case of use of chemical weapons or use of riot control agents as a method of warfare, or humanitarian assistance in case of serious threat of use of chemical weapons or serious threat of use of riot control agents as a method of warfare to the State

Party concerned not later than 12 hours after receipt of the request. The Director-General shall initiate, not later than 24 hours after receipt of the request, an investigation in order to provide foundation for further action. He shall complete the investigation within 72 hours and forward a report to the Executive Council. If additional time is required for completion of the investigation, an interim report shall be submitted within the same time-frame. The additional time required for investigation shall not exceed 72 hours. It may, however, be further extended by similar periods. Reports at the end of each additional period shall be submitted to the Executive Council. The investigation shall, as appropriate and in conformity with the request and the information accompanying the request, establish relevant facts related to the request as well as the type and scope of supplementary assistance and protection needed.

10. The Executive Council shall meet not later than 24 hours after receiving an investigation report to consider the situation and shall take a decision by simple majority within the following 24 hours on whether to instruct the Technical Secretariat to provide supplementary assistance. The Technical Secretariat shall immediately transmit to all States Parties and relevant international organizations the investigation report and the decision taken by the Executive Council. When so decided by the Executive Council, the Director-General shall provide assistance immediately. For this purpose, the Director-General may cooperate with the requesting State Party, other States Parties and relevant international organizations. The States Parties shall make the fullest possible efforts to provide assistance.

11. If the information available from the ongoing investigation or other reliable sources would give sufficient proof that there are victims of use of chemical weapons and immediate action is indispensable, the Director-General shall notify all States Parties and shall take emergency measures of assistance, using the resources the Conference has placed at his disposal for such contingencies. The Director-General shall keep the Executive Council informed of actions undertaken pursuant to this paragraph.

Article XI: Economic and technological development

1. The provisions of this Convention shall be implemented in a manner which avoids hampering the economic or technological development of States Parties, and international cooperation in the field of chemical activities for purposes not prohibited under this Convention including the international exchange of scientific and technical information and chemicals and equipment for the production, processing or use of chemicals for purposes not prohibited under this Convention.

2. Subject to the provisions of this Convention and without prejudice to the principles and applicable rules of international law, the States Parties shall:

(a) Have the right, individually or collectively, to conduct research with, to develop, produce, acquire, retain, transfer, and use chemicals;

(b) Undertake to facilitate, and have the right to participate in, the fullest possible exchange of chemicals, equipment and scientific and technical information relating to the development and application of chemistry for purposes not prohibited under this Convention;

(c) Not maintain among themselves any restrictions, including those in any international agreements, incompatible with the obligations undertaken under this Convention, which would restrict or impede trade and the development and promotion of scientific and technological knowledge in the field of chemistry for industrial, agricultural, research, medical, pharmaceutical or other peaceful purposes;

(d) Not use this Convention as grounds for applying any measures other than those provided for, or permitted, under this Convention nor use any other international agreement for pursuing an objective inconsistent with this Convention;

(e) Undertake to review their existing national regulations in the field of trade in chemicals in order to render them consistent with the object and purpose of this Convention.

Article XII: Measures to redress a situation and to ensure compliance, including sanctions

1. The Conference shall take the necessary measures, as set forth in paragraphs 2, 3 and 4, to ensure compliance with this Convention and to redress and remedy any situation which contravenes the provisions of this Convention. In considering action pursuant to this paragraph, the Conference shall take into account all information and recommendations on the issues submitted by the Executive Council.

2. In cases where a State Party has been requested by the Executive Council to take measures to redress a situation raising problems with regard to its compliance, and where the State Party fails to fulfil the request within the specified time, the Conference may, inter alia, upon the recommendation of the Executive Council, restrict or suspend the State Party's rights and privileges under this Convention until it undertakes the necessary action to conform with its obligations under this Convention.

3. In cases where serious damage to the object and purpose of this Convention may result from activities prohibited under this Convention, in particular by Article I, the Conference may recommend collective measures to States Parties in conformity with international law.

4. The Conference shall, in cases of particular gravity, bring the issue, including relevant information and conclusions, to the attention of the United Nations General Assembly and the United Nations Security Council.

Article XIII: Relation to other international agreements

Nothing in this Convention shall be interpreted as in any way limiting or detracting from the obligations assumed by any State under the Protocol for the Prohibition of the Use in War of Asphyxiating, Poisonous or Other Gases, and of Bacteriological Methods of Warfare, signed at Geneva on 17 June 1925, and under the Convention on the Prohibition of the Development, Production and Stockpiling of Bacteriological (Biological) and Toxin Weapons and on Their Destruction, signed at London, Moscow and Washington on 10 April 1972.

Article XIV: Settlement of disputes

1. Disputes that may arise concerning the application or the interpretation of this Convention shall be settled in accordance with the relevant provisions of this Convention and in conformity with the provisions of the Charter of the United Nations.

2. When a dispute arises between two or more States Parties, or between one or more States Parties and the Organization, relating to the interpretation or application of this Convention, the parties concerned shall consult together with a view to the expeditious settlement of the dispute by negotiation or by other peaceful means of the parties' choice, including recourse to appropriate organs of this Convention and, by mutual consent, referral to the International Court of Justice in conformity with the Statute of the Court. The States Parties involved shall keep the Executive Council informed of actions being taken.

3. The Executive Council may contribute to the settlement of a dispute by whatever means it deems appropriate, including offering its good offices, calling upon the States Parties to a dispute to start the settlement process of their choice and recommending a time-limit for any agreed procedure.

4. The Conference shall consider questions related to disputes raised by States Parties or brought to its attention by the Executive Council. The Conference shall, as it finds necessary, establish or entrust organs with tasks related to the settlement of these disputes in conformity with Article VIII, paragraph 21 (f).

5. The Conference and the Executive Council are separately empowered, subject to authorization from the General Assembly of the United Nations, to request the International Court of Justice to give an advisory opinion on any legal question arising within the scope of the activities of the Organization. An agreement between the Organization and the United Nations shall be concluded for this purpose in accordance with Article VIII, paragraph 34 (a).

6. This Article is without prejudice to Article IX or to the provisions on measures to redress a situation and to ensure compliance, including sanctions.

Article XV: Amendments

1. Any State Party may propose amendments to this Convention. Any State Party may also propose changes, as specified in paragraph 4, to the Annexes of this Convention. Proposals for amendments shall be subject to the procedures in paragraphs 2 and 3. Proposals for changes, as specified in paragraph 4, shall be subject to the procedures in paragraph 5.

2. The text of a proposed amendment shall be submitted to the Director-General for circulation to all States Parties and to the Depositary. The proposed amendment shall be considered only by an Amendment Conference. Such an Amendment Conference shall be convened if one third or more of the States

Parties notify the Director-General not later than 30 days after its circulation that they support further consideration of the proposal. The Amendment Conference shall be held immediately following a regular session of the Conference unless the requesting States Parties ask for an earlier meeting. In no case shall an Amendment Conference be held less than 60 days after the circulation of the proposed amendment.

3. Amendments shall enter into force for all States Parties 30 days after deposit of the instruments of ratification or acceptance by all the States Parties referred to under subparagraph (b) below:

(a) When adopted by the Amendment Conference by a positive vote of a majority of all States Parties with no State Party casting a negative vote; and

(b) Ratified or accepted by all those States Parties casting a positive vote at the Amendment Conference.

4. In order to ensure the viability and the effectiveness of this Convention, provisions in the Annexes shall be subject to changes in accordance with paragraph 5, if proposed changes are related only to matters of an administrative or technical nature. All changes to the Annex on Chemicals shall be made in accordance with paragraph 5. Sections A and C of the Confidentiality Annex, Part X of the Verification Annex, and those definitions in Part I of the Verification Annex which relate exclusively to challenge inspections, shall not be subject to changes in accordance with paragraph 5.

5. Proposed changes referred to in paragraph 4 shall be made in accordance with the following procedures:

(a) The text of the proposed changes shall be transmitted together with the necessary information to the Director-General. Additional information for the evaluation of the proposal may be provided by any State Party and the Director-General. The Director-General shall promptly communicate any such proposals and information to all States Parties, the Executive Council and the Depositary;

(b) Not later than 60 days after its receipt, the Director-General shall evaluate the proposal to determine all its possible consequences for the provisions of this Convention and its implementation and shall communicate any such information to all States Parties and the Executive Council;

(c) The Executive Council shall examine the proposal in the light of all information available to it, including whether the proposal fulfils the requirements of paragraph 4. Not later than 90 days after its receipt, the Executive Council shall notify its recommendation, with appropriate explanations, to all States Parties for consideration. States Parties shall acknowledge receipt within 10 days;

(d) If the Executive Council recommends to all States Parties that the proposal be adopted, it shall be considered approved if no State Party objects to it within 90 days after receipt of the recommendation. If the Executive Council recommends that the proposal be rejected, it shall be considered rejected if no State Party objects to the rejection within 90 days after receipt of the recommendation;

(e) If a recommendation of the Executive Council does not meet with the acceptance required under subparagraph (d), a decision on the proposal, including whether it fulfils the requirements of paragraph 4, shall be taken as a matter of substance by the Conference at its next session;

(f) The Director-General shall notify all States Parties and the Depositary of any decision under this paragraph;

(g) Changes approved under this procedure shall enter into force for all States Parties 180 days after the date of notification by the Director-General of their approval unless another time period is recommended by the Executive Council or decided by the Conference.

Article XVI: Duration and withdrawal

1. This Convention shall be of unlimited duration.

2. Each State Party shall, in exercising its national sovereignty, have the right to withdraw from this Convention if it decides that extraordinary events, related to the subject-matter of this Convention, have jeopardized the supreme interests of its country. It shall give notice of such withdrawal 90 days in advance to all other States Parties, the Executive Council, the Depositary and the United Nations Security Council. Such notice shall include a statement of the extraordinary events it regards as having jeopardized its supreme interests.

3. The withdrawal of a State Party from this Convention shall not in any way affect the duty of States to continue fulfilling the obligations assumed under any relevant rules of international law, particularly the Geneva Protocol of 1925.

Article XVII: Status of the annexes

The Annexes form an integral part of this Convention. Any reference to this Convention includes the Annexes.

Article XVIII: Signature

This Convention shall be open for signature for all States before its entry into force.

Article XIX: Ratification

This Convention shall be subject to ratification by States Signatories according to their respective constitutional processes.

Article XX: Accession

Any State which does not sign this Convention before its entry into force may accede to it at any time thereafter.

Article XXI: Entry into force

1. This Convention shall enter into force 180 days after the date of the deposit of the 65th instrument of ratification, but in no case earlier than two years after its opening for signature.

2. For States whose instruments of ratification or accession are deposited subsequent to the entry into force of this Convention, it shall enter into force on the 30th day following the date of deposit of their instrument of ratification or accession.

Article XXII: Reservations
The Articles of this Convention shall not be subject to reservations. The Annexes of this Convention shall not be subject to reservations incompatible with its object and purpose.

Article XXIII: Depositary
The Secretary-General of the United Nations is hereby designated as the Depositary of this Convention and shall, inter alia:

(a) Promptly inform all signatory and acceding States of the date of each signature, the date of deposit of each instrument of ratification or accession and the date of the entry into force of this Convention, and of the receipt of other notices;

(b) Transmit duly certified copies of this Convention to the Governments of all signatory and acceding States; and

(c) Register this Convention pursuant to Article 102 of the Charter of the United Nations.

Article XIV: Authentic Texts
This Convention, of which the Arabic, Chinese, English, French, Russian and Spanish texts are equally authentic, shall be deposited with the Secretary-General of the United Nations.

IN WITNESS WHEREOF the undersigned, being duly authorized to that effect, have signed this Convention.

Done at Paris on the thirteenth day of January, one thousand nine hundred and ninety-three.

. . . [Annexes not included]

3.5
Comprehensive Nuclear Test-Ban Treaty (CTBT) (1996)

Following the dangerous stand-off during the Cuban Missile Crisis in 1962 talks began in 1963 for a comprehensive nuclear test ban. Verification proved to be a stumbling block and a limited test ban treaty was concluded instead. This was the 1963 Treaty Banning Nuclear Weapon Tests in the Atmosphere, in Outer Space and Under Water (Partial Test Ban Treaty or PTBT). The United States and USSR concluded the Threshold Test Ban Treaty in 1974, which limited the yield of underground nuclear weapon tests to 150 kilotons. A Comprehensive Nuclear Test-Ban Treaty was finally achieved in 1996. It has yet to enter into force, in part because the US has not ratified it, despite having been the first to sign. Many non–nuclear weapon states and campaigners regard entry-into-force of the CTBT as central to the nuclear weapon states fulfilling their disarmament obligations in article VI of the NPT.

On the US failure to ratify the CTBT in the context of US nuclear policy more generally, see Patricia Hewitson, "Nonproliferation and Reduction of Nuclear Weapons: Risks of Weakening the Multilateral Nuclear Nonproliferation Norm," Berkeley Journal of International Law 21 (2003): 405–494. *See also Masahiko Asada, "CTBT: Legal Questions Arising from Its Non-Entry-Into-Force,"* Journal of Conflict and Security Law 7 (2002): 85–122.

The States Parties to this Treaty (hereinafter referred to as "the States Parties"),

Welcoming the international agreements and other positive measures of recent years in the field of nuclear disarmament, including reductions in arsenals of nuclear weapons, as well as in the field of the prevention of nuclear proliferation in all its aspects,

Underlining the importance of the full and prompt implementation of such agreements and measures,

Convinced that the present international situation provides an opportunity to take further effective measures towards nuclear disarmament and against the proliferation of nuclear weapons in all its aspects, and declaring their intention to take such measures,

Stressing therefore the need for continued systematic and progressive efforts to reduce nuclear weapons globally, with the ultimate goal of eliminating those weapons, and of general and complete disarmament under strict and effective international control,

Recognizing that the cessation of all nuclear weapon test explosions and all other nuclear explosions, by constraining the development and qualitative improvement of nuclear weapons and ending the development of advanced new types of nuclear weapons, constitutes an effective measure of nuclear disarmament and non-proliferation in all its aspects,

Further recognizing that an end to all such nuclear explosions will thus constitute a meaningful step in the realization of a systematic process to achieve nuclear disarmament,

Convinced that the most effective way to achieve an end to nuclear testing is through the conclusion of a universal and internationally and effectively verifiable comprehensive nuclear test-ban treaty, which has long been one of the highest priority objectives of the international community in the field of disarmament and non-proliferation,

Noting the aspirations expressed by the Parties to the 1963 Treaty Banning Nuclear Weapon Tests in the Atmosphere, in Outer Space and Under Water to seek to achieve the discontinuance of all test explosions of nuclear weapons for all time,

Noting also the views expressed that this Treaty could contribute to the protection of the environment,

Affirming the purpose of attracting the adherence of all States to this Treaty and its objective to contribute effectively to the prevention of the proliferation of nuclear weapons in all its aspects, to the process of nuclear disarmament and therefore to the enhancement of international peace and security,

Have agreed as follows:

Article I: Basic obligations

1. Each State Party undertakes not to carry out any nuclear weapon test explosion or any other nuclear explosion, and to prohibit and prevent any such nuclear explosion at any place under its jurisdiction or control.

2. Each State Party undertakes, furthermore, to refrain from causing, encouraging, or in any way participating in the carrying out of any nuclear weapon test explosion or any other nuclear explosion.

Article II: The Organization

A. General Provisions

1. The States Parties hereby establish the Comprehensive Nuclear Test-Ban Treaty Organization (hereinafter referred to as "the Organization") to achieve the object and purpose of this Treaty, to ensure the implementation of its provi-

sions, including those for international verification of compliance with it, and to provide a forum for consultation and cooperation among States Parties.

2. All States Parties shall be members of the Organization. A State Party shall not be deprived of its membership in the Organization.

3. The seat of the Organization shall be Vienna, Republic of Austria.

4. There are hereby established as organs of the Organization: the Conference of the States Parties, the Executive Council and the Technical Secretariat, which shall include the International Data Centre.

5. Each State Party shall cooperate with the Organization in the exercise of its functions in accordance with this Treaty. States Parties shall consult, directly among themselves, or through the Organization or other appropriate international procedures, including procedures within the framework of the United Nations and in accordance with its Charter, on any matter which may be raised relating to the object and purpose, or the implementation of the provisions, of this Treaty.

6. The Organization shall conduct its verification activities provided for under this Treaty in the least intrusive manner possible consistent with the timely and efficient accomplishment of their objectives. It shall request only the information and data necessary to fulfil its responsibilities under this Treaty. It shall take every precaution to protect the confidentiality of information on civil and military activities and facilities coming to its knowledge in the implementation of this Treaty and, in particular, shall abide by the confidentiality provisions set forth in this Treaty.

7. Each State Party shall treat as confidential and afford special handling to information and data that it receives in confidence from the Organization in connection with the implementation of this Treaty. It shall treat such information and data exclusively in connection with its rights and obligations under this Treaty.

8. The Organization, as an independent body, shall seek to utilize existing expertise and facilities, as appropriate, and to maximize cost efficiencies, through cooperative arrangements with other international organizations such as the International Atomic Energy Agency. Such arrangements, excluding those of a minor and normal commercial and contractual nature, shall be set out in agreements to be submitted to the Conference of the States Parties for approval.

9. The costs of the activities of the Organization shall be met annually by the States Parties in accordance with the United Nations scale of assessments adjusted to take into account differences in membership between the United Nations and the Organization.

10. Financial contributions of States Parties to the Preparatory Commission shall be deducted in an appropriate way from their contributions to the regular budget.

11. A member of the Organization which is in arrears in the payment of its assessed contribution to the Organization shall have no vote in the Organization if the amount of its arrears equals or exceeds the amount of the

contribution due from it for the preceding two full years. The Conference of the States Parties may, nevertheless, permit such a member to vote if it is satisfied that the failure to pay is due to conditions beyond the control of the member.

B. The Conference of the States Parties

Composition, Procedures and Decision-making

12. The Conference of the States Parties (hereinafter referred to as "the Conference") shall be composed of all States Parties. Each State Party shall have one representative in the Conference, who may be accompanied by alternates and advisers.

13. The initial session of the Conference shall be convened by the Depositary no later than 30 days after the entry into force of this Treaty.

14. The Conference shall meet in regular sessions, which shall be held annually, unless it decides otherwise.

15. A special session of the Conference shall be convened:

   (a) When decided by the Conference;

   (b) When requested by the Executive Council; or

   (c) When requested by any State Party and supported by a majority of the States Parties.

The special session shall be convened no later than 30 days after the decision of the Conference, the request of the Executive Council, or the attainment of the necessary support, unless specified otherwise in the decision or request.

16. The Conference may also be convened in the form of an Amendment Conference, in accordance with Article VII.

17. The Conference may also be convened in the form of a Review Conference, in accordance with Article VIII.

18. Sessions shall take place at the seat of the Organization unless the Conference decides otherwise.

19. The Conference shall adopt its rules of procedure. At the beginning of each session, it shall elect its President and such other officers as may be required. They shall hold office until a new President and other officers are elected at the next session.

20. A majority of the States Parties shall constitute a quorum.

21. Each State Party shall have one vote.

22. The Conference shall take decisions on matters of procedure by a majority of members present and voting. Decisions on matters of substance shall be taken as far as possible by consensus. If consensus is not attainable when an issue comes up for decision, the President of the Conference shall defer any vote for 24 hours and during this period of deferment shall make every effort to facilitate achievement of consensus, and shall report to the Conference before the end of this period. If consensus is not possible at the end of 24

hours, the Conference shall take a decision by a two-thirds majority of members present and voting unless specified otherwise in this Treaty. When the issue arises as to whether the question is one of substance or not, that question shall be treated as a matter of substance unless otherwise decided by the majority required for decisions on matters of substance.

23. When exercising its function under paragraph 26 (k), the Conference shall take a decision to add any State to the list of States contained in Annex 1 to this Treaty in accordance with the procedure for decisions on matters of substance set out in paragraph 22. Notwithstanding paragraph 22, the Conference shall take decisions on any other change to Annex 1 to this Treaty by consensus.

Powers and Functions

24. The Conference shall be the principal organ of the Organization. It shall consider any questions, matters or issues within the scope of this Treaty, including those relating to the powers and functions of the Executive Council and the Technical Secretariat, in accordance with this Treaty. It may make recommendations and take decisions on any questions, matters or issues within the scope of this Treaty raised by a State Party or brought to its attention by the Executive Council.

25. The Conference shall oversee the implementation of, and review compliance with, this Treaty and act in order to promote its object and purpose. It shall also oversee the activities of the Executive Council and the Technical Secretariat and may issue guidelines to either of them for the exercise of their functions.

26. The Conference shall:

(a) Consider and adopt the report of the Organization on the implementation of this Treaty and the annual programme and budget of the Organization, submitted by the Executive Council, as well as consider other reports;

(b) Decide on the scale of financial contributions to be paid by States Parties in accordance with paragraph 9;

(c) Elect the members of the Executive Council;

(d) Appoint the Director-General of the Technical Secretariat (hereinafter referred to as "the Director-General");

(e) Consider and approve the rules of procedure of the Executive Council submitted by the latter;

(f) Consider and review scientific and technological developments that could affect the operation of this Treaty. In this context, the Conference may direct the Director-General to establish a Scientific Advisory Board to enable him or her, in the performance of his or her functions, to render specialized advice in areas of science and technology relevant to this Treaty to the Conference, to the Executive Council, or to States Parties. In that case, the Scientific Advisory Board shall be composed of independent experts serving in their individual capacity and appointed, in accordance with terms of reference adopted by the Conference, on the basis of their expertise and experience in the particular scientific fields relevant to the implementation of this Treaty;

(g) Take the necessary measures to ensure compliance with this Treaty and to redress and remedy any situation that contravenes the provisions of this Treaty, in accordance with Article V;

(h) Consider and approve at its initial session any draft agreements, arrangements, provisions, procedures, operational manuals, guidelines and any other documents developed and recommended by the Preparatory Commission;

(i) Consider and approve agreements or arrangements negotiated by the Technical Secretariat with States Parties, other States and international organizations to be concluded by the Executive Council on behalf of the Organization in accordance with paragraph 38 (h);

(j) Establish such subsidiary organs as it finds necessary for the exercise of its functions in accordance with this Treaty; and

(k) Update Annex 1 to this Treaty, as appropriate, in accordance with paragraph 23.

C. The Executive Council

Composition, Procedures and Decision-making

27. The Executive Council shall consist of 51 members. Each State Party shall have the right, in accordance with the provisions of this Article, to serve on the Executive Council.

28. Taking into account the need for equitable geographical distribution, the Executive Council shall comprise:

(a) Ten States Parties from Africa;

(b) Seven States Parties from Eastern Europe;

(c) Nine States Parties from Latin America and the Caribbean;

(d) Seven States Parties from the Middle East and South Asia;

(e) Ten States Parties from North America and Western Europe; and

(f) Eight States Parties from South–East Asia, the Pacific and the Far East.

All States in each of the above geographical regions are listed in Annex 1 to this Treaty. Annex 1 to this Treaty shall be updated, as appropriate, by the Conference in accordance with paragraphs 23 and 26 (k). It shall not be subject to amendments or changes under the procedures contained in Article VII.

29. The members of the Executive Council shall be elected by the Conference. In this connection, each geographical region shall designate States Parties from that region for election as members of the Executive Council as follows:

(a) At least one-third of the seats allocated to each geographical region shall be filled, taking into account political and security interests, by States Parties in that region designated on the basis of the nuclear capabilities relevant to the Treaty as determined by international data as well as all or any of the following indicative criteria in the order of priority determined by each region: (i) Number of monitoring facilities of the International Monitoring System; (ii) Expertise and experience in monitoring technology; and (iii) Contribution to the annual budget of the Organization;

(b) One of the seats allocated to each geographical region shall be filled on a rotational basis by the State Party that is first in the English alphabetical order among the States Parties in that region that have not served as members of the Executive Council for the longest period of time since becoming States Parties or since their last term, whichever is shorter. A State Party designated on this basis may decide to forgo its seat. In that case, such a State Party shall submit a letter of renunciation to the Director-General, and the seat shall be filled by the State Party following next-in-order according to this sub-paragraph; and

(c) The remaining seats allocated to each geographical region shall be filled by States Parties designated from among all the States Parties in that region by rotation or elections.

30. Each member of the Executive Council shall have one representative on the Executive Council, who may be accompanied by alternates and advisers.

31. Each member of the Executive Council shall hold office from the end of the session of the Conference at which that member is elected until the end of the second regular annual session of the Conference thereafter, except that for the first election of the Executive Council, 26 members shall be elected to hold office until the end of the third regular annual session of the Conference, due regard being paid to the established numerical proportions as described in paragraph 28.

32. The Executive Council shall elaborate its rules of procedure and submit them to the Conference for approval.

33. The Executive Council shall elect its Chairman from among its members.

34. The Executive Council shall meet for regular sessions. Between regular sessions it shall meet as may be required for the fulfilment of its powers and functions.

35. Each member of the Executive Council shall have one vote.

36. The Executive Council shall take decisions on matters of procedure by a majority of all its members. The Executive Council shall take decisions on matters of substance by a two-thirds majority of all its members unless specified otherwise in this Treaty. When the issue arises as to whether the question is one of substance or not, that question shall be treated as a matter of substance unless otherwise decided by the majority required for decisions on matters of substance.

Powers and Functions

37. The Executive Council shall be the executive organ of the Organization. It shall be responsible to the Conference. It shall carry out the powers and functions entrusted to it in accordance with this Treaty. In so doing, it shall act in conformity with the recommendations, decisions and guidelines of the Conference and ensure their continuous and proper implementation.

38. The Executive Council shall:

(a) Promote effective implementation of, and compliance with, this Treaty;

(b) Supervise the activities of the Technical Secretariat;

(c) Make recommendations as necessary to the Conference for consideration of further proposals for promoting the object and purpose of this Treaty;

(d) Cooperate with the National Authority of each State Party;

(e) Consider and submit to the Conference the draft annual programme and budget of the Organization, the draft report of the Organization on the implementation of this Treaty, the report on the performance of its own activities and such other reports as it deems necessary or that the Conference may request;

(f) Make arrangements for the sessions of the Conference, including the preparation of the draft agenda;

(g) Examine proposals for changes, on matters of an administrative or technical nature, to the Protocol or the Annexes thereto, pursuant to Article VII, and make recommendations to the States Parties regarding their adoption;

(h) Conclude, subject to prior approval of the Conference, agreements or arrangements with States Parties, other States and international organizations on behalf of the Organization and supervise their implementation, with the exception of agreements or arrangements referred to in sub-paragraph (i);

(i) Approve and supervise the operation of agreements or arrangements relating to the implementation of verification activities with States Parties and other States; and

(j) Approve any new operational manuals and any changes to the existing operational manuals that may be proposed by the Technical Secretariat.

39. The Executive Council may request a special session of the Conference.

40. The Executive Council shall:

(a) Facilitate cooperation among States Parties, and between States Parties and the Technical Secretariat, relating to the implementation of this Treaty through information exchanges;

(b) Facilitate consultation and clarification among States Parties in accordance with Article IV; and

(c) Receive, consider and take action on requests for, and reports on, on-site inspections in accordance with Article IV.

41. The Executive Council shall consider any concern raised by a State Party about possible non-compliance with this Treaty and abuse of the rights established by this Treaty. In so doing, the Executive Council shall consult

with the States Parties involved and, as appropriate, request a State Party to take measures to redress the situation within a specified time. To the extent that the Executive Council considers further action to be necessary, it shall take, inter alia, one or more of the following measures:

(a) Notify all States Parties of the issue or matter;

(b) Bring the issue or matter to the attention of the Conference;

(c) Make recommendations to the Conference or take action, as appropriate, regarding measures to redress the situation and to ensure compliance in accordance with Article V.

D. The Technical Secretariat

42. The Technical Secretariat shall assist States Parties in the implementation of this Treaty. The Technical Secretariat shall assist the Conference and the Executive Council in the performance of their functions. The Technical Secretariat shall carry out the verification and other functions entrusted to it by this Treaty, as well as those functions delegated to it by the Conference or the Executive Council in accordance with this Treaty. The Technical Secretariat shall include, as an integral part, the International Data Centre.

43. The functions of the Technical Secretariat with regard to verification of compliance with this Treaty shall, in accordance with Article IV and the Protocol, include inter alia:

(a) Being responsible for supervising and coordinating the operation of the International Monitoring System;

(b) Operating the International Data Centre;

(c) Routinely receiving, processing, analysing and reporting on International Monitoring System data;

(d) Providing technical assistance in, and support for, the installation and operation of monitoring stations;

(e) Assisting the Executive Council in facilitating consultation and clarification among States Parties;

(f) Receiving requests for on-site inspections and processing them, facilitating Executive Council consideration of such requests, carrying out the preparations for, and providing technical support during, the conduct of on-site inspections, and reporting to the Executive Council;

(g) Negotiating agreements or arrangements with States Parties, other States and international organizations and concluding, subject to prior approval by the Executive Council, any such agreements or arrangements relating to verification activities with States Parties or other States; and

(h) Assisting the States Parties through their National Authorities on other issues of verification under this Treaty.

44. The Technical Secretariat shall develop and maintain, subject to approval by the Executive Council, operational manuals to guide the operation of the various components of the verification regime, in accordance with Article IV and the Protocol. These manuals shall not constitute integral parts of

this Treaty or the Protocol and may be changed by the Technical Secretariat subject to approval by the Executive Council. The Technical Secretariat shall promptly inform the States Parties of any changes in the operational manuals.

45. The functions of the Technical Secretariat with respect to administrative matters shall include:

(a) Preparing and submitting to the Executive Council the draft programme and budget of the Organization;

(b) Preparing and submitting to the Executive Council the draft report of the Organization on the implementation of this Treaty and such other reports as the Conference or the Executive Council may request;

(c) Providing administrative and technical support to the Conference, the Executive Council and other subsidiary organs;

(d) Addressing and receiving communications on behalf of the Organization relating to the implementation of this Treaty; and

(e) Carrying out the administrative responsibilities related to any agreements between the Organization and other international organizations.

46. All requests and notifications by States Parties to the Organization shall be transmitted through their National Authorities to the Director-General. Requests and notifications shall be in one of the official languages of this Treaty. In response the Director-General shall use the language of the transmitted request or notification.

47. With respect to the responsibilities of the Technical Secretariat for preparing and submitting to the Executive Council the draft programme and budget of the Organization, the Technical Secretariat shall determine and maintain a clear accounting of all costs for each facility established as part of the International Monitoring System. Similar treatment in the draft programme and budget shall be accorded to all other activities of the Organization.

48. The Technical Secretariat shall promptly inform the Executive Council of any problems that have arisen with regard to the discharge of its functions that have come to its notice in the performance of its activities and that it has been unable to resolve through consultations with the State Party concerned.

49. The Technical Secretariat shall comprise a Director-General, who shall be its head and chief administrative officer, and such scientific, technical and other personnel as may be required. The Director-General shall be appointed by the Conference upon the recommendation of the Executive Council for a term of four years, renewable for one further term, but not thereafter. The first Director-General shall be appointed by the Conference at its initial session upon the recommendation of the Preparatory Commission.

50. The Director-General shall be responsible to the Conference and the Executive Council for the appointment of the staff and for the organization and functioning of the Technical Secretariat. The paramount consideration in the employment of the staff and in the determination of the conditions of service shall be the necessity of securing the highest standards of professional expertise, experience, efficiency, competence and integrity. Only citizens of States Parties shall serve as the Director-General, as inspectors or as members of the

professional and clerical staff. Due regard shall be paid to the importance of recruiting the staff on as wide a geographical basis as possible. Recruitment shall be guided by the principle that the staff shall be kept to the minimum necessary for the proper discharge of the responsibilities of the Technical Secretariat.

51. The Director-General may, as appropriate, after consultation with the Executive Council, establish temporary working groups of scientific experts to provide recommendations on specific issues.

52. In the performance of their duties, the Director-General, the inspectors, the inspection assistants and the members of the staff shall not seek or receive instructions from any Government or from any other source external to the Organization. They shall refrain from any action that might reflect adversely on their positions as international officers responsible only to the Organization. The Director-General shall assume responsibility for the activities of an inspection team.

53. Each State Party shall respect the exclusively international character of the responsibilities of the Director-General, the inspectors, the inspection assistants and the members of the staff and shall not seek to influence them in the discharge of their responsibilities.

E. Privileges and Immunities

54. The Organization shall enjoy on the territory and in any other place under the jurisdiction or control of a State Party such legal capacity and such privileges and immunities as are necessary for the exercise of its functions.

55. Delegates of States Parties, together with their alternates and advisers, representatives of members elected to the Executive Council, together with their alternates and advisers, the Director-General, the inspectors, the inspection assistants and the members of the staff of the Organization shall enjoy such privileges and immunities as are necessary in the independent exercise of their functions in connection with the Organization.

56. The legal capacity, privileges and immunities referred to in this Article shall be defined in agreements between the Organization and the States Parties as well as in an agreement between the Organization and the State in which the Organization is seated. Such agreements shall be considered and approved in accordance with paragraph 26 (h) and (i).

57. Notwithstanding paragraphs 54 and 55, the privileges and immunities enjoyed by the Director-General, the inspectors, the inspection assistants and the members of the staff of the Technical Secretariat during the conduct of verification activities shall be those set forth in the Protocol.

Article III: National implementation measures

1. Each State Party shall, in accordance with its constitutional processes, take any necessary measures to implement its obligations under this Treaty. In particular, it shall take any necessary measures:

(a) To prohibit natural and legal persons anywhere on its territory or in any other place under its jurisdiction as recognized by international law from undertaking any activity prohibited to a State Party under this Treaty;

(b) To prohibit natural and legal persons from undertaking any such activity anywhere under its control; and

(c) To prohibit, in conformity with international law, natural persons possessing its nationality from undertaking any such activity anywhere.

2. Each State Party shall cooperate with other States Parties and afford the appropriate form of legal assistance to facilitate the implementation of the obligations under paragraph 1.

3. Each State Party shall inform the Organization of the measures taken pursuant to this Article.

4. In order to fulfil its obligations under the Treaty, each State Party shall designate or set up a National Authority and shall so inform the Organization upon entry into force of the Treaty for it. The National Authority shall serve as the national focal point for liaison with the Organization and with other States Parties.

Article IV: Verification

A. General Provisions

1. In order to verify compliance with this Treaty, a verification regime shall be established consisting of the following elements:
    (a) An International Monitoring System;
    (b) Consultation and clarification;
    (c) On-site inspections; and
    (d) Confidence-building measures.

At entry into force of this Treaty, the verification regime shall be capable of meeting the verification requirements of this Treaty.

2. Verification activities shall be based on objective information, shall be limited to the subject matter of this Treaty, and shall be carried out on the basis of full respect for the sovereignty of States Parties and in the least intrusive manner possible consistent with the effective and timely accomplishment of their objectives. Each State Party shall refrain from any abuse of the right of verification.

3. Each State Party undertakes in accordance with this Treaty to cooperate, through its National Authority established pursuant to Article III, paragraph 4, with the Organization and with other States Parties to facilitate the verification of compliance with this Treaty by, inter alia:

(a) Establishing the necessary facilities to participate in these verification measures and establishing the necessary communication;

(b) Providing data obtained from national stations that are part of the International Monitoring System;

(c) Participating, as appropriate, in a consultation and clarification process;

(d) Permitting the conduct of on-site inspections; and

(e) Participating, as appropriate, in confidence-building measures.

4. All States Parties, irrespective of their technical and financial capabilities, shall enjoy the equal right of verification and assume the equal obligation to accept verification.

5. For the purposes of this Treaty, no State Party shall be precluded from using information obtained by national technical means of verification in a manner consistent with generally recognized principles of international law, including that of respect for the sovereignty of States.

6. Without prejudice to the right of States Parties to protect sensitive installations, activities or locations not related to this Treaty, States Parties shall not interfere with elements of the verification regime of this Treaty or with national technical means of verification operating in accordance with paragraph 5.

7. Each State Party shall have the right to take measures to protect sensitive installations and to prevent disclosure of confidential information and data not related to this Treaty.

8. Moreover, all necessary measures shall be taken to protect the confidentiality of any information related to civil and military activities and facilities obtained during verification activities.

9. Subject to paragraph 8, information obtained by the Organization through the verification regime established by this Treaty shall be made available to all States Parties in accordance with the relevant provisions of this Treaty and the Protocol.

10. The provisions of this Treaty shall not be interpreted as restricting the international exchange of data for scientific purposes.

11. Each State Party undertakes to cooperate with the Organization and with other States Parties in the improvement of the verification regime, and in the examination of the verification potential of additional monitoring technologies such as electromagnetic pulse monitoring or satellite monitoring, with a view to developing, when appropriate, specific measures to enhance the efficient and cost-effective verification of this Treaty. Such measures shall, when agreed, be incorporated in existing provisions in this Treaty, the Protocol or as additional sections of the Protocol, in accordance with Article VII, or, if appropriate, be reflected in the operational manuals in accordance with Article II, paragraph 44.

12. The States Parties undertake to promote cooperation among themselves to facilitate and participate in the fullest possible exchange relating to technologies used in the verification of this Treaty in order to enable all States Parties to strengthen their national implementation of verification measures and to benefit from the application of such technologies for peaceful purposes.

13. The provisions of this Treaty shall be implemented in a manner which avoids hampering the economic and technological development of the States

Parties for further development of the application of atomic energy for peaceful purposes.

Verification Responsibilities of the Technical Secretariat

14. In discharging its responsibilities in the area of verification specified in this Treaty and the Protocol, in cooperation with the States Parties the Technical Secretariat shall, for the purpose of this Treaty:

(a) Make arrangements to receive and distribute data and reporting products relevant to the verification of this Treaty in accordance with its provisions, and to maintain a global communications infrastructure appropriate to this task;

(b) Routinely through its International Data Centre, which shall in principle be the focal point within the Technical Secretariat for data storage and data processing:

(i) Receive and initiate requests for data from the International Monitoring System;

(ii) Receive data, as appropriate, resulting from the process of consultation and clarification, from on-site inspections, and from confidence-building measures; and

(iii) Receive other relevant data from States Parties and international organizations in accordance with this Treaty and the Protocol;

(c) Supervise, coordinate and ensure the operation of the International Monitoring System and its component elements, and of the International Data Centre, in accordance with the relevant operational manuals;

(d) Routinely process, analyse and report on International Monitoring System data according to agreed procedures so as to permit the effective international verification of this Treaty and to contribute to the early resolution of compliance concerns;

(e) Make available all data, both raw and processed, and any reporting products, to all States Parties, each State Party taking responsibility for the use of International Monitoring System data in accordance with Article II, paragraph 7, and with paragraphs 8 and 13 of this Article;

(f) Provide to all States Parties equal, open, convenient and timely access to all stored data;

(g) Store all data, both raw and processed, and reporting products;

(h) Coordinate and facilitate requests for additional data from the International Monitoring System;

(i) Coordinate requests for additional data from one State Party to another State Party;

(j) Provide technical assistance in, and support for, the installation and operation of monitoring facilities and respective communication means, where such assistance and support are required by the State concerned;

(k) Make available to any State Party, upon its request, techniques utilized by the Technical Secretariat and its International Data Centre in compiling, storing, processing, analysing and reporting on data from the verification regime; and

(l) Monitor, assess and report on the overall performance of the International Monitoring System and of the International Data Centre.

15. The agreed procedures to be used by the Technical Secretariat in discharging the verification responsibilities referred to in paragraph 14 and detailed in the Protocol shall be elaborated in the relevant operational manuals.

B. The International Monitoring System

16. The International Monitoring System shall comprise facilities for seismological monitoring, radionuclide monitoring including certified laboratories, hydroacoustic monitoring, infrasound monitoring, and respective means of communication, and shall be supported by the International Data Centre of the Technical Secretariat.

17. The International Monitoring System shall be placed under the authority of the Technical Secretariat. All monitoring facilities of the International Monitoring System shall be owned and operated by the States hosting or otherwise taking responsibility for them in accordance with the Protocol.

18. Each State Party shall have the right to participate in the international exchange of data and to have access to all data made available to the International Data Centre. Each State Party shall cooperate with the International Data Centre through its National Authority.

Funding the International Monitoring System

19. For facilities incorporated into the International Monitoring System and specified in Tables 1-A, 2-A, 3 and 4 of Annex 1 to the Protocol, and for their functioning, to the extent that such facilities are agreed by the relevant State and the Organization to provide data to the International Data Centre in accordance with the technical requirements of the Protocol and relevant operational manuals, the Organization, as specified in agreements or arrangements pursuant to Part I, paragraph 4 of the Protocol, shall meet the costs of:

(a) Establishing any new facilities and upgrading existing facilities, unless the State responsible for such facilities meets these costs itself;

(b) Operating and maintaining International Monitoring System facilities, including facility physical security if appropriate, and application of agreed data authentication procedures;

(c) Transmitting International Monitoring System data (raw or processed) to the International Data Centre by the most direct and cost-effective means available, including, if necessary, via appropriate communications nodes, from monitoring stations, laboratories, analytical facilities or from national data centres; or such data (including samples where appropriate) to laboratory and analytical facilities from monitoring stations; and

(d) Analysing samples on behalf of the Organization.

20. For auxiliary network seismic stations specified in Table 1-B of Annex 1 to the Protocol the Organization, as specified in agreements or arrangements pursuant to Part I, paragraph 4 of the Protocol, shall meet the costs only of:

(a) Transmitting data to the International Data Centre;

(b) Authenticating data from such stations;

(c) Upgrading stations to the required technical standard, unless the State responsible for such facilities meets these costs itself;

(d) If necessary, establishing new stations for the purposes of this Treaty where no appropriate facilities currently exist, unless the State responsible for such facilities meets these costs itself; and

(e) Any other costs related to the provision of data required by the Organization as specified in the relevant operational manuals.

21. The Organization shall also meet the cost of provision to each State Party of its requested selection from the standard range of International Data Centre reporting products and services, as specified in Part I, Section F of the Protocol. The cost of preparation and transmission of any additional data or products shall be met by the requesting State Party.

22. The agreements or, if appropriate, arrangements concluded with States Parties or States hosting or otherwise taking responsibility for facilities of the International Monitoring System shall contain provisions for meeting these costs. Such provisions may include modalities whereby a State Party meets any of the costs referred to in paragraphs 19 (a) and 20 (c) and (d) for facilities which it hosts or for which it is responsible, and is compensated by an appropriate reduction in its assessed financial contribution to the Organization. Such a reduction shall not exceed 50 per cent of the annual assessed financial contribution of a State Party, but may be spread over successive years. A State Party may share such a reduction with another State Party by agreement or arrangement between themselves and with the concurrence of the Executive Council. The agreements or arrangements referred to in this paragraph shall be approved in accordance with Article II, paragraphs 26 (h) and 38 (i).

Changes to the International Monitoring System

23. Any measures referred to in paragraph 11 affecting the International Monitoring System by means of addition or deletion of a monitoring technology shall, when agreed, be incorporated into this Treaty and the Protocol pursuant to Article VII, paragraphs 1 to 6.

24. The following changes to the International Monitoring System, subject to the agreement of those States directly affected, shall be regarded as matters of an administrative or technical nature pursuant to Article VII, paragraphs 7 and 8:

(a) Changes to the number of facilities specified in the Protocol for a given monitoring technology; and

(b) Changes to other details for particular facilities as reflected in the Tables of Annex 1 to the Protocol (including, inter alia, State responsible for the facility; location; name of facility; type of facility; and attribution of a facility between the primary and auxiliary seismic networks).

If the Executive Council recommends, pursuant to Article VII, paragraph 8 (d), that such changes be adopted, it shall as a rule also recommend pursuant to Article VII, paragraph 8 (g), that such changes enter into force upon notification by the Director-General of their approval.

25. The Director-General, in submitting to the Executive Council and States Parties information and evaluation in accordance with Article VII, paragraph 8 (b), shall include in the case of any proposal made pursuant to paragraph 24:

(a) A technical evaluation of the proposal;

(b) A statement on the administrative and financial impact of the proposal; and

(c) A report on consultations with States directly affected by the proposal, including indication of their agreement.

Temporary Arrangements

26. In cases of significant or irretrievable breakdown of a monitoring facility specified in the Tables of Annex 1 to the Protocol, or in order to cover other temporary reductions of monitoring coverage, the Director-General shall, in consultation and agreement with those States directly affected, and with the approval of the Executive Council, initiate temporary arrangements of no more than one year's duration, renewable if necessary by agreement of the Executive Council and of the States directly affected for another year. Such arrangements shall not cause the number of operational facilities of the International Monitoring System to exceed the number specified for the relevant network; shall meet as far as possible the technical and operational requirements specified in the operational manual for the relevant network; and shall be conducted within the budget of the Organization. The Director-General shall furthermore take steps to rectify the situation and make proposals for its permanent resolution. The Director-General shall notify all States Parties of any decision taken pursuant to this paragraph.

Cooperating National Facilities

27. States Parties may also separately establish cooperative arrangements with the Organization, in order to make available to the International Data Centre supplementary data from national monitoring stations that are not formally part of the International Monitoring System.

28. Such cooperative arrangements may be established as follows:

(a) Upon request by a State Party, and at the expense of that State, the Technical Secretariat shall take the steps required to certify that a given monitoring facility meets the technical and operational requirements specified in the relevant operational manuals for an International Monitoring System facility, and make arrangements for the authentication of its data. Subject to the agreement of the Executive Council, the Technical Secretariat shall then formally designate such a facility as a cooperating national facility. The Technical Secretariat shall take the steps required to revalidate its certification as appropriate;

(b) The Technical Secretariat shall maintain a current list of cooperating national facilities and shall distribute it to all States Parties; and

(c) The International Data Centre shall call upon data from cooperating national facilities, if so requested by a State Party, for the purposes of facilitating consultation and clarification and the consideration of on-site inspection requests, data transmission costs being borne by that State Party.

The conditions under which supplementary data from such facilities are made available, and under which the International Data Centre may request further or expedited reporting, or clarifications, shall be elaborated in the operational manual for the respective monitoring network.

C. Consultation and Clarification

29. Without prejudice to the right of any State Party to request an on-site inspection, States Parties should, whenever possible, first make every effort to clarify and resolve, among themselves or with or through the Organization, any matter which may cause concern about possible non-compliance with the basic obligations of this Treaty.

30. A State Party that receives a request pursuant to paragraph 29 directly from another State Party shall provide the clarification to the requesting State Party as soon as possible, but in any case no later than 48 hours after the request. The requesting and requested States Parties may keep the Executive Council and the Director–General informed of the request and the response.

31. A State Party shall have the right to request the Director-General to assist in clarifying any matter which may cause concern about possible non-compliance with the basic obligations of this Treaty. The Director-General shall provide appropriate information in the possession of the Technical Secretariat relevant to such a concern. The Director-General shall inform the Executive Council of the request and of the information provided in response, if so requested by the requesting State Party.

32. A State Party shall have the right to request the Executive Council to obtain clarification from another State Party on any matter which may cause concern about possible non-compliance with the basic obligations of this Treaty. In such a case, the following shall apply:

(a) The Executive Council shall forward the request for clarification to the requested State Party through the Director-General no later than 24 hours after its receipt;

(b) The requested State Party shall provide the clarification to the Executive Council as soon as possible, but in any case no later than 48 hours after receipt of the request;

(c) The Executive Council shall take note of the clarification and forward it to the requesting State Party no later than 24 hours after its receipt;

(d) If the requesting State Party deems the clarification to be inadequate, it shall have the right to request the Executive Council to obtain further clarification from the requested State Party.

The Executive Council shall inform without delay all other States Parties about any request for clarification pursuant to this paragraph as well as any response provided by the requested State Party.

33. If the requesting State Party considers the clarification obtained under paragraph 32 (d) to be unsatisfactory, it shall have the right to request a meeting of the Executive Council in which States Parties involved that are not members of the Executive Council shall be entitled to take part. At such a meeting, the Executive Council shall consider the matter and may recommend any measure in accordance with Article V.

D. On-Site Inspections

Request for an On-Site Inspection

34. Each State Party has the right to request an on-site inspection in accordance with the provisions of this Article and Part II of the Protocol in the territory or in any other place under the jurisdiction or control of any State Party, or in any area beyond the jurisdiction or control of any State.

35. The sole purpose of an on-site inspection shall be to clarify whether a nuclear weapon test explosion or any other nuclear explosion has been carried out in violation of Article I and, to the extent possible, to gather any facts which might assist in identifying any possible violator.

36. The requesting State Party shall be under the obligation to keep the on-site inspection request within the scope of this Treaty and to provide in the request information in accordance with paragraph 37. The requesting State Party shall refrain from unfounded or abusive inspection requests.

37. The on-site inspection request shall be based on information collected by the International Monitoring System, on any relevant technical information obtained by national technical means of verification in a manner consistent with generally recognized principles of international law, or on a combination thereof. The request shall contain information pursuant to Part II, paragraph 41 of the Protocol.

38. The requesting State Party shall present the on-site inspection request to the Executive Council and at the same time to the Director-General for the latter to begin immediate processing.

Follow-up After Submission of an On-Site Inspection Request

39. The Executive Council shall begin its consideration immediately upon receipt of the on-site inspection request.

40. The Director-General, after receiving the on-site inspection request, shall acknowledge receipt of the request to the requesting State Party within two hours and communicate the request to the State Party sought to be inspected within six hours. The Director-General shall ascertain that the request meets the requirements specified in Part II, paragraph 41 of the Protocol, and, if necessary, shall assist the requesting State Party in filing the request accordingly, and shall communicate the request to the Executive Council and to all other States Parties within 24 hours.

41. When the on-site inspection request fulfils the requirements, the Technical Secretariat shall begin preparations for the on-site inspection without delay.

42. The Director-General, upon receipt of an on–site inspection request referring to an inspection area under the jurisdiction or control of a State Party, shall immediately seek clarification from the State Party sought to be inspected in order to clarify and resolve the concern raised in the request.

43. A State Party that receives a request for clarification pursuant to paragraph 42 shall provide the Director-General with explanations and with other relevant information available as soon as possible, but no later than 72 hours after receipt of the request for clarification.

44. The Director-General, before the Executive Council takes a decision on the on-site inspection request, shall transmit immediately to the Executive Council any additional information available from the International Monitoring System or provided by any State Party on the event specified in the request, including any clarification provided pursuant to paragraphs 42 and 43, as well as any other information from within the Technical Secretariat that the Director-General deems relevant or that is requested by the Executive Council.

45. Unless the requesting State Party considers the concern raised in the on-site inspection request to be resolved and withdraws the request, the Executive Council shall take a decision on the request in accordance with paragraph 46.

Executive Council Decisions

46. The Executive Council shall take a decision on the on-site inspection request no later than 96 hours after receipt of the request from the requesting State Party. The decision to approve the on-site inspection shall be made by at least 30 affirmative votes of members of the Executive Council. If the Executive Council does not approve the inspection, preparations shall be stopped and no further action on the request shall be taken.

47. No later than 25 days after the approval of the on-site inspection in accordance with paragraph 46, the inspection team shall transmit to the Executive Council, through the Director-General, a progress inspection report. The continuation of the inspection shall be considered approved unless the Executive Council, no later than 72 hours after receipt of the progress inspection report, decides by a majority of all its members not to continue the inspection. If the Executive Council decides not to continue the inspection, the inspection shall be terminated, and the inspection team shall leave the inspection area and the territory of the inspected State Party as soon as possible in accordance with Part II, paragraphs 109 and 110 of the Protocol.

48. In the course of the on-site inspection, the inspection team may submit to the Executive Council, through the Director-General, a proposal to conduct drilling. The Executive Council shall take a decision on such a proposal no later than 72 hours after receipt of the proposal. The decision to approve drilling shall be made by a majority of all members of the Executive Council.

49. The inspection team may request the Executive Council, through the Director-General, to extend the inspection duration by a maximum of 70 days beyond the 60-day time-frame specified in Part II, paragraph 4 of the Protocol, if the inspection team considers such an extension essential to enable it to fulfil its mandate. The inspection team shall indicate in its request which of the activities and techniques listed in Part II, paragraph 69 of the Protocol it intends to carry out during the extension period. The Executive Council shall take a decision on the extension request no later than 72 hours after receipt of the request. The decision to approve an extension of the inspection duration shall be made by a majority of all members of the Executive Council.

50. Any time following the approval of the continuation of the on-site inspection in accordance with paragraph 47, the inspection team may submit to the Executive Council, through the Director-General, a recommendation to terminate the inspection. Such a recommendation shall be considered approved unless the Executive Council, no later than 72 hours after receipt of the recommendation, decides by a two-thirds majority of all its members not to approve the termination of the inspection. In case of termination of the inspection, the inspection team shall leave the inspection area and the territory of the inspected State Party as soon as possible in accordance with Part II, paragraphs 109 and 110 of the Protocol.

51. The requesting State Party and the State Party sought to be inspected may participate in the deliberations of the Executive Council on the on-site inspection request without voting. The requesting State Party and the inspected State Party may also participate without voting in any subsequent deliberations of the Executive Council related to the inspection.

52. The Director-General shall notify all States Parties within 24 hours about any decision by and reports, proposals, requests and recommendations to the Executive Council pursuant to paragraphs 46 to 50.

Follow-up After Executive Council Approval of an On-Site Inspection

53. An on-site inspection approved by the Executive Council shall be conducted without delay by an inspection team designated by the Director-General and in accordance with the provisions of this Treaty and the Protocol. The inspection team shall arrive at the point of entry no later than six days following the receipt by the Executive Council of the on-site inspection request from the requesting State Party.

54. The Director-General shall issue an inspection mandate for the conduct of the on-site inspection. The inspection mandate shall contain the information specified in Part II, paragraph 42 of the Protocol.

55. The Director-General shall notify the inspected State Party of the inspection no less than 24 hours before the planned arrival of the inspection team at the point of entry, in accordance with Part II, paragraph 43 of the Protocol.

The Conduct of an On-Site Inspection

56. Each State Party shall permit the Organization to conduct an on-site inspection on its territory or at places under its jurisdiction or control in accordance with the provisions of this Treaty and the Protocol. However, no State Party shall have to accept simultaneous on-site inspections on its territory or at places under its jurisdiction or control.

57. In accordance with the provisions of this Treaty and the Protocol, the inspected State Party shall have:

(a) The right and the obligation to make every reasonable effort to demonstrate its compliance with this Treaty and, to this end, to enable the inspection team to fulfil its mandate;

(b) The right to take measures it deems necessary to protect national security interests and to prevent disclosure of confidential information not related to the purpose of the inspection;

(c) The obligation to provide access within the inspection area for the sole purpose of determining facts relevant to the purpose of the inspection, taking into account sub–paragraph (b) and any constitutional obligations it may have with regard to proprietary rights or searches and seizures;

(d) The obligation not to invoke this paragraph or Part II, paragraph 88 of the Protocol to conceal any violation of its obligations under Article I; and

(e) The obligation not to impede the ability of the inspection team to move within the inspection area and to carry out inspection activities in accordance with this Treaty and the Protocol.

Access, in the context of an on-site inspection, means both the physical access of the inspection team and the inspection equipment to, and the conduct of inspection activities within, the inspection area.

58. The on-site inspection shall be conducted in the least intrusive manner

possible, consistent with the efficient and timely accomplishment of the inspection mandate, and in accordance with the procedures set forth in the Protocol. Wherever possible, the inspection team shall begin with the least intrusive procedures and then proceed to more intrusive procedures only as it deems necessary to collect sufficient information to clarify the concern about possible non-compliance with this Treaty. The inspectors shall seek only the information and data necessary for the purpose of the inspection and shall seek to minimize interference with normal operations of the inspected State Party.

59. The inspected State Party shall assist the inspection team throughout the on-site inspection and facilitate its task.

60. If the inspected State Party, acting in accordance with Part II, paragraphs 86 to 96 of the Protocol, restricts access within the inspection area, it shall make every reasonable effort in consultations with the inspection team to demonstrate through alternative means its compliance with this Treaty.

Observer

61. With regard to an observer, the following shall apply:

(a) The requesting State Party, subject to the agreement of the inspected State Party, may send a representative, who shall be a national either of the requesting State Party or of a third State Party, to observe the conduct of the on-site inspection;

(b) The inspected State Party shall notify its acceptance or non–acceptance of the proposed observer to the Director-General within 12 hours after approval of the on-site inspection by the Executive Council;

(c) In case of acceptance, the inspected State Party shall grant access to the observer in accordance with the Protocol;

(d) The inspected State Party shall, as a rule, accept the proposed observer, but if the inspected State Party exercises a refusal, that fact shall be recorded in the inspection report.

There shall be no more than three observers from an aggregate of requesting States Parties.

Reports of an On-Site Inspection

62. Inspection reports shall contain:

(a) A description of the activities conducted by the inspection team;

(b) The factual findings of the inspection team relevant to the purpose of the inspection;

(c) An account of the cooperation granted during the on-site inspection;

(d) A factual description of the extent of the access granted, including the alternative means provided to the team, during the on-site inspection; and

(e) Any other details relevant to the purpose of the inspection.

Differing observations made by inspectors may be attached to the report.

63. The Director-General shall make draft inspection reports available to the inspected State Party. The inspected State Party shall have the right to provide the Director-General within 48 hours with its comments and explanations, and to identify any information and data which, in its view, are not related to the purpose of the inspection and should not be circulated outside the Technical Secretariat. The Director-General shall consider the proposals for changes to the draft inspection report made by the inspected State Party and shall wherever possible incorporate them. The Director-General shall also annex the comments and explanations provided by the inspected State Party to the inspection report.

64. The Director-General shall promptly transmit the inspection report to the requesting State Party, the inspected State Party, the Executive Council and to all other States Parties. The Director-General shall further transmit promptly to the Executive Council and to all other States Parties any results of sample analysis in designated laboratories in accordance with Part II, paragraph 104 of the Protocol, relevant data from the International Monitoring System, the assessments of the requesting and inspected States Parties, as well as any other information that the Director-General deems relevant. In the case of the progress inspection report referred to in paragraph 47, the Director-General shall transmit the report to the Executive Council within the time-frame specified in that paragraph.

65. The Executive Council, in accordance with its powers and functions, shall review the inspection report and any material provided pursuant to paragraph 64, and shall address any concerns as to:

(a) Whether any non-compliance with this Treaty has occurred; and

(b) Whether the right to request an on-site inspection has been abused.

66. If the Executive Council reaches the conclusion, in keeping with its powers and functions, that further action may be necessary with regard to paragraph 65, it shall take the appropriate measures in accordance with Article V.

Frivolous or Abusive On-Site Inspection Requests

67. If the Executive Council does not approve the on-site inspection on the basis that the on-site inspection request is frivolous or abusive, or if the inspection is terminated for the same reasons, the Executive Council shall consider and decide on whether to implement appropriate measures to redress the situation, including the following:

(a) Requiring the requesting State Party to pay for the cost of any preparations made by the Technical Secretariat;

(b) Suspending the right of the requesting State Party to request an on-site inspection for a period of time, as determined by the Executive Council; and

(c) Suspending the right of the requesting State Party to serve on the Executive Council for a period of time.

E. Confidence-Building Measures

68. In order to:

(a) Contribute to the timely resolution of any compliance concerns arising from possible misinterpretation of verification data relating to chemical explosions; and

(b) Assist in the calibration of the stations that are part of the component networks of the International Monitoring System, each State Party undertakes to cooperate with the Organization and with other States Parties in implementing relevant measures as set out in Part III of the Protocol.

Article V: Measures to redress a situation and to ensure compliance, including sanctions

1. The Conference, taking into account, inter alia, the recommendations of the Executive Council, shall take the necessary measures, as set forth in paragraphs 2 and 3, to ensure compliance with this Treaty and to redress and remedy any situation which contravenes the provisions of this Treaty.

2. In cases where a State Party has been requested by the Conference or the Executive Council to redress a situation raising problems with regard to its compliance and fails to fulfil the request within the specified time, the Conference may, inter alia, decide to restrict or suspend the State Party from the exercise of its rights and privileges under this Treaty until the Conference decides otherwise.

3. In cases where damage to the object and purpose of this Treaty may result from non-compliance with the basic obligations of this Treaty, the Conference may recommend to States Parties collective measures which are in conformity with international law.

4. The Conference, or alternatively, if the case is urgent, the Executive Council, may bring the issue, including relevant information and conclusions, to the attention of the United Nations.

Article VI: Settlement of disputes

1. Disputes that may arise concerning the application or the interpretation of this Treaty shall be settled in accordance with the relevant provisions of this Treaty and in conformity with the provisions of the Charter of the United Nations.

2. When a dispute arises between two or more States Parties, or between one or more States Parties and the Organization, relating to the application or interpretation of this Treaty, the parties concerned shall consult together with a view to the expeditious settlement of the dispute by negotiation or by other peaceful means of the parties' choice, including recourse to appropriate organs of this Treaty and, by mutual consent, referral to the International Court of Justice in conformity with the Statute of the Court. The parties involved shall keep the Executive Council informed of actions being taken.

3. The Executive Council may contribute to the settlement of a dispute that may arise concerning the application or interpretation of this Treaty by whatever means it deems appropriate, including offering its good offices, calling upon the States Parties to a dispute to seek a settlement through a process of their own choice, bringing the matter to the attention of the Conference and recommending a time-limit for any agreed procedure.

4. The Conference shall consider questions related to disputes raised by States Parties or brought to its attention by the Executive Council. The Conference shall, as it finds necessary, establish or entrust organs with tasks related to the settlement of these disputes in conformity with Article II, paragraph 26 (j).

5. The Conference and the Executive Council are separately empowered, subject to authorization from the General Assembly of the United Nations, to request the International Court of Justice to give an advisory opinion on any legal question arising within the scope of the activities of the Organization. An agreement between the Organization and the United Nations shall be concluded for this purpose in accordance with Article II, paragraph 38 (h).

6. This Article is without prejudice to Articles IV and V.

Article VII: Amendments

1. At any time after the entry into force of this Treaty, any State Party may propose amendments to this Treaty, the Protocol, or the Annexes to the Protocol. Any State Party may also propose changes, in accordance with paragraph 7, to the Protocol or the Annexes thereto. Proposals for amendments shall be subject to the procedures in paragraphs 2 to 6. Proposals for changes, in accordance with paragraph 7, shall be subject to the procedures in paragraph 8.

2. The proposed amendment shall be considered and adopted only by an Amendment Conference.

3. Any proposal for an amendment shall be communicated to the Director-General, who shall circulate it to all States Parties and the Depositary and seek the views of the States Parties on whether an Amendment Conference should be convened to consider the proposal. If a majority of the States Parties notify the Director-General no later than 30 days after its circulation that they support further consideration of the proposal, the Director-General shall convene an Amendment Conference to which all States Parties shall be invited.

4. The Amendment Conference shall be held immediately following a regular session of the Conference unless all States Parties that support the convening of an Amendment Conference request that it be held earlier. In no case shall an Amendment Conference be held less than 60 days after the circulation of the proposed amendment.

5. Amendments shall be adopted by the Amendment Conference by a positive vote of a majority of the States Parties with no State Party casting a negative vote.

6. Amendments shall enter into force for all States Parties 30 days after

deposit of the instruments of ratification or acceptance by all those States Parties casting a positive vote at the Amendment Conference.

7. In order to ensure the viability and effectiveness of this Treaty, Parts I and III of the Protocol and Annexes 1 and 2 to the Protocol shall be subject to changes in accordance with paragraph 8, if the proposed changes are related only to matters of an administrative or technical nature. All other provisions of the Protocol and the Annexes thereto shall not be subject to changes in accordance with paragraph 8.

8. Proposed changes referred to in paragraph 7 shall be made in accordance with the following procedures:

(a) The text of the proposed changes shall be transmitted together with the necessary information to the Director-General. Additional information for the evaluation of the proposal may be provided by any State Party and the Director-General. The Director-General shall promptly communicate any such proposals and information to all States Parties, the Executive Council and the Depositary;

(b) No later than 60 days after its receipt, the Director-General shall evaluate the proposal to determine all its possible consequences for the provisions of this Treaty and its implementation and shall communicate any such information to all States Parties and the Executive Council;

(c) The Executive Council shall examine the proposal in the light of all information available to it, including whether the proposal fulfils the requirements of paragraph 7. No later than 90 days after its receipt, the Executive Council shall notify its recommendation, with appropriate explanations, to all States Parties for consideration. States Parties shall acknowledge receipt within 10 days;

(d) If the Executive Council recommends to all States Parties that the proposal be adopted, it shall be considered approved if no State Party objects to it within 90 days after receipt of the recommendation. If the Executive Council recommends that the proposal be rejected, it shall be considered rejected if no State Party objects to the rejection within 90 days after receipt of the recommendation;

(e) If a recommendation of the Executive Council does not meet with the acceptance required under sub-paragraph (d), a decision on the proposal, including whether it fulfils the requirements of paragraph 7, shall be taken as a matter of substance by the Conference at its next session;

(f) The Director-General shall notify all States Parties and the Depositary of any decision under this paragraph;

(g) Changes approved under this procedure shall enter into force for all States Parties 180 days after the date of notification by the Director-General of their approval unless another time period is recommended by the Executive Council or decided by the Conference.

Article VIII: Review of the Treaty

1. Unless otherwise decided by a majority of the States Parties, ten years

after the entry into force of this Treaty a Conference of the States Parties shall be held to review the operation and effectiveness of this Treaty, with a view to assuring itself that the objectives and purposes in the Preamble and the provisions of the Treaty are being realized. Such review shall take into account any new scientific and technological developments relevant to this Treaty. On the basis of a request by any State Party, the Review Conference shall consider the possibility of permitting the conduct of underground nuclear explosions for peaceful purposes. If the Review Conference decides by consensus that such nuclear explosions may be permitted, it shall commence work without delay, with a view to recommending to States Parties an appropriate amendment to this Treaty that shall preclude any military benefits of such nuclear explosions. Any such proposed amendment shall be communicated to the Director-General by any State Party and shall be dealt with in accordance with the provisions of Article VII.

2. At intervals of ten years thereafter, further Review Conferences may be convened with the same objective, if the Conference so decides as a matter of procedure in the preceding year. Such Conferences may be convened after an interval of less than ten years if so decided by the Conference as a matter of substance.

3. Normally, any Review Conference shall be held immediately following the regular annual session of the Conference provided for in Article II.

Article IX: Duration and withdrawal

1. This Treaty shall be of unlimited duration.

2. Each State Party shall, in exercising its national sovereignty, have the right to withdraw from this Treaty if it decides that extraordinary events related to the subject matter of this Treaty have jeopardized its supreme interests.

3. Withdrawal shall be effected by giving notice six months in advance to all other States Parties, the Executive Council, the Depositary and the United Nations Security Council. Notice of withdrawal shall include a statement of the extraordinary event or events which a State Party regards as jeopardizing its supreme interests.

Article X: Status of the protocol and the annexes

The Annexes to this Treaty, the Protocol, and the Annexes to the Protocol form an integral part of the Treaty. Any reference to this Treaty includes the Annexes to this Treaty, the Protocol and the Annexes to the Protocol.

Article XI: Signature

This Treaty shall be open to all States for signature before its entry into force.

Article XII: Ratification

This Treaty shall be subject to ratification by States Signatories according to their respective constitutional processes.

Article XIII: Accession

Any State which does not sign this Treaty before its entry into force may accede to it at any time thereafter.

Article XIV: Entry into force

1. This Treaty shall enter into force 180 days after the date of deposit of the instruments of ratification by all States listed in Annex 2 to this Treaty, but in no case earlier than two years after its opening for signature.

2. If this Treaty has not entered into force three years after the date of the anniversary of its opening for signature, the Depositary shall convene a Conference of the States that have already deposited their instruments of ratification upon the request of a majority of those States. That Conference shall examine the extent to which the requirement set out in paragraph 1 has been met and shall consider and decide by consensus what measures consistent with international law may be undertaken to accelerate the ratification process in order to facilitate the early entry into force of this Treaty.

3. Unless otherwise decided by the Conference referred to in paragraph 2 or other such conferences, this process shall be repeated at subsequent anniversaries of the opening for signature of this Treaty, until its entry into force.

4. All States Signatories shall be invited to attend the Conference referred to in paragraph 2 and any subsequent conferences as referred to in paragraph 3, as observers.

5. For States whose instruments of ratification or accession are deposited subsequent to the entry into force of this Treaty, it shall enter into force on the 30th day following the date of deposit of their instruments of ratification or accession.

Article XV: Reservations

The Articles of and the Annexes to this Treaty shall not be subject to reservations. The provisions of the Protocol to this Treaty and the Annexes to the Protocol shall not be subject to reservations incompatible with the object and purpose of this Treaty.

Article XVI: Depositary

1. The Secretary-General of the United Nations shall be the Depositary of this Treaty and shall receive signatures, instruments of ratification and instruments of accession.

2. The Depositary shall promptly inform all States Signatories and acceding States of the date of each signature, the date of deposit of each instrument of ratification or accession, the date of the entry into force of this Treaty and of any amendments and changes thereto, and the receipt of other notices.

3. The Depositary shall send duly certified copies of this Treaty to the Governments of the States Signatories and acceding States.

4. This Treaty shall be registered by the Depositary pursuant to Article 102 of the Charter of the United Nations.

Article XVII: Authentic texts
This Treaty, of which the Arabic, Chinese, English, French, Russian and Spanish texts are equally authentic, shall be deposited with the Secretary-General of the United Nations.

Annex 1:
List of States Pursuant to Article II, Paragraph 28

Africa

Algeria, Angola, Benin, Botswana, Burkina Faso, Burundi, Cameroon, Cape Verde, Central African Republic, Chad, Comoros, Congo, Côte d'Ivoire, Djibouti, Egypt, Equatorial Guinea, Eritrea, Ethiopia, Gabon, Gambia, Ghana, Guinea, Guinea–Bissau, Kenya, Lesotho, Liberia, Libyan Arab Jamahiriya, Madagascar, Malawi, Mali, Mauritania, Mauritius, Morocco, Mozambique, Namibia, Niger, Nigeria, Rwanda, Sao Tome & Principe, Senegal, Seychelles, Sierra Leone, Somalia, South Africa, Sudan, Swaziland, Togo, Tunisia, Uganda, United Republic of Tanzania, Zaire, Zambia, Zimbabwe.

Eastern Europe

Albania, Armenia, Azerbaijan, Belarus, Bosnia and Herzegovina, Bulgaria, Croatia, Czech Republic, Estonia, Georgia, Hungary, Latvia, Lithuania, Poland, Republic of Moldova, Romania, Russian Federation, Slovakia, Slovenia, The former Yugoslav Republic of Macedonia, Ukraine, Yugoslavia.

Latin America and the Caribbean

Antigua and Barbuda, Argentina, Bahamas, Barbados, Belize, Bolivia, Brazil, Chile, Colombia, Costa Rica, Cuba, Dominica, Dominican Republic, Ecuador, El Salvador, Grenada, Guatemala, Guyana, Haiti, Honduras, Jamaica, Mexico, Nicaragua, Panama, Paraguay, Peru, Saint Kitts and Nevis, Saint Lucia, Saint Vincent and the Grenadines, Suriname, Trinidad and Tobago, Uruguay, Venezuela.

Middle East and South Asia

Afghanistan, Bahrain, Bangladesh, Bhutan, India, Iran (Islamic Republic of), Iraq, Israel, Jordan, Kazakstan, Kuwait, Kyrgyzstan, Lebanon, Maldives, Nepal, Oman, Pakistan, Qatar, Saudi Arabia, Sri Lanka, Syrian Arab Republic, Tajikistan, Turkmenistan, United Arab Emirates, Uzbekistan, Yemen.

North America and Western Europe

Andorra, Austria, Belgium, Canada, Cyprus, Denmark, Finland, France, Germany, Greece, Holy See, Iceland, Ireland, Italy, Liechtenstein, Luxembourg, Malta, Monaco, Netherlands, Norway, Portugal, San Marino, Spain, Sweden, Switzerland, Turkey, United Kingdom of Great Britain and Northern Ireland, United States of America.

South East Asia, the Pacific and the Far East

Australia, Brunei Darussalam, Cambodia, China, Cook Islands, Democratic People's Republic of Korea, Fiji, Indonesia, Japan, Kiribati, Lao People's Democratic Republic, Malaysia, Marshall Islands, Micronesia (Federated States of), Mongolia, Myanmar, Nauru, New Zealand, Niue, Palau, Papua New Guinea, Philippines, Republic of Korea, Samoa, Singapore, Solomon Islands, Thailand, Tonga, Tuvalu, Vanuatu, Viet Nam.

Annex 2:
List of States Pursuant to Article XIV

List of States members of the Conference on Disarmament as at 18 June 1996 which formally participated in the work of the 1996 session of the Conference and which appear in Table 1 of the International Atomic Energy Agency's April 1996 edition of "Nuclear Power Reactors in the World," and of States members of the Conference on Disarmament as at 18 June 1996 which formally participated in the work of the 1996 session of the Conference and which appear in Table 1 of the International Atomic Energy Agency's December 1995 edition of "Nuclear Research Reactors in the World": Algeria, Argentina, Australia, Austria, Bangladesh, Belgium, Brazil, Bulgaria, Canada, Chile, China, Colombia, Democratic People's Republic of Korea, Egypt, Finland, France, Germany, Hungary, India, Indonesia, Iran (Islamic Republic of), Israel, Italy, Japan, Mexico, Netherlands, Norway, Pakistan, Peru, Poland, Romania, Republic of Korea, Russian Federation, Slovakia, South Africa, Spain, Sweden, Switzerland, Turkey, Ukraine, United Kingdom of Great Britain and Northern Ireland, United States of America, Viet Nam, Zaire.

3.6
Convention on the Prohibition of the Use, Stockpiling, Production and Transfer of Anti-Personnel Mines and on Their Destruction (Ottawa or Landmines Convention) (1997)

The Ottawa Convention can be classified as a treaty on arms control or of international humanitarian law. Its origins are notable both for the significant role played by an NGO coalition known as the International Campaign to Ban Landmines (ICBL) working in conjunction with the Canadian government, and for the fact that the convention was achieved without the support of the United States.

On the process leading to the conclusion of the convention, see Maxwell A. Cameron *et al., eds.,* To Walk Without Fear: The Global Movement to Ban Landmines *(New York: Oxford University Press, 1998). On the convention text, see Stuart Maslen,* Commentaries on Arms Control Treaties: The Convention on the Prohibition of the Use, Stockpiling, Production and Transfer of Anti-Personnel Mines and on Their Destruction *(Oxford: Oxford University Press, 2004). Up-to-date information on progress in implementing this treaty can be found on the ICBL website at www.icbl.org.*

The States Parties,

Determined to put an end to the suffering and casualties caused by anti-personnel mines, that kill or maim hundreds of people every week, mostly innocent and defenceless civilians and especially children, obstruct economic development and reconstruction, inhibit the repatriation of refugees and internally displaced persons, and have other severe consequences for years after emplacement,

Believing it necessary to do their utmost to contribute in an efficient and coordinated manner to face the challenge of removing anti-personnel mines placed throughout the world, and to assure their destruction,

Wishing to do their utmost in providing assistance for the care and rehabilitation, including the social and economic reintegration of mine victims,

Recognizing that a total ban of anti-personnel mines would also be an important confidence-building measure,

Welcoming the adoption of the Protocol on Prohibitions or Restrictions on the Use of Mines, Booby-Traps and Other Devices, as amended on 3 May 1996, annexed to the Convention on Prohibitions or Restrictions on the Use of Certain Conventional Weapons Which May Be Deemed to Be Excessively Injurious or to Have Indiscriminate Effects, and calling for the early ratification of this Protocol by all States which have not yet done so,

Welcoming also United Nations General Assembly Resolution 51/45 S of 10 December 1996 urging all States to pursue vigorously an effective, legally-binding international agreement to ban the use, stockpiling, production and transfer of anti-personnel landmines,

Welcoming furthermore the measures taken over the past years, both unilaterally and multilaterally, aiming at prohibiting, restricting or suspending the use, stockpiling, production and transfer of anti-personnel mines,

Stressing the role of public conscience in furthering the principles of humanity as evidenced by the call for a total ban of anti-personnel mines and recognizing the efforts to that end undertaken by the International Red Cross and Red Crescent Movement, the International Campaign to Ban Landmines and numerous other non-governmental organizations around the world,

Recalling the Ottawa Declaration of 5 October 1996 and the Brussels Declaration of 27 June 1997 urging the international community to negotiate an international and legally binding agreement prohibiting the use, stockpiling, production and transfer of anti-personnel mines,

Emphasizing the desirability of attracting the adherence of all States to this Convention, and determined to work strenuously towards the promotion of its universalization in all relevant for a including, inter alia, the United Nations, the Conference on Disarmament, regional organizations, and groupings, and review conferences of the Convention on Prohibitions or Restrictions on the Use of Certain Conventional Weapons Which May Be Deemed to Be Excessively Injurious or to Have Indiscriminate Effects,

Basing themselves on the principle of international humanitarian law that the right of the parties to an armed conflict to choose methods or means of warfare is not unlimited, on the principle that prohibits the employment in armed conflicts of weapons, projectiles and materials and methods of warfare of a nature to cause superfluous injury or unnecessary suffering and on the principle that a distinction must be made between civilians and combatants,

Have agreed as follows:

Article 1: General obligations

1. Each State Party undertakes never under any circumstances:

(a) To use anti-personnel mines;

(b) To develop, produce, otherwise acquire, stockpile, retain or transfer to anyone, directly or indirectly, anti-personnel mines;

(c) To assist, encourage or induce, in any way, anyone to engage in any activity prohibited to a State Party under this Convention.

2. Each State Party undertakes to destroy or ensure the destruction of all anti-personnel mines in accordance with the provisions of this Convention.

Article 2: Definitions

1. "Anti-personnel mine" means a mine designed to be exploded by the presence, proximity or contact of a person and that will incapacitate, injure or kill one or more persons. Mines designed to be detonated by the presence, proximity or contact of a vehicle as opposed to a person, that are equipped with anti-handling devices, are not considered anti-personnel mines as a result of being so equipped.

2. "Mine" means a munition designed to be placed under, on or near the ground or other surface area and to be exploded by the presence, proximity or contact of a person or a vehicle.

3. "Anti-handling device" means a device intended to protect a mine and which is part of, linked to, attached to or placed under the mine and which activates when an attempt is made to tamper with or otherwise intentionally disturb the mine.

4. "Transfer" involves, in addition to the physical movement of anti-personnel mines into or from national territory, the transfer of title to and control over the mines, but does not involve the transfer of territory containing emplaced anti-personnel mines.

5. "Mined area" means an area which is dangerous due to the presence or suspected presence of mines.

Article 3: Exceptions

1. Notwithstanding the general obligations under Article 1, the retention or transfer of a number of anti-personnel mines for the development of and training in mine detection, mine clearance, or mine destruction techniques is permitted. The amount of such mines shall not exceed the minimum number absolutely necessary for the above-mentioned purposes.

2. The transfer of anti-personnel mines for the purpose of destruction is permitted.

Article 4: Destruction of stockpiled anti-personnel mines

Except as provided for in Article 3, each State Party undertakes to destroy or ensure the destruction of all stockpiled anti-personnel mines it owns or possesses, or that are under its jurisdiction or control, as soon as possible but not later than four years after the entry into force of this Convention for that State Party.

Article 5: Destruction of anti-personnel mines in mined areas

1. Each State Party undertakes to destroy or ensure the destruction of all anti-personnel mines in mined areas under its jurisdiction or control, as soon as possible but not later than ten years after the entry into force of this Convention for that State Party.

2. Each State Party shall make every effort to identify all areas under its jurisdiction or control in which anti-personnel mines are known or suspected to be emplaced and shall ensure as soon as possible that all anti-personnel mines in mined areas under its jurisdiction or control are perimetermarked, monitored and protected by fencing or other means, to ensure the effective exclusion of civilians, until all anti-personnel mines contained therein have been destroyed. The marking shall at least be to the standards set out in the Protocol on Prohibitions or Restrictions on the Use of Mines, Booby-Traps and Other Devices, as amended on 3 May 1996, annexed to the Convention on Prohibitions or Restrictions on the Use of Certain Conventional Weapons Which May Be Deemed to Be Excessively Injurious or to Have Indiscriminate Effects.

3. If a State Party believes that it will be unable to destroy or ensure the destruction of all antipersonnel mines referred to in paragraph 1 within that time period, it may submit a request to a Meeting of the States Parties or a Review Conference for an extension of the deadline for completing the destruction of such anti-personnel mines, for a period of up to ten years.

4. Each request shall contain:

(a) The duration of the proposed extension;

(b) A detailed explanation of the reasons for the proposed extension, including: (i) The preparation and status of work conducted under national demining programs; (ii) The financial and technical means available to the State Party for the destruction of all the anti-personnel mines; and (iii) Circumstances which impede the ability of the State Party to destroy all the antipersonnel mines in mined areas;

(c) The humanitarian, social, economic, and environmental implications of the extension; and

(d) Any other information relevant to the request for the proposed extension.

5. The Meeting of the States Parties or the Review Conference shall, taking into consideration the factors contained in paragraph 4, assess the request and decide by a majority of votes of States Parties present and voting whether to grant the request for an extension period.

6. Such an extension may be renewed upon the submission of a new request in accordance with paragraphs 3, 4 and 5 of this Article. In requesting a further extension period a State Party shall submit relevant additional information on what has been undertaken in the previous extension period pursuant to this Article.

Article 6: International cooperation and assistance

1. In fulfilling its obligations under this Convention each State Party has the

right to seek and receive assistance, where feasible, from other States Parties to the extent possible.

2. Each State Party undertakes to facilitate and shall have the right to participate in the fullest possible exchange of equipment, material and scientific and technological information concerning the implementation of this Convention. The States Parties shall not impose undue restrictions on the provision of mine clearance equipment and related technological information for humanitarian purposes.

3. Each State Party in a position to do so shall provide assistance for the care and rehabilitation, and social and economic reintegration, of mine victims and for mine awareness programs. Such assistance may be provided, inter alia, through the United Nations system, international, regional or national organizations or institutions, the International Committee of the Red Cross, national Red Cross and Red Crescent societies and their International Federation, non-governmental organizations, or on a bilateral basis.

4. Each State Party in a position to do so shall provide assistance for mine clearance and related activities. Such assistance may be provided, inter alia, through the United Nations system, international or regional organizations or institutions, non-governmental organizations or institutions, or on a bilateral basis, or by contributing to the United Nations Voluntary Trust Fund for Assistance in Mine Clearance, or other regional funds that deal with demining.

5. Each State Party in a position to do so shall provide assistance for the destruction of stockpiled anti-personnel mines.

6. Each State Party undertakes to provide information to the database on mine clearance established within the United Nations system, especially information concerning various means and technologies of mine clearance, and lists of experts, expert agencies or national points of contact on mine clearance.

7. States Parties may request the United Nations, regional organizations, other States Parties or other competent intergovernmental or non-governmental fora to assist its authorities in the elaboration of a national demining program to determine, inter alia:

(a) The extent and scope of the anti-personnel mine problem;

(b) The financial, technological and human resources that are required for the implementation of the program;

(c) The estimated number of years necessary to destroy all anti-personnel mines in mined areas under the jurisdiction or control of the concerned State Party;

(d) Mine awareness activities to reduce the incidence of mine-related injuries or deaths;

(e) Assistance to mine victims;

(f) The relationship between the Government of the concerned State Party and the relevant governmental, inter-governmental or non-governmental entities that will work in the implementation of the program.

8. Each State Party giving and receiving assistance under the provisions of

this Article shall cooperate with a view to ensuring the full and prompt implementation of agreed assistance programs.

Article 7: Transparency measures

1. Each State Party shall report to the Secretary-General of the United Nations as soon as practicable, and in any event not later than 180 days after the entry into force of this Convention for that State Party on:

(a) The national implementation measures referred to in Article 9;

(b) The total of all stockpiled anti-personnel mines owned or possessed by it, or under its jurisdiction or control, to include a breakdown of the type, quantity and, if possible, lot numbers of each type of anti-personnel mine stockpiled;

(c) To the extent possible, the location of all mined areas that contain, or are suspected to contain, anti-personnel mines under its jurisdiction or control, to include as much detail as possible regarding the type and quantity of each type of anti-personnel mine in each mined area and when they were emplaced;

(d) The types, quantities and, if possible, lot numbers of all anti-personnel mines retained or transferred for the development of and training in mine detection, mine clearance or mine destruction techniques, or transferred for the purpose of destruction, as well as the institutions authorized by a State Party to retain or transfer anti-personnel mines, in accordance with Article 3;

(e) The status of programs for the conversion or de-commissioning of anti-personnel mine production facilities;

(f) The status of programs for the destruction of anti-personnel mines in accordance with Articles 4 and 5, including details of the methods which will be used in destruction, the location of all destruction sites and the applicable safety and environmental standards to be observed;

(g) The types and quantities of all anti-personnel mines destroyed after the entry into force of this Convention for that State Party, to include a breakdown of the quantity of each type of antipersonnel mine destroyed, in accordance with Articles 4 and 5, respectively, along with, if possible, the lot numbers of each type of anti-personnel mine in the case of destruction in accordance with Article 4;

(h) The technical characteristics of each type of anti-personnel mine produced, to the extent known, and those currently owned or possessed by a State Party, giving, where reasonably possible, such categories of information as may facilitate identification and clearance of anti-personnel mines; at a minimum, this information shall include the dimensions, fusing, explosive content, metallic content, colour photographs and other information which may facilitate mine clearance; and

(i) The measures taken to provide an immediate and effective warning to the population in relation to all areas identified under paragraph 2 of Article 5.

2. The information provided in accordance with this Article shall be updated by the States Parties annually, covering the last calendar year, and reported to

the Secretary-General of the United Nations not later than 30 April of each year.

3. The Secretary-General of the United Nations shall transmit all such reports received to the States Parties.

Article 8: Facilitation and clarification of compliance

1. The States Parties agree to consult and cooperate with each other regarding the implementation of the provisions of this Convention, and to work together in a spirit of cooperation to facilitate compliance by States Parties with their obligations under this Convention.

2. If one or more States Parties wish to clarify and seek to resolve questions relating to compliance with the provisions of this Convention by another State Party, it may submit, through the Secretary-General of the United Nations, a Request for Clarification of that matter to that State Party. Such a request shall be accompanied by all appropriate information. Each State Party shall refrain from unfounded Requests for Clarification, care being taken to avoid abuse. A State Party that receives a Request for Clarification shall provide, through the Secretary-General of the United Nations, within 28 days to the requesting State Party all information which would assist in clarifying this matter.

3. If the requesting State Party does not receive a response through the Secretary-General of the United Nations within that time period, or deems the response to the Request for Clarification to be unsatisfactory, it may submit the matter through the Secretary-General of the United Nations to the next Meeting of the States Parties. The Secretary-General of the United Nations shall transmit the submission, accompanied by all appropriate information pertaining to the Request for Clarification, to all States Parties. All such information shall be presented to the requested State Party which shall have the right to respond.

4. Pending the convening of any meeting of the States Parties, any of the States Parties concerned may request the Secretary-General of the United Nations to exercise his or her good offices to facilitate the clarification requested.

5. The requesting State Party may propose through the Secretary-General of the United Nations the convening of a Special Meeting of the States Parties to consider the matter. The Secretary-General of the United Nations shall thereupon communicate this proposal and all information submitted by the States Parties concerned, to all States Parties with a request that they indicate whether they favour a Special Meeting of the States Parties, for the purpose of considering the matter. In the event that within 14 days from the date of such communication, at least one-third of the States Parties favours such a Special Meeting, the Secretary-General of the United Nations shall convene this Special Meeting of the States Parties within a further 14 days. A quorum for this Meeting shall consist of a majority of States Parties.

6. The Meeting of the States Parties or the Special Meeting of the States Parties, as the case may be, shall first determine whether to consider the matter

further, taking into account all information submitted by the States Parties concerned. The Meeting of the States Parties or the Special Meeting of the States Parties shall make every effort to reach a decision by consensus. If despite all efforts to that end no agreement has been reached, it shall take this decision by a majority of States Parties present and voting.

7. All States Parties shall cooperate fully with the Meeting of the States Parties or the Special Meeting of the States Parties in the fulfilment of its review of the matter, including any fact-finding missions that are authorized in accordance with paragraph 8.

8. If further clarification is required, the Meeting of the States Parties or the Special Meeting of the States Parties shall authorize a fact-finding mission and decide on its mandate by a majority of States Parties present and voting. At any time the requested State Party may invite a fact-finding mission to its territory. Such a mission shall take place without a decision by a Meeting of the States Parties or a Special Meeting of the States Parties to authorize such a mission. The mission, consisting of up to 9 experts, designated and approved in accordance with paragraphs 9 and 10, may collect additional information on the spot or in other places directly related to the alleged compliance issue under the jurisdiction or control of the requested State Party.

9. The Secretary-General of the United Nations shall prepare and update a list of the names, nationalities and other relevant data of qualified experts provided by States Parties and communicate it to all States Parties. Any expert included on this list shall be regarded as designated for all fact-finding missions unless a State Party declares its non-acceptance in writing. In the event of nonacceptance, the expert shall not participate in fact-finding missions on the territory or any other place under the jurisdiction or control of the objecting State Party, if the non-acceptance was declared prior to the appointment of the expert to such missions.

10. Upon receiving a request from the Meeting of the States Parties or a Special Meeting of the States Parties, the Secretary-General of the United Nations shall, after consultations with the requested State Party, appoint the members of the mission, including its leader. Nationals of States Parties requesting the fact-finding mission or directly affected by it shall not be appointed to the mission. The members of the fact-finding mission shall enjoy privileges and immunities under Article VI of the Convention on the Privileges and Immunities of the United Nations, adopted on 13 February 1946.

11. Upon at least 72 hours notice, the members of the fact-finding mission shall arrive in the territory of the requested State Party at the earliest opportunity. The requested State Party shall take the necessary administrative measures to receive, transport and accommodate the mission, and shall be responsible for ensuring the security of the mission to the maximum extent possible while they are on territory under its control.

12. Without prejudice to the sovereignty of the requested State Party, the fact-finding mission may bring into the territory of the requested State Party the necessary equipment which shall be used exclusively for gathering infor-

mation on the alleged compliance issue. Prior to its arrival, the mission will advise the requested State Party of the equipment that it intends to utilize in the course of its factfinding mission.

13. The requested State Party shall make all efforts to ensure that the fact-finding mission is given the opportunity to speak with all relevant persons who may be able to provide information related to the alleged compliance issue.

14. The requested State Party shall grant access for the fact-finding mission to all areas and installations under its control where facts relevant to the compliance issue could be expected to be collected. This shall be subject to any arrangements that the requested State Party considers necessary for:

(a) The protection of sensitive equipment, information and areas;

(b) The protection of any constitutional obligations the requested State Party may have with regard to proprietary rights, searches and seizures, or other constitutional rights; or

(c) The physical protection and safety of the members of the fact-finding mission.

In the event that the requested State Party makes such arrangements, it shall make every reasonable effort to demonstrate through alternative means its compliance with this Convention.

15. The fact-finding mission may remain in the territory of the State Party concerned for no more than 14 days, and at any particular site no more than 7 days, unless otherwise agreed.

16. All information provided in confidence and not related to the subject matter of the fact-finding mission shall be treated on a confidential basis.

17. The fact-finding mission shall report, through the Secretary-General of the United Nations, to the Meeting of the States Parties or the Special Meeting of the States Parties the results of its findings.

18. The Meeting of the States Parties or the Special Meeting of the States Parties shall consider all relevant information, including the report submitted by the fact-finding mission, and may request the requested State Party to take measures to address the compliance issue within a specified period of time. The requested State Party shall report on all measures taken in response to this request.

19. The Meeting of the States Parties or the Special Meeting of the States Parties may suggest to the States Parties concerned ways and means to further clarify or resolve the matter under consideration, including the initiation of appropriate procedures in conformity with international law. In circumstances where the issue at hand is determined to be due to circumstances beyond the control of the requested State Party, the Meeting of the States Parties or the Special Meeting of the States Parties may recommend appropriate measures, including the use of cooperative measures referred to in Article 6.

20. The Meeting of the States Parties or the Special Meeting of the States Parties shall make every effort to reach its decisions referred to in paragraphs 18 and 19 by consensus, otherwise by a two-thirds majority of States Parties present and voting.

Article 9: National implementation measures

Each State Party shall take all appropriate legal, administrative and other measures, including the imposition of penal sanctions, to prevent and suppress any activity prohibited to a State Party under this Convention undertaken by persons or on territory under its jurisdiction or control.

Article 10: Settlement of disputes

1. The States Parties shall consult and cooperate with each other to settle any dispute that may arise with regard to the application or the interpretation of this Convention. Each State Party may bring any such dispute before the Meeting of the States Parties.

2. The Meeting of the States Parties may contribute to the settlement of the dispute by whatever means it deems appropriate, including offering its good offices, calling upon the States parties to a dispute to start the settlement procedure of their choice and recommending a time-limit for any agreed procedure.

3. This Article is without prejudice to the provisions of this Convention on facilitation and clarification of compliance.

Article 11: Meetings of the States Parties

1. The States Parties shall meet regularly in order to consider any matter with regard to the application or implementation of this Convention, including:

    (a) The operation and status of this Convention;

    (b) Matters arising from the reports submitted under the provisions of this Convention;

    (c) International cooperation and assistance in accordance with Article 6;

    (d) The development of technologies to clear anti-personnel mines;

    (e) Submissions of States Parties under Article 8; and

    (f) Decisions relating to submissions of States Parties as provided for in Article 5.

2. The First Meeting of the States Parties shall be convened by the Secretary-General of the United Nations within one year after the entry into force of this Convention. The subsequent meetings shall be convened by the Secretary-General of the United Nations annually until the first Review Conference.

3. Under the conditions set out in Article 8, the Secretary-General of the United Nations shall convene a Special Meeting of the States Parties.

4. States not parties to this Convention, as well as the United Nations, other relevant international organizations or institutions, regional organizations, the International Committee of the Red Cross and relevant non-governmental organizations may be invited to attend these meetings as observers in accordance with the agreed Rules of Procedure.

Article 12: Review Conferences

1. A Review Conference shall be convened by the Secretary-General of the United Nations five years after the entry into force of this Convention.

Further Review Conferences shall be convened by the Secretary-General of the United Nations if so requested by one or more States Parties, provided that the interval between Review Conferences shall in no case be less than five years. All States Parties to this Convention shall be invited to each Review Conference.

2. The purpose of the Review Conference shall be:

(a) To review the operation and status of this Convention;

(b) To consider the need for and the interval between further Meetings of the States Parties referred to in paragraph 2 of Article 11;

(c) To take decisions on submissions of States Parties as provided for in Article 5; and

(d) To adopt, if necessary, in its final report conclusions related to the implementation of this Convention.

3. States not parties to this Convention, as well as the United Nations, other relevant international organizations or institutions, regional organizations, the International Committee of the Red Cross and relevant non-governmental organizations may be invited to attend each Review Conference as observers in accordance with the agreed Rules of Procedure.

Article 13: Amendments

1. At any time after the entry into force of this Convention any State Party may propose amendments to this Convention. Any proposal for an amendment shall be communicated to the Depositary, who shall circulate it to all States Parties and shall seek their views on whether an Amendment Conference should be convened to consider the proposal. If a majority of the States Parties notify the Depositary no later than 30 days after its circulation that they support further consideration of the proposal, the Depositary shall convene an Amendment Conference to which all States Parties shall be invited.

2. States not parties to this Convention, as well as the United Nations, other relevant international organizations or institutions, regional organizations, the International Committee of the Red Cross and relevant non-governmental organizations may be invited to attend each Amendment Conference as observers in accordance with the agreed Rules of Procedure.

3. The Amendment Conference shall be held immediately following a Meeting of the States Parties or a Review Conference unless a majority of the States Parties request that it be held earlier.

4. Any amendment to this Convention shall be adopted by a majority of two-thirds of the States Parties present and voting at the Amendment Conference. The Depositary shall communicate any amendment so adopted to the States Parties.

5. An amendment to this Convention shall enter into force for all States Parties to this Convention which have accepted it, upon the deposit with the Depositary of instruments of acceptance by a majority of States Parties. Thereafter it shall enter into force for any remaining State Party on the date of deposit of its instrument of acceptance.

Article 14: Costs

1. The costs of the Meetings of the States Parties, the Special Meetings of the States Parties, the Review Conferences and the Amendment Conferences shall be borne by the States Parties and States not parties to this Convention participating therein, in accordance with the United Nations scale of assessment adjusted appropriately.

2. The costs incurred by the Secretary-General of the United Nations under Articles 7 and 8 and the costs of any fact-finding mission shall be borne by the States Parties in accordance with the United Nations scale of assessment adjusted appropriately.

Article 15: Signature

This Convention, done at Oslo, Norway, on 18 September 1997, shall be open for signature at Ottawa, Canada, by all States from 3 December 1997 until 4 December 1997, and at the United Nations Headquarters in New York from 5 December 1997 until its entry into force.

Article 16: Ratification, acceptance, approval or accession

1. This Convention is subject to ratification, acceptance or approval of the Signatories.

2. It shall be open for accession by any State which has not signed the Convention.

3. The instruments of ratification, acceptance, approval or accession shall be deposited with the Depositary.

Article 17: Entry into force

1. This Convention shall enter into force on the first day of the sixth month after the month in which the 40th instrument of ratification, acceptance, approval or accession has been deposited.

2. For any State which deposits its instrument of ratification, acceptance, approval or accession after the date of the deposit of the 40th instrument of ratification, acceptance, approval or accession, this Convention shall enter into force on the first day of the sixth month after the date on which that State has deposited its instrument of ratification, acceptance, approval or accession.

Article 18: Provisional application

Any State may at the time of its ratification, acceptance, approval or accession, declare that it will apply provisionally paragraph 1 of Article 1 of this Convention pending its entry into force.

Article 19: Reservations

The Articles of this Convention shall not be subject to reservations.

Article 20: Duration and withdrawal

1. This Convention shall be of unlimited duration.

2. Each State Party shall, in exercising its national sovereignty, have the right to withdraw from this Convention. It shall give notice of such withdrawal to all other States Parties, to the Depositary and to the United Nations Security Council. Such instrument of withdrawal shall include a full explanation of the reasons motivating this withdrawal.

3. Such withdrawal shall only take effect six months after the receipt of the instrument of withdrawal by the Depositary. If, however, on the expiry of that six-month period, the withdrawing State Party is engaged in an armed conflict, the withdrawal shall not take effect before the end of the armed conflict.

4. The withdrawal of a State Party from this Convention shall not in any way affect the duty of States to continue fulfilling the obligations assumed under any relevant rules of international law.

Article 21: Depositary

The Secretary-General of the United Nations is hereby designated as the Depositary of this Convention.

Article 22: Authentic texts

The original of this Convention, of which the Arabic, Chinese, English, French, Russian and Spanish texts are equally authentic, shall be deposited with the Secretary-General of the United Nations.

3.7
Treaty on Strategic Offensive Reductions (SORT or The Moscow Treaty) (2002)

This treaty differs from previous US-USSR bilateral arms control treaties in that it does not include detailed definitions or monitoring and verification measures.

On the negotiations for the treaty, see the CRS report for Congress by Amy F. Woolf, Nuclear Arms Control: The Strategic Offensive Reductions Treaty, *available at www.fas.org/sgp/crs/nuke/RL31448.pdf. See also the article-by-article analysis of the treaty accompanying the letter of transmittal sent by President George W. Bush to the Senate, reprinted in* Arms Control Today *(July–August 2002) at www.armscontrol.org/act/2002_07-08/docjul_aug02.asp. For fascinating insights into the negotiation of the Cold War bilateral arms control treaties that provide the historical context in which to understand SORT, see the memoirs of Thomas Graham Jr.,* Disarmament Sketches: Three Decades of Arms Control and International Law *(Seattle: University of Washington Press, 2002).*

The United States of America and the Russian Federation, hereinafter referred to as "the Parties,"

Embarking upon the path of new relations for a new century and committed to the goal of strengthening their relationship through cooperation and friendship,

Believing that new global challenges and threats require the building of a qualitatively new foundation for strategic relations between the Parties,

Desiring to establish a genuine partnership based on the principles of mutual security, cooperation, trust, openness, and predictability,

Committed to implementing significant reductions in strategic offensive arms,

Proceeding from the Joint Statements by the President of the United States of America and the President of the Russian Federation on Strategic Issues of July 22, 2001 in Genoa and on a New Relationship between the United States and Russia of November 13, 2001 in Washington,

Mindful of their obligations under the Treaty Between the United States of America and the Union of Soviet Socialist Republics on the Reduction and Limitation of Strategic Offensive Arms of July 31, 1991, hereinafter referred to as the START Treaty,

Mindful of their obligations under Article VI of the Treaty on the Non-Proliferation of Nuclear Weapons of July 1, 1968, and

Convinced that this Treaty will help to establish more favorable conditions for actively promoting security and cooperation, and enhancing international stability,

Have agreed as follows:

Article I

Each Party shall reduce and limit strategic nuclear warheads, as stated by the President of the United States of America on November 13, 2001 and as stated by the President of the Russian Federation on November 13, 2001 and December 13, 2001 respectively, so that by December 31, 2012 the aggregate number of such warheads does not exceed 1700-2200 for each Party. Each Party shall determine for itself the composition and structure of its strategic offensive arms, based on the established aggregate limit for the number of such warheads.

Article II

The Parties agree that the START Treaty remains in force in accordance with its terms.

Article III

For purposes of implementing this Treaty, the Parties shall hold meetings at least twice a year of a Bilateral Implementation Commission.

Article IV

1. This Treaty shall be subject to ratification in accordance with the constitutional procedures of each Party. This Treaty shall enter into force on the date of the exchange of instruments of ratification.

2. This Treaty shall remain in force until December 31, 2012 and may be extended by agreement of the Parties or superseded earlier by a subsequent agreement.

3. Each Party, in exercising its national sovereignty, may withdraw from this Treaty upon three months written notice to the other Party.

Article V

This Treaty shall be registered pursuant to Article 102 of the Charter of the United Nations.

Done at Moscow on May 24, 2002, in two copies, each in the English and Russian languages, both texts being equally authentic.

3.8
Resolution on the Non-Transfer of Weapons of Mass Destruction to Non-State Actors: United Nations Security Council Resolution 1540 (2004)

In resolution 1540 the Security Council drew on its chapter VII powers to require states to take certain specified actions to prevent nonstate actors acquiring weapons of mass destruction. Resolution 1540 also established a committee for a period of no more than two years. The Council stopped short of using its chapter VII powers to require states to report to the committee, which in turn reports to the Security Council. Nevertheless, states were "called" to make their first report within six months of the adoption of the resolution. There has been some criticism that, in legal terms, the resolution was of an inappropriate legislative nature and that, in political terms, the resolution represented the imposition of US policy wishes on the rest of the world.

For discussion, see Merav Datan, "Security Council Resolution 1540: WMD and Non-State Trafficking," Disarmament Diplomacy *79 (2005) at www.acronym.org.uk/dd/index.htm; and Stefan Talman, "The Security Council as World Legislature,"* American Journal of International Law *99 (2005): 175–193. The website of the 1540 committee is at www. disarmament2.un.org/Committee1540/index.html.*

The Security Council,

Affirming that proliferation of nuclear, chemical and biological weapons, as well as their means of delivery,* constitutes a threat to international peace and security,

---

* Definition for the purpose of this resolution only. Means of delivery: missiles, rockets and other unmanned systems capable of delivering nuclear, chemical, or biological weapons, that are specially designed for such use.

Reaffirming, in this context, the Statement of its President adopted at the Council's meeting at the level of Heads of State and Government on 31 January 1992 (S/23500), including the need for all Member States to fulfil their obligations in relation to arms control and disarmament and to prevent proliferation in all its aspects of all weapons of mass destruction,

Recalling also that the Statement underlined the need for all Member States to resolve peacefully in accordance with the Charter any problems in that context threatening or disrupting the maintenance of regional and global stability,

Affirming its resolve to take appropriate and effective actions against any threat to international peace and security caused by the proliferation of nuclear, chemical and biological weapons and their means of delivery, in conformity with its primary responsibilities, as provided for in the United Nations Charter,

Affirming its support for the multilateral treaties whose aim is to eliminate or prevent the proliferation of nuclear, chemical or biological weapons and the importance for all States parties to these treaties to implement them fully in order to promote international stability,

Welcoming efforts in this context by multilateral arrangements which contribute to non-proliferation,

Affirming that prevention of proliferation of nuclear, chemical and biological weapons should not hamper international cooperation in materials, equipment and technology for peaceful purposes while goals of peaceful utilization should not be used as a cover for proliferation,

Gravely concerned by the threat of terrorism and the risk that non-State actors* such as those identified in the United Nations list established and maintained by the Committee established under Security Council resolution 1267 and those to whom resolution 1373 applies, may acquire, develop, traffic in or use nuclear, chemical and biological weapons and their means of delivery,

Gravely concerned by the threat of illicit trafficking in nuclear, chemical, or biological weapons and their means of delivery, and related materials,* which adds a new dimension to the issue of proliferation of such weapons and also poses a threat to international peace and security,

Recognizing the need to enhance coordination of efforts on national, subregional, regional and international levels in order to strengthen a global response to this serious challenge and threat to international security,

Recognizing that most States have undertaken binding legal obligations under treaties to which they are parties, or have made other commitments

---

* Definitions for the purpose of this resolution only. Non-State actor: individual or entity, not acting under the lawful authority of any State in conducting activities which come within the scope of this resolution.

Related materials: materials, equipment and technology covered by relevant multilateral treaties and arrangements, or included on national control lists, which could be used for the design, development, production or use of nuclear, chemical and biological weapons and their means of delivery.

aimed at preventing the proliferation of nuclear, chemical or biological weapons, and have taken effective measures to account for, secure and physically protect sensitive materials, such as those required by the Convention on the Physical Protection of Nuclear Materials and those recommended by the IAEA Code of Conduct on the Safety and Security of Radioactive Sources,

Recognizing further the urgent need for all States to take additional effective measures to prevent the proliferation of nuclear, chemical or biological weapons and their means of delivery,

Encouraging all Member States to implement fully the disarmament treaties and agreements to which they are party,

Reaffirming the need to combat by all means, in accordance with the Charter of the United Nations, threats to international peace and security caused by terrorist acts,

Determined to facilitate henceforth an effective response to global threats in the area of non-proliferation,

Acting under Chapter VII of the Charter of the United Nations,

1. Decides that all States shall refrain from providing any form of support to non-State actors that attempt to develop, acquire, manufacture, possess, transport, transfer or use nuclear, chemical or biological weapons and their means of delivery;

2. Decides also that all States, in accordance with their national procedures, shall adopt and enforce appropriate effective laws which prohibit any non-State actor to manufacture, acquire, possess, develop, transport, transfer or use nuclear, chemical or biological weapons and their means of delivery, in particular for terrorist purposes, as well as attempts to engage in any of the foregoing activities, participate in them as an accomplice, assist or finance them;

3. Decides also that all States shall take and enforce effective measures to establish domestic controls to prevent the proliferation of nuclear, chemical, or biological weapons and their means of delivery, including by establishing appropriate controls over related materials and to this end shall:

(a) Develop and maintain appropriate effective measures to account for and secure such items in production, use, storage or transport;

(b) Develop and maintain appropriate effective physical protection measures;

(c) Develop and maintain appropriate effective border controls and law enforcement efforts to detect, deter, prevent and combat, including through international cooperation when necessary, the illicit trafficking and brokering in such items in accordance with their national legal authorities and legislation and consistent with international law;

(d) Establish, develop, review and maintain appropriate effective national export and trans-shipment controls over such items, including appropriate laws and regulations to control export, transit, trans-shipment and re-export and controls on providing funds and services related to such export and trans-shipment such as financing, and transporting that would contribute to proliferation, as well as establishing end-user controls; and establishing and enforcing appropriate criminal or civil penalties for violations of such export control laws and regulations;

4. Decides to establish, in accordance with rule 28 of its provisional rules of procedure, for a period of no longer than two years, a Committee of the Security Council, consisting of all members of the Council, which will, calling as appropriate on other expertise, report to the Security Council for its examination, on the implementation of this resolution, and to this end calls upon States to present a first report no later than six months from the adoption of this resolution to the Committee on steps they have taken or intend to take to implement this resolution;

5. Decides that none of the obligations set forth in this resolution shall be interpreted so as to conflict with or alter the rights and obligations of State Parties to the Nuclear Non-Proliferation Treaty, the Chemical Weapons Convention and the Biological and Toxin Weapons Convention or alter the responsibilities of the International Atomic Energy Agency or the Organization for the Prohibition of Chemical Weapons;

6. Recognizes the utility in implementing this resolution of effective national control lists and calls upon all Member States, when necessary, to pursue at the earliest opportunity the development of such lists;

7. Recognizes that some States may require assistance in implementing the provisions of this resolution within their territories and invites States in a position to do so to offer assistance as appropriate in response to specific requests to the States lacking the legal and regulatory infrastructure, implementation experience and/or resources for fulfilling the above provisions;

8. Calls upon all States:

(a) To promote the universal adoption and full implementation, and, where necessary, strengthening of multilateral treaties to which they are parties, whose aim is to prevent the proliferation of nuclear, biological or chemical weapons;

(b) To adopt national rules and regulations, where it has not yet been done, to ensure compliance with their commitments under the key multilateral nonproliferation treaties;

(c) To renew and fulfil their commitment to multilateral cooperation, in particular within the framework of the International Atomic Energy Agency, the Organization for the Prohibition of Chemical Weapons and the Biological and Toxin Weapons Convention, as important means of pursuing and achieving their common objectives in the area of non-proliferation and of promoting international cooperation for peaceful purposes;

(d) To develop appropriate ways to work with and inform industry and the public regarding their obligations under such laws;

9. Calls upon all States to promote dialogue and cooperation on nonproliferation so as to address the threat posed by proliferation of nuclear, chemical, or biological weapons, and their means of delivery;

10. Further to counter that threat, calls upon all States, in accordance with their national legal authorities and legislation and consistent with international

law, to take cooperative action to prevent illicit trafficking in nuclear, chemical or biological weapons, their means of delivery, and related materials;

11. Expresses its intention to monitor closely the implementation of this resolution and, at the appropriate level, to take further decisions which may be required to this end;

12. Decides to remain seized of the matter.

4
International
Criminal Law

4.1
Convention on the Prevention and Punishment of the Crime of Genocide (1948)

Raphael Lemkin, a Polish lawyer who emigrated to the United States in 1941, invented the term genocide *from the Greek* genos *meaning race and the Latin* cide *meaning killing. Lemkin sought to galvanize world condemnation of Nazi atrocities. Drafting of the convention in the immediate post–World War II years was closely related to efforts to establish a permanent international criminal court, but this was not to happen for another fifty years. Controversial in the convention is its omission of political groups from the definition of genocide in article II.*

See Raphael Lemkin, "Genocide as a Crime Under International Law," American Journal of International Law *41 (1947): 145–151; M. Lippman, "The Convention on the Prevention and Punishment of the Crime of Genocide: Fifty Years Later,"* Arizona Journal of International and Comparative Law *15 (1998): 415–514; and Sherrie L. Russell-Brown, "Rape as an Act of Genocide,"* Berkeley Journal of International Law *21 (2003): 350–374. On the twentieth-century US policy response to genocide, see Samantha Power,* "A Problem From Hell": America and the Age of Genocide *(New York: Basic Books, 2002).*

The Contracting Parties,

Having considered the declaration made by the General Assembly of the United Nations in its resolution 96 (I) dated 11 December 1946 that genocide is a crime under international law, contrary to the spirit and aims of the United Nations and condemned by the civilized world,

Recognizing that at all periods of history genocide has inflicted great losses on humanity, and

Being convinced that, in order to liberate mankind from such an odious scourge, international co-operation is required,

Hereby agree as hereinafter provided:

Article I

The Contracting Parties confirm that genocide, whether committed in time of peace or in time of war, is a crime under international law which they undertake to prevent and to punish.

Article II

In the present Convention, genocide means any of the following acts committed with intent to destroy, in whole or in part, a national, ethnical, racial or religious group, as such:

    (a) Killing members of the group;

    (b) Causing serious bodily or mental harm to members of the group;

    (c) Deliberately inflicting on the group conditions of life calculated to bring about its physical destruction in whole or in part;

    (d) Imposing measures intended to prevent births within the group;

    (e) Forcibly transferring children of the group to another group.

Article III

The following acts shall be punishable:

    (a) Genocide;

    (b) Conspiracy to commit genocide;

    (c) Direct and public incitement to commit genocide;

    (d) Attempt to commit genocide;

    (e) Complicity in genocide.

Article IV

Persons committing genocide or any of the other acts enumerated in article III shall be punished, whether they are constitutionally responsible rulers, public officials or private individuals.

Article V

The Contracting Parties undertake to enact, in accordance with their respective Constitutions, the necessary legislation to give effect to the provisions of the present Convention, and, in particular, to provide effective penalties for persons guilty of genocide or any of the other acts enumerated in article III.

Article VI

Persons charged with genocide or any of the other acts enumerated in article III shall be tried by a competent tribunal of the State in the territory of which the act was committed, or by such international penal tribunal as may have jurisdiction with respect to those Contracting Parties which shall have accepted its jurisdiction.

Article VII

Genocide and the other acts enumerated in article III shall not be considered as political crimes for the purpose of extradition.

    The Contracting Parties pledge themselves in such cases to grant extradition in accordance with their laws and treaties in force.

Article VIII

Any Contracting Party may call upon the competent organs of the United Nations to take such action under the Charter of the United Nations as they consider appropriate for the prevention and suppression of acts of genocide or any of the other acts enumerated in article III.

Article IX

Disputes between the Contracting Parties relating to the interpretation, application or fulfilment of the present Convention, including those relating to the responsibility of a State for genocide or for any of the other acts enumerated in article III, shall be submitted to the International Court of Justice at the request of any of the parties to the dispute.

Article X

The present Convention, of which the Chinese, English, French, Russian and Spanish texts are equally authentic, shall bear the date of 9 December 1948.

Article XI

The present Convention shall be open until 31 December 1949 for signature on behalf of any Member of the United Nations and of any non-member State to which an invitation to sign has been addressed by the General Assembly.

The present Convention shall be ratified, and the instruments of ratification shall be deposited with the Secretary-General of the United Nations.

After 1 January 1950, the present Convention may be acceded to on behalf of any Member of the United Nations and of any non-member State which has received an invitation as aforesaid.

Instruments of accession shall be deposited with the Secretary-General of the United Nations.

Article XII

Any Contracting Party may at any time, by notification addressed to the Secretary-General of the United Nations, extend the application of the present Convention to all or any of the territories for the conduct of whose foreign relations that Contracting Party is responsible.

Article XIII

On the day when the first twenty instruments of ratification or accession have been deposited, the Secretary-General shall draw up a procès-verbal and transmit a copy thereof to each Member of the United Nations and to each of the non-member States contemplated in article XI.

The present Convention shall come into force on the ninetieth day following the date of deposit of the twentieth instrument of ratification or accession.

Any ratification or accession effected subsequent to the latter date shall become effective on the ninetieth day following the deposit of the instrument of ratification or accession.

Article XIV

The present Convention shall remain in effect for a period of ten years as from the date of its coming into force.

It shall thereafter remain in force for successive periods of five years for such Contracting Parties as have not denounced it at least six months before the expiration of the current period.

Denunciation shall be effected by a written notification addressed to the Secretary-General of the United Nations.

Article XV

If, as a result of denunciations, the number of Parties to the present Convention should become less than sixteen, the Convention shall cease to be in force as from the date on which the last of these denunciations shall become effective.

Article XVI

A request for the revision of the present Convention may be made at any time by any Contracting Party by means of a notification in writing addressed to the Secretary-General.

The General Assembly shall decide upon the steps, if any, to be taken in respect of such request.

Article XVII

The Secretary-General of the United Nations shall notify all Members of the United Nations and the non-member States contemplated in article XI of the following:

(a) Signatures, ratifications and accessions received in accordance with article XI;

(b) Notifications received in accordance with article XII;

(c) The date upon which the present Convention comes into force in accordance with article XIII;

(d) Denunciations received in accordance with article XIV;

(e) The abrogation of the Convention in accordance with article XV;

(f) Notifications received in accordance with article XVI.

Article XVIII

The original of the present Convention shall be deposited in the archives of the United Nations.

A certified copy of the Convention shall be transmitted to each Member of the United Nations and to each of the non-member States contemplated in article XI.

Article XIX

The present Convention shall be registered by the Secretary-General of the United Nations on the date of its coming into force.

4.2
Convention Against Torture and Other Cruel, Inhuman or Degrading Treatment or Punishment (CAT) (1984)

The convention has come into prominence with claims of US abuse of detainees in Iraq, at Guantánamo Bay, and elsewhere. Karen Greenberg and Joshua Dratel have documented the development of protorture policies by the Bush administration in Karen J. Greenberg and Joshua L. Dratel, eds., The Torture Papers: The Road to Abu Ghraib *(Cambridge: Cambridge University Press, 2005). Official US policy, as stated in the 2005 US Report to the convention's monitoring body, has continued to be that the United States is "unequivocally opposed to the use and practice of torture."* The Second Periodic Report of the United States of America to the Committee Against Torture *submitted May 6, 2005, is available at www.state.gov/g/drl/rls/45738.htm. For background on the treaty, see M. Lippman, "The Development and Drafting of the United Nations Convention Against Torture and Other Cruel, Inhuman or Degrading Treatment or Punishment,"* Boston College International and Comparative Law Review *17 (1994): 275–335. See also the websites of Human Rights Watch at www.hrw.org and Amnesty International at www.amnesty.org. The convention has an optional protocol which, once it enters into force, will create a subcommittee and allow in-country visits to places of detention. The text of the protocol can be found on the website of the Committee against Torture, at www.ohchr.org/english/law/ cat-one.htm.*

The States Parties to this Convention,

Considering that, in accordance with the principles proclaimed in the Charter of the United Nations, recognition of the equal and inalienable rights of all members of the human family is the foundation of freedom, justice and peace in the world,

Recognizing that those rights derive from the inherent dignity of the human person,

Considering the obligation of States under the Charter, in particular article 55, to promote universal respect for, and observance of, human rights and fundamental freedoms,

Having regard to article 5 of the Universal Declaration of Human Rights and article 7 of the International Covenant on Civil and Political Rights, both of which provide that no one shall be subjected to torture or to cruel, inhuman or degrading treatment or punishment,

Having regard also to the Declaration on the Protection of All Persons from Being Subjected to Torture and Other Cruel, Inhuman or Degrading Treatment or Punishment, adopted by the General Assembly on 9 December 1975,

Desiring to make more effective the struggle against torture and other cruel, inhuman or degrading treatment or punishment throughout the world,

Have agreed as follows:

Part I

Article 1

1. For the purposes of this Convention, the term "torture" means any act by which severe pain or suffering, whether physical or mental, is intentionally inflicted on a person for such purposes as obtaining from him or a third person information or a confession, punishing him for an act he or a third person has committed or is suspected of having committed, or intimidating or coercing him or a third person, or for any reason based on discrimination of any kind, when such pain or suffering is inflicted by or at the instigation of or with the consent or acquiescence of a public official or other person acting in an official capacity. It does not include pain or suffering arising only from, inherent in or incidental to lawful sanctions.

2. This article is without prejudice to any international instrument or national legislation which does or may contain provisions of wider application.

Article 2

1. Each State Party shall take effective legislative, administrative, judicial or other measures to prevent acts of torture in any territory under its jurisdiction.

2. No exceptional circumstances whatsoever, whether a state of war or a threat of war, internal political in stability or any other public emergency, may be invoked as a justification of torture.

3. An order from a superior officer or a public authority may not be invoked as a justification of torture.

Article 3

1. No State Party shall expel, return ("refouler") or extradite a person to another State where there are substantial grounds for believing that he would be in danger of being subjected to torture.

2. For the purpose of determining whether there are such grounds, the com-

petent authorities shall take into account all relevant considerations including, where applicable, the existence in the State concerned of a consistent pattern of gross, flagrant or mass violations of human rights.

Article 4

1. Each State Party shall ensure that all acts of torture are offences under its criminal law. The same shall apply to an attempt to commit torture and to an act by any person which constitutes complicity or participation in torture.

2. Each State Party shall make these offences punishable by appropriate penalties which take into account their grave nature.

Article 5

1. Each State Party shall take such measures as may be necessary to establish its jurisdiction over the offences referred to in article 4 in the following cases: (a) When the offences are committed in any territory under its jurisdiction or on board a ship or aircraft registered in that State; (b) When the alleged offender is a national of that State; (c) When the victim is a national of that State if that State considers it appropriate.

2. Each State Party shall likewise take such measures as may be necessary to establish its jurisdiction over such offences in cases where the alleged offender is present in any territory under its jurisdiction and it does not extradite him pursuant to article 8 to any of the States mentioned in paragraph 1 of this article.

3. This Convention does not exclude any criminal jurisdiction exercised in accordance with internal law.

Article 6

1. Upon being satisfied, after an examination of information available to it, that the circumstances so warrant, any State Party in whose territory a person alleged to have committed any offence referred to in article 4 is present shall take him into custody or take other legal measures to ensure his presence. The custody and other legal measures shall be as provided in the law of that State but may be continued only for such time as is necessary to enable any criminal or extradition proceedings to be instituted.

2. Such State shall immediately make a preliminary inquiry into the facts.

3. Any person in custody pursuant to paragraph 1 of this article shall be assisted in communicating immediately with the nearest appropriate representative of the State of which he is a national, or, if he is a stateless person, with the representative of the State where he usually resides.

4. When a State, pursuant to this article, has taken a person into custody, it shall immediately notify the States referred to in article 5, paragraph 1, of the fact that such person is in custody and of the circumstances which warrant his detention. The State which makes the preliminary inquiry contemplated in paragraph 2 of this article shall promptly report its findings to the said States and shall indicate whether it intends to exercise jurisdiction.

Article 7

1. The State Party in the territory under whose jurisdiction a person alleged to have committed any offence referred to in article 4 is found shall in the cases contemplated in article 5, if it does not extradite him, submit the case to its competent authorities for the purpose of prosecution.

2. These authorities shall take their decision in the same manner as in the case of any ordinary offence of a serious nature under the law of that State. In the cases referred to in article 5, paragraph 2, the standards of evidence required for prosecution and conviction shall in no way be less stringent than those which apply in the cases referred to in article 5, paragraph 1.

3. Any person regarding whom proceedings are brought in connection with any of the offences referred to in article 4 shall be guaranteed fair treatment at all stages of the proceedings.

Article 8

1. The offences referred to in article 4 shall be deemed to be included as extraditable offences in any extradition treaty existing between States Parties. States Parties undertake to include such offences as extraditable offences in every extradition treaty to be concluded between them.

2. If a State Party which makes extradition conditional on the existence of a treaty receives a request for extradition from another State Party with which it has no extradition treaty, it may consider this Convention as the legal basis for extradition in respect of such offences. Extradition shall be subject to the other conditions provided by the law of the requested State.

3. States Parties which do not make extradition conditional on the existence of a treaty shall recognize such offences as extraditable offences between themselves subject to the conditions provided by the law of the requested State.

4. Such offences shall be treated, for the purpose of extradition between States Parties, as if they had been committed not only in the place in which they occurred but also in the territories of the States required to establish their jurisdiction in accordance with article 5, paragraph 1.

Article 9

1. States Parties shall afford one another the greatest measure of assistance in connection with criminal proceedings brought in respect of any of the offences referred to in article 4, including the supply of all evidence at their disposal necessary for the proceedings.

2. States Parties shall carry out their obligations under paragraph 1 of this article in conformity with any treaties on mutual judicial assistance that may exist between them.

Article 10

1. Each State Party shall ensure that education and information regarding the prohibition against torture are fully included in the training of law enforce-

ment personnel, civil or military, medical personnel, public officials and other persons who may be involved in the custody, interrogation or treatment of any individual subjected to any form of arrest, detention or imprisonment.

2. Each State Party shall include this prohibition in the rules or instructions issued in regard to the duties and functions of any such person.

Article 11

Each State Party shall keep under systematic review interrogation rules, instructions, methods and practices as well as arrangements for the custody and treatment of persons subjected to any form of arrest, detention or imprisonment in any territory under its jurisdiction, with a view to preventing any cases of torture.

Article 12

Each State Party shall ensure that its competent authorities proceed to a prompt and impartial investigation, wherever there is reasonable ground to believe that an act of torture has been committed in any territory under its jurisdiction.

Article 13

Each State Party shall ensure that any individual who alleges he has been subjected to torture in any territory under its jurisdiction has the right to complain to, and to have his case promptly and impartially examined by, its competent authorities. Steps shall be taken to ensure that the complainant and witnesses are protected against all ill-treatment or intimidation as a consequence of his complaint or any evidence given.

Article 14

1. Each State Party shall ensure in its legal system that the victim of an act of torture obtains redress and has an enforceable right to fair and adequate compensation, including the means for as full rehabilitation as possible. In the event of the death of the victim as a result of an act of torture, his dependants shall be entitled to compensation.

2. Nothing in this article shall affect any right of the victim or other persons to compensation which may exist under national law.

Article 15

Each State Party shall ensure that any statement which is established to have been made as a result of torture shall not be invoked as evidence in any proceedings, except against a person accused of torture as evidence that the statement was made.

Article 16

1. Each State Party shall undertake to prevent in any territory under its jurisdiction other acts of cruel, inhuman or degrading treatment or punishment which do not amount to torture as defined in article 1, when such acts are com-

mitted by or at the instigation of or with the consent or acquiescence of a public official or other person acting in an official capacity. In particular, the obligations contained in articles 10, 11, 12 and 13 shall apply with the substitution for references to torture of references to other forms of cruel, inhuman or degrading treatment or punishment.

2. The provisions of this Convention are without prejudice to the provisions of any other international instrument or national law which prohibits cruel, inhuman or degrading treatment or punishment or which relates to extradition or expulsion.

Part II

Article 17

1. There shall be established a Committee against Torture (hereinafter referred to as the Committee) which shall carry out the functions hereinafter provided. The Committee shall consist of ten experts of high moral standing and recognized competence in the field of human rights, who shall serve in their personal capacity. The experts shall be elected by the States Parties, consideration being given to equitable geographical distribution and to the usefulness of the participation of some persons having legal experience.

2. The members of the Committee shall be elected by secret ballot from a list of persons nominated by States Parties. Each State Party may nominate one person from among its own nationals. States Parties shall bear in mind the usefulness of nominating persons who are also members of the Human Rights Committee established under the International Covenant on Civil and Political Rights and who are willing to serve on the Committee against Torture.

3. Elections of the members of the Committee shall be held at biennial meetings of States Parties convened by the Secretary-General of the United Nations. At those meetings, for which two thirds of the States Parties shall constitute a quorum, the persons elected to the Committee shall be those who obtain the largest number of votes and an absolute majority of the votes of the representatives of States Parties present and voting.

4. The initial election shall be held no later than six months after the date of the entry into force of this Convention. At least four months before the date of each election, the Secretary-General of the United Nations shall address a letter to the States Parties inviting them to submit their nominations within three months. The Secretary-General shall prepare a list in alphabetical order of all persons thus nominated, indicating the States Parties which have nominated them, and shall submit it to the States Parties.

5. The members of the Committee shall be elected for a term of four years. They shall be eligible for re-election if renominated. However, the term of five of the members elected at the first election shall expire at the end of two years; immediately after the first election the names of these five members shall be

chosen by lot by the chairman of the meeting referred to in paragraph 3 of this article.

6. If a member of the Committee dies or resigns or for any other cause can no longer perform his Committee duties, the State Party which nominated him shall appoint another expert from among its nationals to serve for the remainder of his term, subject to the approval of the majority of the States Parties. The approval shall be considered given unless half or more of the States Parties respond negatively within six weeks after having been informed by the Secretary-General of the United Nations of the proposed appointment.

7. States Parties shall be responsible for the expenses of the members of the Committee while they are in performance of Committee duties.

Article 18

1. The Committee shall elect its officers for a term of two years. They may be re-elected.

2. The Committee shall establish its own rules of procedure, but these rules shall provide, inter alia, that: (a) Six members shall constitute a quorum; (b) Decisions of the Committee shall be made by a majority vote of the members present.

3. The Secretary-General of the United Nations shall provide the necessary staff and facilities for the effective performance of the functions of the Committee under this Convention.

4. The Secretary-General of the United Nations shall convene the initial meeting of the Committee. After its initial meeting, the Committee shall meet at such times as shall be provided in its rules of procedure.

5. The States Parties shall be responsible for expenses incurred in connection with the holding of meetings of the States Parties and of the Committee, including reimbursement to the United Nations for any expenses, such as the cost of staff and facilities, incurred by the United Nations pursuant to paragraph 3 of this article.

Article 19

1. The States Parties shall submit to the Committee, through the Secretary-General of the United Nations, reports on the measures they have taken to give effect to their undertakings under this Convention, within one year after the entry into force of the Convention for the State Party concerned. Thereafter the States Parties shall submit supplementary reports every four years on any new measures taken and such other reports as the Committee may request.

2. The Secretary-General of the United Nations shall transmit the reports to all States Parties.

3. Each report shall be considered by the Committee which may make such general comments on the report as it may consider appropriate and shall forward these to the State Party concerned. That State Party may respond with any observations it chooses to the Committee.

4. The Committee may, at its discretion, decide to include any comments made by it in accordance with paragraph 3 of this article, together with the observations thereon received from the State Party concerned, in its annual report made in accordance with article 24. If so requested by the State Party concerned, the Committee may also include a copy of the report submitted under paragraph 1 of this article.

Article 20

1. If the Committee receives reliable information which appears to it to contain well-founded indications that torture is being systematically practised in the territory of a State Party, the Committee shall invite that State Party to co-operate in the examination of the information and to this end to submit observations with regard to the information concerned.

2. Taking into account any observations which may have been submitted by the State Party concerned, as well as any other relevant information available to it, the Committee may, if it decides that this is warranted, designate one or more of its members to make a confidential inquiry and to report to the Committee urgently.

3. If an inquiry is made in accordance with paragraph 2 of this article, the Committee shall seek the co-operation of the State Party concerned. In agreement with that State Party, such an inquiry may include a visit to its territory.

4. After examining the findings of its member or members submitted in accordance with paragraph 2 of this article, the Commission shall transmit these findings to the State Party concerned together with any comments or suggestions which seem appropriate in view of the situation.

5. All the proceedings of the Committee referred to in paragraphs 1 to 4 of this article shall be confidential, and at all stages of the proceedings the co-operation of the State Party shall be sought. After such proceedings have been completed with regard to an inquiry made in accordance with paragraph 2, the Committee may, after consultations with the State Party concerned, decide to include a summary account of the results of the proceedings in its annual report made in accordance with article 24.

Article 21

1. A State Party to this Convention may at any time declare under this article that it recognizes the competence of the Committee to receive and consider communications to the effect that a State Party claims that another State Party is not fulfilling its obligations under this Convention. Such communications may be received and considered according to the procedures laid down in this article only if submitted by a State Party which has made a declaration recognizing in regard to itself the competence of the Committee. No communication shall be dealt with by the Committee under this article if it concerns a State Party which has not made such a declaration. Communications received under this article shall be dealt with in accordance with the following procedure; (a) If a State Party considers that another State Party is not giving effect to the

provisions of this Convention, it may, by written communication, bring the matter to the attention of that State Party. Within three months after the receipt of the communication the receiving State shall afford the State which sent the communication an explanation or any other statement in writing clarifying the matter, which should include, to the extent possible and pertinent, reference to domestic procedures and remedies taken, pending or available in the matter; (b) If the matter is not adjusted to the satisfaction of both States Parties concerned within six months after the receipt by the receiving State of the initial communication, either State shall have the right to refer the matter to the Committee, by notice given to the Committee and to the other State; (c) The Committee shall deal with a matter referred to it under this article only after it has ascertained that all domestic remedies have been invoked and exhausted in the matter, in conformity with the generally recognized principles of international law. This shall not be the rule where the application of the remedies is unreasonably prolonged or is unlikely to bring effective relief to the person who is the victim of the violation of this Convention; (d) The Committee shall hold closed meetings when examining communications under this article; (e) Subject to the provisions of subparagraph (c), the Committee shall make available its good offices to the States Parties concerned with a view to a friendly solution of the matter on the basis of respect for the obligations provided for in this Convention. For this purpose, the Committee may, when appropriate, set up an ad hoc conciliation commission; (f) In any matter referred to it under this article, the Committee may call upon the States Parties concerned, referred to in subparagraph (b), to supply any relevant information; (g) The States Parties concerned, referred to in subparagraph (b), shall have the right to be represented when the matter is being considered by the Committee and to make submissions orally and/or in writing; (h) The Committee shall, within twelve months after the date of receipt of notice under subparagraph (b), submit a report: (i) If a solution within the terms of subparagraph (e) is reached, the Committee shall confine its report to a brief statement of the facts and of the solution reached; (ii) If a solution within the terms of subparagraph (e) is not reached, the Committee shall confine its report to a brief statement of the facts; the written submissions and record of the oral submissions made by the States Parties concerned shall be attached to the report.

In every matter, the report shall be communicated to the States Parties concerned.

2. The provisions of this article shall come into force when five States Parties to this Convention have made declarations under paragraph 1 of this article. Such declarations shall be deposited by the States Parties with the Secretary-General of the United Nations, who shall transmit copies thereof to the other States Parties. A declaration may be withdrawn at any time by notification to the Secretary-General. Such a withdrawal shall not prejudice the consideration of any matter which is the subject of a communication already transmitted under this article; no further communication by any State Party shall be received under this article after the notification of withdrawal of the declara-

tion has been received by the Secretary-General, unless the State Party concerned has made a new declaration.

Article 22

1. A State Party to this Convention may at any time declare under this article that it recognizes the competence of the Committee to receive and consider communications from or on behalf of individuals subject to its jurisdiction who claim to be victims of a violation by a State Party of the provisions of the Convention. No communication shall be received by the Committee if it concerns a State Party which has not made such a declaration.

2. The Committee shall consider inadmissible any communication under this article which is anonymous or which it considers to be an abuse of the right of submission of such communications or to be incompatible with the provisions of this Convention.

3. Subject to the provisions of paragraph 2, the Committee shall bring any communications submitted to it under this article to the attention of the State Party to this Convention which has made a declaration under paragraph 1 and is alleged to be violating any provisions of the Convention. Within six months, the receiving State shall submit to the Committee written explanations or statements clarifying the matter and the remedy, if any, that may have been taken by that State.

4. The Committee shall consider communications received under this article in the light of all information made available to it by or on behalf of the individual and by the State Party concerned.

5. The Committee shall not consider any communications from an individual under this article unless it has ascertained that: (a) The same matter has not been, and is not being, examined under another procedure of international investigation or settlement; (b) The individual has exhausted all available domestic remedies; this shall not be the rule where the application of the remedies is unreasonably prolonged or is unlikely to bring effective relief to the person who is the victim of the violation of this Convention.

6. The Committee shall hold closed meetings when examining communications under this article.

7. The Committee shall forward its views to the State Party concerned and to the individual.

8. The provisions of this article shall come into force when five States Parties to this Convention have made declarations under paragraph 1 of this article. Such declarations shall be deposited by the States Parties with the Secretary-General of the United Nations, who shall transmit copies thereof to the other States Parties. A declaration may be withdrawn at any time by notification to the Secretary-General. Such a withdrawal shall not prejudice the consideration of any matter which is the subject of a communication already transmitted under this article; no further communication by or on behalf of an individual shall be received under this article after the notification of with-

drawal of the declaration has been received by the Secretary-General, unless the State Party has made a new declaration.

Article 23

The members of the Committee and of the ad hoc conciliation commissions which may be appointed under article 21, paragraph 1(e), shall be entitled to the facilities, privileges and immunities of experts on mission for the United Nations as laid down in the relevant sections of the Convention on the Privileges and Immunities of the United Nations.

Article 24

The Committee shall submit an annual report on its activities under this Convention to the States Parties and to the General Assembly of the United Nations.

Part III

Article 25

1. This Convention is open for signature by all States.

2. This Convention is subject to ratification. Instruments of ratification shall be deposited with the Secretary-General of the United Nations.

Article 26

This Convention is open to accession by all States. Accession shall be effected by the deposit of an instrument of accession with the Secretary-General of the United Nations.

Article 27

1. This Convention shall enter into force on the thirtieth day after the date of the deposit with the Secretary-General of the United Nations of the twentieth instrument of ratification or accession.

2. For each State ratifying this Convention or acceding to it after the deposit of the twentieth instrument of ratification or accession, the Convention shall enter into force on the thirtieth day after the date of the deposit of its own instrument of ratification or accession.

Article 28

1. Each State may, at the time of signature or ratification of this Convention or accession thereto, declare that it does not recognize the competence of the Committee provided for in article 20.

2. Any State Party having made a reservation in accordance with paragraph 1 of this article may, at any time, withdraw this reservation by notification to the Secretary-General of the United Nations.

Article 29

1. Any State Party to this Convention may propose an amendment and file it with the Secretary-General of the United Nations. The Secretary-General shall thereupon communicate the proposed amendment to the States Parties with a request that they notify him whether they favour a conference of States Parties for the purpose of considering and voting upon the proposal. In the event that within four months from the date of such communication at least one third of the States Parties favours such a conference, the Secretary-General shall convene the conference under the auspices of the United Nations. Any amendment adopted by a majority of the States Parties present and voting at the conference shall be submitted by the Secretary-General to all the States Parties for acceptance.

2. An amendment adopted in accordance with paragraph 1 of this article shall enter into force when two thirds of the States Parties to this Convention have notified the Secretary-General of the United Nations that they have accepted it in accordance with their respective constitutional processes.

3. When amendments enter into force, they shall be binding on those States Parties which have accepted them, other States Parties still being bound by the provisions of this Convention and any earlier amendments which they have accepted.

Article 30

1. Any dispute between two or more States Parties concerning the interpretation or application of this Convention which cannot be settled through negotiation shall, at the request of one of them, be submitted to arbitration. If within six months from the date of the request for arbitration the Parties are unable to agree on the organization of the arbitration, any one of those Parties may refer the dispute to the International Court of Justice by request in conformity with the Statute of the Court.

2. Each State may, at the time of signature or ratification of this Convention or accession thereto, declare that it does not consider itself bound by paragraph 1 of this article. The other States Parties shall not be bound by paragraph 1 of this article with respect to any State Party having made such a reservation.

3. Any State Party having made a reservation in accordance with paragraph 2 of this article may at any time withdraw this reservation by notification to the Secretary-General of the United Nations.

Article 31

1. A State Party may denounce this Convention by written notification to the Secretary-General of the United Nations. Denunciation becomes effective one year after the date of receipt of the notification by the Secretary-General.

2. Such a denunciation shall not have the effect of releasing the State Party from its obligations under this Convention in regard to any act or omission which occurs prior to the date at which the denunciation becomes effective, nor shall denunciation prejudice in any way the continued consideration of any

matter which is already under consideration by the Committee prior to the date at which the denunciation becomes effective.

3. Following the date at which the denunciation of a State Party becomes effective, the Committee shall not commence consideration of any new matter regarding that State.

Article 32

The Secretary-General of the United Nations shall inform all States Members of the United Nations and all States which have signed this Convention or acceded to it of the following:

(a) Signatures, ratifications and accessions under articles 25 and 26;

(b) The date of entry into force of this Convention under article 27 and the date of the entry into force of any amendments under article 29;

(c) Denunciations under article 31.

Article 33

1. This Convention, of which the Arabic, Chinese, English, French, Russian and Spanish texts are equally authentic, shall be deposited with the Secretary-General of the United Nations.

2. The Secretary-General of the United Nations shall transmit certified copies of this Convention to all States.

4.3
International Convention for the Suppression of Terrorist Bombings (1997)

General Assembly Resolution 51/210 of 17 December 1996 established an ad hoc committee "to elaborate an international convention for the suppression of terrorist bombings and, subsequently, an international convention for the suppression of acts of nuclear terrorism, to supplement related existing international instruments, and thereafter to address means of further developing a comprehensive legal framework of conventions dealing with international terrorism." The United States initiated negotiations for this convention, which was adopted by the General Assembly in December 1997. The International Convention for the Suppression of the Financing of Terrorism was adopted by the General Assembly on 9 December 1999, and the International Convention for the Suppression of Acts of Nuclear Terrorism was adopted by the General Assembly on 13 April 2005. Efforts are ongoing to draft a comprehensive convention on terrorism.

On this convention, see Samuel M. Wittens, "The International Convention for the Suppression of Terrorist Bombings," American Journal of International Law *92 (1998): 774–781. For the texts of other counter-terrorism conventions, see the UN publication* International Instruments Related to the Prevention and Suppression of International Terrorism, *available at www.untreaty.un.org/English/Terrorism.asp. Annual reports of the Secretary-General to the General Assembly on measures to eliminate international terrorism are available at the website of the Sixth Committee of the General Assembly at www.un.org/law/cod/sixth/60/sixth60.htm. For documents related to UN efforts to draft a comprehensive convention on terrorism, seewww.un.org/law/terrorism/index.html.*

The States Parties to this Convention,

Having in mind the purposes and principles of the Charter of the United Nations concerning the maintenance of international peace and security and the promotion of good-neighbourliness and friendly relations and cooperation among States,

Deeply concerned about the worldwide escalation of acts of terrorism in all its forms and manifestations,

Recalling the Declaration on the Occasion of the Fiftieth Anniversary of the United Nations of 24 October 1995,

Recalling also the Declaration on Measures to Eliminate International Terrorism, annexed to General Assembly resolution 49/60 of 9 December 1994, in which, inter alia, "the States Members of the United Nations solemnly reaffirm their unequivocal condemnation of all acts, methods and practices of terrorism as criminal and unjustifiable, wherever and by whomever committed, including those which jeopardize the friendly relations among States and peoples and threaten the territorial integrity and security of States,"

Noting that the Declaration also encouraged States "to review urgently the scope of the existing international legal provisions on the prevention, repression and elimination of terrorism in all its forms and manifestations, with the aim of ensuring that there is a comprehensive legal framework covering all aspects of the matter,"

Recalling further General Assembly resolution 51/210 of 17 December 1996 and the Declaration to Supplement the 1994 Declaration on Measures to Eliminate International Terrorism, annexed thereto,

Noting that terrorist attacks by means of explosives or other lethal devices have become increasingly widespread,

Noting also that existing multilateral legal provisions do not adequately address these attacks,

Being convinced of the urgent need to enhance international cooperation between States in devising and adopting effective and practical measures for the prevention of such acts of terrorism, and for the prosecution and punishment of their perpetrators,

Considering that the occurrence of such acts is a matter of grave concern to the international community as a whole,

Noting that the activities of military forces of States are governed by rules of international law outside the framework of this Convention and that the exclusion of certain actions from the coverage of this Convention does not condone or make lawful otherwise unlawful acts, or preclude prosecution under other laws,

Have agreed as follows:

Article 1

For the purposes of this Convention:

1. "State or government facility" includes any permanent or temporary facility or conveyance that is used or occupied by representatives of a State, members of Government, the legislature or the judiciary or by officials or employees of a State or any other public authority or entity or by employees or officials of an intergovernmental organization in connection with their official duties.

2. "Infrastructure facility" means any publicly or privately owned facility

providing or distributing services for the benefit of the public, such as water, sewage, energy, fuel or communications.

3. "Explosive or other lethal device" means:

(a) An explosive or incendiary weapon or device that is designed, or has the capability, to cause death, serious bodily injury or substantial material damage; or

(b) A weapon or device that is designed, or has the capability, to cause death, serious bodily injury or substantial material damage through the release, dissemination or impact of toxic chemicals, biological agents or toxins or similar substances or radiation or radioactive material.

4. "Military forces of a State" means the armed forces of a State which are organized, trained and equipped under its internal law for the primary purpose of national defence or security, and persons acting in support of those armed forces who are under their formal command, control and responsibility.

5. "Place of public use" means those parts of any building, land, street, waterway or other location that are accessible or open to members of the public, whether continuously, periodically or occasionally, and encompasses any commercial, business, cultural, historical, educational, religious, governmental, entertainment, recreational or similar place that is so accessible or open to the public.

6. "Public transportation system" means all facilities, conveyances and instrumentalities, whether publicly or privately owned, that are used in or for publicly available services for the transportation of persons or cargo.

Article 2

1. Any person commits an offence within the meaning of this Convention if that person unlawfully and intentionally delivers, places, discharges or detonates an explosive or other lethal device in, into or against a place of public use, a State or government facility, a public transportation system or an infrastructure facility:

(a) With the intent to cause death or serious bodily injury; or

(b) With the intent to cause extensive destruction of such a place, facility or system, where such destruction results in or is likely to result in major economic loss.

2. Any person also commits an offence if that person attempts to commit an offence as set forth in paragraph 1 of the present article.

3. Any person also commits an offence if that person:

(a) Participates as an accomplice in an offence as set forth in paragraph 1 or 2; or

(b) Organizes or directs others to commit an offence as set forth in paragraph 1 or 2; or

(c) In any other way contributes to the commission of one or more offences as set forth in paragraph 1 or 2 by a group of persons acting with a common purpose; such contribution shall be intentional and either be made with the aim of furthering the general criminal activity or purpose of the group or be made in the knowledge of the intention of the group to commit the offence or offences concerned.

Article 3
This Convention shall not apply where the offence is committed within a single State, the alleged offender and the victims are nationals of that State, the alleged offender is found in the territory of that State and no other State has a basis under article 6, paragraph 1, or article 6, paragraph 2, of this Convention to exercise jurisdiction, except that the provisions of articles 10 to 15 shall, as appropriate, apply in those cases.

Article 4
Each State Party shall adopt such measures as may be necessary:
(a) To establish as criminal offences under its domestic law the offences set forth in article 2 of this Convention;
(b) To make those offences punishable by appropriate penalties which take into account the grave nature of those offences.

Article 5
Each State Party shall adopt such measures as may be necessary, including, where appropriate, domestic legislation, to ensure that criminal acts within the scope of this Convention, in particular where they are intended or calculated to provoke a state of terror in the general public or in a group of persons or particular persons, are under no circumstances justifiable by considerations of a political, philosophical, ideological, racial, ethnic, religious or other similar nature and are punished by penalties consistent with their grave nature.

Article 6
1. Each State Party shall take such measures as may be necessary to establish its jurisdiction over the offences set forth in article 2 when:
(a) The offence is committed in the territory of that State; or
(b) The offence is committed on board a vessel flying the flag of that State or an aircraft which is registered under the laws of that State at the time the offence is committed; or
(c) The offence is committed by a national of that State.
2. A State Party may also establish its jurisdiction over any such offence when:
(a) The offence is committed against a national of that State; or
(b) The offence is committed against a State or government facility of that State abroad, including an embassy or other diplomatic or consular premises of that State; or
(c) The offence is committed by a stateless person who has his or her habitual residence in the territory of that State; or
(d) The offence is committed in an attempt to compel that State to do or abstain from doing any act; or

(e) The offence is committed on board an aircraft which is operated by the Government of that State.

3. Upon ratifying, accepting, approving or acceding to this Convention, each State Party shall notify the Secretary-General of the United Nations of the jurisdiction it has established in accordance with paragraph 2 under its domestic law. Should any change take place, the State Party concerned shall immediately notify the Secretary-General.

4. Each State Party shall likewise take such measures as may be necessary to establish its jurisdiction over the offences set forth in article 2 in cases where the alleged offender is present in its territory and it does not extradite that person to any of the States Parties which have established their jurisdiction in accordance with paragraph 1 or 2.

5. This Convention does not exclude the exercise of any criminal jurisdiction established by a State Party in accordance with its domestic law.

Article 7

1. Upon receiving information that a person who has committed or who is alleged to have committed an offence as set forth in article 2 may be present in its territory, the State Party concerned shall take such measures as may be necessary under its domestic law to investigate the facts contained in the information.

2. Upon being satisfied that the circumstances so warrant, the State Party in whose territory the offender or alleged offender is present shall take the appropriate measures under its domestic law so as to ensure that person's presence for the purpose of prosecution or extradition.

3. Any person regarding whom the measures referred to in paragraph 2 are being taken shall be entitled to:

(a) Communicate without delay with the nearest appropriate representative of the State of which that person is a national or which is otherwise entitled to protect that person's rights or, if that person is a stateless person, the State in the territory of which that person habitually resides;

(b) Be visited by a representative of that State;

(c) Be informed of that person's rights under subparagraphs (a) and (b).

4. The rights referred to in paragraph 3 shall be exercised in conformity with the laws and regulations of the State in the territory of which the offender or alleged offender is present, subject to the provision that the said laws and regulations must enable full effect to be given to the purposes for which the rights accorded under paragraph 3 are intended.

5. The provisions of paragraphs 3 and 4 shall be without prejudice to the right of any State Party having a claim to jurisdiction in accordance with article 6, subparagraph 1 (c) or 2 (c), to invite the International Committee of the Red Cross to communicate with and visit the alleged offender.

6. When a State Party, pursuant to this article, has taken a person into custody, it shall immediately notify, directly or through the Secretary-General of the United Nations, the States Parties which have established jurisdiction in

accordance with article 6, paragraphs 1 and 2, and, if it considers it advisable, any other interested States Parties, of the fact that such person is in custody and of the circumstances which warrant that person's detention. The State which makes the investigation contemplated in paragraph 1 shall promptly inform the said States Parties of its findings and shall indicate whether it intends to exercise jurisdiction.

Article 8

1. The State Party in the territory of which the alleged offender is present shall, in cases to which article 6 applies, if it does not extradite that person, be obliged, without exception whatsoever and whether or not the offence was committed in its territory, to submit the case without undue delay to its competent authorities for the purpose of prosecution, through proceedings in accordance with the laws of that State. Those authorities shall take their decision in the same manner as in the case of any other offence of a grave nature under the law of that State.

2. Whenever a State Party is permitted under its domestic law to extradite or otherwise surrender one of its nationals only upon the condition that the person will be returned to that State to serve the sentence imposed as a result of the trial or proceeding for which the extradition or surrender of the person was sought, and this State and the State seeking the extradition of the person agree with this option and other terms they may deem appropriate, such a conditional extradition or surrender shall be sufficient to discharge the obligation set forth in paragraph 1.

Article 9

1. The offences set forth in article 2 shall be deemed to be included as extraditable offences in any extradition treaty existing between any of the States Parties before the entry into force of this Convention. States Parties undertake to include such offences as extraditable offences in every extradition treaty to be subsequently concluded between them.

2. When a State Party which makes extradition conditional on the existence of a treaty receives a request for extradition from another State Party with which it has no extradition treaty, the requested State Party may, at its option, consider this Convention as a legal basis for extradition in respect of the offences set forth in article 2. Extradition shall be subject to the other conditions provided by the law of the requested State.

3. States Parties which do not make extradition conditional on the existence of a treaty shall recognize the offences set forth in article 2 as extraditable offences between themselves, subject to the conditions provided by the law of the requested State.

4. If necessary, the offences set forth in article 2 shall be treated, for the purposes of extradition between States Parties, as if they had been committed not only in the place in which they occurred but also in the territory of the States that have established jurisdiction in accordance with article 6, paragraphs 1 and 2.

5. The provisions of all extradition treaties and arrangements between States Parties with regard to offences set forth in article 2 shall be deemed to be modified as between State Parties to the extent that they are incompatible with this Convention.

Article 10

1. States Parties shall afford one another the greatest measure of assistance in connection with investigations or criminal or extradition proceedings brought in respect of the offences set forth in article 2, including assistance in obtaining evidence at their disposal necessary for the proceedings.

2. States Parties shall carry out their obligations under paragraph 1 in conformity with any treaties or other arrangements on mutual legal assistance that may exist between them. In the absence of such treaties or arrangements, States Parties shall afford one another assistance in accordance with their domestic law.

Article 11

None of the offences set forth in article 2 shall be regarded, for the purposes of extradition or mutual legal assistance, as a political offence or as an offence connected with a political offence or as an offence inspired by political motives. Accordingly, a request for extradition or for mutual legal assistance based on such an offence may not be refused on the sole ground that it concerns a political offence or an offence connected with a political offence or an offence inspired by political motives.

Article 12

Nothing in this Convention shall be interpreted as imposing an obligation to extradite or to afford mutual legal assistance, if the requested State Party has substantial grounds for believing that the request for extradition for offences set forth in article 2 or for mutual legal assistance with respect to such offences has been made for the purpose of prosecuting or punishing a person on account of that person's race, religion, nationality, ethnic origin or political opinion or that compliance with the request would cause prejudice to that person's position for any of these reasons.

Article 13

1. A person who is being detained or is serving a sentence in the territory of one State Party whose presence in another State Party is requested for purposes of testimony, identification or otherwise providing assistance in obtaining evidence for the investigation or prosecution of offences under this Convention may be transferred if the following conditions are met:

(a) The person freely gives his or her informed consent; and

(b) The competent authorities of both States agree, subject to such conditions as those States may deem appropriate.

2. For the purposes of the present article:

(a) The State to which the person is transferred shall have the authority and obligation to keep the person transferred in custody, unless otherwise requested or authorized by the State from which the person was transferred;

(b) The State to which the person is transferred shall without delay implement its obligation to return the person to the custody of the State from which the person was transferred as agreed beforehand, or as otherwise agreed, by the · competent authorities of both States;

(c) The State to which the person is transferred shall not require the State from which the person was transferred to initiate extradition proceedings for the return of the person;

(d) The person transferred shall receive credit for service of the sentence being served in the State from which he was transferred for time spent in the custody of the State to which he was transferred.

3. Unless the State Party from which a person is to be transferred in accordance with this article so agrees, that person, whatever his or her nationality, shall not be prosecuted or detained or subjected to any other restriction of his or her personal liberty in the territory of the State to which that person is transferred in respect of acts or convictions anterior to his or her departure from the territory of the State from which such person was transferred.

Article 14

Any person who is taken into custody or regarding whom any other measures are taken or proceedings are carried out pursuant to this Convention shall be guaranteed fair treatment, including enjoyment of all rights and guarantees in conformity with the law of the State in the territory of which that person is present and applicable provisions of international law, including international law of human rights.

Article 15

States Parties shall cooperate in the prevention of the offences set forth in article 2, particularly:

(a) By taking all practicable measures, including, if necessary, adapting their domestic legislation, to prevent and counter preparations in their respective territories for the commission of those offences within or outside their territories, including measures to prohibit in their territories illegal activities of persons, groups and organizations that encourage, instigate, organize, knowingly finance or engage in the perpetration of offences as set forth in article 2;

(b) By exchanging accurate and verified information in accordance with their national law, and coordinating administrative and other measures taken as appropriate to prevent the commission of offences as set forth in article 2;

(c) Where appropriate, through research and development regarding methods of detection of explosives and other harmful substances that can cause death or bodily injury, consultations on the development of standards for marking explosives in order to identify their origin in post-blast investigations, exchange of information on preventive measures, cooperation and transfer of technology, equipment and related materials.

Article 16
The State Party where the alleged offender is prosecuted shall, in accordance with its domestic law or applicable procedures, communicate the final outcome of the proceedings to the Secretary-General of the United Nations, who shall transmit the information to the other States Parties.

Article 17
The States Parties shall carry out their obligations under this Convention in a manner consistent with the principles of sovereign equality and territorial integrity of States and that of non-intervention in the domestic affairs of other States.

Article 18
Nothing in this Convention entitles a State Party to undertake in the territory of another State Party the exercise of jurisdiction and performance of functions which are exclusively reserved for the authorities of that other State Party by its domestic law.

Article 19
1. Nothing in this Convention shall affect other rights, obligations and responsibilities of States and individuals under international law, in particular the purposes and principles of the Charter of the United Nations and international humanitarian law.

2. The activities of armed forces during an armed conflict, as those terms are understood under international humanitarian law, which are governed by that law, are not governed by this Convention, and the activities undertaken by military forces of a State in the exercise of their official duties, inasmuch as they are governed by other rules of international law, are not governed by this Convention.

Article 20
1. Any dispute between two or more States Parties concerning the interpretation or application of this Convention which cannot be settled through negotiation within a reasonable time shall, at the request of one of them, be submitted to arbitration. If, within six months from the date of the request for arbitration, the parties are unable to agree on the organization of the arbitration, any one of those parties may refer the dispute to the International Court of Justice, by application, in conformity with the Statute of the Court.

2. Each State may at the time of signature, ratification, acceptance or approval of this Convention or accession thereto declare that it does not consider itself bound by paragraph 1. The other States Parties shall not be

bound by paragraph 1 with respect to any State Party which has made such a reservation.

3. Any State which has made a reservation in accordance with paragraph 2 may at any time withdraw that reservation by notification to the Secretary-General of the United Nations.

Article 21

1. This Convention shall be open for signature by all States from 12 January 1998 until 31 December 1999 at United Nations Headquarters in New York.

2. This Convention is subject to ratification, acceptance or approval. The instruments of ratification, acceptance or approval shall be deposited with the Secretary-General of the United Nations.

3. This Convention shall be open to accession by any State. The instruments of accession shall be deposited with the Secretary-General of the United Nations.

Article 22

1. This Convention shall enter into force on the thirtieth day following the date of the deposit of the twenty-second instrument of ratification, acceptance, approval or accession with the Secretary-General of the United Nations.

2. For each State ratifying, accepting, approving or acceding to the Convention after the deposit of the twenty-second instrument of ratification, acceptance, approval or accession, the Convention shall enter into force on the thirtieth day after deposit by such State of its instrument of ratification, acceptance, approval or accession.

Article 23

1. Any State Party may denounce this Convention by written notification to the Secretary-General of the United Nations.

2. Denunciation shall take effect one year following the date on which notification is received by the Secretary-General of the United Nations.

Article 24

The original of this Convention, of which the Arabic, Chinese, English, French, Russian and Spanish texts are equally authentic, shall be deposited with the Secretary-General of the United Nations, who shall send certified copies thereof to all States.

IN WITNESS WHEREOF, the undersigned, being duly authorized thereto by their respective Governments, have signed this Convention, opened for signature at New York on 12 January 1998.

4.4
The Rome Statute of the International Criminal Court (1998)

The establishment of a permanent international criminal court was one of the most significant developments in international law of the late twentieth century. The court is not intended to replace but to complement national courts, but the fact that the court may be able to exercise jurisdiction if a state is unable or unwilling to do so has prompted the passage in a number of countries of national legislation intended to ensure that the crimes specified in the statute are also crimes in national law.

The statute entered into force on 1 July 2002. The court's website details recent developments (www.icc-cpi.int/home.html). A good starting point for understanding the court is William A. Schabas, An Introduction to the International Criminal Court, *2nd ed. (New York: Cambridge University Press, 2004). On the place of the court in the growing body of international criminal law, see M. Cherif Bassiouni,* Introduction to International Criminal Law *(Ardsley, N.Y.: Transnational, 2003). On US objections to the statute, see Marcella David "Grotius Repudiated: The American Objections to the International Criminal Court and the Commitment to International Law,"* Michigan Journal of International Law *20 (1999): 337–412. For details of the bilateral "immunity agreements" that the US has signed with a number of countries, see www.icc-now.org/documents/otherissuesimpunityagreem.html.*

The States Parties to this Statute,

Conscious that all peoples are united by common bonds, their cultures pieced together in a shared heritage, and concerned that this delicate mosaic may be shattered at any time,

Mindful that during this century millions of children, women and men have been victims of unimaginable atrocities that deeply shock the conscience of humanity,

Recognizing that such grave crimes threaten the peace, security and well-being of the world,

Affirming that the most serious crimes of concern to the international community as a whole must not go unpunished and that their effective prosecution must be ensured by taking measures at the national level and by enhancing international cooperation,

Determined to put an end to impunity for the perpetrators of these crimes and thus to contribute to the prevention of such crimes,

Recalling that it is the duty of every State to exercise its criminal jurisdiction over those responsible for international crimes,

Reaffirming the Purposes and Principles of the Charter of the United Nations, and in particular that all States shall refrain from the threat or use of force against the territorial integrity or political independence of any State, or in any other manner inconsistent with the Purposes of the United Nations,

Emphasizing in this connection that nothing in this Statute shall be taken as authorizing any State Party to intervene in an armed conflict or in the internal affairs of any State,

Determined to these ends and for the sake of present and future generations, to establish an independent permanent International Criminal Court in relationship with the United Nations system, with jurisdiction over the most serious crimes of concern to the international community as a whole,

Emphasizing that the International Criminal Court established under this Statute shall be complementary to national criminal jurisdictions,

Resolved to guarantee lasting respect for and the enforcement of international justice,

Have agreed as follows:

Part 1: Establishment of the Court

Article 1: The Court
An International Criminal Court ("the Court") is hereby established. It shall be a permanent institution and shall have the power to exercise its jurisdiction over persons for the most serious crimes of international concern, as referred to in this Statute, and shall be complementary to national criminal jurisdictions. The jurisdiction and functioning of the Court shall be governed by the provisions of this Statute.

Article 2: Relationship of the Court with the United Nations
The Court shall be brought into relationship with the United Nations through an agreement to be approved by the Assembly of States Parties to this Statute and thereafter concluded by the President of the Court on its behalf.

Article 3: Seat of the Court
1. The seat of the Court shall be established at The Hague in the Netherlands ("the host State").

2. The Court shall enter into a headquarters agreement with the host State, to be approved by the Assembly of States Parties and thereafter concluded by the President of the Court on its behalf.

3. The Court may sit elsewhere, whenever it considers it desirable, as provided in this Statute.

Article 4: Legal status and powers of the Court

1. The Court shall have international legal personality. It shall also have such legal capacity as may be necessary for the exercise of its functions and the fulfilment of its purposes.

2. The Court may exercise its functions and powers, as provided in this Statute, on the territory of any State Party and, by special agreement, on the territory of any other State.

Part 2: Jurisdiction, Admissibiity and Applicable Law

Article 5: Crimes within the jurisdiction of the Court

1. The jurisdiction of the Court shall be limited to the most serious crimes of concern to the international community as a whole. The Court has jurisdiction in accordance with this Statute with respect to the following crimes:

(a) The crime of genocide;

(b) Crimes against humanity;

(c) War crimes;

(d) The crime of aggression.

2. The Court shall exercise jurisdiction over the crime of aggression once a provision is adopted in accordance with articles 121 and 123 defining the crime and setting out the conditions under which the Court shall exercise jurisdiction with respect to this crime. Such a provision shall be consistent with the relevant provisions of the Charter of the United Nations.

Article 6: Genocide

For the purpose of this Statute, "genocide" means any of the following acts committed with intent to destroy, in whole or in part, a national, ethnical, racial or religious group, as such:

(a) Killing members of the group;

(b) Causing serious bodily or mental harm to members of the group;

(c) Deliberately inflicting on the group conditions of life calculated to bring about its physical destruction in whole or in part;

(d) Imposing measures intended to prevent births within the group;

(e) Forcibly transferring children of the group to another group.

Article 7: Crimes against humanity

1. For the purpose of this Statute, "crime against humanity" means any of the following acts when committed as part of a widespread or systematic attack directed against any civilian population, with knowledge of the attack:

(a) Murder;

(b) Extermination;

(c) Enslavement;

(d) Deportation or forcible transfer of population;

(e) Imprisonment or other severe deprivation of physical liberty in violation of fundamental rules of international law;

(f) Torture;

(g) Rape, sexual slavery, enforced prostitution, forced pregnancy, enforced sterilization, or any other form of sexual violence of comparable gravity;

(h) Persecution against any identifiable group or collectivity on political, racial, national, ethnic, cultural, religious, gender as defined in paragraph 3, or other grounds that are universally recognized as impermissible under international law, in connection with any act referred to in this paragraph or any crime within the jurisdiction of the Court;

(i) Enforced disappearance of persons;

(j) The crime of apartheid;

(k) Other inhumane acts of a similar character intentionally causing great suffering, or serious injury to body or to mental or physical health.

2. For the purpose of paragraph 1:

(a) "Attack directed against any civilian population" means a course of conduct involving the multiple commission of acts referred to in paragraph 1 against any civilian population, pursuant to or in furtherance of a State or organizational policy to commit such attack;

(b) "Extermination" includes the intentional infliction of conditions of life, inter alia the deprivation of access to food and medicine, calculated to bring about the destruction of part of a population;

(c) "Enslavement" means the exercise of any or all of the powers attaching to the right of ownership over a person and includes the exercise of such power in the course of trafficking in persons, in particular women and children;

(d) "Deportation or forcible transfer of population" means forced displacement of the persons concerned by expulsion or other coercive acts from the area in which they are lawfully present, without grounds permitted under international law;

(e) "Torture" means the intentional infliction of severe pain or suffering, whether physical or mental, upon a person in the custody or under the control of the accused; except that torture shall not include pain or suffering arising only from, inherent in or incidental to, lawful sanctions;

(f) "Forced pregnancy" means the unlawful confinement of a woman forcibly made pregnant, with the intent of affecting the ethnic composition of any population or carrying out other grave violations of international law. This definition shall not in any way be interpreted as affecting national laws relating to pregnancy;

(g) "Persecution" means the intentional and severe deprivation of fundamental rights contrary to international law by reason of the identity of the group or collectivity;

(h) "The crime of apartheid" means inhuman acts of a character similar to those referred to in paragraph 1, committed in the context of an institutionalized regime of systematic oppression and domination by one racial group over any other racial group or groups and committed with the intention of maintaining that regime;

(i) "Enforced disappearance of persons" means the arrest, detention or abduction of persons by, or with the authorization, support or acquiescence of, a State or a political organization, followed by a refusal to acknowledge that deprivation of freedom or to give information on the fate or whereabouts of those persons, with the intention of removing them from the protection of the law for a prolonged period of time.

3. For the purpose of this Statute, it is understood that the term "gender" refers to the two sexes, male and female, within the context of society. The term "gender" does not indicate any meaning different from the above.

Article 8: War crimes

1. The Court shall have jurisdiction in respect of war crimes in particular when committed as part of a plan or policy or as part of a large-scale commission of such crimes.

2. For the purpose of this Statute, "war crimes" means:

(a) Grave breaches of the Geneva Conventions of 12 August 1949, namely, any of the following acts against persons or property protected under the provisions of the relevant Geneva Convention: (i) Wilful killing; (ii) Torture or inhuman treatment, including biological experiments; (iii) Wilfully causing great suffering, or serious injury to body or health; (iv) Extensive destruction and appropriation of property, not justified by military necessity and carried out unlawfully and wantonly; (v) Compelling a prisoner of war or other protected person to serve in the forces of a hostile Power; (vi) Wilfully depriving a prisoner of war or other protected person of the rights of fair and regular trial; (vii) Unlawful deportation or transfer or unlawful confinement; (viii) Taking of hostages.

(b) Other serious violations of the laws and customs applicable in international armed conflict, within the established framework of international law, namely, any of the following acts: (i) Intentionally directing attacks against the civilian population as such or against individual civilians not taking direct part in hostilities; (ii) Intentionally directing attacks against civilian objects, that is, objects which are not military objectives; (iii) Intentionally directing attacks against personnel, installations, material, units or vehicles involved in a humanitarian assistance or peacekeeping mission in accordance with the Charter of the United Nations, as long as they are entitled to the protection given to civilians or civilian objects under the international law of armed conflict; (iv) Intentionally launching an attack in the knowledge that such attack will cause incidental loss of life or injury to civilians or damage to civilian objects or widespread, long-term and severe damage to the natural environment which would be clearly excessive in relation to the concrete and direct overall military advantage anticipated; (v) Attacking or bombarding, by whatever means, towns, villages, dwellings or buildings which are undefended and which are not military objectives; (vi) Killing or wounding a combatant who, having laid down his arms or having no longer means of defence, has surrendered at discretion; (vii) Making improper use of a flag of truce, of the flag or of the military insignia and uniform of the enemy or of the United Nations, as well as of the distinctive emblems of the Geneva Conventions, resulting in death or serious personal injury; (viii) The transfer, directly or indirectly, by the Occupying Power of parts of its own civilian population into the territory it occupies, or the deportation or transfer of all or parts of the population of the occupied territory within or outside this territory; (ix) Intentionally directing attacks against buildings dedicated to religion, education, art, science or charitable purposes, historic monuments, hospitals and places where the sick and wounded are collected, provided they are not military objectives; (x) Subjecting persons who are in the power of an adverse party to physical mutilation or to medical or scientific experiments of any kind which are neither justified by the medical, dental or hospital treatment of the person concerned nor carried out in his or her interest, and which cause death to or seriously endanger the health of such person or persons; (xi) Killing or wounding treacherously individuals belonging to the hostile nation or army; (xii) Declaring that no quarter will be given; (xiii) Destroying or seizing the enemy's property unless such destruction or seizure be imperatively demanded by the necessities of war; (xiv) Declaring abolished, suspended or inadmissible in a court of law the rights and actions of the nationals of the hostile party; (xv) Compelling the nationals of the hostile party to take part in the operations of war directed against their own country, even if they were in the belligerent's service before the commencement of the war; (xvi) Pillaging a town or place, even when taken by assault; (xvii) Employing poison or poisoned weapons; (xviii) Employing asphyxiating, poisonous or other gases, and all analogous liquids, materials or devices; (xix) Employing bullets which expand or flatten easily in the human body, such as bullets with a hard envelope which does not entirely cover the core or is pierced with incisions; (xx) Employing weapons, projectiles and material and methods of warfare which are of a nature to cause superfluous injury or unnecessary suffering or which are inherently indiscriminate in violation of the international law of armed conflict, provided that such weapons, projectiles and material and methods of warfare are the subject of a comprehensive prohibition and are included in an annex to this Statute, by an amendment in accordance with the relevant provisions set forth in articles 121 and 123; (xxi) Committing outrages upon personal dignity, in particular humiliating and degrading treatment; (xxii) Committing rape, sexual slavery, enforced prostitution, forced pregnancy, as defined in article 7, paragraph 2 (f), enforced sterilization, or any other form of sexual violence also constituting a grave breach of the Geneva Conventions; (xxiii) Utilizing the presence of a civilian or other protected person to render certain points, areas or military forces immune from military operations; (xxiv) Intentionally directing attacks against buildings, material, medical units and transport, and personnel using the distinctive emblems of the Geneva Conventions in conformity with international law; (xxv) Intentionally using starvation of civilians as a method of warfare by depriving them of objects indispensable to their survival, including wilfully impeding relief supplies as provided for under the Geneva Conventions; (xxvi) Conscripting or enlisting children under the age of fifteen years into the national armed forces or using them to participate actively in hostilities.

(c) In the case of an armed conflict not of an international character, serious violations of article 3 common to the four Geneva Conventions of 12 August 1949, namely, any of the following acts committed against persons taking no active part in the hostilities, including members of armed forces who have laid down their arms and those placed hors de combat by sickness, wounds, detention or any other cause: (i) Violence to life and person, in particular murder of all kinds, mutilation, cruel treatment and torture; (ii) Committing outrages upon personal dignity, in particular humiliating and degrading treatment; (iii) Taking of hostages; (iv) The passing of sentences and the carrying out of executions without previous judgement pronounced by a regularly constituted court, affording all judicial guarantees which are generally recognized as indispensable.

(d) Paragraph 2 (c) applies to armed conflicts not of an international character and thus does not apply to situations of internal disturbances and tensions, such as riots, isolated and sporadic acts of violence or other acts of a similar nature.

(e) Other serious violations of the laws and customs applicable in armed conflicts not of an international character, within the established framework of international law, namely, any of the following acts: (i) Intentionally directing attacks against the civilian population as such or against individual civilians not taking direct part in hostilities; (ii) Intentionally directing attacks against buildings, material, medical units and transport, and personnel using the distinctive emblems of the Geneva Conventions in conformity with international law; (iii) Intentionally directing attacks against personnel, installations, material, units or vehicles involved in a humanitarian assistance or peacekeeping mission in accordance with the Charter of the United Nations, as long as they are entitled to the protection given to civilians or civilian objects under the international law of armed conflict; (iv) Intentionally directing attacks against buildings dedicated to religion, education, art, science or charitable purposes, historic monuments, hospitals and places where the sick and wounded are collected, provided they are not military objectives; (v) Pillaging a town or place, even when taken by assault; (vi) Committing rape, sexual slavery, enforced prostitution, forced pregnancy, as defined in article 7, paragraph 2 (f), enforced sterilization, and any other form of sexual violence also constituting a serious violation of article 3 common to the four Geneva Conventions; (vii) Conscripting or enlisting children under the age of fifteen years into armed forces or groups or using them to participate actively in hostilities; (viii) Ordering the displacement of the civilian population for reasons related to the conflict, unless the security of the civilians involved or imperative military reasons so demand; (ix) Killing or wounding treacherously a combatant adversary; (x) Declaring that no quarter will be given; (xi) Subjecting persons who are in the power of another party to the conflict to physical mutilation or to medical or scientific experiments of any kind which are neither justified by the medical, dental or hospital treatment of the person concerned nor carried out in his or her interest, and which cause death to or seriously endanger the health of such person or persons; (xii) Destroying or seizing the property of an adversary unless such destruction or seizure be imperatively demanded by the necessities of the conflict;

(f) Paragraph 2 (e) applies to armed conflicts not of an international character and thus does not apply to situations of internal disturbances and tensions, such as riots, isolated and sporadic acts of violence or other acts of a similar nature. It applies to armed conflicts that take place in the territory of a State when there is protracted armed conflict between governmental authorities and organized armed groups or between such groups.

3. Nothing in paragraph 2 (c) and (d) shall affect the responsibility of a Government to maintain or re-establish law and order in the State or to defend the unity and territorial integrity of the State, by all legitimate means.

Article 9: Elements of Crimes

1. Elements of Crimes shall assist the Court in the interpretation and application of articles 6, 7 and 8. They shall be adopted by a two-thirds majority of the members of the Assembly of States Parties.

2. Amendments to the Elements of Crimes may be proposed by:

(a) Any State Party;

(b) The judges acting by an absolute majority;

(c) The Prosecutor.

Such amendments shall be adopted by a two-thirds majority of the members of the Assembly of States Parties.

3. The Elements of Crimes and amendments thereto shall be consistent with this Statute.

Article 10

Nothing in this Part shall be interpreted as limiting or prejudicing in any way existing or developing rules of international law for purposes other than this Statute.

Article 11: Jurisdiction ratione temporis

1. The Court has jurisdiction only with respect to crimes committed after the entry into force of this Statute.

2. If a State becomes a Party to this Statute after its entry into force, the Court may exercise its jurisdiction only with respect to crimes committed after the entry into force of this Statute for that State, unless that State has made a declaration under article 12, paragraph 3.

Article 12: Preconditions to the exercise of jurisdiction

1. A State which becomes a Party to this Statute thereby accepts the jurisdiction of the Court with respect to the crimes referred to in article 5.

2. In the case of article 13, paragraph (a) or (c), the Court may exercise its jurisdiction if one or more of the following States are Parties to this Statute or have accepted the jurisdiction of the Court in accordance with paragraph 3:

(a) The State on the territory of which the conduct in question occurred or, if the crime was committed on board a vessel or aircraft, the State of registration of that vessel or aircraft;

(b) The State of which the person accused of the crime is a national.

3. If the acceptance of a State which is not a Party to this Statute is required under paragraph 2, that State may, by declaration lodged with the Registrar, accept the exercise of jurisdiction by the Court with respect to the crime in question. The accepting State shall cooperate with the Court without any delay or exception in accordance with Part 9.

Article 13: Exercise of jurisdiction

The Court may exercise its jurisdiction with respect to a crime referred to in article 5 in accordance with the provisions of this Statute if:

(a) A situation in which one or more of such crimes appears to have been committed is referred to the Prosecutor by a State Party in accordance with article 14;

(b) A situation in which one or more of such crimes appears to have been committed is referred to the Prosecutor by the Security Council acting under Chapter VII of the Charter of the United Nations; or

(c) The Prosecutor has initiated an investigation in respect of such a crime in accordance with article 15.

Article 14: Referral of a situation by a State Party

1. A State Party may refer to the Prosecutor a situation in which one or more crimes within the jurisdiction of the Court appear to have been committed requesting the Prosecutor to investigate the situation for the purpose of determining whether one or more specific persons should be charged with the commission of such crimes.

2. As far as possible, a referral shall specify the relevant circumstances and be accompanied by such supporting documentation as is available to the State referring the situation.

Article 15: Prosecutor

1. The Prosecutor may initiate investigations proprio motu on the basis of information on crimes within the jurisdiction of the Court.

2. The Prosecutor shall analyse the seriousness of the information received. For this purpose, he or she may seek additional information from States, organs of the United Nations, intergovernmental or non-governmental organi-

zations, or other reliable sources that he or she deems appropriate, and may receive written or oral testimony at the seat of the Court.

3. If the Prosecutor concludes that there is a reasonable basis to proceed with an investigation, he or she shall submit to the Pre-Trial Chamber a request for authorization of an investigation, together with any supporting material collected. Victims may make representations to the Pre-Trial Chamber, in accordance with the Rules of Procedure and Evidence.

4. If the Pre-Trial Chamber, upon examination of the request and the supporting material, considers that there is a reasonable basis to proceed with an investigation, and that the case appears to fall within the jurisdiction of the Court, it shall authorize the commencement of the investigation, without prejudice to subsequent determinations by the Court with regard to the jurisdiction and admissibility of a case.

5. The refusal of the Pre-Trial Chamber to authorize the investigation shall not preclude the presentation of a subsequent request by the Prosecutor based on new facts or evidence regarding the same situation.

6. If, after the preliminary examination referred to in paragraphs 1 and 2, the Prosecutor concludes that the information provided does not constitute a reasonable basis for an investigation, he or she shall inform those who provided the information. This shall not preclude the Prosecutor from considering further information submitted to him or her regarding the same situation in the light of new facts or evidence.

Article 16: Deferral of investigation or prosecution

No investigation or prosecution may be commenced or proceeded with under this Statute for a period of 12 months after the Security Council, in a resolution adopted under Chapter VII of the Charter of the United Nations, has requested the Court to that effect; that request may be renewed by the Council under the same conditions.

Article 17: Issues of admissibility

1. Having regard to paragraph 10 of the Preamble and article 1, the Court shall determine that a case is inadmissible where:

(a) The case is being investigated or prosecuted by a State which has jurisdiction over it, unless the State is unwilling or unable genuinely to carry out the investigation or prosecution;

(b) The case has been investigated by a State which has jurisdiction over it and the State has decided not to prosecute the person concerned, unless the decision resulted from the unwillingness or inability of the State genuinely to prosecute;

(c) The person concerned has already been tried for conduct which is the subject of the complaint, and a trial by the Court is not permitted under article 20, paragraph 3;

(d) The case is not of sufficient gravity to justify further action by the Court.

2. In order to determine unwillingness in a particular case, the Court shall consider, having regard to the principles of due process recognized by international law, whether one or more of the following exist, as applicable:

(a) The proceedings were or are being undertaken or the national decision was made for the purpose of shielding the person concerned from criminal responsibility for crimes within the jurisdiction of the Court referred to in article 5;

(b) There has been an unjustified delay in the proceedings which in the circumstances is inconsistent with an intent to bring the person concerned to justice;

(c) The proceedings were not or are not being conducted independently or impartially, and they were or are being conducted in a manner which, in the circumstances, is inconsistent with an intent to bring the person concerned to justice.

3. In order to determine inability in a particular case, the Court shall consider whether, due to a total or substantial collapse or unavailability of its national judicial system, the State is unable to obtain the accused or the necessary evidence and testimony or otherwise unable to carry out its proceedings.

Article 18: Preliminary rulings regarding admissibility

1. When a situation has been referred to the Court pursuant to article 13 (a) and the Prosecutor has determined that there would be a reasonable basis to commence an investigation, or the Prosecutor initiates an investigation pursuant to articles 13 (c) and 15, the Prosecutor shall notify all States Parties and those States which, taking into account the information available, would normally exercise jurisdiction over the crimes concerned. The Prosecutor may notify such States on a confidential basis and, where the Prosecutor believes it necessary to protect persons, prevent destruction of evidence or prevent the absconding of persons, may limit the scope of the information provided to States.

2. Within one month of receipt of that notification, a State may inform the Court that it is investigating or has investigated its nationals or others within its jurisdiction with respect to criminal acts which may constitute crimes referred to in article 5 and which relate to the information provided in the notification to States. At the request of that State, the Prosecutor shall defer to the State's investigation of those persons unless the Pre-Trial Chamber, on the application of the Prosecutor, decides to authorize the investigation.

3. The Prosecutor's deferral to a State's investigation shall be open to review by the Prosecutor six months after the date of deferral or at any time when there has been a significant change of circumstances based on the State's unwillingness or inability genuinely to carry out the investigation.

4. The State concerned or the Prosecutor may appeal to the Appeals Chamber against a ruling of the Pre-Trial Chamber, in accordance with article 82. The appeal may be heard on an expedited basis.

5. When the Prosecutor has deferred an investigation in accordance with

paragraph 2, the Prosecutor may request that the State concerned periodically inform the Prosecutor of the progress of its investigations and any subsequent prosecutions. States Parties shall respond to such requests without undue delay.

6. Pending a ruling by the Pre-Trial Chamber, or at any time when the Prosecutor has deferred an investigation under this article, the Prosecutor may, on an exceptional basis, seek authority from the Pre-Trial Chamber to pursue necessary investigative steps for the purpose of preserving evidence where there is a unique opportunity to obtain important evidence or there is a significant risk that such evidence may not be subsequently available.

7. A State which has challenged a ruling of the Pre-Trial Chamber under this article may challenge the admissibility of a case under article 19 on the grounds of additional significant facts or significant change of circumstances.

Article 19: Challenges to the jurisdiction of the Court or the admissibility of a case

1. The Court shall satisfy itself that it has jurisdiction in any case brought before it. The Court may, on its own motion, determine the admissibility of a case in accordance with article 17.

2. Challenges to the admissibility of a case on the grounds referred to in article 17 or challenges to the jurisdiction of the Court may be made by:

(a) An accused or a person for whom a warrant of arrest or a summons to appear has been issued under article 58;

(b) A State which has jurisdiction over a case, on the ground that it is investigating or prosecuting the case or has investigated or prosecuted; or

(c) A State from which acceptance of jurisdiction is required under article 12.

3. The Prosecutor may seek a ruling from the Court regarding a question of jurisdiction or admissibility. In proceedings with respect to jurisdiction or admissibility, those who have referred the situation under article 13, as well as victims, may also submit observations to the Court.

4. The admissibility of a case or the jurisdiction of the Court may be challenged only once by any person or State referred to in paragraph 2. The challenge shall take place prior to or at the commencement of the trial. In exceptional circumstances, the Court may grant leave for a challenge to be brought more than once or at a time later than the commencement of the trial. Challenges to the admissibility of a case, at the commencement of a trial, or subsequently with the leave of the Court, may be based only on article 17, paragraph 1(c).

5. A State referred to in paragraph 2 (b) and (c) shall make a challenge at the earliest opportunity.

6. Prior to the confirmation of the charges, challenges to the admissibility of a case or challenges to the jurisdiction of the Court shall be referred to the Pre-Trial Chamber. After confirmation of the charges, they shall be referred to the

Trial Chamber. Decisions with respect to jurisdiction or admissibility may be appealed to the Appeals Chamber in accordance with article 82.

7. If a challenge is made by a State referred to in paragraph 2 (b) or (c), the Prosecutor shall suspend the investigation until such time as the Court makes a determination in accordance with article 17.

8. Pending a ruling by the Court, the Prosecutor may seek authority from the Court:

(a) To pursue necessary investigative steps of the kind referred to in article 18, paragraph 6;

(b) To take a statement or testimony from a witness or complete the collection and examination of evidence which had begun prior to the making of the challenge; and

(c) In cooperation with the relevant States, to prevent the absconding of persons in respect of whom the Prosecutor has already requested a warrant of arrest under article 58.

9. The making of a challenge shall not affect the validity of any act performed by the Prosecutor or any order or warrant issued by the Court prior to the making of the challenge.

10. If the Court has decided that a case is inadmissible under article 17, the Prosecutor may submit a request for a review of the decision when he or she is fully satisfied that new facts have arisen which negate the basis on which the case had previously been found inadmissible under article 17.

11. If the Prosecutor, having regard to the matters referred to in article 17, defers an investigation, the Prosecutor may request that the relevant State make available to the Prosecutor information on the proceedings. That information shall, at the request of the State concerned, be confidential. If the Prosecutor thereafter decides to proceed with an investigation, he or she shall notify the State to which deferral of the proceedings has taken place.

Article 20: Ne bis in idem

1. Except as provided in this Statute, no person shall be tried before the Court with respect to conduct which formed the basis of crimes for which the person has been convicted or acquitted by the Court.

2. No person shall be tried by another court for a crime referred to in article 5 for which that person has already been convicted or acquitted by the Court.

3. No person who has been tried by another court for conduct also proscribed under article 6, 7 or 8 shall be tried by the Court with respect to the same conduct unless the proceedings in the other court:

(a) Were for the purpose of shielding the person concerned from criminal responsibility for crimes within the jurisdiction of the Court; or

(b) Otherwise were not conducted independently or impartially in accordance with the norms of due process recognized by international law and were conducted in a manner which, in the circumstances, was inconsistent with an intent to bring the person concerned to justice.

Article 21: Applicable law

1. The Court shall apply:

(a) In the first place, this Statute, Elements of Crimes and its Rules of Procedure and Evidence;

(b) In the second place, where appropriate, applicable treaties and the principles and rules of international law, including the established principles of the international law of armed conflict;

(c) Failing that, general principles of law derived by the Court from national laws of legal systems of the world including, as appropriate, the national laws of States that would normally exercise jurisdiction over the crime, provided that those principles are not inconsistent with this Statute and with international law and internationally recognized norms and standards.

2. The Court may apply principles and rules of law as interpreted in its previous decisions.

3. The application and interpretation of law pursuant to this article must be consistent with internationally recognized human rights, and be without any adverse distinction founded on grounds such as gender as defined in article 7, paragraph 3, age, race, colour, language, religion or belief, political or other opinion, national, ethnic or social origin, wealth, birth or other status.

Part 3: General Principles of Criminal Law

Article 22: Nullum crimen sine lege

1. A person shall not be criminally responsible under this Statute unless the conduct in question constitutes, at the time it takes place, a crime within the jurisdiction of the Court.

2. The definition of a crime shall be strictly construed and shall not be extended by analogy. In case of ambiguity, the definition shall be interpreted in favour of the person being investigated, prosecuted or convicted.

3. This article shall not affect the characterization of any conduct as criminal under international law independently of this Statute.

Article 23: Nulla poena sine lege

A person convicted by the Court may be punished only in accordance with this Statute.

Article 24: Non-retroactivity ratione personae

1. No person shall be criminally responsible under this Statute for conduct prior to the entry into force of the Statute.

2. In the event of a change in the law applicable to a given case prior to a final judgement, the law more favourable to the person being investigated, prosecuted or convicted shall apply.

Article 25: Individual criminal responsibility

1. The Court shall have jurisdiction over natural persons pursuant to this Statute.

2. A person who commits a crime within the jurisdiction of the Court shall be individually responsible and liable for punishment in accordance with this Statute.

3. In accordance with this Statute, a person shall be criminally responsible and liable for punishment for a crime within the jurisdiction of the Court if that person:

(a) Commits such a crime, whether as an individual, jointly with another or through another person, regardless of whether that other person is criminally responsible;

(b) Orders, solicits or induces the commission of such a crime which in fact occurs or is attempted;

(c) For the purpose of facilitating the commission of such a crime, aids, abets or otherwise assists in its commission or its attempted commission, including providing the means for its commission;

(d) In any other way contributes to the commission or attempted commission of such a crime by a group of persons acting with a common purpose. Such contribution shall be intentional and shall either: (i) Be made with the aim of furthering the criminal activity or criminal purpose of the group, where such activity or purpose involves the commission of a crime within the jurisdiction of the Court; or (ii) Be made in the knowledge of the intention of the group to commit the crime;

(e) In respect of the crime of genocide, directly and publicly incites others to commit genocide;

(f) Attempts to commit such a crime by taking action that commences its execution by means of a substantial step, but the crime does not occur because of circumstances independent of the person's intentions. However, a person who abandons the effort to commit the crime or otherwise prevents the completion of the crime shall not be liable for punishment under this Statute for the attempt to commit that crime if that person completely and voluntarily gave up the criminal purpose.

4. No provision in this Statute relating to individual criminal responsibility shall affect the responsibility of States under international law.

Article 26: Exclusion of jurisdiction over persons under eighteen

The Court shall have no jurisdiction over any person who was under the age of 18 at the time of the alleged commission of a crime.

Article 27: Irrelevance of official capacity

1. This Statute shall apply equally to all persons without any distinction based on official capacity. In particular, official capacity as a Head of State or Government, a member of a Government or parliament, an elected representative or a government official shall in no case exempt a person from criminal

responsibility under this Statute, nor shall it, in and of itself, constitute a ground for reduction of sentence.

2. Immunities or special procedural rules which may attach to the official capacity of a person, whether under national or international law, shall not bar the Court from exercising its jurisdiction over such a person.

Article 28: Responsibility of commanders and other superiors

In addition to other grounds of criminal responsibility under this Statute for crimes within the jurisdiction of the Court:

(a) A military commander or person effectively acting as a military commander shall be criminally responsible for crimes within the jurisdiction of the Court committed by forces under his or her effective command and control, or effective authority and control as the case may be, as a result of his or her failure to exercise control properly over such forces, where: (i) That military commander or person either knew or, owing to the circumstances at the time, should have known that the forces were committing or about to commit such crimes; and (ii) That military commander or person failed to take all necessary and reasonable measures within his or her power to prevent or repress their commission or to submit the matter to the competent authorities for investigation and prosecution.

(b) With respect to superior and subordinate relationships not described in paragraph (a), a superior shall be criminally responsible for crimes within the jurisdiction of the Court committed by subordinates under his or her effective authority and control, as a result of his or her failure to exercise control properly over such subordinates, where: (i) The superior either knew, or consciously disregarded information which clearly indicated, that the subordinates were committing or about to commit such crimes; (ii) The crimes concerned activities that were within the effective responsibility and control of the superior; and (iii) The superior failed to take all necessary and reasonable measures within his or her power to prevent or repress their commission or to submit the matter to the competent authorities for investigation and prosecution.

Article 29: Non-applicability of statute of limitations

The crimes within the jurisdiction of the Court shall not be subject to any statute of limitations.

Article 30: Mental element

1. Unless otherwise provided, a person shall be criminally responsible and liable for punishment for a crime within the jurisdiction of the Court only if the material elements are committed with intent and knowledge.

2. For the purposes of this article, a person has intent where:

(a) In relation to conduct, that person means to engage in the conduct;

(b) In relation to a consequence, that person means to cause that consequence or is aware that it will occur in the ordinary course of events.

3. For the purposes of this article, "knowledge" means awareness that a cir-

cumstance exists or a consequence will occur in the ordinary course of events. "Know" and "knowingly" shall be construed accordingly.

Article 31: Grounds for excluding criminal responsibility

1. In addition to other grounds for excluding criminal responsibility provided for in this Statute, a person shall not be criminally responsible if, at the time of that person's conduct:

(a) The person suffers from a mental disease or defect that destroys that person's capacity to appreciate the unlawfulness or nature of his or her conduct, or capacity to control his or her conduct to conform to the requirements of law;

(b) The person is in a state of intoxication that destroys that person's capacity to appreciate the unlawfulness or nature of his or her conduct, or capacity to control his or her conduct to conform to the requirements of law, unless the person has become voluntarily intoxicated under such circumstances that the person knew, or disregarded the risk, that, as a result of the intoxication, he or she was likely to engage in conduct constituting a crime within the jurisdiction of the Court;

(c) The person acts reasonably to defend himself or herself or another person or, in the case of war crimes, property which is essential for the survival of the person or another person or property which is essential for accomplishing a military mission, against an imminent and unlawful use of force in a manner proportionate to the degree of danger to the person or the other person or property protected. The fact that the person was involved in a defensive operation conducted by forces shall not in itself constitute a ground for excluding criminal responsibility under this subparagraph;

(d) The conduct which is alleged to constitute a crime within the jurisdiction of the Court has been caused by duress resulting from a threat of imminent death or of continuing or imminent serious bodily harm against that person or another person, and the person acts necessarily and reasonably to avoid this threat, provided that the person does not intend to cause a greater harm than the one sought to be avoided. Such a threat may either be: (i) Made by other persons; or (ii) Constituted by other circumstances beyond that person's control.

2. The Court shall determine the applicability of the grounds for excluding criminal responsibility provided for in this Statute to the case before it.

3. At trial, the Court may consider a ground for excluding criminal responsibility other than those referred to in paragraph 1 where such a ground is derived from applicable law as set forth in article 21. The procedures relating to the consideration of such a ground shall be provided for in the Rules of Procedure and Evidence.

Article 32: Mistake of fact or mistake of law

1. A mistake of fact shall be a ground for excluding criminal responsibility only if it negates the mental element required by the crime.

2. A mistake of law as to whether a particular type of conduct is a crime within the jurisdiction of the Court shall not be a ground for excluding criminal responsibility. A mistake of law may, however, be a ground for excluding criminal responsibility if it negates the mental element required by such a crime, or as provided for in article 33.

Article 33: Superior orders and prescription of law

1. The fact that a crime within the jurisdiction of the Court has been committed by a person pursuant to an order of a Government or of a superior, whether military or civilian, shall not relieve that person of criminal responsibility unless:

(a) The person was under a legal obligation to obey orders of the Government or the superior in question;

(b) The person did not know that the order was unlawful; and

(c) The order was not manifestly unlawful.

2. For the purposes of this article, orders to commit genocide or crimes against humanity are manifestly unlawful.

Part 4: Composition and Administration of the Court

Article 34: Organs of the Court

The Court shall be composed of the following organs:

(a) The Presidency;

(b) An Appeals Division, a Trial Division and a Pre-Trial Division;

(c) The Office of the Prosecutor;

(d) The Registry.

Article 35: Service of judges

1. All judges shall be elected as full-time members of the Court and shall be available to serve on that basis from the commencement of their terms of office.

2. The judges composing the Presidency shall serve on a full-time basis as soon as they are elected.

3. The Presidency may, on the basis of the workload of the Court and in consultation with its members, decide from time to time to what extent the remaining judges shall be required to serve on a full-time basis. Any such arrangement shall be without prejudice to the provisions of article 40.

4. The financial arrangements for judges not required to serve on a full-time basis shall be made in accordance with article 49.

Article 36: Qualifications, nomination and election of judges

1. Subject to the provisions of paragraph 2, there shall be 18 judges of the Court.

2. (a) The Presidency, acting on behalf of the Court, may propose an

increase in the number of judges specified in paragraph 1, indicating the reasons why this is considered necessary and appropriate. The Registrar shall promptly circulate any such proposal to all States Parties.

(b) Any such proposal shall then be considered at a meeting of the Assembly of States Parties to be convened in accordance with article 112. The proposal shall be considered adopted if approved at the meeting by a vote of two thirds of the members of the Assembly of States Parties and shall enter into force at such time as decided by the Assembly of States Parties.

(c) (i) Once a proposal for an increase in the number of judges has been adopted under subparagraph (b), the election of the additional judges shall take place at the next session of the Assembly of States Parties in accordance with paragraphs 3 to 8, and article 37, paragraph 2; (ii) Once a proposal for an increase in the number of judges has been adopted and brought into effect under subparagraphs (b) and (c) (i), it shall be open to the Presidency at any time thereafter, if the workload of the Court justifies it, to propose a reduction in the number of judges, provided that the number of judges shall not be reduced below that specified in paragraph 1. The proposal shall be dealt with in accordance with the procedure laid down in subparagraphs (a) and (b). In the event that the proposal is adopted, the number of judges shall be progressively decreased as the terms of office of serving judges expire, until the necessary number has been reached.

3. (a) The judges shall be chosen from among persons of high moral character, impartiality and integrity who possess the qualifications required in their respective States for appointment to the highest judicial offices.

(b) Every candidate for election to the Court shall: (i) Have established competence in criminal law and procedure, and the necessary relevant experience, whether as judge, prosecutor, advocate or in other similar capacity, in criminal proceedings; or (ii) Have established competence in relevant areas of international law such as international humanitarian law and the law of human rights, and extensive experience in a professional legal capacity which is of relevance to the judicial work of the Court;

(c) Every candidate for election to the Court shall have an excellent knowledge of and be fluent in at least one of the working languages of the Court.

4. (a) Nominations of candidates for election to the Court may be made by any State Party to this Statute, and shall be made either: (i) By the procedure for the nomination of candidates for appointment to the highest judicial offices in the State in question; or (ii) By the procedure provided for the nomination of candidates for the International Court of Justice in the Statute of that Court. Nominations shall be accompanied by a statement in the necessary detail specifying how the candidate fulfils the requirements of paragraph 3.

(b) Each State Party may put forward one candidate for any given election who need not necessarily be a national of that State Party but shall in any case be a national of a State Party.

(c) The Assembly of States Parties may decide to establish, if appropriate, an Advisory Committee on nominations. In that event, the Committee's composition and mandate shall be established by the Assembly of States Parties.

5. For the purposes of the election, there shall be two lists of candidates:

List A containing the names of candidates with the qualifications specified in paragraph 3 (b) (i); and

List B containing the names of candidates with the qualifications specified in paragraph 3 (b) (ii).

A candidate with sufficient qualifications for both lists may choose on which list to appear. At the first election to the Court, at least nine judges shall be elected from list A and at least five judges from list B. Subsequent elections shall be so organized as to maintain the equivalent proportion on the Court of judges qualified on the two lists.

6. (a) The judges shall be elected by secret ballot at a meeting of the Assembly of States Parties convened for that purpose under article 112. Subject to paragraph 7, the persons elected to the Court shall be the 18 candidates who obtain the highest number of votes and a two-thirds majority of the States Parties present and voting.

(b) In the event that a sufficient number of judges is not elected on the first ballot, successive ballots shall be held in accordance with the procedures laid down in subparagraph (a) until the remaining places have been filled.

7. No two judges may be nationals of the same State. A person who, for the purposes of membership of the Court, could be regarded as a national of more than one State shall be deemed to be a national of the State in which that person ordinarily exercises civil and political rights.

8. (a) The States Parties shall, in the selection of judges, take into account the need, within the membership of the Court, for: (i) The representation of the principal legal systems of the world; (ii) Equitable geographical representation; and (iii) A fair representation of female and male judges.

(b) States Parties shall also take into account the need to include judges with legal expertise on specific issues, including, but not limited to, violence against women or children.

9. (a) Subject to subparagraph (b), judges shall hold office for a term of nine years and, subject to subparagraph (c) and to article 37, paragraph 2, shall not be eligible for re-election.

(b) At the first election, one third of the judges elected shall be selected by lot to serve for a term of three years; one third of the judges elected shall be selected by lot to serve for a term of six years; and the remainder shall serve for a term of nine years.

(c) A judge who is selected to serve for a term of three years under subparagraph (b) shall be eligible for re-election for a full term.

10. Notwithstanding paragraph 9, a judge assigned to a Trial or Appeals Chamber in accordance with article 39 shall continue in office to complete any trial or appeal the hearing of which has already commenced before that Chamber.

Article 37: Judicial vacancies

1. In the event of a vacancy, an election shall be held in accordance with article 36 to fill the vacancy.

2. A judge elected to fill a vacancy shall serve for the remainder of the predecessor's term and, if that period is three years or less, shall be eligible for re-election for a full term under article 36.

Article 38: The Presidency

1. The President and the First and Second Vice-Presidents shall be elected by an absolute majority of the judges. They shall each serve for a term of three years or until the end of their respective terms of office as judges, whichever expires earlier. They shall be eligible for re-election once.

2. The First Vice-President shall act in place of the President in the event that the President is unavailable or disqualified. The Second Vice-President shall act in place of the President in the event that both the President and the First Vice-President are unavailable or disqualified.

3. The President, together with the First and Second Vice-Presidents, shall constitute the Presidency, which shall be responsible for:

(a) The proper administration of the Court, with the exception of the Office of the Prosecutor; and

(b) The other functions conferred upon it in accordance with this Statute.

4. In discharging its responsibility under paragraph 3 (a), the Presidency shall coordinate with and seek the concurrence of the Prosecutor on all matters of mutual concern.

Article 39: Chambers

1. As soon as possible after the election of the judges, the Court shall organize itself into the divisions specified in article 34, paragraph (b). The Appeals Division shall be composed of the President and four other judges, the Trial Division of not less than six judges and the Pre-Trial Division of not less than six judges. The assignment of judges to divisions shall be based on the nature of the functions to be performed by each division and the qualifications and experience of the judges elected to the Court, in such a way that each division shall contain an appropriate combination of expertise in criminal law and procedure and in international law. The Trial and Pre-Trial Divisions shall be composed predominantly of judges with criminal trial experience.

2. (a) The judicial functions of the Court shall be carried out in each division by Chambers.

(b) (i) The Appeals Chamber shall be composed of all the judges of the Appeals Division; (ii) The functions of the Trial Chamber shall be carried out by three judges of the Trial Division; (iii) The functions of the Pre-Trial Chamber shall be carried out either by three judges of the Pre-Trial Division or by a single judge of that division in accordance with this Statute and the Rules of Procedure and Evidence;

(c) Nothing in this paragraph shall preclude the simultaneous constitution of more than one Trial Chamber or Pre-Trial Chamber when the efficient management of the Court's workload so requires.

3. (a) Judges assigned to the Trial and Pre-Trial Divisions shall serve in those divisions for a period of three years, and thereafter until the completion of any case the hearing of which has already commenced in the division concerned.

(b) Judges assigned to the Appeals Division shall serve in that division for their entire term of office.

4. Judges assigned to the Appeals Division shall serve only in that division. Nothing in this article shall, however, preclude the temporary attachment of judges from the Trial Division to the Pre-Trial Division or vice versa, if the Presidency considers that the efficient management of the Court's workload so requires, provided that under no circumstances shall a judge who has participated in the pre-trial phase of a case be eligible to sit on the Trial Chamber hearing that case.

Article 40: Independence of the judges

1. The judges shall be independent in the performance of their functions.

2. Judges shall not engage in any activity which is likely to interfere with their judicial functions or to affect confidence in their independence.

3. Judges required to serve on a full-time basis at the seat of the Court shall not engage in any other occupation of a professional nature.

4. Any question regarding the application of paragraphs 2 and 3 shall be decided by an absolute majority of the judges. Where any such question concerns an individual judge, that judge shall not take part in the decision.

Article 41: Excusing and disqualification of judges

1. The Presidency may, at the request of a judge, excuse that judge from the exercise of a function under this Statute, in accordance with the Rules of Procedure and Evidence.

2. (a) A judge shall not participate in any case in which his or her impartiality might reasonably be doubted on any ground. A judge shall be disqualified from a case in accordance with this paragraph if, inter alia, that judge has previously been involved in any capacity in that case before the Court or in a related criminal case at the national level involving the person being investigated or prosecuted. A judge shall also be disqualified on such other grounds as may be provided for in the Rules of Procedure and Evidence.

(b) The Prosecutor or the person being investigated or prosecuted may request the disqualification of a judge under this paragraph.

(c) Any question as to the disqualification of a judge shall be decided by an absolute majority of the judges. The challenged judge shall be entitled to present his or her comments on the matter, but shall not take part in the decision.

Article 42: The Office of the Prosecutor

1. The Office of the Prosecutor shall act independently as a separate organ of the Court. It shall be responsible for receiving referrals and any substantiated information on crimes within the jurisdiction of the Court, for examining them and for conducting investigations and prosecutions before the Court. A member of the Office shall not seek or act on instructions from any external source.

2. The Office shall be headed by the Prosecutor. The Prosecutor shall have full authority over the management and administration of the Office, including the staff, facilities and other resources thereof. The Prosecutor shall be assisted by one or more Deputy Prosecutors, who shall be entitled to carry out any of the acts required of the Prosecutor under this Statute. The Prosecutor and the Deputy Prosecutors shall be of different nationalities. They shall serve on a full-time basis.

3. The Prosecutor and the Deputy Prosecutors shall be persons of high moral character, be highly competent in and have extensive practical experience in the prosecution or trial of criminal cases. They shall have an excellent knowledge of and be fluent in at least one of the working languages of the Court.

4. The Prosecutor shall be elected by secret ballot by an absolute majority of the members of the Assembly of States Parties. The Deputy Prosecutors shall be elected in the same way from a list of candidates provided by the Prosecutor. The Prosecutor shall nominate three candidates for each position of Deputy Prosecutor to be filled. Unless a shorter term is decided upon at the time of their election, the Prosecutor and the Deputy Prosecutors shall hold office for a term of nine years and shall not be eligible for re-election.

5. Neither the Prosecutor nor a Deputy Prosecutor shall engage in any activity which is likely to interfere with his or her prosecutorial functions or to affect confidence in his or her independence. They shall not engage in any other occupation of a professional nature.

6. The Presidency may excuse the Prosecutor or a Deputy Prosecutor, at his or her request, from acting in a particular case.

7. Neither the Prosecutor nor a Deputy Prosecutor shall participate in any matter in which their impartiality might reasonably be doubted on any ground. They shall be disqualified from a case in accordance with this paragraph if, inter alia, they have previously been involved in any capacity in that case before the Court or in a related criminal case at the national level involving the person being investigated or prosecuted.

8. Any question as to the disqualification of the Prosecutor or a Deputy Prosecutor shall be decided by the Appeals Chamber.

(a) The person being investigated or prosecuted may at any time request the disqualification of the Prosecutor or a Deputy Prosecutor on the grounds set out in this article;

(b) The Prosecutor or the Deputy Prosecutor, as appropriate, shall be entitled to present his or her comments on the matter;

9. The Prosecutor shall appoint advisers with legal expertise on specific issues, including, but not limited to, sexual and gender violence and violence against children.

Article 43: The Registry

1. The Registry shall be responsible for the non-judicial aspects of the administration and servicing of the Court, without prejudice to the functions and powers of the Prosecutor in accordance with article 42.

2. The Registry shall be headed by the Registrar, who shall be the principal administrative officer of the Court. The Registrar shall exercise his or her functions under the authority of the President of the Court.

3. The Registrar and the Deputy Registrar shall be persons of high moral character, be highly competent and have an excellent knowledge of and be fluent in at least one of the working languages of the Court.

4. The judges shall elect the Registrar by an absolute majority by secret ballot, taking into account any recommendation by the Assembly of States Parties. If the need arises and upon the recommendation of the Registrar, the judges shall elect, in the same manner, a Deputy Registrar.

5. The Registrar shall hold office for a term of five years, shall be eligible for re-election once and shall serve on a full-time basis. The Deputy Registrar shall hold office for a term of five years or such shorter term as may be decided upon by an absolute majority of the judges, and may be elected on the basis that the Deputy Registrar shall be called upon to serve as required.

6. The Registrar shall set up a Victims and Witnesses Unit within the Registry. This Unit shall provide, in consultation with the Office of the Prosecutor, protective measures and security arrangements, counselling and other appropriate assistance for witnesses, victims who appear before the Court, and others who are at risk on account of testimony given by such witnesses. The Unit shall include staff with expertise in trauma, including trauma related to crimes of sexual violence.

Article 44: Staff

1. The Prosecutor and the Registrar shall appoint such qualified staff as may be required to their respective offices. In the case of the Prosecutor, this shall include the appointment of investigators.

2. In the employment of staff, the Prosecutor and the Registrar shall ensure the highest standards of efficiency, competency and integrity, and shall have regard, mutatis mutandis, to the criteria set forth in article 36, paragraph 8.

3. The Registrar, with the agreement of the Presidency and the Prosecutor, shall propose Staff Regulations which include the terms and conditions upon which the staff of the Court shall be appointed, remunerated and dismissed. The Staff Regulations shall be approved by the Assembly of States Parties.

4. The Court may, in exceptional circumstances, employ the expertise of gratis personnel offered by States Parties, intergovernmental organizations or non-governmental organizations to assist with the work of any of the organs of

the Court. The Prosecutor may accept any such offer on behalf of the Office of the Prosecutor. Such gratis personnel shall be employed in accordance with guidelines to be established by the Assembly of States Parties.

Article 45: Solemn undertaking

Before taking up their respective duties under this Statute, the judges, the Prosecutor, the Deputy Prosecutors, the Registrar and the Deputy Registrar shall each make a solemn undertaking in open court to exercise his or her respective functions impartially and conscientiously.

Article 46: Removal from office

1. A judge, the Prosecutor, a Deputy Prosecutor, the Registrar or the Deputy Registrar shall be removed from office if a decision to this effect is made in accordance with paragraph 2, in cases where that person:

(a) Is found to have committed serious misconduct or a serious breach of his or her duties under this Statute, as provided for in the Rules of Procedure and Evidence; or

(b) Is unable to exercise the functions required by this Statute.

2. A decision as to the removal from office of a judge, the Prosecutor or a Deputy Prosecutor under paragraph 1 shall be made by the Assembly of States Parties, by secret ballot:

(a) In the case of a judge, by a two-thirds majority of the States Parties upon a recommendation adopted by a two-thirds majority of the other judges;

(b) In the case of the Prosecutor, by an absolute majority of the States Parties;

(c) In the case of a Deputy Prosecutor, by an absolute majority of the States Parties upon the recommendation of the Prosecutor.

3. A decision as to the removal from office of the Registrar or Deputy Registrar shall be made by an absolute majority of the judges.

4. A judge, Prosecutor, Deputy Prosecutor, Registrar or Deputy Registrar whose conduct or ability to exercise the functions of the office as required by this Statute is challenged under this article shall have full opportunity to present and receive evidence and to make submissions in accordance with the Rules of Procedure and Evidence. The person in question shall not otherwise participate in the consideration of the matter.

Article 47: Disciplinary measures

A judge, Prosecutor, Deputy Prosecutor, Registrar or Deputy Registrar who has committed misconduct of a less serious nature than that set out in article 46, paragraph 1, shall be subject to disciplinary measures, in accordance with the Rules of Procedure and Evidence.

Article 48: Privileges and immunities

1. The Court shall enjoy in the territory of each State Party such privileges and immunities as are necessary for the fulfilment of its purposes.

2. The judges, the Prosecutor, the Deputy Prosecutors and the Registrar shall, when engaged on or with respect to the business of the Court, enjoy the same privileges and immunities as are accorded to heads of diplomatic missions and shall, after the expiry of their terms of office, continue to be accorded immunity from legal process of every kind in respect of words spoken or written and acts performed by them in their official capacity.

3. The Deputy Registrar, the staff of the Office of the Prosecutor and the staff of the Registry shall enjoy the privileges and immunities and facilities necessary for the performance of their functions, in accordance with the agreement on the privileges and immunities of the Court.

4. Counsel, experts, witnesses or any other person required to be present at the seat of the Court shall be accorded such treatment as is necessary for the proper functioning of the Court, in accordance with the agreement on the privileges and immunities of the Court.

5. The privileges and immunities of:

(a) A judge or the Prosecutor may be waived by an absolute majority of the judges;

(b) The Registrar may be waived by the Presidency;

(c) The Deputy Prosecutors and staff of the Office of the Prosecutor may be waived by the Prosecutor;

(d) The Deputy Registrar and staff of the Registry may be waived by the Registrar.

Article 49: Salaries, allowances and expenses

The judges, the Prosecutor, the Deputy Prosecutors, the Registrar and the Deputy Registrar shall receive such salaries, allowances and expenses as may be decided upon by the Assembly of States Parties. These salaries and allowances shall not be reduced during their terms of office.

Article 50: Official and working languages

1. The official languages of the Court shall be Arabic, Chinese, English, French, Russian and Spanish. The judgements of the Court, as well as other decisions resolving fundamental issues before the Court, shall be published in the official languages. The Presidency shall, in accordance with the criteria established by the Rules of Procedure and Evidence, determine which decisions may be considered as resolving fundamental issues for the purposes of this paragraph.

2. The working languages of the Court shall be English and French. The Rules of Procedure and Evidence shall determine the cases in which other official languages may be used as working languages.

3. At the request of any party to a proceeding or a State allowed to intervene in a proceeding, the Court shall authorize a language other than English or French to be used by such a party or State, provided that the Court considers such authorization to be adequately justified.

Article 51: Rules of Procedure and Evidence

1. The Rules of Procedure and Evidence shall enter into force upon adoption by a two-thirds majority of the members of the Assembly of States Parties.

2. Amendments to the Rules of Procedure and Evidence may be proposed by:

(a) Any State Party;

(b) The judges acting by an absolute majority; or

(c) The Prosecutor.

Such amendments shall enter into force upon adoption by a two-thirds majority of the members of the Assembly of States Parties.

3. After the adoption of the Rules of Procedure and Evidence, in urgent cases where the Rules do not provide for a specific situation before the Court, the judges may, by a two-thirds majority, draw up provisional Rules to be applied until adopted, amended or rejected at the next ordinary or special session of the Assembly of States Parties.

4. The Rules of Procedure and Evidence, amendments thereto and any provisional Rule shall be consistent with this Statute. Amendments to the Rules of Procedure and Evidence as well as provisional Rules shall not be applied retroactively to the detriment of the person who is being investigated or prosecuted or who has been convicted.

5. In the event of conflict between the Statute and the Rules of Procedure and Evidence, the Statute shall prevail.

Article 52: Regulations of the Court

1. The judges shall, in accordance with this Statute and the Rules of Procedure and Evidence, adopt, by an absolute majority, the Regulations of the Court necessary for its routine functioning.

2. The Prosecutor and the Registrar shall be consulted in the elaboration of the Regulations and any amendments thereto.

3. The Regulations and any amendments thereto shall take effect upon adoption unless otherwise decided by the judges. Immediately upon adoption, they shall be circulated to States Parties for comments. If within six months there are no objections from a majority of States Parties, they shall remain in force.

Part 5: Investigation and Prosecution

Article 53: Initiation of an investigation

1. The Prosecutor shall, having evaluated the information made available to him or her, initiate an investigation unless he or she determines that there is no reasonable basis to proceed under this Statute. In deciding whether to initiate an investigation, the Prosecutor shall consider whether:

(a) The information available to the Prosecutor provides a reasonable basis to believe that a crime within the jurisdiction of the Court has been or is being committed;

(b) The case is or would be admissible under article 17; and

(c) Taking into account the gravity of the crime and the interests of victims, there are nonetheless substantial reasons to believe that an investigation would not serve the interests of justice.

If the Prosecutor determines that there is no reasonable basis to proceed and his or her determination is based solely on subparagraph (c) above, he or she shall inform the Pre-Trial Chamber.

2. If, upon investigation, the Prosecutor concludes that there is not a sufficient basis for a prosecution because:

(a) There is not a sufficient legal or factual basis to seek a warrant or summons under article 58;

(b) The case is inadmissible under article 17; or

(c) A prosecution is not in the interests of justice, taking into account all the circumstances, including the gravity of the crime, the interests of victims and the age or infirmity of the alleged perpetrator, and his or her role in the alleged crime; the Prosecutor shall inform the Pre-Trial Chamber and the State making a referral under article 14 or the Security Council in a case under article 13, paragraph (b), of his or her conclusion and the reasons for the conclusion.

3. (a) At the request of the State making a referral under article 14 or the Security Council under article 13, paragraph (b), the Pre-Trial Chamber may review a decision of the Prosecutor under paragraph 1 or 2 not to proceed and may request the Prosecutor to reconsider that decision.

(b) In addition, the Pre-Trial Chamber may, on its own initiative, review a decision of the Prosecutor not to proceed if it is based solely on paragraph 1 (c) or 2 (c). In such a case, the decision of the Prosecutor shall be effective only if confirmed by the Pre-Trial Chamber.

4. The Prosecutor may, at any time, reconsider a decision whether to initiate an investigation or prosecution based on new facts or information.

Article 54: Duties and powers of the Prosecutor with respect to investigations

1. The Prosecutor shall:

(a) In order to establish the truth, extend the investigation to cover all facts and evidence relevant to an assessment of whether there is criminal responsibility under this Statute, and, in doing so, investigate incriminating and exonerating circumstances equally;

(b) Take appropriate measures to ensure the effective investigation and prosecution of crimes within the jurisdiction of the Court, and in doing so, respect the interests and personal circumstances of victims and witnesses, including age, gender as defined in article 7, paragraph 3, and health, and take into account the nature of the crime, in particular where it involves sexual violence, gender violence or violence against children; and

(c) Fully respect the rights of persons arising under this Statute.

2. The Prosecutor may conduct investigations on the territory of a State:

(a) In accordance with the provisions of Part 9; or

(b) As authorized by the Pre-Trial Chamber under article 57, paragraph 3 (d).

3. The Prosecutor may:

(a) Collect and examine evidence;

(b) Request the presence of and question persons being investigated, victims and witnesses;

(c) Seek the cooperation of any State or intergovernmental organization or arrangement in accordance with its respective competence and/or mandate;

(d) Enter into such arrangements or agreements, not inconsistent with this Statute, as may be necessary to facilitate the cooperation of a State, intergovernmental organization or person;

(e) Agree not to disclose, at any stage of the proceedings, documents or information that the Prosecutor obtains on the condition of confidentiality and solely for the purpose of generating new evidence, unless the provider of the information consents; and

(f) Take necessary measures, or request that necessary measures be taken, to ensure the confidentiality of information, the protection of any person or the preservation of evidence.

Article 55: Rights of persons during an investigation

1. In respect of an investigation under this Statute, a person:

(a) Shall not be compelled to incriminate himself or herself or to confess guilt;

(b) Shall not be subjected to any form of coercion, duress or threat, to torture or to any other form of cruel, inhuman or degrading treatment or punishment;

(c) Shall, if questioned in a language other than a language the person fully understands and speaks, have, free of any cost, the assistance of a competent interpreter and such translations as are necessary to meet the requirements of fairness; and

(d) Shall not be subjected to arbitrary arrest or detention, and shall not be deprived of his or her liberty except on such grounds and in accordance with such procedures as are established in this Statute.

2. Where there are grounds to believe that a person has committed a crime within the jurisdiction of the Court and that person is about to be questioned either by the Prosecutor, or by national authorities pursuant to a request made under Part 9, that person shall also have the following rights of which he or she shall be informed prior to being questioned:

(a) To be informed, prior to being questioned, that there are grounds to believe that he or she has committed a crime within the jurisdiction of the Court;

(b) To remain silent, without such silence being a consideration in the determination of guilt or innocence;

(c) To have legal assistance of the person's choosing, or, if the person does not have legal assistance, to have legal assistance assigned to him or her, in any case where the interests of justice so require, and without payment by the person in any such case if the person does not have sufficient means to pay for it; and

(d) To be questioned in the presence of counsel unless the person has voluntarily waived his or her right to counsel.

Article 56: Role of the Pre-Trial Chamber in relation to a unique investigative opportunity

1. (a) Where the Prosecutor considers an investigation to present a unique opportunity to take testimony or a statement from a witness or to examine, collect or test evidence, which may not be available subsequently for the purposes of a trial, the Prosecutor shall so inform the Pre-Trial Chamber.

(b) In that case, the Pre-Trial Chamber may, upon request of the Prosecutor, take such measures as may be necessary to ensure the efficiency and integrity of the proceedings and, in particular, to protect the rights of the defence.

(c) Unless the Pre-Trial Chamber orders otherwise, the Prosecutor shall provide the relevant information to the person who has been arrested or appeared in response to a summons in connection with the investigation referred to in subparagraph (a), in order that he or she may be heard on the matter.

2. The measures referred to in paragraph 1 (b) may include:

(a) Making recommendations or orders regarding procedures to be followed;

(b) Directing that a record be made of the proceedings;

(c) Appointing an expert to assist;

(d) Authorizing counsel for a person who has been arrested, or appeared before the Court in response to a summons, to participate, or where there has not yet been such an arrest or appearance or counsel has not been designated, appointing another counsel to attend and represent the interests of the defence;

(e) Naming one of its members or, if necessary, another available judge of the Pre-Trial or Trial Division to observe and make recommendations or orders regarding the collection and preservation of evidence and the questioning of persons;

(f) Taking such other action as may be necessary to collect or preserve evidence.

3. (a) Where the Prosecutor has not sought measures pursuant to this article but the Pre-Trial Chamber considers that such measures are required to preserve evidence that it deems would be essential for the defence at trial, it shall consult with the Prosecutor as to whether there is good reason for the Prosecutor's failure to request the measures. If upon consultation, the Pre-Trial Chamber concludes that the Prosecutor's failure to request such measures is unjustified, the Pre-Trial Chamber may take such measures on its own initiative.

(b) A decision of the Pre-Trial Chamber to act on its own initiative under this paragraph may be appealed by the Prosecutor. The appeal shall be heard on an expedited basis.

4. The admissibility of evidence preserved or collected for trial pursuant to this article, or the record thereof, shall be governed at trial by article 69, and given such weight as determined by the Trial Chamber.

Article 57: Functions and powers of the Pre-Trial Chamber

1. Unless otherwise provided in this Statute, the Pre-Trial Chamber shall exercise its functions in accordance with the provisions of this article.

2. (a) Orders or rulings of the Pre-Trial Chamber issued under articles 15, 18, 19, 54, paragraph 2, 61, paragraph 7, and 72 must be concurred in by a majority of its judges.

(b) In all other cases, a single judge of the Pre-Trial Chamber may exercise the functions provided for in this Statute, unless otherwise provided for in the Rules of Procedure and Evidence or by a majority of the Pre-Trial Chamber.

3. In addition to its other functions under this Statute, the Pre-Trial Chamber may:

(a) At the request of the Prosecutor, issue such orders and warrants as may be required for the purposes of an investigation;

(b) Upon the request of a person who has been arrested or has appeared pursuant to a summons under article 58, issue such orders, including measures such as those described in article 56, or seek such cooperation pursuant to Part 9 as may be necessary to assist the person in the preparation of his or her defence;

(c) Where necessary, provide for the protection and privacy of victims and witnesses, the preservation of evidence, the protection of persons who have been arrested or appeared in response to a summons, and the protection of national security information;

(d) Authorize the Prosecutor to take specific investigative steps within the territory of a State Party without having secured the cooperation of that State under Part 9 if, whenever possible having regard to the views of the State concerned, the Pre-Trial Chamber has determined in that case that the State is clearly unable to execute a request for cooperation due to the unavailability of any authority or any component of its judicial system competent to execute the request for cooperation under Part 9.

(e) Where a warrant of arrest or a summons has been issued under article 58, and having due regard to the strength of the evidence and the rights of the parties concerned, as provided for in this Statute and the Rules of Procedure and Evidence, seek the cooperation of States pursuant to article 93, paragraph 1 (k), to take protective measures for the purpose of forfeiture, in particular for the ultimate benefit of victims.

Article 58: Issuance by the Pre-Trial Chamber
of a warrant of arrest or a summons to appear

1. At any time after the initiation of an investigation, the Pre-Trial Chamber shall, on the application of the Prosecutor, issue a warrant of arrest of a person if, having examined the application and the evidence or other information submitted by the Prosecutor, it is satisfied that:

(a) There are reasonable grounds to believe that the person has committed a crime within the jurisdiction of the Court; and

(b) The arrest of the person appears necessary: (i) To ensure the person's appearance at trial, (ii) To ensure that the person does not obstruct or endanger the investigation or the court proceedings, or (iii) Where applicable, to prevent the person from continuing with the commission of that crime or a related crime which is within the jurisdiction of the Court and which arises out of the same circumstances.

2. The application of the Prosecutor shall contain:

(a) The name of the person and any other relevant identifying information;

(b) A specific reference to the crimes within the jurisdiction of the Court which the person is alleged to have committed;

(c) A concise statement of the facts which are alleged to constitute those crimes;

(d) A summary of the evidence and any other information which establish reasonable grounds to believe that the person committed those crimes; and

(e) The reason why the Prosecutor believes that the arrest of the person is necessary.

3. The warrant of arrest shall contain:

(a) The name of the person and any other relevant identifying information;

(b) A specific reference to the crimes within the jurisdiction of the Court for which the person's arrest is sought; and

(c) A concise statement of the facts which are alleged to constitute those crimes.

4. The warrant of arrest shall remain in effect until otherwise ordered by the Court.

5. On the basis of the warrant of arrest, the Court may request the provisional arrest or the arrest and surrender of the person under Part 9.

6. The Prosecutor may request the Pre-Trial Chamber to amend the warrant of arrest by modifying or adding to the crimes specified therein. The Pre-Trial Chamber shall so amend the warrant if it is satisfied that there are reasonable grounds to believe that the person committed the modified or additional crimes.

7. As an alternative to seeking a warrant of arrest, the Prosecutor may submit an application requesting that the Pre-Trial Chamber issue a summons for the person to appear. If the Pre-Trial Chamber is satisfied that there are reason-

able grounds to believe that the person committed the crime alleged and that a summons is sufficient to ensure the person's appearance, it shall issue the summons, with or without conditions restricting liberty (other than detention) if provided for by national law, for the person to appear. The summons shall contain:

(a) The name of the person and any other relevant identifying information;

(b) The specified date on which the person is to appear;

(c) A specific reference to the crimes within the jurisdiction of the Court which the person is alleged to have committed; and

(d) A concise statement of the facts which are alleged to constitute the crime.

The summons shall be served on the person.

Article 59: Arrest proceedings in the custodial State

1. A State Party which has received a request for provisional arrest or for arrest and surrender shall immediately take steps to arrest the person in question in accordance with its laws and the provisions of Part 9.

2. A person arrested shall be brought promptly before the competent judicial authority in the custodial State which shall determine, in accordance with the law of that State, that:

(a) The warrant applies to that person;

(b) The person has been arrested in accordance with the proper process; and

(c) The person's rights have been respected.

3. The person arrested shall have the right to apply to the competent authority in the custodial State for interim release pending surrender.

4. In reaching a decision on any such application, the competent authority in the custodial State shall consider whether, given the gravity of the alleged crimes, there are urgent and exceptional circumstances to justify interim release and whether necessary safeguards exist to ensure that the custodial State can fulfil its duty to surrender the person to the Court. It shall not be open to the competent authority of the custodial State to consider whether the warrant of arrest was properly issued in accordance with article 58, paragraph 1 (a) and (b).

5. The Pre-Trial Chamber shall be notified of any request for interim release and shall make recommendations to the competent authority in the custodial State. The competent authority in the custodial State shall give full consideration to such recommendations, including any recommendations on measures to prevent the escape of the person, before rendering its decision.

6. If the person is granted interim release, the Pre-Trial Chamber may request periodic reports on the status of the interim release.

7. Once ordered to be surrendered by the custodial State, the person shall be delivered to the Court as soon as possible.

Article 60: Initial proceedings before the Court

1. Upon the surrender of the person to the Court, or the person's appearance before the Court voluntarily or pursuant to a summons, the Pre-Trial Chamber shall satisfy itself that the person has been informed of the crimes which he or she is alleged to have committed, and of his or her rights under this Statute, including the right to apply for interim release pending trial.

2. A person subject to a warrant of arrest may apply for interim release pending trial. If the Pre-Trial Chamber is satisfied that the conditions set forth in article 58, paragraph 1, are met, the person shall continue to be detained. If it is not so satisfied, the Pre-Trial Chamber shall release the person, with or without conditions.

3. The Pre-Trial Chamber shall periodically review its ruling on the release or detention of the person, and may do so at any time on the request of the Prosecutor or the person. Upon such review, it may modify its ruling as to detention, release or conditions of release, if it is satisfied that changed circumstances so require.

4. The Pre-Trial Chamber shall ensure that a person is not detained for an unreasonable period prior to trial due to inexcusable delay by the Prosecutor. If such delay occurs, the Court shall consider releasing the person, with or without conditions.

5. If necessary, the Pre-Trial Chamber may issue a warrant of arrest to secure the presence of a person who has been released.

Article 61: Confirmation of the charges before trial

1. Subject to the provisions of paragraph 2, within a reasonable time after the person's surrender or voluntary appearance before the Court, the Pre-Trial Chamber shall hold a hearing to confirm the charges on which the Prosecutor intends to seek trial. The hearing shall be held in the presence of the Prosecutor and the person charged, as well as his or her counsel.

2. The Pre-Trial Chamber may, upon request of the Prosecutor or on its own motion, hold a hearing in the absence of the person charged to confirm the charges on which the Prosecutor intends to seek trial when the person has:

(a) Waived his or her right to be present; or

(b) Fled or cannot be found and all reasonable steps have been taken to secure his or her appearance before the Court and to inform the person of the charges and that a hearing to confirm those charges will be held.

In that case, the person shall be represented by counsel where the Pre-Trial Chamber determines that it is in the interests of justice.

3. Within a reasonable time before the hearing, the person shall:

(a) Be provided with a copy of the document containing the charges on which the Prosecutor intends to bring the person to trial; and

(b) Be informed of the evidence on which the Prosecutor intends to rely at the hearing.

The Pre-Trial Chamber may issue orders regarding the disclosure of information for the purposes of the hearing.

4. Before the hearing, the Prosecutor may continue the investigation and may amend or withdraw any charges. The person shall be given reasonable notice before the hearing of any amendment to or withdrawal of charges. In case of a withdrawal of charges, the Prosecutor shall notify the Pre-Trial Chamber of the reasons for the withdrawal.

5. At the hearing, the Prosecutor shall support each charge with sufficient evidence to establish substantial grounds to believe that the person committed the crime charged. The Prosecutor may rely on documentary or summary evidence and need not call the witnesses expected to testify at the trial.

6. At the hearing, the person may:

(a) Object to the charges;

(b) Challenge the evidence presented by the Prosecutor; and

(c) Present evidence.

7. The Pre-Trial Chamber shall, on the basis of the hearing, determine whether there is sufficient evidence to establish substantial grounds to believe that the person committed each of the crimes charged. Based on its determination, the Pre-Trial Chamber shall:

(a) Confirm those charges in relation to which it has determined that there is sufficient evidence, and commit the person to a Trial Chamber for trial on the charges as confirmed;

(b) Decline to confirm those charges in relation to which it has determined that there is insufficient evidence;

(c) Adjourn the hearing and request the Prosecutor to consider: (i) Providing further evidence or conducting further investigation with respect to a particular charge; or (ii) Amending a charge because the evidence submitted appears to establish a different crime within the jurisdiction of the Court.

8. Where the Pre-Trial Chamber declines to confirm a charge, the Prosecutor shall not be precluded from subsequently requesting its confirmation if the request is supported by additional evidence.

9. After the charges are confirmed and before the trial has begun, the Prosecutor may, with the permission of the Pre-Trial Chamber and after notice to the accused, amend the charges. If the Prosecutor seeks to add additional charges or to substitute more serious charges, a hearing under this article to confirm those charges must be held. After commencement of the trial, the Prosecutor may, with the permission of the Trial Chamber, withdraw the charges.

10. Any warrant previously issued shall cease to have effect with respect to any charges which have not been confirmed by the Pre-Trial Chamber or which have been withdrawn by the Prosecutor.

11. Once the charges have been confirmed in accordance with this article, the Presidency shall constitute a Trial Chamber which, subject to paragraph 8 and to article 64, paragraph 4, shall be responsible for the conduct of subse-

quent proceedings and may exercise any function of the Pre-Trial Chamber that is relevant and capable of application in those proceedings.

Part 6: The Trial

Article 62: Place of trial
Unless otherwise decided, the place of the trial shall be the seat of the Court.

Article 63: Trial in the presence of the accused
1. The accused shall be present during the trial.

2. If the accused, being present before the Court, continues to disrupt the trial, the Trial Chamber may remove the accused and shall make provision for him or her to observe the trial and instruct counsel from outside the courtroom, through the use of communications technology, if required. Such measures shall be taken only in exceptional circumstances after other reasonable alternatives have proved inadequate, and only for such duration as is strictly required.

Article 64: Functions and powers of the Trial Chamber
1. The functions and powers of the Trial Chamber set out in this article shall be exercised in accordance with this Statute and the Rules of Procedure and Evidence.

2. The Trial Chamber shall ensure that a trial is fair and expeditious and is conducted with full respect for the rights of the accused and due regard for the protection of victims and witnesses.

3. Upon assignment of a case for trial in accordance with this Statute, the Trial Chamber assigned to deal with the case shall:

(a) Confer with the parties and adopt such procedures as are necessary to facilitate the fair and expeditious conduct of the proceedings;

(b) Determine the language or languages to be used at trial; and

(c) Subject to any other relevant provisions of this Statute, provide for disclosure of documents or information not previously disclosed, sufficiently in advance of the commencement of the trial to enable adequate preparation for trial.

4. The Trial Chamber may, if necessary for its effective and fair functioning, refer preliminary issues to the Pre-Trial Chamber or, if necessary, to another available judge of the Pre-Trial Division.

5. Upon notice to the parties, the Trial Chamber may, as appropriate, direct that there be joinder or severance in respect of charges against more than one accused.

6. In performing its functions prior to trial or during the course of a trial, the Trial Chamber may, as necessary:

(a) Exercise any functions of the Pre-Trial Chamber referred to in article 61, paragraph 11;

(b) Require the attendance and testimony of witnesses and production of documents and other evidence by obtaining, if necessary, the assistance of States as provided in this Statute;

(c) Provide for the protection of confidential information;

(d) Order the production of evidence in addition to that already collected prior to the trial or presented during the trial by the parties;

(e) Provide for the protection of the accused, witnesses and victims; and

(f) Rule on any other relevant matters.

7. The trial shall be held in public. The Trial Chamber may, however, determine that special circumstances require that certain proceedings be in closed session for the purposes set forth in article 68, or to protect confidential or sensitive information to be given in evidence.

8. (a) At the commencement of the trial, the Trial Chamber shall have read to the accused the charges previously confirmed by the Pre-Trial Chamber. The Trial Chamber shall satisfy itself that the accused understands the nature of the charges. It shall afford him or her the opportunity to make an admission of guilt in accordance with article 65 or to plead not guilty.

(b) At the trial, the presiding judge may give directions for the conduct of proceedings, including to ensure that they are conducted in a fair and impartial manner. Subject to any directions of the presiding judge, the parties may submit evidence in accordance with the provisions of this Statute.

9. The Trial Chamber shall have, inter alia, the power on application of a party or on its own motion to:

(a) Rule on the admissibility or relevance of evidence; and

(b) Take all necessary steps to maintain order in the course of a hearing.

10. The Trial Chamber shall ensure that a complete record of the trial, which accurately reflects the proceedings, is made and that it is maintained and preserved by the Registrar.

Article 65: Proceedings on an admission of guilt

1. Where the accused makes an admission of guilt pursuant to article 64, paragraph 8 (a), the Trial Chamber shall determine whether:

(a) The accused understands the nature and consequences of the admission of guilt;

(b) The admission is voluntarily made by the accused after sufficient consultation with defence counsel; and

(c) The admission of guilt is supported by the facts of the case that are contained in: (i) The charges brought by the Prosecutor and admitted by the accused; (ii) Any materials presented by the Prosecutor which supplement the charges and which the accused accepts; and (iii) Any other evidence, such as the testimony of witnesses, presented by the Prosecutor or the accused.

2. Where the Trial Chamber is satisfied that the matters referred to in paragraph 1 are established, it shall consider the admission of guilt, together with any additional evidence presented, as establishing all the essential facts that

are required to prove the crime to which the admission of guilt relates, and may convict the accused of that crime.

3. Where the Trial Chamber is not satisfied that the matters referred to in paragraph 1 are established, it shall consider the admission of guilt as not having been made, in which case it shall order that the trial be continued under the ordinary trial procedures provided by this Statute and may remit the case to another Trial Chamber.

4. Where the Trial Chamber is of the opinion that a more complete presentation of the facts of the case is required in the interests of justice, in particular the interests of the victims, the Trial Chamber may:

(a) Request the Prosecutor to present additional evidence, including the testimony of witnesses; or

(b) Order that the trial be continued under the ordinary trial procedures provided by this Statute, in which case it shall consider the admission of guilt as not having been made and may remit the case to another Trial Chamber.

5. Any discussions between the Prosecutor and the defence regarding modification of the charges, the admission of guilt or the penalty to be imposed shall not be binding on the Court.

Article 66: Presumption of innocence

1. Everyone shall be presumed innocent until proved guilty before the Court in accordance with the applicable law.

2. The onus is on the Prosecutor to prove the guilt of the accused.

3. In order to convict the accused, the Court must be convinced of the guilt of the accused beyond reasonable doubt.

Article 67: Rights of the accused

1. In the determination of any charge, the accused shall be entitled to a public hearing, having regard to the provisions of this Statute, to a fair hearing conducted impartially, and to the following minimum guarantees, in full equality:

(a) To be informed promptly and in detail of the nature, cause and content of the charge, in a language which the accused fully understands and speaks;

(b) To have adequate time and facilities for the preparation of the defence and to communicate freely with counsel of the accused's choosing in confidence;

(c) To be tried without undue delay;

(d) Subject to article 63, paragraph 2, to be present at the trial, to conduct the defence in person or through legal assistance of the accused's choosing, to be informed, if the accused does not have legal assistance, of this right and to have legal assistance assigned by the Court in any case where the interests of justice so require, and without payment if the accused lacks sufficient means to pay for it;

(e) To examine, or have examined, the witnesses against him or her and to obtain the attendance and examination of witnesses on his or her behalf under the same conditions as witnesses against him or her. The accused shall also be entitled to raise defences and to present other evidence admissible under this Statute;

(f) To have, free of any cost, the assistance of a competent interpreter and such translations as are necessary to meet the requirements of fairness, if any of the proceedings of or documents presented to the Court are not in a language which the accused fully understands and speaks;

(g) Not to be compelled to testify or to confess guilt and to remain silent, without such silence being a consideration in the determination of guilt or innocence;

(h) To make an unsworn oral or written statement in his or her defence; and

(i) Not to have imposed on him or her any reversal of the burden of proof or any onus of rebuttal.

2. In addition to any other disclosure provided for in this Statute, the Prosecutor shall, as soon as practicable, disclose to the defence evidence in the Prosecutor's possession or control which he or she believes shows or tends to show the innocence of the accused, or to mitigate the guilt of the accused, or which may affect the credibility of prosecution evidence. In case of doubt as to the application of this paragraph, the Court shall decide.

Article 68: Protection of the victims and witnesses and their participation in the proceedings

1. The Court shall take appropriate measures to protect the safety, physical and psychological well-being, dignity and privacy of victims and witnesses. In so doing, the Court shall have regard to all relevant factors, including age, gender as defined in article 7, paragraph 3, and health, and the nature of the crime, in particular, but not limited to, where the crime involves sexual or gender violence or violence against children. The Prosecutor shall take such measures particularly during the investigation and prosecution of such crimes. These measures shall not be prejudicial to or inconsistent with the rights of the accused and a fair and impartial trial.

2. As an exception to the principle of public hearings provided for in article 67, the Chambers of the Court may, to protect victims and witnesses or an accused, conduct any part of the proceedings in camera or allow the presentation of evidence by electronic or other special means. In particular, such measures shall be implemented in the case of a victim of sexual violence or a child who is a victim or a witness, unless otherwise ordered by the Court, having regard to all the circumstances, particularly the views of the victim or witness.

3. Where the personal interests of the victims are affected, the Court shall permit their views and concerns to be presented and considered at stages of the proceedings determined to be appropriate by the Court and in a manner which is not prejudicial to or inconsistent with the rights of the accused and a fair and impartial trial. Such views and concerns may be presented by the legal repre-

sentatives of the victims where the Court considers it appropriate, in accordance with the Rules of Procedure and Evidence.

4. The Victims and Witnesses Unit may advise the Prosecutor and the Court on appropriate protective measures, security arrangements, counselling and assistance as referred to in article 43, paragraph 6.

5. Where the disclosure of evidence or information pursuant to this Statute may lead to the grave endangerment of the security of a witness or his or her family, the Prosecutor may, for the purposes of any proceedings conducted prior to the commencement of the trial, withhold such evidence or information and instead submit a summary thereof. Such measures shall be exercised in a manner which is not prejudicial to or inconsistent with the rights of the accused and a fair and impartial trial.

6. A State may make an application for necessary measures to be taken in respect of the protection of its servants or agents and the protection of confidential or sensitive information.

Article 69: Evidence

1. Before testifying, each witness shall, in accordance with the Rules of Procedure and Evidence, give an undertaking as to the truthfulness of the evidence to be given by that witness.

2. The testimony of a witness at trial shall be given in person, except to the extent provided by the measures set forth in article 68 or in the Rules of Procedure and Evidence. The Court may also permit the giving of viva voce (oral) or recorded testimony of a witness by means of video or audio technology, as well as the introduction of documents or written transcripts, subject to this Statute and in accordance with the Rules of Procedure and Evidence. These measures shall not be prejudicial to or inconsistent with the rights of the accused.

3. The parties may submit evidence relevant to the case, in accordance with article 64. The Court shall have the authority to request the submission of all evidence that it considers necessary for the determination of the truth.

4. The Court may rule on the relevance or admissibility of any evidence, taking into account, inter alia, the probative value of the evidence and any prejudice that such evidence may cause to a fair trial or to a fair evaluation of the testimony of a witness, in accordance with the Rules of Procedure and Evidence.

5. The Court shall respect and observe privileges on confidentiality as provided for in the Rules of Procedure and Evidence.

6. The Court shall not require proof of facts of common knowledge but may take judicial notice of them.

7. Evidence obtained by means of a violation of this Statute or internationally recognized human rights shall not be admissible if:

(a) The violation casts substantial doubt on the reliability of the evidence; or

(b) The admission of the evidence would be antithetical to and would seriously damage the integrity of the proceedings.

8. When deciding on the relevance or admissibility of evidence collected by a State, the Court shall not rule on the application of the State's national law.

Article 70: Offences against the administration of justice

1. The Court shall have jurisdiction over the following offences against its administration of justice when committed intentionally:

(a) Giving false testimony when under an obligation pursuant to article 69, paragraph 1, to tell the truth;

(b) Presenting evidence that the party knows is false or forged;

(c) Corruptly influencing a witness, obstructing or interfering with the attendance or testimony of a witness, retaliating against a witness for giving testimony or destroying, tampering with or interfering with the collection of evidence;

(d) Impeding, intimidating or corruptly influencing an official of the Court for the purpose of forcing or persuading the official not to perform, or to perform improperly, his or her duties;

(e) Retaliating against an official of the Court on account of duties performed by that or another official;

(f) Soliciting or accepting a bribe as an official of the Court in connection with his or her official duties.

2. The principles and procedures governing the Court's exercise of jurisdiction over offences under this article shall be those provided for in the Rules of Procedure and Evidence. The conditions for providing international cooperation to the Court with respect to its proceedings under this article shall be governed by the domestic laws of the requested State.

3. In the event of conviction, the Court may impose a term of imprisonment not exceeding five years, or a fine in accordance with the Rules of Procedure and Evidence, or both.

4. (a) Each State Party shall extend its criminal laws penalizing offences against the integrity of its own investigative or judicial process to offences against the administration of justice referred to in this article, committed on its territory, or by one of its nationals;

(b) Upon request by the Court, whenever it deems it proper, the State Party shall submit the case to its competent authorities for the purpose of prosecution. Those authorities shall treat such cases with diligence and devote sufficient resources to enable them to be conducted effectively.

Article 71: Sanctions for misconduct before the Court

1. The Court may sanction persons present before it who commit misconduct, including disruption of its proceedings or deliberate refusal to comply with its directions, by administrative measures other than imprisonment, such as temporary or permanent removal from the courtroom, a fine or other similar measures provided for in the Rules of Procedure and Evidence.

2. The procedures governing the imposition of the measures set forth in

paragraph 1 shall be those provided for in the Rules of Procedure and Evidence.

Article 72: Protection of national security information

1. This article applies in any case where the disclosure of the information or documents of a State would, in the opinion of that State, prejudice its national security interests. Such cases include those falling within the scope of article 56, paragraphs 2 and 3, article 61, paragraph 3, article 64, paragraph 3, article 67, paragraph 2, article 68, paragraph 6, article 87, paragraph 6 and article 93, as well as cases arising at any other stage of the proceedings where such disclosure may be at issue.

2. This article shall also apply when a person who has been requested to give information or evidence has refused to do so or has referred the matter to the State on the ground that disclosure would prejudice the national security interests of a State and the State concerned confirms that it is of the opinion that disclosure would prejudice its national security interests.

3. Nothing in this article shall prejudice the requirements of confidentiality applicable under article 54, paragraph 3 (e) and (f), or the application of article 73.

4. If a State learns that information or documents of the State are being, or are likely to be, disclosed at any stage of the proceedings, and it is of the opinion that disclosure would prejudice its national security interests, that State shall have the right to intervene in order to obtain resolution of the issue in accordance with this article.

5. If, in the opinion of a State, disclosure of information would prejudice its national security interests, all reasonable steps will be taken by the State, acting in conjunction with the Prosecutor, the defence or the Pre-Trial Chamber or Trial Chamber, as the case may be, to seek to resolve the matter by cooperative means. Such steps may include:

(a) Modification or clarification of the request;

(b) A determination by the Court regarding the relevance of the information or evidence sought, or a determination as to whether the evidence, though relevant, could be or has been obtained from a source other than the requested State;

(c) Obtaining the information or evidence from a different source or in a different form; or

(d) Agreement on conditions under which the assistance could be provided including, among other things, providing summaries or redactions, limitations on disclosure, use of in camera or ex parte proceedings, or other protective measures permissible under the Statute and the Rules.

6. Once all reasonable steps have been taken to resolve the matter through cooperative means, and if the State considers that there are no means or conditions under which the information or documents could be provided or disclosed without prejudice to its national security interests, it shall so notify the Prosecutor or the Court of the specific reasons for its decision, unless a specif-

ic description of the reasons would itself necessarily result in such prejudice to the State's national security interests.

7. Thereafter, if the Court determines that the evidence is relevant and necessary for the establishment of the guilt or innocence of the accused, the Court may undertake the following actions:

(a) Where disclosure of the information or document is sought pursuant to a request for cooperation under Part 9 or the circumstances described in paragraph 2, and the State has invoked the ground for refusal referred to in article 93, paragraph 4: (i) The Court may, before making any conclusion referred to in subparagraph 7 (a) (ii), request further consultations for the purpose of considering the State's representations, which may include, as appropriate, hearings in camera and ex parte; (ii) If the Court concludes that, by invoking the ground for refusal under article 93, paragraph 4, in the circumstances of the case, the requested State is not acting in accordance with its obligations under this Statute, the Court may refer the matter in accordance with article 87, paragraph 7, specifying the reasons for its conclusion; and (iii) The Court may make such inference in the trial of the accused as to the existence or non-existence of a fact, as may be appropriate in the circumstances; or

(b) In all other circumstances: (i) Order disclosure; or (ii) To the extent it does not order disclosure, make such inference in the trial of the accused as to the existence or non-existence of a fact, as may be appropriate in the circumstances.

Article 73: Third-party information or documents

If a State Party is requested by the Court to provide a document or information in its custody, possession or control, which was disclosed to it in confidence by a State, intergovernmental organization or international organization, it shall seek the consent of the originator to disclose that document or information. If the originator is a State Party, it shall either consent to disclosure of the information or document or undertake to resolve the issue of disclosure with the Court, subject to the provisions of article 72. If the originator is not a State Party and refuses to consent to disclosure, the requested State shall inform the Court that it is unable to provide the document or information because of a pre-existing obligation of confidentiality to the originator.

Article 74: Requirements for the decision

1. All the judges of the Trial Chamber shall be present at each stage of the trial and throughout their deliberations. The Presidency may, on a case-by-case basis, designate, as available, one or more alternate judges to be present at each stage of the trial and to replace a member of the Trial Chamber if that member is unable to continue attending.

2. The Trial Chamber's decision shall be based on its evaluation of the evidence and the entire proceedings. The decision shall not exceed the facts and circumstances described in the charges and any amendments to the charges.

The Court may base its decision only on evidence submitted and discussed before it at the trial.

3. The judges shall attempt to achieve unanimity in their decision, failing which the decision shall be taken by a majority of the judges.

4. The deliberations of the Trial Chamber shall remain secret.

5. The decision shall be in writing and shall contain a full and reasoned statement of the Trial Chamber's findings on the evidence and conclusions. The Trial Chamber shall issue one decision. When there is no unanimity, the Trial Chamber's decision shall contain the views of the majority and the minority. The decision or a summary thereof shall be delivered in open court.

Article 75: Reparations to victims

1. The Court shall establish principles relating to reparations to, or in respect of, victims, including restitution, compensation and rehabilitation. On this basis, in its decision the Court may, either upon request or on its own motion in exceptional circumstances, determine the scope and extent of any damage, loss and injury to, or in respect of, victims and will state the principles on which it is acting.

2. The Court may make an order directly against a convicted person specifying appropriate reparations to, or in respect of, victims, including restitution, compensation and rehabilitation.

Where appropriate, the Court may order that the award for reparations be made through the Trust Fund provided for in article 79.

3. Before making an order under this article, the Court may invite and shall take account of representations from or on behalf of the convicted person, victims, other interested persons or interested States.

4. In exercising its power under this article, the Court may, after a person is convicted of a crime within the jurisdiction of the Court, determine whether, in order to give effect to an order which it may make under this article, it is necessary to seek measures under article 93, paragraph 1.

5. A State Party shall give effect to a decision under this article as if the provisions of article 109 were applicable to this article.

6. Nothing in this article shall be interpreted as prejudicing the rights of victims under national or international law.

Article 76: Sentencing

1. In the event of a conviction, the Trial Chamber shall consider the appropriate sentence to be imposed and shall take into account the evidence presented and submissions made during the trial that are relevant to the sentence.

2. Except where article 65 applies and before the completion of the trial, the Trial Chamber may on its own motion and shall, at the request of the Prosecutor or the accused, hold a further hearing to hear any additional evi-

dence or submissions relevant to the sentence, in accordance with the Rules of Procedure and Evidence.

3. Where paragraph 2 applies, any representations under article 75 shall be heard during the further hearing referred to in paragraph 2 and, if necessary, during any additional hearing.

4. The sentence shall be pronounced in public and, wherever possible, in the presence of the accused.

Part 7: Penalties

Article 77: Applicable penalties

1. Subject to article 110, the Court may impose one of the following penalties on a person convicted of a crime referred to in article 5 of this Statute:

(a) Imprisonment for a specified number of years, which may not exceed a maximum of 30 years; or

(b) A term of life imprisonment when justified by the extreme gravity of the crime and the individual circumstances of the convicted person.

2. In addition to imprisonment, the Court may order:

(a) A fine under the criteria provided for in the Rules of Procedure and Evidence;

(b) A forfeiture of proceeds, property and assets derived directly or indirectly from that crime, without prejudice to the rights of bona fide third parties.

Article 78: Determination of the sentence

1. In determining the sentence, the Court shall, in accordance with the Rules of Procedure and Evidence, take into account such factors as the gravity of the crime and the individual circumstances of the convicted person.

2. In imposing a sentence of imprisonment, the Court shall deduct the time, if any, previously spent in detention in accordance with an order of the Court. The Court may deduct any time otherwise spent in detention in connection with conduct underlying the crime.

3. When a person has been convicted of more than one crime, the Court shall pronounce a sentence for each crime and a joint sentence specifying the total period of imprisonment. This period shall be no less than the highest individual sentence pronounced and shall not exceed 30 years imprisonment or a sentence of life imprisonment in conformity with article 77, paragraph 1 (b).

Article 79: Trust Fund

1. A Trust Fund shall be established by decision of the Assembly of States Parties for the benefit of victims of crimes within the jurisdiction of the Court, and of the families of such victims.

2. The Court may order money and other property collected through fines or forfeiture to be transferred, by order of the Court, to the Trust Fund.

3. The Trust Fund shall be managed according to criteria to be determined by the Assembly of States Parties.

Article 80: Non-prejudice to national
application of penalties and national laws

Nothing in this Part affects the application by States of penalties prescribed by their national law, nor the law of States which do not provide for penalties prescribed in this Part.

Part 8: Appeal and Revision

Article 81: Appeal against decision of
acquittal or conviction or against sentence

1. A decision under article 74 may be appealed in accordance with the Rules of Procedure and Evidence as follows:

(a) The Prosecutor may make an appeal on any of the following grounds: (i) Procedural error, (ii) Error of fact, or (iii) Error of law;

(b) The convicted person, or the Prosecutor on that person's behalf, may make an appeal on any of the following grounds: (i) Procedural error, (ii) Error of fact, (iii) Error of law, or (iv) Any other ground that affects the fairness or reliability of the proceedings or decision.

2. (a) A sentence may be appealed, in accordance with the Rules of Procedure and Evidence, by the Prosecutor or the convicted person on the ground of disproportion between the crime and the sentence;

(b) If on an appeal against sentence the Court considers that there are grounds on which the conviction might be set aside, wholly or in part, it may invite the Prosecutor and the convicted person to submit grounds under article 81, paragraph 1 (a) or (b), and may render a decision on conviction in accordance with article 83;

(c) The same procedure applies when the Court, on an appeal against conviction only, considers that there are grounds to reduce the sentence under paragraph 2 (a).

3. (a) Unless the Trial Chamber orders otherwise, a convicted person shall remain in custody pending an appeal;

(b) When a convicted person's time in custody exceeds the sentence of imprisonment imposed, that person shall be released, except that if the Prosecutor is also appealing, the release may be subject to the conditions under subparagraph (c) below;

(c) In case of an acquittal, the accused shall be released immediately, subject to the following: (i) Under exceptional circumstances, and having regard, inter alia, to the concrete risk of flight, the seriousness of the offence charged and the probability of success on appeal, the Trial Chamber, at the request of the Prosecutor, may maintain the detention of the person pending appeal; (ii) A decision by the Trial Chamber under subparagraph (c) (i) may be appealed in accordance with the Rules of Procedure and Evidence.

4. Subject to the provisions of paragraph 3 (a) and (b), execution of the decision or sentence shall be suspended during the period allowed for appeal and for the duration of the appeal proceedings.

Article 82: Appeal against other decisions

1. Either party may appeal any of the following decisions in accordance with the Rules of Procedure and Evidence:

(a) A decision with respect to jurisdiction or admissibility;

(b) A decision granting or denying release of the person being investigated or prosecuted;

(c) A decision of the Pre-Trial Chamber to act on its own initiative under article 56, paragraph 3;

(d) A decision that involves an issue that would significantly affect the fair and expeditious conduct of the proceedings or the outcome of the trial, and for which, in the opinion of the Pre-Trial or Trial Chamber, an immediate resolution by the Appeals Chamber may materially advance the proceedings.

2. A decision of the Pre-Trial Chamber under article 57, paragraph 3 (d), may be appealed against by the State concerned or by the Prosecutor, with the leave of the Pre-Trial Chamber. The appeal shall be heard on an expedited basis.

3. An appeal shall not of itself have suspensive effect unless the Appeals Chamber so orders, upon request, in accordance with the Rules of Procedure and Evidence.

4. A legal representative of the victims, the convicted person or a bona fide owner of property adversely affected by an order under article 75 may appeal against the order for reparations, as provided in the Rules of Procedure and Evidence.

Article 83: Proceedings on appeal

1. For the purposes of proceedings under article 81 and this article, the Appeals Chamber shall have all the powers of the Trial Chamber.

2. If the Appeals Chamber finds that the proceedings appealed from were unfair in a way that affected the reliability of the decision or sentence, or that the decision or sentence appealed from was materially affected by error of fact or law or procedural error, it may:

(a) Reverse or amend the decision or sentence; or

(b) Order a new trial before a different Trial Chamber.

For these purposes, the Appeals Chamber may remand a factual issue to the original Trial Chamber for it to determine the issue and to report back accordingly, or may itself call evidence to determine the issue. When the decision or sentence has been appealed only by the person convicted, or the Prosecutor on that person's behalf, it cannot be amended to his or her detriment.

3. If in an appeal against sentence the Appeals Chamber finds that the sen-

tence is disproportionate to the crime, it may vary the sentence in accordance with Part 7.

4. The judgement of the Appeals Chamber shall be taken by a majority of the judges and shall be delivered in open court. The judgement shall state the reasons on which it is based. When there is no unanimity, the judgement of the Appeals Chamber shall contain the views of the majority and the minority, but a judge may deliver a separate or dissenting opinion on a question of law.

5. The Appeals Chamber may deliver its judgement in the absence of the person acquitted or convicted.

Article 84: Revision of conviction or sentence

1. The convicted person or, after death, spouses, children, parents or one person alive at the time of the accused's death who has been given express written instructions from the accused to bring such a claim, or the Prosecutor on the person's behalf, may apply to the Appeals Chamber to revise the final judgement of conviction or sentence on the grounds that:

(a) New evidence has been discovered that: (i) Was not available at the time of trial, and such unavailability was not wholly or partially attributable to the party making application; and (ii) Is sufficiently important that had it been proved at trial it would have been likely to have resulted in a different verdict;

(b) It has been newly discovered that decisive evidence, taken into account at trial and upon which the conviction depends, was false, forged or falsified;

(c) One or more of the judges who participated in conviction or confirmation of the charges has committed, in that case, an act of serious misconduct or serious breach of duty of sufficient gravity to justify the removal of that judge or those judges from office under article 46.

2. The Appeals Chamber shall reject the application if it considers it to be unfounded. If it determines that the application is meritorious, it may, as appropriate:

(a) Reconvene the original Trial Chamber;

(b) Constitute a new Trial Chamber; or

(c) Retain jurisdiction over the matter, with a view to, after hearing the parties in the manner set forth in the Rules of Procedure and Evidence, arriving at a determination on whether the judgement should be revised.

Article 85: Compensation to an arrested or convicted person

1. Anyone who has been the victim of unlawful arrest or detention shall have an enforceable right to compensation.

2. When a person has by a final decision been convicted of a criminal offence, and when subsequently his or her conviction has been reversed on the ground that a new or newly discovered fact shows conclusively that there has been a miscarriage of justice, the person who has suffered punishment as a result of such conviction shall be compensated according to law, unless it is

proved that the non-disclosure of the unknown fact in time is wholly or partly attributable to him or her.

3. In exceptional circumstances, where the Court finds conclusive facts showing that there has been a grave and manifest miscarriage of justice, it may in its discretion award compensation, according to the criteria provided in the Rules of Procedure and Evidence, to a person who has been released from detention following a final decision of acquittal or a termination of the proceedings for that reason.

Part 9:
International Cooperation and Judicial Assistance

Article 86: General obligation to cooperate
States Parties shall, in accordance with the provisions of this Statute, cooperate fully with the Court in its investigation and prosecution of crimes within the jurisdiction of the Court.

Article 87: Requests for cooperation: general provisions
1. (a) The Court shall have the authority to make requests to States Parties for cooperation. The requests shall be transmitted through the diplomatic channel or any other appropriate channel as may be designated by each State Party upon ratification, acceptance, approval or accession. Subsequent changes to the designation shall be made by each State Party in accordance with the Rules of Procedure and Evidence.

(b) When appropriate, without prejudice to the provisions of subparagraph (a), requests may also be transmitted through the International Criminal Police Organization or any appropriate regional organization.

2. Requests for cooperation and any documents supporting the request shall either be in or be accompanied by a translation into an official language of the requested State or one of the working languages of the Court, in accordance with the choice made by that State upon ratification, acceptance, approval or accession.

Subsequent changes to this choice shall be made in accordance with the Rules of Procedure and Evidence.

3. The requested State shall keep confidential a request for cooperation and any documents supporting the request, except to the extent that the disclosure is necessary for execution of the request.

4. In relation to any request for assistance presented under this Part, the Court may take such measures, including measures related to the protection of information, as may be necessary to ensure the safety or physical or psychological well-being of any victims, potential witnesses and their families. The Court may request that any information that is made available under this Part shall be provided and handled in a manner that protects the safety and physical

or psychological well-being of any victims, potential witnesses and their families.

5. The Court may invite any State not party to this Statute to provide assistance under this Part on the basis of an ad hoc arrangement, an agreement with such State or any other appropriate basis.

Where a State not party to this Statute, which has entered into an ad hoc arrangement or an agreement with the Court, fails to cooperate with requests pursuant to any such arrangement or agreement, the Court may so inform the Assembly of States Parties or, where the Security Council referred the matter to the Court, the Security Council.

6. The Court may ask any intergovernmental organization to provide information or documents. The Court may also ask for other forms of cooperation and assistance which may be agreed upon with such an organization and which are in accordance with its competence or mandate.

7. Where a State Party fails to comply with a request to cooperate by the Court contrary to the provisions of this Statute, thereby preventing the Court from exercising its functions and powers under this Statute, the Court may make a finding to that effect and refer the matter to the Assembly of States Parties or, where the Security Council referred the matter to the Court, to the Security Council.

Article 88: Availability of procedures under national law

States Parties shall ensure that there are procedures available under their national law for all of the forms of cooperation which are specified under this Part.

Article 89: Surrender of persons to the Court

1. The Court may transmit a request for the arrest and surrender of a person, together with the material supporting the request outlined in article 91, to any State on the territory of which that person may be found and shall request the cooperation of that State in the arrest and surrender of such a person. States Parties shall, in accordance with the provisions of this Part and the procedure under their national law, comply with requests for arrest and surrender.

2. Where the person sought for surrender brings a challenge before a national court on the basis of the principle of ne bis in idem as provided in article 20, the requested State shall immediately consult with the Court to determine if there has been a relevant ruling on admissibility. If the case is admissible, the requested State shall proceed with the execution of the request. If an admissibility ruling is pending, the requested State may postpone the execution of the request for surrender of the person until the Court makes a determination on admissibility.

3. (a) A State Party shall authorize, in accordance with its national procedural law, transportation through its territory of a person being surrendered to the Court by another State, except where transit through that State would impede or delay the surrender.

(b) A request by the Court for transit shall be transmitted in accordance with article 87. The request for transit shall contain: (i) A description of the person being transported; (ii) A brief statement of the facts of the case and their legal characterization; and (iii) The warrant for arrest and surrender;

(c) A person being transported shall be detained in custody during the period of transit;

(d) No authorization is required if the person is transported by air and no landing is scheduled on the territory of the transit State;

(e) If an unscheduled landing occurs on the territory of the transit State, that State may require a request for transit from the Court as provided for in subparagraph (b). The transit State shall detain the person being transported until the request for transit is received and the transit is effected, provided that detention for purposes of this subparagraph may not be extended beyond 96 hours from the unscheduled landing unless the request is received within that time.

4. If the person sought is being proceeded against or is serving a sentence in the requested State for a crime different from that for which surrender to the Court is sought, the requested State, after making its decision to grant the request, shall consult with the Court.

Article 90: Competing requests

1. A State Party which receives a request from the Court for the surrender of a person under article 89 shall, if it also receives a request from any other State for the extradition of the same person for the same conduct which forms the basis of the crime for which the Court seeks the person's surrender, notify the Court and the requesting State of that fact.

2. Where the requesting State is a State Party, the requested State shall give priority to the request from the Court if:

(a) The Court has, pursuant to article 18 or 19, made a determination that the case in respect of which surrender is sought is admissible and that determination takes into account the investigation or prosecution conducted by the requesting State in respect of its request for extradition; or

(b) The Court makes the determination described in subparagraph (a) pursuant to the requested State's notification under paragraph 1.

3. Where a determination under paragraph 2 (a) has not been made, the requested State may, at its discretion, pending the determination of the Court under paragraph 2 (b), proceed to deal with the request for extradition from the requesting State but shall not extradite the person until the Court has determined that the case is inadmissible. The Court's determination shall be made on an expedited basis.

4. If the requesting State is a State not Party to this Statute the requested State, if it is not under an international obligation to extradite the person to the requesting State, shall give priority to the request for surrender from the Court, if the Court has determined that the case is admissible.

5. Where a case under paragraph 4 has not been determined to be admissible

by the Court, the requested State may, at its discretion, proceed to deal with the request for extradition from the requesting State.

6. In cases where paragraph 4 applies except that the requested State is under an existing international obligation to extradite the person to the requesting State not Party to this Statute, the requested State shall determine whether to surrender the person to the Court or extradite the person to the requesting State. In making its decision, the requested State shall consider all the relevant factors, including but not limited to:

(a) The respective dates of the requests;

(b) The interests of the requesting State including, where relevant, whether the crime was committed in its territory and the nationality of the victims and of the person sought; and

(c) The possibility of subsequent surrender between the Court and the requesting State.

7. Where a State Party which receives a request from the Court for the surrender of a person also receives a request from any State for the extradition of the same person for conduct other than that which constitutes the crime for which the Court seeks the person's surrender:

(a) The requested State shall, if it is not under an existing international obligation to extradite the person to the requesting State, give priority to the request from the Court;

(b) The requested State shall, if it is under an existing international obligation to extradite the person to the requesting State, determine whether to surrender the person to the Court or to extradite the person to the requesting State. In making its decision, the requested State shall consider all the relevant factors, including but not limited to those set out in paragraph 6, but shall give special consideration to the relative nature and gravity of the conduct in question.

8. Where pursuant to a notification under this article, the Court has determined a case to be inadmissible, and subsequently extradition to the requesting State is refused, the requested State shall notify the Court of this decision.

Article 91: Contents of request for arrest and surrender

1. A request for arrest and surrender shall be made in writing. In urgent cases, a request may be made by any medium capable of delivering a written record, provided that the request shall be confirmed through the channel provided for in article 87, paragraph 1 (a).

2. In the case of a request for the arrest and surrender of a person for whom a warrant of arrest has been issued by the Pre-Trial Chamber under article 58, the request shall contain or be supported by:

(a) Information describing the person sought, sufficient to identify the person, and information as to that person's probable location;

(b) A copy of the warrant of arrest; and

(c) Such documents, statements or information as may be necessary to meet the requirements for the surrender process in the requested State, except that those requirements should not be more burdensome than those applicable to requests for extradition pursuant to treaties or arrangements between the requested State and other States and should, if possible, be less burdensome, taking into account the distinct nature of the Court.

3. In the case of a request for the arrest and surrender of a person already convicted, the request shall contain or be supported by:

(a) A copy of any warrant of arrest for that person;

(b) A copy of the judgement of conviction;

(c) Information to demonstrate that the person sought is the one referred to in the judgement of conviction; and

(d) If the person sought has been sentenced, a copy of the sentence imposed and, in the case of a sentence for imprisonment, a statement of any time already served and the time remaining to be served.

4. Upon the request of the Court, a State Party shall consult with the Court, either generally or with respect to a specific matter, regarding any requirements under its national law that may apply under paragraph 2(c). During the consultations, the State Party shall advise the Court of the specific requirements of its national law.

Article 92: Provisional arrest

1. In urgent cases, the Court may request the provisional arrest of the person sought, pending presentation of the request for surrender and the documents supporting the request as specified in article 91.

2. The request for provisional arrest shall be made by any medium capable of delivering a written record and shall contain:

(a) Information describing the person sought, sufficient to identify the person, and information as to that person's probable location;

(b) A concise statement of the crimes for which the person's arrest is sought and of the facts which are alleged to constitute those crimes, including, where possible, the date and location of the crime;

(c) A statement of the existence of a warrant of arrest or a judgement of conviction against the person sought; and

(d) A statement that a request for surrender of the person sought will follow.

3. A person who is provisionally arrested may be released from custody if the requested State has not received the request for surrender and the documents supporting the request as specified in article 91 within the time limits specified in the Rules of Procedure and Evidence. However, the person may consent to surrender before the expiration of this period if permitted by the law of the requested State. In such a case, the requested State shall proceed to surrender the person to the Court as soon as possible.

4. The fact that the person sought has been released from custody pursuant to paragraph 3 shall not prejudice the subsequent arrest and surrender of that person if the request for surrender and the documents supporting the request are delivered at a later date.

Article 93: Other forms of cooperation

1. States Parties shall, in accordance with the provisions of this Part and under procedures of national law, comply with requests by the Court to provide the following assistance in relation to investigations or prosecutions:

(a) The identification and whereabouts of persons or the location of items;

(b) The taking of evidence, including testimony under oath, and the production of evidence, including expert opinions and reports necessary to the Court;

(c) The questioning of any person being investigated or prosecuted;

(d) The service of documents, including judicial documents;

(e) Facilitating the voluntary appearance of persons as witnesses or experts before the Court;

(f) The temporary transfer of persons as provided in paragraph 7;

(g) The examination of places or sites, including the exhumation and examination of grave sites;

(h) The execution of searches and seizures;

(i) The provision of records and documents, including official records and documents;

(j) The protection of victims and witnesses and the preservation of evidence;

(k) The identification, tracing and freezing or seizure of proceeds, property and assets and instrumentalities of crimes for the purpose of eventual forfeiture, without prejudice to the rights of bona fide third parties; and

(l) Any other type of assistance which is not prohibited by the law of the requested State, with a view to facilitating the investigation and prosecution of crimes within the jurisdiction of the Court.

2. The Court shall have the authority to provide an assurance to a witness or an expert appearing before the Court that he or she will not be prosecuted, detained or subjected to any restriction of personal freedom by the Court in respect of any act or omission that preceded the departure of that person from the requested State.

3. Where execution of a particular measure of assistance detailed in a request presented under paragraph 1, is prohibited in the requested State on the basis of an existing fundamental legal principle of general application, the requested State shall promptly consult with the Court to try to resolve the matter. In the consultations, consideration should be given to whether the assistance can be rendered in another manner or subject to conditions. If after consultations the matter cannot be resolved, the Court shall modify the request as necessary.

4. In accordance with article 72, a State Party may deny a request for assistance, in whole or in part, only if the request concerns the production of any documents or disclosure of evidence which relates to its national security.

5. Before denying a request for assistance under paragraph 1 (l), the requested State shall consider whether the assistance can be provided subject to specified conditions, or whether the assistance can be provided at a later

date or in an alternative manner, provided that if the Court or the Prosecutor accepts the assistance subject to conditions, the Court or the Prosecutor shall abide by them.

6. If a request for assistance is denied, the requested State Party shall promptly inform the Court or the Prosecutor of the reasons for such denial.

7. (a) The Court may request the temporary transfer of a person in custody for purposes of identification or for obtaining testimony or other assistance. The person may be transferred if the following conditions are fulfilled: (i) The person freely gives his or her informed consent to the transfer; and (ii) The requested State agrees to the transfer, subject to such conditions as that State and the Court may agree.

(b) The person being transferred shall remain in custody. When the purposes of the transfer have been fulfilled, the Court shall return the person without delay to the requested State.

8. (a) The Court shall ensure the confidentiality of documents and information, except as required for the investigation and proceedings described in the request.

(b) The requested State may, when necessary, transmit documents or information to the Prosecutor on a confidential basis. The Prosecutor may then use them solely for the purpose of generating new evidence.

(c) The requested State may, on its own motion or at the request of the Prosecutor, subsequently consent to the disclosure of such documents or information. They may then be used as evidence pursuant to the provisions of Parts 5 and 6 and in accordance with the Rules of Procedure and Evidence.

9. (a) (i) In the event that a State Party receives competing requests, other than for surrender or extradition, from the Court and from another State pursuant to an international obligation, the State Party shall endeavour, in consultation with the Court and the other State, to meet both requests, if necessary by postponing or attaching conditions to one or the other request. (ii) Failing that, competing requests shall be resolved in accordance with the principles established in article 90.

(b) Where, however, the request from the Court concerns information, property or persons which are subject to the control of a third State or an international organization by virtue of an international agreement, the requested States shall so inform the Court and the Court shall direct its request to the third State or international organization.

10. (a) The Court may, upon request, cooperate with and provide assistance to a State Party conducting an investigation into or trial in respect of conduct which constitutes a crime within the jurisdiction of the Court or which constitutes a serious crime under the national law of the requesting State.

(b) (i) The assistance provided under subparagraph (a) shall include, inter alia: (1). The transmission of statements, documents or other types of evidence obtained in the course of an investigation or a trial conducted by the Court; and (2) The questioning of any person detained by order of the Court; (ii) In the case of assistance under subparagraph (b) (i) (1): (1) If the documents or other types of evidence have been obtained with the assistance of a State, such transmission shall require the consent of that State; (2) If the statements, documents or other types of evidence have been provided by a witness or expert, such transmission shall be subject to the provisions of article 68.

(c) The Court may, under the conditions set out in this paragraph, grant a request for assistance under this paragraph from a State which is not a Party to this Statute.

Article 94: Postponement of execution of a
request in respect of ongoing investigation or prosecution

1. If the immediate execution of a request would interfere with an ongoing investigation or prosecution of a case different from that to which the request relates, the requested State may postpone the execution of the request for a period of time agreed upon with the Court. However, the postponement shall be no longer than is necessary to complete the relevant investigation or prosecution in the requested State. Before making a decision to postpone, the requested State should consider whether the assistance may be immediately provided subject to certain conditions.

2. If a decision to postpone is taken pursuant to paragraph 1, the Prosecutor may, however, seek measures to preserve evidence, pursuant to article 93, paragraph 1 (j).

Article 95: Postponement of execution of
a request in respect of an admissibility challenge

Without prejudice to article 53, paragraph 2, where there is an admissibility challenge under consideration by the Court pursuant to article 18 or 19, the requested State may postpone the execution of a request under this Part pending a determination by the Court, unless the Court has specifically ordered that the Prosecutor may pursue the collection of such evidence pursuant to article 18 or 19.

Article 96: Contents of request for
other forms of assistance under article 93

1. A request for other forms of assistance referred to in article 93 shall be made in writing. In urgent cases, a request may be made by any medium capable of delivering a written record, provided that the request shall be confirmed through the channel provided for in article 87, paragraph 1 (a).

2. The request shall, as applicable, contain or be supported by the following:

(a) A concise statement of the purpose of the request and the assistance sought, including the legal basis and the grounds for the request;

(b) As much detailed information as possible about the location or identification of any person or place that must be found or identified in order for the assistance sought to be provided;

(c) A concise statement of the essential facts underlying the request;

(d) The reasons for and details of any procedure or requirement to be followed;

(e) Such information as may be required under the law of the requested State in order to execute the request; and

(f) Any other information relevant in order for the assistance sought to be provided.

3. Upon the request of the Court, a State Party shall consult with the Court, either generally or with respect to a specific matter, regarding any requirements under its national law that may apply under paragraph 2 (e). During the consultations, the State Party shall advise the Court of the specific requirements of its national law.

4. The provisions of this article shall, where applicable, also apply in respect of a request for assistance made to the Court.

Article 97: Consultations

Where a State Party receives a request under this Part in relation to which it identifies problems which may impede or prevent the execution of the request, that State shall consult with the Court without delay in order to resolve the matter. Such problems may include, inter alia:

(a) Insufficient information to execute the request;

(b) In the case of a request for surrender, the fact that despite best efforts, the person sought cannot be located or that the investigation conducted has determined that the person in the requested State is clearly not the person named in the warrant; or

(c) The fact that execution of the request in its current form would require the requested State to breach a pre-existing treaty obligation undertaken with respect to another State.

Article 98: Cooperation with respect to
waiver of immunity and consent to surrender

1. The Court may not proceed with a request for surrender or assistance which would require the requested State to act inconsistently with its obligations under international law with respect to the State or diplomatic immunity of a person or property of a third State, unless the Court can first obtain the cooperation of that third State for the waiver of the immunity.

2. The Court may not proceed with a request for surrender which would require the requested State to act inconsistently with its obligations under international agreements pursuant to which the consent of a sending State is required to surrender a person of that State to the Court, unless the Court can first obtain the cooperation of the sending State for the giving of consent for the surrender.

Article 99: Execution of requests under articles 93 and 96

1. Requests for assistance shall be executed in accordance with the relevant procedure under the law of the requested State and, unless prohibited by such law, in the manner specified in the request, including following any procedure

outlined therein or permitting persons specified in the request to be present at and assist in the execution process.

2. In the case of an urgent request, the documents or evidence produced in response shall, at the request of the Court, be sent urgently.

3. Replies from the requested State shall be transmitted in their original language and form.

4. Without prejudice to other articles in this Part, where it is necessary for the successful execution of a request which can be executed without any compulsory measures, including specifically the interview of or taking evidence from a person on a voluntary basis, including doing so without the presence of the authorities of the requested State Party if it is essential for the request to be executed, and the examination without modification of a public site or other public place, the Prosecutor may execute such request directly on the territory of a State as follows:

(a) When the State Party requested is a State on the territory of which the crime is alleged to have been committed, and there has been a determination of admissibility pursuant to article 18 or 19, the Prosecutor may directly execute such request following all possible consultations with the requested State Party;

(b) In other cases, the Prosecutor may execute such request following consultations with the requested State Party and subject to any reasonable conditions or concerns raised by that State Party. Where the requested State Party identifies problems with the execution of a request pursuant to this subparagraph it shall, without delay, consult with the Court to resolve the matter.

5. Provisions allowing a person heard or examined by the Court under article 72 to invoke restrictions designed to prevent disclosure of confidential information connected with national security shall also apply to the execution of requests for assistance under this article.

Article 100: Costs

1. The ordinary costs for execution of requests in the territory of the requested State shall be borne by that State, except for the following, which shall be borne by the Court:

(a) Costs associated with the travel and security of witnesses and experts or the transfer under article 93 of persons in custody;

(b) Costs of translation, interpretation and transcription;

(c) Travel and subsistence costs of the judges, the Prosecutor, the Deputy Prosecutors, the Registrar, the Deputy Registrar and staff of any organ of the Court;

(d) Costs of any expert opinion or report requested by the Court;

(e) Costs associated with the transport of a person being surrendered to the Court by a custodial State; and

(f) Following consultations, any extraordinary costs that may result from the execution of a request.

2. The provisions of paragraph 1 shall, as appropriate, apply to requests from States Parties to the Court. In that case, the Court shall bear the ordinary costs of execution.

Article 101: Rule of speciality

1. A person surrendered to the Court under this Statute shall not be proceeded against, punished or detained for any conduct committed prior to surrender, other than the conduct or course of conduct which forms the basis of the crimes for which that person has been surrendered.

2. The Court may request a waiver of the requirements of paragraph 1 from the State which surrendered the person to the Court and, if necessary, the Court shall provide additional information in accordance with article 91. States Parties shall have the authority to provide a waiver to the Court and should endeavour to do so.

Article 102: Use of terms

For the purposes of this Statute:

(a) "surrender" means the delivering up of a person by a State to the Court, pursuant to this Statute.

(b) "extradition" means the delivering up of a person by one State to another as provided by treaty, convention or national legislation.

Part 10: Enforcement

Article 103: Role of States in enforcement of sentences of imprisonment

1. (a) A sentence of imprisonment shall be served in a State designated by the Court from a list of States which have indicated to the Court their willingness to accept sentenced persons.

(b) At the time of declaring its willingness to accept sentenced persons, a State may attach conditions to its acceptance as agreed by the Court and in accordance with this Part.

(c) A State designated in a particular case shall promptly inform the Court whether it accepts the Court's designation.

2. (a) The State of enforcement shall notify the Court of any circumstances, including the exercise of any conditions agreed under paragraph 1, which could materially affect the terms or extent of the imprisonment. The Court shall be given at least 45 days' notice of any such known or foreseeable circumstances. During this period, the State of enforcement shall take no action that might prejudice its obligations under article 110.

(b) Where the Court cannot agree to the circumstances referred to in subparagraph (a), it shall notify the State of enforcement and proceed in accordance with article 104, paragraph 1.

3. In exercising its discretion to make a designation under paragraph 1, the Court shall take into account the following:

(a) The principle that States Parties should share the responsibility for enforcing sentences of imprisonment, in accordance with principles of equitable distribution, as provided in the Rules of Procedure and Evidence;

(b) The application of widely accepted international treaty standards governing the treatment of prisoners;

(c) The views of the sentenced person;

(d) The nationality of the sentenced person;

(e) Such other factors regarding the circumstances of the crime or the person sentenced, or the effective enforcement of the sentence, as may be appropriate in designating the State of enforcement.

4. If no State is designated under paragraph 1, the sentence of imprisonment shall be served in a prison facility made available by the host State, in accordance with the conditions set out in the headquarters agreement referred to in article 3, paragraph 2. In such a case, the costs arising out of the enforcement of a sentence of imprisonment shall be borne by the Court.

Article 104: Change in designation of State of enforcement

1. The Court may, at any time, decide to transfer a sentenced person to a prison of another State.

2. A sentenced person may, at any time, apply to the Court to be transferred from the State of enforcement.

Article 105: Enforcement of the sentence

1. Subject to conditions which a State may have specified in accordance with article 103, paragraph 1 (b), the sentence of imprisonment shall be binding on the States Parties, which shall in no case modify it.

2. The Court alone shall have the right to decide any application for appeal and revision. The State of enforcement shall not impede the making of any such application by a sentenced person.

Article 106: Supervision of enforcement
of sentences and conditions of imprisonment

1. The enforcement of a sentence of imprisonment shall be subject to the supervision of the Court and shall be consistent with widely accepted international treaty standards governing treatment of prisoners.

2. The conditions of imprisonment shall be governed by the law of the State of enforcement and shall be consistent with widely accepted international treaty standards governing treatment of prisoners; in no case shall such conditions be more or less favourable than those available to prisoners convicted of similar offences in the State of enforcement.

3. Communications between a sentenced person and the Court shall be unimpeded and confidential.

Article 107: Transfer of the person upon completion of sentence

1. Following completion of the sentence, a person who is not a national of the State of enforcement may, in accordance with the law of the State of enforcement, be transferred to a State which is obliged to receive him or her, or to another State which agrees to receive him or her, taking into account any wishes of the person to be transferred to that State, unless the State of enforcement authorizes the person to remain in its territory.

2. If no State bears the costs arising out of transferring the person to another State pursuant to paragraph 1, such costs shall be borne by the Court.

3. Subject to the provisions of article 108, the State of enforcement may also, in accordance with its national law, extradite or otherwise surrender the person to a State which has requested the extradition or surrender of the person for purposes of trial or enforcement of a sentence.

Article 108: Limitation on the
prosecution or punishment of other offences

1. A sentenced person in the custody of the State of enforcement shall not be subject to prosecution or punishment or to extradition to a third State for any conduct engaged in prior to that person's delivery to the State of enforcement, unless such prosecution, punishment or extradition has been approved by the Court at the request of the State of enforcement.

2. The Court shall decide the matter after having heard the views of the sentenced person.

3. Paragraph 1 shall cease to apply if the sentenced person remains voluntarily for more than 30 days in the territory of the State of enforcement after having served the full sentence imposed by the Court, or returns to the territory of that State after having left it.

Article 109: Enforcement of fines and forfeiture measures

1. States Parties shall give effect to fines or forfeitures ordered by the Court under Part 7, without prejudice to the rights of bona fide third parties, and in accordance with the procedure of their national law.

2. If a State Party is unable to give effect to an order for forfeiture, it shall take measures to recover the value of the proceeds, property or assets ordered by the Court to be forfeited, without prejudice to the rights of bona fide third parties.

3. Property, or the proceeds of the sale of real property or, where appropriate, the sale of other property, which is obtained by a State Party as a result of its enforcement of a judgement of the Court shall be transferred to the Court.

Article 110: Review by the Court concerning reduction of sentence

1. The State of enforcement shall not release the person before expiry of the sentence pronounced by the Court.

2. The Court alone shall have the right to decide any reduction of sentence, and shall rule on the matter after having heard the person.

3. When the person has served two thirds of the sentence, or 25 years in the case of life imprisonment, the Court shall review the sentence to determine whether it should be reduced. Such a review shall not be conducted before that time.

4. In its review under paragraph 3, the Court may reduce the sentence if it finds that one or more of the following factors are present:

(a) The early and continuing willingness of the person to cooperate with the Court in its investigations and prosecutions;

(b) The voluntary assistance of the person in enabling the enforcement of the judgements and orders of the Court in other cases, and in particular providing assistance in locating assets subject to orders of fine, forfeiture or reparation which may be used for the benefit of victims; or

(c) Other factors establishing a clear and significant change of circumstances sufficient to justify the reduction of sentence, as provided in the Rules of Procedure and Evidence.

5. If the Court determines in its initial review under paragraph 3 that it is not appropriate to reduce the sentence, it shall thereafter review the question of reduction of sentence at such intervals and applying such criteria as provided for in the Rules of Procedure and Evidence.

Article 111: Escape

If a convicted person escapes from custody and flees the State of enforcement, that State may, after consultation with the Court, request the person's surrender from the State in which the person is located pursuant to existing bilateral or multilateral arrangements, or may request that the Court seek the person's surrender, in accordance with Part 9. It may direct that the person be delivered to the State in which he or she was serving the sentence or to another State designated by the Court.

Part 11: Assembly of States Parties

Article 112: Assembly of States Parties

1. An Assembly of States Parties to this Statute is hereby established. Each State Party shall have one representative in the Assembly who may be accompanied by alternates and advisers. Other States which have signed this Statute or the Final Act may be observers in the Assembly.

2. The Assembly shall:

(a) Consider and adopt, as appropriate, recommendations of the Preparatory Commission;

(b) Provide management oversight to the Presidency, the Prosecutor and the Registrar regarding the administration of the Court;

(c) Consider the reports and activities of the Bureau established under paragraph 3 and take appropriate action in regard thereto;

(d) Consider and decide the budget for the Court;

(e) Decide whether to alter, in accordance with article 36, the number of judges;

(f) Consider pursuant to article 87, paragraphs 5 and 7, any question relating to non-cooperation;

(g) Perform any other function consistent with this Statute or the Rules of Procedure and Evidence.

3. (a) The Assembly shall have a Bureau consisting of a President, two Vice-Presidents and 18 members elected by the Assembly for three-year terms.

(b) The Bureau shall have a representative character, taking into account, in particular, equitable geographical distribution and the adequate representation of the principal legal systems of the world.

(c) The Bureau shall meet as often as necessary, but at least once a year. It shall assist the Assembly in the discharge of its responsibilities.

4. The Assembly may establish such subsidiary bodies as may be necessary, including an independent oversight mechanism for inspection, evaluation and investigation of the Court, in order to enhance its efficiency and economy.

5. The President of the Court, the Prosecutor and the Registrar or their representatives may participate, as appropriate, in meetings of the Assembly and of the Bureau.

6. The Assembly shall meet at the seat of the Court or at the Headquarters of the United Nations once a year and, when circumstances so require, hold special sessions. Except as otherwise specified in this Statute, special sessions shall be convened by the Bureau on its own initiative or at the request of one third of the States Parties.

7. Each State Party shall have one vote. Every effort shall be made to reach decisions by consensus in the Assembly and in the Bureau. If consensus cannot be reached, except as otherwise provided in the Statute:

(a) Decisions on matters of substance must be approved by a two-thirds majority of those present and voting provided that an absolute majority of States Parties constitutes the quorum for voting;

(b) Decisions on matters of procedure shall be taken by a simple majority of States Parties present and voting.

8. A State Party which is in arrears in the payment of its financial contributions towards the costs of the Court shall have no vote in the Assembly and in the Bureau if the amount of its arrears equals or exceeds the amount of the contributions due from it for the preceding two full years. The Assembly may, nevertheless, permit such a State Party to vote in the Assembly and in the Bureau if it is satisfied that the failure to pay is due to conditions beyond the control of the State Party.

9. The Assembly shall adopt its own rules of procedure.

10. The official and working languages of the Assembly shall be those of the General Assembly of the United Nations.

Part 12: Financing

Article 113: Financial Regulations
Except as otherwise specifically provided, all financial matters related to the Court and the meetings of the Assembly of States Parties, including its Bureau and subsidiary bodies, shall be governed by this Statute and the Financial Regulations and Rules adopted by the Assembly of States Parties.

Article 114: Payment of expenses
Expenses of the Court and the Assembly of States Parties, including its Bureau and subsidiary bodies, shall be paid from the funds of the Court.

Article 115: Funds of the Court and of the Assembly of States Parties
The expenses of the Court and the Assembly of States Parties, including its Bureau and subsidiary bodies, as provided for in the budget decided by the Assembly of States Parties, shall be provided by the following sources:

(a) Assessed contributions made by States Parties;

(b) Funds provided by the United Nations, subject to the approval of the General Assembly, in particular in relation to the expenses incurred due to referrals by the Security Council.

Article 116: Voluntary contributions
Without prejudice to article 115, the Court may receive and utilize, as additional funds, voluntary contributions from Governments, international organizations, individuals, corporations and other entities, in accordance with relevant criteria adopted by the Assembly of States Parties.

Article 117: Assessment of contributions
The contributions of States Parties shall be assessed in accordance with an agreed scale of assessment, based on the scale adopted by the United Nations for its regular budget and adjusted in accordance with the principles on which that scale is based.

Article 118: Annual audit
The records, books and accounts of the Court, including its annual financial statements, shall be audited annually by an independent auditor.

Part 13: Final Clauses

Article 119: Settlement of disputes
1. Any dispute concerning the judicial functions of the Court shall be settled by the decision of the Court.

2. Any other dispute between two or more States Parties relating to the

interpretation or application of this Statute which is not settled through negotiations within three months of their commencement shall be referred to the Assembly of States Parties. The Assembly may itself seek to settle the dispute or may make recommendations on further means of settlement of the dispute, including referral to the International Court of Justice in conformity with the Statute of that Court.

Article 120: Reservations

No reservations may be made to this Statute.

Article 121: Amendments

1. After the expiry of seven years from the entry into force of this Statute, any State Party may propose amendments thereto. The text of any proposed amendment shall be submitted to the Secretary-General of the United Nations, who shall promptly circulate it to all States Parties.

2. No sooner than three months from the date of notification, the Assembly of States Parties, at its next meeting, shall, by a majority of those present and voting, decide whether to take up the proposal. The Assembly may deal with the proposal directly or convene a Review Conference if the issue involved so warrants.

3. The adoption of an amendment at a meeting of the Assembly of States Parties or at a Review Conference on which consensus cannot be reached shall require a two-thirds majority of States Parties.

4. Except as provided in paragraph 5, an amendment shall enter into force for all States Parties one year after instruments of ratification or acceptance have been deposited with the Secretary-General of the United Nations by seven-eighths of them.

5. Any amendment to articles 5, 6, 7 and 8 of this Statute shall enter into force for those States Parties which have accepted the amendment one year after the deposit of their instruments of ratification or acceptance. In respect of a State Party which has not accepted the amendment, the Court shall not exercise its jurisdiction regarding a crime covered by the amendment when committed by that State Party's nationals or on its territory.

6. If an amendment has been accepted by seven-eighths of States Parties in accordance with paragraph 4, any State Party which has not accepted the amendment may withdraw from this Statute with immediate effect, notwithstanding article 127, paragraph 1, but subject to article 127, paragraph 2, by giving notice no later than one year after the entry into force of such amendment.

7. The Secretary-General of the United Nations shall circulate to all States Parties any amendment adopted at a meeting of the Assembly of States Parties or at a Review Conference.

Article 122: Amendments to provisions of an institutional nature

1. Amendments to provisions of this Statute which are of an exclusively

institutional nature, namely, article 35, article 36, paragraphs 8 and 9, article 37, article 38, article 39, paragraphs 1 (first two sentences), 2 and 4, article 42, paragraphs 4 to 9, article 43, paragraphs 2 and 3, and articles 44, 46, 47 and 49, may be proposed at any time, notwithstanding article 121, paragraph 1, by any State Party. The text of any proposed amendment shall be submitted to the Secretary-General of the United Nations or such other person designated by the Assembly of States Parties who shall promptly circulate it to all States Parties and to others participating in the Assembly.

2. Amendments under this article on which consensus cannot be reached shall be adopted by the Assembly of States Parties or by a Review Conference, by a two-thirds majority of States Parties. Such amendments shall enter into force for all States Parties six months after their adoption by the Assembly or, as the case may be, by the Conference.

Article 123: Review of the Statute

1. Seven years after the entry into force of this Statute the Secretary-General of the United Nations shall convene a Review Conference to consider any amendments to this Statute. Such review may include, but is not limited to, the list of crimes contained in article 5. The Conference shall be open to those participating in the Assembly of States Parties and on the same conditions.

2. At any time thereafter, at the request of a State Party and for the purposes set out in paragraph 1, the Secretary-General of the United Nations shall, upon approval by a majority of States Parties, convene a Review Conference.

3. The provisions of article 121, paragraphs 3 to 7, shall apply to the adoption and entry into force of any amendment to the Statute considered at a Review Conference.

Article 124: Transitional Provision

Notwithstanding article 12, paragraph 1, a State, on becoming a party to this Statute, may declare that, for a period of seven years after the entry into force of this Statute for the State concerned, it does not accept the jurisdiction of the Court with respect to the category of crimes referred to in article 8 when a crime is alleged to have been committed by its nationals or on its territory. A declaration under this article may be withdrawn at any time. The provisions of this article shall be reviewed at the Review Conference convened in accordance with article 123, paragraph 1.

Article 125: Signature, ratification, acceptance, approval or accession

1. This Statute shall be open for signature by all States in Rome, at the headquarters of the Food and Agriculture Organization of the United Nations, on 17 July 1998. Thereafter, it shall remain open for signature in Rome at the Ministry of Foreign Affairs of Italy until 17 October 1998. After that date, the Statute shall remain open for signature in New York, at United Nations Headquarters, until 31 December 2000.

2. This Statute is subject to ratification, acceptance or approval by signatory

States. Instruments of ratification, acceptance or approval shall be deposited with the Secretary-General of the United Nations.

3. This Statute shall be open to accession by all States. Instruments of accession shall be deposited with the Secretary-General of the United Nations.

Article 126: Entry into force

1. This Statute shall enter into force on the first day of the month after the 60th day following the date of the deposit of the 60th instrument of ratification, acceptance, approval or accession with the Secretary-General of the United Nations.

2. For each State ratifying, accepting, approving or acceding to this Statute after the deposit of the 60th instrument of ratification, acceptance, approval or accession, the Statute shall enter into force on the first day of the month after the 60th day following the deposit by such State of its instrument of ratification, acceptance, approval or accession.

Article 127: Withdrawal

1. A State Party may, by written notification addressed to the Secretary-General of the United Nations, withdraw from this Statute. The withdrawal shall take effect one year after the date of receipt of the notification, unless the notification specifies a later date.

2. A State shall not be discharged, by reason of its withdrawal, from the obligations arising from this Statute while it was a Party to the Statute, including any financial obligations which may have accrued. Its withdrawal shall not affect any cooperation with the Court in connection with criminal investigations and proceedings in relation to which the withdrawing State had a duty to cooperate and which were commenced prior to the date on which the withdrawal became effective, nor shall it prejudice in any way the continued consideration of any matter which was already under consideration by the Court prior to the date on which the withdrawal became effective.

Article 128: Authentic texts

The original of this Statute, of which the Arabic, Chinese, English, French, Russian and Spanish texts are equally authentic, shall be deposited with the Secretary-General of the United Nations, who shall send certified copies thereof to all States.

IN WITNESS WHEREOF, the undersigned, being duly authorized thereto by their respective Governments, have signed this Statute.

DONE at Rome, this 17th day of July 1998.

4.5
International Convention for the Suppression of the Financing of Terrorism (1999)

France initiated negotiations for this convention following identification by the Group of 8 of the issue of suppressing financing as a priority in combating terrorism. The convention follows the approach of other UN counterterrorism conventions in requiring states parties to criminalize and to establish jurisdiction over the offenses listed in the convention and to extradite or submit to prosecution persons accused of committing or aiding in the commission of such offenses.

For discussion of this convention in the context of other international law measures against terrorism, see Clifton M. Johnson, "Introductory Note," 39 ILM 268 (2000); and Jean-Marc Sorel, "Some Questions About the Definition of Terrorism and the Fight Against Its Financing," European Journal of International Law *14 (2003): 365–378. On the diffi-culties of the task, see John D. G. Waszak, "The Obstacles to Suppressing Radical Islamic Terrorist Financing,"* Case Western Reserve Journal of International Law *36 (2004): 673–710.*

The States Parties to this Convention,

Bearing in mind the purposes and principles of the Charter of the United Nations concerning the maintenance of international peace and security and the promotion of good-neighbourliness and friendly relations and cooperation among States,

Deeply concerned about the worldwide escalation of acts of terrorism in all its forms and manifestations,

Recalling the Declaration on the Occasion of the Fiftieth Anniversary of the United Nations, contained in General Assembly resolution 50/6 of 24 October 1995,

Recalling also all the relevant General Assembly resolutions on the matter, including resolution 49/60 of 9 December 1994 and the annex thereto on the Declaration on Measures to Eliminate International Terrorism, in which the States Members of the United Nations solemnly reaffirmed their unequivocal condemnation of all acts, methods and practices of terrorism as criminal and unjustifiable, wherever and by whomever committed, including those which jeopardize the friendly relations among States and peoples and threaten the territorial integrity and security of States,

Noting that the Declaration on Measures to Eliminate International Terrorism also encouraged States to review urgently the scope of the existing international legal provisions on the prevention, repression and elimination of terrorism in all its forms and manifestations, with the aim of ensuring that there is a comprehensive legal framework covering all aspects of the matter,

Recalling paragraph 3 (f) of General Assembly resolution 51/210 of 17 December 1996, in which the Assembly called upon all States to take steps to prevent and counteract, through appropriate domestic measures, the financing of terrorists and terrorist organizations, whether such financing is direct or indirect through organizations which also have or claim to have charitable, social or cultural goals or which are also engaged in unlawful activities such as illicit arms trafficking, drug dealing and racketeering, including the exploitation of persons for purposes of funding terrorist activities, and in particular to consider, where appropriate, adopting regulatory measures to prevent and counteract movements of funds suspected to be intended for terrorist purposes without impeding in any way the freedom of legitimate capital movements and to intensify the exchange of information concerning international movements of such funds,

Recalling also General Assembly resolution 52/165 of 15 December 1997, in which the Assembly called upon States to consider, in particular, the implementation of the measures set out in paragraphs 3 (a) to (f) of its resolution 51/210 of 17 December 1996,

Recalling further General Assembly resolution 53/108 of 8 December 1998, in which the Assembly decided that the Ad Hoc Committee established by General Assembly resolution 51/210 of 17 December 1996 should elaborate a draft international convention for the suppression of terrorist financing to supplement related existing international instruments,

Considering that the financing of terrorism is a matter of grave concern to the international community as a whole,

Noting that the number and seriousness of acts of international terrorism depend on the financing that terrorists may obtain,

Noting also that existing multilateral legal instruments do not expressly address such financing,

Being convinced of the urgent need to enhance international cooperation among States in devising and adopting effective measures for the prevention of the financing of terrorism, as well as for its suppression through the prosecution and punishment of its perpetrators,

Have agreed as follows:

Article 1
For the purposes of this Convention:

1. "Funds" means assets of every kind, whether tangible or intangible, movable or immovable, however acquired, and legal documents or instruments in

any form, including electronic or digital, evidencing title to, or interest in, such assets, including, but not limited to, bank credits, travellers cheques, bank cheques, money orders, shares, securities, bonds, drafts and letters of credit.

2. "State or government facility" means any permanent or temporary facility or conveyance that is used or occupied by representatives of a State, members of Government, the legislature or the judiciary or by officials or employees of a State or any other public authority or entity or by employees or officials of an intergovernmental organization in connection with their official duties.

3. "Proceeds" means any funds derived from or obtained, directly or indirectly, through the commission of an offence set forth in article 2.

Article 2

1. Any person commits an offence within the meaning of this Convention if that person by any means, directly or indirectly, unlawfully and wilfully, provides or collects funds with the intention that they should be used or in the knowledge that they are to be used, in full or in part, in order to carry out:

(a) An act which constitutes an offence within the scope of and as defined in one of the treaties listed in the annex; or

(b) Any other act intended to cause death or serious bodily injury to a civilian, or to any other person not taking an active part in the hostilities in a situation of armed conflict, when the purpose of such act, by its nature or context, is to intimidate a population, or to compel a Government or an international organization to do or to abstain from doing any act.

2. (a) On depositing its instrument of ratification, acceptance, approval or accession, a State Party which is not a party to a treaty listed in the annex may declare that, in the application of this Convention to the State Party, the treaty shall be deemed not to be included in the annex referred to in paragraph 1, subparagraph (a). The declaration shall cease to have effect as soon as the treaty enters into force for the State Party, which shall notify the depositary of this fact;

(b) When a State Party ceases to be a party to a treaty listed in the annex, it may make a declaration as provided for in this article, with respect to that treaty.

3. For an act to constitute an offence set forth in paragraph 1, it shall not be necessary that the funds were actually used to carry out an offence referred to in paragraph 1, subparagraph (a) or (b).

4. Any person also commits an offence if that person attempts to commit an offence as set forth in paragraph 1 of this article.

5. Any person also commits an offence if that person:

(a) Participates as an accomplice in an offence as set forth in paragraph 1 or 4 of this article;

(b) Organizes or directs others to commit an offence as set forth in paragraph 1 or 4 of this article;

(c) Contributes to the commission of one or more offences as set forth in paragraph 1 or 4 of this article by a group of persons acting with a common purpose. Such contribution shall be intentional and shall either: (i) Be made with the aim of furthering the criminal activity or criminal purpose of the group, where such activity or purpose involves the commission of an offence as set forth in paragraph 1 of this article; or (ii) Be made in the knowledge of the intention of the group to commit an offence as set forth in paragraph 1 of this article.

Article 3

This Convention shall not apply where the offence is committed within a single State, the alleged offender is a national of that State and is present in the territory of that State and no other State has a basis under article 7, paragraph 1 or 2, to exercise jurisdiction, except that the provisions of articles 12 to 18 shall, as appropriate, apply in those cases.

Article 4

Each State Party shall adopt such measures as may be necessary:

(a) To establish as criminal offences under its domestic law the offences as set forth in article 2;

(b) To make those offences punishable by appropriate penalties which take into account the grave nature of the offences.

Article 5

1. Each State Party, in accordance with its domestic legal principles, shall take the necessary measures to enable a legal entity located in its territory or organized under its laws to be held liable when a person responsible for the management or control of that legal entity has, in that capacity, committed an offence as set forth in article 2. Such liability may be criminal, civil or administrative.

2. Such liability is incurred without prejudice to the criminal liability of individuals who have committed the offences.

3. Each State Party shall ensure, in particular, that legal entities liable in accordance with paragraph 1 above are subject to effective, proportionate and dissuasive criminal, civil or administrative sanctions. Such sanctions may include monetary sanctions.

Article 6

Each State Party shall adopt such measures as may be necessary, including, where appropriate, domestic legislation, to ensure that criminal acts within the scope of this Convention are under no circumstances justifiable by considerations of a political, philosophical, ideological, racial, ethnic, religious or other similar nature.

Article 7

1. Each State Party shall take such measures as may be necessary to establish its jurisdiction over the offences set forth in article 2 when:

(a) The offence is committed in the territory of that State;

(b) The offence is committed on board a vessel flying the flag of that State or an aircraft registered under the laws of that State at the time the offence is committed;

(c) The offence is committed by a national of that State.

2. A State Party may also establish its jurisdiction over any such offence when:

(a) The offence was directed towards or resulted in the carrying out of an offence referred to in article 2, paragraph 1, subparagraph (a) or (b), in the territory of or against a national of that State;

(b) The offence was directed towards or resulted in the carrying out of an offence referred to in article 2, paragraph 1, subparagraph (a) or (b), against a State or government facility of that State abroad, including diplomatic or consular premises of that State;

(c) The offence was directed towards or resulted in an offence referred to in article 2, paragraph 1, subparagraph (a) or (b), committed in an attempt to compel that State to do or abstain from doing any act;

(d) The offence is committed by a stateless person who has his or her habitual residence in the territory of that State;

(e) The offence is committed on board an aircraft which is operated by the Government of that State.

3. Upon ratifying, accepting, approving or acceding to this Convention, each State Party shall notify the Secretary-General of the United Nations of the jurisdiction it has established in accordance with paragraph 2. Should any change take place, the State Party concerned shall immediately notify the Secretary-General.

4. Each State Party shall likewise take such measures as may be necessary to establish its jurisdiction over the offences set forth in article 2 in cases where the alleged offender is present in its territory and it does not extradite that person to any of the States Parties that have established their jurisdiction in accordance with paragraphs 1 or 2.

5. When more than one State Party claims jurisdiction over the offences set forth in article 2, the relevant States Parties shall strive to coordinate their actions appropriately, in particular concerning the conditions for prosecution and the modalities for mutual legal assistance.

6. Without prejudice to the norms of general international law, this Convention does not exclude the exercise of any criminal jurisdiction established by a State Party in accordance with its domestic law.

Article 8

1. Each State Party shall take appropriate measures, in accordance with its domestic legal principles, for the identification, detection and freezing or seizure of any funds used or allocated for the purpose of committing the offences set forth in article 2 as well as the proceeds derived from such offences, for purposes of possible forfeiture.

2. Each State Party shall take appropriate measures, in accordance with its domestic legal principles, for the forfeiture of funds used or allocated for the purpose of committing the offences set forth in article 2 and the proceeds derived from such offences.

3. Each State Party concerned may give consideration to concluding agreements on the sharing with other States Parties, on a regular or case-by-case basis, of the funds derived from the forfeitures referred to in this article.

4. Each State Party shall consider establishing mechanisms whereby the funds derived from the forfeitures referred to in this article are utilized to compensate the victims of offences referred to in article 2, paragraph 1, subparagraph (a) or (b), or their families.

5. The provisions of this article shall be implemented without prejudice to the rights of third parties acting in good faith.

Article 9

1. Upon receiving information that a person who has committed or who is alleged to have committed an offence set forth in article 2 may be present in its territory, the State Party concerned shall take such measures as may be necessary under its domestic law to investigate the facts contained in the information.

2. Upon being satisfied that the circumstances so warrant, the State Party in whose territory the offender or alleged offender is present shall take the appropriate measures under its domestic law so as to ensure that person's presence for the purpose of prosecution or extradition.

3. Any person regarding whom the measures referred to in paragraph 2 are being taken shall be entitled to:

(a) Communicate without delay with the nearest appropriate representative of the State of which that person is a national or which is otherwise entitled to protect that person's rights or, if that person is a stateless person, the State in the territory of which that person habitually resides;

(b) Be visited by a representative of that State;

(c) Be informed of that person's rights under subparagraphs (a) and (b).

4. The rights referred to in paragraph 3 shall be exercised in conformity with the laws and regulations of the State in the territory of which the offender or alleged offender is present, subject to the provision that the said laws and regulations must enable full effect to be given to the purposes for which the rights accorded under paragraph 3 are intended.

5. The provisions of paragraphs 3 and 4 shall be without prejudice to the right of any State Party having a claim to jurisdiction in accordance with article 7, paragraph 1, subparagraph (b), or paragraph 2, subparagraph (b), to invite the International Committee of the Red Cross to communicate with and visit the alleged offender.

6. When a State Party, pursuant to the present article, has taken a person into custody, it shall immediately notify, directly or through the Secretary-General of the United Nations, the States Parties which have established juris-

diction in accordance with article 7, paragraph 1 or 2, and, if it considers it advisable, any other interested States Parties, of the fact that such person is in custody and of the circumstances which warrant that person's detention. The State which makes the investigation contemplated in paragraph 1 shall promptly inform the said States Parties of its findings and shall indicate whether it intends to exercise jurisdiction.

Article 10

1. The State Party in the territory of which the alleged offender is present shall, in cases to which article 7 applies, if it does not extradite that person, be obliged, without exception whatsoever and whether or not the offence was committed in its territory, to submit the case without undue delay to its competent authorities for the purpose of prosecution, through proceedings in accordance with the laws of that State. Those authorities shall take their decision in the same manner as in the case of any other offence of a grave nature under the law of that State.

2. Whenever a State Party is permitted under its domestic law to extradite or otherwise surrender one of its nationals only upon the condition that the person will be returned to that State to serve the sentence imposed as a result of the trial or proceeding for which the extradition or surrender of the person was sought, and this State and the State seeking the extradition of the person agree with this option and other terms they may deem appropriate, such a conditional extradition or surrender shall be sufficient to discharge the obligation set forth in paragraph 1.

Article 11

1. The offences set forth in article 2 shall be deemed to be included as extraditable offences in any extradition treaty existing between any of the States Parties before the entry into force of this Convention. States Parties undertake to include such offences as extraditable offences in every extradition treaty to be subsequently concluded between them.

2. When a State Party which makes extradition conditional on the existence of a treaty receives a request for extradition from another State Party with which it has no extradition treaty, the requested State Party may, at its option, consider this Convention as a legal basis for extradition in respect of the offences set forth in article 2. Extradition shall be subject to the other conditions provided by the law of the requested State.

3. States Parties which do not make extradition conditional on the existence of a treaty shall recognize the offences set forth in article 2 as extraditable offences between themselves, subject to the conditions provided by the law of the requested State.

4. If necessary, the offences set forth in article 2 shall be treated, for the purposes of extradition between States Parties, as if they had been committed not only in the place in which they occurred but also in the territory of the States that have established jurisdiction in accordance with article 7, paragraphs 1 and 2.

5. The provisions of all extradition treaties and arrangements between States Parties with regard to offences set forth in article 2 shall be deemed to be modified as between States Parties to the extent that they are incompatible with this Convention.

Article 12

1. States Parties shall afford one another the greatest measure of assistance in connection with criminal investigations or criminal or extradition proceedings in respect of the offences set forth in article 2, including assistance in obtaining evidence in their possession necessary for the proceedings.

2. States Parties may not refuse a request for mutual legal assistance on the ground of bank secrecy.

3. The requesting Party shall not transmit or use information or evidence furnished by the requested Party for investigations, prosecutions or proceedings other than those stated in the request without the prior consent of the requested Party.

4. Each State Party may give consideration to establishing mechanisms to share with other States Parties information or evidence needed to establish criminal, civil or administrative liability pursuant to article 5.

5. States Parties shall carry out their obligations under paragraphs 1 and 2 in conformity with any treaties or other arrangements on mutual legal assistance or information exchange that may exist between them. In the absence of such treaties or arrangements, States Parties shall afford one another assistance in accordance with their domestic law.

Article 13

None of the offences set forth in article 2 shall be regarded, for the purposes of extradition or mutual legal assistance, as a fiscal offence. Accordingly, States Parties may not refuse a request for extradition or for mutual legal assistance on the sole ground that it concerns a fiscal offence.

Article 14

None of the offences set forth in article 2 shall be regarded for the purposes of extradition or mutual legal assistance as a political offence or as an offence connected with a political offence or as an offence inspired by political motives. Accordingly, a request for extradition or for mutual legal assistance based on such an offence may not be refused on the sole ground that it concerns a political offence or an offence connected with a political offence or an offence inspired by political motives.

Article 15

Nothing in this Convention shall be interpreted as imposing an obligation to extradite or to afford mutual legal assistance, if the requested State Party has substantial grounds for believing that the request for extradition for offences set forth in article 2 or for mutual legal assistance with respect to such offences has been made for the purpose of prosecuting or punishing a person on account of that person's race, religion, nationality, ethnic origin or political opinion or that compliance with the request would cause prejudice to that person's position for any of these reasons.

Article 16

1. A person who is being detained or is serving a sentence in the territory of one State Party whose presence in another State Party is requested for purposes of identification, testimony or otherwise providing assistance in obtaining evidence for the investigation or prosecution of offences set forth in article 2 may be transferred if the following conditions are met:

(a) The person freely gives his or her informed consent;

(b) The competent authorities of both States agree, subject to such conditions as those States may deem appropriate.

2. For the purposes of the present article:

(a) The State to which the person is transferred shall have the authority and obligation to keep the person transferred in custody, unless otherwise requested or authorized by the State from which the person was transferred;

(b) The State to which the person is transferred shall without delay implement its obligation to return the person to the custody of the State from which the person was transferred as agreed beforehand, or as otherwise agreed, by the competent authorities of both States;

(c) The State to which the person is transferred shall not require the State from which the person was transferred to initiate extradition proceedings for the return of the person;

(d) The person transferred shall receive credit for service of the sentence being served in the State from which he or she was transferred for time spent in the custody of the State to which he or she was transferred.

3. Unless the State Party from which a person is to be transferred in accordance with the present article so agrees, that person, whatever his or her nationality, shall not be prosecuted or detained or subjected to any other restriction of his or her personal liberty in the territory of the State to which that person is transferred in respect of acts or convictions anterior to his or her departure from the territory of the State from which such person was transferred.

Article 17

Any person who is taken into custody or regarding whom any other measures are taken or proceedings are carried out pursuant to this Convention shall be guaranteed fair treatment, including enjoyment of all rights and guarantees in conformity with the law of the State in the territory of which that person is present and applicable provisions of international law, including international human rights law.

Article 18

1. States Parties shall cooperate in the prevention of the offences set forth in article 2 by taking all practicable measures, inter alia, by adapting their domestic legislation, if necessary, to prevent and counter preparations in their respective territories for the commission of those offences within or outside their territories, including:

(a) Measures to prohibit in their territories illegal activities of persons and organizations that knowingly encourage, instigate, organize or engage in the commission of offences set forth in article 2;

(b) Measures requiring financial institutions and other professions involved in financial transactions to utilize the most efficient measures available for the identification of their usual or occasional customers, as well as customers in whose interest accounts are opened, and to pay special attention to unusual or suspicious transactions and report transactions suspected of stemming from a criminal activity. For this purpose, States Parties shall consider: (i) Adopting regulations prohibiting the opening of accounts, the holders or beneficiaries of which are unidentified or unidentifiable, and measures to ensure that such institutions verify the identity of the real owners of such transactions; (ii) With respect to the identification of legal entities, requiring financial institutions, when necessary, to take measures to verify the legal existence and the structure of the customer by obtaining, either from a public register or from the customer or both, proof of incorporation, including information concerning the customer's name, legal form, address, directors and provisions regulating the power to bind the entity; (iii) Adopting regulations imposing on financial institutions the obligation to report promptly to the competent authorities all complex, unusual large transactions and unusual patterns of transactions, which have no apparent economic or obviously lawful purpose, without fear of assuming criminal or civil liability for breach of any restriction on disclosure of information if they report their suspicions in good faith; (iv) Requiring financial institutions to maintain, for at least five years, all necessary records on transactions, both domestic and international.

2. States Parties shall further cooperate in the prevention of offences set forth in article 2 by considering:

(a) Measures for the supervision, including, for example, the licensing, of all money-transmission agencies;

(b) Feasible measures to detect or monitor the physical cross-border transportation of cash and bearer negotiable instruments, subject to strict safeguards to ensure proper use of information and without impeding in any way the freedom of capital movements.

3. States Parties shall further cooperate in the prevention of the offences set forth in article 2 by exchanging accurate and verified information in accordance with their domestic law and coordinating administrative and other measures taken, as appropriate, to prevent the commission of offences set forth in article 2, in particular by:

(a) Establishing and maintaining channels of communication between their competent agencies and services to facilitate the secure and rapid exchange of information concerning all aspects of offences set forth in article 2;

(b) Cooperating with one another in conducting inquiries, with respect to the offences set forth in article 2, concerning: (i) The identity, whereabouts and activities of persons in respect of whom reasonable suspicion exists that they are involved in such offences; (ii) The movement of funds relating to the commission of such offences.

4. States Parties may exchange information through the International Criminal Police Organization (Interpol).

Article 19
The State Party where the alleged offender is prosecuted shall, in accordance with its domestic law or applicable procedures, communicate the final outcome of the proceedings to the Secretary-General of the United Nations, who shall transmit the information to the other States Parties.

Article 20
The States Parties shall carry out their obligations under this Convention in a manner consistent with the principles of sovereign equality and territorial integrity of States and that of non-intervention in the domestic affairs of other States.

Article 21
Nothing in this Convention shall affect other rights, obligations and responsibilities of States and individuals under international law, in particular the purposes of the Charter of the United Nations, international humanitarian law and other relevant conventions.

Article 22
Nothing in this Convention entitles a State Party to undertake in the territory of another State Party the exercise of jurisdiction or performance of functions which are exclusively reserved for the authorities of that other State Party by its domestic law.

Article 23
1. The annex may be amended by the addition of relevant treaties that:
    (a) Are open to the participation of all States;
    (b) Have entered into force;
    (c) Have been ratified, accepted, approved or acceded to by at least twenty-two States Parties to the present Convention.

2. After the entry into force of this Convention, any State Party may propose such an amendment. Any proposal for an amendment shall be communicated to the depositary in written form. The depositary shall notify proposals that meet the requirements of paragraph 1 to all States Parties and seek their views on whether the proposed amendment should be adopted.

3. The proposed amendment shall be deemed adopted unless one third of the States Parties object to it by a written notification not later than 180 days after its circulation.

4. The adopted amendment to the annex shall enter into force 30 days after the deposit of the twenty-second instrument of ratification, acceptance or approval of such amendment for all those States Parties that have deposited such an instrument. For each State Party ratifying, accepting or approving the amendment after the deposit of the twenty-second instrument, the amendment shall enter into force on the thirtieth day after deposit by such State Party of its instrument of ratification, acceptance or approval.

Article 24

1. Any dispute between two or more States Parties concerning the interpretation or application of this Convention which cannot be settled through negotiation within a reasonable time shall, at the request of one of them, be submitted to arbitration. If, within six months from the date of the request for arbitration, the parties are unable to agree on the organization of the arbitration, any one of those parties may refer the dispute to the International Court of Justice, by application, in conformity with the Statute of the Court.

2. Each State may at the time of signature, ratification, acceptance or approval of this Convention or accession thereto declare that it does not consider itself bound by paragraph 1. The other States Parties shall not be bound by paragraph 1 with respect to any State Party which has made such a reservation.

3. Any State which has made a reservation in accordance with paragraph 2 may at any time withdraw that reservation by notification to the Secretary-General of the United Nations.

Article 25

1. This Convention shall be open for signature by all States from 10 January 2000 to 31 December 2001 at United Nations Headquarters in New York.

2. This Convention is subject to ratification, acceptance or approval. The instruments of ratification, acceptance or approval shall be deposited with the Secretary-General of the United Nations.

3. This Convention shall be open to accession by any State. The instruments of accession shall be deposited with the Secretary-General of the United Nations.

Article 26

1. This Convention shall enter into force on the thirtieth day following the date of the deposit of the twenty-second instrument of ratification, acceptance, approval or accession with the Secretary-General of the United Nations.

2. For each State ratifying, accepting, approving or acceding to the Convention after the deposit of the twenty-second instrument of ratification, acceptance, approval or accession, the Convention shall enter into force on the

thirtieth day after deposit by such State of its instrument of ratification, acceptance, approval or accession.

Article 27

1. Any State Party may denounce this Convention by written notification to the Secretary-General of the United Nations.

2. Denunciation shall take effect one year following the date on which notification is received by the Secretary-General of the United Nations.

Article 28

The original of this Convention, of which the Arabic, Chinese, English, French, Russian and Spanish texts are equally authentic, shall be deposited with the Secretary-General of the United Nations who shall send certified copies thereof to all States.

IN WITNESS WHEREOF, the undersigned, being duly authorized thereto by their respective Governments, have signed this Convention, opened for signature at United Nations Headquarters in New York on 10 January 2000.

Annex

1. Convention for the Suppression of Unlawful Seizure of Aircraft, done at The Hague on 16 December 1970.

2. Convention for the Suppression of Unlawful Acts against the Safety of Civil Aviation, done at Montreal on 23 September 1971.

3. Convention on the Prevention and Punishment of Crimes against Internationally Protected Persons, including Diplomatic Agents, adopted by the General Assembly of the United Nations on 14 December 1973.

4. International Convention against the Taking of Hostages, adopted by the General Assembly of the United Nations on 17 December 1979.

5. Convention on the Physical Protection of Nuclear Material, adopted at Vienna on 3 March 1980.

6. Protocol for the Suppression of Unlawful Acts of Violence at Airports Serving International Civil Aviation, supplementary to the Convention for the Suppression of Unlawful Acts against the Safety of Civil Aviation, done at Montreal on 24 February 1988.

7. Convention for the Suppression of Unlawful Acts against the Safety of Maritime Navigation, done at Rome on 10 March 1988.

8. Protocol for the Suppression of Unlawful Acts against the Safety of Fixed Platforms located on the Continental Shelf, done at Rome on 10 March 1988.

9. International Convention for the Suppression of Terrorist Bombings, adopted by the General Assembly of the United Nations on 15 December 1997.

4.6
Establishing the Counter-Terrorism Committee: Security Council Resolution 1373 (2001)

This resolution, adopted on 28 September 2001, is the centerpiece of the counterterrorism efforts of the Security Council. It requires states to take wide-ranging legislative and executive actions, including improving border security, to prevent states from becoming a haven for terrorists. The resolution established a Counter-Terrorism Committee (CTC) to monitor the implementation of the obligations. The move to supplement jointly-negotiated treaties on terrorism with Security Council–imposed obligations may have been generally accepted as effective in addressing the issue, but it has given rise to claims that the Security Council is usurping a role akin to that of a legislature.

The CTC has a website at www.un.org/Docs/sc/committees/1373/index.html. For commentary on the work of the CTC, see Eric Rosand, "Security Council Resolution 1373, the Counter-Terrorism Committee, and the Fight Against Terrorism," American Journal of International Law 97 (2003): 333–341. *On the legislative nature of resolution 1373, see Paul C. Szasz, "The Security Council Starts Legislating,"* American Journal of International Law 96, no. 4 (2002): 901–905.

The Security Council,

Reaffirming its resolutions 1269 (1999) of 19 October 1999 and 1368 (2001) of 12 September 2001,

Reaffirming also its unequivocal condemnation of the terrorist attacks which took place in New York, Washington, D.C., and Pennsylvania on 11 September 2001, and expressing its determination to prevent all such acts,

Reaffirming further that such acts, like any act of international terrorism, constitute a threat to international peace and security,

Reaffirming the inherent right of individual or collective self-defence as recognized by the Charter of the United Nations as reiterated in resolution 1368 (2001),

Reaffirming the need to combat by all means, in accordance with the

Charter of the United Nations, threats to international peace and security caused by terrorist acts,

Deeply concerned by the increase, in various regions of the world, of acts of terrorism motivated by intolerance or extremism,

Calling on States to work together urgently to prevent and suppress terrorist acts, including through increased cooperation and full implementation of the relevant international conventions relating to terrorism,

Recognizing the need for States to complement international cooperation by taking additional measures to prevent and suppress, in their territories through all lawful means, the financing and preparation of any acts of terrorism,

Reaffirming the principle established by the General Assembly in its declaration of October 1970 (resolution 2625 (XXV)) and reiterated by the Security Council in its resolution 1189 (1998) of 13 August 1998, namely that every State has the duty to refrain from organizing, instigating, assisting or participating in terrorist acts in another State or acquiescing in organized activities within its territory directed towards the commission of such acts,

Acting under Chapter VII of the Charter of the United Nations,

1. Decides that all States shall:

(a) Prevent and suppress the financing of terrorist acts;

(b) Criminalize the wilful provision or collection, by any means, directly or indirectly, of funds by their nationals or in their territories with the intention that the funds should be used, or in the knowledge that they are to be used, in order to carry out terrorist acts;

(c) Freeze without delay funds and other financial assets or economic resources of persons who commit, or attempt to commit, terrorist acts or participate in or facilitate the commission of terrorist acts; of entities owned or controlled directly or indirectly by such persons; and of persons and entities acting on behalf of, or at the direction of such persons and entities, including funds derived or generated from property owned or controlled directly or indirectly by such persons and associated persons and entities;

(d) Prohibit their nationals or any persons and entities within their territories from making any funds, financial assets or economic resources or financial or other related services available, directly or indirectly, for the benefit of persons who commit or attempt to commit or facilitate or participate in the commission of terrorist acts, of entities owned or controlled, directly or indirectly, by such persons and of persons and entities acting on behalf of or at the direction of such persons;

2. Decides also that all States shall:

(a) Refrain from providing any form of support, active or passive, to entities or persons involved in terrorist acts, including by suppressing recruitment of members of terrorist groups and eliminating the supply of weapons to terrorists;

(b) Take the necessary steps to prevent the commission of terrorist acts, including by provision of early warning to other States by exchange of information;

(c) Deny safe haven to those who finance, plan, support, or commit terrorist acts, or provide safe havens;

(d) Prevent those who finance, plan, facilitate or commit terrorist acts from using their respective territories for those purposes against other States or their citizens;

(e) Ensure that any person who participates in the financing, planning, preparation or perpetration of terrorist acts or in supporting terrorist acts is brought to justice and ensure that, in addition to any other measures against them, such terrorist acts are established as serious criminal offences in domestic laws and regulations and that the punishment duly reflects the seriousness of such terrorist acts;

(f) Afford one another the greatest measure of assistance in connection with criminal investigations or criminal proceedings relating to the financing or support of terrorist acts, including assistance in obtaining evidence in their possession necessary for the proceedings;

(g) Prevent the movement of terrorists or terrorist groups by effective border controls and controls on issuance of identity papers and travel documents, and through measures for preventing counterfeiting, forgery or fraudulent use of identity papers and travel documents;

3. Calls upon all States to:

(a) Find ways of intensifying and accelerating the exchange of operational information, especially regarding actions or movements of terrorist persons or networks; forged or falsified travel documents; traffic in arms, explosives or sensitive materials; use of communications technologies by terrorist groups; and the threat posed by the possession of weapons of mass destruction by terrorist groups;

(b) Exchange information in accordance with international and domestic law and cooperate on administrative and judicial matters to prevent the commission of terrorist acts;

(c) Cooperate, particularly through bilateral and multilateral arrangements and agreements, to prevent and suppress terrorist attacks and take action against perpetrators of such acts;

(d) Become parties as soon as possible to the relevant international conventions and protocols relating to terrorism, including the International Convention for the Suppression of the Financing of Terrorism of 9 December 1999;

(e) Increase cooperation and fully implement the relevant international conventions and protocols relating to terrorism and Security Council resolutions 1269 (1999) and 1368 (2001);

(f) Take appropriate measures in conformity with the relevant provisions of national and international law, including international standards of human rights, before granting refugee status, for the purpose of ensuring that the asylum-seeker has not planned, facilitated or participated in the commission of terrorist acts;

(g) Ensure, in conformity with international law, that refugee status is not abused by the perpetrators, organizers or facilitators of terrorist acts, and that claims of political motivation are not recognized as grounds for refusing requests for the extradition of alleged terrorists;

4. Notes with concern the close connection between international terrorism and transnational organized crime, illicit drugs, money-laundering, illegal arms-strafficking, and illegal movement of nuclear, chemical, biological and other potentially deadly materials, and in this regard emphasizes the need to enhance coordination of efforts on national, subregional, regional and international levels in order to strengthen a global response to this serious challenge and threat to international security;

5. Declares that acts, methods, and practices of terrorism are contrary to the purposes and principles of the United Nations and that knowingly financing, planning and inciting terrorist acts are also contrary to the purposes and principles of the United Nations;

6. Decides to establish, in accordance with rule 28 of its provisional rules of procedure, a Committee of the Security Council, consisting of all the members of the Council, to monitor implementation of this resolution, with the assistance of appropriate expertise, and calls upon all States to report to the Committee, no later than 90 days from the date of adoption of this resolution and thereafter according to a timetable to be proposed by the Committee, on the steps they have taken to implement this resolution;

7. Directs the Committee to delineate its tasks, submit a work programme within 30 days of the adoption of this resolution, and to consider the support it requires, in consultation with the Secretary-General;

8. Expresses its determination to take all necessary steps in order to ensure the full implementation of this resolution, in accordance with its responsibilities under the Charter;

9. Decides to remain seized of this matter.

5
International
Human Rights Law

5.1
Universal Declaration of Human Rights (UDHR) (1948)

Regarded as the foundation of modern human rights law, this declaration was drafted by a committee chaired by Eleanor Roosevelt. The UDHR, the International Covenant on Civil and Political Rights (ICCPR), and the International Covenant on Economic, Social, and Cultural Rights (ICESCR) are together referred to as the International Bill of Rights.

On the philosophy of human rights, see J. J. Shestack, "The Philosophic Foundations of Human Rights," Human Rights Quarterly *20 (1998): 201–234. On the origins and drafting of the UDHR, see Mary Ann Glendon,* A World Made New: Eleanor Roosevelt and the Universal Declaration of Human Rights *(New York: Random House, 2001). For commentary on the declaration, see A. Eide, ed.,* The Universal Declaration of Human Rights: A Commentary *(Oslo: Scandinavian University Press, 1992). For case study examples of the specific rights covered by the Universal Declaration, see www.bbc.co.uk/worldservice/ people/features/ihavearightto/four_b/all_rights.shtml.*

Whereas recognition of the inherent dignity and of the equal and inalienable rights of all members of the human family is the foundation of freedom, justice and peace in the world,

Whereas disregard and contempt for human rights have resulted in barbarous acts which have outraged the conscience of mankind, and the advent of a world in which human beings shall enjoy freedom of speech and belief and freedom from fear and want has been proclaimed as the highest aspiration of the common people,

Whereas it is essential, if man is not to be compelled to have recourse, as a last resort, to rebellion against tyranny and oppression, that human rights should be protected by the rule of law,

Whereas it is essential to promote the development of friendly relations between nations,

Whereas the peoples of the United Nations have in the Charter reaffirmed their faith in fundamental human rights, in the dignity and worth of the human person and in the equal rights of men and women and have determined to promote social progress and better standards of life in larger freedom,

Whereas Member States have pledged themselves to achieve, in co-operation with the United Nations, the promotion of universal respect for and observance of human rights and fundamental freedoms,

Whereas a common understanding of these rights and freedoms is of the greatest importance for the full realization of this pledge,

Now, therefore THE GENERAL ASSEMBLY proclaims THIS UNIVERSAL DECLARATION OF HUMAN RIGHTS as a common standard of achievement for all peoples and all nations, to the end that every individual and every organ of society, keeping this Declaration constantly in mind, shall strive by teaching and education to promote respect for these rights and freedoms and by progressive measures, national and international, to secure their universal and effective recognition and observance, both among the peoples of Member States themselves and among the peoples of territories under their jurisdiction.

Article 1

All human beings are born free and equal in dignity and rights. They are endowed with reason and conscience and should act towards one another in a spirit of brotherhood.

Article 2

Everyone is entitled to all the rights and freedoms set forth in this Declaration, without distinction of any kind, such as race, colour, sex, language, religion, political or other opinion, national or social origin, property, birth or other status. Furthermore, no distinction shall be made on the basis of the political, jurisdictional or international status of the country or territory to which a person belongs, whether it be independent, trust, non–self-governing or under any other limitation of sovereignty.

Article 3

Everyone has the right to life, liberty and security of person.

Article 4

No one shall be held in slavery or servitude; slavery and the slave trade shall be prohibited in all their forms.

Article 5

No one shall be subjected to torture or to cruel, inhuman or degrading treatment or punishment.

Article 6

Everyone has the right to recognition everywhere as a person before the law.

Article 7

All are equal before the law and are entitled without any discrimination to equal protection of the law. All are entitled to equal protection against any discrimination in violation of this Declaration and against any incitement to such discrimination.

Article 8

Everyone has the right to an effective remedy by the competent national tribunals for acts violating the fundamental rights granted him by the constitution or by law.

Article 9

No one shall be subjected to arbitrary arrest, detention or exile.

Article 10

Everyone is entitled in full equality to a fair and public hearing by an independent and impartial tribunal, in the determination of his rights and obligations and of any criminal charge against him.

Article 11

(1) Everyone charged with a penal offence has the right to be presumed innocent until proved guilty according to law in a public trial at which he has had all the guarantees necessary for his defence.

(2) No one shall be held guilty of any penal offence on account of any act or omission which did not constitute a penal offence, under national or international law, at the time when it was committed. Nor shall a heavier penalty be imposed than the one that was applicable at the time the penal offence was committed.

Article 12

No one shall be subjected to arbitrary interference with his privacy, family, home or correspondence, nor to attacks upon his honour and reputation. Everyone has the right to the protection of the law against such interference or attacks.

Article 13

(1) Everyone has the right to freedom of movement and residence within the borders of each state.

(2) Everyone has the right to leave any country, including his own, and to return to his country.

Article 14

(1) Everyone has the right to seek and to enjoy in other countries asylum from persecution.

(2) This right may not be invoked in the case of prosecutions genuinely aris-

ing from non-political crimes or from acts contrary to the purposes and principles of the United Nations.

Article 15

(1) Everyone has the right to a nationality.

(2) No one shall be arbitrarily deprived of his nationality nor denied the right to change his nationality.

Article 16

(1) Men and women of full age, without any limitation due to race, nationality or religion, have the right to marry and to found a family. They are entitled to equal rights as to marriage, during marriage and at its dissolution.

(2) Marriage shall be entered into only with the free and full consent of the intending spouses.

(3) The family is the natural and fundamental group unit of society and is entitled to protection by society and the State.

Article 17

(1) Everyone has the right to own property alone as well as in association with others.

(2) No one shall be arbitrarily deprived of his property.

Article 18

Everyone has the right to freedom of thought, conscience and religion; this right includes freedom to change his religion or belief, and freedom, either alone or in community with others and in public or private, to manifest his religion or belief in teaching, practice, worship and observance.

Article 19

Everyone has the right to freedom of opinion and expression; this right includes freedom to hold opinions without interference and to seek, receive and impart information and ideas through any media and regardless of frontiers.

Article 20

(1) Everyone has the right to freedom of peaceful assembly and association.

(2) No one may be compelled to belong to an association.

Article 21

(1) Everyone has the right to take part in the government of his country, directly or through freely chosen representatives.

(2) Everyone has the right of equal access to public service in his country.

(3) The will of the people shall be the basis of the authority of government; this will shall be expressed in periodic and genuine elections which shall be by

universal and equal suffrage and shall be held by secret vote or by equivalent free voting procedures.

Article 22

Everyone, as a member of society, has the right to social security and is entitled to realization, through national effort and international co-operation and in accordance with the organization and resources of each State, of the economic, social and cultural rights indispensable for his dignity and the free development of his personality.

Article 23

(1) Everyone has the right to work, to free choice of employment, to just and favourable conditions of work and to protection against unemployment.

(2) Everyone, without any discrimination, has the right to equal pay for equal work.

(3) Everyone who works has the right to just and favourable remuneration ensuring for himself and his family an existence worthy of human dignity, and supplemented, if necessary, by other means of social protection.

(4) Everyone has the right to form and to join trade unions for the protection of his interests.

Article 24

Everyone has the right to rest and leisure, including reasonable limitation of working hours and periodic holidays with pay.

Article 25

(1) Everyone has the right to a standard of living adequate for the health and well-being of himself and of his family, including food, clothing, housing and medical care and necessary social services, and the right to security in the event of unemployment, sickness, disability, widowhood, old age or other lack of livelihood in circumstances beyond his control.

(2) Motherhood and childhood are entitled to special care and assistance. All children, whether born in or out of wedlock, shall enjoy the same social protection.

Article 26

(1) Everyone has the right to education. Education shall be free, at least in the elementary and fundamental stages. Elementary education shall be compulsory. Technical and professional education shall be made generally available and higher education shall be equally accessible to all on the basis of merit.

(2) Education shall be directed to the full development of the human personality and to the strengthening of respect for human rights and fundamental freedoms. It shall promote understanding, tolerance and friendship among all

nations, racial or religious groups, and shall further the activities of the United Nations for the maintenance of peace.

(3) Parents have a prior right to choose the kind of education that shall be given to their children.

Article 27

(1) Everyone has the right freely to participate in the cultural life of the community, to enjoy the arts and to share in scientific advancement and its benefits.

(2) Everyone has the right to the protection of the moral and material interests resulting from any scientific, literary or artistic production of which he is the author.

Article 28

Everyone is entitled to a social and international order in which the rights and freedoms set forth in this Declaration can be fully realized.

Article 29

(1) Everyone has duties to the community in which alone the free and full development of his personality is possible.

(2) In the exercise of his rights and freedoms, everyone shall be subject only to such limitations as are determined by law solely for the purpose of securing due recognition and respect for the rights and freedoms of others and of meeting the just requirements of morality, public order and the general welfare in a democratic society.

(3) These rights and freedoms may in no case be exercised contrary to the purposes and principles of the United Nations.

Article 30

Nothing in this Declaration may be interpreted as implying for any State, group or person any right to engage in any activity or to perform any act aimed at the destruction of any of the rights and freedoms set forth herein.

5.2
Convention Relating to the Status of Refugees (1951)

Negotiated during the early years of the Cold War, the convention has in recent years come under scrutiny for whether it is adequate to address contemporary concerns, including the sheer numbers of involuntary immigrants, issues specific to female refugees, and the problems of those displaced within their own countries.

On the context in which the treaty was negotiated, see James C. Hathaway, "A Reconsideration of the Underlying Premise of Refugee Law," Harvard International Law Journal *31 (1990): 129–183. See also James C. Hathaway,* The Rights of Refugees Under International Law *(Cambridge: Cambridge University Press, 2005); Susan Kneebone, ed.,* The Refugee Convention 50 Years On: Globalization and International Law *(Burlington, Vt.: Ashgate, 2003); Catherine Phuong,* The International Protection of Internally Displaced Persons *(Cambridge: Cambridge University Press, 2004); and Thomas Spijkerboer,* Gender and Refugee Status *(Burlington: Aldershot, 2000). A key journal in this field is the* International Journal of Refugee Law.

The High Contracting Parties,

Considering that the Charter of the United Nations and the Universal Declaration of Human Rights approved on 10 December 1948 by the General Assembly have affirmed the principle that human beings shall enjoy fundamental rights and freedoms without discrimination,

Considering that the United Nations has, on various occasions, manifested its profound concern for refugees and endeavoured to assure refugees the widest possible exercise of these fundamental rights and freedoms,

Considering that it is desirable to revise and consolidate previous international agreements relating to the status of refugees and to extend the scope of and the protection accorded by such instruments by means of a new agreement,

Considering that the grant of asylum may place unduly heavy burdens on certain countries, and that a satisfactory solution of a problem of which the United Nations has recognized the international scope and nature cannot therefore be achieved without international co-operation,

Expressing the wish that all States, recognizing the social and humanitarian nature of the problem of refugees, will do everything within their power to prevent this problem from becoming a cause of tension between States,

Noting that the United Nations High Commissioner for Refugees is charged with the task of supervising international conventions providing for the protection of refugees, and recognizing that the effective co-ordination of measures taken to deal with this problem will depend upon the co-operation of States with the High Commissioner,

Have agreed as follows:

Chapter I: General Provisions

Article 1: Definition of the term "refugee"

A. For the purposes of the present Convention, the term "refugee" shall apply to any person who:

(1) Has been considered a refugee under the Arrangements of 12 May 1926 and 30 June 1928 or under the Conventions of 28 October 1933 and 10 February 1938, the Protocol of 14 September 1939 or the Constitution of the International Refugee Organization;

Decisions of non-eligibility taken by the International Refugee Organization during the period of its activities shall not prevent the status of refugee being accorded to persons who fulfil the conditions of paragraph 2 of this section;

(2) As a result of events occurring before 1 January 1951 and owing to well-founded fear of being persecuted for reasons of race, religion, nationality, membership of a particular social group or political opinion, is outside the country of his nationality and is unable or, owing to such fear, is unwilling to avail himself of the protection of that country; or who, not having a nationality and being outside the country of his former habitual residence as a result of such events, is unable or, owing to such fear, is unwilling to return to it.

In the case of a person who has more than one nationality, the term "the country of his nationality" shall mean each of the countries of which he is a national, and a person shall not be deemed to be lacking the protection of the country of his nationality if, without any valid reason based on well-founded fear, he has not availed himself of the protection of one of the countries of which he is a national.

B. (1) For the purposes of this Convention, the words "events occurring before 1 January 1951" in article 1, section A, shall be understood to mean either (a) "events occurring in Europe before 1 January 1951"; or (b) "events occurring in Europe or elsewhere before 1 January 1951"; and each Contracting State shall make a declaration at the time of signature, ratification or accession, specifying which of these meanings it applies for the purpose of its obligations under this Convention.

(2) Any Contracting State which has adopted alternative (a) may at any

time extend its obligations by adopting alternative (b) by means of a notification addressed to the Secretary-General of the United Nations.

C. This Convention shall cease to apply to any person falling under the terms of section A if:

(1) He has voluntarily re-availed himself of the protection of the country of his nationality; or

(2) Having lost his nationality, he has voluntarily reacquired it; or

(3) He has acquired a new nationality, and enjoys the protection of the country of his new nationality; or

(4) He has voluntarily re-established himself in the country which he left or outside which he remained owing to fear of persecution; or

(5) He can no longer, because the circumstances in connection with which he has been recognized as a refugee have ceased to exist, continue to refuse to avail himself of the protection of the country of his nationality;

Provided that this paragraph shall not apply to a refugee falling under section A (1) of this article who is able to invoke compelling reasons arising out of previous persecution for refusing to avail himself of the protection of the country of nationality;

(6) Being a person who has no nationality he is, because the circumstances in connection with which he has been recognized as a refugee have ceased to exist, able to return to the country of his former habitual residence;

Provided that this paragraph shall not apply to a refugee falling under section A (1) of this article who is able to invoke compelling reasons arising out of previous persecution for refusing to return to the country of his former habitual residence.

D. This Convention shall not apply to persons who are at present receiving from organs or agencies of the United Nations other than the United Nations High Commissioner for Refugees protection or assistance.

When such protection or assistance has ceased for any reason, without the position of such persons being definitively settled in accordance with the relevant resolutions adopted by the General Assembly of the United Nations, these persons shall ipso facto be entitled to the benefits of this Convention.

E. This Convention shall not apply to a person who is recognized by the competent authorities of the country in which he has taken residence as having the rights and obligations which are attached to the possession of the nationality of that country.

F. The provisions of this Convention shall not apply to any person with respect to whom there are serious reasons for considering that:

(a) He has committed a crime against peace, a war crime, or a crime against humanity, as defined in the international instruments drawn up to make provision in respect of such crimes;

(b) He has committed a serious non-political crime outside the country of refuge prior to his admission to that country as a refugee;

(c) He has been guilty of acts contrary to the purposes and principles of the United Nations.

Article 2: General obligations

Every refugee has duties to the country in which he finds himself, which require in particular that he conform to its laws and regulations as well as to measures taken for the maintenance of public order.

Article 3: Non-discrimination

The Contracting States shall apply the provisions of this Convention to refugees without discrimination as to race, religion or country of origin.

Article 4: Religion

The Contracting States shall accord to refugees within their territories treatment at least as favourable as that accorded to their nationals with respect to freedom to practise their religion and freedom as regards the religious education of their children.

Article 5: Rights granted apart from this Convention

Nothing in this Convention shall be deemed to impair any rights and benefits granted by a Contracting State to refugees apart from this Convention.

Article 6: The term "in the same circumstances"

For the purposes of this Convention, the term "in the same circumstances" implies that any requirements (including requirements as to length and conditions of sojourn or residence) which the particular individual would have to fulfil for the enjoyment of the right in question, if he were not a refugee, must be fulfilled by him, with the exception of requirements which by their nature a refugee is incapable of fulfilling.

Article 7: Exemption from reciprocity

1. Except where this Convention contains more favourable provisions, a Contracting State shall accord to refugees the same treatment as is accorded to aliens generally.

2. After a period of three years' residence, all refugees shall enjoy exemption from legislative reciprocity in the territory of the Contracting States.

3. Each Contracting State shall continue to accord to refugees the rights and benefits to which they were already entitled, in the absence of reciprocity, at the date of entry into force of this Convention for that State.

4. The Contracting States shall consider favourably the possibility of according to refugees, in the absence of reciprocity, rights and benefits beyond those to which they are entitled according to paragraphs 2 and 3, and to extending exemption from reciprocity to refugees who do not fulfil the conditions provided for in paragraphs 2 and 3.

5. The provisions of paragraphs 2 and 3 apply both to the rights and benefits referred to in articles 13, 18, 19, 21 and 22 of this Convention and to rights and benefits for which this Convention does not provide.

Article 8: Exemption from exceptional measures

With regard to exceptional measures which may be taken against the person, property or interests of nationals of a foreign State, the Contracting States shall not apply such measures to a refugee who is formally a national of the said State solely on account of such nationality. Contracting States which, under their legislation, are prevented from applying the general principle expressed in this article, shall, in appropriate cases, grant exemptions in favour of such refugees.

Article 9: Provisional measures

Nothing in this Convention shall prevent a Contracting State, in time of war or other grave and exceptional circumstances, from taking provisionally measures which it considers to be essential to the national security in the case of a particular person, pending a determination by the Contracting State that that person is in fact a refugee and that the continuance of such measures is necessary in his case in the interests of national security.

Article 10: Continuity of residence

1. Where a refugee has been forcibly displaced during the Second World War and removed to the territory of a Contracting State, and is resident there, the period of such enforced sojourn shall be considered to have been lawful residence within that territory.

2. Where a refugee has been forcibly displaced during the Second World War from the territory of a Contracting State and has, prior to the date of entry into force of this Convention, returned there for the purpose of taking up residence, the period of residence before and after such enforced displacement shall be regarded as one uninterrupted period for any purposes for which uninterrupted residence is required.

Article 11: Refugee seamen

In the case of refugees regularly serving as crew members on board a ship flying the flag of a Contracting State, that State shall give sympathetic consideration to their establishment on its territory and the issue of travel documents to them or their temporary admission to its territory particularly with a view to facilitating their establishment in another country.

Chapter II: Juridical Status

Article 12: Personal status

1. The personal status of a refugee shall be governed by the law of the country of his domicile or, if he has no domicile, by the law of the country of his residence.

2. Rights previously acquired by a refugee and dependent on personal sta-

tus, more particularly rights attaching to marriage, shall be respected by a Contracting State, subject to compliance, if this be necessary, with the formalities required by the law of that State, provided that the right in question is one which would have been recognized by the law of that State had he not become a refugee.

Article 13: Movable and immovable property
The Contracting States shall accord to a refugee treatment as favourable as possible and, in any event, not less favourable than that accorded to aliens generally in the same circumstances, as regards the acquisition of movable and immovable property and other rights pertaining thereto, and to leases and other contracts relating to movable and immovable property.

Article 14: Artistic rights and industrial property
In respect of the protection of industrial property, such as inventions, designs or models, trade marks, trade names, and of rights in literary, artistic and scientific works, a refugee shall be accorded in the country in which he has his habitual residence the same protection as is accorded to nationals of that country. In the territory of any other Contracting States, he shall be accorded the same protection as is accorded in that territory to nationals of the country in which he has his habitual residence.

Article 15: Right of association
As regards non-political and non-profit-making associations and trade unions the Contracting States shall accord to refugees lawfully staying in their territory the most favourable treatment accorded to nationals of a foreign country, in the same circumstances.

Article 16: Access to courts
1. A refugee shall have free access to the courts of law on the territory of all Contracting States.

2. A refugee shall enjoy in the Contracting State in which he has his habitual residence the same treatment as a national in matters pertaining to access to the courts, including legal assistance and exemption from cautio judicatum solvi.

3. A refugee shall be accorded in the matters referred to in paragraph 2 in countries other than that in which he has his habitual residence the treatment granted to a national of the country of his habitual residence.

Chapter III: Gainful Employment

Article 17: Wage-earning employment
1. The Contracting States shall accord to refugees lawfully staying in their territory the most favourable treatment accorded to nationals of a foreign coun-

try in the same circumstances, as regards the right to engage in wage-earning employment.

2. In any case, restrictive measures imposed on aliens or the employment of aliens for the protection of the national labour market shall not be applied to a refugee who was already exempt from them at the date of entry into force of this Convention for the Contracting State concerned, or who fulfils one of the following conditions:

(a) He has completed three years' residence in the country;

(b) He has a spouse possessing the nationality of the country of residence. A refugee may not invoke the benefit of this provision if he has abandoned his spouse;

(c) He has one or more children possessing the nationality of the country of residence.

3. The Contracting States shall give sympathetic consideration to assimilating the rights of all refugees with regard to wage-earning employment to those of nationals, and in particular of those refugees who have entered their territory pursuant to programmes of labour recruitment or under immigration schemes.

Article 18: Self-employment

The Contracting States shall accord to a refugee lawfully in their territory treatment as favourable as possible and, in any event, not less favourable than that accorded to aliens generally in the same circumstances, as regards the right to engage on his own account in agriculture, industry, handicrafts and commerce and to establish commercial and industrial companies.

Article 19: Liberal professions

1. Each Contracting State shall accord to refugees lawfully staying in their territory who hold diplomas recognized by the competent authorities of that State, and who are desirous of practising a liberal profession, treatment as favourable as possible and, in any event, not less favourable than that accorded to aliens generally in the same circumstances.

2. The Contracting States shall use their best endeavours consistently with their laws and constitutions to secure the settlement of such refugees in the territories, other than the metropolitan territory, for whose international relations they are responsible.

Chapter IV: Welfare

Article 20: Rationing

Where a rationing system exists, which applies to the population at large and regulates the general distribution of products in short supply, refugees shall be accorded the same treatment as nationals.

Article 21: Housing

As regards housing, the Contracting States, in so far as the matter is regulated by laws or regulations or is subject to the control of public authorities, shall accord to refugees lawfully staying in their territory treatment as favourable as possible and, in any event, not less favourable than that accorded to aliens generally in the same circumstances.

Article 22: Public education

1. The Contracting States shall accord to refugees the same treatment as is accorded to nationals with respect to elementary education.

2. The Contracting States shall accord to refugees treatment as favourable as possible, and, in any event, not less favourable than that accorded to aliens generally in the same circumstances, with respect to education other than elementary education and, in particular, as regards access to studies, the recognition of foreign school certificates, diplomas and degrees, the remission of fees and charges and the award of scholarships.

Article 23: Public relief

The Contracting States shall accord to refugees lawfully staying in their territory the same treatment with respect to public relief and assistance as is accorded to their nationals.

Article 24: Labour legislation and social security

1. The Contracting States shall accord to refugees lawfully staying in their territory the same treatment as is accorded to nationals in respect of the following matters;

(a) In so far as such matters are governed by laws or regulations or are subject to the control of administrative authorities: remuneration, including family allowances where these form part of remuneration, hours of work, overtime arrangements, holidays with pay, restrictions on home work, minimum age of employment, apprenticeship and training, women's work and the work of young persons, and the enjoyment of the benefits of collective bargaining;

(b) Social security (legal provisions in respect of employment injury, occupational diseases, maternity, sickness, disability, old age, death, unemployment, family responsibilities and any other contingency which, according to national laws or regulations, is covered by a social security scheme), subject to the following limitations: (i) There may be appropriate arrangements for the maintenance of acquired rights and rights in course of acquisition; (ii) National laws or regulations of the country of residence may prescribe special arrangements concerning benefits or portions of benefits which are payable wholly out of public funds, and concerning allowances paid to persons who do not fulfil the contribution conditions prescribed for the award of a normal pension.

2. The right to compensation for the death of a refugee resulting from employment injury or from occupational disease shall not be affected by the

fact that the residence of the beneficiary is outside the territory of the Contracting State.

3. The Contracting States shall extend to refugees the benefits of agreements concluded between them, or which may be concluded between them in the future, concerning the maintenance of acquired rights and rights in the process of acquisition in regard to social security, subject only to the conditions which apply to nationals of the States signatory to the agreements in question.

4. The Contracting States will give sympathetic consideration to extending to refugees so far as possible the benefits of similar agreements which may at any time be in force between such Contracting States and non-contracting States.

Chapter V: Administrative Measures

Article 25: Administrative assistance

1. When the exercise of a right by a refugee would normally require the assistance of authorities of a foreign country to whom he cannot have recourse, the Contracting States in whose territory he is residing shall arrange that such assistance be afforded to him by their own authorities or by an international authority.

2. The authority or authorities mentioned in paragraph 1 shall deliver or cause to be delivered under their supervision to refugees such documents or certifications as would normally be delivered to aliens by or through their national authorities.

3. Documents or certifications so delivered shall stand in the stead of the official instruments delivered to aliens by or through their national authorities, and shall be given credence in the absence of proof to the contrary.

4. Subject to such exceptional treatment as may be granted to indigent persons, fees may be charged for the services mentioned herein, but such fees shall be moderate and commensurate with those charged to nationals for similar services.

5. The provisions of this article shall be without prejudice to articles 27 and 28.

Article 26: Freedom of movement

Each Contracting State shall accord to refugees lawfully in its territory the right to choose their place of residence and to move freely within its territory subject to any regulations applicable to aliens generally in the same circumstances.

Article 27: Identity papers

The Contracting States shall issue identity papers to any refugee in their territory who does not possess a valid travel document.

Article 28: Travel documents

1. The Contracting States shall issue to refugees lawfully staying in their territory travel documents for the purpose of travel outside their territory, unless compelling reasons of national security or public order otherwise require, and the provisions of the Schedule to this Convention shall apply with respect to such documents. The Contracting States may issue such a travel document to any other refugee in their territory; they shall in particular give sympathetic consideration to the issue of such a travel document to refugees in their territory who are unable to obtain a travel document from the country of their lawful residence.

2. Travel documents issued to refugees under previous international agreements by Parties thereto shall be recognized and treated by the Contracting States in the same way as if they had been issued pursuant to this article.

Article 29: Fiscal charges

1. The Contracting States shall not impose upon refugees duties, charges or taxes, of any description whatsoever, other or higher than those which are or may be levied on their nationals in similar situations.

2. Nothing in the above paragraph shall prevent the application to refugees of the laws and regulations concerning charges in respect of the issue to aliens of administrative documents including identity papers.

Article 30: Transfer of assets

1. A Contracting State shall, in conformity with its laws and regulations, permit refugees to transfer assets which they have brought into its territory, to another country where they have been admitted for the purposes of resettlement.

2. A Contracting State shall give sympathetic consideration to the application of refugees for permission to transfer assets wherever they may be and which are necessary for their resettlement in another country to which they have been admitted.

Article 31: Refugees unlawfully in the country of refuge

1. The Contracting States shall not impose penalties, on account of their illegal entry or presence, on refugees who, coming directly from a territory where their life or freedom was threatened in the sense of article 1, enter or are present in their territory without authorization, provided they present themselves without delay to the authorities and show good cause for their illegal entry or presence.

2. The Contracting States shall not apply to the movements of such refugees restrictions other than those which are necessary and such restrictions shall only be applied until their status in the country is regularized or they obtain admission into another country. The Contracting States shall allow such refugees a reasonable period and all the necessary facilities to obtain admission into another country.

Article 32: Expulsion

1. The Contracting States shall not expel a refugee lawfully in their territory save on grounds of national security or public order.

2. The expulsion of such a refugee shall be only in pursuance of a decision reached in accordance with due process of law. Except where compelling reasons of national security otherwise require, the refugee shall be allowed to submit evidence to clear himself, and to appeal to and be represented for the purpose before competent authority or a person or persons specially designated by the competent authority.

3. The Contracting States shall allow such a refugee a reasonable period within which to seek legal admission into another country. The Contracting States reserve the right to apply during that period such internal measures as they may deem necessary.

Article 33: Prohibition of expulsion or return ("refoulement")

1. No Contracting State shall expel or return ("refouler") a refugee in any manner whatsoever to the frontiers of territories where his life or freedom would be threatened on account of his race, religion, nationality, membership of a particular social group or political opinion.

2. The benefit of the present provision may not, however, be claimed by a refugee whom there are reasonable grounds for regarding as a danger to the security of the country in which he is, or who, having been convicted by a final judgement of a particularly serious crime, constitutes a danger to the community of that country.

Article 34: Naturalization

The Contracting States shall as far as possible facilitate the assimilation and naturalization of refugees. They shall in particular make every effort to expedite naturalization proceedings and to reduce as far as possible the charges and costs of such proceedings.

Chapter VI:
Executory and Transitory Provisions

Article 35: Co-operation of the
national authorities with the United Nations

1. The Contracting States undertake to co-operate with the Office of the United Nations High Commissioner for Refugees, or any other agency of the United Nations which may succeed it, in the exercise of its functions, and shall in particular facilitate its duty of supervising the application of the provisions of this Convention.

2. In order to enable the Office of the High Commissioner or any other agency of the United Nations which may succeed it, to make reports to the competent organs of the United Nations, the Contracting States undertake to

provide them in the appropriate form with information and statistical data requested concerning:

(a) The condition of refugees,

(b) The implementation of this Convention, and

(c) Laws, regulations and decrees which are, or may hereafter be, in force relating to refugees.

Article 36: Information on national legislation

The Contracting States shall communicate to the Secretary-General of the United Nations the laws and regulations which they may adopt to ensure the application of this Convention.

Article 37: Relation to previous conventions

Without prejudice to article 28, paragraph 2, of this Convention, this Convention replaces, as between Parties to it, the Arrangements of 5 July 1922, 31 May 1924, 12 May 1926, 30 June 1928 and 30 July 1935, the Conventions of 28 October 1933 and 10 February 1938, the Protocol of 14 September 1939 and the Agreement of 15 October 1946.

Chapter VII: Final Clauses

Article 38: Settlement of disputes

Any dispute between Parties to this Convention relating to its interpretation or application, which cannot be settled by other means, shall be referred to the International Court of Justice at the request of any one of the parties to the dispute.

Article 39: Signature, ratification and accession

1. This Convention shall be opened for signature at Geneva on 28 July 1951 and shall thereafter be deposited with the Secretary-General of the United Nations. It shall be open for signature at the European Office of the United Nations from 28 July to 31 August 1951 and shall be re-opened for signature at the Headquarters of the United Nations from 17 September 1951 to 31 December 1952.

2. This Convention shall be open for signature on behalf of all States Members of the United Nations, and also on behalf of any other State invited to attend the Conference of Plenipotentiaries on the Status of Refugees and Stateless Persons or to which an invitation to sign will have been addressed by the General Assembly. It shall be ratified and the instruments of ratification shall be deposited with the Secretary-General of the United Nations.

3. This Convention shall be open from 28 July 1951 for accession by the States referred to in paragraph 2 of this article. Accession shall be effected by the deposit of an instrument of accession with the Secretary-General of the United Nations.

Article 40: Territorial application clause

1. Any State may, at the time of signature, ratification or accession, declare that this Convention shall extend to all or any of the territories for the international relations of which it is responsible. Such a declaration shall take effect when the Convention enters into force for the State concerned.

2. At any time thereafter any such extension shall be made by notification addressed to the Secretary-General of the United Nations and shall take effect as from the ninetieth day after the day of receipt by the Secretary-General of the United Nations of this notification, or as from the date of entry into force of the Convention for the State concerned, whichever is the later.

3. With respect to those territories to which this Convention is not extended at the time of signature, ratification or accession, each State concerned shall consider the possibility of taking the necessary steps in order to extend the application of this Convention to such territories, subject, where necessary for constitutional reasons, to the consent of the Governments of such territories.

Article 41: Federal clause

In the case of a Federal or non-unitary State, the following provisions shall apply:

(a) With respect to those articles of this Convention that come within the legislative jurisdiction of the federal legislative authority, the obligations of the Federal Government shall to this extent be the same as those of parties which are not Federal States;

(b) With respect to those articles of this Convention that come within the legislative jurisdiction of constituent States, provinces or cantons which are not, under the constitutional system of the Federation, bound to take legislative action, the Federal Government shall bring such articles with a favourable recommendation to the notice of the appropriate authorities of States, provinces or cantons at the earliest possible moment;

(c) A Federal State Party to this Convention shall, at the request of any other Contracting State transmitted through the Secretary-General of the United Nations, supply a statement of the law and practice of the Federation and its constituent units in regard to any particular provision of the Convention showing the extent to which effect has been given to that provision by legislative or other action.

Article 42: Reservations

1. At the time of signature, ratification or accession, any State may make reservations to articles of the Convention other than to articles 1, 3, 4, 16 (1), 33, 36–46 inclusive.

2. Any State making a reservation in accordance with paragraph 1 of this article may at any time withdraw the reservation by a communication to that effect addressed to the Secretary-General of the United Nations.

Article 43: Entry into force

1. This Convention shall come into force on the ninetieth day following the day of deposit of the sixth instrument of ratification or accession.

2. For each State ratifying or acceding to the Convention after the deposit of the sixth instrument of ratification or accession, the Convention shall enter into force on the ninetieth day following the date of deposit by such State of its instrument of ratification or accession.

Article 44: Denunciation

1. Any Contracting State may denounce this Convention at any time by a notification addressed to the Secretary-General of the United Nations.

2. Such denunciation shall take effect for the Contracting State concerned one year from the date upon which it is received by the Secretary-General of the United Nations.

3. Any State which has made a declaration or notification under article 40 may, at any time thereafter, by a notification to the Secretary-General of the United Nations, declare that the Convention shall cease to extend to such territory one year after the date of receipt of the notification by the Secretary-General.

Article 45: Revision

1. Any Contracting State may request revision of this Convention at any time by a notification addressed to the Secretary-General of the United Nations.

2. The General Assembly of the United Nations shall recommend the steps, if any, to be taken in respect of such request.

Article 46: Notifications by the Secretary-General of the United Nations

The Secretary-General of the United Nations shall inform all Members of the United Nations and non-member States referred to in article 39:

(a) Of declarations and notifications in accordance with section B of article 1;

(b) Of signatures, ratifications and accessions in accordance with article 39;

(c) Of declarations and notifications in accordance with article 40;

(d) Of reservations and withdrawals in accordance with article 42;

(e) Of the date on which this Convention will come into force in accordance with article 43;

(f) Of denunciations and notifications in accordance with article 44;

(g) Of requests for revision in accordance with article 45.

IN FAITH WHEREOF the undersigned, duly authorized, have signed this Convention on behalf of their respective Governments.

DONE at Geneva, this twenty-eighth day of July, one thousand nine hundred and fifty-one, in a single copy, of which the English and French texts are equally authentic and which shall remain deposited in the archives of the

United Nations, and certified true copies of which shall be delivered to all Members of the United Nations and to the non-member States referred to in article 39.

Protocol Relating to the Status of Refugees (1967)

This protocol revised the limitations on the definition of "refugee" in the 1951 Convention Relating to the Status of Refugees. For an historical perspective on the negotiation of the protocol, see Kazimierz Bem, "The Coming of a "Blank Cheque"—Europe, the 1951 Convention, and the 1967 Protocol," International Journal of Refugee Law 16 (2004): 609–627. The convention definition of "refugee" continues to be a question of practical importance and scholarly discussion. See Kristen Walker, "Defending the 1951 Convention Definition of Refugee," Georgetown Immigration Law Journal 17 (2003): 583–609; and Daniel J. Steinbock, "Interpreting the Refugee Definition," UCLA Law Review 45 (1998): 733–816.

The States Parties to the present Protocol,

Considering that the Convention relating to the Status of Refugees done at Geneva on 28 July 1951 (hereinafter referred to as the Convention) covers only those persons who have become refugees as a result of events occurring before I January 1951,

Considering that new refugee situations have arisen since the Convention was adopted and that the refugees concerned may therefore not fall within the scope of the Convention,

Considering that it is desirable that equal status should be enjoyed by all refugees covered by the definition in the Convention irrespective of the dateline I January 1951,

Have agreed as follows:

Article I: General provision

1. The States Parties to the present Protocol undertake to apply articles 2 to 34 inclusive of the Convention to refugees as hereinafter defined.

2. For the purpose of the present Protocol, the term "refugee" shall, except as regards the application of paragraph 3 of this article, mean any person within the definition of article I of the Convention as if the words "As a result of events occurring before 1 January 1951 and . . ." and the words ". . . as a result of such events," in article 1 A (2) were omitted.

3. The present Protocol shall be applied by the States Parties hereto without any geographic limitation, save that existing declarations made by States already Parties to the Convention in accordance with article I B (I) (a) of the Convention, shall, unless extended under article I B (2) thereof, apply also under the present Protocol.

Article II: Co-operation of the national authorities with the United Nations

1. The States Parties to the present Protocol undertake to co-operate with the Office of the United Nations High Commissioner for Refugees, or any other agency of the United Nations which may succeed it, in the exercise of its functions, and shall in particular facilitate its duty of supervising the application of the provisions of the present Protocol.

2. In order to enable the Office of the High Commissioner or any other agency of the United Nations which may succeed it, to make reports to the competent organs of the United Nations, the States Parties to the present Protocol undertake to provide them with the information and statistical data requested, in the appropriate form, concerning:

(a) The condition of refugees;

(b) The implementation of the present Protocol;

(c) Laws, regulations and decrees which are, or may hereafter be, in force relating to refugees.

Article III: Information on national legislation

The States Parties to the present Protocol shall communicate to the Secretary-General of the United Nations the laws and regulations which they may adopt to ensure the application of the present Protocol.

Article IV: Settlement of disputes

Any dispute between States Parties to the present Protocol which relates to its interpretation or application and which cannot be settled by other means shall be referred to the International Court of Justice at the request of any one of the parties to the dispute.

Article V: Accession

The present Protocol shall be open for accession on behalf of all States Parties to the Convention and of any other State Member of the United Nations or member of any of the specialized agencies or to which an invitation to accede may have been addressed by the General Assembly of the United Nations. Accession shall be effected by the deposit of an instrument of accession with the Secretary-General of the United Nations.

Article VI: Federal clause

In the case of a Federal or non-unitary State, the following provisions shall apply:

(a) With respect to those articles of the Convention to be applied in accordance with article I, paragraph 1, of the present Protocol that come within the legislative jurisdiction of the federal legislative authority, the obligations of the Federal Government shall to this extent be the same as those of States Parties which are not Federal States;

(b) With respect to those articles of the Convention to be applied in accordance with article I, paragraph 1, of the present Protocol that come within the legislative jurisdiction of constituent States, provinces or cantons which are not, under the constitutional system of the Federation, bound to take legislative action, the Federal Government shall bring such articles with a favourable recommendation to the notice of the appropriate authorities of States, provinces or cantons at the earliest possible moment;

(c) A Federal State Party to the present Protocol shall, at the request of any other State Party hereto transmitted through the Secretary-General of the United Nations, supply a statement of the law and practice of the Federation and its constituent units in regard to any particular provision of the Convention to be applied in accordance with article I, paragraph 1, of the present Protocol, showing the extent to which effect has been given to that provision by legislative or other action.

Article VII: Reservations and declarations

1. At the time of accession, any State may make reservations in respect of article IV of the present Protocol and in respect of the application in accordance with article I of the present Protocol of any provisions of the Convention other than those contained in articles 1, 3, 4, 16 (1) and 33 thereof, provided that in the case of a State Party to the Convention reservations made under this article shall not extend to refugees in respect of whom the Convention applies.

2. Reservations made by States Parties to the Convention in accordance with article 42 thereof shall, unless withdrawn, be applicable in relation to their obligations under the present Protocol.

3. Any State making a reservation in accordance with paragraph 1 of this article may at any time withdraw such reservation by a communication to that effect addressed to the Secretary-General of the United Nations.

4. Declarations made under article 40, paragraphs 1 and 2, of the Convention by a State Party thereto which accedes to the present Protocol shall be deemed to apply in respect of the present Protocol, unless upon accession a notification to the contrary is addressed by the State Party concerned to the Secretary-General of the United Nations. The provisions of article 40, paragraphs 2 and 3, and of article 44, paragraph 3, of the Convention shall be deemed to apply mutatis mutandis to the present Protocol.

Article VIII: Entry into force

1. The present Protocol shall come into force on the day of deposit of the sixth instrument of accession.

2. For each State acceding to the Protocol after the deposit of the sixth

instrument of accession, the Protocol shall come into force on the date of deposit by such State of its instrument of accession.

Article IX: Denunciation

1. Any State Party hereto may denounce this Protocol at any time by a notification addressed to the Secretary-General of the United Nations.

2. Such denunciation shall take effect for the State Party concerned one year from the date on which it is received by the Secretary-General of the United Nations.

Article X: Notifications by the Secretary-General of the United Nations

The Secretary-General of the United Nations shall inform the States referred to in article V above of the date of entry into force, accessions, reservations and withdrawals of reservations to and denunciations of the present Protocol, and of declarations and notifications relating hereto.

Article XI: Deposit in the archives of the Secretariat of the United Nations

A copy of the present Protocol, of which the Chinese, English, French, Russian and Spanish texts are equally authentic, signed by the President of the General Assembly and by the Secretary-General of the United Nations, shall be deposited in the archives of the Secretariat of the United Nations. The Secretary-General will transmit certified copies thereof to all States Members of the United Nations and to the other States referred to in article V above.

5.3
International Convention on the Elimination of All Forms of Racial Discrimination (CERD) (1965)

The convention was preceded by the 1963 United Nations Declaration on the Elimination of All Forms of Racial Discrimination. The CERD was the first UN human rights instrument to set up an international monitoring system in the form of a committee whose work would include receiving "communications" from individuals or groups of individuals claiming to have had their convention rights violated.

On the negotiation of the convention, see Egon Schwelb, "The International Convention on the Elimination of All forms of Racial Discrimination," International and Comparative Law Quarterly *15 (1966): 996–1068. On the operation of the convention and the work of its committee, see Michael Banton,* International Action Against Racial Discrimination *(New York: Oxford University Press, 1996).*

The States Parties to this Convention,

Considering that the Charter of the United Nations is based on the principles of the dignity and equality inherent in all human beings, and that all Member States have pledged themselves to take joint and separate action, in co-operation with the Organization, for the achievement of one of the purposes of the United Nations which is to promote and encourage universal respect for and observance of human rights and fundamental freedoms for all, without distinction as to race, sex, language or religion,

Considering that the Universal Declaration of Human Rights proclaims that all human beings are born free and equal in dignity and rights and that everyone is entitled to all the rights and freedoms set out therein, without distinction of any kind, in particular as to race, colour or national origin,

Considering that all human beings are equal before the law and are entitled to equal protection of the law against any discrimination and against any incitement to discrimination,

Considering that the United Nations has condemned colonialism and all practices of segregation and discrimination associated therewith, in whatever form and wherever they exist, and that the Declaration on the Granting of Independence to Colonial Countries and Peoples of 14 December 1960 (General Assembly resolution 1514 (XV)) has affirmed and solemnly proclaimed the necessity of bringing them to a speedy and unconditional end,

Considering that the United Nations Declaration on the Elimination of All Forms of Racial Discrimination of 20 November 1963 (General Assembly resolution 1904 (XVIII)) solemnly affirms the necessity of speedily eliminating racial discrimination throughout the world in all its forms and manifestations and of securing understanding of and respect for the dignity of the human person,

Convinced that any doctrine of superiority based on racial differentiation is scientifically false, morally condemnable, socially unjust and dangerous, and that there is no justification for racial discrimination, in theory or in practice, anywhere,

Reaffirming that discrimination between human beings on the grounds of race, colour or ethnic origin is an obstacle to friendly and peaceful relations among nations and is capable of disturbing peace and security among peoples and the harmony of persons living side by side even within one and the same State,

Convinced that the existence of racial barriers is repugnant to the ideals of any human society,

Alarmed by manifestations of racial discrimination still in evidence in some areas of the world and by governmental policies based on racial superiority or hatred, such as policies of apartheid, segregation or separation,

Resolved to adopt all necessary measures for speedily eliminating racial discrimination in all its forms and manifestations, and to prevent and combat racist doctrines and practices in order to promote understanding between races and to build an international community free from all forms of racial segregation and racial discrimination,

Bearing in mind the Convention concerning Discrimination in respect of Employment and Occupation adopted by the International Labour Organisation in 1958, and the Convention against Discrimination in Education adopted by the United Nations Educational, Scientific and Cultural Organization in 1960,

Desiring to implement the principles embodied in the United Nations Declaration on the Elimination of All Forms of Racial Discrimination and to secure the earliest adoption of practical measures to that end,

Have agreed as follows:

Part I

Article I

1. In this Convention, the term "racial discrimination" shall mean any distinction, exclusion, restriction or preference based on race, colour, descent, or

national or ethnic origin which has the purpose or effect of nullifying or impairing the recognition, enjoyment or exercise, on an equal footing, of human rights and fundamental freedoms in the political, economic, social, cultural or any other field of public life.

2. This Convention shall not apply to distinctions, exclusions, restrictions or preferences made by a State Party to this Convention between citizens and non-citizens.

3. Nothing in this Convention may be interpreted as affecting in any way the legal provisions of States Parties concerning nationality, citizenship or naturalization, provided that such provisions do not discriminate against any particular nationality.

4. Special measures taken for the sole purpose of securing adequate advancement of certain racial or ethnic groups or individuals requiring such protection as may be necessary in order to ensure such groups or individuals equal enjoyment or exercise of human rights and fundamental freedoms shall not be deemed racial discrimination, provided, however, that such measures do not, as a consequence, lead to the maintenance of separate rights for different racial groups and that they shall not be continued after the objectives for which they were taken have been achieved.

Article 2

1. States Parties condemn racial discrimination and undertake to pursue by all appropriate means and without delay a policy of eliminating racial discrimination in all its forms and promoting understanding among all races, and, to this end:

(a) Each State Party undertakes to engage in no act or practice of racial discrimination against persons, groups of persons or institutions and to ensure that all public authorities and public institutions, national and local, shall act in conformity with this obligation;

(b) Each State Party undertakes not to sponsor, defend or support racial discrimination by any persons or organizations;

(c) Each State Party shall take effective measures to review governmental, national and local policies, and to amend, rescind or nullify any laws and regulations which have the effect of creating or perpetuating racial discrimination wherever it exists;

(d) Each State Party shall prohibit and bring to an end, by all appropriate means, including legislation as required by circumstances, racial discrimination by any persons, group or organization;

(e) Each State Party undertakes to encourage, where appropriate, integrationist multiracial organizations and movements and other means of eliminating barriers between races, and to discourage anything which tends to strengthen racial division.

2. States Parties shall, when the circumstances so warrant, take, in the social, economic, cultural and other fields, special and concrete measures to ensure the adequate development and protection of certain racial groups or

individuals belonging to them, for the purpose of guaranteeing them the full and equal enjoyment of human rights and fundamental freedoms. These measures shall in no case entail as a consequence the maintenance of unequal or separate rights for different racial groups after the objectives for which they were taken have been achieved.

Article 3
States Parties particularly condemn racial segregation and apartheid and undertake to prevent, prohibit and eradicate all practices of this nature in territories under their jurisdiction.

Article 4
States Parties condemn all propaganda and all organizations which are based on ideas or theories of superiority of one race or group of persons of one colour or ethnic origin, or which attempt to justify or promote racial hatred and discrimination in any form, and undertake to adopt immediate and positive measures designed to eradicate all incitement to, or acts of, such discrimination and, to this end, with due regard to the principles embodied in the Universal Declaration of Human Rights and the rights expressly set forth in article 5 of this Convention, inter alia:

(a) Shall declare an offence punishable by law all dissemination of ideas based on racial superiority or hatred, incitement to racial discrimination, as well as all acts of violence or incitement to such acts against any race or group of persons of another colour or ethnic origin, and also the provision of any assistance to racist activities, including the financing thereof;

(b) Shall declare illegal and prohibit organizations, and also organized and all other propaganda activities, which promote and incite racial discrimination, and shall recognize participation in such organizations or activities as an offence punishable by law;

(c) Shall not permit public authorities or public institutions, national or local, to promote or incite racial discrimination.

Article 5
In compliance with the fundamental obligations laid down in article 2 of this Convention, States Parties undertake to prohibit and to eliminate racial discrimination in all its forms and to guarantee the right of everyone, without distinction as to race, colour, or national or ethnic origin, to equality before the law, notably in the enjoyment of the following rights:

(a) The right to equal treatment before the tribunals and all other organs administering justice;

(b) The right to security of person and protection by the State against violence or bodily harm, whether inflicted by government officials or by any individual group or institution;

(c) Political rights, in particular the right to participate in elections—to vote and to stand for election—on the basis of universal and equal suffrage, to take part in the Government as well as in the conduct of public affairs at any level and to have equal access to public service;

(d) Other civil rights, in particular:

(i) The right to freedom of movement and residence within the border of the State;

(ii) The right to leave any country, including one's own, and to return to one's country;

(iii) The right to nationality;

(iv) The right to marriage and choice of spouse;

(v) The right to own property alone as well as in association with others;

(vi) The right to inherit;

(vii) The right to freedom of thought, conscience and religion;

(viii) The right to freedom of opinion and expression;

(ix) The right to freedom of peaceful assembly and association;

(e) Economic, social and cultural rights, in particular:

(i) The rights to work, to free choice of employment, to just and favourable conditions of work, to protection against unemployment, to equal pay for equal work, to just and favourable remuneration; (ii) The right to form and join trade unions;

(iii) The right to housing;

(iv) The right to public health, medical care, social security and social services;

(v) The right to education and training;

(vi) The right to equal participation in cultural activities;

(f) The right of access to any place or service intended for use by the general public, such as transport hotels, restaurants, cafes, theatres and parks.

Article 6

States Parties shall assure to everyone within their jurisdiction effective protection and remedies, through the competent national tribunals and other State institutions, against any acts of racial discrimination which violate his human rights and fundamental freedoms contrary to this Convention, as well as the right to seek from such tribunals just and adequate reparation or satisfaction for any damage suffered as a result of such discrimination.

Article 7

States Parties undertake to adopt immediate and effective measures, particularly in the fields of teaching, education, culture and information, with a view to combating prejudices which lead to racial discrimination and to promoting understanding, tolerance and friendship among nations and racial or ethnical groups, as well as to propagating the purposes and principles of the Charter of the United Nations, the Universal Declaration of Human Rights, the United Nations Declaration on the Elimination of All Forms of Racial Discrimination, and this Convention.

Part II

Article 8

1. There shall be established a Committee on the Elimination of Racial Discrimination (hereinafter referred to as the Committee) consisting of eighteen experts of high moral standing and acknowledged impartiality elected by States Parties from among their nationals, who shall serve in their personal capacity, consideration being given to equitable geographical distribution and to the representation of the different forms of civilization as well as of the principal legal systems.

2. The members of the Committee shall be elected by secret ballot from a list of persons nominated by the States Parties. Each State Party may nominate one person from among its own nationals.

3. The initial election shall be held six months after the date of the entry into force of this Convention. At least three months before the date of each election the Secretary-General of the United Nations shall address a letter to the States Parties inviting them to submit their nominations within two months. The Secretary-General shall prepare a list in alphabetical order of all persons thus nominated, indicating the States Parties which have nominated them, and shall submit it to the States Parties.

4. Elections of the members of the Committee shall be held at a meeting of States Parties convened by the Secretary-General at United Nations Headquarters. At that meeting, for which two thirds of the States Parties shall constitute a quorum, the persons elected to the Committee shall be nominees who obtain the largest number of votes and an absolute majority of the votes of the representatives of States Parties present and voting.

5. (a) The members of the Committee shall be elected for a term of four years. However, the terms of nine of the members elected at the first election shall expire at the end of two years; immediately after the first election the names of these nine members shall be chosen by lot by the Chairman of the Committee;

(b) For the filling of casual vacancies, the State Party whose expert has ceased to function as a member of the Committee shall appoint another expert from among its nationals, subject to the approval of the Committee.

6. States Parties shall be responsible for the expenses of the members of the Committee while they are in performance of Committee duties.

Article 9

1. States Parties undertake to submit to the Secretary-General of the United Nations, for consideration by the Committee, a report on the legislative, judicial, administrative or other measures which they have adopted and which give effect to the provisions of this Convention:

(a) within one year after the entry into force of the Convention for the State concerned; and

(b) thereafter every two years and whenever the Committee so requests. The Committee may request further information from the States Parties.

2. The Committee shall report annually, through the Secretary General, to the General Assembly of the United Nations on its activities and may make suggestions and general recommendations based on the examination of the reports and information received from the States Parties. Such suggestions and general recommendations shall be reported to the General Assembly together with comments, if any, from States Parties.

Article 10

1. The Committee shall adopt its own rules of procedure.

2. The Committee shall elect its officers for a term of two years.

3. The secretariat of the Committee shall be provided by the Secretary General of the United Nations.

4. The meetings of the Committee shall normally be held at United Nations Headquarters.

Article 11

1. If a State Party considers that another State Party is not giving effect to the provisions of this Convention, it may bring the matter to the attention of the Committee. The Committee shall then transmit the communication to the State Party concerned. Within three months, the receiving State shall submit to the Committee written explanations or statements clarifying the matter and the remedy, if any, that may have been taken by that State.

2. If the matter is not adjusted to the satisfaction of both parties, either by bilateral negotiations or by any other procedure open to them, within six months after the receipt by the receiving State of the initial communication, either State shall have the right to refer the matter again to the Committee by notifying the Committee and also the other State.

3. The Committee shall deal with a matter referred to it in accordance with paragraph 2 of this article after it has ascertained that all available domestic remedies have been invoked and exhausted in the case, in conformity with the generally recognized principles of international law. This shall not be the rule where the application of the remedies is unreasonably prolonged.

4. In any matter referred to it, the Committee may call upon the States Parties concerned to supply any other relevant information.

5. When any matter arising out of this article is being considered by the Committee, the States Parties concerned shall be entitled to send a representative to take part in the proceedings of the Committee, without voting rights, while the matter is under consideration.

Article 12

1. (a) After the Committee has obtained and collated all the information it deems necessary, the Chairman shall appoint an ad hoc Conciliation

Commission (hereinafter referred to as the Commission) comprising five persons who may or may not be members of the Committee. The members of the Commission shall be appointed with the unanimous consent of the parties to the dispute, and its good offices shall be made available to the States concerned with a view to an amicable solution of the matter on the basis of respect for this Convention;

(b) If the States parties to the dispute fail to reach agreement within three months on all or part of the composition of the Commission, the members of the Commission not agreed upon by the States parties to the dispute shall be elected by secret ballot by a two-thirds majority vote of the Committee from among its own members.

2. The members of the Commission shall serve in their personal capacity. They shall not be nationals of the States parties to the dispute or of a State not Party to this Convention.

3. The Commission shall elect its own Chairman and adopt its own rules of procedure.

4. The meetings of the Commission shall normally be held at United Nations Headquarters or at any other convenient place as determined by the Commission.

5. The secretariat provided in accordance with article 10, paragraph 3, of this Convention shall also service the Commission whenever a dispute among States Parties brings the Commission into being.

6. The States parties to the dispute shall share equally all the expenses of the members of the Commission in accordance with estimates to be provided by the Secretary-General of the United Nations.

7. The Secretary-General shall be empowered to pay the expenses of the members of the Commission, if necessary, before reimbursement by the States parties to the dispute in accordance with paragraph 6 of this article.

8. The information obtained and collated by the Committee shall be made available to the Commission, and the Commission may call upon the States concerned to supply any other relevant information.

Article 13

1. When the Commission has fully considered the matter, it shall prepare and submit to the Chairman of the Committee a report embodying its findings on all questions of fact relevant to the issue between the parties and containing such recommendations as it may think proper for the amicable solution of the dispute.

2. The Chairman of the Committee shall communicate the report of the Commission to each of the States parties to the dispute. These States shall, within three months, inform the Chairman of the Committee whether or not they accept the recommendations contained in the report of the Commission.

3. After the period provided for in paragraph 2 of this article, the Chairman of the Committee shall communicate the report of the Commission and the declarations of the States Parties concerned to the other States Parties to this Convention.

Article 14

1. A State Party may at any time declare that it recognizes the competence of the Committee to receive and consider communications from individuals or groups of individuals within its jurisdiction claiming to be victims of a violation by that State Party of any of the rights set forth in this Convention. No communication shall be received by the Committee if it concerns a State Party which has not made such a declaration.

2. Any State Party which makes a declaration as provided for in paragraph 1 of this article may establish or indicate a body within its national legal order which shall be competent to receive and consider petitions from individuals and groups of individuals within its jurisdiction who claim to be victims of a violation of any of the rights set forth in this Convention and who have exhausted other available local remedies.

3. A declaration made in accordance with paragraph 1 of this article and the name of any body established or indicated in accordance with paragraph 2 of this article shall be deposited by the State Party concerned with the Secretary-General of the United Nations, who shall transmit copies thereof to the other States Parties. A declaration may be withdrawn at any time by notification to the Secretary-General, but such a withdrawal shall not affect communications pending before the Committee.

4. A register of petitions shall be kept by the body established or indicated in accordance with paragraph 2 of this article, and certified copies of the register shall be filed annually through appropriate channels with the Secretary-General on the understanding that the contents shall not be publicly disclosed.

5. In the event of failure to obtain satisfaction from the body established or indicated in accordance with paragraph 2 of this article, the petitioner shall have the right to communicate the matter to the Committee within six months.

6. (a) The Committee shall confidentially bring any communication referred to it to the attention of the State Party alleged to be violating any provision of this Convention, but the identity of the individual or groups of individuals concerned shall not be revealed without his or their express consent. The Committee shall not receive anonymous communications;

(b) Within three months, the receiving State shall submit to the Committee written explanations or statements clarifying the matter and the remedy, if any, that may have been taken by that State.

7. (a) The Committee shall consider communications in the light of all information made available to it by the State Party concerned and by the petitioner. The Committee shall not consider any communication from a petitioner unless it has ascertained that the petitioner has exhausted all available domestic remedies. However, this shall not be the rule where the application of the remedies is unreasonably prolonged;

(b) The Committee shall forward its suggestions and recommendations, if any, to the State Party concerned and to the petitioner.

8. The Committee shall include in its annual report a summary of such com-

munications and, where appropriate, a summary of the explanations and statements of the States Parties concerned and of its own suggestions and recommendations.

9. The Committee shall be competent to exercise the functions provided for in this article only when at least ten States Parties to this Convention are bound by declarations in accordance with paragraph 1 of this article.

Article 15

1. Pending the achievement of the objectives of the Declaration on the Granting of Independence to Colonial Countries and Peoples, contained in General Assembly resolution 1514 (XV) of 14 December 1960, the provisions of this Convention shall in no way limit the right of petition granted to these peoples by other international instruments or by the United Nations and its specialized agencies.

2. (a) The Committee established under article 8, paragraph 1, of this Convention shall receive copies of the petitions from, and submit expressions of opinion and recommendations on these petitions to, the bodies of the United Nations which deal with matters directly related to the principles and objectives of this Convention in their consideration of petitions from the inhabitants of Trust and Non-Self-Governing Territories and all other territories to which General Assembly resolution 1514 (XV) applies, relating to matters covered by this Convention which are before these bodies;

(b) The Committee shall receive from the competent bodies of the United Nations copies of the reports concerning the legislative, judicial, administrative or other measures directly related to the principles and objectives of this Convention applied by the administering Powers within the Territories mentioned in subparagraph (a) of this paragraph, and shall express opinions and make recommendations to these bodies.

3. The Committee shall include in its report to the General Assembly a summary of the petitions and reports it has received from United Nations bodies, and the expressions of opinion and recommendations of the Committee relating to the said petitions and reports.

4. The Committee shall request from the Secretary-General of the United Nations all information relevant to the objectives of this Convention and available to him regarding the Territories mentioned in paragraph 2 (a) of this article.

Article 16

The provisions of this Convention concerning the settlement of disputes or complaints shall be applied without prejudice to other procedures for settling disputes or complaints in the field of discrimination laid down in the constituent instruments of, or conventions adopted by, the United Nations and its specialized agencies, and shall not prevent the States Parties from having recourse to other procedures for settling a dispute in accordance with general or special international agreements in force between them.

Part III

Article 17

1. This Convention is open for signature by any State Member of the United Nations or member of any of its specialized agencies, by any State Party to the Statute of the International Court of Justice, and by any other State which has been invited by the General Assembly of the United Nations to become a Party to this Convention.

2. This Convention is subject to ratification. Instruments of ratification shall be deposited with the Secretary-General of the United Nations.

Article 18

1. This Convention shall be open to accession by any State referred to in article 17, paragraph 1, of the Convention.

2. Accession shall be effected by the deposit of an instrument of accession with the Secretary-General of the United Nations.

Article 19

1. This Convention shall enter into force on the thirtieth day after the date of the deposit with the Secretary-General of the United Nations of the twenty-seventh instrument of ratification or instrument of accession.

2. For each State ratifying this Convention or acceding to it after the deposit of the twenty-seventh instrument of ratification or instrument of accession, the Convention shall enter into force on the thirtieth day after the date of the deposit of its own instrument of ratification or instrument of accession.

Article 20

1. The Secretary-General of the United Nations shall receive and circulate to all States which are or may become Parties to this Convention reservations made by States at the time of ratification or accession. Any State which objects to the reservation shall, within a period of ninety days from the date of the said communication, notify the Secretary-General that it does not accept it.

2. A reservation incompatible with the object and purpose of this Convention shall not be permitted, nor shall a reservation the effect of which would inhibit the operation of any of the bodies established by this Convention be allowed. A reservation shall be considered incompatible or inhibitive if at least two thirds of the States Parties to this Convention object to it.

3. Reservations may be withdrawn at any time by notification to this effect addressed to the Secretary-General. Such notification shall take effect on the date on which it is received.

Article 21

A State Party may denounce this Convention by written notification to the Secretary-General of the United Nations. Denunciation shall take effect one year after the date of receipt of the notification by the Secretary General.

Article 22

Any dispute between two or more States Parties with respect to the interpretation or application of this Convention, which is not settled by negotiation or by the procedures expressly provided for in this Convention, shall, at the request of any of the parties to the dispute, be referred to the International Court of Justice for decision, unless the disputants agree to another mode of settlement.

Article 23

1. A request for the revision of this Convention may be made at any time by any State Party by means of a notification in writing addressed to the Secretary-General of the United Nations.

2. The General Assembly of the United Nations shall decide upon the steps, if any, to be taken in respect of such a request.

Article 24

The Secretary-General of the United Nations shall inform all States referred to in article 17, paragraph 1, of this Convention of the following particulars:
   (a) Signatures, ratifications and accessions under articles 17 and 18;
   (b) The date of entry into force of this Convention under article 19;
   (c) Communications and declarations received under articles 14, 20 and 23;
   (d) Denunciations under article 21.

Article 25

1. This Convention, of which the Chinese, English, French, Russian and Spanish texts are equally authentic, shall be deposited in the archives of the United Nations.

2. The Secretary-General of the United Nations shall transmit certified copies of this Convention to all States belonging to any of the categories mentioned in article 17, paragraph 1, of the Convention.

IN FAITH WHEREOF the undersigned, being duly authorized thereto by their respective Governments, have signed the present Convention, opened for signature at New York, on the seventh day of March, one thousand nine hundred and sixty-six.

5.4
International Covenant on Civil and Political Rights (ICCPR) (1966)

This is the first of two treaties to flow directly from the Universal Declaration of Human Rights. On the covenant in general, see Sarah Joseph, Jenny Schultz, and Melissa Castan, The International Covenant on Civil and Political Rights: Cases, Materials, and Commentary, *2nd ed. (Oxford: Oxford University Press, 2005).*

The US ratified the ICCPR in 1992, but with a number of reservations, understandings, and declarations. The report of the US Senate Committee on Foreign Relations on the covenant is reprinted in International Legal Materials *31 (1992): 645. For analysis of the US ratification, see John Henry Stone, "The International Covenant on Civil and Political Rights and the United States Reservations: The American Conception of International Human Rights,"* U.C. Davis Journal of International Law and Policy *7 (2001): 1–39. The texts of all declarations and reservations are found at www.ohchr.org/english/countries/ratification/4_1.htm.*

The States Parties to the present Covenant,

Considering that, in accordance with the principles proclaimed in the Charter of the United Nations, recognition of the inherent dignity and of the equal and inalienable rights of all members of the human family is the foundation of freedom, justice and peace in the world,

Recognizing that these rights derive from the inherent dignity of the human person,

Recognizing that, in accordance with the Universal Declaration of Human Rights, the ideal of free human beings enjoying civil and political freedom and freedom from fear and want can only be achieved if conditions are created whereby everyone may enjoy his civil and political rights, as well as his economic, social and cultural rights,

Considering the obligation of States under the Charter of the United Nations to promote universal respect for, and observance of, human rights and freedoms,

Realizing that the individual, having duties to other individuals and to the community to which he belongs, is under a responsibility to strive for the promotion and observance of the rights recognized in the present Covenant,

Agree upon the following articles:

Part I

Article 1

1. All peoples have the right of self-determination. By virtue of that right they freely determine their political status and freely pursue their economic, social and cultural development.

2. All peoples may, for their own ends, freely dispose of their natural wealth and resources without prejudice to any obligations arising out of international economic co-operation, based upon the principle of mutual benefit, and international law. In no case may a people be deprived of its own means of subsistence.

3. The States Parties to the present Covenant, including those having responsibility for the administration of Non-Self-Governing and Trust Territories, shall promote the realization of the right of self-determination, and shall respect that right, in conformity with the provisions of the Charter of the United Nations.

Part II

Article 2

1. Each State Party to the present Covenant undertakes to respect and to ensure to all individuals within its territory and subject to its jurisdiction the rights recognized in the present Covenant, without distinction of any kind, such as race, colour, sex, language, religion, political or other opinion, national or social origin, property, birth or other status.

2. Where not already provided for by existing legislative or other measures, each State Party to the present Covenant undertakes to take the necessary steps, in accordance with its constitutional processes and with the provisions of the present Covenant, to adopt such laws or other measures as may be necessary to give effect to the rights recognized in the present Covenant.

3. Each State Party to the present Covenant undertakes:

(a) To ensure that any person whose rights or freedoms as herein recognized are violated shall have an effective remedy, notwithstanding that the violation has been committed by persons acting in an official capacity;

(b) To ensure that any person claiming such a remedy shall have his right thereto determined by competent judicial, administrative or legislative authorities, or by any other competent authority provided for by the legal system of the State, and to develop the possibilities of judicial remedy;

(c) To ensure that the competent authorities shall enforce such remedies when granted.

Article 3

The States Parties to the present Covenant undertake to ensure the equal right of men and women to the enjoyment of all civil and political rights set forth in the present Covenant.

Article 4

1. In time of public emergency which threatens the life of the nation and the existence of which is officially proclaimed, the States Parties to the present Covenant may take measures derogating from their obligations under the present Covenant to the extent strictly required by the exigencies of the situation, provided that such measures are not inconsistent with their other obligations under international law and do not involve discrimination solely on the ground of race, colour, sex, language, religion or social origin.

2. No derogation from articles 6, 7, 8 (paragraphs 1 and 2), 11, 15, 16 and 18 may be made under this provision.

3. Any State Party to the present Covenant availing itself of the right of derogation shall immediately inform the other States Parties to the present Covenant, through the intermediary of the Secretary-General of the United Nations, of the provisions from which it has derogated and of the reasons by which it was actuated. A further communication shall be made, through the same intermediary, on the date on which it terminates such derogation.

Article 5

1. Nothing in the present Covenant may be interpreted as implying for any State, group or person any right to engage in any activity or perform any act aimed at the destruction of any of the rights and freedoms recognized herein or at their limitation to a greater extent than is provided for in the present Covenant.

2. There shall be no restriction upon or derogation from any of the fundamental human rights recognized or existing in any State Party to the present Covenant pursuant to law, conventions, regulations or custom on the pretext that the present Covenant does not recognize such rights or that it recognizes them to a lesser extent.

Part III

Article 6

1. Every human being has the inherent right to life. This right shall be protected by law. No one shall be arbitrarily deprived of his life.

2. In countries which have not abolished the death penalty, sentence of death may be imposed only for the most serious crimes in accordance with the law in force at the time of the commission of the crime and not contrary to the

provisions of the present Covenant and to the Convention on the Prevention and Punishment of the Crime of Genocide. This penalty can only be carried out pursuant to a final judgement rendered by a competent court.

3. When deprivation of life constitutes the crime of genocide, it is understood that nothing in this article shall authorize any State Party to the present Covenant to derogate in any way from any obligation assumed under the provisions of the Convention on the Prevention and Punishment of the Crime of Genocide.

4. Anyone sentenced to death shall have the right to seek pardon or commutation of the sentence. Amnesty, pardon or commutation of the sentence of death may be granted in all cases.

5. Sentence of death shall not be imposed for crimes committed by persons below eighteen years of age and shall not be carried out on pregnant women.

6. Nothing in this article shall be invoked to delay or to prevent the abolition of capital punishment by any State Party to the present Covenant.

Article 7
No one shall be subjected to torture or to cruel, inhuman or degrading treatment or punishment. In particular, no one shall be subjected without his free consent to medical or scientific experimentation.

Article 8
1. No one shall be held in slavery; slavery and the slave-trade in all their forms shall be prohibited.

2. No one shall be held in servitude.

3. (a) No one shall be required to perform forced or compulsory labour;

(b) Paragraph 3 (a) shall not be held to preclude, in countries where imprisonment with hard labour may be imposed as a punishment for a crime, the performance of hard labour in pursuance of a sentence to such punishment by a competent court;

(c) For the purpose of this paragraph the term "forced or compulsory labour" shall not include: (i) Any work or service, not referred to in subparagraph (b), normally required of a person who is under detention in consequence of a lawful order of a court, or of a person during conditional release from such detention; (ii) Any service of a military character and, in countries where conscientious objection is recognized, any national service required by law of conscientious objectors; (iii) Any service exacted in cases of emergency or calamity threatening the life or well-being of the community; (iv) Any work or service which forms part of normal civil obligations.

Article 9
1. Everyone has the right to liberty and security of person. No one shall be subjected to arbitrary arrest or detention. No one shall be deprived of his liberty except on such grounds and in accordance with such procedure as are established by law.

2. Anyone who is arrested shall be informed, at the time of arrest, of the reasons for his arrest and shall be promptly informed of any charges against him.

3. Anyone arrested or detained on a criminal charge shall be brought promptly before a judge or other officer authorized by law to exercise judicial power and shall be entitled to trial within a reasonable time or to release. It shall not be the general rule that persons awaiting trial shall be detained in custody, but release may be subject to guarantees to appear for trial, at any other stage of the judicial proceedings, and, should occasion arise, for execution of the judgement.

4. Anyone who is deprived of his liberty by arrest or detention shall be entitled to take proceedings before a court, in order that that court may decide without delay on the lawfulness of his detention and order his release if the detention is not lawful.

5. Anyone who has been the victim of unlawful arrest or detention shall have an enforceable right to compensation.

Article 10

1. All persons deprived of their liberty shall be treated with humanity and with respect for the inherent dignity of the human person.

2. (a) Accused persons shall, save in exceptional circumstances, be segregated from convicted persons and shall be subject to separate treatment appropriate to their status as unconvicted persons;

(b) Accused juvenile persons shall be separated from adults and brought as speedily as possible for adjudication.

3. The penitentiary system shall comprise treatment of prisoners the essential aim of which shall be their reformation and social rehabilitation. Juvenile offenders shall be segregated from adults and be accorded treatment appropriate to their age and legal status.

Article 11

No one shall be imprisoned merely on the ground of inability to fulfil a contractual obligation.

Article 12

1. Everyone lawfully within the territory of a State shall, within that territory, have the right to liberty of movement and freedom to choose his residence.

2. Everyone shall be free to leave any country, including his own.

3. The above-mentioned rights shall not be subject to any restrictions except those which are provided by law, are necessary to protect national security, public order (ordre public), public health or morals or the rights and freedoms of others, and are consistent with the other rights recognized in the present Covenant.

4. No one shall be arbitrarily deprived of the right to enter his own country.

Article 13

An alien lawfully in the territory of a State Party to the present Covenant may be expelled therefrom only in pursuance of a decision reached in accordance with law and shall, except where compelling reasons of national security otherwise require, be allowed to submit the reasons against his expulsion and to have his case reviewed by, and be represented for the purpose before, the competent authority or a person or persons especially designated by the competent authority.

Article 14

1. All persons shall be equal before the courts and tribunals. In the determination of any criminal charge against him, or of his rights and obligations in a suit at law, everyone shall be entitled to a fair and public hearing by a competent, independent and impartial tribunal established by law. The press and the public may be excluded from all or part of a trial for reasons of morals, public order (ordre public) or national security in a democratic society, or when the interest of the private lives of the parties so requires, or to the extent strictly necessary in the opinion of the court in special circumstances where publicity would prejudice the interests of justice; but any judgement rendered in a criminal case or in a suit at law shall be made public except where the interest of juvenile persons otherwise requires or the proceedings concern matrimonial disputes or the guardianship of children.

2. Everyone charged with a criminal offence shall have the right to be presumed innocent until proved guilty according to law.

3. In the determination of any criminal charge against him, everyone shall be entitled to the following minimum guarantees, in full equality:

(a) To be informed promptly and in detail in a language which he understands of the nature and cause of the charge against him;

(b) To have adequate time and facilities for the preparation of his defence and to communicate with counsel of his own choosing;

(c) To be tried without undue delay;

(d) To be tried in his presence, and to defend himself in person or through legal assistance of his own choosing; to be informed, if he does not have legal assistance, of this right; and to have legal assistance assigned to him, in any case where the interests of justice so require, and without payment by him in any such case if he does not have sufficient means to pay for it;

(e) To examine, or have examined, the witnesses against him and to obtain the attendance and examination of witnesses on his behalf under the same conditions as witnesses against him;

(f) To have the free assistance of an interpreter if he cannot understand or speak the language used in court;

(g) Not to be compelled to testify against himself or to confess guilt.

4. In the case of juvenile persons, the procedure shall be such as will take account of their age and the desirability of promoting their rehabilitation.

5. Everyone convicted of a crime shall have the right to his conviction and sentence being reviewed by a higher tribunal according to law.

6. When a person has by a final decision been convicted of a criminal offence and when subsequently his conviction has been reversed or he has been pardoned on the ground that a new or newly discovered fact shows conclusively that there has been a miscarriage of justice, the person who has suffered punishment as a result of such conviction shall be compensated according to law, unless it is proved that the non-disclosure of the unknown fact in time is wholly or partly attributable to him.

7. No one shall be liable to be tried or punished again for an offence for which he has already been finally convicted or acquitted in accordance with the law and penal procedure of each country.

Article 15

1. No one shall be held guilty of any criminal offence on account of any act or omission which did not constitute a criminal offence, under national or international law, at the time when it was committed. Nor shall a heavier penalty be imposed than the one that was applicable at the time when the criminal offence was committed. If, subsequent to the commission of the offence, provision is made by law for the imposition of the lighter penalty, the offender shall benefit thereby.

2. Nothing in this article shall prejudice the trial and punishment of any person for any act or omission which, at the time when it was committed, was criminal according to the general principles of law recognized by the community of nations.

Article 16

Everyone shall have the right to recognition everywhere as a person before the law.

Article 17

1. No one shall be subjected to arbitrary or unlawful interference with his privacy, family, home or correspondence, nor to unlawful attacks on his honour and reputation.

2. Everyone has the right to the protection of the law against such interference or attacks.

Article 18

1. Everyone shall have the right to freedom of thought, conscience and religion. This right shall include freedom to have or to adopt a religion or belief of his choice, and freedom, either individually or in community with others and in public or private, to manifest his religion or belief in worship, observance, practice and teaching.

2. No one shall be subject to coercion which would impair his freedom to have or to adopt a religion or belief of his choice.

3. Freedom to manifest one's religion or beliefs may be subject only to such limitations as are prescribed by law and are necessary to protect public safety, order, health, or morals or the fundamental rights and freedoms of others.

4. The States Parties to the present Covenant undertake to have respect for the liberty of parents and, when applicable, legal guardians to ensure the religious and moral education of their children in conformity with their own convictions.

Article 19

1. Everyone shall have the right to hold opinions without interference.

2. Everyone shall have the right to freedom of expression; this right shall include freedom to seek, receive and impart information and ideas of all kinds, regardless of frontiers, either orally, in writing or in print, in the form of art, or through any other media of his choice.

3. The exercise of the rights provided for in paragraph 2 of this article carries with it special duties and responsibilities. It may therefore be subject to certain restrictions, but these shall only be such as are provided by law and are necessary:

(a) For respect of the rights or reputations of others;

(b) For the protection of national security or of public order (ordre public), or of public health or morals.

Article 20

1. Any propaganda for war shall be prohibited by law.

2. Any advocacy of national, racial or religious hatred that constitutes incitement to discrimination, hostility or violence shall be prohibited by law.

Article 21

The right of peaceful assembly shall be recognized. No restrictions may be placed on the exercise of this right other than those imposed in conformity with the law and which are necessary in a democratic society in the interests of national security or public safety, public order (ordre public), the protection of public health or morals or the protection of the rights and freedoms of others.

Article 22

1. Everyone shall have the right to freedom of association with others, including the right to form and join trade unions for the protection of his interests.

2. No restrictions may be placed on the exercise of this right other than those which are prescribed by law and which are necessary in a democratic society in the interests of national security or public safety, public order (ordre public), the protection of public health or morals or the protection of the rights and freedoms of others. This article shall not prevent the imposition of lawful restrictions on members of the armed forces and of the police in their exercise of this right.

3. Nothing in this article shall authorize States Parties to the International Labour Organisation Convention of 1948 concerning Freedom of Association and Protection of the Right to Organize to take legislative measures which would prejudice, or to apply the law in such a manner as to prejudice, the guarantees provided for in that Convention.

Article 23

1. The family is the natural and fundamental group unit of society and is entitled to protection by society and the State.

2. The right of men and women of marriageable age to marry and to found a family shall be recognized.

3. No marriage shall be entered into without the free and full consent of the intending spouses.

4. States Parties to the present Covenant shall take appropriate steps to ensure equality of rights and responsibilities of spouses as to marriage, during marriage and at its dissolution. In the case of dissolution, provision shall be made for the necessary protection of any children.

Article 24

1. Every child shall have, without any discrimination as to race, colour, sex, language, religion, national or social origin, property or birth, the right to such measures of protection as are required by his status as a minor, on the part of his family, society and the State.

2. Every child shall be registered immediately after birth and shall have a name.

3. Every child has the right to acquire a nationality.

Article 25

Every citizen shall have the right and the opportunity, without any of the distinctions mentioned in article 2 and without unreasonable restrictions:

(a) To take part in the conduct of public affairs, directly or through freely chosen representatives;

(b) To vote and to be elected at genuine periodic elections which shall be by universal and equal suffrage and shall be held by secret ballot, guaranteeing the free expression of the will of the electors;

(c) To have access, on general terms of equality, to public service in his country.

Article 26

All persons are equal before the law and are entitled without any discrimination to the equal protection of the law. In this respect, the law shall prohibit any discrimination and guarantee to all persons equal and effective protection against discrimination on any ground such as race, colour, sex, language, religion, political or other opinion, national or social origin, property, birth or other status.

Article 27

In those States in which ethnic, religious or linguistic minorities exist, persons belonging to such minorities shall not be denied the right, in community with the other members of their group, to enjoy their own culture, to profess and practise their own religion, or to use their own language.

Part IV

Article 28

1. There shall be established a Human Rights Committee (hereafter referred to in the present Covenant as the Committee). It shall consist of eighteen members and shall carry out the functions hereinafter provided.

2. The Committee shall be composed of nationals of the States Parties to the present Covenant who shall be persons of high moral character and recognized competence in the field of human rights, consideration being given to the usefulness of the participation of some persons having legal experience.

3. The members of the Committee shall be elected and shall serve in their personal capacity.

Article 29

1. The members of the Committee shall be elected by secret ballot from a list of persons possessing the qualifications prescribed in article 28 and nominated for the purpose by the States Parties to the present Covenant.

2. Each State Party to the present Covenant may nominate not more than two persons. These persons shall be nationals of the nominating State.

3. A person shall be eligible for renomination.

Article 30

1. The initial election shall be held no later than six months after the date of the entry into force of the present Covenant.

2. At least four months before the date of each election to the Committee, other than an election to fill a vacancy declared in accordance with article 34, the Secretary-General of the United Nations shall address a written invitation to the States Parties to the present Covenant to submit their nominations for membership of the Committee within three months.

3. The Secretary-General of the United Nations shall prepare a list in alphabetical order of all the persons thus nominated, with an indication of the States Parties which have nominated them, and shall submit it to the States Parties to the present Covenant no later than one month before the date of each election.

4. Elections of the members of the Committee shall be held at a meeting of the States Parties to the present Covenant convened by the Secretary General of the United Nations at the Headquarters of the United Nations. At that meeting, for which two thirds of the States Parties to the present Covenant shall constitute a quorum, the persons elected to the Committee shall be those nomi-

nees who obtain the largest number of votes and an absolute majority of the votes of the representatives of States Parties present and voting.

Article 31

1. The Committee may not include more than one national of the same State.

2. In the election of the Committee, consideration shall be given to equitable geographical distribution of membership and to the representation of the different forms of civilization and of the principal legal systems.

Article 32

1. The members of the Committee shall be elected for a term of four years. They shall be eligible for re-election if renominated. However, the terms of nine of the members elected at the first election shall expire at the end of two years; immediately after the first election, the names of these nine members shall be chosen by lot by the Chairman of the meeting referred to in article 30, paragraph 4.

2. Elections at the expiry of office shall be held in accordance with the preceding articles of this part of the present Covenant.

Article 33

1. If, in the unanimous opinion of the other members, a member of the Committee has ceased to carry out his functions for any cause other than absence of a temporary character, the Chairman of the Committee shall notify the Secretary-General of the United Nations, who shall then declare the seat of that member to be vacant.

2. In the event of the death or the resignation of a member of the Committee, the Chairman shall immediately notify the Secretary-General of the United Nations, who shall declare the seat vacant from the date of death or the date on which the resignation takes effect.

Article 34

1. When a vacancy is declared in accordance with article 33 and if the term of office of the member to be replaced does not expire within six months of the declaration of the vacancy, the Secretary-General of the United Nations shall notify each of the States Parties to the present Covenant, which may within two months submit nominations in accordance with article 29 for the purpose of filling the vacancy.

2. The Secretary-General of the United Nations shall prepare a list in alphabetical order of the persons thus nominated and shall submit it to the States Parties to the present Covenant. The election to fill the vacancy shall then take place in accordance with the relevant provisions of this part of the present Covenant.

3. A member of the Committee elected to fill a vacancy declared in accordance with article 33 shall hold office for the remainder of the term of the

member who vacated the seat on the Committee under the provisions of that article.

Article 35

The members of the Committee shall, with the approval of the General Assembly of the United Nations, receive emoluments from United Nations resources on such terms and conditions as the General Assembly may decide, having regard to the importance of the Committee's responsibilities.

Article 36

The Secretary-General of the United Nations shall provide the necessary staff and facilities for the effective performance of the functions of the Committee under the present Covenant.

Article 37

1. The Secretary-General of the United Nations shall convene the initial meeting of the Committee at the Headquarters of the United Nations.

2. After its initial meeting, the Committee shall meet at such times as shall be provided in its rules of procedure.

3. The Committee shall normally meet at the Headquarters of the United Nations or at the United Nations Office at Geneva.

Article 38

Every member of the Committee shall, before taking up his duties, make a solemn declaration in open committee that he will perform his functions impartially and conscientiously.

Article 39

1. The Committee shall elect its officers for a term of two years. They may be re-elected.

2. The Committee shall establish its own rules of procedure, but these rules shall provide, inter alia, that:

(a) Twelve members shall constitute a quorum;

(b) Decisions of the Committee shall be made by a majority vote of the members present.

Article 40

1. The States Parties to the present Covenant undertake to submit reports on the measures they have adopted which give effect to the rights recognized herein and on the progress made in the enjoyment of those rights:

(a) Within one year of the entry into force of the present Covenant for the States Parties concerned;

(b) Thereafter whenever the Committee so requests.

2. All reports shall be submitted to the Secretary-General of the United Nations, who shall transmit them to the Committee for consideration. Reports

shall indicate the factors and difficulties, if any, affecting the implementation of the present Covenant.

3. The Secretary-General of the United Nations may, after consultation with the Committee, transmit to the specialized agencies concerned copies of such parts of the reports as may fall within their field of competence.

4. The Committee shall study the reports submitted by the States Parties to the present Covenant. It shall transmit its reports, and such general comments as it may consider appropriate, to the States Parties. The Committee may also transmit to the Economic and Social Council these comments along with the copies of the reports it has received from States Parties to the present Covenant.

5. The States Parties to the present Covenant may submit to the Committee observations on any comments that may be made in accordance with paragraph 4 of this article.

Article 41

1. A State Party to the present Covenant may at any time declare under this article that it recognizes the competence of the Committee to receive and consider communications to the effect that a State Party claims that another State Party is not fulfilling its obligations under the present Covenant. Communications under this article may be received and considered only if submitted by a State Party which has made a declaration recognizing in regard to itself the competence of the Committee. No communication shall be received by the Committee if it concerns a State Party which has not made such a declaration. Communications received under this article shall be dealt with in accordance with the following procedure:

(a) If a State Party to the present Covenant considers that another State Party is not giving effect to the provisions of the present Covenant, it may, by written communication, bring the matter to the attention of that State Party. Within three months after the receipt of the communication the receiving State shall afford the State which sent the communication an explanation, or any other statement in writing clarifying the matter which should include, to the extent possible and pertinent, reference to domestic procedures and remedies taken, pending, or available in the matter;

(b) If the matter is not adjusted to the satisfaction of both States Parties concerned within six months after the receipt by the receiving State of the initial communication, either State shall have the right to refer the matter to the Committee, by notice given to the Committee and to the other State;

(c) The Committee shall deal with a matter referred to it only after it has ascertained that all available domestic remedies have been invoked and exhausted in the matter, in conformity with the generally recognized principles of international law. This shall not be the rule where the application of the remedies is unreasonably prolonged;

(d) The Committee shall hold closed meetings when examining communications under this article;

(e) Subject to the provisions of subparagraph (c), the Committee shall make available its good offices to the States Parties concerned with a view to a friendly solution of the matter on the basis of respect for human rights and fundamental freedoms as recognized in the present Covenant;

(f) In any matter referred to it, the Committee may call upon the States Parties concerned, referred to in subparagraph (b), to supply any relevant information;

(g) The States Parties concerned, referred to in subparagraph (b), shall have the right to be represented when the matter is being considered in the Committee and to make submissions orally and/or in writing;

(h) The Committee shall, within twelve months after the date of receipt of notice under subparagraph (b), submit a report: (i) If a solution within the terms of subparagraph (e) is reached, the Committee shall confine its report to a brief statement of the facts and of the solution reached; (ii) If a solution within the terms of subparagraph (e) is not reached, the Committee shall confine its report to a brief statement of the facts; the written submissions and record of the oral submissions made by the States Parties concerned shall be attached to the report.

In every matter, the report shall be communicated to the States Parties concerned.

2. The provisions of this article shall come into force when ten States Parties to the present Covenant have made declarations under paragraph 1 of this article. Such declarations shall be deposited by the States Parties with the Secretary-General of the United Nations, who shall transmit copies thereof to the other States Parties. A declaration may be withdrawn at any time by notification to the Secretary-General. Such a withdrawal shall not prejudice the consideration of any matter which is the subject of a communication already transmitted under this article; no further communication by any State Party shall be received after the notification of withdrawal of the declaration has been received by the Secretary-General, unless the State Party concerned has made a new declaration.

Article 42

1. (a) If a matter referred to the Committee in accordance with article 41 is not resolved to the satisfaction of the States Parties concerned, the Committee may, with the prior consent of the States Parties concerned, appoint an ad hoc Conciliation Commission (hereinafter referred to as the Commission). The good offices of the Commission shall be made available to the States Parties concerned with a view to an amicable solution of the matter on the basis of respect for the present Covenant;

(b) The Commission shall consist of five persons acceptable to the States Parties concerned. If the States Parties concerned fail to reach agreement within three months on all or part of the composition of the Commission, the members of the Commission concerning whom no agreement has been reached shall be elected by secret ballot by a two-thirds majority vote of the Committee from among its members.

2. The members of the Commission shall serve in their personal capacity. They shall not be nationals of the States Parties concerned, or of a State not Party to the present Covenant, or of a State Party which has not made a declaration under article 41.

3. The Commission shall elect its own Chairman and adopt its own rules of procedure.

4. The meetings of the Commission shall normally be held at the Headquarters of the United Nations or at the United Nations Office at Geneva. However, they may be held at such other convenient places as the Commission may determine in consultation with the Secretary-General of the United Nations and the States Parties concerned.

5. The secretariat provided in accordance with article 36 shall also service the commissions appointed under this article.

6. The information received and collated by the Committee shall be made available to the Commission and the Commission may call upon the States Parties concerned to supply any other relevant information.

7. When the Commission has fully considered the matter, but in any event not later than twelve months after having been seized of the matter, it shall submit to the Chairman of the Committee a report for communication to the States Parties concerned:

(a) If the Commission is unable to complete its consideration of the matter within twelve months, it shall confine its report to a brief statement of the status of its consideration of the matter;

(b) If an amicable solution to the matter on tie basis of respect for human rights as recognized in the present Covenant is reached, the Commission shall confine its report to a brief statement of the facts and of the solution reached;

(c) If a solution within the terms of subparagraph (b) is not reached, the Commission's report shall embody its findings on all questions of fact relevant to the issues between the States Parties concerned, and its views on the possibilities of an amicable solution of the matter. This report shall also contain the written submissions and a record of the oral submissions made by the States Parties concerned;

(d) If the Commission's report is submitted under subparagraph (c), the States Parties concerned shall, within three months of the receipt of the report, notify the Chairman of the Committee whether or not they accept the contents of the report of the Commission.

8. The provisions of this article are without prejudice to the responsibilities of the Committee under article 41.

9. The States Parties concerned shall share equally all the expenses of the members of the Commission in accordance with estimates to be provided by the Secretary-General of the United Nations.

10. The Secretary-General of the United Nations shall be empowered to pay

the expenses of the members of the Commission, if necessary, before reimbursement by the States Parties concerned, in accordance with paragraph 9 of this article.

Article 43
The members of the Committee, and of the ad hoc conciliation commissions which may be appointed under article 42, shall be entitled to the facilities, privileges and immunities of experts on mission for the United Nations as laid down in the relevant sections of the Convention on the Privileges and Immunities of the United Nations.

Article 44
The provisions for the implementation of the present Covenant shall apply without prejudice to the procedures prescribed in the field of human rights by or under the constituent instruments and the conventions of the United Nations and of the specialized agencies and shall not prevent the States Parties to the present Covenant from having recourse to other procedures for settling a dispute in accordance with general or special international agreements in force between them.

Article 45
The Committee shall submit to the General Assembly of the United Nations, through the Economic and Social Council, an annual report on its activities.

Part V

Article 46
Nothing in the present Covenant shall be interpreted as impairing the provisions of the Charter of the United Nations and of the constitutions of the specialized agencies which define the respective responsibilities of the various organs of the United Nations and of the specialized agencies in regard to the matters dealt with in the present Covenant.

Article 47
Nothing in the present Covenant shall be interpreted as impairing the inherent right of all peoples to enjoy and utilize fully and freely their natural wealth and resources.

Part VI

Article 48
1. The present Covenant is open for signature by any State Member of the United Nations or member of any of its specialized agencies, by any State

Party to the Statute of the International Court of Justice, and by any other State which has been invited by the General Assembly of the United Nations to become a Party to the present Covenant.

2. The present Covenant is subject to ratification. Instruments of ratification shall be deposited with the Secretary-General of the United Nations.

3. The present Covenant shall be open to accession by any State referred to in paragraph 1 of this article.

4. Accession shall be effected by the deposit of an instrument of accession with the Secretary-General of the United Nations.

5. The Secretary-General of the United Nations shall inform all States which have signed this Covenant or acceded to it of the deposit of each instrument of ratification or accession.

Article 49

1. The present Covenant shall enter into force three months after the date of the deposit with the Secretary-General of the United Nations of the thirty-fifth instrument of ratification or instrument of accession.

2. For each State ratifying the present Covenant or acceding to it after the deposit of the thirty-fifth instrument of ratification or instrument of accession, the present Covenant shall enter into force three months after the date of the deposit of its own instrument of ratification or instrument of accession.

Article 50

The provisions of the present Covenant shall extend to all parts of federal States without any limitations or exceptions.

Article 51

1. Any State Party to the present Covenant may propose an amendment and file it with the Secretary-General of the United Nations. The Secretary-General of the United Nations shall thereupon communicate any proposed amendments to the States Parties to the present Covenant with a request that they notify him whether they favour a conference of States Parties for the purpose of considering and voting upon the proposals. In the event that at least one third of the States Parties favours such a conference, the Secretary-General shall convene the conference under the auspices of the United Nations. Any amendment adopted by a majority of the States Parties present and voting at the conference shall be submitted to the General Assembly of the United Nations for approval.

2. Amendments shall come into force when they have been approved by the General Assembly of the United Nations and accepted by a two-thirds majority of the States Parties to the present Covenant in accordance with their respective constitutional processes.

3. When amendments come into force, they shall be binding on those States Parties which have accepted them, other States Parties still being bound by the provisions of the present Covenant and any earlier amendment which they have accepted.

Article 52

1. Irrespective of the notifications made under article 48, paragraph 5, the Secretary-General of the United Nations shall inform all States referred to in paragraph I of the same article of the following particulars:

(a) Signatures, ratifications and accessions under article 48;

(b) The date of the entry into force of the present Covenant under article 49 and the date of the entry into force of any amendments under article 51.

Article 53

1. The present Covenant, of which the Chinese, English, French, Russian and Spanish texts are equally authentic, shall be deposited in the archives of the United Nations.

2. The Secretary-General of the United Nations shall transmit certified copies of the present Covenant to all States referred to in article 48.

(First) Optional Protocol to the International Covenant on Civil and Political Rights (1966)

The First Optional Protocol, providing for individual complaints to the Human Rights Committee established by the ICCPR, was adopted at the same time as the Convention on 16 December 1966.

On the operation of the committee, see P. R. Ghandi, The Human Rights Committee and the Right of Individual Communication: Law and Practice *(Aldershot, Hants.: Ashgate, 1998). The UN Treaty Bodies Database contains up-to-date information and documents for all of the international human rights treaty bodies at www.unhchr.ch/tbs/doc.nsf.*

The States Parties to the present Protocol,

Considering that in order further to achieve the purposes of the International Covenant on Civil and Political Rights (hereinafter referred to as the Covenant) and the implementation of its provisions it would be appropriate to enable the Human Rights Committee set up in part IV of the Covenant (hereinafter referred to as the Committee) to receive and consider, as provided in the present Protocol, communications from individuals claiming to be victims of violations of any of the rights set forth in the Covenant.

Have agreed as follows:

Article 1

A State Party to the Covenant that becomes a Party to the present Protocol recognizes the competence of the Committee to receive and consider communications from individuals subject to its jurisdiction who claim to be victims of a violation by that State Party of any of the rights set forth in the Covenant. No communication shall be received by the Committee if it concerns a State Party to the Covenant which is not a Party to the present Protocol.

Article 2

Subject to the provisions of article 1, individuals who claim that any of their rights enumerated in the Covenant have been violated and who have exhausted all available domestic remedies may submit a written communication to the Committee for consideration.

Article 3

The Committee shall consider inadmissible any communication under the present Protocol which is anonymous, or which it considers to be an abuse of the right of submission of such communications or to be incompatible with the provisions of the Covenant.

Article 4

1. Subject to the provisions of article 3, the Committee shall bring any communications submitted to it under the present Protocol to the attention of the State Party to the present Protocol alleged to be violating any provision of the Covenant.

2. Within six months, the receiving State shall submit to the Committee written explanations or statements clarifying the matter and the remedy, if any, that may have been taken by that State.

Article 5

1. The Committee shall consider communications received under the present Protocol in the light of all written information made available to it by the individual and by the State Party concerned.

2. The Committee shall not consider any communication from an individual unless it has ascertained that:

(a) The same matter is not being examined under another procedure of international investigation or settlement;

(b) The individual has exhausted all available domestic remedies. This shall not be the rule where the application of the remedies is unreasonably prolonged.

3. The Committee shall hold closed meetings when examining communications under the present Protocol.

4. The Committee shall forward its views to the State Party concerned and to the individual.

Article 6

The Committee shall include in its annual report under article 45 of the Covenant a summary of its activities under the present Protocol.

Article 7

Pending the achievement of the objectives of resolution 1514 (XV) adopted by the General Assembly of the United Nations on 14 December 1960 concerning the Declaration on the Granting of Independence to Colonial Countries and Peoples, the provisions of the present Protocol shall in no way limit the right of petition granted to these peoples by the Charter of the United Nations and other international conventions and instruments under the United Nations and its specialized agencies.

Article 8

1. The present Protocol is open for signature by any State which has signed the Covenant.

2. The present Protocol is subject to ratification by any State which has ratified or acceded to the Covenant. Instruments of ratification shall be deposited with the Secretary-General of the United Nations.

3. The present Protocol shall be open to accession by any State which has ratified or acceded to the Covenant.

4. Accession shall be effected by the deposit of an instrument of accession with the Secretary-General of the United Nations.

5. The Secretary-General of the United Nations shall inform all States which have signed the present Protocol or acceded to it of the deposit of each instrument of ratification or accession.

Article 9

1. Subject to the entry into force of the Covenant, the present Protocol shall enter into force three months after the date of the deposit with the Secretary-General of the United Nations of the tenth instrument of ratification or instrument of accession.

2. For each State ratifying the present Protocol or acceding to it after the deposit of the tenth instrument of ratification or instrument of accession, the present Protocol shall enter into force three months after the date of the deposit of its own instrument of ratification or instrument of accession.

Article 10

The provisions of the present Protocol shall extend to all parts of federal States without any limitations or exceptions.

Article 11

1. Any State Party to the present Protocol may propose an amendment and file it with the Secretary-General of the United Nations. The Secretary-General shall thereupon communicate any proposed amendments to the States Parties

to the present Protocol with a request that they notify him whether they favour a conference of States Parties for the purpose of considering and voting upon the proposal. In the event that at least one third of the States Parties favours such a conference, the Secretary-General shall convene the conference under the auspices of the United Nations. Any amendment adopted by a majority of the States Parties present and voting at the conference shall be submitted to the General Assembly of the United Nations for approval.

2. Amendments shall come into force when they have been approved by the General Assembly of the United Nations and accepted by a two-thirds majority of the States Parties to the present Protocol in accordance with their respective constitutional processes.

3. When amendments come into force, they shall be binding on those States Parties which have accepted them, other States Parties still being bound by the provisions of the present Protocol and any earlier amendment which they have accepted.

Article 12

1. Any State Party may denounce the present Protocol at any time by written notification addressed to the Secretary-General of the United Nations. Denunciation shall take effect three months after the date of receipt of the notification by the Secretary-General.

2. Denunciation shall be without prejudice to the continued application of the provisions of the present Protocol to any communication submitted under article 2 before the effective date of denunciation.

Article 13

Irrespective of the notifications made under article 8, paragraph 5, of the present Protocol, the Secretary-General of the United Nations shall inform all States referred to in article 48, paragraph 1, of the Covenant of the following particulars:

(a) Signatures, ratifications and accessions under article 8;

(b) The date of the entry into force of the present Protocol under article 9 and the date of the entry into force of any amendments under article 11;

(c) Denunciations under article 12.

Article 14

1. The present Protocol, of which the Chinese, English, French, Russian and Spanish texts are equally authentic, shall be deposited in the archives of the United Nations.

2. The Secretary-General of the United Nations shall transmit certified copies of the present Protocol to all States referred to in article 48 of the Covenant.

IN FAITH WHEREOF the undersigned, being duly authorised thereto by their respective Governments, have signed the present Protocol, opened for signature at New York, on the nineteenth day of December, one thousand nine hundred and sixty-six.

Second Optional Protocol to the International Covenant on Civil and Political Rights (1989)

The text of this protocol was adopted by the General Assembly by 59 votes in favor, 26 against, and 48 abstentions. The protocol can be understood as part of a growing international trend against the death penalty.

On the development of an international abolitionist norm, see William Schabas, The Abolition of the Death Penalty in International Law, *3rd ed. (Cambridge: Cambridge University Press, 2002). The United States stands out for being a Western democracy that has not accepted the norm. When the US ratified the ICCPR it did so with a reservation for the death penalty, and it has not signed this protocol nor the protocol to the American Convention on Human Rights to Abolish the Death Penalty. For a historical perspective on the retention of the death penalty in the United States, see Stuart Banner,* The Death Penalty: An American History *(Cambridge, Mass.: Harvard University Press, 2002). Amnesty International USA's Program to Abolish the Death Penalty has a website at www.amnestyusa.org/abolish/index.do.*

The States Parties to the present Protocol,

Believing that abolition of the death penalty contributes to enhancement of human dignity and progressive development of human rights,

Recalling article 3 of the Universal Declaration of Human Rights, adopted on 10 December 1948, and article 6 of the International Covenant on Civil and Political Rights, adopted on 16 December 1966,

Noting that article 6 of the International Covenant on Civil and Political Rights refers to abolition of the death penalty in terms that strongly suggest that abolition is desirable,

Convinced that all measures of abolition of the death penalty should be considered as progress in the enjoyment of the right to life,

Desirous to undertake hereby an international commitment to abolish the death penalty,

Have agreed as follows:

Article 1

1. No one within the jurisdiction of a State Party to the present Protocol shall be executed.

2. Each State Party shall take all necessary measures to abolish the death penalty within its jurisdiction.

Article 2

1. No reservation is admissible to the present Protocol, except for a reservation made at the time of ratification or accession that provides for the application of the death penalty in time of war pursuant to a conviction for a most serious crime of a military nature committed during wartime.

2. The State Party making such a reservation shall at the time of ratification or accession communicate to the Secretary-General of the United Nations the relevant provisions of its national legislation applicable during wartime.

3. The State Party having made such a reservation shall notify the Secretary-General of the United Nations of any beginning or ending of a state of war applicable to its territory.

Article 3

The States Parties to the present Protocol shall include in the reports they submit to the Human Rights Committee, in accordance with article 40 of the Covenant, information on the measures that they have adopted to give effect to the present Protocol.

Article 4

With respect to the States Parties to the Covenant that have made a declaration under article 41, the competence of the Human Rights Committee to receive and consider communications when a State Party claims that another State Party is not fulfilling its obligations shall extend to the provisions of the present Protocol, unless the State Party concerned has made a statement to the contrary at the moment of ratification or accession.

Article 5

With respect to the States Parties to the first Optional Protocol to the International Covenant on Civil and Political Rights adopted on 16 December 1966, the competence of the Human Rights Committee to receive and consider communications from individuals subject to its jurisdiction shall extend to the provisions of the present Protocol, unless the State Party concerned has made a statement to the contrary at the moment of ratification or accession.

Article 6

1. The provisions of the present Protocol shall apply as additional provisions to the Covenant.

2. Without prejudice to the possibility of a reservation under article 2 of the present Protocol, the right guaranteed in article 1, paragraph 1, of the present Protocol shall not be subject to any derogation under article 4 of the Covenant.

Article 7
1. The present Protocol is open for signature by any State that has signed the Covenant.

2. The present Protocol is subject to ratification by any State that has ratified the Covenant or acceded to it. Instruments of ratification shall be deposited with the Secretary-General of the United Nations.

3. The present Protocol shall be open to accession by any State that has ratified the Covenant or acceded to it.

4. Accession shall be effected by the deposit of an instrument of accession with the Secretary-General of the United Nations.

5. The Secretary-General of the United Nations shall inform all States that have signed the present Protocol or acceded to it of the deposit of each instrument of ratification or accession.

Article 8
1. The present Protocol shall enter into force three months after the date of the deposit with the Secretary-General of the United Nations of the tenth instrument of ratification or accession.

2. For each State ratifying the present Protocol or acceding to it after the deposit of the tenth instrument of ratification or accession, the present Protocol shall enter into force three months after the date of the deposit of its own instrument of ratification or accession.

Article 9
The provisions of the present Protocol shall extend to all parts of federal States without any limitations or exceptions.

Article 10
The Secretary-General of the United Nations shall inform all States referred to in article 48, paragraph 1, of the Covenant of the following particulars:

(a) Reservations, communications and notifications under article 2 of the present Protocol;

(b) Statements made under articles 4 or 5 of the present Protocol;

(c) Signatures, ratifications and accessions under article 7 of the present Protocol:

(d) The date of the entry into force of the present Protocol under article 8 thereof.

Article 11
1. The present Protocol, of which the Arabic, Chinese, English, French,

Russian and Spanish texts are equally authentic, shall be deposited in the archives of the United Nations.

2. The Secretary-General of the United Nations shall transmit certified copies of the present Protocol to all States referred to in article 48 of the Covenant.

5.5
International Covenant on Economic, Social and Cultural Rights (ICESCR) (1966)

This is the second of two treaties to flow directly from the UDHR. Implementation of the ICESCR is monitored by the United Nations Committee on Economic, Social, and Cultural Rights, which the Economic and Social Council (ECOSOC) established in 1985. Unlike the ICCPR, there is no individual complaints mechanism for the ICESCR.

On the ICESCR in general, see Matthew Craven, The International Covenant on Economic, Social, and Cultural Rights: A Perspective on Its Development *(Oxford: Clarendon, 1998). Documents of the Committee on Economic, Social and Cultural Rights can be accessed from the UN Treaty Bodies Database at www.unhchr.ch/tbs/doc.nsf. On the enforcement of rights in the ICESCR, see Michael J. Dennis and David P. Stewart, "Justiciability of Economic, Social, and Cultural Rights: Should There Be an International Complaints Mechanism to Adjudicate the Rights to Food, Water, Housing, and Health?* American Journal of International Law *98 (2004): 462–515.*

The States Parties to the present Covenant,

Considering that, in accordance with the principles proclaimed in the Charter of the United Nations, recognition of the inherent dignity and of the equal and inalienable rights of all members of the human family is the foundation of freedom, justice and peace in the world,

Recognizing that these rights derive from the inherent dignity of the human person,

Recognizing that, in accordance with the Universal Declaration of Human Rights, the ideal of free human beings enjoying freedom from fear and want can only be achieved if conditions are created whereby everyone may enjoy his economic, social and cultural rights, as well as his civil and political rights,

Considering the obligation of States under the Charter of the United Nations to promote universal respect for, and observance of, human rights and freedoms,

Realizing that the individual, having duties to other individuals and to the community to which he belongs, is under a responsibility to strive for the promotion and observance of the rights recognized in the present Covenant,

Agree upon the following articles:

Part I

Article 1

1. All peoples have the right of self-determination. By virtue of that right they freely determine their political status and freely pursue their economic, social and cultural development.

2. All peoples may, for their own ends, freely dispose of their natural wealth and resources without prejudice to any obligations arising out of international economic co-operation, based upon the principle of mutual benefit, and international law. In no case may a people be deprived of its own means of subsistence.

3. The States Parties to the present Covenant, including those having responsibility for the administration of Non-Self-Governing and Trust Territories, shall promote the realization of the right of self-determination, and shall respect that right, in conformity with the provisions of the Charter of the United Nations.

Part II

Article 2

1. Each State Party to the present Covenant undertakes to take steps, individually and through international assistance and co-operation, especially economic and technical, to the maximum of its available resources, with a view to achieving progressively the full realization of the rights recognized in the present Covenant by all appropriate means, including particularly the adoption of legislative measures.

2. The States Parties to the present Covenant undertake to guarantee that the rights enunciated in the present Covenant will be exercised without discrimination of any kind as to race, colour, sex, language, religion, political or other opinion, national or social origin, property, birth or other status.

3. Developing countries, with due regard to human rights and their national economy, may determine to what extent they would guarantee the economic rights recognized in the present Covenant to non-nationals.

Article 3

The States Parties to the present Covenant undertake to ensure the equal right of men and women to the enjoyment of all economic, social and cultural rights set forth in the present Covenant.

Article 4

The States Parties to the present Covenant recognize that, in the enjoyment of those rights provided by the State in conformity with the present Covenant, the State may subject such rights only to such limitations as are determined by law only in so far as this may be compatible with the nature of these rights and solely for the purpose of promoting the general welfare in a democratic society.

Article 5

1. Nothing in the present Covenant may be interpreted as implying for any State, group or person any right to engage in any activity or to perform any act aimed at the destruction of any of the rights or freedoms recognized herein, or at their limitation to a greater extent than is provided for in the present Covenant.

2. No restriction upon or derogation from any of the fundamental human rights recognized or existing in any country in virtue of law, conventions, regulations or custom shall be admitted on the pretext that the present Covenant does not recognize such rights or that it recognizes them to a lesser extent.

Part III

Article 6

1. The States Parties to the present Covenant recognize the right to work, which includes the right of everyone to the opportunity to gain his living by work which he freely chooses or accepts, and will take appropriate steps to safeguard this right.

2. The steps to be taken by a State Party to the present Covenant to achieve the full realization of this right shall include technical and vocational guidance and training programmes, policies and techniques to achieve steady economic, social and cultural development and full and productive employment under conditions safeguarding fundamental political and economic freedoms to the individual.

Article 7

The States Parties to the present Covenant recognize the right of everyone to the enjoyment of just and favourable conditions of work which ensure, in particular:

(a) Remuneration which provides all workers, as a minimum, with: (i) Fair wages and equal remuneration for work of equal value without distinction of any kind, in particular women being guaranteed conditions of work not inferior to those enjoyed by men, with equal pay for equal work; (ii) A decent living for themselves and their families in accordance with the provisions of the present Covenant;

(b) Safe and healthy working conditions;

(c) Equal opportunity for everyone to be promoted in his employment to an appropriate higher level, subject to no considerations other than those of seniority and competence;

(d) Rest, leisure and reasonable limitation of working hours and periodic holidays with pay, as well as remuneration for public holidays.

Article 8

1. The States Parties to the present Covenant undertake to ensure:

(a) The right of everyone to form trade unions and join the trade union of his choice, subject only to the rules of the organization concerned, for the promotion and protection of his economic and social interests. No restrictions may be placed on the exercise of this right other than those prescribed by law and which are necessary in a democratic society in the interests of national security or public order or for the protection of the rights and freedoms of others;

(b) The right of trade unions to establish national federations or confederations and the right of the latter to form or join international trade-union organizations;

(c) The right of trade unions to function freely subject to no limitations other than those prescribed by law and which are necessary in a democratic society in the interests of national security or public order or for the protection of the rights and freedoms of others;

(d) The right to strike, provided that it is exercised in conformity with the laws of the particular country.

2. This article shall not prevent the imposition of lawful restrictions on the exercise of these rights by members of the armed forces or of the police or of the administration of the State.

3. Nothing in this article shall authorize States Parties to the International Labour Organisation Convention of 1948 concerning Freedom of Association and Protection of the Right to Organize to take legislative measures which would prejudice, or apply the law in such a manner as would prejudice, the guarantees provided for in that Convention.

Article 9

The States Parties to the present Covenant recognize the right of everyone to social security, including social insurance.

Article 10

The States Parties to the present Covenant recognize that:

1. The widest possible protection and assistance should be accorded to the family, which is the natural and fundamental group unit of society, particularly for its establishment and while it is responsible for the care and education of dependent children. Marriage must be entered into with the free consent of the intending spouses.

2. Special protection should be accorded to mothers during a reasonable period before and after childbirth. During such period working mothers

should be accorded paid leave or leave with adequate social security benefits.

3. Special measures of protection and assistance should be taken on behalf of all children and young persons without any discrimination for reasons of parentage or other conditions. Children and young persons should be protected from economic and social exploitation. Their employment in work harmful to their morals or health or dangerous to life or likely to hamper their normal development should be punishable by law. States should also set age limits below which the paid employment of child labour should be prohibited and punishable by law.

Article 11

1. The States Parties to the present Covenant recognize the right of everyone to an adequate standard of living for himself and his family, including adequate food, clothing and housing, and to the continuous improvement of living conditions. The States Parties will take appropriate steps to ensure the realization of this right, recognizing to this effect the essential importance of international co-operation based on free consent.

2. The States Parties to the present Covenant, recognizing the fundamental right of everyone to be free from hunger, shall take, individually and through international co-operation, the measures, including specific programmes, which are needed:

(a) To improve methods of production, conservation and distribution of food by making full use of technical and scientific knowledge, by disseminating knowledge of the principles of nutrition and by developing or reforming agrarian systems in such a way as to achieve the most efficient development and utilization of natural resources;

(b) Taking into account the problems of both food-importing and food-exporting countries, to ensure an equitable distribution of world food supplies in relation to need.

Article 12

1. The States Parties to the present Covenant recognize the right of everyone to the enjoyment of the highest attainable standard of physical and mental health.

2. The steps to be taken by the States Parties to the present Covenant to achieve the full realization of this right shall include those necessary for:

(a) The provision for the reduction of the stillbirth-rate and of infant mortality and for the healthy development of the child;

(b) The improvement of all aspects of environmental and industrial hygiene;

(c) The prevention, treatment and control of epidemic, endemic, occupational and other diseases;

(d) The creation of conditions which would assure to all medical service and medical attention in the event of sickness.

Article 13

1. The States Parties to the present Covenant recognize the right of everyone to education. They agree that education shall be directed to the full development of the human personality and the sense of its dignity, and shall strengthen the respect for human rights and fundamental freedoms. They further agree that education shall enable all persons to participate effectively in a free society, promote understanding, tolerance and friendship among all nations and all racial, ethnic or religious groups, and further the activities of the United Nations for the maintenance of peace.

2. The States Parties to the present Covenant recognize that, with a view to achieving the full realization of this right:

(a) Primary education shall be compulsory and available free to all;

(b) Secondary education in its different forms, including technical and vocational secondary education, shall be made generally available and accessible to all by every appropriate means, and in particular by the progressive introduction of free education;

(c) Higher education shall be made equally accessible to all, on the basis of capacity, by every appropriate means, and in particular by the progressive introduction of free education;

(d) Fundamental education shall be encouraged or intensified as far as possible for those persons who have not received or completed the whole period of their primary education;

(e) The development of a system of schools at all levels shall be actively pursued, an adequate fellowship system shall be established, and the material conditions of teaching staff shall be continuously improved.

3. The States Parties to the present Covenant undertake to have respect for the liberty of parents and, when applicable, legal guardians to choose for their children schools, other than those established by the public authorities, which conform to such minimum educational standards as may be laid down or approved by the State and to ensure the religious and moral education of their children in conformity with their own convictions.

4. No part of this article shall be construed so as to interfere with the liberty of individuals and bodies to establish and direct educational institutions, subject always to the observance of the principles set forth in paragraph 1 of this article and to the requirement that the education given in such institutions shall conform to such minimum standards as may be laid down by the State.

Article 14

Each State Party to the present Covenant which, at the time of becoming a Party, has not been able to secure in its metropolitan territory or other territories under its jurisdiction compulsory primary education, free of charge, undertakes, within two years, to work out and adopt a detailed plan of action for the progressive implementation, within a reasonable number of years, to be fixed in the plan, of the principle of compulsory education free of charge for all.

Article 15

1. The States Parties to the present Covenant recognize the right of everyone:

(a) To take part in cultural life;

(b) To enjoy the benefits of scientific progress and its applications;

(c) To benefit from the protection of the moral and material interests resulting from any scientific, literary or artistic production of which he is the author.

2. The steps to be taken by the States Parties to the present Covenant to achieve the full realization of this right shall include those necessary for the conservation, the development and the diffusion of science and culture.

3. The States Parties to the present Covenant undertake to respect the freedom indispensable for scientific research and creative activity.

4. The States Parties to the present Covenant recognize the benefits to be derived from the encouragement and development of international contacts and co-operation in the scientific and cultural fields.

Part IV

Article 16

1. The States Parties to the present Covenant undertake to submit in conformity with this part of the Covenant reports on the measures which they have adopted and the progress made in achieving the observance of the rights recognized herein.

2. (a) All reports shall be submitted to the Secretary-General of the United Nations, who shall transmit copies to the Economic and Social Council for consideration in accordance with the provisions of the present Covenant;

(b) The Secretary-General of the United Nations shall also transmit to the specialized agencies copies of the reports, or any relevant parts therefrom, from States Parties to the present Covenant which are also members of these specialized agencies in so far as these reports, or parts therefrom, relate to any matters which fall within the responsibilities of the said agencies in accordance with their constitutional instruments.

Article 17

1. The States Parties to the present Covenant shall furnish their reports in stages, in accordance with a programme to be established by the Economic and Social Council within one year of the entry into force of the present Covenant after consultation with the States Parties and the specialized agencies concerned.

2. Reports may indicate factors and difficulties affecting the degree of fulfilment of obligations under the present Covenant.

3. Where relevant information has previously been furnished to the United Nations or to any specialized agency by any State Party to the present Covenant, it will not be necessary to reproduce that information, but a precise reference to the information so furnished will suffice.

Article 18
Pursuant to its responsibilities under the Charter of the United Nations in the field of human rights and fundamental freedoms, the Economic and Social Council may make arrangements with the specialized agencies in respect of their reporting to it on the progress made in achieving the observance of the provisions of the present Covenant falling within the scope of their activities. These reports may include particulars of decisions and recommendations on such implementation adopted by their competent organs.

Article 19
The Economic and Social Council may transmit to the Commission on Human Rights for study and general recommendation or, as appropriate, for information the reports concerning human rights submitted by States in accordance with articles 16 and 17, and those concerning human rights submitted by the specialized agencies in accordance with article 18.

Article 20
The States Parties to the present Covenant and the specialized agencies concerned may submit comments to the Economic and Social Council on any general recommendation under article 19 or reference to such general recommendation in any report of the Commission on Human Rights or any documentation referred to therein.

Article 21
The Economic and Social Council may submit from time to time to the General Assembly reports with recommendations of a general nature and a summary of the information received from the States Parties to the present Covenant and the specialized agencies on the measures taken and the progress made in achieving general observance of the rights recognized in the present Covenant.

Article 22
The Economic and Social Council may bring to the attention of other organs of the United Nations, their subsidiary organs and specialized agencies concerned with furnishing technical assistance any matters arising out of the reports referred to in this part of the present Covenant which may assist such bodies in deciding, each within its field of competence, on the advisability of international measures likely to contribute to the effective progressive implementation of the present Covenant.

Article 23

The States Parties to the present Covenant agree that international action for the achievement of the rights recognized in the present Covenant includes such methods as the conclusion of conventions, the adoption of recommendations, the furnishing of technical assistance and the holding of regional meetings and technical meetings for the purpose of consultation and study organized in conjunction with the Governments concerned.

Article 24

Nothing in the present Covenant shall be interpreted as impairing the provisions of the Charter of the United Nations and of the constitutions of the specialized agencies which define the respective responsibilities of the various organs of the United Nations and of the specialized agencies in regard to the matters dealt with in the present Covenant.

Article 25

Nothing in the present Covenant shall be interpreted as impairing the inherent right of all peoples to enjoy and utilize fully and freely their natural wealth and resources.

Part V

Article 26

1. The present Covenant is open for signature by any State Member of the United Nations or member of any of its specialized agencies, by any State Party to the Statute of the International Court of Justice, and by any other State which has been invited by the General Assembly of the United Nations to become a party to the present Covenant.

2. The present Covenant is subject to ratification. Instruments of ratification shall be deposited with the Secretary-General of the United Nations.

3. The present Covenant shall be open to accession by any State referred to in paragraph 1 of this article.

4. Accession shall be effected by the deposit of an instrument of accession with the Secretary-General of the United Nations.

5. The Secretary-General of the United Nations shall inform all States which have signed the present Covenant or acceded to it of the deposit of each instrument of ratification or accession.

Article 27

1. The present Covenant shall enter into force three months after the date of the deposit with the Secretary-General of the United Nations of the thirty-fifth instrument of ratification or instrument of accession.

2. For each State ratifying the present Covenant or acceding to it after the deposit of the thirty-fifth instrument of ratification or instrument of accession,

the present Covenant shall enter into force three months after the date of the deposit of its own instrument of ratification or instrument of accession.

Article 28
The provisions of the present Covenant shall extend to all parts of federal States without any limitations or exceptions.

Article 29
1. Any State Party to the present Covenant may propose an amendment and file it with the Secretary-General of the United Nations. The Secretary-General shall thereupon communicate any proposed amendments to the States Parties to the present Covenant with a request that they notify him whether they favour a conference of States Parties for the purpose of considering and voting upon the proposals. In the event that at least one third of the States Parties favours such a conference, the Secretary-General shall convene the conference under the auspices of the United Nations. Any amendment adopted by a majority of the States Parties present and voting at the conference shall be submitted to the General Assembly of the United Nations for approval.

2. Amendments shall come into force when they have been approved by the General Assembly of the United Nations and accepted by a two-thirds majority of the States Parties to the present Covenant in accordance with their respective constitutional processes.

3. When amendments come into force they shall be binding on those States Parties which have accepted them, other States Parties still being bound by the provisions of the present Covenant and any earlier amendment which they have accepted.

Article 30
Irrespective of the notifications made under article 26, paragraph 5, the Secretary-General of the United Nations shall inform all States referred to in paragraph I of the same article of the following particulars:

(a) Signatures, ratifications and accessions under article 26;

(b) The date of the entry into force of the present Covenant under article 27 and the date of the entry into force of any amendments under article 29.

Article 31
1. The present Covenant, of which the Chinese, English, French, Russian and Spanish texts are equally authentic, shall be deposited in the archives of the United Nations.

2. The Secretary-General of the United Nations shall transmit certified copies of the present Covenant to all States referred to in article 26.

5.6
Convention on the Elimination of All Forms of Discrimination Against Women (CEDAW) (1979)

This convention owes much to the efforts of NGOs to place the issue of women's rights on the international agenda. The convention was built on the 1967 Declaration on the Elimination of Discrimination Against Women, which proclaimed that discrimination against women, denying or limiting as it does their equality of rights with men, is fundamentally unjust and constitutes an offense against human dignity. The convention is widely ratified, but with many reservations. An optional protocol providing for individual and group complaints to the committee established by CEDAW, as well as an enquiry procedure, was adopted by the General Assembly on 6 October 1999 and entered into force on 22 December 2000.

On the question of reservations to CEDAW, see R. Cook, "Reservations to the Convention on the Elimination of all Forms of Discrimination Against Women," Virginia Journal of International Law *30 no. 3 (1990): 643–716. Texts of the reservations and the protocol are available at www.un.org/womenwatch/daw/cedaw. On the optional protocol, see H. Gilchrist, "The Optional Protocol to the Women's Convention,"* Columbia Journal of Transnational Law *39, no. 3 (2001): 763–783.*

The States Parties to the present Convention,

Noting that the Charter of the United Nations reaffirms faith in fundamental human rights, in the dignity and worth of the human person and in the equal rights of men and women,

Noting that the Universal Declaration of Human Rights affirms the principle of the inadmissibility of discrimination and proclaims that all human beings are born free and equal in dignity and rights and that everyone is entitled to all the rights and freedoms set forth therein, without distinction of any kind, including distinction based on sex,

Noting that the States Parties to the International Covenants on Human Rights have the obligation to ensure the equal rights of men and women to enjoy all economic, social, cultural, civil and political rights,

Considering the international conventions concluded under the auspices of the United Nations and the specialized agencies promoting equality of rights of men and women,

Noting also the resolutions, declarations and recommendations adopted by the United Nations and the specialized agencies promoting equality of rights of men and women,

Concerned, however, that despite these various instruments extensive discrimination against women continues to exist,

Recalling that discrimination against women violates the principles of equality of rights and respect for human dignity, is an obstacle to the participation of women, on equal terms with men, in the political, social, economic and cultural life of their countries, hampers the growth of the prosperity of society and the family and makes more difficult the full development of the potentialities of women in the service of their countries and of humanity,

Concerned that in situations of poverty women have the least access to food, health, education, training and opportunities for employment and other needs,

Convinced that the establishment of the new international economic order based on equity and justice will contribute significantly towards the promotion of equality between men and women,

Emphasizing that the eradication of apartheid, all forms of racism, racial discrimination, colonialism, neo-colonialism, aggression, foreign occupation and domination and interference in the internal affairs of States is essential to the full enjoyment of the rights of men and women,

Affirming that the strengthening of international peace and security, the relaxation of international tension, mutual co-operation among all States irrespective of their social and economic systems, general and complete disarmament, in particular nuclear disarmament under strict and effective international control, the affirmation of the principles of justice, equality and mutual benefit in relations among countries and the realization of the right of peoples under alien and colonial domination and foreign occupation to self-determination and independence, as well as respect for national sovereignty and territorial integrity, will promote social progress and development and as a consequence will contribute to the attainment of full equality between men and women,

Convinced that the full and complete development of a country, the welfare of the world and the cause of peace require the maximum participation of women on equal terms with men in all fields,

Bearing in mind the great contribution of women to the welfare of the family and to the development of society, so far not fully recognized, the social significance of maternity and the role of both parents in the family and in the upbringing of children, and aware that the role of women in procreation should not be a basis for discrimination but that the upbringing of children requires a sharing of responsibility between men and women and society as a whole,

Aware that a change in the traditional role of men as well as the role of women in society and in the family is needed to achieve full equality between men and women,

Determined to implement the principles set forth in the Declaration on the Elimination of Discrimination against Women and, for that purpose, to adopt the measures required for the elimination of such discrimination in all its forms and manifestations,

Have agreed on the following:

Part I

Article 1

For the purposes of the present Convention, the term "discrimination against women" shall mean any distinction, exclusion or restriction made on the basis of sex which has the effect or purpose of impairing or nullifying the recognition, enjoyment or exercise by women, irrespective of their marital status, on a basis of equality of men and women, of human rights and fundamental freedoms in the political, economic, social, cultural, civil or any other field.

Article 2

States Parties condemn discrimination against women in all its forms, agree to pursue by all appropriate means and without delay a policy of eliminating discrimination against women and, to this end, undertake:

(a) To embody the principle of the equality of men and women in their national constitutions or other appropriate legislation if not yet incorporated therein and to ensure, through law and other appropriate means, the practical realization of this principle;

(b) To adopt appropriate legislative and other measures, including sanctions where appropriate, prohibiting all discrimination against women;

(c) To establish legal protection of the rights of women on an equal basis with men and to ensure through competent national tribunals and other public institutions the effective protection of women against any act of discrimination;

(d) To refrain from engaging in any act or practice of discrimination against women and to ensure that public authorities and institutions shall act in conformity with this obligation;

(e) To take all appropriate measures to eliminate discrimination against women by any person, organization or enterprise;

(f) To take all appropriate measures, including legislation, to modify or abolish existing laws, regulations, customs and practices which constitute discrimination against women;

(g) To repeal all national penal provisions which constitute discrimination against women.

Article 3

States Parties shall take in all fields, in particular in the political, social, economic and cultural fields, all appropriate measures, including legislation, to ensure the full development and advancement of women, for the purpose of guaranteeing them the exercise and enjoyment of human rights and fundamental freedoms on a basis of equality with men.

Article 4

1. Adoption by States Parties of temporary special measures aimed at accelerating de facto equality between men and women shall not be considered discrimination as defined in the present Convention, but shall in no way entail as a consequence the maintenance of unequal or separate standards; these measures shall be discontinued when the objectives of equality of opportunity and treatment have been achieved.

2. Adoption by States Parties of special measures, including those measures contained in the present Convention, aimed at protecting maternity shall not be considered discriminatory.

Article 5

States Parties shall take all appropriate measures:

(a) To modify the social and cultural patterns of conduct of men and women, with a view to achieving the elimination of prejudices and customary and all other practices which are based on the idea of the inferiority or the superiority of either of the sexes or on stereotyped roles for men and women;

(b) To ensure that family education includes a proper understanding of maternity as a social function and the recognition of the common responsibility of men and women in the upbringing and development of their children, it being understood that the interest of the children is the primordial consideration in all cases.

Article 6

States Parties shall take all appropriate measures, including legislation, to suppress all forms of traffic in women and exploitation of prostitution of women.

Part II

Article 7

States Parties shall take all appropriate measures to eliminate discrimination against women in the political and public life of the country and, in particular, shall ensure to women, on equal terms with men, the right:

(a) To vote in all elections and public referenda and to be eligible for election to all publicly elected bodies;

(b) To participate in the formulation of government policy and the implementation thereof and to hold public office and perform all public functions at all levels of government;

(c) To participate in non-governmental organizations and associations concerned with the public and political life of the country.

Article 8

States Parties shall take all appropriate measures to ensure to women, on equal terms with men and without any discrimination, the opportunity to represent their Governments at the international level and to participate in the work of international organizations.

Article 9

1. States Parties shall grant women equal rights with men to acquire, change or retain their nationality. They shall ensure in particular that neither marriage to an alien nor change of nationality by the husband during marriage shall automatically change the nationality of the wife, render her stateless or force upon her the nationality of the husband.

2. States Parties shall grant women equal rights with men with respect to the nationality of their children.

Part III

Article 10

States Parties shall take all appropriate measures to eliminate discrimination against women in order to ensure to them equal rights with men in the field of education and in particular to ensure, on a basis of equality of men and women:

(a) The same conditions for career and vocational guidance, for access to studies and for the achievement of diplomas in educational establishments of all categories in rural as well as in urban areas; this equality shall be ensured in pre-school, general, technical, professional and higher technical education, as well as in all types of vocational training;

(b) Access to the same curricula, the same examinations, teaching staff with qualifications of the same standard and school premises and equipment of the same quality;

(c) The elimination of any stereotyped concept of the roles of men and women at all levels and in all forms of education by encouraging coeducation and other types of education which will help to achieve this aim and, in particular, by the revision of textbooks and school programmes and the adaptation of teaching methods;

(d) The same opportunities to benefit from scholarships and other study grants;

(e) The same opportunities for access to programmes of continuing education, including adult and functional literacy programmes, particularly those aimed at reducing, at the earliest possible time, any gap in education existing between men and women;

(f) The reduction of female student drop-out rates and the organization of programmes for girls and women who have left school prematurely;

(g) The same opportunities to participate actively in sports and physical education;

(h) Access to specific educational information to help to ensure the health and well-being of families, including information and advice on family planning.

Article 11

1. States Parties shall take all appropriate measures to eliminate discrimination against women in the field of employment in order to ensure, on a basis of equality of men and women, the same rights, in particular:

(a) The right to work as an inalienable right of all human beings;

(b) The right to the same employment opportunities, including the application of the same criteria for selection in matters of employment;

(c) The right to free choice of profession and employment, the right to promotion, job security and all benefits and conditions of service and the right to receive vocational training and retraining, including apprenticeships, advanced vocational training and recurrent training;

(d) The right to equal remuneration, including benefits, and to equal treatment in respect of work of equal value, as well as equality of treatment in the evaluation of the quality of work;

(e) The right to social security, particularly in cases of retirement, unemployment, sickness, invalidity and old age and other incapacity to work, as well as the right to paid leave;

(f) The right to protection of health and to safety in working conditions, including the safeguarding of the function of reproduction.

2. In order to prevent discrimination against women on the grounds of marriage or maternity and to ensure their effective right to work, States Parties shall take appropriate measures:

(a) To prohibit, subject to the imposition of sanctions, dismissal on the grounds of pregnancy or of maternity leave and discrimination in dismissals on the basis of marital status;

(b) To introduce maternity leave with pay or with comparable social benefits without loss of former employment, seniority or social allowances;

(c) To encourage the provision of the necessary supporting social services to enable parents to combine family obligations with work responsibilities and participation in public life, in particular through promoting the establishment and development of a network of child-care facilities;

(d) To provide special protection to women during pregnancy in types of work proved to be harmful to them.

3. Protective legislation relating to matters covered in this article shall be reviewed periodically in the light of scientific and technological knowledge and shall be revised, repealed or extended as necessary.

Article 12

1. States Parties shall take all appropriate measures to eliminate discrimina-

tion against women in the field of health care in order to ensure, on a basis of equality of men and women, access to health care services, including those related to family planning.

2. Notwithstanding the provisions of paragraph 1 of this article, States Parties shall ensure to women appropriate services in connection with pregnancy, confinement and the post-natal period, granting free services where necessary, as well as adequate nutrition during pregnancy and lactation.

Article 13

States Parties shall take all appropriate measures to eliminate discrimination against women in other areas of economic and social life in order to ensure, on a basis of equality of men and women, the same rights, in particular:

(a) The right to family benefits;

(b) The right to bank loans, mortgages and other forms of financial credit;

(c) The right to participate in recreational activities, sports and all aspects of cultural life.

Article 14

1. States Parties shall take into account the particular problems faced by rural women and the significant roles which rural women play in the economic survival of their families, including their work in the non-monetized sectors of the economy, and shall take all appropriate measures to ensure the application of the provisions of the present Convention to women in rural areas.

2. States Parties shall take all appropriate measures to eliminate discrimination against women in rural areas in order to ensure, on a basis of equality of men and women, that they participate in and benefit from rural development and, in particular, shall ensure to such women the right:

(a) To participate in the elaboration and implementation of development planning at all levels;

(b) To have access to adequate health care facilities, including information, counselling and services in family planning;

(c) To benefit directly from social security programmes;

(d) To obtain all types of training and education, formal and non-formal, including that relating to functional literacy, as well as, inter alia, the benefit of all community and extension services, in order to increase their technical proficiency;

(e) To organize self-help groups and co-operatives in order to obtain equal access to economic opportunities through employment or self employment;

(f) To participate in all community activities;

(g) To have access to agricultural credit and loans, marketing facilities, appropriate technology and equal treatment in land and agrarian reform as well as in land resettlement schemes;

(h) To enjoy adequate living conditions, particularly in relation to housing, sanitation, electricity and water supply, transport and communications.

Part IV

Article 15

1. States Parties shall accord to women equality with men before the law.

2. States Parties shall accord to women, in civil matters, a legal capacity identical to that of men and the same opportunities to exercise that capacity. In particular, they shall give women equal rights to conclude contracts and to administer property and shall treat them equally in all stages of procedure in courts and tribunals.

3. States Parties agree that all contracts and all other private instruments of any kind with a legal effect which is directed at restricting the legal capacity of women shall be deemed null and void.

4. States Parties shall accord to men and women the same rights with regard to the law relating to the movement of persons and the freedom to choose their residence and domicile.

Article 16

1. States Parties shall take all appropriate measures to eliminate discrimination against women in all matters relating to marriage and family relations and in particular shall ensure, on a basis of equality of men and women:

(a) The same right to enter into marriage;

(b) The same right freely to choose a spouse and to enter into marriage only with their free and full consent;

(c) The same rights and responsibilities during marriage and at its dissolution;

(d) The same rights and responsibilities as parents, irrespective of their marital status, in matters relating to their children; in all cases the interests of the children shall be paramount;

(e) The same rights to decide freely and responsibly on the number and spacing of their children and to have access to the information, education and means to enable them to exercise these rights;

(f) The same rights and responsibilities with regard to guardianship, wardship, trusteeship and adoption of children, or similar institutions where these concepts exist in national legislation; in all cases the interests of the children shall be paramount;

(g) The same personal rights as husband and wife, including the right to choose a family name, a profession and an occupation;

(h) The same rights for both spouses in respect of the ownership, acquisition, management, administration, enjoyment and disposition of property, whether free of charge or for a valuable consideration.

2. The betrothal and the marriage of a child shall have no legal effect, and all necessary action, including legislation, shall be taken to specify a minimum age for marriage and to make the registration of marriages in an official registry compulsory.

Part V

Article 17

1. For the purpose of considering the progress made in the implementation of the present Convention, there shall be established a Committee on the Elimination of Discrimination against Women (hereinafter referred to as the Committee) consisting, at the time of entry into force of the Convention, of eighteen and, after ratification of or accession to the Convention by the thirty-fifth State Party, of twenty-three experts of high moral standing and competence in the field covered by the Convention. The experts shall be elected by States Parties from among their nationals and shall serve in their personal capacity, consideration being given to equitable geographical distribution and to the representation of the different forms of civilization as well as the principal legal systems.

2. The members of the Committee shall be elected by secret ballot from a list of persons nominated by States Parties. Each State Party may nominate one person from among its own nationals.

3. The initial election shall be held six months after the date of the entry into force of the present Convention. At least three months before the date of each election the Secretary-General of the United Nations shall address a letter to the States Parties inviting them to submit their nominations within two months. The Secretary-General shall prepare a list in alphabetical order of all persons thus nominated, indicating the States Parties which have nominated them, and shall submit it to the States Parties.

4. Elections of the members of the Committee shall be held at a meeting of States Parties convened by the Secretary-General at United Nations Headquarters. At that meeting, for which two thirds of the States Parties shall constitute a quorum, the persons elected to the Committee shall be those nominees who obtain the largest number of votes and an absolute majority of the votes of the representatives of States Parties present and voting.

5. The members of the Committee shall be elected for a term of four years. However, the terms of nine of the members elected at the first election shall expire at the end of two years; immediately after the first election the names of these nine members shall be chosen by lot by the Chairman of the Committee.

6. The election of the five additional members of the Committee shall be held in accordance with the provisions of paragraphs 2, 3 and 4 of this article, following the thirty-fifth ratification or accession. The terms of two of the additional members elected on this occasion shall expire at the end of two years, the names of these two members having been chosen by lot by the Chairman of the Committee.

7. For the filling of casual vacancies, the State Party whose expert has ceased to function as a member of the Committee shall appoint another expert from among its nationals, subject to the approval of the Committee.

8. The members of the Committee shall, with the approval of the General

Assembly, receive emoluments from United Nations resources on such terms and conditions as the Assembly may decide, having regard to the importance of the Committee's responsibilities.

9. The Secretary-General of the United Nations shall provide the necessary staff and facilities for the effective performance of the functions of the Committee under the present Convention.

Article 18

1. States Parties undertake to submit to the Secretary-General of the United Nations, for consideration by the Committee, a report on the legislative, judicial, administrative or other measures which they have adopted to give effect to the provisions of the present Convention and on the progress made in this respect:

(a) Within one year after the entry into force for the State concerned;

(b) Thereafter at least every four years and further whenever the Committee so requests.

2. Reports may indicate factors and difficulties affecting the degree of fulfilment of obligations under the present Convention.

Article 19

1. The Committee shall adopt its own rules of procedure.

2. The Committee shall elect its officers for a term of two years.

Article 20

1. The Committee shall normally meet for a period of not more than two weeks annually in order to consider the reports submitted in accordance with article 18 of the present Convention.

2. The meetings of the Committee shall normally be held at United Nations Headquarters or at any other convenient place as determined by the Committee.

Article 21

1. The Committee shall, through the Economic and Social Council, report annually to the General Assembly of the United Nations on its activities and may make suggestions and general recommendations based on the examination of reports and information received from the States Parties. Such suggestions and general recommendations shall be included in the report of the Committee together with comments, if any, from States Parties.

2. The Secretary-General of the United Nations shall transmit the reports of the Committee to the Commission on the Status of Women for its information.

Article 22

The specialized agencies shall be entitled to be represented at the consideration of the implementation of such provisions of the present Convention as fall within the scope of their activities. The Committee may invite the specialized agencies to submit reports on the implementation of the Convention in areas falling within the scope of their activities.

Part VI

Article 23
Nothing in the present Convention shall affect any provisions that are more conducive to the achievement of equality between men and women which may be contained:

(a) In the legislation of a State Party; or

(b) In any other international convention, treaty or agreement in force for that State.

Article 24
States Parties undertake to adopt all necessary measures at the national level aimed at achieving the full realization of the rights recognized in the present Convention.

Article 25
1. The present Convention shall be open for signature by all States.

2. The Secretary-General of the United Nations is designated as the depositary of the present Convention.

3. The present Convention is subject to ratification. Instruments of ratification shall be deposited with the Secretary-General of the United Nations.

4. The present Convention shall be open to accession by all States. Accession shall be effected by the deposit of an instrument of accession with the Secretary-General of the United Nations.

Article 26
1. A request for the revision of the present Convention may be made at any time by any State Party by means of a notification in writing addressed to the Secretary-General of the United Nations.

2. The General Assembly of the United Nations shall decide upon the steps, if any, to be taken in respect of such a request.

Article 27
1. The present Convention shall enter into force on the thirtieth day after the date of deposit with the Secretary-General of the United Nations of the twentieth instrument of ratification or accession.

2. For each State ratifying the present Convention or acceding to it after the deposit of the twentieth instrument of ratification or accession, the Convention shall enter into force on the thirtieth day after the date of the deposit of its own instrument of ratification or accession.

Article 28

1. The Secretary-General of the United Nations shall receive and circulate to all States the text of reservations made by States at the time of ratification or accession.

2. A reservation incompatible with the object and purpose of the present Convention shall not be permitted.

3. Reservations may be withdrawn at any time by notification to this effect addressed to the Secretary-General of the United Nations, who shall then inform all States thereof. Such notification shall take effect on the date on which it is received.

Article 29

1. Any dispute between two or more States Parties concerning the interpretation or application of the present Convention which is not settled by negotiation shall, at the request of one of them, be submitted to arbitration. If within six months from the date of the request for arbitration the parties are unable to agree on the organization of the arbitration, any one of those parties may refer the dispute to the International Court of Justice by request in conformity with the Statute of the Court.

2. Each State Party may at the time of signature or ratification of the present Convention or accession thereto declare that it does not consider itself bound by paragraph 1 of this article. The other States Parties shall not be bound by that paragraph with respect to any State Party which has made such a reservation.

3. Any State Party which has made a reservation in accordance with paragraph 2 of this article may at any time withdraw that reservation by notification to the Secretary-General of the United Nations.

Article 30

The present Convention, the Arabic, Chinese, English, French, Russian and Spanish texts of which are equally authentic, shall be deposited with the Secretary-General of the United Nations.

IN WITNESS WHEREOF the undersigned, duly authorized, have signed the present Convention.

5.7
Convention on the Rights of the Child (CROC) (1989)

CROC was preceded by the 1924 Geneva Declaration of the Rights of the Child and the Declaration of the Rights of the Child of 1959, both of which proclaimed that "mankind owes to the Child the best that it has to give." Further momentum toward conclusion of the convention came from the 1979 UN Year of the Child, and the convention was adopted by the General Assembly on 20 November 1989. It has been almost universally ratified, with the notable exception of the United States. Article 37(a) of the convention prohibits capital punishment for offenses committed by those under the age of 18; the United States is one of a few countries retaining the juvenile death penalty. For discussion of the convention, see S. Detrick, A Commentary on the United Nations Convention on the Rights of the Child *(The Hague: M. Nijhoff, 1999). Nancy E. Walker draws on CROC to argue for abolition of the juvenile death penalty in the United States in "The United Nations Convention on the Rights of the Child: A Basis for* Jus Cogens *Prohibition of Juvenile Capital Punishment in the United States,"* Behavioral Sciences and the Law *19 (January 2001): 143–169.*

The convention has two optional protocols. The Optional Protocol on the Involvement of Children in Armed Conflict was adopted by the General Assembly on 25 May 2000 and entered into force on 12 February 2002. The Optional Protocol on the Sale of Children, Child Prostitution and Child Pornography was adopted on 25 May 2000 and entered into force on 18 January 2002. The texts of the protocols, together with documents of the Committee on the Rights of the Child are available at www.ohchr.org/english/bodies/crc.

The States Parties to the present Convention,

Considering that, in accordance with the principles proclaimed in the Charter of the United Nations, recognition of the inherent dignity and of the equal and inalienable rights of all members of the human family is the foundation of freedom, justice and peace in the world,

Bearing in mind that the peoples of the United Nations have, in the Charter, reaffirmed their faith in fundamental human rights and in the dignity and worth of the human person, and have determined to promote social progress and better standards of life in larger freedom,

Recognizing that the United Nations has, in the Universal Declaration of Human Rights and in the International Covenants on Human Rights, proclaimed and agreed that everyone is entitled to all the rights and freedoms set forth therein, without distinction of any kind, such as race, colour, sex, language, religion, political or other opinion, national or social origin, property, birth or other status,

Recalling that, in the Universal Declaration of Human Rights, the United Nations has proclaimed that childhood is entitled to special care and assistance,

Convinced that the family, as the fundamental group of society and the natural environment for the growth and well-being of all its members and particularly children, should be afforded the necessary protection and assistance so that it can fully assume its responsibilities within the community,

Recognizing that the child, for the full and harmonious development of his or her personality, should grow up in a family environment, in an atmosphere of happiness, love and understanding,

Considering that the child should be fully prepared to live an individual life in society, and brought up in the spirit of the ideals proclaimed in the Charter of the United Nations, and in particular in the spirit of peace, dignity, tolerance, freedom, equality and solidarity,

Bearing in mind that the need to extend particular care to the child has been stated in the Geneva Declaration of the Rights of the Child of 1924 and in the Declaration of the Rights of the Child adopted by the General Assembly on 20 November 1959 and recognized in the Universal Declaration of Human Rights, in the International Covenant on Civil and Political Rights (in particular in articles 23 and 24), in the International Covenant on Economic, Social and Cultural Rights (in particular in article 10) and in the statutes and relevant instruments of specialized agencies and international organizations concerned with the welfare of children,

Bearing in mind that, as indicated in the Declaration of the Rights of the Child, "the child, by reason of his physical and mental immaturity, needs special safeguards and care, including appropriate legal protection, before as well as after birth,"

Recalling the provisions of the Declaration on Social and Legal Principles relating to the Protection and Welfare of Children, with Special Reference to Foster Placement and Adoption Nationally and Internationally; the United Nations Standard Minimum Rules for the Administration of Juvenile Justice (The Beijing Rules); and the Declaration on the Protection of Women and Children in Emergency and Armed Conflict,

Recognizing that, in all countries in the world, there are children living in exceptionally difficult conditions, and that such children need special consideration,

Taking due account of the importance of the traditions and cultural values

of each people for the protection and harmonious development of the child,
Recognizing the importance of international co-operation for improving the
living conditions of children in every country, in particular in the developing
countries,

Have agreed as follows:

Part I

Article 1

For the purposes of the present Convention, a child means every human being
below the age of eighteen years unless under the law applicable to the child,
majority is attained earlier.

Article 2

1. States Parties shall respect and ensure the rights set forth in the present
Convention to each child within their jurisdiction without discrimination of
any kind, irrespective of the child's or his or her parent's or legal guardian's
race, colour, sex, language, religion, political or other opinion, national, ethnic
or social origin, property, disability, birth or other status.

2. States Parties shall take all appropriate measures to ensure that the child
is protected against all forms of discrimination or punishment on the basis of
the status, activities, expressed opinions, or beliefs of the child's parents, legal
guardians, or family members.

Article 3

1. In all actions concerning children, whether undertaken by public or private social welfare institutions, courts of law, administrative authorities or legislative bodies, the best interests of the child shall be a primary consideration.

2. States Parties undertake to ensure the child such protection and care as is
necessary for his or her well-being, taking into account the rights and duties of
his or her parents, legal guardians, or other individuals legally responsible for
him or her, and, to this end, shall take all appropriate legislative and administrative measures.

3. States Parties shall ensure that the institutions, services and facilities
responsible for the care or protection of children shall conform with the standards established by competent authorities, particularly in the areas of safety,
health, in the number and suitability of their staff, as well as competent supervision.

Article 4

States Parties shall undertake all appropriate legislative, administrative, and
other measures for the implementation of the rights recognized in the present
Convention. With regard to economic, social and cultural rights, States
Parties shall undertake such measures to the maximum extent of their avail-

able resources and, where needed, within the framework of international co-operation.

Article 5

States Parties shall respect the responsibilities, rights and duties of parents or, where applicable, the members of the extended family or community as provided for by local custom, legal guardians or other persons legally responsible for the child, to provide, in a manner consistent with the evolving capacities of the child, appropriate direction and guidance in the exercise by the child of the rights recognized in the present Convention.

Article 6

1. States Parties recognize that every child has the inherent right to life.

2. States Parties shall ensure to the maximum extent possible the survival and development of the child.

Article 7

1. The child shall be registered immediately after birth and shall have the right from birth to a name, the right to acquire a nationality and. as far as possible, the right to know and be cared for by his or her parents.

2. States Parties shall ensure the implementation of these rights in accordance with their national law and their obligations under the relevant international instruments in this field, in particular where the child would otherwise be stateless.

Article 8

1. States Parties undertake to respect the right of the child to preserve his or her identity, including nationality, name and family relations as recognized by law without unlawful interference.

2. Where a child is illegally deprived of some or all of the elements of his or her identity, States Parties shall provide appropriate assistance and protection, with a view to re-establishing speedily his or her identity.

Article 9

1. States Parties shall ensure that a child shall not be separated from his or her parents against their will, except when competent authorities subject to judicial review determine, in accordance with applicable law and procedures, that such separation is necessary for the best interests of the child. Such determination may be necessary in a particular case such as one involving abuse or neglect of the child by the parents, or one where the parents are living separately and a decision must be made as to the child's place of residence.

2. In any proceedings pursuant to paragraph 1 of the present article, all interested parties shall be given an opportunity to participate in the proceedings and make their views known.

3. States Parties shall respect the right of the child who is separated from

one or both parents to maintain personal relations and direct contact with both parents on a regular basis, except if it is contrary to the child's best interests.

4. Where such separation results from any action initiated by a State Party, such as the detention, imprisonment, exile, deportation or death (including death arising from any cause while the person is in the custody of the State) of one or both parents or of the child, that State Party shall, upon request, provide the parents, the child or, if appropriate, another member of the family with the essential information concerning the whereabouts of the absent member(s) of the family unless the provision of the information would be detrimental to the well-being of the child. States Parties shall further ensure that the submission of such a request shall of itself entail no adverse consequences for the person(s) concerned.

Article 10

1. In accordance with the obligation of States Parties under article 9, paragraph 1, applications by a child or his or her parents to enter or leave a State Party for the purpose of family reunification shall be dealt with by States Parties in a positive, humane and expeditious manner. States Parties shall further ensure that the submission of such a request shall entail no adverse consequences for the applicants and for the members of their family.

2. A child whose parents reside in different States shall have the right to maintain on a regular basis, save in exceptional circumstances personal relations and direct contacts with both parents. Towards that end and in accordance with the obligation of States Parties under article 9, paragraph 1, States Parties shall respect the right of the child and his or her parents to leave any country, including their own, and to enter their own country. The right to leave any country shall be subject only to such restrictions as are prescribed by law and which are necessary to protect the national security, public order (ordre public), public health or morals or the rights and freedoms of others and are consistent with the other rights recognized in the present Convention.

Article 11

1. States Parties shall take measures to combat the illicit transfer and non-return of children abroad.

2. To this end, States Parties shall promote the conclusion of bilateral or multilateral agreements or accession to existing agreements.

Article 12

1. States Parties shall assure to the child who is capable of forming his or her own views the right to express those views freely in all matters affecting the child, the views of the child being given due weight in accordance with the age and maturity of the child.

2. For this purpose, the child shall in particular be provided the opportunity

to be heard in any judicial and administrative proceedings affecting the child, either directly, or through a representative or an appropriate body, in a manner consistent with the procedural rules of national law.

Article 13

1. The child shall have the right to freedom of expression; this right shall include freedom to seek, receive and impart information and ideas of all kinds, regardless of frontiers, either orally, in writing or in print, in the form of art, or through any other media of the child's choice.

2. The exercise of this right may be subject to certain restrictions, but these shall only be such as are provided by law and are necessary:

(a) For respect of the rights or reputations of others; or

(b) For the protection of national security or of public order (ordre public), or of public health or morals.

Article 14

1. States Parties shall respect the right of the child to freedom of thought, conscience and religion.

2. States Parties shall respect the rights and duties of the parents and, when applicable, legal guardians, to provide direction to the child in the exercise of his or her right in a manner consistent with the evolving capacities of the child.

3. Freedom to manifest one's religion or beliefs may be subject only to such limitations as are prescribed by law and are necessary to protect public safety, order, health or morals, or the fundamental rights and freedoms of others.

Article 15

1. States Parties recognize the rights of the child to freedom of association and to freedom of peaceful assembly.

2. No restrictions may be placed on the exercise of these rights other than those imposed in conformity with the law and which are necessary in a democratic society in the interests of national security or public safety, public order (ordre public), the protection of public health or morals or the protection of the rights and freedoms of others.

Article 16

1. No child shall be subjected to arbitrary or unlawful interference with his or her privacy, family, home or correspondence, nor to unlawful attacks on his or her honour and reputation.

2. The child has the right to the protection of the law against such interference or attacks.

Article 17

States Parties recognize the important function performed by the mass media and shall ensure that the child has access to information and material from a diversity of national and international sources, especially those aimed at the promotion of his or her social, spiritual and moral well-being and physical and mental health.

To this end, States Parties shall:

(a) Encourage the mass media to disseminate information and material of social and cultural benefit to the child and in accordance with the spirit of article 29;

(b) Encourage international co-operation in the production, exchange and dissemination of such information and material from a diversity of cultural, national and international sources;

(c) Encourage the production and dissemination of children's books;

(d) Encourage the mass media to have particular regard to the linguistic needs of the child who belongs to a minority group or who is indigenous;

(e) Encourage the development of appropriate guidelines for the protection of the child from information and material injurious to his or her well-being, bearing in mind the provisions of articles 13 and 18.

Article 18

1. States Parties shall use their best efforts to ensure recognition of the principle that both parents have common responsibilities for the upbringing and development of the child. Parents or, as the case may be, legal guardians, have the primary responsibility for the upbringing and development of the child. The best interests of the child will be their basic concern.

2. For the purpose of guaranteeing and promoting the rights set forth in the present Convention, States Parties shall render appropriate assistance to parents and legal guardians in the performance of their child-rearing responsibilities and shall ensure the development of institutions, facilities and services for the care of children.

3. States Parties shall take all appropriate measures to ensure that children of working parents have the right to benefit from child-care services and facilities for which they are eligible.

Article 19

1. States Parties shall take all appropriate legislative, administrative, social and educational measures to protect the child from all forms of physical or mental violence, injury or abuse, neglect or negligent treatment, maltreatment or exploitation, including sexual abuse, while in the care of parent(s), legal guardian(s) or any other person who has the care of the child.

2. Such protective measures should, as appropriate, include effective procedures for the establishment of social programmes to provide necessary support for the child and for those who have the care of the child, as well as for other forms of prevention and for identification, reporting, referral, investigation, treatment and follow-up of instances of child maltreatment described heretofore, and, as appropriate, for judicial involvement.

Article 20

1. A child temporarily or permanently deprived of his or her family environment, or in whose own best interests cannot be allowed to remain in that environment, shall be entitled to special protection and assistance provided by the State.

2. States Parties shall in accordance with their national laws ensure alternative care for such a child.

3. Such care could include, inter alia, foster placement, kafalah of Islamic law, adoption or if necessary placement in suitable institutions for the care of children. When considering solutions, due regard shall be paid to the desirability of continuity in a child's upbringing and to the child's ethnic, religious, cultural and linguistic background.

Article 21

States Parties that recognize and/or permit the system of adoption shall ensure that the best interests of the child shall be the paramount consideration and they shall:

(a) Ensure that the adoption of a child is authorized only by competent authorities who determine, in accordance with applicable law and procedures and on the basis of all pertinent and reliable information, that the adoption is permissible in view of the child's status concerning parents, relatives and legal guardians and that, if required, the persons concerned have given their informed consent to the adoption on the basis of such counselling as may be necessary;

(b) Recognize that inter-country adoption may be considered as an alternative means of child's care, if the child cannot be placed in a foster or an adoptive family or cannot in any suitable manner be cared for in the child's country of origin;

(c) Ensure that the child concerned by inter-country adoption enjoys safeguards and standards equivalent to those existing in the case of national adoption;

(d) Take all appropriate measures to ensure that, in inter-country adoption, the placement does not result in improper financial gain for those involved in it;

(e) Promote, where appropriate, the objectives of the present article by concluding bilateral or multilateral arrangements or agreements, and endeavour, within this framework, to ensure that the placement of the child in another country is carried out by competent authorities or organs.

Article 22

1. States Parties shall take appropriate measures to ensure that a child who is seeking refugee status or who is considered a refugee in accordance with applicable international or domestic law and procedures shall, whether unaccompanied or accompanied by his or her parents or by any other person, receive appropriate protection and humanitarian assistance in the enjoyment

of applicable rights set forth in the present Convention and in other international human rights or humanitarian instruments to which the said States are Parties.

2. For this purpose, States Parties shall provide, as they consider appropriate, co-operation in any efforts by the United Nations and other competent intergovernmental organizations or non-governmental organizations co-operating with the United Nations to protect and assist such a child and to trace the parents or other members of the family of any refugee child in order to obtain information necessary for reunification with his or her family. In cases where no parents or other members of the family can be found, the child shall be accorded the same protection as any other child permanently or temporarily deprived of his or her family environment for any reason, as set forth in the present Convention.

Article 23

1. States Parties recognize that a mentally or physically disabled child should enjoy a full and decent life, in conditions which ensure dignity, promote self-reliance and facilitate the child's active participation in the community.

2. States Parties recognize the right of the disabled child to special care and shall encourage and ensure the extension, subject to available resources, to the eligible child and those responsible for his or her care, of assistance for which application is made and which is appropriate to the child's condition and to the circumstances of the parents or others caring for the child.

3. Recognizing the special needs of a disabled child, assistance extended in accordance with paragraph 2 of the present article shall be provided free of charge, whenever possible, taking into account the financial resources of the parents or others caring for the child, and shall be designed to ensure that the disabled child has effective access to and receives education, training, health care services, rehabilitation services, preparation for employment and recreation opportunities in a manner conducive to the child's achieving the fullest possible social integration and individual development, including his or her cultural and spiritual development

4. States Parties shall promote, in the spirit of international cooperation, the exchange of appropriate information in the field of preventive health care and of medical, psychological and functional treatment of disabled children, including dissemination of and access to information concerning methods of rehabilitation, education and vocational services, with the aim of enabling States Parties to improve their capabilities and skills and to widen their experience in these areas. In this regard, particular account shall be taken of the needs of developing countries.

Article 24

1. States Parties recognize the right of the child to the enjoyment of the highest attainable standard of health and to facilities for the treatment of illness

and rehabilitation of health. States Parties shall strive to ensure that no child is deprived of his or her right of access to such health care services.

2. States Parties shall pursue full implementation of this right and, in particular, shall take appropriate measures:

(a) To diminish infant and child mortality;

(b) To ensure the provision of necessary medical assistance and health care to all children with emphasis on the development of primary health care;

(c) To combat disease and malnutrition, including within the framework of primary health care, through, inter alia, the application of readily available technology and through the provision of adequate nutritious foods and clean drinking-water, taking into consideration the dangers and risks of environmental pollution;

(d) To ensure appropriate pre-natal and post-natal health care for mothers;

(e) To ensure that all segments of society, in particular parents and children, are informed, have access to education and are supported in the use of basic knowledge of child health and nutrition, the advantages of breastfeeding, hygiene and environmental sanitation and the prevention of accidents;

(f) To develop preventive health care, guidance for parents and family planning education and services.

3. States Parties shall take all effective and appropriate measures with a view to abolishing traditional practices prejudicial to the health of children.

4. States Parties undertake to promote and encourage international co-operation with a view to achieving progressively the full realization of the right recognized in the present article. In this regard, particular account shall be taken of the needs of developing countries.

Article 25

States Parties recognize the right of a child who has been placed by the competent authorities for the purposes of care, protection or treatment of his or her physical or mental health, to a periodic review of the treatment provided to the child and all other circumstances relevant to his or her placement.

Article 26

1. States Parties shall recognize for every child the right to benefit from social security, including social insurance, and shall take the necessary measures to achieve the full realization of this right in accordance with their national law.

2. The benefits should, where appropriate, be granted, taking into account the resources and the circumstances of the child and persons having responsibility for the maintenance of the child, as well as any other consideration relevant to an application for benefits made by or on behalf of the child.

Article 27

1. States Parties recognize the right of every child to a standard of liv-

ing adequate for the child's physical, mental, spiritual, moral and social development.

2. The parent(s) or others responsible for the child have the primary responsibility to secure, within their abilities and financial capacities, the conditions of living necessary for the child's development.

3. States Parties, in accordance with national conditions and within their means, shall take appropriate measures to assist parents and others responsible for the child to implement this right and shall in case of need provide material assistance and support programmes, particularly with regard to nutrition, clothing and housing.

4. States Parties shall take all appropriate measures to secure the recovery of maintenance for the child from the parents or other persons having financial responsibility for the child, both within the State Party and from abroad. In particular, where the person having financial responsibility for the child lives in a State different from that of the child, States Parties shall promote the accession to international agreements or the conclusion of such agreements, as well as the making of other appropriate arrangements.

Article 28

1. States Parties recognize the right of the child to education, and with a view to achieving this right progressively and on the basis of equal opportunity, they shall, in particular:

(a) Make primary education compulsory and available free to all;

(b) Encourage the development of different forms of secondary education, including general and vocational education, make them available and accessible to every child, and take appropriate measures such as the introduction of free education and offering financial assistance in case of need;

(c) Make higher education accessible to all on the basis of capacity by every appropriate means;

(d) Make educational and vocational information and guidance available and accessible to all children;

(e) Take measures to encourage regular attendance at schools and the reduction of drop-out rates.

2. States Parties shall take all appropriate measures to ensure that school discipline is administered in a manner consistent with the child's human dignity and in conformity with the present Convention.

3. States Parties shall promote and encourage international cooperation in matters relating to education, in particular with a view to contributing to the elimination of ignorance and illiteracy throughout the world and facilitating access to scientific and technical knowledge and modern teaching methods. In this regard, particular account shall be taken of the needs of developing countries.

Article 29

1. States Parties agree that the education of the child shall be directed to:

(a) The development of the child's personality, talents and mental and physical abilities to their fullest potential;

(b) The development of respect for human rights and fundamental freedoms, and for the principles enshrined in the Charter of the United Nations;

(c) The development of respect for the child's parents, his or her own cultural identity, language and values, for the national values of the country in which the child is living, the country from which he or she may originate, and for civilizations different from his or her own;

(d) The preparation of the child for responsible life in a free society, in the spirit of understanding, peace, tolerance, equality of sexes, and friendship among all peoples, ethnic, national and religious groups and persons of indigenous origin;

(e) The development of respect for the natural environment.

2. No part of the present article or article 28 shall be construed so as to interfere with the liberty of individuals and bodies to establish and direct educational institutions, subject always to the observance of the principle set forth in paragraph 1 of the present article and to the requirements that the education given in such institutions shall conform to such minimum standards as may be laid down by the State.

Article 30

In those States in which ethnic, religious or linguistic minorities or persons of indigenous origin exist, a child belonging to such a minority or who is indigenous shall not be denied the right, in community with other members of his or her group, to enjoy his or her own culture, to profess and practise his or her own religion, or to use his or her own language.

Article 31

1. States Parties recognize the right of the child to rest and leisure, to engage in play and recreational activities appropriate to the age of the child and to participate freely in cultural life and the arts.

2. States Parties shall respect and promote the right of the child to participate fully in cultural and artistic life and shall encourage the provision of appropriate and equal opportunities for cultural, artistic, recreational and leisure activity.

Article 32

1. States Parties recognize the right of the child to be protected from economic exploitation and from performing any work that is likely to be hazardous or to interfere with the child's education, or to be harmful to the child's health or physical, mental, spiritual, moral or social development.

2. States Parties shall take legislative, administrative, social and educational measures to ensure the implementation of the present article. To this end, and having regard to the relevant provisions of other international instruments, States Parties shall in particular:

(a) Provide for a minimum age or minimum ages for admission to employment;

(b) Provide for appropriate regulation of the hours and conditions of employment;

(c) Provide for appropriate penalties or other sanctions to ensure the effective enforcement of the present article.

Article 33

States Parties shall take all appropriate measures, including legislative, administrative, social and educational measures, to protect children from the illicit use of narcotic drugs and psychotropic substances as defined in the relevant international treaties, and to prevent the use of children in the illicit production and trafficking of such substances.

Article 34

States Parties undertake to protect the child from all forms of sexual exploitation and sexual abuse. For these purposes, States Parties shall in particular take all appropriate national, bilateral and multilateral measures to prevent:

(a) The inducement or coercion of a child to engage in any unlawful sexual activity;

(b) The exploitative use of children in prostitution or other unlawful sexual practices;

(c) The exploitative use of children in pornographic performances and materials.

Article 35

States Parties shall take all appropriate national, bilateral and multilateral measures to prevent the abduction of, the sale of or traffic in children for any purpose or in any form.

Article 36

States Parties shall protect the child against all other forms of exploitation prejudicial to any aspects of the child's welfare.

Article 37

States Parties shall ensure that:

(a) No child shall be subjected to torture or other cruel, inhuman or degrading treatment or punishment. Neither capital punishment nor life imprisonment without possibility of release shall be imposed for offences committed by persons below eighteen years of age;

(b) No child shall be deprived of his or her liberty unlawfully or arbitrarily. The arrest, detention or imprisonment of a child shall be in conformity with the law and shall be used only as a measure of last resort and for the shortest appropriate period of time;

(c) Every child deprived of liberty shall be treated with humanity and respect for the inherent dignity of the human person, and in a manner which takes into account the needs of persons of his or her age. In particular, every child deprived of liberty shall be separated from adults unless it is considered in the child's best interest not to do so and shall have the right to maintain contact with his or her family through correspondence and visits, save in exceptional circumstances;

(d) Every child deprived of his or her liberty shall have the right to prompt access to legal and other appropriate assistance, as well as the right to challenge the legality of the deprivation of his or her liberty before a court or other competent, independent and impartial authority, and to a prompt decision on any such action.

Article 38

1. States Parties undertake to respect and to ensure respect for rules of international humanitarian law applicable to them in armed conflicts which are relevant to the child.

2. States Parties shall take all feasible measures to ensure that persons who have not attained the age of fifteen years do not take a direct part in hostilities.

3. States Parties shall refrain from recruiting any person who has not attained the age of fifteen years into their armed forces. In recruiting among those persons who have attained the age of fifteen years but who have not attained the age of eighteen years, States Parties shall endeavour to give priority to those who are oldest.

4. In accordance with their obligations under international humanitarian law to protect the civilian population in armed conflicts, States Parties shall take all feasible measures to ensure protection and care of children who are affected by an armed conflict.

Article 39

States Parties shall take all appropriate measures to promote physical and psychological recovery and social reintegration of a child victim of: any form of neglect, exploitation, or abuse; torture or any other form of cruel, inhuman or degrading treatment or punishment; or armed conflicts. Such recovery and reintegration shall take place in an environment which fosters the health, self-respect and dignity of the child.

Article 40

1. States Parties recognize the right of every child alleged as, accused of, or recognized as having infringed the penal law to be treated in a manner consistent with the promotion of the child's sense of dignity and worth, which reinforces the child's respect for the human rights and fundamental freedoms of others and which takes into account the child's age and the desirability of promoting the child's reintegration and the child's assuming a constructive role in society.

2. To this end, and having regard to the relevant provisions of international instruments, States Parties shall, in particular, ensure that:

(a) No child shall be alleged as, be accused of, or recognized as having infringed the penal law by reason of acts or omissions that were not prohibited by national or international law at the time they were committed;

(b) Every child alleged as or accused of having infringed the penal law has at least the following guarantees: (i) To be presumed innocent until proven guilty according to law; (ii) To be informed promptly and directly of the charges against him or her, and, if appropriate, through his or her parents or legal guardians, and to have legal or other appropriate assistance in the preparation and presentation of his or her defence; (iii) To have the matter determined without delay by a competent, independent and impartial authority or judicial body in a fair hearing according to law, in the presence of legal or other appropriate assistance and, unless it is considered not to be in the best interest of the child, in particular, taking into account his or her age or situation, his or her parents or legal guardians; (iv) Not to be compelled to give testimony or to confess guilt; to examine or have examined adverse witnesses and to obtain the participation and examination of witnesses on his or her behalf under conditions of equality; (v) If considered to have infringed the penal law, to have this decision and any measures imposed in consequence thereof reviewed by a higher competent, independent and impartial authority or judicial body according to law; (vi) To have the free assistance of an interpreter if the child cannot understand or speak the language used; (vii) To have his or her privacy fully respected at all stages of the proceedings.

3. States Parties shall seek to promote the establishment of laws, procedures, authorities and institutions specifically applicable to children alleged as, accused of, or recognized as having infringed the penal law, and, in particular:

(a) The establishment of a minimum age below which children shall be presumed not to have the capacity to infringe the penal law;

(b) Whenever appropriate and desirable, measures for dealing with such children without resorting to judicial proceedings, providing that human rights and legal safeguards are fully respected.

4. A variety of dispositions, such as care, guidance and supervision orders; counselling; probation; foster care; education and vocational training programmes and other alternatives to institutional care shall be available to ensure that children are dealt with in a manner appropriate to their well-being and proportionate both to their circumstances and the offence.

Article 41

Nothing in the present Convention shall affect any provisions which are more conducive to the realization of the rights of the child and which may be contained in:

(a) The law of a State party; or

(b) International law in force for that State.

Part II

Article 42

States Parties undertake to make the principles and provisions of the Convention widely known, by appropriate and active means, to adults and children alike.

Article 43

1. For the purpose of examining the progress made by States Parties in achieving the realization of the obligations undertaken in the present Convention, there shall be established a Committee on the Rights of the Child, which shall carry out the functions hereinafter provided.

2. The Committee shall consist of ten experts of high moral standing and recognized competence in the field covered by this Convention. The members of the Committee shall be elected by States Parties from among their nationals and shall serve in their personal capacity, consideration being given to equitable geographical distribution, as well as to the principal legal systems.

3. The members of the Committee shall be elected by secret ballot from a list of persons nominated by States Parties. Each State Party may nominate one person from among its own nationals.

4. The initial election to the Committee shall be held no later than six months after the date of the entry into force of the present Convention and thereafter every second year. At least four months before the date of each election, the Secretary-General of the United Nations shall address a letter to States Parties inviting them to submit their nominations within two months. The Secretary-General shall subsequently prepare a list in alphabetical order of all persons thus nominated, indicating States Parties which have nominated them, and shall submit it to the States Parties to the present Convention.

5. The elections shall be held at meetings of States Parties convened by the Secretary-General at United Nations Headquarters. At those meetings, for which two thirds of States Parties shall constitute a quorum, the persons elected to the Committee shall be those who obtain the largest number of votes and an absolute majority of the votes of the representatives of States Parties present and voting.

6. The members of the Committee shall be elected for a term of four years. They shall be eligible for re-election if renominated. The term of five of the members elected at the first election shall expire at the end of two years; immediately after the first election, the names of these five members shall be chosen by lot by the Chairman of the meeting.

7. If a member of the Committee dies or resigns or declares that for any other cause he or she can no longer perform the duties of the Committee, the State Party which nominated the member shall appoint another expert from among its nationals to serve for the remainder of the term, subject to the approval of the Committee.

8. The Committee shall establish its own rules of procedure.

9. The Committee shall elect its officers for a period of two years.

10. The meetings of the Committee shall normally be held at United Nations Headquarters or at any other convenient place as determined by the Committee. The Committee shall normally meet annually. The duration of the meetings of the Committee shall be determined, and reviewed, if necessary, by a meeting of the States Parties to the present Convention, subject to the approval of the General Assembly.

11. The Secretary-General of the United Nations shall provide the necessary staff and facilities for the effective performance of the functions of the Committee under the present Convention.

12. With the approval of the General Assembly, the members of the Committee established under the present Convention shall receive emoluments from United Nations resources on such terms and conditions as the Assembly may decide.

Article 44

1. States Parties undertake to submit to the Committee, through the Secretary-General of the United Nations, reports on the measures they have adopted which give effect to the rights recognized herein and on the progress made on the enjoyment of those rights

(a) Within two years of the entry into force of the Convention for the State Party concerned;

(b) Thereafter every five years.

2. Reports made under the present article shall indicate factors and difficulties, if any, affecting the degree of fulfilment of the obligations under the present Convention. Reports shall also contain sufficient information to provide the Committee with a comprehensive understanding of the implementation of the Convention in the country concerned.

3. A State Party which has submitted a comprehensive initial report to the Committee need not, in its subsequent reports submitted in accordance with paragraph 1 (b) of the present article, repeat basic information previously provided.

4. The Committee may request from States Parties further information relevant to the implementation of the Convention.

5. The Committee shall submit to the General Assembly, through the Economic and Social Council, every two years, reports on its activities.

6. States Parties shall make their reports widely available to the public in their own countries.

Article 45

In order to foster the effective implementation of the Convention and to encourage international co-operation in the field covered by the Convention:

(a) The specialized agencies, the United Nations Children's Fund, and other

United Nations organs shall be entitled to be represented at the consideration of the implementation of such provisions of the present Convention as fall within the scope of their mandate. The Committee may invite the specialized agencies, the United Nations Children's Fund and other competent bodies as it may consider appropriate to provide expert advice on the implementation of the Convention in areas falling within the scope of their respective mandates. The Committee may invite the specialized agencies, the United Nations Children's Fund, and other United Nations organs to submit reports on the implementation of the Convention in areas falling within the scope of their activities;

(b) The Committee shall transmit, as it may consider appropriate, to the specialized agencies, the United Nations Children's Fund and other competent bodies, any reports from States Parties that contain a request, or indicate a need, for technical advice or assistance, along with the Committee's observations and suggestions, if any, on these requests or indications;

(c) The Committee may recommend to the General Assembly to request the Secretary-General to undertake on its behalf studies on specific issues relating to the rights of the child;

(d) The Committee may make suggestions and general recommendations based on information received pursuant to articles 44 and 45 of the present Convention. Such suggestions and general recommendations shall be transmitted to any State Party concerned and reported to the General Assembly, together with comments, if any, from States Parties.

Part III

Article 46
The present Convention shall be open for signature by all States.

Article 47
The present Convention is subject to ratification. Instruments of ratification shall be deposited with the Secretary-General of the United Nations.

Article 48
The present Convention shall remain open for accession by any State. The instruments of accession shall be deposited with the Secretary-General of the United Nations.

Article 49
1. The present Convention shall enter into force on the thirtieth day following the date of deposit with the Secretary-General of the United Nations of the twentieth instrument of ratification or accession.

2. For each State ratifying or acceding to the Convention after the deposit of

the twentieth instrument of ratification or accession, the Convention shall enter into force on the thirtieth day after the deposit by such State of its instrument of ratification or accession.

Article 50

1. Any State Party may propose an amendment and file it with the Secretary-General of the United Nations. The Secretary-General shall thereupon communicate the proposed amendment to States Parties, with a request that they indicate whether they favour a conference of States Parties for the purpose of considering and voting upon the proposals. In the event that, within four months from the date of such communication, at least one third of the States Parties favour such a conference, the Secretary-General shall convene the conference under the auspices of the United Nations. Any amendment adopted by a majority of States Parties present and voting at the conference shall be submitted to the General Assembly for approval.

2. An amendment adopted in accordance with paragraph 1 of the present article shall enter into force when it has been approved by the General Assembly of the United Nations and accepted by a two-thirds majority of States Parties.

3. When an amendment enters into force, it shall be binding on those States Parties which have accepted it, other States Parties still being bound by the provisions of the present Convention and any earlier amendments which they have accepted.

Article 51

1. The Secretary-General of the United Nations shall receive and circulate to all States the text of reservations made by States at the time of ratification or accession.

2. A reservation incompatible with the object and purpose of the present Convention shall not be permitted.

3. Reservations may be withdrawn at any time by notification to that effect addressed to the Secretary-General of the United Nations, who shall then inform all States. Such notification shall take effect on the date on which it is received by the Secretary-General.

Article 52

A State Party may denounce the present Convention by written notification to the Secretary-General of the United Nations. Denunciation becomes effective one year after the date of receipt of the notification by the Secretary-General.

Article 53

The Secretary-General of the United Nations is designated as the depositary of the present Convention.

Article 54

The original of the present Convention, of which the Arabic, Chinese, English, French, Russian and Spanish texts are equally authentic, shall be deposited with the Secretary-General of the United Nations.

IN WITNESS THEREOF the undersigned plenipotentiaries, being duly authorized thereto by their respective governments, have signed the present Convention.

6
International
Humanitarian Law

6.1
Geneva Convention Relative to the Treatment of Prisoners of War (Third Geneva Convention) (1949)

This convention revised and extended the provisions of the 1929 Geneva Convention on the Treatment of Prisoners of War. It came into renewed prominence with the Bush administration's controversial announcement that captured Taliban and Al-Qaida fighters were not entitled to prisoner-of-war status under this convention. The International Committee of the Red Cross (ICRC) clarified its position on this and related questions in an official statement entitled "The Relevance of International Humanitarian Law in the Context of Terrorism," issued on 21 July 2005. This statement, together with commentary on the four 1949 Geneva Conventions, and other useful materials is available from the website of the International Committee of the Red Cross at www.icrc.org/eng/ihl. See also George H. Aldrich, "The Taliban, Al Qaeda, and the Determination of Illegal Combatants," American Journal of International Law 96 (2002): 891–898.

Part I: General Provisions

Article 1
The High Contracting Parties undertake to respect and to ensure respect for the present Convention in all circumstances.

Article 2
In addition to the provisions which shall be implemented in peacetime, the present Convention shall apply to all cases of declared war or of any other armed conflict which may arise between two or more of the High Contracting Parties, even if the state of war is not recognized by one of them.

The Convention shall also apply to all cases of partial or total occupation of the territory of a High Contracting Party, even if the said occupation meets with no armed resistance.

Although one of the Powers in conflict may not be a party to the present Convention, the Powers who are parties thereto shall remain bound by it in their mutual relations. They shall furthermore be bound by the Convention in relation to the said Power, if the latter accepts and applies the provisions thereof.

Article 3

In the case of armed conflict not of an international character occurring in the territory of one of the High Contracting Parties, each party to the conflict shall be bound to apply, as a minimum, the following provisions:

1. Persons taking no active part in the hostilities, including members of armed forces who have laid down their arms and those placed hors de combat by sickness, wounds, detention, or any other cause, shall in all circumstances be treated humanely, without any adverse distinction founded on race, colour, religion or faith, sex, birth or wealth, or any other similar criteria.

To this end the following acts are and shall remain prohibited at any time and in any place whatsoever with respect to the above-mentioned persons:

(a) Violence to life and person, in particular murder of all kinds, mutilation, cruel treatment and torture;

(b) Taking of hostages;

(c) Outrages upon personal dignity, in particular, humiliating and degrading treatment;

(d) The passing of sentences and the carrying out of executions without previous judgment pronounced by a regularly constituted court affording all the judicial guarantees which are recognized as indispensable by civilized peoples.

2. The wounded and sick shall be collected and cared for.

An impartial humanitarian body, such as the International Committee of the Red Cross, may offer its services to the Parties to the conflict.

The Parties to the conflict should further endeavour to bring into force, by means of special agreements, all or part of the other provisions of the present Convention.

The application of the preceding provisions shall not affect the legal status of the Parties to the conflict.

Article 4

A. Prisoners of war, in the sense of the present Convention, are persons belonging to one of the following categories, who have fallen into the power of the enemy:

1. Members of the armed forces of a Party to the conflict as well as members of militias or volunteer corps forming part of such armed forces.

2. Members of other militias and members of other volunteer corps, including those of organized resistance movements, belonging to a Party to the conflict and operating in or outside their own territory, even if this territory is occupied, provided that such militias or volunteer corps, including such organized resistance movements, fulfil the following conditions:

(a) That of being commanded by a person responsible for his subordinates;

(b) That of having a fixed distinctive sign recognizable at a distance;

(c) That of carrying arms openly;

(d) That of conducting their operations in accordance with the laws and customs of war.

3. Members of regular armed forces who profess allegiance to a government or an authority not recognized by the Detaining Power:

4. Persons who accompany the armed forces without actually being members thereof, such as civilian members of military aircraft crews, war correspondents, supply contractors, members of labour units or of services responsible for the welfare of the armed forces, provided that they have received authorization from the armed forces which they accompany, who shall provide them for that purpose with an identity card similar to the annexed model.

5. Members of crews, including masters, pilots and apprentices, of the merchant marine and the crews of civil aircraft of the Parties to the conflict, who do not benefit by more favourable treatment under any other provisions of international law.

6. Inhabitants of a non-occupied territory, who on the approach of the enemy spontaneously take up arms to resist the invading forces, without having had time to form themselves into regular armed units, provided they carry arms openly and respect the laws and customs of war.

B. The following shall likewise be treated as prisoners of war under the present Convention:

1. Persons belonging, or having belonged, to the armed forces of the occupied country, if the occupying Power considers it necessary by reason of such allegiance to intern them, even though it has originally liberated them while hostilities were going on outside the territory it occupies, in particular where such persons have made an unsuccessful attempt to rejoin the armed forces to which they belong and which are engaged in combat, or where they fail to comply with a summons made to them with a view to internment.

2. The persons belonging to one of the categories enumerated in the present Article, who have been received by neutral or non-belligerent Powers on their territory and whom these Powers are required to intern under international law, without prejudice to any more favourable treatment which these Powers may choose to give and with the exception of Articles 8, 10, 15, 30, fifth paragraph, 58-67, 92, 126 and, where diplomatic relations exist between the Parties to the conflict and the neutral or non-belligerent Power concerned, those Articles concerning the Protecting Power. Where such diplomatic relations exist, the Parties to a conflict on whom these persons depend shall be allowed to perform towards them the functions of a Protecting Power as provided in the present Convention, without prejudice to the functions which these Parties normally exercise in conformity with diplomatic and consular usage and treaties.

C. This Article shall in no way affect the status of medical personnel and chaplains as provided for in Article 33 of the present Convention.

Article 5

The present Convention shall apply to the persons referred to in Article 4 from the time they fall into the power of the enemy and until their final release and repatriation.

Should any doubt arise as to whether persons, having committed a belligerent act and having fallen into the hands of the enemy, belong to any of the categories enumerated in Article 4, such persons shall enjoy the protection of the present Convention until such time as their status has been determined by a competent tribunal.

Article 6

In addition to the agreements expressly provided for in Articles 10, 23, 28, 33, 60, 65, 66, 67, 72, 73, 75, 109, 110, 118, 119, 122 and 132, the High Contracting Parties may conclude other special agreements for all matters concerning which they may deem it suitable to make separate provision. No special agreement shall adversely affect the situation of prisoners of war, as defined by the present Convention, nor restrict the rights which it confers upon them.

Prisoners of war shall continue to have the benefit of such agreements as long as the Convention is applicable to them, except where express provisions to the contrary are contained in the aforesaid or in subsequent agreements, or where more favourable measures have been taken with regard to them by one or other of the Parties to the conflict.

Article 7

Prisoners of war may in no circumstances renounce in part or in entirety the rights secured to them by the present Convention, and by the special agreements referred to in the foregoing Article, if such there be.

Article 8

The present Convention shall be applied with the cooperation and under the scrutiny of the Protecting Powers whose duty it is to safeguard the interests of the Parties to the conflict. For this purpose, the Protecting Powers may appoint, apart from their diplomatic or consular staff, delegates from amongst their own nationals or the nationals of other neutral Powers. The said delegates shall be subject to the approval of the Power with which they are to carry out their duties.

The Parties to the conflict shall facilitate to the greatest extent possible the task of the representatives or delegates of the Protecting Powers.

The representatives or delegates of the Protecting Powers shall not in any case exceed their mission under the present Convention. They shall, in particular, take account of the imperative necessities of security of the State wherein they carry out their duties.

Article 9

The provisions of the present Convention constitute no obstacle to the humanitarian activities which the International Committee of the Red Cross or any other impartial humanitarian organization may, subject to the consent of the Parties to the conflict concerned, undertake for the protection of prisoners of war and for their relief.

Article 10

The High Contracting Parties may at any time agree to entrust to an organization which offers all guarantees of impartiality and efficacy the duties incumbent on the Protecting Powers by virtue of the present Convention.

When prisoners of war do not benefit or cease to benefit, no matter for what reason, by the activities of a Protecting Power or of an organization provided for in the first paragraph above, the Detaining Power shall request a neutral State, or such an organization, to undertake the functions performed under the present Convention by a Protecting Power designated by the Parties to a conflict.

If protection cannot be arranged accordingly, the Detaining Power shall request or shall accept, subject to the provisions of this Article, the offer of the services of a humanitarian organization, such as the International Committee of the Red Cross, to assume the humanitarian functions performed by Protecting Powers under the present Convention.

Any neutral Power or any organization invited by the Power concerned or offering itself for these purposes, shall be required to act with a sense of responsibility towards the Party to the conflict on which persons protected by the present Convention depend, and shall be required to furnish sufficient assurances that it is in a position to undertake the appropriate functions and to discharge them impartially.

No derogation from the preceding provisions shall be made by special agreements between Powers one of which is restricted, even temporarily, in its freedom to negotiate with the other Power or its allies by reason of military events, more particularly where the whole, or a substantial part, of the territory of the said Power is occupied.

Whenever in the present Convention mention is made of a Protecting Power, such mention applies to substitute organizations in the sense of the present Article.

Article 11

In cases where they deem it advisable in the interest of protected persons, particularly in cases of disagreement between the Parties to the conflict as to the application or interpretation of the provisions of the present Convention, the Protecting Powers shall lend their good offices with a view to settling the disagreement.

For this purpose, each of the Protecting Powers may, either at the invitation of one Party or on its own initiative, propose to the Parties to the conflict a meeting of their representatives, and in particular of the authorities responsible for prisoners of war, possibly on neutral territory suitably chosen. The Parties to the conflict shall be bound to give effect to the proposals made to them for this purpose. The Protecting Powers may, if necessary, propose for approval by the Parties to the conflict a person belonging to a neutral Power, or delegated by the International Committee of the Red Cross, who shall be invited to take part in such a meeting.

Part II: General Protection of Prisoners of War

Article 12
Prisoners of war are in the hands of the enemy Power, but not of the individuals or military units who have captured them. Irrespective of the individual responsibilities that may exist, the Detaining Power is responsible for the treatment given them.

Prisoners of war may only be transferred by the Detaining Power to a Power which is a party to the Convention and after the Detaining Power has satisfied itself of the willingness and ability of such transferee Power to apply the Convention. When prisoners of war are transferred under such circumstances, responsibility for the application of the Convention rests on the Power accepting them while they are in its custody.

Nevertheless if that Power fails to carry out the provisions of the Convention in any important respect, the Power by whom the prisoners of war were transferred shall, upon being notified by the Protecting Power, take effective measures to correct the situation or shall request the return of the prisoners of war. Such requests must be complied with.

Article 13
Prisoners of war must at all times be humanely treated. Any unlawful act or omission by the Detaining Power causing death or seriously endangering the health of a prisoner of war in its custody is prohibited, and will be regarded as a serious breach of the present Convention. In particular, no prisoner of war may be subjected to physical mutilation or to medical or scientific experiments of any kind which are not justified by the medical, dental or hospital treatment of the prisoner concerned and carried out in his interest.

Likewise, prisoners of war must at all times be protected, particularly against acts of violence or intimidation and against insults and public curiosity.

Measures of reprisal against prisoners of war are prohibited.

Article 14
Prisoners of war are entitled in all circumstances to respect for their persons and their honour.

Women shall be treated with all the regard due to their sex and shall in all cases benefit by treatment as favourable as that granted to men.

Prisoners of war shall retain the full civil capacity which they enjoyed at the time of their capture. The Detaining Power may not restrict the exercise, either within or without its own territory, of the rights such capacity confers except in so far as the captivity requires.

Article 15
The Power detaining prisoners of war shall be bound to provide free of charge for their maintenance and for the medical attention required by their state of health.

Article 16
Taking into consideration the provisions of the present Convention relating to rank and sex, and subject to any privileged treatment which may be accorded to them by reason of their state of health, age or professional qualifications, all prisoners of war shall be treated alike by the Detaining Power, without any adverse distinction based on race, nationality, religious belief or political opinions, or any other distinction founded on similar criteria.

Part III: Captivity

Section I: Beginning of Captivity

Article 17
Every prisoner of war, when questioned on the subject, is bound to give only his surname, first names and rank, date of birth, and army, regimental, personal or serial number, or failing this, equivalent information.

If he wilfully infringes this rule, he may render himself liable to a restriction of the privileges accorded to his rank or status.

Each Party to a conflict is required to furnish the persons under its jurisdiction who are liable to become prisoners of war, with an identity card showing the owner's surname, first names, rank, army, regimental, personal or serial number or equivalent information, and date of birth. The identity card may, furthermore, bear the signature or the fingerprints, or both, of the owner, and may bear, as well, any other information the Party to the conflict may wish to add concerning persons belonging to its armed forces. As far as possible the card shall measure 6.5 x 10 cm. and shall be issued in duplicate. The identity card shall be shown by the prisoner of war upon demand, but may in no case be taken away from him.

No physical or mental torture, nor any other form of coercion, may be inflicted on prisoners of war to secure from them information of any kind whatever. Prisoners of war who refuse to answer may not be threatened, insulted, or exposed to any unpleasant or disadvantageous treatment of any kind.

Prisoners of war who, owing to their physical or mental condition, are unable to state their identity, shall be handed over to the medical service. The identity of such prisoners shall be established by all possible means, subject to the provisions of the preceding paragraph.

The questioning of prisoners of war shall be carried out in a language which they understand.

Article 18

All effects and articles of personal use, except arms, horses, military equipment and military documents shall remain in the possession of prisoners of war, likewise their metal helmets and gas masks and like articles issued for personal protection. Effects and articles used for their clothing or feeding shall likewise remain in their possession, even if such effects and articles belong to their regulation military equipment.

At no time should prisoners of war be without identity documents. The Detaining Power shall supply such documents to prisoners of war who possess none.

Badges of rank and nationality, decorations and articles having above all a personal or sentimental value may not be taken from prisoners of war.

Sums of money carried by prisoners of war may not be taken away from them except by order of an officer, and after the amount and particulars of the owner have been recorded in a special register and an itemized receipt has been given, legibly inscribed with the name, rank and unit of the person issuing the said receipt. Sums in the currency of the Detaining Power, or which are changed into such currency at the prisoner's request, shall be placed to the credit of the prisoner's account as provided in Article 64.

The Detaining Power may withdraw articles of value from prisoners of war only for reasons of security; when such articles are withdrawn, the procedure laid down for sums of money impounded shall apply.

Such objects, likewise the sums taken away in any currency other than that of the Detaining Power and the conversion of which has not been asked for by the owners, shall be kept in the custody of the Detaining Power and shall be returned in their initial shape to prisoners of war at the end of their captivity.

Article 19

Prisoners of war shall be evacuated, as soon as possible after their capture, to camps situated in an area far enough from the combat zone for them to be out of danger.

Only those prisoners of war who, owing to wounds or sickness, would run greater risks by being evacuated than by remaining where they are, may be temporarily kept back in a danger zone.

Prisoners of war shall not be unnecessarily exposed to danger while awaiting evacuation from a fighting zone.

Article 20

The evacuation of prisoners of war shall always be effected humanely and in conditions similar to those for the forces of the Detaining Power in their changes of station.

The Detaining Power shall supply prisoners of war who are being evacuated with sufficient food and potable water, and with the necessary clothing and medical attention. The Detaining Power shall take all suitable precautions to ensure their safety during evacuation, and shall establish as soon as possible a list of the prisoners of war who are evacuated.

If prisoners of war must, during evacuation, pass through transit camps, their stay in such camps shall be as brief as possible.

Section II: Internment of Prisoners of War

Chapter I: General Observations

Article 21

The Detaining Power may subject prisoners of war to internment. It may impose on them the obligation of not leaving, beyond certain limits, the camp where they are interned, or if the said camp is fenced in, of not going outside its perimeter. Subject to the provisions of the present Convention relative to penal and disciplinary sanctions, prisoners of war may not be held in close confinement except where necessary to safeguard their health and then only during the continuation of the circumstances which make such confinement necessary.

Prisoners of war may be partially or wholly released on parole or promise, in so far as is allowed by the laws of the Power on which they depend. Such measures shall be taken particularly in cases where this may contribute to the improvement of their state of health. No prisoner of war shall be compelled to accept liberty on parole or promise.

Upon the outbreak of hostilities, each Party to the conflict shall notify the adverse Party of the laws and regulations allowing or forbidding its own nationals to accept liberty on parole or promise. Prisoners of war who are paroled or who have given their promise in conformity with the laws and regulations so notified, are bound on their personal honour scrupulously to fulfil, both towards the Power on which they depend and towards the Power which has captured them, the engagements of their paroles or promises. In such cases, the Power on which they depend is bound neither to require nor to accept from them any service incompatible with the parole or promise given.

Article 22

Prisoners of war may be interned only in premises located on land and affording every guarantee of hygiene and healthfulness. Except in particular cases which are justified by the interest of the prisoners themselves, they shall not be interned in penitentiaries.

Prisoners of war interned in unhealthy areas, or where the climate is injurious for them, shall be removed as soon as possible to a more favourable climate.

The Detaining Power shall assemble prisoners of war in camps or camp compounds according to their nationality, language and customs, provided that such prisoners shall not be separated from prisoners of war belonging to the armed forces with which they were serving at the time of their capture, except with their consent.

Article 23

No prisoner of war may at any time be sent to or detained in areas where he may be exposed to the fire of the combat zone, nor may his presence be used to render certain points or areas immune from military operations.

Prisoners of war shall have shelters against air bombardment and other hazards of war, to the same extent as the local civilian population. With the exception of those engaged in the protection of their quarters against the aforesaid hazards, they may enter such shelters as soon as possible after the giving of the alarm. Any other protective measure taken in favour of the population shall also apply to them.

Detaining Powers shall give the Powers concerned, through the intermediary of the Protecting Powers, all useful information regarding the geographical location of prisoner of war camps.

Whenever military considerations permit, prisoner of war camps shall be indicated in the day-time by the letters PW or PG, placed so as to be clearly visible from the air. The Powers concerned may, however, agree upon any other system of marking. Only prisoner of war camps shall be marked as such.

Article 24

Transit or screening camps of a permanent kind shall be fitted out under conditions similar to those described in the present Section, and the prisoners therein shall have the same treatment as in other camps.

Chapter II: Quarters, Food and Clothing of Prisoners of War

Article 25

Prisoners of war shall be quartered under conditions as favourable as those for the forces of the Detaining Power who are billeted in the same area. The said conditions shall make allowance for the habits and customs of the prisoners and shall in no case be prejudicial to their health.

The foregoing provisions shall apply in particular to the dormitories of prisoners of war as regards both total surface and minimum cubic space, and the general installations, bedding and blankets.

The premises provided for the use of prisoners of war individually or collectively, shall be entirely protected from dampness and adequately heated and lighted, in particular between dusk and lights out. All precautions must be taken against the danger of fire.

In any camps in which women prisoners of war, as well as men, are accommodated, separate dormitories shall be provided for them.

Article 26

The basic daily food rations shall be sufficient in quantity, quality and variety to keep prisoners of war in good health and to prevent loss of weight or the development of nutritional deficiencies. Account shall also be taken of the habitual diet of the prisoners.

The Detaining Power shall supply prisoners of war who work with such additional rations as are necessary for the labour on which they are employed.

Sufficient drinking water shall be supplied to prisoners of war. The use of tobacco shall be permitted.

Prisoners of war shall, as far as possible, be associated with the preparation of their meals; they may be employed for that purpose in the kitchens. Furthermore, they shall be given the means of preparing, themselves, the additional food in their possession.

Adequate premises shall be provided for messing.

Collective disciplinary measures affecting food are prohibited.

Article 27

Clothing, underwear and footwear shall be supplied to prisoners of war in sufficient quantities by the Detaining Power, which shall make allowance for the climate of the region where the prisoners are detained. Uniforms of enemy armed forces captured by the Detaining Power should, if suitable for the climate, be made available to clothe prisoners of war.

The regular replacement and repair of the above articles shall be assured by the Detaining Power. In addition, prisoners of war who work shall receive appropriate clothing, wherever the nature of the work demands.

Article 28

Canteens shall be installed in all camps, where prisoners of war may procure foodstuffs, soap and tobacco and ordinary articles in daily use. The tariff shall never be in excess of local market prices.

The profits made by camp canteens shall be used for the benefit of the prisoners; a special fund shall be created for this purpose. The prisoners' representative shall have the right to collaborate in the management of the canteen and of this fund.

When a camp is closed down, the credit balance of the special fund shall be handed to an international welfare organization, to be employed for the benefit of prisoners of war of the same nationality as those who have contributed to the fund. In case of a general repatriation, such profits shall be kept by the Detaining Power, subject to any agreement to the contrary between the Powers concerned.

Chapter III: Hygiene and Medical Attention

Article 29

The Detaining Power shall be bound to take all sanitary measures necessary to ensure the cleanliness and healthfulness of camps and to prevent epidemics.

Prisoners of war shall have for their use, day and night, conveniences which conform to the rules of hygiene and are maintained in a constant state of cleanliness. In any camps in which women prisoners of war are accommodated, separate conveniences shall be provided for them.

Also, apart from the baths and showers with which the camps shall be furnished, prisoners of war shall be provided with sufficient water and soap for their personal toilet and for washing their personal laundry; the necessary installations, facilities and time shall be granted them for that purpose.

Article 30

Every camp shall have an adequate infirmary where prisoners of war may have the attention they require, as well as appropriate diet. Isolation wards shall, if necessary, be set aside for cases of contagious or mental disease.

Prisoners of war suffering from serious disease, or whose condition necessitates special treatment, a surgical operation or hospital care, must be admitted to any military or civilian medical unit where such treatment can be given, even if their repatriation is contemplated in the near future. Special facilities shall be afforded for the care to be given to the disabled, in particular to the blind, and for their rehabilitation, pending repatriation.

Prisoners of war shall have the attention, preferably, of medical personnel of the Power on which they depend and, if possible, of their nationality.

Prisoners of war may not be prevented from presenting themselves to the medical authorities for examination. The detaining authorities shall, upon request, issue to every prisoner who has undergone treatment, an official certificate indicating the nature of his illness or injury, and the duration and kind of treatment received. A duplicate of this certificate shall be forwarded to the Central Prisoners of War Agency.

The costs of treatment, including those of any apparatus necessary for the maintenance of prisoners of war in good health, particularly dentures and other artificial appliances, and spectacles, shall be borne by the Detaining Power.

Article 31

Medical inspections of prisoners of war shall be held at least once a month. They shall include the checking and the recording of the weight of each prisoner of war. Their purpose shall be, in particular, to supervise the general state of health, nutrition and cleanliness of prisoners and to detect contagious diseases, especially tuberculosis, malaria and venereal disease. For this purpose the most efficient methods available shall be employed, e.g. periodic mass miniature radiography for the early detection of tuberculosis.

Article 32

Prisoners of war who, though not attached to the medical service of their armed forces, are physicians, surgeons, dentists, nurses or medical orderlies, may be required by the Detaining Power to exercise their medical functions in the interests of prisoners of war dependent on the same Power. In that case they shall continue to be prisoners of war, but shall receive the same treatment as corresponding medical personnel retained by the Detaining Power. They shall be exempted from any other work under Article 49.

Chapter IV: Medical Personnel and Chaplains Retained to Assist Prisoners of War

Article 33

Members of the medical personnel and chaplains while retained by the Detaining Power with a view to assisting prisoners of war, shall not be considered as prisoners of war. They shall, however, receive as a minimum the benefits and protection of the present Convention, and shall also be granted all facilities necessary to provide for the medical care of, and religious ministration to, prisoners of war.

They shall continue to exercise their medical and spiritual functions for the benefit of prisoners of war, preferably those belonging to the armed forces upon which they depend, within the scope of the military laws and regulations of the Detaining Power and under the control of its competent services, in accordance with their professional etiquette. They shall also benefit by the following facilities in the exercise of their medical or spiritual functions:

(a) They shall be authorized to visit periodically prisoners of war situated in working detachments or in hospitals outside the camp. For this purpose, the Detaining Power shall place at their disposal the necessary means of transport.

(b) The senior medical officer in each camp shall be responsible to the camp military authorities for everything connected with the activities of retained medical personnel. For this purpose, Parties to the conflict shall agree at the outbreak of hostilities on the subject of the corresponding ranks of the medical personnel, including that of societies mentioned in Article 26 of the Geneva Convention for the Amelioration of the Condition of the Wounded and Sick in Armed Forces in the Field of August 12, 1949. This senior medical officer, as well as chaplains, shall have the right to deal with the competent authorities of the camp on all questions relating to their duties. Such authorities shall afford them all necessary facilities for correspondence relating to these questions.

(c) Although they shall be subject to the internal discipline of the camp in which they are retained, such personnel may not be compelled to carry out any work other than that concerned with their medical or religious duties.

During hostilities, the Parties to the conflict shall agree concerning the possible relief of retained personnel and shall settle the procedure to be followed.

None of the preceding provisions shall relieve the Detaining Power of its obligations with regard to prisoners of war from the medical or spiritual point of view.

Chapter V: Religious, Intellectual and Physical Activities

Article 34

Prisoners of war shall enjoy complete latitude in the exercise of their religious duties, including attendance at the service of their faith, on condition that they comply with the disciplinary routine prescribed by the military authorities.

Adequate premises shall be provided where religious services may be held.

Article 35

Chaplains who fall into the hands of the enemy Power and who remain or are retained with a view to assisting prisoners of war, shall be allowed to minister to them and to exercise freely their ministry amongst prisoners of war of the same religion, in accordance with their religious conscience. They shall be allocated among the various camps and labour detachments containing prisoners of war belonging to the same forces, speaking the same language or practising the same religion. They shall enjoy the necessary facilities, including the means of transport provided for in Article 33, for visiting the prisoners of war outside their camp. They shall be free to correspond, subject to censorship, on matters concerning their religious duties with the ecclesiastical authorities in the country of detention and with international religious organizations. Letters and cards which they may send for this purpose shall be in addition to the quota provided for in Article 71.

Article 36

Prisoners of war who are ministers of religion, without having officiated as chaplains to their own forces, shall be at liberty, whatever their denomination, to minister freely to the members of their community. For this purpose, they shall receive the same treatment as the chaplains retained by the Detaining Power. They shall not be obliged to do any other work.

Article 37

When prisoners of war have not the assistance of a retained chaplain or of a prisoner of war minister of their faith, a minister belonging to the prisoners' or a similar denomination, or in his absence a qualified layman, if such a course is feasible from a confessional point of view, shall be appointed, at the request of the prisoners concerned, to fill this office. This appointment, subject to the approval of the Detaining Power, shall take place with the agreement of the community of prisoners concerned and, wherever necessary, with the approval of the local religious authorities of the same faith. The person thus appointed shall comply with all regulations established by the Detaining Power in the interests of discipline and military security.

Article 38

While respecting the individual preferences of every prisoner, the Detaining Power shall encourage the practice of intellectual, educational, and recreational pursuits, sports and games amongst prisoners, and shall take the measures necessary to ensure the exercise thereof by providing them with adequate premises and necessary equipment.

Prisoners shall have opportunities for taking physical exercise, including sports and games, and for being out of doors. Sufficient open spaces shall be provided for this purpose in all camps.

Chapter VI: Discipline

Article 39

Every prisoner of war camp shall be put under the immediate authority of a responsible commissioned officer belonging to the regular armed forces of the Detaining Power. Such officer shall have in his possession a copy of the present Convention; he shall ensure that its provisions are known to the camp staff and the guard and shall be responsible, under the direction of his government, for its application.

Prisoners of war, with the exception of officers, must salute and show to all officers of the Detaining Power the external marks of respect provided for by the regulations applying in their own forces.

Officer prisoners of war are bound to salute only officers of a higher rank of the Detaining Power; they must, however, salute the camp commander regardless of his rank.

Article 40

The wearing of badges of rank and nationality, as well as of decorations, shall be permitted.

Article 41

In every camp the text of the present Convention and its Annexes and the contents of any special agreement provided for in Article 6, shall be posted, in the prisoners' own language, at places where all may read them. Copies shall be supplied, on request, to the prisoners who cannot have access to the copy which has been posted.

Regulations, orders, notices and publications of every kind relating to the conduct of prisoners of war shall be issued to them in a language which they understand. Such regulations, orders and publications shall be posted in the manner described above and copies shall be handed to the prisoners' representative. Every order and command addressed to prisoners of war individually must likewise be given in a language which they understand.

Article 42

The use of weapons against prisoners of war, especially against those who are escaping or attempting to escape, shall constitute an extreme measure, which shall always be preceded by warnings appropriate to the circumstances.

Chapter VII: Rank of Prisoners of War

Article 43

Upon the outbreak of hostilities, the Parties to the conflict shall communicate to one another the titles and ranks of all the persons mentioned in Article 4 of the present Convention, in order to ensure equality of treatment between prisoners of equivalent rank. Titles and ranks which are subsequently created shall form the subject of similar communications.

The Detaining Power shall recognize promotions in rank which have been accorded to prisoners of war and which have been duly notified by the Power on which these prisoners depend.

Article 44

Officers and prisoners of equivalent status shall be treated with the regard due to their rank and age.

In order to ensure service in officers' camps, other ranks of the same armed forces who, as far as possible, speak the same language, shall be assigned in sufficient numbers, account being taken of the rank of officers and prisoners of equivalent status. Such orderlies shall not be required to perform any other work.

Supervision of the mess by the officers themselves shall be facilitated in every way.

Article 45

Prisoners of war other than officers and prisoners of equivalent status shall be treated with the regard due to their rank and age.

Supervision of the mess by the prisoners themselves shall be facilitated in every way.

Chapter VIII: Transfer of Prisoners of War After Their Arrival in Camp

Article 46

The Detaining Power, when deciding upon the transfer of prisoners of war, shall take into account the interests of the prisoners themselves, more especially so as not to increase the difficulty of their repatriation.

The transfer of prisoners of war shall always be effected humanely and in conditions not less favourable than those under which the forces of the Detaining Power are transferred. Account shall always be taken of the climatic conditions to which the prisoners of war are accustomed and the conditions of transfer shall in no case be prejudicial to their health.

The Detaining Power shall supply prisoners of war during transfer with sufficient food and drinking water to keep them in good health, likewise with the necessary clothing, shelter and medical attention. The Detaining Power shall take adequate precautions especially in case of transport by sea or by air, to ensure their safety during transfer, and shall draw up a complete list of all transferred prisoners before their departure.

Article 47
Sick or wounded prisoners of war shall not be transferred as long as their recovery may be endangered by the journey, unless their safety imperatively demands it.

If the combat zone draws closer to a camp, the prisoners of war in the said camp shall not be transferred unless their transfer can be carried out in adequate conditions of safety, or if they are exposed to greater risks by remaining on the spot than by being transferred.

Article 48
In the event of transfer, prisoners of war shall be officially advised of their departure and of their new postal address. Such notifications shall be given in time for them to pack their luggage and inform their next of kin.

They shall be allowed to take with them their personal effects, and the correspondence and parcels which have arrived for them. The weight of such baggage may be limited, if the conditions of transfer so require, to what each prisoner can reasonably carry, which shall in no case be more than twenty-five kilograms per head.

Mail and parcels addressed to their former camp shall be forwarded to them without delay. The camp commander shall take, in agreement with the prisoners' representative, any measures needed to ensure the transport of the prisoners' community property and of the luggage they are unable to take with them in consequence of restrictions imposed by virtue of the second paragraph of this Article.

The costs of transfers shall be borne by the Detaining Power.

Section III: Labour of Prisoners of War

Article 49
The Detaining Power may utilize the labour of prisoners of war who are physically fit, taking into account their age, sex, rank and physical aptitude, and with a view particularly to maintaining them in a good state of physical and mental health.

Non-commissioned officers who are prisoners of war shall only be required to do supervisory work. Those not so required may ask for other suitable work which shall, so far as possible, be found for them.

If officers or persons of equivalent status ask for suitable work, it shall be found for them, so far as possible, but they may in no circumstances be compelled to work.

Article 50

Besides work connected with camp administration, installation or maintenance, prisoners of war may be compelled to do only such work as is included in the following classes:

(a) Agriculture;

(b) Industries connected with the production or the extraction of raw materials, and manufacturing industries, with the exception of metallurgical, machinery and chemical industries; public works and building operations which have no military character or purpose;

(c) Transport and handling of stores which are not military in character or purpose;

(d) Commercial business, and arts and crafts;

(e) Domestic service;

(f) Public utility services having no military character or purpose.

Should the above provisions be infringed, prisoners of war shall be allowed to exercise their right of complaint, in conformity with Article 78.

Article 51

Prisoners of war must be granted suitable working conditions, especially as regards accommodation, food, clothing and equipment; such conditions shall not be inferior to those enjoyed by nationals of the Detaining Power employed in similar work; account shall also be taken of climatic conditions.

The Detaining Power, in utilizing the labour of prisoners of war, shall ensure that in areas in which prisoners are employed, the national legislation concerning the protection of labour, and, more particularly, the regulations for the safety of workers, are duly applied.

Prisoners of war shall receive training and be provided with the means of protection suitable to the work they will have to do and similar to those accorded to the nationals of the Detaining Power. Subject to the provisions of Article 52, prisoners may be submitted to the normal risks run by these civilian workers.

Conditions of labour shall in no case be rendered more arduous by disciplinary measures.

Article 52

Unless he be a volunteer, no prisoner of war may be employed on labour which is of an unhealthy or dangerous nature.

No prisoner of war shall be assigned to labour which would be looked upon as humiliating for a member of the Detaining Power's own forces.

The removal of mines or similar devices shall be considered as dangerous labour.

Article 53

The duration of the daily labour of prisoners of war, including the time of the journey to and fro, shall not be excessive, and must in no case exceed that permitted for civilian workers in the district, who are nationals of the Detaining Power and employed on the same work.

Prisoners of war must be allowed, in the middle of the day's work, a rest of not less than one hour. This rest will be the same as that to which workers of the Detaining Power are entitled, if the latter is of longer duration. They shall be allowed in addition a rest of twenty-four consecutive hours every week, preferably on Sunday or the day of rest in their country of origin. Furthermore, every prisoner who has worked for one year shall be granted a rest of eight consecutive days, during which his working pay shall be paid him.

If methods of labour such as piece-work are employed, the length of the working period shall not be rendered excessive thereby.

Article 54

The working pay due to prisoners of war shall be fixed in accordance with the provisions of Article 62 of the present Convention.

Prisoners of war who sustain accidents in connection with work, or who contract a disease in the course, or in consequence of their work, shall receive all the care their condition may require. The Detaining Power shall furthermore deliver to such prisoners of war a medical certificate enabling them to submit their claims to the Power on which they depend, and shall send a duplicate to the Central Prisoners of War Agency provided for in Article 123.

Article 55

The fitness of prisoners of war for work shall be periodically verified by medical examinations at least once a month. The examinations shall have particular regard to the nature of the work which prisoners of war are required to do.

If any prisoner of war considers himself incapable of working, he shall be permitted to appear before the medical authorities of his camp. Physicians or surgeons may recommend that the prisoners who are, in their opinion, unfit for work, be exempted therefrom.

Article 56

The organization and administration of labour detachments shall be similar to those of prisoner of war camps.

Every labour detachment shall remain under the control of and administratively part of a prisoner of war camp. The military authorities and the commander of the said camp shall be responsible, under the direction of their government, for the observance of the provisions of the present Convention in labour detachments.

The camp commander shall keep an up-to-date record of the labour detachments dependent on his camp, and shall communicate it to the delegates of the Protecting Power, of the International Committee of the Red Cross, or of other agencies giving relief to prisoners of war, who may visit the camp.

Article 57

The treatment of prisoners of war who work for private persons, even if the latter are responsible for guarding and protecting them, shall not be inferior to that which is provided for by the present Convention. The Detaining Power, the military authorities and the commander of the camp to which such prisoners belong shall be entirely responsible for the maintenance, care, treatment, and payment of the working pay of such prisoners of war.

Such prisoners of war shall have the right to remain in communication with the prisoners' representatives in the camps on which they depend.

Section IV: Financial Resources of Prisoners of War

Article 58

Upon the outbreak of hostilities, and pending an arrangement on this matter with the Protecting Power, the Detaining Power may determine the maximum amount of money in cash or in any similar form, that prisoners may have in their possession. Any amount in excess, which was properly in their possession and which has been taken or withheld from them, shall be placed to their account, together with any monies deposited by them, and shall not be converted into any other currency without their consent.

If prisoners of war are permitted to purchase services or commodities outside the camp against payment in cash, such payments shall be made by the prisoner himself or by the camp administration who will charge them to the accounts of the prisoners concerned. The Detaining Power will establish the necessary rules in this respect.

Article 59

Cash which was taken from prisoners of war, in accordance with Article 18, at the time of their capture, and which is in the currency of the Detaining Power, shall be placed to their separate accounts, in accordance with the provisions of Article 64 of the present Section.

The amounts, in the currency of the Detaining Power, due to the conversion of sums in other currencies that are taken from the prisoners of war at the same time, shall also be credited to their separate accounts.

Article 60

The Detaining Power shall grant all prisoners of war a monthly advance of pay, the amount of which shall be fixed by conversion, into the currency of the said Power, of the following amounts:

Category I: Prisoners ranking below sergeant: eight Swiss francs.

Category II: Sergeants and other non-commissioned officers, or prisoners of equivalent rank: twelve Swiss francs.

Category III: Warrant officers and commissioned officers below the rank of major or prisoners of equivalent rank: fifty Swiss francs.

Category IV: Majors, lieutenant-colonels, colonels or prisoners of equivalent rank: sixty Swiss francs.

Category V: General officers or prisoners of equivalent rank: seventy-five Swiss francs.

However, the Parties to the conflict concerned may by special agreement modify the amount of advances of pay due to prisoners of the preceding categories.

Furthermore, if the amounts indicated in the first paragraph above would be unduly high compared with the pay of the Detaining Power's armed forces or would, for any reason, seriously embarrass the Detaining Power, then, pending the conclusion of a special agreement with the Power on which the prisoners depend to vary the amounts indicated above, the Detaining Power:

(a) Shall continue to credit the accounts of the prisoners with the amounts indicated in the first paragraph above.

(b) May temporarily limit the amount made available from these advances of pay to prisoners of war for their own use, to sums which are reasonable, but which, for Category I, shall never be inferior to the amount that the Detaining Power gives to the members of its own armed forces.

The reasons for any limitations will be given without delay to the Protecting Power.

Article 61

The Detaining Power shall accept for distribution as supplementary pay to prisoners of war sums which the Power on which the prisoners depend may forward to them, on condition that the sums to be paid shall be the same for each prisoner of the same category, shall be payable to all prisoners of that category depending on that Power, and shall be placed in their separate accounts, at the earliest opportunity, in accordance with the provisions of Article 64. Such supplementary pay shall not relieve the Detaining Power of any obligation under this Convention.

Article 62

Prisoners of war shall be paid a fair working rate of pay by the detaining authorities direct. The rate shall be fixed by the said authorities, but shall at no time be less than one-fourth of one Swiss franc for a full working day. The Detaining Power shall inform prisoners of war, as well as the Power on which they depend, through the intermediary of the Protecting Power, of the rate of daily working pay that it has fixed.

Working pay shall likewise be paid by the detaining authorities to prisoners of war permanently detailed to duties or to a skilled or semi-skilled occupation in connection with the administration, installation or maintenance of camps, and to the prisoners who are required to carry out spiritual or medical duties on behalf of their comrades.

The working pay of the prisoners' representative, of his advisers, if any, and of his assistants, shall be paid out of the fund maintained by canteen profits.

The scale of this working pay shall be fixed by the prisoners' representative and approved by the camp commander. If there is no such fund, the detaining authorities shall pay these prisoners a fair working rate of pay.

Article 63

Prisoners of war shall be permitted to receive remittances of money addressed to them individually or collectively.

Every prisoner of war shall have at his disposal the credit balance of his account as provided for in the following Article, within the limits fixed by the Detaining Power, which shall make such payments as are requested. Subject to financial or monetary restrictions which the Detaining Power regards as essential, prisoners of war may also have payments made abroad. In this case payments addressed by prisoners of war to dependants shall be given priority.

In any event, and subject to the consent of the Power on which they depend, prisoners may have payments made in their own country, as follows: the Detaining Power shall send to the aforesaid Power through the Protecting Power a notification giving all the necessary particulars concerning the prisoners of war, the beneficiaries of the payments, and the amount of the sums to be paid, expressed in the Detaining Power's currency. The said notification shall be signed by the prisoners and countersigned by the camp commander. The Detaining Power shall debit the prisoners' account by a corresponding amount; the sums thus debited shall be placed by it to the credit of the Power on which the prisoners depend.

To apply the foregoing provisions, the Detaining Power may usefully consult the Model Regulations in Annex V of the present Convention.

Article 64

The Detaining Power shall hold an account for each prisoner of war, showing at least the following:

1. The amounts due to the prisoner or received by him as advances of pay, as working pay or derived from any other source; the sums in the currency of the Detaining Power which were taken from him; the sums taken from him and converted at his request into the currency of the said Power.

2. The payments made to the prisoner in cash, or in any other similar form; the payments made on his behalf and at his request; the sums transferred under Article 63, third paragraph.

Article 65

Every item entered in the account of a prisoner of war shall be countersigned or initialled by him, or by the prisoners' representative acting on his behalf.

Prisoners of war shall at all times be afforded reasonable facilities for consulting and obtaining copies of their accounts, which may likewise be inspected by the representatives of the Protecting Powers at the time of visits to the camp.

When prisoners of war are transferred from one camp to another, their personal accounts will follow them. In case of transfer from one Detaining Power to another, the monies which are their property and are not in the currency of the Detaining Power will follow them. They shall be given certificates for any other monies standing to the credit of their accounts.

The Parties to the conflict concerned may agree to notify to each other at specific intervals through the Protecting Power, the amount of the accounts of the prisoners of war.

Article 66

On the termination of captivity, through the release of a prisoner of war or his repatriation, the Detaining Power shall give him a statement, signed by an authorized officer of that Power, showing the credit balance then due to him. The Detaining Power shall also send through the Protecting Power to the government upon which the prisoner of war depends, lists giving all appropriate particulars of all prisoners of war whose captivity has been terminated by repatriation, release, escape, death or any other means, and showing the amount of their credit balances. Such lists shall be certified on each sheet by an authorized representative of the Detaining Power.

Any of the above provisions of this Article may be varied by mutual agreement between any two Parties to the conflict.

The Power on which the prisoner of war depends shall be responsible for settling with him any credit balance due to him from the Detaining Power on the termination of his captivity.

Article 67

Advances of pay, issued to prisoners of war in conformity with Article 60, shall be considered as made on behalf of the Power on which they depend. Such advances of pay, as well as all payments made by the said Power under Article 63, third paragraph, and Article 68, shall form the subject of arrangements between the Powers concerned, at the close of hostilities.

Article 68

Any claim by a prisoner of war for compensation in respect of any injury or other disability arising out of work shall be referred to the Power on which he depends, through the Protecting Power. In accordance with Article 54, the Detaining Power will, in all cases, provide the prisoner of war concerned with a statement showing the nature of the injury or disability, the circumstances in which it arose and particulars of medical or hospital treatment given for it. This statement will be signed by a responsible officer of the Detaining Power and the medical particulars certified by a medical officer.

Any claim by a prisoner of war for compensation in respect of personal effects, monies or valuables impounded by the Detaining Power under Article 18 and not forthcoming on his repatriation, or in respect of loss alleged to be due to the fault of the Detaining Power or any of its servants, shall likewise be referred to the Power on which he depends. Nevertheless, any such personal effects required for use by the prisoners of war whilst in captivity shall be replaced at the expense of the Detaining Power. The Detaining Power will, in all cases, provide the prisoner of war with a statement, signed by a responsible officer, showing all available information regarding the reasons why such effects, monies or valuables have not been restored to him. A copy of this statement will be forwarded to the Power on which he depends through the Central Prisoners of War Agency provided for in Article 123.

Section V: Relations of Prisoners of War with the Exterior

Article 69
Immediately upon prisoners of war falling into its power, the Detaining Power shall inform them and the Powers on which they depend, through the Protecting Power, of the measures taken to carry out the provisions of the present Section. They shall likewise inform the parties concerned of any subsequent modifications of such measures.

Article 70
Immediately upon capture, or not more than one week after arrival at a camp, even if it is a transit camp, likewise in case of sickness or transfer to hospital or another camp, every prisoner of war shall be enabled to write direct to his family, on the one hand, and to the Central Prisoners of War Agency provided for in Article 123, on the other hand, a card similar, if possible, to the model annexed to the present Convention, informing his relatives of his capture, address and state of health. The said cards shall be forwarded as rapidly as possible and may not be delayed in any manner.

Article 71
Prisoners of war shall be allowed to send and receive letters and cards. If the Detaining Power deems it necessary to limit the number of letters and cards sent by each prisoner of war, the said number shall not be less than two letters and four cards monthly, exclusive of the capture cards provided for in Article 70, and conforming as closely as possible to the models annexed to the present Convention. Further limitations may be imposed only if the Protecting Power is satisfied that it would be in the interests of the prisoners of war concerned to do so owing to difficulties of translation caused by the Detaining Power's inability to find sufficient qualified linguists to carry out the necessary censorship. If limitations must be placed on the correspondence addressed to prisoners of war, they may be ordered only by the Power on which the prisoners depend, possibly at the request of the Detaining Power. Such letters and cards must be conveyed by the most rapid method at the disposal of the Detaining Power; they may not be delayed or retained for disciplinary reasons.

Prisoners of war who have been without news for a long period, or who are unable to receive news from their next of kin or to give them news by the ordinary postal route, as well as those who are at a great distance from their homes, shall be permitted to send telegrams, the fees being charged against the prisoners of war's accounts with the Detaining Power or paid in the currency at their disposal. They shall likewise benefit by this measure in cases of urgency.

As a general rule, the correspondence of prisoners of war shall be written in their native language. The Parties to the conflict may allow correspondence in other languages.

Sacks containing prisoner of war mail must be securely sealed and labelled so as clearly to indicate their contents, and must be addressed to offices of destination.

Article 72

Prisoners of war shall be allowed to receive by post or by any other means individual parcels or collective shipments containing, in particular, foodstuffs, clothing, medical supplies and articles of a religious, educational or recreational character which may meet their needs, including books, devotional articles, scientific equipment, examination papers, musical instruments, sports outfits and materials allowing prisoners of war to pursue their studies or their cultural activities.

Such shipments shall in no way free the Detaining Power from the obligations imposed upon it by virtue of the present Convention.

The only limits which may be placed on these shipments shall be those proposed by the Protecting Power in the interest of the prisoners themselves, or by the International Committee of the Red Cross or any other organization giving assistance to the prisoners, in respect of their own shipments only, on account of exceptional strain on transport or communications.

The conditions for the sending of individual parcels and collective relief shall, if necessary, be the subject of special agreements between the Powers concerned, which may in no case delay the receipt by the prisoners of relief supplies. Books may not be included in parcels of clothing and foodstuffs. Medical supplies shall, as a rule, be sent in collective parcels.

Article 73

In the absence of special agreements between the Powers concerned on the conditions for the receipt and distribution of collective relief shipments, the rules and regulations concerning collective shipments, which are annexed to the present Convention, shall be applied.

The special agreements referred to above shall in no case restrict the right of prisoners' representatives to take possession of collective relief shipments intended for prisoners of war, to proceed to their distribution or to dispose of them in the interest of the prisoners.

Nor shall such agreements restrict the right of representatives of the Protecting Power, the International Committee of the Red Cross or any other organization giving assistance to prisoners of war and responsible for the forwarding of collective shipments, to supervise their distribution to the recipients.

Article 74

All relief shipments for prisoners of war shall be exempt from import, customs and other dues.

Correspondence, relief shipments and authorized remittances of money addressed to prisoners of war or despatched by them through the post office, either direct or through the Information Bureaux provided for in Article 122 and the Central Prisoners of War Agency provided for in Article 123, shall be exempt from any postal dues, both in the countries of origin and destination, and in intermediate countries.

If relief shipments intended for prisoners of war cannot be sent through the post office by reason of weight or for any other cause, the cost of transportation shall be borne by the Detaining Power in all the territories under its control. The other Powers party to the Convention shall bear the cost of transport in their respective territories. In the absence of special agreements between the Parties concerned, the costs connected with transport of such shipments, other than costs covered by the above exemption, shall be charged to the senders.

The High Contracting Parties shall endeavour to reduce, so far as possible, the rates charged for telegrams sent by prisoners of war, or addressed to them.

Article 75

Should military operations prevent the Powers concerned from fulfilling their obligation to assure the transport of the shipments referred to in Articles 70, 71, 72 and 77, the Protecting Powers concerned, the International Committee of the Red Cross or any other organization duly approved by the Parties to the conflict may undertake to ensure the conveyance of such shipments by suitable means (railway wagons, motor vehicles, vessels or aircraft, etc.). For this purpose, the High Contracting Parties shall endeavour to supply them with such transport and to allow its circulation, especially by granting the necessary safe-conducts.

Such transport may also be used to convey:

(a) correspondence, lists and reports exchanged between the Central Information Agency referred to in Article 123 and the National Bureaux referred to in Article 122;

(b) correspondence and reports relating to prisoners of war which the Protecting Powers, the International Committee of the Red Cross or any other body assisting the prisoners, exchange either with their own delegates or with the Parties to the conflict.

These provisions in no way detract from the right of any Party to the conflict to arrange other means of transport, if it should so prefer, nor preclude the granting of safe-conducts, under mutually agreed conditions, to such means of transport.

In the absence of special agreements, the costs occasioned by the use of such means of transport shall be borne proportionally by the Parties to the conflict whose nationals are benefited thereby.

Article 76

The censoring of correspondence addressed to prisoners of war or despatched by them shall be done as quickly as possible. Mail shall be censored only by the despatching State and the receiving State, and once only by each.

The examination of consignments intended for prisoners of war shall not be carried out under conditions that will expose the goods contained in them to deterioration; except in the case of written or printed matter, it shall be done in the presence of the addressee, or of a fellow-prisoner duly delegated by him. The delivery to prisoners of individual or collective consignments shall not be delayed under the pretext of difficulties of censorship.

Any prohibition of correspondence ordered by Parties to the conflict, either for military or political reasons, shall be only temporary and its duration shall be as short as possible.

Article 77

The Detaining Powers shall provide all facilities for the transmission, through the Protecting Power or the Central Prisoners of War Agency provided for in Article 123 of instruments, papers or documents intended for prisoners of war or despatched by them, especially powers of attorney and wills.

In all cases they shall facilitate the preparation and execution of such documents on behalf of prisoners of war; in particular, they shall allow them to consult a lawyer and shall take what measures are necessary for the authentication of their signatures.

Section VI: Relations Between Prisoners of War and the Authorities

Chapter I: Complaints of Prisoners of War Respecting the Conditions of Captivity

Article 78

Prisoners of war shall have the right to make known to the military authorities in whose power they are, their requests regarding the conditions of captivity to which they are subjected.

They shall also have the unrestricted right to apply to the representatives of the Protecting Powers either through their prisoners' representative or, if they consider it necessary, direct, in order to draw their attention to any points on which they may have complaints to make regarding their conditions of captivity.

These requests and complaints shall not be limited nor considered to be a part of the correspondence quota referred to in Article 71. They must be transmitted immediately. Even if they are recognized to be unfounded, they may not give rise to any punishment.

Prisoners' representatives may send periodic reports on the situation in the camps and the needs of the prisoners of war to the representatives of the Protecting Powers.

Chapter II: Prisoner of War Representatives

Article 79

In all places where there are prisoners of war, except in those where there are officers, the prisoners shall freely elect by secret ballot, every six months, and also in case of vacancies, prisoners' representatives entrusted with representing them before the military authorities, the Protecting Powers, the International Committee of the Red Cross and any other organization which may assist them. These prisoners' representatives shall be eligible for re-election.

In camps for officers and persons of equivalent status or in mixed camps, the senior officer among the prisoners of war shall be recognized as the camp prisoners' representative. In camps for officers, he shall be assisted by one or more advisers chosen by the officers; in mixed camps, his assistants shall be chosen from among the prisoners of war who are not officers and shall be elected by them.

Officer prisoners of war of the same nationality shall be stationed in labour camps for prisoners of war, for the purpose of carrying out the camp administration duties for which the prisoners of war are responsible. These officers may be elected as prisoners' representatives under the first paragraph of this Article. In such a case the assistants to the prisoners' representatives shall be chosen from among those prisoners of war who are not officers.

Every representative elected must be approved by the Detaining Power before he has the right to commence his duties. Where the Detaining Power refuses to approve a prisoner of war elected by his fellow prisoners of war, it must inform the Protecting Power of the reason for such refusal.

In all cases the prisoners' representative must have the same nationality, language and customs as the prisoners of war whom he represents. Thus, prisoners of war distributed in different sections of a camp, according to their nationality, language or customs, shall have for each section their own prisoners' representative, in accordance with the foregoing paragraphs.

Article 80

Prisoners' representatives shall further the physical, spiritual and intellectual well-being of prisoners of war.

In particular, where the prisoners decide to organize amongst themselves a system of mutual assistance, this organization will be within the province of the prisoners' representative, in addition to the special duties entrusted to him by other provisions of the present Convention.

Prisoners' representatives shall not be held responsible, simply by reason of their duties, for any offences committed by prisoners of war.

Article 81

Prisoners' representatives shall not be required to perform any other work, if the accomplishment of their duties is thereby made more difficult.

Prisoners' representatives may appoint from amongst the prisoners such assistants as they may require. All material facilities shall be granted them, particularly a certain freedom of movement necessary for the accomplishment of their duties (inspection of labour detachments, receipt of supplies, etc.).

Prisoners' representatives shall be permitted to visit premises where prisoners of war are detained, and every prisoner of war shall have the right to consult freely his prisoners' representative.

All facilities shall likewise be accorded to the prisoners' representatives for communication by post and telegraph with the detaining authorities, the Protecting Powers, the International Committee of the Red Cross and their delegates, the Mixed Medical Commissions and the bodies which give assistance to prisoners of war. Prisoners' representatives of labour detachments shall enjoy the same facilities for communication with the prisoners' representatives of the principal camp. Such communications shall not be restricted, nor considered as forming a part of the quota mentioned in Article 71.

Prisoners' representatives who are transferred shall be allowed a reasonable time to acquaint their successors with current affairs.

In case of dismissal, the reasons therefore shall be communicated to the Protecting Power.

Chapter III: Penal and Disciplinary Sanctions

I. General Provisions

Article 82

A prisoner of war shall be subject to the laws, regulations and orders in force in the armed forces of the Detaining Power; the Detaining Power shall be justified in taking judicial or disciplinary measures in respect of any offence committed by a prisoner of war against such laws, regulations or orders. However, no proceedings or punishments contrary to the provisions of this Chapter shall be allowed.

If any law, regulation or order of the Detaining Power shall declare acts committed by a prisoner of war to be punishable, whereas the same acts would not be punishable if committed by a member of the forces of the Detaining Power, such acts shall entail disciplinary punishments only.

Article 83

In deciding whether proceedings in respect of an offence alleged to have been committed by a prisoner of war shall be judicial or disciplinary, the Detaining Power shall ensure that the competent authorities exercise the greatest leniency and adopt, wherever possible, disciplinary rather than judicial measures.

Article 84

A prisoner of war shall be tried only by a military court, unless the existing laws of the Detaining Power expressly permit the civil courts to try a member of the armed forces of the Detaining Power in respect of the particular offence alleged to have been committed by the prisoner of war.

In no circumstances whatever shall a prisoner of war be tried by a court of any kind which does not offer the essential guarantees of independence and impartiality as generally recognized, and, in particular, the procedure of which does not afford the accused the rights and means of defence provided for in Article 105.

Article 85

Prisoners of war prosecuted under the laws of the Detaining Power for acts committed prior to capture shall retain, even if convicted, the benefits of the present Convention.

Article 86

No prisoner of war may be punished more than once for the same act or on the same charge.

Article 87

Prisoners of war may not be sentenced by the military authorities and courts of the Detaining Power to any penalties except those provided for in respect of members of the armed forces of the said Power who have committed the same acts.

When fixing the penalty, the courts or authorities of the Detaining Power shall take into consideration, to the widest extent possible, the fact that the accused, not being a national of the Detaining Power, is not bound to it by any duty of allegiance, and that he is in its power as the result of circumstances independent of his own will. The said courts or authorities shall be at liberty to reduce the penalty provided for the violation of which the prisoner of war is accused, and shall therefore not be bound to apply the minimum penalty prescribed.

Collective punishment for individual acts, corporal punishment, imprisonment in premises without daylight and, in general, any form of torture or cruelty, are forbidden.

No prisoner of war may be deprived of his rank by the Detaining Power, or prevented from wearing his badges.

Article 88

Officers, non-commissioned officers and men who are prisoners of war undergoing a disciplinary or judicial punishment, shall not be subjected to more severe treatment than that applied in respect of the same punishment to members of the armed forces of the Detaining Power of equivalent rank.

A woman prisoner of war shall not be awarded or sentenced to a punishment more severe, or treated whilst undergoing punishment more severely, than a woman member of the armed forces of the Detaining Power dealt with for a similar offence.

In no case may a woman prisoner of war be awarded or sentenced to a punishment more severe, or treated whilst undergoing punishment more severely, than a male member of the armed forces of the Detaining Power dealt with for a similar offence.

Prisoners of war who have served disciplinary or judicial sentences may not be treated differently from other prisoners of war.

II. Disciplinary Sanctions

Article 89

The disciplinary punishments applicable to prisoners of war are the following:

(1) A fine which shall not exceed 50 per cent of the advances of pay and working pay which the prisoner of war would otherwise receive under the provisions of Articles 60 and 62 during a period of not more than thirty days.

(2) Discontinuance of privileges granted over and above the treatment provided for by the present Convention.

(3) Fatigue duties not exceeding two hours daily.

(4) Confinement.

The punishment referred to under (3) shall not be applied to officers.

In no case shall disciplinary punishments be inhuman, brutal or dangerous to the health of prisoners of war.

Article 90

The duration of any single punishment shall in no case exceed thirty days. Any period of confinement awaiting the hearing of a disciplinary offence or the award of disciplinary punishment shall be deducted from an award pronounced against a prisoner of war.

The maximum of thirty days provided above may not be exceeded, even if the prisoner of war is answerable for several acts at the same time when he is awarded punishment, whether such acts are related or not.

The period between the pronouncing of an award of disciplinary punishment and its execution shall not exceed one month.

When a prisoner of war is awarded a further disciplinary punishment, a period of at least three days shall elapse between the execution of any two of the punishments, if the duration of one of these is ten days or more.

Article 91

The escape of a prisoner of war shall be deemed to have succeeded when:

(1) he has joined the armed forces of the Power on which he depends, or those of an allied Power;

(2) he has left the territory under the control of the Detaining Power, or of an ally of the said Power;

(3) he has joined a ship flying the flag of the Power on which he depends, or of an allied Power, in the territorial waters of the Detaining Power, the said ship not being under the control of the last named Power.

Prisoners of war who have made good their escape in the sense of this Article and who are recaptured, shall not be liable to any punishment in respect of their previous escape.

Article 92

A prisoner of war who attempts to escape and is recaptured before having made good his escape in the sense of Article 91 shall be liable only to a disciplinary punishment in respect of this act, even if it is a repeated offence.

A prisoner of war who is recaptured shall be handed over without delay to the competent military authority.

Article 88, fourth paragraph, notwithstanding, prisoners of war punished as a result of an unsuccessful escape may be subjected to special surveillance. Such surveillance must not affect the state of their health, must be undergone in a prisoner of war camp, and must not entail the suppression of any of the safeguards granted them by the present Convention.

Article 93

Escape or attempt to escape, even if it is a repeated offence, shall not be deemed an aggravating circumstance if the prisoner of war is subjected to trial by judicial proceedings in respect of an offence committed during his escape or attempt to escape.

In conformity with the principle stated in Article 83, offences committed by prisoners of war with the sole intention of facilitating their escape and which do not entail any violence against life or limb, such as offences against public property, theft without intention of self-enrichment, the drawing up or use of false papers, or the wearing of civilian clothing, shall occasion disciplinary punishment only.

Prisoners of war who aid or abet an escape or an attempt to escape shall be liable on this count to disciplinary punishment only.

Article 94

If an escaped prisoner of war is recaptured, the Power on which he depends shall be notified thereof in the manner defined in Article 122, provided notification of his escape has been made.

Article 95

A prisoner of war accused of an offence against discipline shall not be kept in confinement pending the hearing unless a member of the armed forces of the Detaining Power would be so kept if he were accused of a similar offence, or if it is essential in the interests of camp order and discipline.

Any period spent by a prisoner of war in confinement awaiting the disposal of an offence against discipline shall be reduced to an absolute minimum and shall not exceed fourteen days.

The provisions of Articles 97 and 98 of this Chapter shall apply to prisoners of war who are in confinement awaiting the disposal of offences against discipline.

Article 96
Acts which constitute offences against discipline shall be investigated immediately.

Without prejudice to the competence of courts and superior military authorities, disciplinary punishment may be ordered only by an officer having disciplinary powers in his capacity as camp commander, or by a responsible officer who replaces him or to whom he has delegated his disciplinary powers.

In no case may such powers be delegated to a prisoner of war or be exercised by a prisoner of war.

Before any disciplinary award is pronounced, the accused shall be given precise information regarding the offences of which he is accused, and given an opportunity of explaining his conduct and of defending himself. He shall be permitted, in particular, to call witnesses and to have recourse, if necessary, to the services of a qualified interpreter. The decision shall be announced to the accused prisoner of war and to the prisoners' representative.

A record of disciplinary punishments shall be maintained by the camp commander and shall be open to inspection by representatives of the Protecting Power.

Article 97
Prisoners of war shall not in any case be transferred to penitentiary establishments (prisons, penitentiaries, convict prisons, etc.) to undergo disciplinary punishment therein.

All premises in which disciplinary punishments are undergone shall conform to the sanitary requirements set forth in Article 25. A prisoner of war undergoing punishment shall be enabled to keep himself in a state of cleanliness, in conformity with Article 29.

Officers and persons of equivalent status shall not be lodged in the same quarters as non-commissioned officers or men.

Women prisoners of war undergoing disciplinary punishment shall be confined in separate quarters from male prisoners of war and shall be under the immediate supervision of women.

Article 98
A prisoner of war undergoing confinement as a disciplinary punishment, shall continue to enjoy the benefits of the provisions of this Convention except in so far as these are necessarily rendered inapplicable by the mere fact that he is confined. In no case may he be deprived of the benefits of the provisions of Articles 78 and 126.

A prisoner of war awarded disciplinary punishment may not be deprived of the prerogatives attached to his rank.

Prisoners of war awarded disciplinary punishment shall be allowed to exercise and to stay in the open air at least two hours daily.

They shall be allowed, on their request, to be present at the daily medical inspections. They shall receive the attention which their state of health requires and, if necessary, shall be removed to the camp infirmary or to a hospital.

They shall have permission to read and write, likewise to send and receive letters. Parcels and remittances of money however, may be withheld from them until the completion of the punishment; they shall meanwhile be entrusted to the prisoners' representative, who will hand over to the infirmary the perishable goods contained in such parcels.

III. Juridicial Proceedings

Article 99

No prisoner of war may be tried or sentenced for an act which is not forbidden by the law of the Detaining Power or by international law, in force at the time the said act was committed.

No moral or physical coercion may be exerted on a prisoner of war in order to induce him to admit himself guilty of the act of which he is accused.

No prisoner of war may be convicted without having had an opportunity to present his defence and the assistance of a qualified advocate or counsel.

Article 100

Prisoners of war and the Protecting Powers shall be informed as soon as possible of the offences which are punishable by the death sentence under the laws of the Detaining Power.

Other offences shall not thereafter be made punishable by the death penalty without the concurrence of the Power on which the prisoners of war depend.

The death sentence cannot be pronounced on a prisoner of war unless the attention of the court has, in accordance with Article 87, second paragraph, been particularly called to the fact that since the accused is not a national of the Detaining Power, he is not bound to it by any duty of allegiance, and that he is in its power as the result of circumstances independent of his own will.

Article 101

If the death penalty is pronounced on a prisoner of war, the sentence shall not be executed before the expiration of a period of at least six months from the date when the Protecting Power receives, at an indicated address, the detailed communication provided for in Article 107.

Article 102

A prisoner of war can be validly sentenced only if the sentence has been pronounced by the same courts according to the same procedure as in the case of members of the armed forces of the Detaining Power, and if, furthermore, the provisions of the present Chapter have been observed.

Article 103

Judicial investigations relating to a prisoner of war shall be conducted as rapidly as circumstances permit and so that his trial shall take place as soon as possible. A prisoner of war shall not be confined while awaiting trial unless a member of the armed forces of the Detaining Power would be so confined if he were accused of a similar offence, or if it is essential to do so in the interests of national security. In no circumstances shall this confinement exceed three months.

Any period spent by a prisoner of war in confinement awaiting trial shall be deducted from any sentence of imprisonment passed upon him and taken into account in fixing any penalty.

The provisions of Articles 97 and 98 of this Chapter shall apply to a prisoner of war whilst in confinement awaiting trial.

Article 104

In any case in which the Detaining Power has decided to institute judicial proceedings against a prisoner of war, it shall notify the Protecting Power as soon as possible and at least three weeks before the opening of the trial. This period of three weeks shall run as from the day on which such notification reaches the Protecting Power at the address previously indicated by the latter to the Detaining Power.

The said notification shall contain the following information:

(1) Surname and first names of the prisoner of war, his rank, his army, regimental, personal or serial number, his date of birth, and his profession or trade, if any;

(2) Place of internment or confinement;

(3) Specification of the charge or charges on which the prisoner of war is to be arraigned, giving the legal provisions applicable;

(4) Designation of the court which will try the case, likewise the date and place fixed for the opening of the trial.

The same communication shall be made by the Detaining Power to the prisoners' representative.

If no evidence is submitted, at the opening of a trial, that the notification referred to above was received by the Protecting Power, by the prisoner of war and by the prisoners' representative concerned, at least three weeks before the opening of the trial, then the latter cannot take place and must be adjourned.

Article 105

The prisoner of war shall be entitled to assistance by one of his prisoner comrades, to defence by a qualified advocate or counsel of his own choice, to the calling of witnesses and, if he deems necessary, to the services of a competent interpreter. He shall be advised of these rights by the Detaining Power in due time before the trial.

Failing a choice by the prisoner of war, the Protecting Power shall find him an advocate or counsel, and shall have at least one week at its disposal for the purpose. The Detaining Power shall deliver to the said Power, on request, a list of persons qualified to present the defence. Failing a choice of an advocate or counsel by the prisoner of war or the Protecting Power, the Detaining Power shall appoint a competent advocate or counsel to conduct the defence.

The advocate or counsel conducting the defence on behalf of the prisoner of war shall have at his disposal a period of two weeks at least before the opening of the trial, as well as the necessary facilities to prepare the defence of the accused. He may, in particular, freely visit the accused and interview him in private. He may also confer with any witnesses for the defence, including prisoners of war. He shall have the benefit of these facilities until the term of appeal or petition has expired.

Particulars of the charge or charges on which the prisoner of war is to be arraigned, as well as the documents which are generally communicated to the accused by virtue of the laws in force in the armed forces of the Detaining Power, shall be communicated to the accused prisoner of war in a language which he understands, and in good time before the opening of the trial. The same communication in the same circumstances shall be made to the advocate or counsel conducting the defence on behalf of the prisoner of war.

The representatives of the Protecting Power shall be entitled to attend the trial of the case, unless, exceptionally, this is held in camera in the interest of State security. In such a case the Detaining Power shall advise the Protecting Power accordingly.

Article 106

Every prisoner of war shall have, in the same manner as the members of the armed forces of the Detaining Power, the right of appeal or petition from any sentence pronounced upon him, with a view to the quashing or revising of the sentence or the reopening of the trial. He shall be fully informed of his right to appeal or petition and of the time limit within which he may do so.

Article 107

Any judgment and sentence pronounced upon a prisoner of war shall be immediately reported to the Protecting Power in the form of a summary communication, which shall also indicate whether he has the right of appeal with a view to the quashing of the sentence or the reopening of the trial. This communication shall likewise be sent to the prisoners' representative concerned. It shall also be sent to the accused prisoner of war in a language he understands, if the sentence was not pronounced in his presence. The Detaining Power shall also immediately communicate to the Protecting Power the decision of the prisoner of war to use or to waive his right of appeal.

Furthermore, if a prisoner of war is finally convicted or if a sentence pronounced on a prisoner of war in the first instance is a death sentence, the Detaining Power shall as soon as possible address to the Protecting Power a detailed communication containing:

(1) the precise wording of the finding and sentence;

(2) a summarized report of any preliminary investigation and of the trial, emphasizing in particular the elements of the prosecution and the defence;

(3) notification, where applicable, of the establishment where the sentence will be served.

The communications provided for in the foregoing sub-paragraphs shall be sent to the Protecting Power at the address previously made known to the Detaining Power.

Article 108

Sentences pronounced on prisoners of war after a conviction has become duly enforceable, shall be served in the same establishments and under the same conditions as in the case of members of the armed forces of the Detaining Power. These conditions shall in all cases conform to the requirements of health and humanity.

A woman prisoner of war on whom such a sentence has been pronounced shall be confined in separate quarters and shall be under the supervision of women.

In any case, prisoners of war sentenced to a penalty depriving them of their liberty shall retain the benefit of the provisions of Articles 78 and 126 of the present Convention. Furthermore, they shall be entitled to receive and despatch correspondence, to receive at least one relief parcel monthly, to take regular exercise in the open air, to have the medical care required by their state of health, and the spiritual assistance they may desire. Penalties to which they may be subjected shall be in accordance with the provisions of Article 87, third paragraph.

Part IV: Termination of Captivity

Section I: Direct Repatriation and Accommodation in Neutral Countries

Article 109

Subject to the provisions of the third paragraph of this Article, Parties to the conflict are bound to send back to their own country, regardless of number or rank, seriously wounded and seriously sick prisoners of war, after having cared for them until they are fit to travel, in accordance with the first paragraph of the following Article.

Throughout the duration of hostilities, Parties to the conflict shall endeavour, with the cooperation of the neutral Powers concerned, to make arrangements for the accommodation in neutral countries of the sick and wounded prisoners of war referred to in the second paragraph of the following Article. They may, in addition, conclude agreements with a view to the direct repatriation or internment in a neutral country of able-bodied prisoners of war who have undergone a long period of captivity.

No sick or injured prisoner of war who is eligible for repatriation under the first paragraph of this Article, may be repatriated against his will during hostilities.

Article 110

The following shall be repatriated direct:

(1) Incurably wounded and sick whose mental or physical fitness seems to have been gravely diminished.

(2) Wounded and sick who, according to medical opinion, are not likely to recover within one year, whose condition requires treatment and whose mental or physical fitness seems to have been gravely diminished.

(3) Wounded and sick who have recovered, but whose mental or physical fitness seems to have been gravely and permanently diminished.

The following may be accommodated in a neutral country:

(1) Wounded and sick whose recovery may be expected within one year of the date of the wound or the beginning of the illness, if treatment in a neutral country might increase the prospects of a more certain and speedy recovery.

(2) Prisoners of war whose mental or physical health, according to medical opinion, is seriously threatened by continued captivity, but whose accommodation in a neutral country might remove such a threat.

The conditions which prisoners of war accommodated in a neutral country must fulfil in order to permit their repatriation shall be fixed, as shall likewise their status, by agreement between the Powers concerned. In general, prisoners of war who have been accommodated in a neutral country, and who belong to the following categories, should be repatriated:

(1) Those whose state of health has deteriorated so as to fulfil the condition laid down for direct repatriation;

(2) Those whose mental or physical powers remain, even after treatment, considerably impaired.

If no special agreements are concluded between the Parties to the conflict concerned, to determine the cases of disablement or sickness entailing direct repatriation or accommodation in a neutral country, such cases shall be settled in accordance with the principles laid down in the Model Agreement concerning direct repatriation and accommodation in neutral countries of wounded and sick prisoners of war and in the Regulations concerning Mixed Medical Commissions annexed to the present Convention.

Article 111

The Detaining Power, the Power on which the prisoners of war depend, and a neutral Power agreed upon by these two Powers, shall endeavour to conclude agreements which will enable prisoners of war to be interned in the territory of the said neutral Power until the close of hostilities.

Article 112

Upon the outbreak of hostilities, Mixed Medical Commissions shall be appointed to examine sick and wounded prisoners of war, and to make all appropriate decisions regarding them. The appointment, duties and functioning of these Commissions shall be in conformity with the provisions of the Regulations annexed to the present Convention.

However, prisoners of war who, in the opinion of the medical authorities of the Detaining Power, are manifestly seriously injured or seriously sick, may be repatriated without having to be examined by a Mixed Medical Commission.

Article 113

Besides those who are designated by the medical authorities of the Detaining Power, wounded or sick prisoners of war belonging to the categories listed below shall be entitled to present themselves for examination by the Mixed Medical Commissions provided for in the foregoing Article:

(1) Wounded and sick proposed by a physician or surgeon who is of the same nationality, or a national of a Party to the conflict allied with the Power on which the said prisoners depend, and who exercises his functions in the camp.

(2) Wounded and sick proposed by their prisoners' representative.

(3) Wounded and sick proposed by the Power on which they depend, or by an organization duly recognized by the said Power and giving assistance to the prisoners.

Prisoners of war who do not belong to one of the three foregoing categories may nevertheless present themselves for examination by Mixed Medical Commissions, but shall be examined only after those belonging to the said categories.

The physician or surgeon of the same nationality as the prisoners who present themselves for examination by the Mixed Medical Commission, likewise the prisoners' representative of the said prisoners, shall have permission to be present at the examination.

Article 114

Prisoners of war who meet with accidents shall, unless the injury is self-inflicted, have the benefit of the provisions of this Convention as regards repatriation or accommodation in a neutral country.

Article 115

No prisoner of war on whom a disciplinary punishment has been imposed and who is eligible for repatriation or for accommodation in a neutral country, may be kept back on the plea that he has not undergone his punishment.

Prisoners of war detained in connection with a judicial prosecution or conviction, and who are designated for repatriation or accommodation in a neutral country, may benefit by such measures before the end of the proceedings or the completion of the punishment, if the Detaining Power consents.

Parties to the conflict shall communicate to each other the names of those who will be detained until the end of the proceedings or the completion of the punishment.

Article 116
The cost of repatriating prisoners of war or of transporting them to a neutral country shall be borne, from the frontiers of the Detaining Power, by the Power on which the said prisoners depend.

Article 117
No repatriated person may be employed on active military service.

Section II: Release and Repatriation of Prisoners of War at the Close of Hostilities

Article 118
Prisoners of war shall be released and repatriated without delay after the cessation of active hostilities.

In the absence of stipulations to the above effect in any agreement concluded between the Parties to the conflict with a view to the cessation of hostilities, or failing any such agreement, each of the Detaining Powers shall itself establish and execute without delay a plan of repatriation in conformity with the principle laid down in the foregoing paragraph.

In either case, the measures adopted shall be brought to the knowledge of the prisoners of war.

The costs of repatriation of prisoners of war shall in all cases be equitably apportioned between the Detaining Power and the Power on which the prisoners depend. This apportionment shall be carried out on the following basis:

(a) If the two Powers are contiguous, the Power on which the prisoners of war depend shall bear the costs of repatriation from the frontiers of the Detaining Power.

(b) If the two Powers are not contiguous, the Detaining Power shall bear the costs of transport of prisoners of war over its own territory as far as its frontier or its port of embarkation nearest to the territory of the Power on which the prisoners of war depend. The Parties concerned shall agree between themselves as to the equitable apportionment of the remaining costs of the repatriation. The conclusion of this agreement shall in no circumstances justify any delay in the repatriation of the prisoners of war.

Article 119
Repatriation shall be effected in conditions similar to those laid down in Articles 46 to 48 inclusive of the present Convention for the transfer of prisoners of war, having regard to the provisions of Article 118 and to those of the following paragraphs.

On repatriation, any articles of value impounded from prisoners of war under Article 18, and any foreign currency which has not been converted into the currency of the Detaining Power, shall be restored to them. Articles of value and foreign currency which, for any reason whatever, are not restored to prisoners of war on repatriation, shall be despatched to the Information Bureau set up under Article 122.

Prisoners of war shall be allowed to take with them their personal effects, and any correspondence and parcels which have arrived for them. The weight of such baggage may be limited, if the conditions of repatriation so require, to what each prisoner can reasonably carry. Each prisoner shall in all cases be authorized to carry at least twenty-five kilograms.

The other personal effects of the repatriated prisoner shall be left in the charge of the Detaining Power which shall have them forwarded to him as soon as it has concluded an agreement to this effect, regulating the conditions of transport and the payment of the costs involved, with the Power on which the prisoner depends.

Prisoners of war against whom criminal proceedings for an indictable offence are pending may be detained until the end of such proceedings, and, if necessary, until the completion of the punishment. The same shall apply to prisoners of war already convicted for an indictable offence.

Parties to the conflict shall communicate to each other the names of any prisoners of war who are detained until the end of the proceedings or until punishment has been completed.

By agreement between the Parties to the conflict, commissions shall be established for the purpose of searching for dispersed prisoners of war and of assuring their repatriation with the least possible delay.

Section III: Death of Prisoners of War

Article 120

Wills of prisoners of war shall be drawn up so as to satisfy the conditions of validity required by the legislation of their country of origin, which will take steps to inform the Detaining Power of its requirements in this respect. At the request of the prisoner of war and, in all cases, after death, the will shall be transmitted without delay to the Protecting Power; a certified copy shall be sent to the Central Agency.

Death certificates, in the form annexed to the present Convention, or lists certified by a responsible officer, of all persons who die as prisoners of war shall be forwarded as rapidly as possible to the Prisoner of War Information Bureau established in accordance with Article 122. The death certificates or certified lists shall show particulars of identity as set out in the third paragraph of Article 17, and also the date and place of death, the cause of death, the date and place of burial and all particulars necessary to identify the graves.

The burial or cremation of a prisoner of war shall be preceded by a medical examination of the body with a view to confirming death and enabling a report to be made and, where necessary, establishing identity.

The detaining authorities shall ensure that prisoners of war who have died in captivity are honourably buried, if possible according to the rites of the religion to which they belonged, and that their graves are respected, suitably maintained and marked so as to be found at any time. Wherever possible, deceased prisoners of war who depended on the same Power shall be interred in the same place.

Deceased prisoners of war shall be buried in individual graves unless unavoidable circumstances require the use of collective graves. Bodies may be cremated only for imperative reasons of hygiene, on account of the religion of the deceased or in accordance with his express wish to this effect. In case of cremation, the fact shall be stated and the reasons given in the death certificate of the deceased.

In order that graves may always be found, all particulars of burials and graves shall be recorded with a Graves Registration Service established by the Detaining Power. Lists of graves and particulars of the prisoners of war interred in cemeteries and elsewhere shall be transmitted to the Power on which such prisoners of war depended. Responsibility for the care of these graves and for records of any subsequent moves of the bodies shall rest on the Power controlling the territory, if a Party to the present Convention. These provisions shall also apply to the ashes, which shall be kept by the Graves Registration Service until proper disposal thereof in accordance with the wishes of the home country.

Article 121

Every death or serious injury of a prisoner of war caused or suspected to have been caused by a sentry, another prisoner of war, or any other person, as well as any death the cause of which is unknown, shall be immediately followed by an official enquiry by the Detaining Power.

A communication on this subject shall be sent immediately to the Protecting Power. Statements shall be taken from witnesses, especially from those who are prisoners of war, and a report including such statements shall be forwarded to the Protecting Power.

If the enquiry indicates the guilt of one or more persons, the Detaining Power shall take all measures for the prosecution of the person or persons responsible.

Part V: Information Bureaux and Relief Societies for Prisoners of War

Article 122

Upon the outbreak of a conflict and in all cases of occupation, each of the Parties to the conflict shall institute an official Information Bureau for prisoners of war who are in its power. Neutral or non-belligerent Powers who may have received within their territory persons belonging to one of the categories referred to in Article 4, shall take the same action with respect to such persons. The Power concerned shall ensure that the Prisoners of War Information Bureau is provided with the necessary accommodation, equipment and staff to ensure its efficient working. It shall be at liberty to employ prisoners of war in such a Bureau under the conditions laid down in the Section of the present Convention dealing with work by prisoners of war.

Within the shortest possible period, each of the Parties to the conflict shall give its Bureau the information referred to in the fourth, fifth and sixth paragraphs of this Article regarding any enemy person belonging to one of the categories referred to in Article 4, who has fallen into its power. Neutral or non-belligerent Powers shall take the same action with regard to persons belonging to such categories whom they have received within their territory.

The Bureau shall immediately forward such information by the most rapid means to the Powers concerned, through the intermediary of the Protecting Powers and likewise of the Central Agency provided for in Article 123.

This information shall make it possible quickly to advise the next of kin concerned. Subject to the provisions of Article 17, the information shall include, in so far as available to the Information Bureau, in respect of each prisoner of war, his surname, first names, rank, army, regimental, personal or serial number, place and full date of birth, indication of the Power on which he depends, first name of the father and maiden name of the mother, name and address of the person to be informed and the address to which correspondence for the prisoner may be sent.

The Information Bureau shall receive from the various departments concerned information regarding transfers, releases, repatriations, escapes, admissions to hospital, and deaths, and shall transmit such information in the manner described in the third paragraph above.

Likewise, information regarding the state of health of prisoners of war who are seriously ill or seriously wounded shall be supplied regularly, every week if possible.

The Information Bureau shall also be responsible for replying to all enquiries sent to it concerning prisoners of war, including those who have died in captivity; it will make any enquiries necessary to obtain the information which is asked for if this is not in its possession.

All written communications made by the Bureau shall be authenticated by a signature or a seal.

The Information Bureau shall furthermore be charged with collecting all personal valuables, including sums in currencies other than that of the Detaining Power and documents of importance to the next of kin, left by prisoners of war who have been repatriated or released, or who have escaped or died, and shall forward the said valuables to the Powers concerned. Such articles shall be sent by the Bureau in sealed packets which shall be accompanied by statements giving clear and full particulars of the identity of the person to whom the articles belonged, and by a complete list of the contents of the parcel. Other personal effects of such prisoners of war shall be transmitted under arrangements agreed upon between the Parties to the conflict concerned.

Article 123

A Central Prisoners of War Information Agency shall be created in a neutral country. The International Committee of the Red Cross shall, if it deems necessary, propose to the Powers concerned the organization of such an Agency.

The function of the Agency shall be to collect all the information it may obtain through official or private channels respecting prisoners of war, and to transmit it as rapidly as possible to the country of origin of the prisoners of war or to the Power on which they depend. It shall receive from the Parties to the conflict all facilities for effecting such transmissions.

The High Contracting Parties, and in particular those whose nationals benefit by the services of the Central Agency, are requested to give the said Agency the financial aid it may require.

The foregoing provisions shall in no way be interpreted as restricting the humanitarian activities of the International Committee of the Red Cross, or of the relief societies provided for in Article 125.

Article 124

The national Information Bureaux and the Central Information Agency shall enjoy free postage for mail, likewise all the exemptions provided for in Article 74, and further, so far as possible, exemption from telegraphic charges or, at least, greatly reduced rates.

Article 125

Subject to the measures which the Detaining Powers may consider essential to ensure their security or to meet any other reasonable need, the representatives of religious organizations, relief societies, or any other organization assisting prisoners of war, shall receive from the said Powers, for themselves and their duly accredited agents, all necessary facilities for visiting the prisoners, for distributing relief supplies and material, from any source, intended for religious, educational or recreative purposes, and for assisting them in organizing their leisure time within the camps. Such societies or organizations may be constituted in the territory of the Detaining Power or in any other country, or they may have an international character.

The Detaining Power may limit the number of societies and organizations whose delegates are allowed to carry out their activities in its territory and under its supervision, on condition, however, that such limitation shall not hinder the effective operation of adequate relief to all prisoners of war.

The special position of the International Committee of the Red Cross in this field shall be recognized and respected at all times.

As soon as relief supplies or material intended for the above-mentioned purposes are handed over to prisoners of war, or very shortly afterwards, receipts for each consignment, signed by the prisoners' representative, shall be forwarded to the relief society or organization making the shipment. At the same time, receipts for these consignments shall be supplied by the administrative authorities responsible for guarding the prisoners.

Part VI: Execution of the Convention

Section I: General Provisions

Article 126
Representatives or delegates of the Protecting Powers shall have permission to go to all places where prisoners of war may be, particularly to places of internment, imprisonment and labour, and shall have access to all premises occupied by prisoners of war; they shall also be allowed to go to the places of departure, passage and arrival of prisoners who are being transferred. They shall be able to interview the prisoners, and in particular the prisoners' representatives, without witnesses, either personally or through an interpreter.

Representatives and delegates of the Protecting Powers shall have full liberty to select the places they wish to visit. The duration and frequency of these visits shall not be restricted. Visits may not be prohibited except for reasons of imperative military necessity, and then only as an exceptional and temporary measure.

The Detaining Power and the Power on which the said prisoners of war depend may agree, if necessary, that compatriots of these prisoners of war be permitted to participate in the visits.

The delegates of the International Committee of the Red Cross shall enjoy the same prerogatives. The appointment of such delegates shall be submitted to the approval of the Power detaining the prisoners of war to be visited.

Article 127
The High Contracting Parties undertake, in time of peace as in time of war, to disseminate the text of the present Convention as widely as possible in their respective countries, and, in particular, to include the study thereof in their programmes of military and, if possible, civil instruction, so that the principles thereof may become known to all their armed forces and to the entire population.

Any military or other authorities, who in time of war assume responsibilities in respect of prisoners of war, must possess the text of the Convention and be specially instructed as to its provisions.

Article 128
The High Contracting Parties shall communicate to one another through the Swiss Federal Council and, during hostilities, through the Protecting Powers,

the official translations of the present Convention, as well as the laws and regulations which they may adopt to ensure the application thereof.

Article 129

The High Contracting Parties undertake to enact any legislation necessary to provide effective penal sanctions for persons committing, or ordering to be committed, any of the grave breaches of the present Convention defined in the following Article.

Each High Contracting Party shall be under the obligation to search for persons alleged to have committed, or to have ordered to be committed, such grave breaches, and shall bring such persons, regardless of their nationality, before its own courts. It may also, if it prefers, and in accordance with the provisions of its own legislation, hand such persons over for trial to another High Contracting Party concerned, provided such High Contracting Party has made out a prima facie case.

Each High Contracting Party shall take measures necessary for the suppression of all acts contrary to the provisions of the present Convention other than the grave breaches defined in the following Article.

In all circumstances, the accused persons shall benefit by safeguards of proper trial and defence, which shall not be less favourable than those provided by Article 105 and those following of the present Convention.

Article 130

Grave breaches to which the preceding Article relates shall be those involving any of the following acts, if committed against persons or property protected by the Convention: wilful killing, torture or inhuman treatment, including biological experiments, wilfully causing great suffering or serious injury to body or health, compelling a prisoner of war to serve in the forces of the hostile Power, or wilfully depriving a prisoner of war of the rights of fair and regular trial prescribed in this Convention.

Article 131

No High Contracting Party shall be allowed to absolve itself or any other High Contracting Party of any liability incurred by itself or by another High Contracting Party in respect of breaches referred to in the preceding Article.

Article 132

At the request of a Party to the conflict, an enquiry shall be instituted, in a manner to be decided between the interested Parties, concerning any alleged violation of the Convention.

If agreement has not been reached concerning the procedure for the enquiry, the Parties should agree on the choice of an umpire who will decide upon the procedure to be followed.

Once the violation has been established, the Parties to the conflict shall put an end to it and shall repress it with the least possible delay.

Section II: Final Provisions

Article 133
The present Convention is established in English and in French. Both texts are equally authentic.

The Swiss Federal Council shall arrange for official translations of the Convention to be made in the Russian and Spanish languages.

Article 134
The present Convention replaces the Convention of July 27, 1929, in relations between the High Contracting Parties.

Article 135
In the relations between the Powers which are bound by the Hague Convention respecting the Laws and Customs of War on Land, whether that of July 29, 1899, or that of October 18, 1907, and which are parties to the present Convention, this last Convention shall be complementary to Chapter II of the Regulations annexed to the above-mentioned Conventions of the Hague.

Article 136
The present Convention, which bears the date of this day, is open to signature until February 12, 1950, in the name of the Powers represented at the Conference which opened at Geneva on April 21, 1949; furthermore, by Powers not represented at that Conference, but which are parties to the Convention of July 27, 1929.

Article 137
The present Convention shall be ratified as soon as possible and the ratifications shall be deposited at Berne.

A record shall be drawn up of the deposit of each instrument of ratification and certified copies of this record shall be transmitted by the Swiss Federal Council to all the Powers in whose name the Convention has been signed, or whose accession has been notified.

Article 138
The present Convention shall come into force six months after not less than two instruments of ratification have been deposited. Thereafter, it shall come into force for each High Contracting Party six months after the deposit of the instrument of ratification.

Article 139
From the date of its coming into force, it shall be open to any Power in whose name the present Convention has not been signed, to accede to this Convention.

Article 140

Accessions shall be notified in writing to the Swiss Federal Council, and shall take effect six months after the date on which they are received.

The Swiss Federal Council shall communicate the accessions to all the Powers in whose name the Convention has been signed, or whose accession has been notified.

Article 141

The situations provided for in Articles 2 and 3 shall give immediate effect to ratifications deposited and accessions notified by the Parties to the conflict before or after the beginning of hostilities or occupation. The Swiss Federal Council shall communicate by the quickest method any ratifications or accessions received from Parties to the conflict.

Article 142

Each of the High Contracting Parties shall be at liberty to denounce the present Convention.

The denunciation shall be notified in writing to the Swiss Federal Council, which shall transmit it to the Governments of all the High Contracting Parties.

The denunciation shall take effect one year after the notification thereof has been made to the Swiss Federal Council. However, a denunciation of which notification has been made at a time when the denouncing Power is involved in a conflict shall not take effect until peace has been concluded, and until after operations connected with release and repatriation of the persons protected by the present Convention have been terminated.

The denunciation shall have effect only in respect of the denouncing Power. It shall in no way impair the obligations which the Parties to the conflict shall remain bound to fulfil by virtue of the principles of the law of nations, as they result from the usages established among civilized peoples, from the laws of humanity and the dictates of the public conscience.

Article 143

The Swiss Federal Council shall register the present Convention with the Secretariat of the United Nations. The Swiss Federal Council shall also inform the Secretariat of the United Nations of all ratifications, accessions and denunciations received by it with respect to the present Convention.

IN WITNESS WHEREOF the undersigned, having deposited their respective full powers, have signed the present Convention.

DONE at Geneva this twelfth day of August 1949, in the English and French languages. The original shall be deposited in the Archives of the Swiss Confederation. The Swiss Federal Council shall transmit certified copies thereof to each of the signatory and acceding States.

. . . [Annexes not included]

6.2
Geneva Convention Relative to the Protection of Civilian Persons in Time of War (Fourth Geneva Convention) (1949)

The proportion of the casualties in armed conflicts who are civilians has steadily increased over the last century. Following World War II there was a recognized need to bring to a conclusion interwar efforts to develop a convention on the treatment of civilians in wartime and this became the Fourth Geneva Convention. For commentary on the convention, see the website of the International Committee of the Red Cross at www.icrc.org/eng/ihl. See also Simon Chesterman, ed., Civilians in War *(Boulder: Lynne Rienner, 2001).*

On 9 July 2004 the ICJ gave an advisory opinion on "the legal consequences arising from the construction of the wall being built by Israel, the occupying Power, in the Occupied Palestinian Territory . . . , considering the rules and principles of international law, including the Fourth Geneva Convention of 1949." The text of the opinion is available at www.icj-cij.org. For commentary on the IHL dimensions of the case, see Ardi Imseis, "Critical Reflections on the International Humanitarian Aspects of the ICJ Wall Advisory Opinion," American Journal of International Law *99 (2005): 102–118.*

Part I: General Provisions

Article 1
The High Contracting Parties undertake to respect and to ensure respect for the present Convention in all circumstances.

Article 2
In addition to the provisions which shall be implemented in peacetime, the present Convention shall apply to all cases of declared war or of any other

armed conflict which may arise between two or more of the High Contracting Parties, even if the state of war is not recognized by one of them.

The Convention shall also apply to all cases of partial or total occupation of the territory of a High Contracting Party, even if the said occupation meets with no armed resistance.

Although one of the Powers in conflict may not be a party to the present Convention, the Powers who are parties thereto shall remain bound by it in their mutual relations. They shall furthermore be bound by the Convention in relation to the said Power, if the latter accepts and applies the provisions thereof.

Article 3

In the case of armed conflict not of an international character occurring in the territory of one of the High Contracting Parties, each Party to the conflict shall be bound to apply, as a minimum, the following provisions:

1. Persons taking no active part in the hostilities, including members of armed forces who have laid down their arms and those placed hors de combat by sickness, wounds, detention, or any other cause, shall in all circumstances be treated humanely, without any adverse distinction founded on race, colour, religion or faith, sex, birth or wealth, or any other similar criteria.

To this end, the following acts are and shall remain prohibited at any time and in any place whatsoever with respect to the above-mentioned persons:

(a) Violence to life and person, in particular murder of all kinds, mutilation, cruel treatment and torture;

(b) Taking of hostages;

(c) Outrages upon personal dignity, in particular humiliating and degrading treatment;

(d) The passing of sentences and the carrying out of executions without previous judgment pronounced by a regularly constituted court, affording all the judicial guarantees which are recognized as indispensable by civilized peoples.

2. The wounded and sick shall be collected and cared for.

An impartial humanitarian body, such as the International Committee of the Red Cross, may offer its services to the Parties to the conflict.

The Parties to the conflict should further endeavour to bring into force, by means of special agreements, all or part of the other provisions of the present Convention.

The application of the preceding provisions shall not affect the legal status of the Parties to the conflict.

Article 4

Persons protected by the Convention are those who, at a given moment and in any manner whatsoever, find themselves, in case of a conflict or occupation, in the hands of a Party to the conflict or Occupying Power of which they are not nationals.

Nationals of a State which is not bound by the Convention are not protected by it. Nationals of a neutral State who find themselves in the territory of a belligerent State, and nationals of a co-belligerent State, shall not be regarded as protected persons while the State of which they are nationals has normal diplomatic representation in the State in whose hands they are.

The provisions of Part II are, however, wider in application, as defined in Article 13.

Persons protected by the Geneva Convention for the Amelioration of the Condition of the Wounded and Sick in Armed Forces in the Field of August 12, 1949, or by the Geneva Convention for the Amelioration of the Condition of Wounded, Sick and Shipwrecked Members of Armed Forces at Sea of August 12, 1949, or by the Geneva Convention relative to the Treatment of Prisoners of War of August 12, 1949, shall not be considered as protected persons within the meaning of the present Convention.

Article 5

Where, in the territory of a Party to the conflict, the latter is satisfied that an individual protected person is definitely suspected of or engaged in activities hostile to the security of the State, such individual person shall not be entitled to claim such rights and privileges under the present Convention as would, if exercised in the favour of such individual person, be prejudicial to the security of such State.

Where in occupied territory an individual protected person is detained as a spy or saboteur, or as a person under definite suspicion of activity hostile to the security of the Occupying Power, such person shall, in those cases where absolute military security so requires, be regarded as having forfeited rights of communication under the present Convention.

In each case, such persons shall nevertheless be treated with humanity, and in case of trial, shall not be deprived of the rights of fair and regular trial prescribed by the present Convention. They shall also be granted the full rights and privileges of a protected person under the present Convention at the earliest date consistent with the security of the State or Occupying Power, as the case may be.

Article 6

The present Convention shall apply from the outset of any conflict or occupation mentioned in Article 2.

In the territory of Parties to the conflict, the application of the present Convention shall cease on the general close of military operations.

In the case of occupied territory, the application of the present Convention shall cease one year after the general close of military operations; however, the Occupying Power shall be bound, for the duration of the occupation, to the extent that such Power exercises the functions of government in such territory, by the provisions of the following Articles of the present Convention: 1 to 12, 27, 29 to 34, 47, 49, 51, 52, 53, 59, 61 to 77, and 143.

Protected persons whose release, repatriation or re-establishment may take place after such dates shall meanwhile continue to benefit by the present Convention.

Article 7

In addition to the agreements expressly provided for in Articles 11, 14, 15, 17, 36, 108, 109, 132, 133 and 149, the High Contracting Parties may conclude other special agreements for all matters concerning which they may deem it suitable to make separate provision. No special agreement shall adversely affect the situation of protected persons, as defined by the present Convention, nor restrict the rights which it confers upon them.

Protected persons shall continue to have the benefit of such agreements as long as the Convention is applicable to them, except where express provisions to the contrary are contained in the aforesaid or in subsequent agreements, or where more favourable measures have been taken with regard to them by one or other of the Parties to the conflict.

Article 8

Protected persons may in no circumstances renounce in part or in entirety the rights secured to them by the present Convention, and by the special agreements referred to in the foregoing Article, if such there be.

Article 9

The present Convention shall be applied with the cooperation and under the scrutiny of the Protecting Powers whose duty it is to safeguard the interests of the Parties to the conflict. For this purpose, the Protecting Powers may appoint, apart from their diplomatic or consular staff, delegates from amongst their own nationals or the nationals of other neutral Powers. The said delegates shall be subject to the approval of the Power with which they are to carry out their duties.

The Parties to the conflict shall facilitate to the greatest extent possible the task of the representatives or delegates of the Protecting Powers.

The representatives or delegates of the Protecting Powers shall not in any case exceed their mission under the present Convention. They shall, in particular, take account of the imperative necessities of security of the State wherein they carry out their duties.

Article 10

The provisions of the present Convention constitute no obstacle to the humanitarian activities which the International Committee of the Red Cross or any other impartial humanitarian organization may, subject to the consent of the Parties to the conflict concerned, undertake for the protection of civilian persons and for their relief.

Article 11

The High Contracting Parties may at any time agree to entrust to an organization which offers all guarantees of impartiality and efficacy the duties incumbent on the Protecting Powers by virtue of the present Convention.

When persons protected by the present Convention do not benefit or cease to benefit, no matter for what reason, by the activities of a Protecting Power or of an organization provided for in the first paragraph above, the Detaining Power shall request a neutral State, or such an organization, to undertake the functions performed under the present Convention by a Protecting Power designated by the Parties to a conflict.

If protection cannot be arranged accordingly, the Detaining Power shall request or shall accept, subject to the provisions of this Article, the offer of the services of a humanitarian organization, such as the International Committee of the Red Cross, to assume the humanitarian functions performed by Protecting Powers under the present Convention.

Any neutral Power, or any organization invited by the Power concerned or offering itself for these purposes, shall be required to act with a sense of responsibility towards the Party to the conflict on which persons protected by the present Convention depend, and shall be required to furnish sufficient assurances that it is in a position to undertake the appropriate functions and to discharge them impartially.

No derogation from the preceding provisions shall be made by special agreements between Powers one of which is restricted, even temporarily, in its freedom to negotiate with the other Power or its allies by reason of military events, more particularly where the whole, or a substantial part, of the territory of the said Power is occupied.

Whenever in the present Convention mention is made of a Protecting Power, such mention applies to substitute organizations in the sense of the present Article.

The provisions of this Article shall extend and be adapted to cases of nationals of a neutral State who are in occupied territory or who find themselves in the territory of a belligerent State with which the State of which they are nationals has not normal diplomatic representation.

Article 12

In cases where they deem it advisable in the interest of protected persons, particularly in cases of disagreement between the Parties to the conflict as to the application or interpretation of the provisions of the present Convention, the Protecting Powers shall lend their good offices with a view to settling the disagreement. For this purpose, each of the Protecting Powers may, either at the invitation of one Party or on its own initiative, propose to the Parties to the conflict a meeting of their representatives, and in particular of the authorities responsible for protected person, possibly on neutral territory suitably chosen. The Parties to the conflict shall be bound to give effect to the proposals made to them for this purpose. The Protecting Powers may, if necessary, propose for approval by the Parties to the conflict, a person belonging to a neutral Power or delegated by the International Committee of the Red Cross who shall be invited to take part in such a meeting.

Part II: General Protection of Populations Against Certain Consequences of War

Article 13

The provisions of Part II cover the whole of the populations of the countries in conflict, without any adverse distinction based, in particular, on race, nationality, religion or political opinion, and are intended to alleviate the sufferings caused by war.

Article 14

In time of peace, the High Contracting Parties and, after the outbreak of hostilities, the Parties thereto, may establish in their own territory and, if the need arises, in occupied areas, hospital and safety zones and localities so organized as to protect from the effects of war, wounded, sick and aged persons, children under fifteen, expectant mothers and mothers of children under seven.

Upon the outbreak and during the course of hostilities, the Parties concerned may conclude agreements on mutual recognition of the zones and localities they have created. They may for this purpose implement the provisions of the Draft Agreement annexed to the present Convention, with such amendments as they may consider necessary.

The Protecting Powers and the International Committee of the Red Cross are invited to lend their good offices in order to facilitate the institution and recognition of these hospital and safety zones and localities.

Article 15

Any Party to the conflict may, either directly or through a neutral State or some humanitarian organization, propose to the adverse Party to establish, in the regions where fighting is taking place, neutralized zones intended to shelter from the effects of war the following persons, without distinction:

(a) wounded and sick combatants or non-combatants;

(b) civilian persons who take no part in hostilities, and who, while they reside in the zones, perform no work of a military character.

When the Parties concerned have agreed upon the geographical position, administration, food supply and supervision of the proposed neutralized zone, a written agreement shall be concluded and signed by the representatives of the Parties to the conflict. The agreement shall fix the beginning and the duration of the neutralization of the zone.

Article 16

The wounded and sick, as well as the infirm, and expectant mothers, shall be the object of particular protection and respect.

As far as military considerations allow, each Party to the conflict shall facilitate the steps taken to search for the killed and wounded, to assist the shipwrecked and other persons exposed to grave danger, and to protect them against pillage and ill-treatment.

Article 17
The Parties to the conflict shall endeavour to conclude local agreements for the removal from besieged or encircled areas, of wounded, sick, infirm, and aged persons, children and maternity cases, and for the passage of ministers of all religions, medical personnel and medical equipment on their way to such areas.

Article 18
Civilian hospitals organized to give care to the wounded and sick, the infirm and maternity cases, may in no circumstances be the object of attack, but shall at all times be respected and protected by the Parties to the conflict.

States which are Parties to a conflict shall provide all civilian hospitals with certificates showing that they are civilian hospitals and that the buildings which they occupy are not used for any purpose which would deprive these hospitals of protection in accordance with Article 19.

Civilian hospitals shall be marked by means of the emblem provided for in Article 38 of the Geneva Convention for the Amelioration of the Condition of the Wounded and Sick in Armed Forces in the Field of August 12, 1949, but only if so authorized by the State.

The Parties to the conflict shall, in so far as military considerations permit, take the necessary steps to make the distinctive emblems indicating civilian hospitals clearly visible to the enemy land, air and naval forces in order to obviate the possibility of any hostile action.

In view of the dangers to which hospitals may be exposed by being close to military objectives, it is recommended that such hospitals be situated as far as possible from such objectives.

Article 19
The protection to which civilian hospitals are entitled shall not cease unless they are used to commit, outside their humanitarian duties, acts harmful to the enemy. Protection may, however, cease only after due warning has been given, naming, in all appropriate cases, a reasonable time limit, and after such warning has remained unheeded.

The fact that sick or wounded members of the armed forces are nursed in these hospitals, or the presence of small arms and ammunition taken from such combatants which have not yet been handed to the proper service, shall not be considered to be acts harmful to the enemy.

Article 20
Persons regularly and solely engaged in the operation and administration of

civilian hospitals, including the personnel engaged in the search for, removal and transporting of and caring for wounded and sick civilians, the infirm and maternity cases, shall be respected and protected.

In occupied territory and in zones of military operations, the above personnel shall be recognizable by means of an identity card certifying their status, bearing the photograph of the holder and embossed with the stamp of the responsible authority, and also by means of a stamped, water-resistant armlet which they shall wear on the left arm while carrying out their duties. This armlet shall be issued by the State and shall bear the emblem provided for in Article 38 of the Geneva Convention for the Amelioration of the Condition of the Wounded and Sick in Armed Forces in the Field of August 12, 1949.

Other personnel who are engaged in the operation and administration of civilian hospitals shall be entitled to respect and protection and to wear the armlet, as provided in and under the conditions prescribed in this Article, while they are employed on such duties. The identity card shall state the duties on which they are employed.

The management of each hospital shall at all times hold at the disposal of the competent national or occupying authorities an up-to-date list of such personnel.

Article 21

Convoys of vehicles or hospital trains on land or specially provided vessels on sea, conveying wounded and sick civilians, the infirm and maternity cases, shall be respected and protected in the same manner as the hospitals provided for in Article 18, and shall be marked, with the consent of the State, by the display of the distinctive emblem provided for in Article 38 of the Geneva Convention for the Amelioration of the Condition of the Wounded and Sick in Armed Forces in the Field of August 12, 1949.

Article 22

Aircraft exclusively employed for the removal of wounded and sick civilians, the infirm and maternity cases, or for the transport of medical personnel and equipment, shall not be attacked, but shall be respected while flying at heights, times and on routes specifically agreed upon between all the Parties to the conflict concerned.

They may be marked with the distinctive emblem provided for in Article 38 of the Geneva Convention for the Amelioration of the Condition of the Wounded and Sick in Armed Forces in the Field of August 12, 1949.

Unless agreed otherwise, flights over enemy or enemy-occupied territory are prohibited.

Such aircraft shall obey every summons to land. In the event of a landing thus imposed, the aircraft with its occupants may continue its flight after examination, if any.

Article 23

Each High Contracting Party shall allow the free passage of all consignments of medical and hospital stores and objects necessary for religious worship intended only for civilians of another High Contracting Party, even if the latter is its adversary. It shall likewise permit the free passage of all consignments of essential foodstuffs, clothing and tonics intended for children under fifteen, expectant mothers and maternity cases.

The obligation of a High Contracting Party to allow the free passage of the consignments indicated in the preceding paragraph is subject to the condition that this Party is satisfied that there are no serious reasons for fearing:

(a) That the consignments may be diverted from their destination;

(b) That the control may not be effective; or

(c) That a definite advantage may accrue to the military efforts or economy of the enemy through the substitution of the above-mentioned consignments for goods which would otherwise be provided or produced by the enemy or through the release of such material, services or facilities as would otherwise be required for the production of such goods.

The Power which allows the passage of the consignments indicated in the first paragraph of this Article may make such permission conditional on the distribution to the persons benefited there by being made under the local supervision of the Protecting Powers.

Such consignments shall be forwarded as rapidly as possible, and the Power which permits their free passage shall have the right to prescribe the technical arrangements under which such passage is allowed.

Article 24

The Parties to the conflict shall take the necessary measures to ensure that children under fifteen, who are orphaned or are separated from their families as a result of the war, are not left to their own resources, and that their maintenance, the exercise of their religion and their education are facilitated in all circumstances. Their education shall, as far as possible, be entrusted to persons of a similar cultural tradition.

The Parties to the conflict shall facilitate the reception of such children in a neutral country for the duration of the conflict with the consent of the Protecting Power, if any, and under due safeguards for the observance of the principles stated in the first paragraph.

They shall, furthermore, endeavour to arrange for all children under twelve to be identified by the wearing of identity discs, or by some other means.

Article 25

All persons in the territory of a Party to the conflict, or in a territory occupied by it, shall be enabled to give news of a strictly personal nature to members of their families, wherever they may be, and to receive news from them. This correspondence shall be forwarded speedily and without undue delay.

If, as a result of circumstances, it becomes difficult or impossible to exchange family correspondence by the ordinary post, the Parties to the conflict concerned shall apply to a neutral intermediary, such as the Central

Agency provided for in Article 140, and shall decide in consultation with it how to ensure the fulfilment of their obligations under the best possible conditions, in particular with the cooperation of the National Red Cross (Red Crescent, Red Lion and Sun) Societies.

If the Parties to the conflict deem it necessary to restrict family correspondence, such restrictions shall be confined to the compulsory use of standard forms containing twenty-five freely chosen words, and to the limitation of the number of these forms despatched to one each month.

Article 26

Each Party to the conflict shall facilitate enquiries made by members of families dispersed owing to the war, with the object of renewing contact with one another and of meeting, if possible. It shall encourage, in particular, the work of organizations engaged on this task provided they are acceptable to it and conform to its security regulations.

Part III: Status and Treatment of Protected Persons

Section I: Provisions Common to the Territories of the Parties to the Conflict and to Occupied Territories

Article 27

Protected persons are entitled, in all circumstances, to respect for their persons, their honour, their family rights, their religious convictions and practices, and their manners and customs. They shall at all times be humanely treated, and shall be protected especially against all acts of violence or threats thereof and against insults and public curiosity.

Women shall be especially protected against any attack on their honour, in particular against rape, enforced prostitution, or any form of indecent assault.

Without prejudice to the provisions relating to their state of health, age and sex, all protected persons shall be treated with the same consideration by the Party to the conflict in whose power they are, without any adverse distinction based, in particular, on race, religion or political opinion.

However, the Parties to the conflict may take such measures of control and security in regard to protected persons as may be necessary as a result of the war.

Article 28

The presence of a protected person may not be used to render certain points or areas immune from military operations.

Article 29

The Party to the conflict in whose hands protected persons may be is responsible for the treatment accorded to them by its agents, irrespective of any individual responsibility which may be incurred.

Article 30

Protected persons shall have every facility for making application to the Protecting Powers, the International Committee of the Red Cross, the National Red Cross (Red Crescent, Red Lion and Sun) Society of the country where they may be, as well as to any organization that might assist them.

These several organizations shall be granted all facilities for that purpose by the authorities, within the bounds set by military or security considerations.

Apart from the visits of the delegates of the Protecting Powers and of the International Committee of the Red Cross, provided for by Article 143, the Detaining or Occupying Powers shall facilitate as much as possible visits to protected persons by the representatives of other organizations whose object is to give spiritual aid or material relief to such persons.

Article 31

No physical or moral coercion shall be exercised against protected persons, in particular to obtain information from them or from third parties.

Article 32

The High Contracting Parties specifically agree that each of them is prohibited from taking any measure of such a character as to cause the physical suffering or extermination of protected persons in their hands. This prohibition applies not only to murder, torture, corporal punishment, mutilation and medical or scientific experiments not necessitated by the medical treatment of a protected person but also to any other measures of brutality whether applied by civilian or military agents.

Article 33

No protected person may be punished for an offence he or she has not personally committed. Collective penalties and likewise all measures of intimidation or of terrorism are prohibited.

Pillage is prohibited.

Reprisals against protected persons and their property are prohibited.

Article 34

The taking of hostages is prohibited.

Section II: Aliens in the Territory of a Party to the Conflict

Article 35

All protected persons who may desire to leave the territory at the outset of, or during a conflict, shall be entitled to do so, unless their departure is contrary to the national interests of the State. The applications of such persons to leave shall be decided in accordance with regularly established procedures and the decision shall be taken as rapidly as possible. Those persons permitted to leave may provide themselves with the necessary funds for their journey and take with them a reasonable amount of their effects and articles of personal use.

If any such person is refused permission to leave the territory, he shall be entitled to have such refusal reconsidered as soon as possible by an appropriate court or administrative board designated by the Detaining Power for that purpose.

Upon request, representatives of the Protecting Power shall, unless reasons of security prevent it, or the persons concerned object, be furnished with the reasons for refusal of any request for permission to leave the territory and be given, as expeditiously as possible, the names of all persons who have been denied permission to leave.

Article 36

Departures permitted under the foregoing Article shall be carried out in satisfactory conditions as regards safety, hygiene, sanitation and food. All costs in connection therewith, from the point of exit in the territory of the Detaining Power, shall be borne by the country of destination, or, in the case of accommodation in a neutral country, by the Power whose nationals are benefited. The practical details of such movements may, if necessary, be settled by special agreements between the Powers concerned.

The foregoing shall not prejudice such special agreements as may be concluded between Parties to the conflict concerning the exchange and repatriation of their nationals in enemy hands.

Article 37

Protected persons who are confined pending proceedings or serving a sentence involving loss of liberty shall during their confinement be humanely treated.

As soon as they are released, they may ask to leave the territory in conformity with the foregoing Articles.

Article 38

With the exception of special measures authorized by the present Convention, in particular by Articles 27 and 41 thereof, the situation of protected persons shall continue to be regulated, in principle, by the provisions concerning aliens in time of peace. In any case, the following rights shall be granted to them:

1. They shall be enabled to receive the individual or collective relief that may be sent to them.

2. They shall, if their state of health so requires, receive medical attention and hospital treatment to the same extent as the nationals of the State concerned.

3. They shall be allowed to practise their religion and to receive spiritual assistance from ministers of their faith.

4. If they reside in an area particularly exposed to the dangers of war, they shall be authorized to move from that area to the same extent as the nationals of the State concerned.

5. Children under fifteen years, pregnant women and mothers of children under seven years shall benefit by any preferential treatment to the same extent as the nationals of the State concerned.

Article 39

Protected persons who, as a result of the war, have lost their gainful employment, shall be granted the opportunity to find paid employment. That opportunity shall, subject to security considerations and to the provisions of Article 40, be equal to that enjoyed by the nationals of the Power in whose territory they are.

Where a Party to the conflict applies to a protected person methods of control which result in his being unable to support himself, and especially if such a person is prevented for reasons of security from finding paid employment on reasonable conditions, the said Party shall ensure his support and that of his dependents.

Protected persons may in any case receive allowances from their home country, the Protecting Power, or the relief societies referred to in Article 30.

Article 40

Protected persons may be compelled to work only to the same extent as nationals of the Party to the conflict in whose territory they are.

If protected persons are of enemy nationality, they may only be compelled to do work which is normally necessary to ensure the feeding, sheltering, clothing, transport and health of human beings and which is not directly related to the conduct of military operations.

In the cases mentioned in the two preceding paragraphs, protected persons compelled to work shall have the benefit of the same working conditions and of the same safeguards as national workers, in particular as regards wages, hours of labour, clothing and equipment, previous training and compensation for occupational accidents and diseases.

If the above provisions are infringed, protected persons shall be allowed to exercise their right of complaint in accordance with Article 30.

Article 41

Should the Power in whose hands protected persons may be consider the measures of control mentioned in the present Convention to be inadequate, it may not have recourse to any other measure of control more severe than that of assigned residence or internment, in accordance with the provisions of Articles 42 and 43.

In applying the provisions of Article 39, second paragraph, to the cases of persons required to leave their usual places of residences by virtue of a decision placing them in assigned residence elsewhere. the Detaining Power shall be guided as closely as possible by the standards of welfare set forth in Part III, Section IV of this Convention.

Article 42

The internment or placing in assigned residence of protected persons may be ordered only if the security of the Detaining Power makes it absolutely necessary.

If any person, acting through the representatives of the Protecting Power, voluntarily demands internment, and if his situation renders this step necessary, he shall be interned by the Power in whose hands he may be.

Article 43

Any protected person who has been interned or placed in assigned residence shall be entitled to have such action reconsidered as soon as possible by an appropriate court or administrative board designated by the Detaining Power for that purpose. If the internment or placing in assigned residence is maintained, the court or administrative board shall periodically, and at least twice yearly, give consideration to his or her case, with a view to the favourable amendment of the initial decision, if circumstances permit.

Unless the protected persons concerned object, the Detaining Power shall, as rapidly as possible, give the Protecting Power the names of any protected persons who have been interned or subjected to assigned residence, or who have been released from internment or assigned residence. The decisions of the courts or boards mentioned in the first paragraph of the present Article shall also, subject to the same conditions, be notified as rapidly as possible to the Protecting Power.

Article 44

In applying the measures of control mentioned in the present Convention, the Detaining Power shall not treat as enemy aliens exclusively on the basis of their nationality de jure of an enemy State, refugees who do not, in fact, enjoy the protection of any government.

Article 45

Protected persons shall not be transferred to a Power which is not a party to the Convention.

This provision shall in no way constitute an obstacle to the repatriation of protected persons, or to their return to their country of residence after the cessation of hostilities.

Protected persons may be transferred by the Detaining Power only to a Power which is a party to the present Convention and after the Detaining Power has satisfied itself of the willingness and ability of such transferee Power to apply the present Convention. If protected persons are transferred under such circumstances, responsibility for the application of the present Convention rests on the Power accepting them, while they are in its custody.

Nevertheless, if that Power fails to carry out the provisions of the present Convention in any important respect, the Power by which the protected persons were transferred shall, upon being so notified by the Protecting Power, take effective measures to correct the situation or shall request the return of the protected persons. Such request must be complied with.

In no circumstances shall a protected person be transferred to a country where he or she may have reason to fear persecution for his or her political opinions or religious beliefs.

The provisions of this Article do not constitute an obstacle to the extradition, in pursuance of extradition treaties concluded before the outbreak of hostilities, of protected persons accused of offences against ordinary criminal law.

Article 46

In so far as they have not been previously withdrawn, restrictive measures taken regarding protected persons shall be cancelled as soon as possible after the close of hostilities.

Restrictive measures affecting their property shall be cancelled, in accordance with the law of the Detaining Power, as soon as possible after the close of hostilities.

Section III: Occupied Territories

Article 47

Protected persons who are in occupied territory shall not be deprived, in any case or in any manner whatsoever, of the benefits of the present Convention by any change introduced, as the result of the occupation of a territory, into the institutions or government of the said territory, nor by any agreement concluded between the authorities of the occupied territories and the Occupying Power, nor by any annexation by the latter of the whole or part of the occupied territory.

Article 48

Protected persons who are not nationals of the Power whose territory is occupied may avail themselves of the right to leave the territory subject to the provisions of Article 35, and decisions thereon shall be taken according to the procedure which the Occupying Power shall establish in accordance with the said Article.

Article 49

Individual or mass forcible transfers, as well as deportations of protected persons from occupied territory to the territory of the Occupying Power or to that of any other country, occupied or not, are prohibited, regardless of their motive.

Nevertheless, the Occupying Power may undertake total or partial evacuation of a given area if the security of the population or imperative military reasons do demand. Such evacuations may not involve the displacement of protected persons outside the bounds of the occupied territory except when for material reasons it is impossible to avoid such displacement. Persons thus evacuated shall be transferred back to their homes as soon as hostilities in the area in question have ceased.

The Occupying Power undertaking such transfers or evacuations shall ensure, to the greatest practicable extent, that proper accommodation is provided to receive the protected persons, that the removals are effected in satisfactory conditions of hygiene, health, safety and nutrition, and that members of the same family are not separated.

The Protecting Power shall be informed of any transfers and evacuations as soon as they have taken place.

The Occupying Power shall not detain protected persons in an area particularly exposed to the dangers of war unless the security of the population or imperative military reasons so demand.

The Occupying Power shall not deport or transfer parts of its own civilian population into the territory it occupies.

Article 50

The Occupying Power shall, with the cooperation of the national and local authorities, facilitate the proper working of all institutions devoted to the care and education of children.

The Occupying Power shall take all necessary steps to facilitate the identification of children and the registration of their parentage. It may not, in any case, change their personal status, nor enlist them in formations or organizations subordinate to it.

Should the local institutions be inadequate for the purpose, the Occupying Power shall make arrangements for the maintenance and education, if possible by persons of their own nationality, language and religion, of children who are orphaned or separated from their parents as a result of the war and who cannot be adequately cared for by a near relative or friend.

A special section of the Bureau set up in accordance with Article 136 shall be responsible for taking all necessary steps to identify children whose identity is in doubt. Particulars of their parents or other near relatives should always be recorded if available.

The Occupying Power shall not hinder the application of any preferential measures in regard to food, medical care and protection against the effects of war, which may have been adopted prior to the occupation in favour of children under fifteen years, expectant mothers, and mothers of children under seven years.

Article 51

The Occupying Power may not compel protected persons to serve in its armed or auxiliary forces. No pressure or propaganda which aims at securing voluntary enlistment is permitted.

The Occupying Power may not compel protected persons to work unless they are over eighteen years of age, and then only on work which is necessary either for the needs of the army of occupation, or for the public utility services, or for the feeding, sheltering, clothing, transportation or health of the population of the occupied country. Protected persons may not be compelled to undertake any work which would involve them in the obligation of taking part in military operations. The Occupying Power may not compel protected persons to employ forcible means to ensure the security of the installations where they are performing compulsory labour.

The work shall be carried out only in the occupied territory where the persons whose services have been requisitioned are. Every such person shall, so far as possible, be kept in his usual place of employment. Workers shall be paid a fair wage and the work shall be proportionate to their physical and intellectual capacities. The legislation in force in the occupied country concerning working conditions, and safeguards as regards, in particular, such matters as wages, hours of work, equipment, preliminary training and compensation for occupational accidents and diseases, shall be applicable to the protected persons assigned to the work referred to in this Article.

In no case shall requisition of labour lead to a mobilization of workers in an organization of a military or semi-military character.

Article 52

No contract, agreement or regulation shall impair the right of any worker, whether voluntary or not and wherever he may be, to apply to the representatives of the Protecting Power in order to request the said Power's intervention.

All measures aiming at creating unemployment or at restricting the opportunities offered to workers in an occupied territory, in order to induce them to work for the Occupying Power, are prohibited.

Article 53

Any destruction by the Occupying Power of real or personal property belonging individually or collectively to private persons, or to the State, or to other public authorities, or to social or cooperative organizations, is prohibited, except where such destruction is rendered absolutely necessary by military operations.

Article 54

The Occupying Power may not alter the status of public officials or judges in the occupied territories, or in any way apply sanctions to or take any measures of coercion or discrimination against them, should they abstain from fulfilling their functions for reasons of conscience.

This prohibition does not prejudice the application of the second paragraph of Article 51. It does not affect the right of the Occupying Power to remove public officials from their posts.

Article 55

To the fullest extent of the means available to it the Occupying Power has the duty of ensuring the food and medical supplies of the population; it should, in particular, bring in the necessary foodstuffs, medical stores and other articles if the resources of the occupied territory are inadequate.

The Occupying Power may not requisition foodstuffs, articles or medical supplies available in the occupied territory, except for use by the occupation forces and administration personnel, and then only if the requirements of the civilian population have been taken into account. Subject to the provisions of other international Conventions, the Occupying Power shall make arrangements to ensure that fair value is paid for any requisitioned goods.

The Protecting Power shall, at any time, be at liberty to verify the state of the food and medical supplies in occupied territories, except where temporary restrictions are made necessary by imperative military requirements.

Article 56

To the fullest extent of the means available to it, the Occupying Power has the duty of ensuring and maintaining, with the cooperation of national and local authorities, the medical and hospital establishments and services, public health and hygiene in the occupied territory, with particular reference to the adoption and application of the prophylactic and preventive measures necessary to combat the spread of contagious diseases and epidemics. Medical personnel of all categories shall be allowed to carry out their duties.

If new hospitals are set up in occupied territory and if the competent organs of the occupied State are not operating there, the occupying authorities shall, if necessary, grant them the recognition provided for in Article 18. In similar circumstances, the occupying authorities shall also grant recognition to hospital personnel and transport vehicles under the provisions of Articles 20 and 21.

In adopting measures of health and hygiene and in their implementation, the Occupying Power shall take into consideration the moral and ethical susceptibilities of the population of the occupied territory.

Article 57

The Occupying Power may requisition civilian hospitals only temporarily and only in cases of urgent necessity for the care of military wounded and sick, and then on condition that suitable arrangements are made in due time for the care and treatment of the patients and for the needs of the civilian population for hospital accommodation.

The material and stores of civilian hospitals cannot be requisitioned so long as they are necessary for the needs of the civilian population.

Article 58

The Occupying Power shall permit ministers of religion to give spiritual assistance to the members of their religious communities.

The Occupying Power shall also accept consignments of books and articles required for religious needs and shall facilitate their distribution in occupied territory.

Article 59

If the whole or part of the population of an occupied territory is inadequately supplied, the Occupying Power shall agree to relief schemes on behalf of the said population, and shall facilitate them by all the means at its disposal.

Such schemes, which may be undertaken either by States or by impartial humanitarian organizations such as the International Committee of the Red Cross, shall consist, in particular, of the provision of consignments of foodstuffs, medical supplies and clothing.

All Contracting Parties shall permit the free passage of these consignments and shall guarantee their protection.

A Power granting free passage to consignments on their way to territory occupied by an adverse Party to the conflict shall, however, have the right to search the consignments, to regulate their passage according to prescribed times and routes, and to be reasonably satisfied through the Protecting Power that these consignments are to be used for the relief of the needy population and are not to be used for the benefit of the Occupying Power.

Article 60

Relief consignments shall in no way relieve the Occupying Power of any of its responsibilities under Articles 55, 56 and 59. The Occupying Power shall in no way whatsoever divert relief consignments from the purpose for which they are intended, except in cases of urgent necessity, in the interests of the population of the occupied territory and with the consent of the Protecting Power.

Article 61

The distribution of the relief consignments referred to in the foregoing Articles shall be carried out with the cooperation and under the supervision of the Protecting Power. This duty may also be delegated, by agreement between the Occupying Power and the Protecting Power, to a neutral Power, to the International Committee of the Red Cross or to any other impartial humanitarian body.

Such consignments shall be exempt in occupied territory from all charges, taxes or customs duties unless these are necessary in the interests of the economy of the territory. The Occupying Power shall facilitate the rapid distribution of these consignments.

All Contracting Parties shall endeavour to permit the transit and transport, free of charge, of such relief consignments on their way to occupied territories.

Article 62

Subject to imperative reasons of security, protected persons in occupied territories shall be permitted to receive the individual relief consignments sent to them.

Article 63

Subject to temporary and exceptional measures imposed for urgent reasons of security by the Occupying Power:

(a) Recognized National Red Cross (Red Crescent, Red Lion and Sun) Societies shall be able to pursue their activities in accordance with Red Cross principles, as defined by the International Red Cross Conferences. Other relief societies shall be permitted to continue their humanitarian activities under similar conditions;

(b) The Occupying Power may not require any changes in the personnel or structure of these societies, which would prejudice the aforesaid activities.

The same principles shall apply to the activities and personnel of special organizations of a non-military character, which already exist or which may be established, for the purpose of ensuring the living conditions of the civilian population by the maintenance of the essential public utility services, by the distribution of relief and by the organization of rescues.

Article 64

The penal laws of the occupied territory shall remain in force, with the exception that they may be repealed or suspended by the Occupying Power in cases where they constitute a threat to its security or an obstacle to the application of the present Convention. Subject to the latter consideration and to the necessity for ensuring the effective administration of justice, the tribunals of the occupied territory shall continue to function in respect of all offences covered by the said laws.

The Occupying Power may, however, subject the population of the occupied territory to provisions which are essential to enable the Occupying Power to fulfil its obligations under the present Convention, to maintain the orderly government of the territory, and to ensure the security of the Occupying Power, of the members and property of the occupying forces or administration, and likewise of the establishments and lines of communication used by them.

Article 65

The penal provisions enacted by the Occupying Power shall not come into force before they have been published and brought to the knowledge of the inhabitants in their own language. The effect of these penal provisions shall not be retroactive.

Article 66

In case of a breach of the penal provisions promulgated by it by virtue of the second paragraph of Article 64, the Occupying Power may hand over the accused to its properly constituted, non-political military courts, on condition that the said courts sit in the occupied country. Courts of appeal shall preferably sit in the occupied country.

Article 67

The courts shall apply only those provisions of law which were applicable prior to the offence, and which are in accordance with general principles of law, in particular the principle that the penalty shall be proportioned to the offence. They shall take into consideration the fact that the accused is not a national of the Occupying Power.

Article 68

Protected persons who commit an offence which is solely intended to harm the Occupying Power, but which does not constitute an attempt on the life or limb of members of the occupying forces or administration, nor a grave collective danger, nor seriously damage the property of the occupying forces or administration or the installations used by them, shall be liable to internment or simple imprisonment, provided the duration of such internment or imprisonment is proportionate to the offence committed. Furthermore, internment or imprisonment shall, for such offences, be the only measure adopted for depriving protected persons of liberty. The courts provided for under Article 66 of the present Convention may at their discretion convert a sentence of imprisonment to one of internment for the same period.

The penal provisions promulgated by the Occupying Power in accordance with Articles 64 and 65 may impose the death penalty on a protected person only in cases where the person is guilty of espionage, of serious acts of sabotage against the military installations of the Occupying Power or of intentional offences which have caused the death of one or more persons, provided that such offences were punishable by death under the law of the occupied territory in force before the occupation began.

The death penalty may not be pronounced against a protected person unless the attention of the court has been particularly called to the fact that, since the accused is not a national of the Occupying Power, he is not bound to it by any duty of allegiance.

In any case, the death penalty may not be pronounced against a protected person who was under eighteen years of age at the time of the offence.

Article 69

In all cases, the duration of the period during which a protected person accused of an offence is under arrest awaiting trial or punishment shall be deducted from any period of imprisonment awarded.

Article 70

Protected persons shall not be arrested, prosecuted or convicted by the Occupying Power for acts committed or for opinions expressed before the occupation, or during a temporary interruption thereof, with the exception of breaches of the laws and customs of war.

Nationals of the Occupying Power who, before the outbreak of hostilities, have sought refuge in the territory of the occupied State, shall not be arrested, prosecuted, convicted or deported from the occupied territory, except for offences committed after the outbreak of hostilities, or for offences under common law committed before the outbreak of hostilities which, according to the law of the occupied State, would have justified extradition in time of peace.

Article 71

No sentence shall be pronounced by the competent courts of the Occupying Power except after a regular trial.

Accused persons who are prosecuted by the Occupying Power shall be promptly informed, in writing, in a language which they understand, of the particulars of the charges preferred against them, and shall be brought to trial as rapidly as possible. The Protecting Power shall be informed of all proceedings instituted by the Occupying Power against protected persons in respect of charges involving the death penalty or imprisonment for two years or more; it shall be enabled, at any time, to obtain information regarding the state of such proceedings. Furthermore, the Protecting Power shall be entitled, on request, to be furnished with all particulars of these and of any other proceedings instituted by the Occupying Power against protected persons.

The notification to the Protecting Power, as provided for in the second paragraph above, shall be sent immediately, and shall in any case reach the Protecting Power three weeks before the date of the first hearing. Unless, at the opening of the trial, evidence is submitted that the provisions of this Article are fully complied with, the trial shall not proceed. The notification shall include the following particulars:

(a) Description of the accused;

(b) Place of residence or detention;

(c) Specification of the charge or charges (with mention of the penal provisions under which it is brought);

(d) Designation of the court which will hear the case;

(e) Place and date of the first hearing.

Article 72

Accused persons shall have the right to present evidence necessary to their defence and may, in particular, call witnesses. They shall have the right to be assisted by a qualified advocate or counsel of their own choice, who shall be able to visit them freely and shall enjoy the necessary facilities for preparing the defence.

Failing a choice by the accused, the Protecting Power may provide him with an advocate or counsel. When an accused person has to meet a serious charge and the Protecting Power is not functioning, the Occupying Power, subject to the consent of the accused, shall provide an advocate or counsel.

Accused persons shall, unless they freely waive such assistance, be aided by an interpreter, both during preliminary investigation and during the hearing in court. They shall have the right at any time to object to the interpreter and to ask for his replacement.

Article 73

A convicted person shall have the right of appeal provided for by the laws applied by the court. He shall be fully informed of his right to appeal or petition and of the time limit within which he may do so.

The penal procedure provided in the present Section shall apply, as far as it is applicable, to appeals. Where the laws applied by the Court make no provision for appeals, the convicted person shall have the right to petition against the finding and sentence to the competent authority of the Occupying Power.

Article 74

Representatives of the Protecting Power shall have the right to attend the trial of any protected person, unless the hearing has, as an exceptional measure, to be held in camera in the interests of the security of the Occupying Power, which shall then notify the Protecting Power. A notification in respect of the date and place of trial shall be sent to the Protecting Power.

Any judgment involving a sentence of death, or imprisonment for two years or more, shall be communicated, with the relevant grounds, as rapidly as possible to the Protecting Power. The notification shall contain a reference to the notification made under Article 71, and in the case of sentences of imprisonment, the name of the place where the sentence is to be served. A record of judgments other than those referred to above shall be kept by the court and shall be open to inspection by representatives of the Protecting Power. Any period allowed for appeal in the case of sentences involving the death penalty, or imprisonment for two years or more, shall not run until notification of judgment has been received by the Protecting Power.

Article 75

In no case shall persons condemned to death be deprived of the right of petition for pardon or reprieve.

No death sentence shall be carried out before the expiration of a period of at least six months from the date of receipt by the Protecting Power of the notification of the final judgment confirming such death sentence, or of an order denying pardon or reprieve.

The six months period of suspension of the death sentence herein prescribed may be reduced in individual cases in circumstances of grave emergency involving an organized threat to the security of the Occupying Power or its forces, provided always that the Protecting Power is notified of such reduction and is given reasonable time and opportunity to make representations to the competent occupying authorities in respect of such death sentences.

Article 76

Protected persons accused of offences shall be detained in the occupied country, and if convicted they shall serve their sentences therein. They shall, if possible, be separated from other detainees and shall enjoy conditions of food and hygiene which will be sufficient to keep them in good health, and which will be at least equal to those obtaining in prisons in the occupied country.

They shall receive the medical attention required by their state of health.

They shall also have the right to receive any spiritual assistance which they may require.

Women shall be confined in separate quarters and shall be under the direct supervision of women.

Proper regard shall be paid to the special treatment due to minors.

Protected persons who are detained shall have the right to be visited by delegates of the Protecting Power and of the International Committee of the Red Cross, in accordance with the provisions of Article 143.

Such persons shall have the right to receive at least one relief parcel monthly.

Article 77

Protected persons who have been accused of offences or convicted by the courts in occupied territory shall be handed over at the close of occupation, with the relevant records, to the authorities of the liberated territory.

Article 78

If the Occupying Power considers it necessary, for imperative reasons of security, to take safety measures concerning protected persons, it may, at the most, subject them to assigned residence or to internment.

Decisions regarding such assigned residence or internment shall be made according to a regular procedure to be prescribed by the Occupying Power in accordance with the provisions of the present Convention. This procedure shall include the right of appeal for the parties concerned. Appeals shall be decided with the least possible delay. In the event of the decision being upheld, it shall be subject to periodical review, if possible every six months, by a competent body set up by the said Power.

Protected persons made subject to assigned residence and thus required to leave their homes shall enjoy the full benefit of Article 39 of the present Convention.

. . . [Section IV: Regulations for the Treatment of Internees, and Section V: Information Bureaux and Central Agency not included]

Part IV: Execution of the Convention

Section I: General Provisions

Article 142

Subject to the measures which the Detaining Powers may consider essential to ensure their security or to meet any other reasonable need, the representatives of religious organizations, relief societies, or any other organizations assisting the protected persons, shall receive from these Powers, for themselves or their duly accredited agents, all facilities for visiting the protected persons, for distributing relief supplies and material from any source, intended for educational, recreational or religious purposes, or for assisting them in organizing their leisure time within the places of internment. Such societies or organizations may be constituted in the territory of the Detaining Power, or in any other country, or they may have an international character.

The Detaining Power may limit the number of societies and organizations whose delegates are allowed to carry out their activities in its territory and under its supervision, on condition, however, that such limitation shall not hinder the supply of effective and adequate relief to all protected persons.

The special position of the International Committee of the Red Cross in this field shall be recognized and respected at all times.

Article 143

Representatives or delegates of the Protecting Powers shall have permission to go to all places where protected persons are, particularly to places of internment, detention and work.

They shall have access to all premises occupied by protected persons and shall be able to interview the latter without witnesses, personally or through an interpreter.

Such visits may not be prohibited except for reasons of imperative military necessity, and then only as an exceptional and temporary measure. Their duration and frequency shall not be restricted.

Such representatives and delegates shall have full liberty to select the places they wish to visit. The Detaining or Occupying Power, the Protecting Power and when occasion arises the Power of origin of the persons to be visited, may agree that compatriots of the internees shall be permitted to participate in the visits.

The delegates of the International Committee of the Red Cross shall also enjoy the above prerogatives. The appointment of such delegates shall be submitted to the approval of the Power governing the territories where they will carry out their duties.

Article 144

The High Contracting Parties undertake, in time of peace as in time of war, to disseminate the text of the present Convention as widely as possible in their respective countries, and, in particular, to include the study thereof in their programmes of military and, if possible, civil instruction, so that the principles thereof may become known to the entire population.

Any civilian, military, police or other authorities, who in time of war assume responsibilities in respect of protected persons, must possess the text of the Convention and be specially instructed as to its provisions.

Article 145

The High Contracting Parties shall communicate to one another through the Swiss Federal Council and, during hostilities, through the Protecting Powers, the official translations of the present Convention, as well as the laws and regulations which they may adopt to ensure the application thereof.

Article 146

The High Contracting Parties undertake to enact any legislation necessary to provide effective penal sanctions for persons committing, or ordering to be committed, any of the grave breaches of the present Convention defined in the following Article.

Each High Contracting Party shall be under the obligation to search for persons alleged to have committed, or to have ordered to be committed, such grave breaches, and shall bring such persons, regardless of their nationality, before its own courts. It may also, if it prefers, and in accordance with the provisions of its own legislation, hand such persons over for trial to another High Contracting Party concerned, provided such High Contracting Party has made out a prima facie case.

Each High Contracting Party shall take measures necessary for the suppression of all acts contrary to the provisions of the present Convention other than the grave breaches defined in the following Article.

In all circumstances, the accused persons shall benefit by safeguards of proper trial and defence, which shall not be less favourable than those provided by Article 105 and those following of the Geneva Convention relative to the Treatment of Prisoners of War of August 12, 1949.

Article 147

Grave breaches to which the preceding Article relates shall be those involving any of the following acts, if committed against persons or property protected by the present Convention: wilful killing, torture or inhuman treatment, including biological experiments, wilfully causing great suffering or serious injury to body or health, unlawful deportation or transfer or unlawful confinement of a protected person, compelling a protected person to serve in the forces of a hostile Power, or wilfully depriving a protected person of the rights of fair and regular trial prescribed in the present Convention, taking of hostages and extensive destruction and appropriation of property, not justified by military necessity and carried out unlawfully and wantonly.

Article 148

No High Contracting Party shall be allowed to absolve itself or any other High Contracting Party of any liability incurred by itself or by another High Contracting Party in respect of breaches referred to in the preceding Article.

Article 149

At the request of a Party to the conflict, an enquiry shall be instituted, in a manner to be decided between the interested Parties, concerning any alleged violation of the Convention.

If agreement has not been reached concerning the procedure for the enquiry, the Parties should agree on the choice of an umpire who will decide upon the procedure to be followed.

Once the violation has been established, the Parties to the conflict shall put an end to it and shall repress it with the least possible delay.

Section II: Final Provisions

Article 150

The present Convention is established in English and in French. Both texts are equally authentic.

The Swiss Federal Council shall arrange for official translations of the Convention to be made in the Russian and Spanish languages.

Article 151

The present Convention, which bears the date of this day, is open to signature until February 12, 1950, in the name of the Powers represented at the Conference which opened at Geneva on April 21, 1949.

Article 152

The present Convention shall be ratified as soon as possible and the ratifications shall be deposited at Berne.

A record shall be drawn up of the deposit of each instrument of ratification and certified copies of this record shall be transmitted by the Swiss Federal Council to all the Powers in whose name the Convention has been signed, or whose accession has been notified.

Article 153

The present Convention shall come into force six months after not less than two instruments of ratification have been deposited.

Thereafter, it shall come into force for each High Contracting Party six months after the deposit of the instrument of ratification.

Article 154

In the relations between the Powers who are bound by The Hague Conventions respecting the Laws and Customs of War on Land, whether that of 29 July, 1899, or that of 18 October, 1907, and who are parties to the present Convention, this last Convention shall be supplementary to Sections II and III of the Regulations annexed to the above-mentioned Conventions of The Hague.

Article 155

From the date of its coming into force, it shall be open to any Power in whose name the present Convention has not been signed, to accede to this Convention.

Article 156

Accessions shall be notified in writing to the Swiss Federal Council, and shall take effect six months after the date on which they are received.

The Swiss Federal Council shall communicate the accessions to all the Powers in whose name the Convention has been signed, or whose accession has been notified.

Article 157

The situations provided for in Articles 2 and 3 shall give immediate effect to ratifications deposited and accessions notified by the Parties to the conflict before or after the beginning of hostilities or occupation. The Swiss Federal Council shall communicate by the quickest method any ratifications or accessions received from Parties to the conflict.

Article 158

Each of the High Contracting Parties shall be at liberty to denounce the present Convention.

The denunciation shall be notified in writing to the Swiss Federal Council, which shall transmit it to the Governments of all the High Contracting Parties.

The denunciation shall take effect one year after the notification thereof has been made to the Swiss Federal Council. However, a denunciation of which notification has been made at a time when the denouncing Power is involved in a conflict shall not take effect until peace has been concluded, and until after operations connected with the release, repatriation and re-establishment of the persons protected by the present Convention have been terminated.

The denunciation shall have effect only in respect of the denouncing Power. It shall in no way impair the obligations which the Parties to the conflict shall remain bound to fulfil by virtue of the principles of the law of nations, as they result from the usages established among civilized peoples, from the laws of humanity and the dictates of the public conscience.

Article 159

The Swiss Federal Council shall register the present Convention with the Secretariat of the United Nations. The Swiss Federal Council shall also inform the Secretariat of the United Nations of all ratifications, accessions and denunciations received by it with respect to the present Convention.

IN WITNESS WHEREOF the undersigned, having deposited their respective full powers, have signed the present Convention.

DONE at Geneva this twelfth day of August 1949, in the English and French languages. The original shall be deposited in the Archives of the Swiss Confederation. The Swiss Federal Council shall transmit certified copies thereof to each of the signatory and acceding States.

. . . [Annexes not included]

6.3
Protocol Additional to the Geneva Conventions of 12 August 1949, and Relating to the Protection of Victims of International Armed Conflicts (Protocol I) (1977)

This is one of three protocols additional to the 1949 Geneva Conventions. Protocols I and II were adopted and opened for signature on 8 June 1977. Protocol I expands protection for the civilian population as well as military and civilian medical workers in international armed conflict. Protocol II expands and complements the protections for those involved in noninternational armed conflict. The Third Additional Protocol, creating the red crystal as an additional emblem for the International Red Cross and Red Crescent Movement, was adopted on 8 December 2005.

On the negotiating history of the First Additional Protocol, see Howard S. Levie, ed., Protection for War Victims: Protocol I to the 1949 Geneva Conventions, *4 vols. (Dobbs Ferry, N.Y.: Oceana, 1979–1981). On the reasons for US nonratification, see "Agora: The US Decision Not to Ratify Protocol I to the Geneva Conventions on the Protection of War Victims,"* American Journal of International Law *81 (1987): 910–925; and George H. Aldrich, "Prospects for United States Ratification of Additional Protocol I to the 1949 Geneva Conventions,"* American Journal of International Law *85 (1991): 1–20. For commentary on the protocol, see M. Bothe, K. Partsch, and W. Solf,* New Rules for Victims of Armed Conflict: Commentary on the Two 1977 Protocols Additional to the Geneva Conventions of 1949 *(The Hague: M. Nijhoff, 1982).*

The High Contracting Parties,

Proclaiming their earnest wish to see peace prevail among peoples,

Recalling that every State has the duty, in conformity with the Charter of the United Nations, to refrain in its international relations from the threat or use of force against the sovereignty, territorial integrity or political independence of any State, or in any other manner inconsistent with the purposes of the United Nations,

Believing it necessary nevertheless to reaffirm and develop the provisions protecting the victims of armed conflicts and to supplement measures intended to reinforce their application,

Expressing their conviction that nothing in this Protocol or in the Geneva Conventions of 12 August 1949 can be construed as legitimizing or authorizing any act of aggression or any other use of force inconsistent with the Charter of the United Nations,

Reaffirming further that the provisions of the Geneva Conventions of 12 August 1949 and of this Protocol must be fully applied in all circumstances to all persons who are protected by those instruments, without any adverse distinction based on the nature or origin of the armed conflict or on the causes espoused by or attributed to the Parties to the conflicts,

Have agreed on the following:

Part I: General Provisions

Article 1: General principles and scope of application

1. The High Contracting Parties undertake to respect and to ensure respect for this Protocol in all circumstances.

2. In cases not covered by this Protocol or by other international agreements, civilians and combatants remain under the protection and authority of the principles of international law derived from established custom, from the principles of humanity and from the dictates of public conscience.

3. This Protocol, which supplements the Geneva Conventions of 12 August 1949 for the protection of war victims, shall apply in the situations referred to in Article 2 common to those Conventions.

4. The situations referred to in the preceding paragraph include armed conflicts in which peoples are fighting against colonial domination and alien occupation and against racist regimes in the exercise of their right of self-determination, as enshrined in the Charter of the United Nations and the Declaration on Principles of International Law concerning Friendly Relations and Co-operation among States in accordance with the Charter of the United Nations.

Article 2: Definitions

For the purposes of this Protocol:

(a) "First Convention," "Second Convention," "Third Convention" and "Fourth Convention" mean, respectively, the Geneva Convention for the Amelioration of the Condition of the Wounded and Sick in Armed Forces in the Field of 12 August 1949; the Geneva Convention for the Amelioration of the Condition of Wounded, Sick and Shipwrecked Members of Armed Forces at Sea of 12 August 1949; the Geneva Convention relative to the Treatment of Prisoners of War of 12 August 1949; the Geneva Convention relative to the Protection of Civilian Persons in Time of War of 12 August 1949; "the Conventions" means the four Geneva Conventions of 12 August 1949 for the protection of war victims;

(b) "Rules of international law applicable in armed conflict" means the rules applicable in armed conflict set forth in international agreements to which the Parties to the conflict are Parties and the generally recognized principles and rules of international law which are applicable to armed conflict;

(c) "Protecting Power" means a neutral or other State not a Party to the conflict which has been designated by a Party to the conflict and accepted by the adverse Party and has agreed to carry out the functions assigned to a Protecting Power under the Conventions and this Protocol;

(d) "Substitute" means an organization acting in place of a Protecting Power in accordance with Article 5.

Article 3: Beginning and end of application

Without prejudice to the provisions which are applicable at all times:

(a) The Conventions and this Protocol shall apply from the beginning of any situation referred to in Article 1 of this Protocol;

(b) The application of the Conventions and of this Protocol shall cease, in the territory of Parties to the conflict, on the general close of military operations and, in the case of occupied territories, on the termination of the occupation, except, in either circumstance, for those persons whose final release, repatriation or re-establishment takes place thereafter. These persons shall continue to benefit from the relevant provisions of the Conventions and of this Protocol until their final release, repatriation or re-establishment.

Article 4: Legal status of the Parties to the conflict

The application of the Conventions and of this Protocol, as well as the conclusion of the agreements provided for therein, shall not affect the legal status of the Parties to the conflict. Neither the occupation of a territory nor the application of the Conventions and this Protocol shall affect the legal status of the territory in question.

Article 5: Appointment of Protecting Powers and of their substitute

1. It is the duty of the Parties to a conflict from the beginning of that conflict to secure the supervision and implementation of the Conventions and of this Protocol by the application of the system of Protecting Powers, including inter alia the designation and acceptance of those Powers, in accordance with the following paragraphs. Protecting Powers shall have the duty of safeguarding the interests of the Parties to the conflict.

2. From the beginning of a situation referred to in Article 1, each Party to the conflict shall without delay designate a Protecting Power for the purpose of applying the Conventions and this Protocol and shall, likewise without delay

and for the same purpose, permit the activities of a Protecting Power which has been accepted by it as such after designation by the adverse Party.

3. If a Protecting Power has not been designated or accepted from the beginning of a situation referred to in Article 1, the International Committee of the Red Cross, without prejudice to the right of any other impartial humanitarian organization to do likewise, shall offer its good offices to the Parties to the conflict with a view to the designation without delay of a Protecting Power to which the Parties to the conflict consent. For that purpose it may, inter alia, ask each Party to provide it with a list of at least five States which that Party considers acceptable to act as Protecting Power on its behalf in relation to an adverse Party, and ask each adverse Party to provide a list of at least five States which it would accept as the Protecting Power of the first Party; these lists shall be communicated to the Committee within two weeks after the receipt of the request; it shall compare them and seek the agreement of any proposed State named on both lists.

4. If, despite the foregoing, there is no Protecting Power, the Parties to the conflict shall accept without delay an offer which may be made by the International Committee of the Red Cross or by any other organization which offers all guarantees of impartiality and efficacy, after due consultations with the said Parties and taking into account the result of these consultations, to act as a substitute. The functioning of such a substitute is subject to the consent of the Parties to the conflict; every effort shall be made by the Parties to the conflict to facilitate the operations of the substitute in the performance of its tasks under the Conventions and this Protocol.

5. In accordance with Article 4, the designation and acceptance of Protecting Powers for the purpose of applying the Conventions and this Protocol shall not affect the legal status of the Parties to the conflict or of any territory, including occupied territory.

6. The maintenance of diplomatic relations between Parties to the conflict or the entrusting of the protection of a Party's interests and those of its nationals to a third State in accordance with the rules of international law relating to diplomatic relations is no obstacle to the designation of Protecting Powers for the purpose of applying the Conventions and this Protocol.

7. Any subsequent mention in this Protocol of a Protecting Power includes also a substitute.

Article 6: Qualified persons
1. The High Contracting Parties shall, also in peacetime, endeavour, with the assistance of the national Red Cross (Red Crescent, Red Lion and Sun) Societies, to train qualified personnel to facilitate the application of the Conventions and of this Protocol, and in particular the activities of the Protecting Powers.

2. The recruitment and training of such personnel are within domestic jurisdiction.

3. The International Committee of the Red Cross shall hold at the disposal

of the High Contracting Parties the lists of persons so trained which the High Contracting Parties may have established and may have transmitted to it for that purpose.

4. The conditions governing the employment of such personnel outside the national territory shall, in each case, be the subject of special agreements between the Parties concerned.

Article 7: Meetings

The depositary of this Protocol shall convene a meeting of the High Contracting Parties, at the request of one or more of the said Parties and upon the approval of the majority of the said Parties, to consider general problems concerning the application of the Conventions and of the Protocol.

Part II: Wounded, Sick and Shipwrecked

Section I: General Protection

Article 8: Terminology

For the purposes of this Protocol:

(a) "Wounded" and "sick" mean persons, whether military or civilian, who, because of trauma, disease or other physical or mental disorder or disability, are in need of medical assistance or care and who refrain from any act of hostility. These terms also cover maternity cases, new-born babies and other persons who may be in need of immediate medical assistance or care, such as the infirm or expectant mothers, and who refrain from any act of hostility;

(b) "Shipwrecked" means persons, whether military or civilian, who are in peril at sea or in other waters as a result of misfortune affecting them or the vessel or aircraft carrying them and who refrain from any act of hostility. These persons, provided that they continue to refrain from any act of hostility, shall continue to be considered shipwrecked during their rescue until they acquire another status under the Conventions or this Protocol;

(c) "Medical personnel" means those persons assigned, by a Party to the conflict, exclusively to the medical purposes enumerated under subparagraph (e) or to the administration of medical units or to the operation or administration of medical transports. Such assignments may be either permanent or temporary. The term includes: (i) Medical personnel of a Party to the conflict, whether military or civilian, including those described in the First and Second Conventions, and those assigned to civil defence organizations; (ii) Medical personnel of national Red Cross (Red Crescent, Red Lion and Sun) Societies and other national voluntary aid societies duly recognized and authorized by a Party to the conflict; (iii) Medical personnel of medical units or medical transports described in Article 9, paragraph 2;

(d) "Religious personnel" means military or civilian persons, such as chaplains, who are exclusively engaged in the work of their ministry and attached:

(i) To the armed forces of a Party to the conflict; (ii) To medical units or medical transports of a Party to the conflict; (iii) To medical units or medical transports described in Article 9, paragraph 2; or (iv) To civil defence organizations of a Party to the conflict.

The attachment of religious personnel may be either permanent or temporary, and the relevant provisions mentioned under sub-paragraph (k) apply to them;

(e) "Medical units" means establishments and other units, whether military or civilian, organized for medical purposes, namely the search for, collection, transportation, diagnosis or treatment—including first-aid treatment—of the wounded, sick and shipwrecked, or for the prevention of disease. The term includes, for example, hospitals and other similar units, blood transfusion centres, preventive medicine centres and institutes, medical depots and the medical and pharmaceutical stores of such units. Medical units may be fixed or mobile, permanent or temporary;

(f) "Medical transportation" means the conveyance by land, water or air of the wounded, sick, shipwrecked, medical personnel, religious personnel, medical equipment or medical supplies protected by the Conventions and by this Protocol;

(g) "Medical transports" means any means of transportation, whether military or civilian, permanent or temporary, assigned exclusively to medical transportation and under the control of a competent authority of a Party to the conflict;

(h) "Medical vehicles" means any medical transports by land;

(i) "Medical ships and craft" means any medical transports by water;

(j) "Medical aircraft" means any medical transports by air;

(k) "Permanent medical personnel," "permanent medical units" and "permanent medical transports" mean those assigned exclusively to medical purposes for an indeterminate period. "Temporary medical personnel," "temporary medical units" and "temporary medical transports" mean those devoted exclusively to medical purposes for limited periods during the whole of such periods. Unless otherwise specified, the terms "medical personnel," "medical units" and "medical transports" cover both permanent and temporary categories;

(l) "Distinctive emblem" means the distinctive emblem of the red cross, red crescent or red lion and sun on a white ground when used for the protection of medical units and transports, or medical and religious personnel, equipment or supplies;

(m) "Distinctive signal" means any signal or message specified for the identification exclusively of medical units or transports in Chapter III of Annex I to this Protocol.

Article 9: Field of application

1. This Part, the provisions of which are intended to ameliorate the condition of the wounded, sick and shipwrecked, shall apply to all those affected by

a situation referred to in Article 1, without any adverse distinction founded on race, colour, sex, language, religion or belief, political or other opinion, national or social origin, wealth, birth or other status, or on any other similar criteria.

2. The relevant provisions of Articles 27 and 32 of the First Convention shall apply to permanent medical units and transports (other than hospital ships, to which Article 25 of the Second Convention applies) and their personnel made available to a Party to the conflict for humanitarian purposes:

(a) by a neutral or other State which is not a Party to that conflict;

(b) by a recognized and authorized aid society of such a State;

(c) by an impartial international humanitarian organization.

Article 10: Protection and care

1. All the wounded, sick and shipwrecked, to whichever Party they belong, shall be respected and protected.

2. In all circumstances they shall be treated humanely and shall receive, to the fullest extent practicable and with the least possible delay, the medical care and attention required by their condition. There shall be no distinction among them founded on any grounds other than medical ones.

Article 11: Protection of persons

1. The physical or mental health and integrity of persons who are in the power of the adverse Party or who are interned, detained or otherwise deprived of liberty as a result of a situation referred to in Article 1 shall not be endangered by any unjustified act or omission. Accordingly, it is prohibited to subject the persons described in this Article to any medical procedure which is not indicated by the state of health of the person concerned and which is not consistent with generally accepted medical standards which would be applied under similar medical circumstances to persons who are nationals of the Party conducting the procedure and who are in no way deprived of liberty.

2. It is, in particular, prohibited to carry out on such persons, even with their consent:

(a) Physical mutilations;

(b) Medical or scientific experiments;

(c) Removal of tissue or organs for transplantation, except where these acts are justified in conformity with the conditions provided for in paragraph 1.

3. Exceptions to the prohibition in paragraph 2 (c) may be made only in the case of donations of blood for transfusion or of skin for grafting, provided that they are given voluntarily and without any coercion or inducement, and then only for therapeutic purposes, under conditions consistent with generally accepted medical standards and controls designed for the benefit of both the donor and the recipient.

4. Any wilful act or omission which seriously endangers the physical or mental health or integrity of any person who is in the power of a Party other than the one on which he depends and which either violates any of the prohibi-

tions in paragraphs 1 and 2 or fails to comply with the requirements of paragraph 3 shall be a grave breach of this Protocol.

5. The persons described in paragraph 1 have the right to refuse any surgical operation. In case of refusal, medical personnel shall endeavour to obtain a written statement to that effect, signed or acknowledged by the patient.

6. Each Party to the conflict shall keep a medical record for every donation of blood for transfusion or skin for grafting by persons referred to in paragraph 1, if that donation is made under the responsibility of that Party. In addition, each Party to the conflict shall endeavour to keep a record of all medical procedures undertaken with respect to any person who is interned, detained or otherwise deprived of liberty as a result of a situation referred to in Article 1. These records shall be available at all times for inspection by the Protecting Power.

Article 12: Protection of medical units

1. Medical units shall be respected and protected at all times and shall not be the object of attack.

2. Paragraph 1 shall apply to civilian medical units, provided that they:

(a) Belong to one of the Parties to the conflict;

(b) Are recognized and authorized by the competent authority of one of the Parties to the conflict; or

(c) Are authorized in conformity with Article 9, paragraph 2, of this Protocol or Article 27 of the First Convention.

3. The Parties to the conflict are invited to notify each other of the location of their fixed medical units. The absence of such notification shall not exempt any of the Parties from the obligation to comply with the provisions of paragraph 1.

4. Under no circumstances shall medical units be used in an attempt to shield military objectives from attack. Whenever possible, the Parties to the conflict shall ensure that medical units are so sited that attacks against military objectives do not imperil their safety.

Article 13: Discontinuance of protection of civilian medical units

1. The protection to which civilian medical units are entitled shall not cease unless they are used to commit, outside their humanitarian function, acts harmful to the enemy. Protection may, however, cease only after a warning has been given setting, whenever appropriate, a reasonable time-limit, and after such warning has remained unheeded.

2. The following shall not be considered as acts harmful to the enemy;

(a) That the personnel of the unit are equipped with light individual weapons for their own defence or for that of the wounded and sick in their charge;

(b) That the unit is guarded by a picket or by sentries or by an escort;

(c) That small arms and ammunition taken from the wounded and sick, and not yet handed to the proper service, are found in the units;

(d) That members of the armed forces or other combatants are in the unit for medical reasons.

Article 14: Limitations on requisition of civilian medical units

1. The Occupying Power has the duty to ensure that the medical needs of the civilian population in occupied territory continue to be satisfied.

2. The Occupying Power shall not, therefore, requisition civilian medical units, their equipment, their matériel or the services of their personnel, so long as these resources are necessary for the provision of adequate medical services for the civilian population and for the continuing medical care of any wounded and sick already under treatment.

3. Provided that the general rule in paragraph 2 continues to be observed, the Occupying Power may requisition the said resources, subject to the following particular conditions:

(a) That the resources are necessary for the adequate and immediate medical treatment of the wounded and sick members of the armed forces of the Occupying Power or of prisoners of war;

(b) That the requisition continues only while such necessity exists; and

(c) That immediate arrangements are made to ensure that the medical needs of the civilian population, as well as those of any wounded and sick under treatment who are affected by the requisition, continue to be satisfied.

Article 15: Protection of civilian medical and religious personnel

1. Civilian medical personnel shall be respected and protected.

2. If needed, all available help shall be afforded to civilian medical personnel in an area where civilian medical services are disrupted by reason of combat activity.

3. The Occupying Power shall afford civilian medical personnel in occupied territories every assistance to enable them to perform, to the best of their ability, their humanitarian functions. The Occupying Power may not require that, in the performance of those functions, such personnel shall give priority to the treatment of any person except on medical grounds. They shall not be compelled to carry out tasks which are not compatible with their humanitarian mission.

4. Civilian medical personnel shall have access to any place where their services are essential, subject to such supervisory and safety measures as the relevant Party to the conflict may deem necessary.

5. Civilian religious personnel shall be respected and protected. The provisions of the Conventions and of this Protocol concerning the protection and identification of medical personnel shall apply equally to such persons.

Article 16: General protection of medical duties

1. Under no circumstances shall any person be punished for carrying out medical activities compatible with medical ethics, regardless of the person benefiting therefrom.

2. Persons engaged in medical activities shall not be compelled to perform acts or to carry out work contrary to the rules of medical ethics or to other medical rules designed for the benefit of the wounded and sick or to the provisions of the Conventions or of this Protocol, or to refrain from performing acts or from carrying out work required by those rules and provisions.

3. No person engaged in medical activities shall be compelled to give to anyone belonging either to an adverse Party, or to his own Party except as required by the law of the latter Party, any information concerning the wounded and sick who are, or who have been, under his care, if such information would, in his opinion, prove harmful to the patients concerned or to their families. Regulations for the compulsory notification of communicable diseases shall, however, be respected.

Article 17: Role of the civilian population and of aid societies

1. The civilian population shall respect the wounded, sick and shipwrecked, even if they belong to the adverse Party, and shall commit no act of violence against them. The civilian population and aid societies, such as national Red Cross (Red Crescent, Red Lion and Sun) Societies, shall be permitted, even on their own initiative, to collect and care for the wounded, sick and shipwrecked, even in invaded or occupied areas. No one shall be harmed, prosecuted, convicted or punished for such humanitarian acts.

2. The Parties to the conflict may appeal to the civilian population and the aid societies referred to in paragraph 1 to collect and care for the wounded, sick and shipwrecked, and to search for the dead and report their location; they shall grant both protection and the necessary facilities to those who respond to this appeal. If the adverse Party gains or regains control of the area, that Party also shall afford the same protection and facilities for so long as they are needed.

Article 18: Identification

1. Each Party to the conflict shall endeavour to ensure that medical and religious personnel and medical units and transports are identifiable.

2. Each Party to the conflict shall also endeavour to adopt and to implement methods and procedures which will make it possible to recognize medical units and transports which use the distinctive emblem and distinctive signals.

3. In occupied territory and in areas where fighting is taking place or is likely to take place, civilian medical personnel and civilian religious personnel should be recognizable by the distinctive emblem and an identity card certifying their status.

4. With the consent of the competent authority, medical units and transports shall be marked by the distinctive emblem. The ships and craft referred to in Article 22 of this Protocol shall be marked in accordance with the provisions of the Second Convention.

5. In addition to the distinctive emblem, a Party to the conflict may, as provided in Chapter III of Annex I to this Protocol, authorize the use of distinctive signals to identify medical units and transports. Exceptionally, in the special

cases covered in that Chapter, medical transports may use distinctive signals without displaying the distinctive emblem.

6. The application of the provisions of paragraphs 1 to 5 of this Article is governed by Chapters I to III of Annex I to this Protocol. Signals designated in Chapter III of the Annex for the exclusive use of medical units and transports shall not, except as provided therein, be used for any purpose other than to identify the medical units and transports specified in that Chapter.

7. This Article does not authorize any wider use of the distinctive emblem in peacetime than is prescribed in Article 44 of the First Convention.

8. The provisions of the Conventions and of this Protocol relating to supervision of the use of the distinctive emblem and to the prevention and repression of any misuse thereof shall be applicable to distinctive signals.

Article 19: Neutral and other States not Parties to the conflict

Neutral and other States not Parties to the conflict shall apply the relevant provisions of this Protocol to persons protected by this Part who may be received or interned within their territory, and to any dead of the Parties to that conflict whom they may find.

Article 20: Prohibition of reprisals

Reprisals against the persons and objects protected by this Part are prohibited.

Section II: Medical Transportation

Article 21: Medical vehicles

Medical vehicles shall be respected and protected in the same way as mobile medical units under the Conventions and this Protocol.

Article 22: Hospitals ships and coastal rescue craft

1. The provisions of the Conventions relating to:

(a) Vessels described in Articles 22, 24, 25 and 27 of the Second Convention,

(b) Their lifeboats and small craft,

(c) Their personnel and crews; and

(d) The wounded, sick and shipwrecked on board,

shall also apply where these vessels carry civilian wounded, sick and shipwrecked who do not belong to any of the categories mentioned in Article 13 of the Second Convention. Such civilians shall not, however, be subject to surrender to any Party which is not their own, or to capture at sea. If they find themselves in the power of a Party to the conflict other than their own they shall be covered by the Fourth Convention and by this Protocol.

2. The protection provided by the Conventions to vessels described in Article 25 of the Second Convention shall extend to hospital ships made available for humanitarian purposes to a Party to the conflict:

(a) By a neutral or other State which is not a Party to that conflict; or

(b) By an impartial international humanitarian organization,

provided that, in either case, the requirements set out in that Article are complied with.

3. Small craft described in Article 27 of the Second Convention shall be protected even if the notification envisaged by that Article has not been made. The Parties to the conflict are, nevertheless, invited to inform each other of any details of such craft which will facilitate their identification and recognition.

Article 23: Other medical ships and craft

1. Medical ships and craft other than those referred to in Article 22 of this Protocol and Article 38 of the Second Convention shall, whether at sea or in other waters, be respected and protected in the same way as mobile medical units under the Conventions and this Protocol. Since this protection can only be effective if they can be identified and recognized as medical ships or craft, such vessels should be marked with the distinctive emblem and as far as possible comply with the second paragraph of Article 43 of the Second Convention.

2. The ships and craft referred to in paragraph 1 shall remain subject to the laws of war. Any warship on the surface able immediately to enforce its command may order them to stop, order them off, or make them take a certain course, and they shall obey every such command. Such ships and craft may not in any other way be diverted from their medical mission so long as they are needed for the wounded, sick and shipwrecked on board.

3. The protection provided in paragraph 1 shall cease only under the conditions set out in Articles 34 and 35 of the Second Convention. A clear refusal to obey a command given in accordance with paragraph 2 shall be an act harmful to the enemy under Article 34 of the Second Convention.

4. A Party to the conflict may notify any adverse Party as far in advance of sailing as possible of the name, description, expected time of sailing, course and estimated speed of the medical ship or craft, particularly in the case of ships of over 2,000 gross tons, and may provide any other information which would facilitate identification and recognition. The adverse Party shall acknowledge receipt of such information.

5. The provisions of Article 37 of the Second Convention shall apply to medical and religious personnel in such ships and craft.

6. The provisions of the Second Convention shall apply to the wounded, sick and shipwrecked belonging to the categories referred to in Article 13 of the Second Convention and in Article 44 of this Protocol who may be on board such medical ships and craft. Wounded, sick and shipwrecked civilians who do not belong to any of the categories mentioned in Article 13 of the Second Convention shall not be subject, at sea, either to surrender to any Party which is not their own, or to removal from such ships or craft; if they find themselves in the power of a Party to the conflict other than their own, they shall be covered by the Fourth Convention and by this Protocol.

Article 24: Protection of medical aircraft

Medical aircraft shall be respected and protected, subject to the provisions of this Part.

Article 25: Medical aircraft in areas not controlled by an adverse Party

In and over land areas physically controlled by friendly forces, or in and over sea areas not physically controlled by an adverse Party, the respect and protection of medical aircraft of a Party to the conflict is not dependent on any agreement with an adverse Party. For greater safety, however, a Party to the conflict operating its medical aircraft in these areas may notify the adverse Party, as provided in Article 29, in particular when such aircraft are making flights bringing them within range of surface-to-air weapons systems of the adverse Party.

Article 26: Medical aircraft in contact or similar zones

1. In and over those parts of the contact zone which are physically controlled by friendly forces and in and over those areas the physical control of which is not clearly established, protection for medical aircraft can be fully effective only by prior agreement between the competent military authorities of the Parties to the conflict, as provided for in Article 29. Although, in the absence of such an agreement, medical aircraft operate at their own risk, they shall nevertheless be respected after they have been recognized as such.

2. "Contact zone" means any area on land where the forward elements of opposing forces are in contact with each other, especially where they are exposed to direct fire from the ground.

Article 27: Medical aircraft in areas controlled by an adverse Party

1. The medical aircraft of a Party to the conflict shall continue to be protected while flying over land or sea areas physically controlled by an adverse Patty, provided that prior agreement to such flights has been obtained from the competent authority of the adverse Party.

2. A medical aircraft which flies over an area physically controlled by an adverse Party without, or in deviation from the terms of, an agreement provided for in paragraph 1, either through navigational error or because of an emergency affecting the safety of the flight, shall make every effort to identify itself and to inform the adverse Party of the circumstances. As soon as such medical aircraft has been recognized by the adverse Party, that Party shall make all reasonable efforts to give the order to land or to alight on water, referred to in Article 30, paragraph 1, or to take other measures to safeguard its own interests, and, in either case, to allow the aircraft time for compliance, before resorting to an attack against the aircraft.

Article 28: Restrictions on operations of medical aircraft

1. The Parties to the conflict are prohibited from using their medical aircraft to attempt to acquire any military advantage over an adverse Party. The pres-

ence of medical aircraft shall not be used in an attempt to render military objectives immune from attack.

2. Medical aircraft shall not be used to collect or transmit intelligence data and shall not carry any equipment intended for such purposes. They are prohibited from carrying any persons or cargo not included within the definition in Article 8, subparagraph (f). The carrying on board of the personal effects of the occupants or of equipment intended solely to facilitate navigation, communication or identification shall not be considered as prohibited.

3. Medical aircraft shall not carry any armament except small arms and ammunition taken from the wounded, sick and shipwrecked on board and not yet handed to the proper service, and such light individual weapons as may be necessary to enable the medical personnel on board to defend themselves and the wounded, sick and shipwrecked in their charge.

4. While carrying out the flights referred to in Articles 26 and 27, medical aircraft shall not, except by prior agreement with the adverse Party, be used to search for the wounded, sick and shipwrecked

Article 29: Notifications and agreements concerning medical aircraft

1. Notifications under Article 25, or requests for prior agreement under Articles 26, 27, 28 (paragraph 4), or 31 shall state the proposed number of medical aircraft, their flight plans and means of identification, and shall be understood to mean that every flight will be carried out in compliance with Article 28.

2. A Party which receives a notification given under Article 25 shall at once acknowledge receipt of such notification.

3. A Party which receives a request for prior agreement under Articles 26, 27, 28 (paragraph 4), or 31 shall, as rapidly as possible, notify the requesting Party:

    (a) That the request is agreed to;

    (b) That the request is denied; or

    (c) Of reasonable alternative proposals to the request. It may also propose a prohibition or restriction of other flights in the area during the time involved. If the Party which submitted the request accepts the alternative proposals, it shall notify the other Party of such acceptance.

4. The Parties shall take the necessary measures to ensure that notifications and agreements can be made rapidly.

5. The Parties shall also take the necessary measures to disseminate rapidly the substance of any such notifications and agreements to the military units concerned and shall instruct those units regarding the means of identification that will be used by the medical aircraft in question.

Article 30: Landing and inspection of medical aircraft

1. Medical aircraft flying over areas which are physically controlled by an adverse Party, or over areas the physical control of which is not clearly established, may be ordered to land or to alight on water, as appropriate, to permit

inspection in accordance with the following paragraphs. Medical aircraft shall obey any such order.

2. If such an aircraft lands or alights on water, whether ordered to do so or for other reasons, it may be subjected to inspection solely to determine the matters referred to in paragraphs 3 and 4. Any such inspection shall be commenced without delay and shall be conducted expeditiously. The inspecting Party shall not require the wounded and sick to be removed from the aircraft unless their removal is essential for the inspection. That Party shall in any event ensure that the condition of the wounded and sick is not adversely affected by the inspection or by the removal.

3. If the inspection discloses that the aircraft:

(a) Is a medical aircraft within the meaning of Article 8, subparagraph (j);

(b) Is not in violation of the conditions prescribed in Article 28; and

(c) Has not flown without or in breach of a prior agreement where such agreement is required;

the aircraft and those of its occupants who belong to the adverse Party or to a neutral or other State not a Party to the conflict shall be authorized to continue the flight without delay.

4. If the inspection discloses that the aircraft:

(a) Is not a medical aircraft within the meaning of Article 8, subparagraph (j);

(b) Is in violation of the conditions prescribed in Article 28; or,

(c) Has flown without or in breach of a prior agreement where such agreement is required;

the aircraft may be seized. Its occupants shall be treated in conformity with the relevant provisions of the Conventions and of this Protocol. Any aircraft seized which had been assigned as a permanent medical aircraft may be used thereafter only as a medical aircraft.

Article 31: Neutral or other States not Parties to the conflict

1. Except by prior agreement, medical aircraft shall not fly over or land in the territory of a neutral or other State not a Party to the conflict. However, with such an agreement, they shall be respected throughout their flight and also for the duration of any calls in the territory. Nevertheless they shall obey any summons to land or to alight on water, as appropriate.

2. Should a medical aircraft, in the absence of an agreement or in deviation from the terms of an agreement, fly over the territory of a neutral or other State not a Party to the conflict, either through navigational error or because of an emergency affecting the safety of the flight, it shall make every effort to give notice of the flight and to identify itself. As soon as such medical aircraft is recognized, that State shall make all reasonable efforts to give the order to land or to alight on water referred to in Article 30, paragraph 1, or to take other measures to safeguard its own interests, and in either case, to allow the aircraft time for compliance, before resorting to an attack against the aircraft.

3. If a medical aircraft, either by agreement or in the circumstances men-

tioned in paragraph 2, lands or alights on water in the territory of a neutral or other State not Party to the conflict, whether ordered to do so or for other reasons, the aircraft shall be subject to inspection for the purposes of determining whether it is in fact a medical aircraft. The inspection shall be commenced without delay and shall be conducted expeditiously. The inspecting Party shall not require the wounded and sick of the Party operating the aircraft to be removed from it unless their removal is essential for the inspection. The inspecting Party shall in any event ensure that the condition of the wounded and sick is not adversely affected by the inspection or the removal. If the inspection discloses that the aircraft is in fact a medical aircraft, the aircraft with its occupants, other than those who must be detained in accordance with the rules of international law applicable in armed conflict, shall be allowed to resume its flight, and reasonable facilities shall be given for the continuation of the flight. If the inspection discloses that the aircraft is not a medical aircraft, it shall be seized and the occupants treated in accordance with paragraph 4.

4. The wounded, sick and shipwrecked disembarked, otherwise than temporarily, from a medical aircraft with the consent of the local authorities in the territory of a neutral or other State not a Party to the conflict shall, unless agreed otherwise between that State and the Parties to the conflict, be detained by that State where so required by the rules of international law applicable in armed conflict, in such a manner that they cannot again take part in the hostilities. The cost of hospital treatment and internment shall be borne by the State to which those persons belong.

5. Neutral or other States not Parties to the conflict shall apply any conditions and restrictions on the passage of medical aircraft over, or on the landing of medical aircraft in, their territory equally to all Parties to the conflict.

Section III: Missing and Dead Persons

Article 32: General principles
In the implementation of this Section, the activities of the High Contracting Parties, of the Parties to the conflict and of the international humanitarian organizations mentioned in the Conventions and in this Protocol shall be prompted mainly by the right of families to know the fate of their relatives.

Article 33: Missing persons
1. As soon as circumstances permit, and at the latest from the end of active hostilities, each Party to the conflict shall search for the persons who have been reported missing by an adverse Party. Such adverse Party shall transmit all relevant information concerning such persons in order to facilitate such searches.

2. In order to facilitate the gathering of information pursuant to the preceding paragraph, each Party to the conflict shall, with respect to persons who would not receive more favourable consideration under the Conventions and this Protocol:

(a) Record the information specified in Article 138 of the Fourth Convention in respect of such persons who have been detained, imprisoned or otherwise held in captivity for more than two weeks as a result of hostilities or occupation, or who have died during any period of detention;

(b) To the fullest extent possible, facilitate and, if need be, carry out the search for and the recording of information concerning such persons if they have died in other circumstances as a result of hostilities or occupation.

3. Information concerning persons reported missing pursuant to paragraph 1 and requests for such information shall be transmitted either directly or through the Protecting Power or the Central Tracing Agency of the International Committee of the Red Cross or national Red Cross (Red Crescent, Red Lion and Sun) Societies. Where the information is not transmitted through the International Committee of the Red Cross and its Central Tracing Agency, each Party to the conflict shall ensure that such information is also supplied to the Central Tracing Agency.

4. The Parties to the conflict shall endeavour to agree on arrangements for teams to search for, identify and recover the dead from battlefield areas, including arrangements, if appropriate, for such teams to be accompanied by personnel of the adverse Party while carrying out the missions in areas controlled by the adverse Party. Personnel of such teams shall be respected and protected while exclusively carrying out these duties.

Article 34: Remains of deceased

1. The remains of persons who have died for reasons related to occupation or in detention resulting from occupation or hostilities and those of persons not nationals of the country in which they have died as a result of hostilities shall be respected, and the gravesites of all such persons shall be respected, maintained and marked as provided for in Article 130 of the Fourth Convention, where their remains or gravesites would not receive more favourable consideration under the Conventions and this Protocol.

2. As soon as circumstances and the relations between the adverse Parties permit, the High Contracting Parties in whose territories graves and, as the case may be, other locations of the remains of persons who have died as a result of hostilities or during occupation or in detention are situated, shall conclude agreements in order:

(a) To facilitate access to the gravesites by relatives of the deceased and by representatives of official graves registration services and to regulate the practical arrangements for such access;

(b) To protect and maintain such gravesites permanently;

(c) To facilitate the return of the remains of the deceased and of personal effects to the home country upon its request or, unless that country objects, upon the request of the next of kin.

3. In the absence of the agreements provided for in paragraph 2 (b) or (c) and if the home country of such deceased is not willing to arrange at its expense for the maintenance of such gravesites, the High Contracting Party

in whose territory the gravesites are situated may offer to facilitate the return of the remains of the deceased to the home country. Where such an offer has not been accepted the High Contracting Party may, after the expiry of five years from the date of the offer and upon due notice to the home country, adopt the arrangements laid down in its own laws relating to cemeteries and graves.

4. A High Contracting Party in whose territory the gravesites referred to in this Article are situated shall be permitted to exhume the remains only:

(a) In accordance with paragraphs 2 (c) and 3; or

(b) Where exhumation is a matter of overriding public necessity, including cases of medical and investigative necessity, in which case the High Contracting Party shall at all times respect the remains, and shall give notice to the home country of its intention to exhume the remains together with details of the intended place of reinterment.

Part III: Methods and Means of Warfare Combatant and Prisoner-of-War Status

Section I: Methods and Means of Warfare

Article 35: Basic rules

1. In any armed conflict, the right of the Parties to the conflict to choose methods or means of warfare is not unlimited.

2. It is prohibited to employ weapons, projectiles and material and methods of warfare of a nature to cause superfluous injury or unnecessary suffering.

3. It is prohibited to employ methods or means of warfare which are intended, or may be expected, to cause widespread, long-term and severe damage to the natural environment.

Article 36: New weapons

In the study, development, acquisition or adoption of a new weapon, means or method of warfare, a High Contracting Party is under an obligation to determine whether its employment would, in some or all circumstances, be prohibited by this Protocol or by any other rule of international law applicable to the High Contracting Party.

Article 37: Prohibition of perfidy

1. It is prohibited to kill, injure or capture an adversary by resort to perfidy. Acts inviting the confidence of an adversary to lead him to believe that he is entitled to, or is obliged to accord, protection under the rules of international law applicable in armed conflict, with intent to betray that confidence, shall constitute perfidy. The following acts are examples of perfidy:

(a) The feigning of an intent to negotiate under a flag of truce or of a surrender;

(b) The feigning of an incapacitation by wounds or sickness;

(c) The feigning of civilian, non-combatant status; and

(d) The feigning of protected status by the use of signs, emblems or uniforms of the United Nations or of neutral or other States not Parties to the conflict.

2. Ruses of war are not prohibited. Such ruses are acts which are intended to mislead an adversary or to induce him to act recklessly but which infringe no rule of international law applicable in armed conflict and which are not perfidious because they do not invite the confidence of an adversary with respect to protection under that law. The following are examples of such ruses: the use of camouflage, decoys, mock operations and misinformation.

Article 38: Recognized emblems

1. It is prohibited to make improper use of the distinctive emblem of the red cross, red crescent or red lion and sun or of other emblems, signs or signals provided for by the Conventions or by this Protocol. It is also prohibited to misuse deliberately in an armed conflict other internationally recognized protective emblems, signs or signals, including the flag of truce, and the protective emblem of cultural property.

2. It is prohibited to make use of the distinctive emblem of the United Nations, except as authorized by that Organization.

Article 39: Emblems of nationality

1. It is prohibited to make use in an armed conflict of the flags or military emblems, insignia or uniforms of neutral or other States not Parties to the conflict.

2. It is prohibited to make use of the flags or military emblems, insignia or uniforms of adverse Parties while engaging in attacks or in order to shield, favour, protect or impede military operations.

3. Nothing in this Article or in Article 37, paragraph 1 (d), shall affect the existing generally recognized rules of international law applicable to espionage or to the use of flags in the conduct of armed conflict at sea.

Article 40: Quarter

It is prohibited to order that there shall be no survivors, to threaten an adversary therewith or to conduct hostilities on this basis.

Article 41: Safeguard of an enemy hors de combat

1. A person who is recognized or who, in the circumstances, should be recognized to be hors de combat shall not be made the object of attack.

2. A person is hors de combat if:

(a) He is in the power of an adverse Party;

(b) He clearly expresses an intention to surrender; or

(c) He has been rendered unconscious or is otherwise incapacitated by wounds or sickness, and therefore is incapable of defending himself; provided that in any of these cases he abstains from any hostile act and does not attempt to escape.

3. When persons entitled to protection as prisoners of war have fallen into the power of an adverse Party under unusual conditions of combat which prevent their evacuation as provided for in Part III, Section I, of the Third Convention, they shall be released and all feasible precautions shall be taken to ensure their safety.

Article 42: Occupants of aircraft

1. No person parachuting from an aircraft in distress shall be made the object of attack during his descent.

2. Upon reaching the ground in territory controlled by an adverse Party, a person who has parachuted from an aircraft in distress shall be given an opportunity to surrender before being made the object of attack, unless it is apparent that he is engaging in a hostile act.

3. Airborne troops are not protected by this Article.

Section II: Combatant and Prisoner-of-War Status

Article 43: Armed forces

1. The armed forces of a Party to a conflict consist of all organized armed forces, groups and units which are under a command responsible to that Party for the conduct of its subordinates, even if that Party is represented by a government or an authority not recognized by an adverse Party. Such armed forces shall be subject to an internal disciplinary system which, inter alia, shall enforce compliance with the rules of international law applicable in armed conflict.

2. Members of the armed forces of a Party to a conflict (other than medical personnel and chaplains covered by Article 33 of the Third Convention) are combatants, that is to say, they have the right to participate directly in hostilities.

3. Whenever a Party to a conflict incorporates a paramilitary or armed law enforcement agency into its armed forces it shall so notify the other Parties to the conflict.

Article 44: Combatants and prisoners of war

1. Any combatant, as defined in Article 43, who falls into the power of an adverse Party shall be a prisoner of war.

2. While all combatants are obliged to comply with the rules of international law applicable in armed conflict, violations of these rules shall not deprive a combatant of his right to be a combatant or, if he falls into the power of an adverse Party, of his right to be a prisoner of war, except as provided in paragraphs 3 and 4.

3. In order to promote the protection of the civilian population from the

effects of hostilities, combatants are obliged to distinguish themselves from the civilian population while they are engaged in an attack or in a military operation preparatory to an attack. Recognizing, however, that there are situations in armed conflicts where, owing to the nature of the hostilities an armed combatant cannot so distinguish himself, he shall retain his status as a combatant, provided that, in such situations, he carries his arms openly:

(a) During each military engagement, and

(b) During such time as he is visible to the adversary while he is engaged in a military deployment preceding the launching of an attack in which he is to participate.

Acts which comply with the requirements of this paragraph shall not be considered as perfidious within the meaning of Article 37, paragraph 1 (c).

4. A combatant who falls into the power of an adverse Party while failing to meet the requirements set forth in the second sentence of paragraph 3 shall forfeit his right to be a prisoner of war, but he shall, nevertheless, be given protections equivalent in all respects to those accorded to prisoners of war by the Third Convention and by this Protocol. This protection includes protections equivalent to those accorded to prisoners of war by the Third Convention in the case where such a person is tried and punished for any offences he has committed.

5. Any combatant who falls into the power of an adverse Party while not engaged in an attack or in a military operation preparatory to an attack shall not forfeit his rights to be a combatant and a prisoner of war by virtue of his prior activities.

6. This Article is without prejudice to the right of any person to be a prisoner of war pursuant to Article 4 of the Third Convention.

7. This Article is not intended to change the generally accepted practice of States with respect to the wearing of the uniform by combatants assigned to the regular, uniformed armed units of a Party to the conflict.

8. In addition to the categories of persons mentioned in Article 13 of the First and Second Conventions, all members of the armed forces of a Party to the conflict, as defined in Article 43 of this Protocol, shall be entitled to protection under those Conventions if they are wounded or sick or, in the case of the Second Convention, shipwrecked at sea or in other waters.

Article 45: Protection of persons who have taken part in hostilities

1. A person who takes part in hostilities and falls into the power of an adverse Party shall be presumed to be a prisoner of war, and therefore shall be protected by the Third Convention, if he claims the status of prisoner of war, or if he appears to be entitled to such status, or if the Party on which he depends claims such status on his behalf by notification to the detaining Power or to the Protecting Power. Should any doubt arise as to whether any such person is entitled to the status of prisoner of war, he shall continue to have such status

and, therefore, to be protected by the Third Convention and this Protocol until such time as his status has been determined by a competent tribunal.

2. If a person who has fallen into the power of an adverse Party is not held as a prisoner of war and is to be tried by that Party for an offence arising out of the hostilities, he shall have the right to assert his entitlement to prisoner-of-war status before a judicial tribunal and to have that question adjudicated. Whenever possible under the applicable procedure, this adjudication shall occur before the trial for the offence. The representatives of the Protecting Power shall be entitled to attend the proceedings in which that question is adjudicated, unless, exceptionally, the proceedings are held in camera in the interest of State security. In such a case the detaining Power shall advise the Protecting Power accordingly.

3. Any person who has taken part in hostilities, who is not entitled to prisoner-of-war status and who does not benefit from more favourable treatment in accordance with the Fourth Convention shall have the right at all times to the protection of Article 75 of this Protocol. In occupied territory, any such person, unless he is held as a spy, shall also be entitled, notwithstanding Article 5 of the Fourth Convention, to his rights of communication under that Convention.

Article 46: Spies

1. Notwithstanding any other provision of the Conventions or of this Protocol, any member of the armed forces of a Party to the conflict who falls into the power of an adverse Party while engaging in espionage shall not have the right to the status of prisoner of war and may be treated as a spy.

2. A member of the armed forces of a Party to the conflict who, on behalf of that Party and in territory controlled by an adverse Party, gathers or attempts to gather information shall not be considered as engaging in espionage if, while so acting, he is in the uniform of his armed forces.

3. A member of the armed forces of a Party to the conflict who is a resident of territory occupied by an adverse Party and who, on behalf of the Party on which he depends, gathers or attempts to gather information of military value within that territory shall not be considered as engaging in espionage unless he does so through an act of false pretences or deliberately in a clandestine manner. Moreover, such a resident shall not lose his right to the status of prisoner of war and may not be treated as a spy unless he is captured while engaging in espionage.

4. A member of the armed forces of a Party to the conflict who is not a resident of territory occupied by an adverse Party and who has engaged in espionage in that territory shall not lose his right to the status of prisoner of war and may not be treated as a spy unless he is captured before he has rejoined the armed forces to which he belongs.

Article 47: Mercenaries

1. A mercenary shall not have the right to be a combatant or a prisoner of war.

2. A mercenary is any person who:

(a) Is specially recruited locally or abroad in order to fight in an armed conflict;

(b) Does, in fact, take a direct part in the hostilities;

(c) Is motivated to take part in the hostilities essentially by the desire for private gain and, in fact, is promised, by or on behalf of a Party to the conflict, material compensation substantially in excess of that promised or paid to combatants of similar ranks and functions in the armed forces of that Party;

(d) Is neither a national of a Party to the conflict nor a resident of territory controlled by a Party to the conflict;

(e) Is not a member of the armed forces of a Party to the conflict; and

(f) Has not been sent by a State which is not a Party to the conflict on official duty as a member of its armed forces.

Part IV: Civilian Population

Section I: General Protection Against Effects of Hostilities

Chapter I: Basic Rule and Field of Application

Article 48: Basic rule

In order to ensure respect for and protection of the civilian population and civilian objects, the Parties to the conflict shall at all times distinguish between the civilian population and combatants and between civilian objects and military objectives and accordingly shall direct their operations only against military objectives.

Article 49: Definition of attacks and scope of application

1. "Attacks" means acts of violence against the adversary, whether in offence or in defence.

2. The provisions of this Protocol with respect to attacks apply to all attacks in whatever territory conducted, including the national territory belonging to a Party to the conflict but under the control of an adverse Party.

3. The provisions of this Section apply to any land, air or sea warfare which may affect the civilian population, individual civilians or civilian objects on land. They further apply to all attacks from the sea or from the air against objectives on land but do not otherwise affect the rules of international law applicable in armed conflict at sea or in the air.

4. The provisions of this Section are additional to the rules concerning humanitarian protection contained in the Fourth Convention, particularly in Part II thereof, and in other international agreements binding upon the High Contracting Parties, as well as to other rules of international law relating to the protection of civilians and civilian objects on land, at sea or in the air against the effects of hostilities.

Chapter II: Civilians and Civilian Population

Article 50: Definition of civilians and civilian population

1. A civilian is any person who does not belong to one of the categories of persons referred to in Article 4 A (1), (2), (3) and (6) of the Third Convention and in Article 43 of this Protocol. In case of doubt whether a person is a civilian, that person shall be considered to be a civilian.

2. The civilian population comprises all persons who are civilians.

3. The presence within the civilian population of individuals who do not come within the definition of civilians does not deprive the population of its civilian character.

Article 51: Protection of the civilian population

1. The civilian population and individual civilians shall enjoy general protection against dangers arising from military operations. To give effect to this protection, the following rules, which are additional to other applicable rules of international law, shall be observed in circumstances.

2. The civilian population as such, as well as individual civilians, shall not be the object of attack. Acts or threats of violence the primary purpose of which is to spread terror among the civilian population are prohibited.

3. Civilians shall enjoy the protection afforded by this Section, unless and for such time as they take a direct part in hostilities.

4. Indiscriminate attacks are prohibited. Indiscriminate attacks are:

(a) Those which are not directed at a specific military objective;

(b) Those which employ a method or means of combat which cannot be directed at a specific military objective; or

(c) Those which employ a method or means of combat the effects of which cannot be limited as required by this Protocol; and consequently, in each such case, are of a nature to strike military objectives and civilians or civilian objects without distinction.

5. Among others, the following types of attacks are to be considered as indiscriminate:

(a) An attack by bombardment by any methods or means which treats as a single military objective a number of clearly separated and distinct military objectives located in a city, town, village or other area containing a similar concentration of civilians or civilian objects; and

(b) An attack which may be expected to cause incidental loss of civilian life, injury to civilians, damage to civilian objects, or a combination thereof, which would be excessive in relation to the concrete and direct military advantage anticipated.

6. Attacks against the civilian population or civilians by way of reprisals are prohibited.

7. The presence or movements of the civilian population or individual civilians shall not be used to render certain points or areas immune from military operations, in particular in attempts to shield military objectives from attacks

or to shield, favour or impede military operations. The Parties to the conflict shall not direct the movement of the civilian population or individual civilians in order to attempt to shield military objectives from attacks or to shield military operations.

8. Any violation of these prohibitions shall not release the Parties to the conflict from their legal obligations with respect to the civilian population and civilians, including the obligation to take the precautionary measures provided for in Article 57.

Chapter III: Civilian Objects

Article 52: General protection of civilian objects
1. Civilian objects shall not be the object of attack or of reprisals. Civilian objects are all objects which are not military objectives as defined in paragraph 2.

2. Attacks shall be limited strictly to military objectives. In so far as objects are concerned, military objectives are limited to those objects which by their nature, location, purpose or use make an effective contribution to military action and whose total or partial destruction, capture or neutralization, in the circumstances ruling at the time, offers a definite military of advantage.

3. In case of doubt whether an object which is normally dedicated to civilian purposes, such as a place of worship, a house or other dwelling or a school, is being used to make an effective contribution to military action, it shall be presumed not to be so used.

Article 53: Protection of cultural objects and of places of worship
Without prejudice to the provisions of the Hague Convention for the Protection of Cultural Property in the Event of Armed Conflict of 14 May 1954, and of other relevant international instruments, it is prohibited:

(a) To commit any acts of hostility directed against the historic monuments, works of art or places of worship which constitute the cultural or spiritual heritage of peoples;

(b) To use such objects in support of the military effort;

(c) To make such objects the object of reprisals.

Article 54: Protection of objects
indispensable to the survival of the civilian population
1. Starvation of civilians as a method of warfare is prohibited.

2. It is prohibited to attack, destroy, remove or render useless objects indispensable to the survival of the civilian population, such as foodstuffs, agricultural areas for the production of foodstuffs, crops, livestock, drinking water installations and supplies and irrigation works, for the specific purpose of denying them for their sustenance value to the civilian population or to the adverse Party, whatever the motive, whether in order to starve out civilians, to cause them to move away, or for any other motive.

3. The prohibitions in paragraph 2 shall not apply to such of the objects covered by it as are used by an adverse Party:

(a) As sustenance solely for the members of its armed forces; or

(b) If not as sustenance, then in direct support of military action, provided, however, that in no event shall actions against these objects be taken which may be expected to leave the civilian population with such inadequate food or water as to cause its starvation or force its movement.

4. These objects shall not be made the object of reprisals.

5. In recognition of the vital requirements of any Party to the conflict in the defence of its national territory against invasion, derogation from the prohibitions contained in paragraph 2 may be made by a Party to the conflict within such territory under its own control where required by imperative military necessity.

Article 55: Protection of the natural environment

1. Care shall be taken in warfare to protect the natural environment against widespread, long-term and severe damage. This protection includes a prohibition of the use of methods or means of warfare which are intended or may be expected to cause such damage to the natural environment and thereby to prejudice the health or survival of the population.

2. Attacks against the natural environment by way of reprisals are prohibited.

Article 56: Protection of works and
installations containing dangerous forces

1. Works or installations containing dangerous forces, namely dams, dykes and nuclear electrical generating stations, shall not be made the object of attack, even where these objects are military objectives, if such attack may cause the release of dangerous forces and consequent severe losses among the civilian population. Other military objectives located at or in the vicinity of these works or installations shall not be made the object of attack if such attack may cause the release of dangerous forces from the works or installations and consequent severe losses among the civilian population.

2. The special protection against attack provided by paragraph 1 shall cease:

(a) For a dam or a dyke only if it is used for other than its normal function and in regular, significant and direct support of military operations and if such attack is the only feasible way to terminate such support;

(b) For a nuclear electrical generating station only if it provides electric power in regular, significant and direct support of military operations and if such attack is the only feasible way to terminate such support;

(c) For other military objectives located at or in the vicinity of these works or installations only if they are used in regular, significant and direct support of military operations and if such attack is the only feasible way to terminate such support.

3. In all cases, the civilian population and individual civilians shall remain entitled to all the protection accorded them by international law, including the

protection of the precautionary measures provided for in Article 57. If the protection ceases and any of the works, installations or military objectives mentioned in paragraph 1 is attacked, all practical precautions shall be taken to avoid the release of the dangerous forces.

4. It is prohibited to make any of the works, installations or military objectives mentioned in paragraph 1 the object of reprisals.

5. The Parties to the conflict shall endeavour to avoid locating any military objectives in the vicinity of the works or installations mentioned in paragraph 1. Nevertheless, installations erected for the sole purpose of defending the protected works or installations from attack are permissible and shall not themselves be made the object of attack, provided that they are not used in hostilities except for defensive actions necessary to respond to attacks against the protected works or installations and that their armament is limited to weapons capable only of repelling hostile action against the protected works or installations.

6. The High Contracting Parties and the Parties to the conflict are urged to conclude further agreements among themselves to provide additional protection for objects containing dangerous forces.

7. In order to facilitate the identification of the objects protected by this article, the Parties to the conflict may mark them with a special sign consisting of a group of three bright orange circles placed on the same axis, as specified in Article 16 of Annex I to this Protocol. The absence of such marking in no way relieves any Party to the conflict of its obligations under this Article.

Chapter IV: Precautionary Measures

Article 57: Precautions in attack

1. In the conduct of military operations, constant care shall be taken to spare the civilian population, civilians and civilian objects.

2. With respect to attacks, the following precautions shall be taken:

(a) Those who plan or decide upon an attack shall: (i) Do everything feasible to verify that the objectives to be attacked are neither civilians nor civilian objects and are not subject to special protection but are military objectives within the meaning of paragraph 2 of Article 52 and that it is not prohibited by the provisions of this Protocol to attack them; (ii) Take all feasible precautions in the choice of means and methods of attack with a view to avoiding, and in any event to minimizing, incidental loss of civilian life, injury to civilians and damage to civilian objects; (iii) Refrain from deciding to launch any attack which may be expected to cause incidental loss of civilian life, injury to civilians, damage to civilian objects, or a combination thereof, which would be excessive in relation to the concrete and direct military advantage anticipated;

(b) An attack shall be cancelled or suspended if it becomes apparent that the objective is not a military one or is subject to special protection or that the attack may be expected to cause incidental loss of civilian life, injury to civilians, damage to civilian objects, or a combination thereof, which would be excessive in relation to the concrete and direct military advantage anticipated;

(c) Effective advance warning shall be given of attacks which may affect the civilian population, unless circumstances do not permit.

3. When a choice is possible between several military objectives for obtaining a similar military advantage, the objective to be selected shall be that the attack on which may be expected to cause the least danger to civilian lives and to civilian objects.

4. In the conduct of military operations at sea or in the air, each Party to the conflict shall, in conformity with its rights and duties under the rules of international law applicable in armed conflict, take all reasonable precautions to avoid losses of civilian lives and damage to civilian objects.

5. No provision of this Article may be construed as authorizing any attacks against the civilian population, civilians or civilian objects.

Article 58: Precautions against the effects of attacks

The Parties to the conflict shall, to the maximum extent feasible:

(a) Without prejudice to Article 49 of the Fourth Convention, endeavour to remove the civilian population, individual civilians and civilian objects under their control from the vicinity of military objectives;

(b) Avoid locating military objectives within or near densely populated areas;

(c) Take the other necessary precautions to protect the civilian population, individual civilians and civilian objects under their control against the dangers resulting from military operations.

Chapter V: Localities and Zones Under Special Protection

Article 59: Non-defended localities

1. It is prohibited for the Parties to the conflict to attack, by any means whatsoever, non-defended localities.

2. The appropriate authorities of a Party to the conflict may declare as a non-defended locality any inhabited place near or in a zone where armed forces are in contact which is open for occupation by an adverse Party. Such a locality shall fulfil the following conditions:

(a) All combatants, as well as mobile weapons and mobile military equipment must have been evacuated;

(b) No hostile use shall be made of fixed military installations or establishments;

(c) No acts of hostility shall be committed by the authorities or by the population; and

(d) No activities in support of military operations shall be undertaken.

3. The presence, in this locality, of persons specially protected under the

Conventions and this Protocol, and of police forces retained for the sole purpose of maintaining law and order, is not contrary to the conditions laid down in paragraph 2.

4. The declaration made under paragraph 2 shall be addressed to the adverse Party and shall define and describe, as precisely as possible, the limits of the non-defended locality. The Party to the conflict to which the declaration is addressed shall acknowledge its receipt and shall treat the locality as a non-defended locality unless the conditions laid down in paragraph 2 are not in fact fulfilled, in which event it shall immediately so inform the Party making the declaration. Even if the conditions laid down in paragraph 2 are not fulfilled, the locality shall continue to enjoy the protection provided by the other provisions of this Protocol and the other rules of international law applicable in armed conflict.

5. The Parties to the conflict may agree on the establishment of non-defended localities even if such localities do not fulfil the conditions laid down in paragraph 2. The agreement should define and describe, as precisely as possible, the limits of the non-defended locality; if necessary, it may lay down the methods of supervision.

6. The Party which is in control of a locality governed by such an agreement shall mark it, so far as possible, by such signs as may be agreed upon with the other Party, which shall be displayed where they are clearly visible, especially on its perimeter and limits and on highways.

7. A locality loses its status as a non-defended locality when it ceases to fulfil the conditions laid down in paragraph 2 or in the agreement referred to in paragraph 5. In such an eventuality, the locality shall continue to enjoy the protection provided by the other provisions of this Protocol and the other rules of international law applicable in armed conflict.

Article 60: Demilitarized zones

1. It is prohibited for the Parties to the conflict to extend their military operations to zones on which they have conferred by agreement the status of demilitarized zone, if such extension is contrary to the terms of this agreement.

2. The agreement shall be an express agreement, may be concluded verbally or in writing, either directly or through a Protecting Power or any impartial humanitarian organization, and may consist of reciprocal and concordant declarations. The agreement may be concluded in peacetime, as well as after the outbreak of hostilities, and should define and describe, as precisely as possible, the limits of the demilitarized zone and, if necessary, lay down the methods of supervision.

3. The subject of such an agreement shall normally be any zone which fulfils the following conditions:

(a) All combatants, as well as mobile weapons and mobile military equipment, must have been evacuated;

(b) No hostile use shall be made of fixed military installations or establishments;

(c) No acts of hostility shall be committed by the authorities or by the population; and

(d) Any activity linked to the military effort must have ceased.

The Parties to the conflict shall agree upon the interpretation to be given to the condition laid down in sub-paragraph (d) and upon persons to be admitted to the demilitarized zone other than those mentioned in paragraph 4.

4. The presence, in this zone, of persons specially protected under the Conventions and this Protocol, and of police forces retained for the sole purpose of maintaining law and order, is not contrary to the conditions laid down in paragraph 3.

5. The Party which is in control of such a zone shall mark it, so far as possible, by such signs as may be agreed upon with the other Party, which shall be displayed where they are clearly visible, especially on its perimeter and limits and on highways.

6. If the fighting draws near to a demilitarized zone, and if the Parties to the conflict have so agreed, none of them may use the zone for purposes related to the conduct of military operations or unilaterally revoke its status.

7. If one of the Parties to the conflict commits a material breach of the provisions of paragraphs 3 or 6, the other Party shall be released from its obligations under the agreement conferring upon the zone the status of demilitarized zone. In such an eventuality, the zone loses its status but shall continue to enjoy the protection provided by the other provisions of this Protocol and the other rules of international law applicable in armed conflict.

Chapter VI: Civil Defence

Article 61: Definitions and scope

For the purposes of this Protocol:

(a) "Civil defence" means the performance of some or all of the undermentioned humanitarian tasks intended to protect the civilian population against the dangers, and to help it to recover from the immediate effects, of hostilities or disasters and also to provide the conditions necessary for its survival. These tasks are: (i) Warning; (ii) Evacuation; (iii) Management of shelters; (iv) Management of blackout measures; (v) Rescue; (vi) Medical services, including first aid, and religious assistance; (vii) Fire-fighting; (viii) Detection and marking of danger areas; (ix) Decontamination and similar protective measures; (x) Provision of emergency accommodation and supplies; (xi) Emergency assistance in the restoration and maintenance of order in distressed areas; (xii) Emergency repair of indispensable public utilities; (xiii) Emergency disposal of the dead; (xiv) Assistance in the preservation of objects essential for survival; (xv) Complementary activities necessary to carry out any of the tasks mentioned above, including, but not limited to, planning and organization;

(b) "Civil defence organizations" means those establishments and other units which are organized or authorized by the competent authorities of a Party to the conflict to perform any of the tasks mentioned under subparagraph (a), and which are assigned and devoted exclusively to such tasks;

(c) "Personnel" of civil defence organizations means those persons assigned by a Party to the conflict exclusively to the performance of the tasks mentioned under sub-paragraph (a), including personnel assigned by the competent authority of that Party exclusively to the administration of these organizations;

(d) "Matériel" of civil defence organizations means equipment, supplies and transports used by these organizations for the performance of the tasks mentioned under sub-paragraph (a).

Article 62: General protection

1. Civilian civil defence organizations and their personnel shall be respected and protected, subject to the provisions of this Protocol, particularly the provisions of this Section. They shall be entitled to perform their civil defence tasks except in case of imperative military necessity.

2. The provisions of paragraph 1 shall also apply to civilians who, although not members of civilian civil defence organizations, respond to an appeal from the competent authorities and perform civil defence tasks under their control.

3. Buildings and matériel used for civil defence purposes and shelters provided for the civilian population are covered by Article 52. Objects used for civil defence purposes may not be destroyed or diverted from their proper use except by the Party to which they belong.

Article 63: Civil defence in occupied territories

1. In occupied territories, civilian civil defence organizations shall receive from the authorities the facilities necessary for the performance of their tasks. In no circumstances shall their personnel be compelled to perform activities which would interfere with the proper performance of these tasks. The Occupying Power shall not change the structure or personnel of such organizations in any way which might jeopardize the efficient performance of their mission. These organizations shall not be required to give priority to the nationals or interests of that Power.

2. The Occupying Power shall not compel, coerce or induce civilian civil defense organizations to perform their tasks in any manner prejudicial to the interests of the civilian population.

3. The Occupying Power may disarm civil defense personnel for reasons of security.

4. The Occupying Power shall neither divert from their proper use nor requisition buildings or matériel belonging to or used by civil defense organizations if such diversion or requisition would be harmful to the civilian population.

5. Provided that the general rule in paragraph 4 continues to be observed, the occupying Power may requisition or divert these resources, subject to the following particular conditions:

(a) That the buildings or matériel are necessary for other needs of the civilian population; and

(b) That the requisition or diversion continues only while such necessity exists.

6. The Occupying Power shall neither divert nor requisition shelters provided for the use of the civilian population or needed by such population.

Article 64: Civilian civil defence organizations of neutral or other States not Parties to the conflict and international co-ordinating organizations

1. Articles 62, 63, 65 and 66 shall also apply to the personnel and matériel of civilian civil defence organizations of neutral or other States not Parties to the conflict which perform civil defense tasks mentioned in Article 61 in the territory of a Party to the conflict, with the consent and under the control of that Party. Notification of such assistance shall be given as soon as possible to any adverse Party concerned. In no circumstances shall this activity be deemed to be an interference in the conflict. This activity should, however, be performed with due regard to the security interests of the Parties to the conflict concerned.

2. The Parties to the conflict receiving the assistance referred to in paragraph 1 and the High Contracting Parties granting it should facilitate international co-ordination of such civil defence actions when appropriate. In such cases the relevant international organizations are covered by the provisions of this Chapter.

3. In occupied territories, the Occupying Power may only exclude or restrict the activities of civilian civil defence organizations of neutral or other States not Parties to the conflict and of international co-ordinating organizations if it can ensure the adequate performance of civil defence tasks from its own resources or those of the occupied territory.

Article 65: Cessation of protection

1. The protection to which civilian civil defence organizations, their personnel, buildings, shelters and matériel are entitled shall not cease unless they commit or are used to commit, outside their proper tasks, acts harmful to the enemy. Protection may, however, cease only after a warning has been given setting, whenever appropriate, a reasonable time-limit, and after such warning has remained unheeded.

2. The following shall not be considered as acts harmful to the enemy:

(a) That civil defence tasks are carried out under the direction or control of military authorities;

(b) That civilian civil defence personnel co-operate with military personnel in the performance of civil defence tasks, or that some military personnel are attached to civilian civil defence organizations;

(c) That the performance of civil defence tasks may incidentally benefit military victims, particularly those who are hors de combat.

3. It shall also not be considered as an act harmful to the enemy that civilian

defence personnel bear light individual weapons for the purpose of maintaining order or for self-defence. However, in areas where land fighting it taking place or is likely to take place, the Parties to the conflict shall undertake the appropriate measures to limit these weapons to handguns, such as pistols or revolvers, in order to assist in distinguishing between civil defence personnel and combatants. Although civil defence personnel bear other light individual weapons in such areas, they shall nevertheless be respected and protected as soon as they have been recognized as such.

4. The formation of civilian civil defence organizations along military lines, and compulsory service in them, shall also not deprive them of the protection conferred by this Chapter.

Article 66: Identification

1. Each Party to the conflict shall endeavour to ensure that its civil defence organizations, their personnel, buildings and matériel, are identifiable while they are exclusively devoted to the performance of civil defence tasks. Shelters provided for the civilian population should be similarly identifiable.

2. Each Party to the conflict shall also endeavour to adopt and implement methods and procedures which will make it possible to recognize civilian shelters as well as civil defence personnel, buildings and matériel on which the international distinctive sign of civil defence is displayed.

3. In occupied territories and in areas where fighting is taking place or is likely to take place, civilian civil defence personnel should be recognizable by the international distinctive sign of civil defence and by an identity and certifying their status.

4. The international distinctive sign of civil defence is an equilateral blue triangle on an orange ground when used for the protection of civil defence organizations, their personnel, buildings and matériel and for civilian shelters.

5. In addition to the distinctive sign, Parties to the conflict may agree upon the use of distinctive signals for civil defence identification purposes.

6. The application of the provisions of paragraphs 1 to 4 is governed by Chapter V of Annex I to this Protocol.

7. In time of peace, the sign described in paragraph 4 may, with the consent of the competent national authorities, be used for civil defence identification purposes.

8. The High Contracting Parties and the Parties to the conflict shall take the measures necessary to supervise the display of the international distinctive sign of civil defence and to prevent and repress any misuse thereof.

9. The identification of civil defence medical and religious personnel, medical units and medical transports is also governed by Article 18.

Article 67: Members of the armed forces and
military units assigned to civil defence organizations

1. Members of the armed forces and military units assigned to civil defence organizations shall be respected and protected, provided that:

(a) Such personnel and such units are permanently assigned and exclusively devoted to the performance of any of the tasks mentioned in Article 61;

(b) If so assigned, such personnel do not perform any other military duties during the conflict;

(c) Such personnel are clearly distinguishable from the other members of the armed forces by prominently displaying the international distinctive sign of civil defence, which shall be as large as appropriate, and such personnel are provided with the identity card referred to in Chapter V of Annex I to this Protocol certifying their status;

(d) Such personnel and such units are equipped only with light individual weapons for the purpose of maintaining order or for self-defence. The provisions of Article 65, paragraph 3 shall also apply in this case;

(e) Such personnel do not participate directly in hostilities, and do not commit, or are not used to commit, outside their civil defence tasks, acts harmful to the adverse Party;

(f) Such personnel and such units perform their civil defence tasks only within the national territory of their Party.

The non-observance of the conditions stated in (e) above by any member of the armed forces who is bound by the conditions prescribed in (a) and (b) above is prohibited.

2. Military personnel serving within civil defence organizations shall, if they fall into the power of an adverse Party, be prisoners of war. In occupied territory they may, but only in the interest of the civilian population of that territory, be employed on civil defence tasks in so far as the need arises, provided however that, if such work is dangerous, they volunteer for such tasks.

3. The buildings and major items of equipment and transports of military units assigned to civil defence organizations shall be clearly marked with the international distinctive sign of civil defence. This distinctive sign shall be as large as appropriate.

4. The matériel and buildings of military units permanently assigned to civil defence organizations and exclusively devoted to the performance of civil defence tasks shall, if they fall into the hands of an adverse Party, remain subject to the laws of war. They may not be diverted from their civil defence purpose so long as they are required for the performance of civil defence tasks, except in case of imperative military necessity, unless previous arrangements have been made for adequate provision for the needs of the civilian population.

Section II: Relief in Favour of the Civilian Population

Article 68: Field of application
The provisions of this Section apply to the civilian population as defined in this Protocol and are supplementary to Articles 23, 55, 59, 60, 61 and 62 and other relevant provisions of the Fourth Convention.

Article 69: Basic needs in occupied territories

1. In addition to the duties specified in Article 55 of the Fourth Convention concerning food and medical supplies, the Occupying Power shall, to the fullest extent of the means available to it and without any adverse distinction, also ensure the provision of clothing, bedding, means of shelter, other supplies essential to the survival of the civilian population of the occupied territory and objects necessary for religious worship.

2. Relief actions for the benefit of the civilian population of occupied territories are governed by Articles 59, 60, 61, 62, 108, 109, 110 and 111 of the Fourth Convention, and by Article 71 of this Protocol, and shall be implemented without delay.

Article 70: Relief actions

1. If the civilian population of any territory under the control of a Party to the conflict, other than occupied territory, is not adequately provided with the supplies mentioned in Article 69, relief actions which are humanitarian and impartial in character and conducted without any adverse distinction shall be undertaken, subject to the agreement of the Parties concerned in such relief actions. Offers of such relief shall not be regarded as interference in the armed conflict or as unfriendly acts. In the distribution of relief consignments, priority shall be given to those persons, such as children, expectant mothers, maternity cases and nursing mothers, who, under the Fourth Convention or under this Protocol, are to be accorded privileged treatment or special protection.

2. The Parties to the conflict and each High Contracting Party shall allow and facilitate rapid and unimpeded passage of all relief consignments, equipment and personnel provided in accordance with this Section, even if such assistance is destined for the civilian population of the adverse Party.

3. The Parties to the conflict and each High Contracting Party which allow the passage of relief consignments, equipment and personnel in accordance with paragraph 2:

   (a) Shall have the right to prescribe the technical arrangements, including search, under which such passage is permitted;

   (b) May make such permission conditional on the distribution of this assistance being made under the local supervision of a Protecting Power;

   (c) Shall, in no way whatsoever, divert relief consignments from the purpose for which they are intended nor delay their forwarding, except in cases of urgent necessity in the interest of the civilian population concerned.

4. The Parties to the conflict shall protect relief consignments and facilitate their rapid distribution.

5. The Parties to the conflict and each High Contracting Party concerned shall encourage and facilitate effective international co-ordination of the relief actions referred to in paragraph 1.

Article 71: Personnel participating in relief actions

1. Where necessary, relief personnel may form part of the assistance pro-

vided in any relief action, in particular for the transportation and distribution of relief consignments; the participation of such personnel shall be subject to the approval of the Party in whose territory they will carry out their duties.

2. Such personnel shall be respected and protected.

3. Each Party in receipt of relief consignments shall, to the fullest extent practicable, assist the relief personnel referred to in paragraph 1 in carrying out their relief mission. Only in case of imperative military necessity may the activities of the relief personnel be limited or their movements temporarily restricted.

4. Under no circumstances may relief personnel exceed the terms of their mission under this Protocol. In particular they shall take account of the security requirements of the Party in whose territory they are carrying out their duties. The mission of any of the personnel who do not respect these conditions may be terminated.

Section III: Treatment of Persons in the Power of a Party to the Conflict

Chapter I: Field of Application and Protection of Persons and Objects

Article 72: Field of application

The provisions of this Section are additional to the rules concerning humanitarian protection of civilians and civilian objects in the power of a Party to the conflict contained in the Fourth Convention, particularly Parts I and III thereof, as well as to other applicable rules of international law relating to the protection of fundamental human rights during international armed conflict.

Article 73: Refugees and stateless persons

Persons who, before the beginning of hostilities, were considered as stateless persons or refugees under the relevant international instruments accepted by the Parties concerned or under the national legislation of the State of refuge or State of residence shall be protected persons within the meaning of Parts I and III of the Fourth Convention, in all circumstances and without any adverse distinction.

Article 74: Reunion of dispersed families

The High Contracting Parties and the Parties to the conflict shall facilitate in every possible way the reunion of families dispersed as a result of armed conflicts and shall encourage in particular the work of the humanitarian organizations engaged in this task in accordance with the provisions of the Conventions and of this Protocol and in conformity with their respective security regulations.

Article 75: Fundamental guarantees

1. In so far as they are affected by a situation referred to in Article 1 of this Protocol, persons who are in the power of a Party to the conflict and who do not benefit from more favourable treatment under the Conventions or under this Protocol shall be treated humanely in all circumstances and shall enjoy, as a minimum, the protection provided by this Article without any adverse distinction based upon race, colour, sex, language, religion or belief, political or other opinion, national or social origin, wealth, birth or other status, or on any other similar criteria. Each Party shall respect the person, honour, convictions and religious practices of all such persons.

2. The following acts are and shall remain prohibited at any time and in any place whatsoever, whether committed by civilian or by military agents:

(a) Violence to the life, health, or physical or mental well-being of persons, in particular: (i) murder; (ii) torture of all kinds, whether physical or mental; (iii) corporal punishment; and (iv) mutilation;

(b) outrages upon personal dignity, in particular humiliating and degrading treatment, enforced prostitution and any form of indecent assault;

(c) the taking of hostages;

(d) collective punishments; and

(e) threats to commit any of the foregoing acts.

3. Any person arrested, detained or interned for actions related to the armed conflict shall be informed promptly, in a language he understands, of the reasons why these measures have been taken. Except in cases of arrest or detention for penal offences, such persons shall be released with the minimum delay possible and in any event as soon as the circumstances justifying the arrest, detention or internment have ceased to exist.

4. No sentence may be passed and no penalty may be executed on a person found guilty of a penal offence related to the armed conflict except pursuant to a conviction pronounced by an impartial and regularly constituted court respecting the generally recognized principles of regular judicial procedure, which include the following:

(a) the procedure shall provide for an accused to be informed without delay of the particulars of the offence alleged against him and shall afford the accused before and during his trial all necessary rights and means of defence;

(b) no one shall be convicted of an offence except on the basis of individual penal responsibility;

(c) no one shall be accused or convicted of a criminal offence on account of any act or omission which did not constitute a criminal offence under the national or international law to which he was subject at the time when it was committed; nor shall a heavier penalty be imposed than that which was applicable at the time when the criminal offence was committed; if, after the commission of the offence, provision is made by law for the imposition of a lighter penalty, the offender shall benefit thereby;

(d) anyone charged with an offence is presumed innocent until proved guilty according to law;

(e) anyone charged with an offence shall have the right to be tried in his presence;

(f) no one shall be compelled to testify against himself or to confess guilt;

(g) anyone charged with an offence shall have the right to examine, or have examined, the witnesses against him and to obtain the attendance and examination of witnesses on his behalf under the same conditions as witnesses against him;

(h) no one shall be prosecuted or punished by the same Party for an offence in respect of which a final judgement acquitting or convicting that person has been previously pronounced under the same law and judicial procedure;

(i) anyone prosecuted for an offence shall have the right to have the judgement pronounced publicly; and

(i) a convicted person shall be advised on conviction of his judicial and other remedies and of the time-limits within which they may be exercised.

5. Women whose liberty has been restricted for reasons related to the armed conflict shall be held in quarters separated from men's quarters. They shall be under the immediate supervision of women. Nevertheless, in cases where families are detained or interned, they shall, whenever possible, be held in the same place and accommodated as family units.

6. Persons who are arrested, detained or interned for reasons related to the armed conflict shall enjoy the protection provided by this Article until their final release, repatriation or re-establishment, even after the end of the armed conflict.

7. In order to avoid any doubt concerning the prosecution and trial of persons accused of war crimes or crimes against humanity, the following principles shall apply:

(a) Persons who are accused of such crimes should be submitted for the purpose of prosecution and trial in accordance with the applicable rules of international law; and

(b) Any such persons who do not benefit from more favourable treatment under the Conventions or this Protocol shall be accorded the treatment provided by this Article, whether or not the crimes of which they are accused constitute grave breaches of the Conventions or of this Protocol.

8. No provision of this Article may be construed as limiting or infringing any other more favourable provision granting greater protection, under any applicable rules of international law, to persons covered by paragraph 1.

Chapter II: Measures in Favour of Women and Children

Article 76: Protection of women

1. Women shall be the object of special respect and shall be protected in particular against rape, forced prostitution and any other form of indecent assault.

2. Pregnant women and mothers having dependent infants who are arrested, detained or interned for reasons related to the armed conflict, shall have their cases considered with the utmost priority.

3. To the maximum extent feasible, the Parties to the conflict shall endeavour to avoid the pronouncement of the death penalty on pregnant women or mothers having dependent infants, for an offence related to the armed conflict. The death penalty for such offences shall not be executed on such women.

Article 77: Protection of children

1. Children shall be the object of special respect and shall be protected against any form of indecent assault. The Parties to the conflict shall provide them with the care and aid they require, whether because of their age or for any other reason.

2. The Parties to the conflict shall take all feasible measures in order that children who have not attained the age of fifteen years do not take a direct part in hostilities and, in particular, they shall refrain from recruiting them into their armed forces. In recruiting among those persons who have attained the age of fifteen years but who have not attained the age of eighteen years, the Parties to the conflict shall endeavour to give priority to those who are oldest.

3. If, in exceptional cases, despite the provisions of paragraph 2, children who have not attained the age of fifteen years take a direct part in hostilities and fall into the power of an adverse Party, they shall continue to benefit from the special protection accorded by this Article, whether or not they are prisoners of war.

4. If arrested, detained or interned for reasons related to the armed conflict, children shall be held in quarters separate from the quarters of adults, except where families are accommodated as family units as provided in Article 75, paragraph 5.

5. The death penalty for an offence related to armed conflict shall not be executed on persons who had not attained the age of eighteen years at the time the offence was committed.

Article 78: Evacuation of children

1. No Party to the conflict shall arrange for the evacuation of children, other than its own nationals, to a foreign country except for a temporary evacuation where compelling reasons of the health or medical treatment of the children or, except in occupied territory, their safety, so require. Where the parents or legal guardians can be found, their written consent to such evacuation is required. If these persons cannot be found, the written consent to such evacuation of the persons who by law or custom are primarily responsible for the care of the children is required. Any such evacuation shall be supervised by the Protecting Power in agreement with the Parties concerned, namely, the Party arranging for the evacuation, the Party receiving the children and any Parties whose nationals are being evacuated. In each case, all Parties to the conflict shall take all feasible precautions to avoid endangering the evacuation.

2. Whenever an evacuation occurs pursuant to paragraph 1, each child's education, including his religious and moral education as his parents desire, shall be provided while he is away with the greatest possible continuity.

3. With a view to facilitating the return to their families and country of children evacuated pursuant to this Article, the authorities of the Party arranging for the evacuation and, as appropriate, the authorities of the receiving country shall establish for each child a card with photographs, which they shall send to the Central Tracing Agency of the International Committee of the Red Cross. Each card shall bear, whenever possible, and whenever it involves no risk of harm to the child, the following information: (a) surname(s) of the child; (b) the child's first name(s); (c) the child's sex; (d) the place and date of birth (or, if that date is not known, the approximate age); (e) the father's full name; (f) the mother's full name and her maiden name; (g) the child's next-of-kin; (h) the child's nationality; (i) the child's native language, and any other languages he speaks; (j) the address of the child's family; (k) any identification number for the child; (I) the child's state of health; (m) the child's blood group; (n) any distinguishing features; (o) the date on which and the place where the child was found; (p) the date on which and the place from which the child left the country; (q) the child's religion, if any; (r) the child's present address in the receiving country; (s) should the child die before his return, the date, place and circumstances of death and place of interment.

Chapter III: Journalists

Article 79: Measures of protection for journalists

1. Journalists engaged in dangerous professional missions in areas of armed conflict shall be considered as civilians within the meaning of Article 50, paragraph 1.

2. They shall be protected as such under the Conventions and this Protocol, provided that they take no action adversely affecting their status as civilians, and without prejudice to the right of war correspondents accredited to the armed forces to the status provided for in Article 4 A (4) of the Third Convention.

3. They may obtain an identity card similar to the model in Annex II of this Protocol. This card, which shall be issued by the government of the State of which the journalist is a national or in whose territory he resides or in which the news medium employing him is located, shall attest to his status as a journalist.

Part V: Execution of the Conventions and of this Protocol

Section I: General Provisions

Article 80: Measures for execution

1. The High Contracting Parties and the Parties to the conflict shall without delay take all necessary measures for the execution of their obligations under the Conventions and this Protocol.

2. The High Contracting Parties and the Parties to the conflict shall give orders and instructions to ensure observance of the Conventions and this Protocol, and shall supervise their execution.

Article 81: Activities of the Red Cross and other humanitarian organizations

1. The Parties to the conflict shall grant to the International Committee of the Red Cross all facilities within their power so as to enable it to carry out the humanitarian functions assigned to it by the Conventions and this Protocol in order to ensure protection and assistance to the victims of conflicts; the International Committee of the Red Cross may also carry out any other humanitarian activities in favour of these victims, subject to the consent of the Parties to the conflict concerned.

2. The Parties to the conflict shall grant to their respective Red Cross (Red Crescent, Red Lion and Sun) organizations the facilities necessary for carrying out their humanitarian activities in favour of the victims of the conflict, in accordance with the provisions of the Conventions and this Protocol and the fundamental principles of the Red Cross as formulated by the International Conferences of the Red Cross.

3. The High Contracting Parties and the Parties to the conflict shall facilitate in every possible way the assistance which Red Cross (Red Crescent, Red Lion and Sun) organizations and the League of Red Cross Societies extend to the victims of conflicts in accordance with the provisions of the Conventions and this Protocol and with the fundamental principles of the Red Cross as formulated by the International Conferences of the Red Cross.

4. The High Contracting Parties and the Parties to the conflict shall, as far as possible, make facilities similar to those mentioned in paragraphs 2 and 3 available to the other humanitarian organizations referred to in the Conventions and this Protocol which are duly authorized by the respective Parties to the conflict and which perform their humanitarian activities in accordance with the provisions of the Conventions and this Protocol.

Article 82: Legal advisers in armed forces

The High Contracting Parties at all times, and the Parties to the conflict in time of armed conflict, shall ensure that legal advisers are available, when necessary, to advise military commanders at the appropriate level on the application of the Conventions and this Protocol and on the appropriate instruction to be given to the armed forces on this subject.

Article 83: Dissemination

1. The High Contracting Parties undertake, in time of peace as in time of armed conflict, to disseminate the Conventions and this Protocol as widely as possible in their respective countries and, in particular, to include the study thereof in their programmes of military instruction and to encourage the study

thereof by the civilian population, so that those instruments may become known to the armed forces and to the civilian population.

2. Any military or civilian authorities who, in time of armed conflict, assume responsibilities in respect of the application of the Conventions and this Protocol shall be fully acquainted with the text thereof.

Article 84: Rules of application

The High Contracting Parties shall communicate to one another, as soon as possible, through the depositary and, as appropriate, through the Protecting Powers, their official translations of this Protocol, as well as the laws and regulations which they may adopt to ensure its application.

Section II: Repression of Breaches of the Conventions and of this Protocol

Article 85: Repression of breaches of this Protocol

1. The provisions of the Conventions relating to the repression of breaches and grave breaches, supplemented by this Section, shall apply to the repression of breaches and grave breaches of this Protocol.

2. Acts described as grave breaches in the Conventions are grave breaches of this Protocol if committed against persons in the power of an adverse Party protected by Articles 44, 45 and 73 of this Protocol, or against the wounded, sick and shipwrecked of the adverse Party who are protected by this Protocol, or against those medical or religious personnel, medical units or medical transports which are under the control of the adverse Party and are protected by this Protocol.

3. In addition to the grave breaches defined in Article 11, the following acts shall be regarded as grave breaches of this Protocol, when committed wilfully, in violation of the relevant provisions of this Protocol, and causing death or serious injury to body or health:

(a) making the civilian population or individual civilians the object of attack;

(b) launching an indiscriminate attack affecting the civilian population or civilian objects in the knowledge that such attack will cause excessive loss of life, injury to civilians or damage to civilian objects, as defined in Article 57, paragraph 2 (a) (iii);

(c) launching an attack against works or installations containing dangerous forces in the knowledge that such attack will cause excessive loss of life, injury to civilians or damage to civilian objects, as defined in Article 57, paragraph 2 (a) (iii);

(d) making non-defended localities and demilitarized zones the object of attack;

(e) making a person the object of attack in the knowledge that he is hors de combat;

(f) the perfidious use, in violation of Article 37, of the distinctive emblem of the red cross, red crescent or red lion and sun or of other protective signs recognized by the Conventions or this Protocol.

4. In addition to the grave breaches defined in the preceding paragraphs and in the Conventions, the following shall be regarded as grave breaches of this Protocol, when committed wilfully and in violation of the Conventions of the Protocol;

(a) the transfer by the Occupying Power of parts of its own civilian population into the territory it occupies, or the deportation or transfer of all or parts of the population of the occupied territory within or outside this territory, in violation of Article 49 of the Fourth Convention;

(b) unjustifiable delay in the repatriation of prisoners of war or civilians;

(c) practices of apartheid and other inhuman and degrading practices involving outrages upon personal dignity, based on racial discrimination;

(d) making the clearly-recognized historic monuments, works of art or places of worship which constitute the cultural or spiritual heritage of peoples and to which special protection has been given by special arrangement, for example, within the framework of a competent international organization, the object of attack, causing as a result extensive destruction thereof, where there is no evidence of the violation by the adverse Party of Article 53, sub-paragraph (b), and when such historic monuments, works of art and places of worship are not located in the immediate proximity of military objectives:

(e) depriving a person protected by the Conventions or referred to in paragraph 2 of this Article of the rights of fair and regular trial.

5. Without prejudice to the application of the Conventions and of this Protocol, grave breaches of these instruments shall be regarded as war crimes.

Article 86: Failure to act

1. The High Contracting Parties and the Parties to the conflict shall repress grave breaches, and take measures necessary to suppress all other breaches, of the Conventions or of this Protocol which result from a failure to act when under a duty to do so.

2. The fact that a breach of the Conventions or of this Protocol was committed by a subordinate does not absolve his superiors from penal or disciplinary responsibility, as the case may be, if they knew, or had information which should have enabled them to conclude in the circumstances at the time, that he was committing or was going to commit such a breach and if they did not take all feasible measures within their power to prevent or repress the breach.

Article 87: Duty of commanders

1. The High Contracting Parties and the Parties to the conflict shall require military commanders, with respect to members of the armed forces under their command and other persons under their control, to prevent and, where necessary, to suppress and to report to competent authorities breaches of the Conventions and of this Protocol.

2. In order to prevent and suppress breaches, High Contracting Parties and Parties to the conflict shall require that, commensurate with their level of responsibility, commanders ensure that members of the armed forces under their command are aware of their obligations under the Conventions and this Protocol.

3. The High Contracting Parties and Parties to the conflict shall require any commander who is aware that subordinates or other persons under his control are going to commit or have committed a breach of the Conventions or of this Protocol, to initiate such steps as are necessary to prevent such violations of the Conventions or this Protocol, and, where appropriate, to initiate disciplinary or penal action against violators thereof.

Article 88: Mutual assistance in criminal matters

1. The High Contracting Parties shall afford one another the greatest measure of assistance in connexion with criminal proceedings brought in respect of grave breaches of the Conventions or of this Protocol.

2. Subject to the rights and obligations established in the Conventions and in Article 85, paragraph 1, of this Protocol, and when circumstances permit, the High Contracting Parties shall co-operate in the matter of extradition. They shall give due consideration to the request of the State in whose territory the alleged offence has occurred.

3. The law of the High Contracting Party requested shall apply in all cases. The provisions of the preceding paragraphs shall not, however, affect the obligations arising from the provisions of any other treaty of a bilateral or multilateral nature which governs or will govern the whole or part of the subject of mutual assistance in criminal matters.

Article 89: Co-operation

In situations of serious violations of the Conventions or of this Protocol, the High Contracting Parties undertake to act, jointly or individually, in co-operation with the United Nations and in conformity with the United Nations Charter.

Article 90: International Fact-Finding Commission

1. (a) An International Fact-Finding Commission (hereinafter referred to as "the Commission") consisting of fifteen members of high moral standing and acknowledged impartiality shall be established.

(b) When not less than twenty High Contracting Parties have agreed to accept the competence of the Commission pursuant to paragraph 2, the depositary shall then, and at intervals of five years thereafter, convene a meeting of representatives of those High Contracting Parties for the purpose of electing the members of the Commission. At the meeting, the representatives shall elect the members of the Commission by secret ballot from a list of person s to which each of those High Contracting Parties may nominate one person.

(c) The members of the Commission shall serve in their personal capacity and shall hold office until the election of new members at the ensuing meeting.

(d) At the election, the High Contracting Parties shall ensure that the persons to be elected to the Commission individually possess the qualifications required and that, in the Commission as a whole, equitable geographical representation is assured.

(e) In the case of a casual vacancy, the Commission itself shall fill the vacancy, having due regard to the provisions of the preceding sub paragraphs.

(f) The depositary shall make available to the Commission the necessary administrative facilities for the performance of its functions.

2. (a) The High Contracting Parties may at the time of signing, ratifying or acceding to the Protocol, or at any other subsequent time, declare that they recognize ipso facto and without special agreement, in relation to any other High Contracting Party accepting the same obligation, the competence of the Commission to enquire into allegations by such other Party, as authorized by this Article.

(b) The declarations referred to above shall be deposited with the depositary, which shall transmit copies thereof to the High Contracting Parties.

(c) The Commission shall be competent to: (i) enquire into any facts alleged to be a grave breach as defined in the Conventions and this Protocol or other serious violation of the Conventions or of this Protocol; (ii) facilitate, through its good offices, the restoration of an attitude of respect for the Conventions and this Protocol.

(d) In other situations, the Commission shall institute an enquiry at the request of a Party to the conflict only with the consent of the other Party or Parties concerned.

(e) Subject to-the foregoing provisions of this paragraph, the provisions of Article 52 of the First Convention, Article 53 of the Second Convention, Article 132 of the Third Convention and Article 149 of the Fourth Convention shall continue to apply to any alleged violation of the Conventions and shall extend to any alleged violation of this Protocol.

3. (a) Unless otherwise agreed by the Parties concerned, all enquiries shall be undertaken by a Chamber consisting of seven members appointed as follows: (i) five members of the Commission, not nationals of any Party to the conflict, appointed by the President of the Commission on the basis of equitable representation of the geographical areas, after consultation with the Parties to the conflict; (ii) two ad hoc members, not nationals of any Party to the conflict, one to be appointed by each side.

(b) Upon receipt of the request for an enquiry, the President of the Commission shall specify an appropriate time limit for setting up a Chamber. If any ad hoc member has not been appointed within the time limit, the President shall immediately appoint such additional member or members of the Commission as may be necessary to complete the membership of the Chamber.

4. (a) The Chamber set up under paragraph 3 to undertake an enquiry shall invite the Parties to the conflict to assist it and to present evidence. The Chamber may also seek such other evidence as it deems appropriate and may carry out an investigation of the situation in loco.

(b) All evidence shall be fully disclosed to the Parties, which shall have the right to comment on it to the Commission.

(c) Each Party shall have the right to challenge such evidence.

5. (a) The Commission shall submit to the Parties a report on the findings of fact of the Chamber, with such recommendations as it may deem appropriate.

(b) If the Chamber is unable to secure sufficient evidence for factual and impartial findings, the Commission shall state the reasons for that inability.

(c) The Commission shall not report its findings publicly, unless all the Parties to the conflict have requested the Commission to do so.

6. The Commission shall establish its own rules, including rules for the presidency of the Commission and the presidency of the Chamber. Those rules shall ensure that the functions of the President of the Commission are exercised at all times and that, in the case of an enquiry, they are exercised by a person who is not a national of a Party to the conflict.

7. The administrative expenses of the Commission shall be met by contributions from the High Contracting Parties which made declarations under paragraph 2, and by voluntary contributions. The Party or Parties to the conflict requesting an enquiry shall advance the necessary funds for expenses incurred by a Chamber and shall be reimbursed by the Party or Parties against which the allegations are made to the extent of fifty per cent of the costs of the Chamber. Where there are counter-allegations before the Chamber each side shall advance fifty per cent of the necessary funds.

Article 91: Responsibility

A Party to the conflict which violates the provisions of the Conventions or of this Protocol shall, if the case demands, be liable to pay compensation. It shall be responsible for all acts committed by persons forming part of its armed forces.

Part VI: Final Provisions

Article 92: Signature

This Protocol shall be open for signature by the Parties to the Conventions six months after the signing of the Final Act and will remain open for a period of twelve months.

Article 93: Ratification

This Protocol shall be ratified as soon as possible. The instruments of ratification shall be deposited with the Swiss Federal Council, depositary of the Conventions.

Article 94: Accession

This Protocol shall be open for accession by any Party to the Conventions which has not signed it. The instruments of accession shall be deposited with the depositary.

Article 95: Entry into force

1. This Protocol shall enter into force six months after two instruments of ratification or accession have been deposited.

2. For each Party to the Conventions thereafter ratifying or acceding to this Protocol, it shall enter into force six months after the deposit by such Party of its instrument of ratification or accession.

Article 96: Treaty relations upon entry into force of this Protocol

1. When the Parties to the Conventions are also Parties to this Protocol, the Conventions shall apply as supplemented by this Protocol.

2. When one of the Parties to the conflict is not bound by this Protocol, the Parties to the Protocol shall remain bound by it in their mutual relations. They shall furthermore be bound by this Protocol in relation to each of the Parties which are not bound by it, if the latter accepts and applies the provisions thereof.

3. The authority representing a people engaged against a High Contracting Party in an armed conflict of the type referred to in Article 1, paragraph 4, may undertake to apply the Conventions and this Protocol in relation to that conflict by means of a unilateral declaration addressed to the depositary. Such declaration shall, upon its receipt by the depositary, have in relation to that conflict the following effects:

(a) the Conventions and this Protocol are brought into force for the said authority as a Party to the conflict with immediate effect;

(b) the said authority assumes the same rights and obligations as those which have been assumed by a High Contracting Party to the Conventions and this Protocol; and

(c) the Conventions and this Protocol are equally binding upon all Parties to the conflict.

Article 97: Amendment

1. Any High Contracting Party may propose amendments to this Protocol. The text of any proposed amendment shall be communicated to the depositary, which shall decide, after consultation with all the High Contracting Parties and the International Committee of the Red Cross, whether a conference should be convened to consider the proposed amendment.

2. The depositary shall invite to that conference all the High Contracting Parties as well as the Parties to the Conventions, whether or not they are signatories of this Protocol.

Article 98: Revision of Annex I

1. Not later than four years after the entry into force of this Protocol and

thereafter at intervals of not less than four years, the International Committee of the Red Cross shall consult the High Contracting Parties concerning Annex I to this Protocol and, if it considers it necessary, may propose a meeting of technical experts to review Annex I and to propose such amendments to it as may appear to be desirable. Unless, within six months of the communication of a proposal for such a meeting to the High Contracting Parties, one third of them object, the International Committee of the Red Cross shall convene the meeting, inviting also observers of appropriate international organizations. Such a meeting shall also be convened by the International Committee of the Red Cross at any time at the request of one third of the High Contracting Parties.

2. The depositary shall convene a conference of the High Contracting Parties and the Parties to the Conventions to consider amendments proposed by the meeting of technical experts if, after that meeting, the International Committee of the Red Cross or one third of the High Contracting Parties so request.

3. Amendments to Annex I may be adopted at such a conference by a two-thirds majority of the High Contracting Parties present and voting.

4. The depositary shall communicate any amendment so adopted to the High Contracting Parties and to the Parties to the Conventions. The amendment shall be considered to have been accepted at the end of a period of one year after it has been so communicated, unless within that period a declaration of non-acceptance of the amendment has been communicated to the depositary by not less than one third of the High Contracting Parties.

5. An amendment considered to have been accepted in accordance with paragraph 4 shall enter into force three months after its acceptance for all High Contracting Parties other than those which have made a declaration of non-acceptance in accordance with that paragraph. Any Party making such a declaration may at any time withdraw it and the amendment shall then enter into force for that Party three months thereafter.

6. The depositary shall notify the High Contracting Parties and the Parties to the Conventions of the entry into force of any amendment, of the Parties bound thereby, of the date of its entry into force in relation to each Party, of declarations of non-acceptance made in accordance with paragraph 4, and of withdrawals of such declarations.

Article 99: Denunciation

1. In case a High Contracting Party should denounce this Protocol, the denunciation shall only take effect one year after receipt of the instrument of denunciation. If, however, on the expiry of that year the denouncing Party is engaged in one of the situations referred to in Article 1, the denunciation shall not take effect before the end of the armed conflict or occupation and not, in any case, before operations connected with the final release, repatriation or re-establishment of the persons protected by the Conventions or this Protocol have been terminated.

2. The denunciation shall be notified in writing to the depositary, which shall transmit it to all the High Contracting Parties.

3. The denunciation shall have effect only in respect of the denouncing Party.

4. Any denunciation under paragraph 1 shall not affect the obligations already incurred, by reason of the armed conflict, under this Protocol by such denouncing Party in respect of any act committed before this denunciation becomes effective.

Article 100: Notifications

The depositary shall inform the High Contracting Parties as well as the Parties to the Conventions, whether or not they are signatories of this Protocol, of:

(a) signatures affixed to this Protocol and the deposit of instruments of ratification and accession under Articles 93 and 94;

(b) the date of entry into force of this Protocol under Article 95;

(c) communications and declarations received under Articles 84, 90 and 97.

(d) declarations received under Article 96, paragraph 3, which shall be communicated by the quickest methods; and

(e) denunciations under Article 99.

Article 101: Registration

1. After its entry into force, this Protocol shall be transmitted by the depositary to the Secretariat of the United Nations for registration and publication, in accordance with Article 102 of the Charter of the United Nations.

2. The depositary shall also inform the Secretariat of the United Nations of all ratifications, accessions and denunciations received by it with respect to this Protocol.

Article 102: Authentic texts

The original of this Protocol, of which the Arabic, Chinese, English, French, Russian and Spanish texts are equally authentic, shall be deposited with the depositary, which shall transmit certified true copies thereof to all the Parties to the Conventions.

. . . [Annexes not included]

6.4
Protocol Additional to the Geneva Conventions of 12 August 1949, and Relating to the Protection of Victims of Non-International Armed Conflicts (Protocol II) (1977)

Additional Protocol II builds on the common article 3 in the 1949 Geneva Conventions, although its application requires a higher threshold of armed conflict. The United States signed Additional Protocols I and II on the day they were opened for signature, but has ratified neither.

For an introduction to the protocol and its relationship to article 3 of the 1949 Geneva Conventions, see Sylvie Junod, "Additional Protocol II: History and Scope," American University Law Review *33 (1983): 29–40. For detailed negotiating history, see Howard S. Levie, ed.,* The Law of Non-International Armed Conflict: Protocol II to the 1949 Geneva Conventions *(Dordrecht: M. Nijhoff, 1987). On the United States and the protocol, see Walter L. Jacobsen, "A Discussion of Protocol II to the Geneva Conventions of 1949,"* Proceedings of the American Society of International Law at its Annual Meeting *88 (1988): 613–625. As on all matters of international humanitarian law, see also the website of the ICRC at www.icrc.org/eng/ihl.*

The High Contracting Parties,

Recalling that the humanitarian principles enshrined in Article 3 common to the Geneva Conventions of 12 August 1949 constitute the foundation of respect for the human person in cases of armed conflict not of an international character,

Recalling furthermore that international instruments relating to human rights offer a basic protection to the human person,

Emphasizing the need to ensure a better protection for the victims of those armed conflicts,

Recalling that, in cases not covered by the law in force, the human person remains under the protection of the principles of humanity and the dictates of the public conscience,

Have agreed on the following:

Part I: Scope of this Protocol

Article 1: Material field of application

1. This Protocol, which develops and supplements Article 3 common to the Geneva Conventions of 12 August 1949 without modifying its existing conditions of application, shall apply to all armed conflicts which are not covered by Article 1 of the Protocol Additional to the Geneva Conventions of 12 August 1949, and relating to the Protection of Victims of International Armed Conflicts (Protocol I) and which take place in the territory of a High Contracting Party between its armed forces and dissident armed forces or other organized armed groups which, under responsible command, exercise such control over a part of its territory as to enable them to carry out sustained and concerted military operations and to implement this Protocol.

2. This Protocol shall not apply to situations of internal disturbances and tensions, such as riots, isolated and sporadic acts of violence and other acts of a similar nature, as not being armed conflicts.

Article 2: Personal field of application

1. This Protocol shall be applied without any adverse distinction founded on race, colour, sex, language, religion or belief, political or other opinion, national or social origin, wealth, birth or other status, or on any other similar criteria (hereinafter referred to as "adverse distinction") to all persons affected by an armed conflict as defined in Article 1.

2. At the end of the armed conflict, all the persons who have been deprived of their liberty or whose liberty has been restricted for reasons related to such conflict, as well as those deprived of their liberty or whose liberty is restricted after the conflict for the same reasons, shall enjoy the protection of Articles 5 and 6 until the end of such deprivation or restriction of liberty.

Article 3: Non-intervention

1. Nothing in this Protocol shall be invoked for the purpose of affecting the sovereignty of a State or the responsibility of the government, by all legitimate means, to maintain or re-establish law and order in the State or to defend the national unity and territorial integrity of the State.

2. Nothing in this Protocol shall be invoked as a justification for intervening, directly or indirectly, for any reason whatever, in the armed conflict or in

the internal or external affairs of the High Contracting Party in the territory of which that conflict occurs.

Part II: Humane Treatment

Article 4: Fundamental guarantees

1. All persons who do not take a direct part or who have ceased to take part in hostilities, whether or not their liberty has been restricted, are entitled to respect for their person, honour and convictions and religious practices. They shall in all circumstances be treated humanely, without any adverse distinction. It is prohibited to order that there shall be no survivors.

2. Without prejudice to the generality of the foregoing, the following acts against the persons referred to in paragraph I are and shall remain prohibited at any time and in any place whatsoever:

(a) violence to the life, health and physical or mental well-being of persons, in particular murder as well as cruel treatment such as torture, mutilation or any form of corporal punishment;

(b) collective punishments;

(c) taking of hostages;

(d) acts of terrorism;

(e) outrages upon personal dignity, in particular humiliating and degrading treatment, rape, enforced prostitution and any form of indecent assault;

(f) slavery and the slave trade in all their forms;

(g) pillage;

(h) threats to commit any of the foregoing acts.

3. Children shall be provided with the care and aid they require, and in particular:

(a) they shall receive an education, including religious and moral education, in keeping with the wishes of their parents, or in the absence of parents, of those responsible for their care;

(b) all appropriate steps shall be taken to facilitate the reunion of families temporarily separated;

(c) children who have not attained the age of fifteen years shall neither be recruited in the armed forces or groups nor allowed to take part in hostilities;

(d) the special protection provided by this Article to children who have not attained the age of fifteen years shall remain applicable to them if they take a direct part in hostilities despite the provisions of sub-paragraph (c) and are captured;

(e) measures shall be taken, if necessary, and whenever possible with the consent of their parents or persons who by law or custom are primarily responsible for their care, to remove children temporarily from the area in which hostilities are taking place to a safer area within the country and ensure that they are accompanied by persons responsible for their safety and well-being.

Article 5: Persons whose liberty has been restricted

1. In addition to the provisions of Article 4, the following provisions shall be respected as a minimum with regard to persons deprived of their liberty for reasons related to the armed conflict, whether they are interned or detained:

(a) the wounded and the sick shall be treated in accordance with Article 7;

(b) the persons referred to in this paragraph shall, to the same extent as the local civilian population, be provided with food and drinking water and be afforded safeguards as regards health and hygiene and protection against the rigours of the climate and the dangers of the armed conflict;

(c) they shall be allowed to receive individual or collective relief;

(d) they shall be allowed to practise their religion and, if requested and appropriate, to receive spiritual assistance from persons, such as chaplains, performing religious functions;

(e) they shall, if made to work, have the benefit of working conditions and safeguards similar to those enjoyed by the local civilian population.

2. Those who are responsible for the internment or detention of the persons referred to in paragraph 1 shall also, within the limits of their capabilities, respect the following provisions relating to such persons:

(a) except when men and women of a family are accommodated together, women shall be held in quarters separated from those of men and shall be under the immediate supervision of women;

(b) they shall be allowed to send and receive letters and cards, the number of which may be limited by the competent authority if it deems necessary;

(c) places of internment and detention shall not be located close to the combat zone. The persons referred to in paragraph 1 shall be evacuated when the places where they are interned or detained become particularly exposed to danger arising out of the armed conflict, if their evacuation can be carried out under adequate conditions of safety;

(d) they shall have the benefit of medical examinations;

(e) their physical or mental health and integrity shall not be endangered by an unjustified act or omission. Accordingly, it is prohibited to subject the persons described in this Article to any medical procedure which is not indicated by the state of health of the person concerned, and which is not consistent with the generally accepted medical standards applied to free persons under similar medical circumstances.

3. Persons who are not covered by paragraph 1 but whose liberty has been restricted in any way whatsoever for reasons related to the armed conflict shall be treated humanely in accordance with Article 4 and with paragraphs 1 (a), (c) and (d), and 2 (b) of this Article.

4. If it is decided to release persons deprived of their liberty, necessary measures to ensure their safety shall be taken by those so deciding.

Article 6: Penal prosecutions

1. This Article applies to the prosecution and punishment of criminal offences related to the armed conflict.

2. No sentence shall be passed and no penalty shall be executed on a person found guilty of an offence except pursuant to a conviction pronounced by a court offering the essential guarantees of independence and impartiality. In particular:

(a) the procedure shall provide for an accused to be informed without delay of the particulars of the offence alleged against him and shall afford the accused before and during his trial all necessary rights and means of defence;

(b) no one shall be convicted of an offence except on the basis of individual penal responsibility;

(c) no one shall be held guilty of any criminal offence on account of any act or omission which did not constitute a criminal offence, under the law, at the time when it was committed; nor shall a heavier penalty be imposed than that which was applicable at the time when the criminal offence was committed; if, after the commission of the offence, provision is made by law for the imposition of a lighter penalty, the offender shall benefit thereby;

(d) anyone charged with an offence is presumed innocent until proved guilty according to law;

(e) anyone charged with an offence shall have the right to be tried in his presence;

(f) no one shall be compelled to testify against himself or to confess guilt.

3. A convicted person shall be advised on conviction of his judicial and other remedies and of the time-limits within which they may be exercised.

4. The death penalty shall not be pronounced on persons who were under the age of eighteen years at the time of the offence and shall not be carried out on pregnant women or mothers of young children.

5. At the end of hostilities, the authorities in power shall endeavour to grant the broadest possible amnesty to persons who have participated in the armed conflict, or those deprived of their liberty for reasons related to the armed conflict, whether they are interned or detained.

Part III: Wounded, Sick and Shipwrecked

Article 7: Protection and care

1. All the wounded, sick and shipwrecked, whether or not they have taken part in the armed conflict, shall be respected and protected.

2. In all circumstances they shall be treated humanely and shall receive, to the fullest extent practicable and with the least possible delay, the medical care and attention required by their condition. There shall be no distinction among them founded on any grounds other than medical ones.

Article 8: Search

Whenever circumstances permit, and particularly after an engagement, all possible measures shall be taken, without delay, to search for and collect the wounded, sick and shipwrecked, to protect them against pillage and ill-treatment, to ensure their adequate care, and to search for the dead, prevent their being despoiled, and decently dispose of them.

Article 9: Protection of medical and religious personnel

1. Medical and religious personnel shall be respected and protected and shall be granted all available help for the performance of their duties. They shall not be compelled to carry out tasks which are not compatible with their humanitarian mission.

2. In the performance of their duties medical personnel may not be required to give priority to any person except on medical grounds.

Article 10: General protection of medical duties

1. Under no circumstances shall any person be punished for having carried out medical activities compatible with medical ethics, regardless of the person benefiting therefrom.

2. Persons engaged in medical activities shall neither be compelled to perform acts or to carry out work contrary to, nor be compelled to refrain from acts required by, the rules of medical ethics or other rules designed for the benefit of the wounded and sick, or this Protocol.

3. The professional obligations of persons engaged in medical activities regarding information which they may acquire concerning the wounded and sick under their care shall, subject to national law, be respected.

4. Subject to national law, no person engaged in medical activities may be penalized in any way for refusing or failing to give information concerning the wounded and sick who are, or who have been, under his care.

Article 11: Protection of medical units and transports

1. Medical units and transports shall be respected and protected at all times and shall not be the object of attack.

2. The protection to which medical units and transports are entitled shall not cease unless they are used to commit hostile acts, outside their humanitarian function. Protection may, however, cease only after a warning has been given setting, whenever appropriate, a reasonable time-limit, and after such warning has remained unheeded.

Article 12: The distinctive emblem

Under the direction of the competent authority concerned, the distinctive emblem of the red cross, red crescent or red lion and sun on a white ground shall be displayed by medical and religious personnel and medical units, and on medical transports. It shall be respected in all circumstances. It shall not be used improperly.

Part IV: Civilian Population

Article 13: Protection of the civilian population

1. The civilian population and individual civilians shall enjoy general protection against the dangers arising from military operations. To give effect to this protection, the following rules shall be observed in all circumstances.

2. The civilian population as such, as well as individual civilians, shall not be the object of attack. Acts or threats of violence the primary purpose of which is to spread terror among the civilian population are prohibited.

3. Civilians shall enjoy the protection afforded by this Part, unless and for such time as they take a direct part in hostilities.

Article 14: Protection of objects
indispensable to the survival of the civilian population

Starvation of civilians as a method of combat is prohibited. It is therefore prohibited to attack, destroy, remove or render useless, for that purpose, objects indispensable to the survival of the civilian population, such as foodstuffs, agricultural areas for the production of foodstuffs, crops, livestock, drinking water installations and supplies and irrigation works.

Article 15: Protection of works and
installations containing dangerous forces

Works or installations containing dangerous forces, namely dams, dykes and nuclear electrical generating stations, shall not be made the object of attack, even where these objects are military objectives, if such attack may cause the release of dangerous forces and consequent severe losses among the civilian population.

Article 16: Protection of cultural objects and of places of worship

Without prejudice to the provisions of The Hague Convention for the Protection of Cultural Property in the Event of Armed Conflict of 14 May 1954, it is prohibited to commit any acts of hostility directed against historic monuments, works of art or places of worship which constitute the cultural or spiritual heritage of peoples, and to use them in support of the military effort.

Article 17: Prohibition of forced movement of civilians

1. The displacement of the civilian population shall not be ordered for reasons related to the conflict unless the security of the civilians involved or imperative military reasons so demand. Should such displacements have to be carried out, all possible measures shall be taken in order that the civilian population may be received under satisfactory conditions of shelter, hygiene, health, safety and nutrition.

2. Civilians shall not be compelled to leave their own territory for reasons connected with the conflict.

Article 18: Relief societies and relief actions

1. Relief societies located in the territory of the High Contracting Party, such as Red Cross (Red Crescent, Red Lion and Sun) organizations, may offer their services for the performance of their traditional functions in relation to the victims of the armed conflict. The civilian population may, even on its own initiative, offer to collect and care for the wounded, sick and shipwrecked.

2. If the civilian population is suffering undue hardship owing to a lack of the supplies essential for its survival, such as foodstuffs and medical supplies, relief actions for the civilian population which are of an exclusively humanitarian and impartial nature and which are conducted without any adverse distinction shall be undertaken subject to the consent of the High Contracting Party concerned.

Part V: Final Provisions

Article 19: Dissemination

This Protocol shall be disseminated as widely as possible.

Article 20: Signature

This Protocol shall be open for signature by the Parties to the Conventions six months after the signing of the Final Act and will remain open for a period of twelve months.

Article 21: Ratification

This Protocol shall be ratified as soon as possible. The instruments of ratification shall be deposited with the Swiss Federal Council, depositary of the Conventions.

Article 22: Accession

This Protocol shall be open for accession by any Party to the Conventions which has not signed it. The instruments of accession shall be deposited with the depositary.

Article 23: Entry into force

1. This Protocol shall enter into force six months after two instruments of ratification or accession have been deposited.

2. For each Party to the Conventions thereafter ratifying or acceding to this Protocol, it shall enter into force six months after the deposit by such Party of its instrument of ratification or accession.

Article 24: Amendment

1. Any High Contracting Party may propose amendments to this Protocol. The text of any proposed amendment shall be communicated to the depositary

which shall decide, after consultation with all the High Contracting Parties and the International Committee of the Red Cross, whether a conference should be convened to consider the proposed amendment.

2. The depositary shall invite to that conference all the High Contracting Parties as well as the Parties to the Conventions, whether or not they are signatories of this Protocol.

Article 25: Denunciation

1. In case a High Contracting Party should denounce this Protocol, the denunciation shall only take effect six months after receipt of the instrument of denunciation. If, however, on the expiry of six months, the denouncing Party is engaged in the situation referred to in Article 1, the denunciation shall not take effect before the end of the armed conflict. Persons who have been deprived of liberty, or whose liberty has been restricted, for reasons related to the conflict shall nevertheless continue to benefit from the provisions of this Protocol until their final release.

2. The denunciation shall be notified in writing to the depositary, which shall transmit it to all the High Contracting Parties.

Article 26: Notifications

The depositary shall inform the High Contracting Parties as well as the Parties to the Conventions, whether or not they are signatories of this Protocol, of:

(a) signatures affixed to this Protocol and the deposit of instruments of ratification and accession under Articles 21 and 22;

(b) the date of entry into force of this Protocol under Article 23; and

(c) communications and declarations received under Article 24.

Article 27: Registration

1. After its entry into force, this Protocol shall be transmitted by the depositary to the Secretariat of the United Nations for registration and publication, in accordance with Article 102 of the Charter of the United Nations.

2. The depositary shall also inform the Secretariat of the United Nations of all ratifications and accessions received by it with respect to this Protocol.

Article 28: Authentic texts

The original of this Protocol, of which the Arabic, Chinese, English, French, Russian and Spanish texts are equally authentic shall be deposited with the depositary, which shall transmit certified true copies thereof to all the Parties to the Conventions.

7
International Law and the Environment

7.1
Basel Convention on the Control of Transboundary Movements of Hazardous Wastes and Their Disposal (1989)

The United Nations Environment Programme has responded to growing concern at the effects on human health and the environment of hazardous substances through the negotiation of several treaties. The Basel Convention originated with the concerns of developing countries and countries with economies in transition at the dumping in their countries of toxic waste from industrialized countries. The 1998 Rotterdam Convention on the Prior Informed Consent Procedure for Certain Hazardous Chemicals and Pesticides in International Trade (which entered into force in 2004) aims to give countries the power to make informed decisions as to which chemicals to accept for import. The Stockholm Convention on Persistent Organic Pollutants, adopted in 2001, seeks to eliminate or minimize the production and use of highly toxic chemicals.

For analysis of the Basel Convention, see Katharina Kummer, International Management of Hazardous Wastes: The Basel Convention and Related Legal Rules *(Oxford: Oxford University Press, 1995). The secretariat of the Basel Convention has a website at www.basel.int. See also the website of the Basel Action Network (BAN), a US-based, international activist network "seeking to prevent the globalization of the toxic chemical crisis," at www.ban.org. On the US attitude toward the convention and its protocol, see Sejal Choksi, "The Basel Convention on the Control of Transboundary Movements of Hazardous Wastes and Their Disposal: 1999 Protocol on Liability and Compensation,"* Ecology Law Quarterly *28 (2001): 509–545.*

The Parties to this Convention,

Aware of the risk of damage to human health and the environment caused by hazardous wastes and other wastes and the transboundary movement thereof,

Mindful of the growing threat to human health and the environment posed by the increased generation and complexity, and transboundary movement of hazardous wastes and other wastes,

Mindful also that the most effective way of protecting human health and the environment from the dangers posed by such wastes is the reduction of their generation to a minimum in terms of quantity and/or hazard potential,

Convinced that States should take necessary measures to ensure that the management of hazardous wastes and other wastes including their transboundary movement and disposal is consistent with the protection of human health and the environment whatever the place of disposal,

Noting that States should ensure that the generator should carry out duties with regard to the transport and disposal of hazardous wastes and other wastes in a manner that is consistent with the protection of the environment, whatever the place of disposal,

Fully recognizing that any State has the sovereign right to ban the entry or disposal of foreign hazardous wastes and other wastes in its territory,

Recognizing also the increasing desire for the prohibition of transboundary movements of hazardous wastes and their disposal in other States, especially developing countries,

Convinced that hazardous wastes and other wastes should, as far as is compatible with environmentally sound and efficient management, be disposed of in the State where they were generated,

Aware also that transboundary movements of such wastes from the State of their generation to any other State should be permitted only when conducted under conditions which do not endanger human health and the environment, and under conditions in conformity with the provisions of this Convention,

Considering that enhanced control of transboundary movement of hazardous wastes and other wastes will act as an incentive for their environmentally sound management and for the reduction of the volume of such transboundary movement,

Convinced that States should take measures for the proper exchange of information on and control of the transboundary movement of hazardous wastes and other wastes from and to those States,

Noting that a number of international and regional agreements have addressed the issue of protection and preservation of the environment with regard to the transit of dangerous goods,

Taking into account the Declaration of the United Nations Conference on the Human Environment (Stockholm, 1972), the Cairo Guidelines and Principles for the Environmentally Sound Management of Hazardous Wastes adopted by the Governing Council of the United Nations Environment Programme (UNEP) by decision 14/30 of 17 June 1987, the Recommendations of the United Nations Committee of Experts on the Transport of Dangerous Goods (formulated in 1957 and updated biennially), relevant recommendations, declarations, instruments and regulations adopted within the United Nations system and the work and studies done within other international and regional organizations,

Mindful of the spirit, principles, aims and functions of the World Charter for Nature adopted by the General Assembly of the United Nations at its thirty-seventh session (1982) as the rule of ethics in respect of the protection of the human environment and the conservation of natural resources,

Affirming that States are responsible for the fulfilment of their international obligations concerning the protection of human health and protection and preservation of the environment, and are liable in accordance with international law,

Recognizing that in the case of a material breach of the provisions of this Convention or any protocol thereto the relevant international law of treaties shall apply,

Aware of the need to continue the development and implementation of environmentally sound low-waste technologies, recycling options, good housekeeping and management systems with a view to reducing to a minimum the generation of hazardous wastes and other wastes,

Aware also of the growing international concern about the need for stringent control of transboundary movement of hazardous wastes and other wastes, and of the need as far as possible to reduce such movement to a minimum,

Concerned about the problem of illegal transboundary traffic in hazardous wastes and other wastes,

Taking into account also the limited capabilities of the developing countries to manage hazardous wastes and other wastes,

Recognizing the need to promote the transfer of technology for the sound management of hazardous wastes and other wastes produced locally, particularly to the developing countries in accordance with the spirit of the Cairo Guidelines and decision 14/16 of the Governing Council of UNEP on Promotion of the transfer of environmental protection technology,

Recognizing also that hazardous wastes and other wastes should be transported in accordance with relevant international conventions and recommendations,

Convinced also that the transboundary movement of hazardous wastes and other wastes should be permitted only when the transport and the ultimate disposal of such wastes is environmentally sound, and

Determined to protect, by strict control, human health and the environment against the adverse effects which may result from the generation and management of hazardous wastes and other wastes,

HAVE AGREED AS FOLLOWS:

Article 1: Scope of the Convention

1. The following wastes that are subject to transboundary movement shall be "hazardous wastes" for the purposes of this Convention:

(a) Wastes that belong to any category contained in Annex I, unless they do not possess any of the characteristics contained in Annex III; and

(b) Wastes that are not covered under paragraph (a) but are defined as, or are considered to be, hazardous wastes by the domestic legislation of the Party of export, import or transit.

2. Wastes that belong to any category contained in Annex II that are subject to transboundary movement shall be "other wastes" for the purposes of this Convention.

3. Wastes which, as a result of being radioactive, are subject to other international control systems, including international instruments, applying specifically to radioactive materials, are excluded from the scope of this Convention.

4. Wastes which derive from the normal operations of a ship, the discharge of which is covered by another international instrument, are excluded from the scope of this Convention.

Article 2: Definitions
For the purposes of this Convention:

1. "Wastes" are substances or objects which are disposed of or are intended to be disposed of or are required to be disposed of by the provisions of national law;

2. "Management" means the collection, transport and disposal of hazardous wastes or other wastes, including after-care of disposal sites;

3. "Transboundary movement" means any movement of hazardous wastes or other wastes from an area under the national jurisdiction of one State to or through an area under the national jurisdiction of another State or to or through an area not under the national jurisdiction of any State, provided at least two States are involved in the movement;

4. "Disposal" means any operation specified in Annex IV to this Convention;

5. "Approved site or facility" means a site or facility for the disposal of hazardous wastes or other wastes which is authorized or permitted to operate for this purpose by a relevant authority of the State where the site or facility is located;

6. "Competent authority" means one governmental authority designated by a Party to be responsible, within such geographical areas as the Party may think fit, for receiving the notification of a transboundary movement of hazardous wastes or other wastes, and any information related to it, and for responding to such a notification, as provided in Article 6;

7. "Focal point" means the entity of a Party referred to in Article 5 responsible for receiving and submitting information as provided for in Articles 13 and 16;

8. "Environmentally sound management of hazardous wastes or other wastes" means taking all practicable steps to ensure that hazardous wastes or other wastes are managed in a manner which will protect human health and the environment against the adverse effects which may result from such wastes;

9. "Area under the national jurisdiction of a State" means any land, marine area or airspace within which a State exercises administrative and regulatory responsibility in accordance with international law in regard to the protection of human health or the environment;

10. "State of export" means a Party from which a transboundary movement of hazardous wastes or other wastes is planned to be initiated or is initiated;

11. "State of import" means a Party to which a transboundary movement of hazardous wastes or other wastes is planned or takes place for the purpose of disposal therein or for the purpose of loading prior to disposal in an area not under the national jurisdiction of any State;

12. "State of transit" means any State, other than the State of export or import, through which a movement of hazardous wastes or other wastes is planned or takes place;

13. "States concerned" means Parties which are States of export or import, or transit States, whether or not Parties;

14. "Person" means any natural or legal person;

15. "Exporter" means any person under the jurisdiction of the State of export who arranges for hazardous wastes or other wastes to be exported;

16. "Importer" means any person under the jurisdiction of the State of import who arranges for hazardous wastes or other wastes to be imported;

17. "Carrier" means any person who carries out the transport of hazardous wastes or other wastes;

18. "Generator" means any person whose activity produces hazardous wastes or other wastes or, if that person is not known, the person who is in possession and/or control of those wastes;

19. "Disposer" means any person to whom hazardous wastes or other wastes are shipped and who carries out the disposal of such wastes;

20. "Political and/or economic integration organization" means an organization constituted by sovereign States to which its member States have transferred competence in respect of matters governed by this Convention and which has been duly authorized, in accordance with its internal procedures, to sign, ratify, accept, approve, formally confirm or accede to it;

21. "Illegal traffic" means any transboundary movement of hazardous wastes or other wastes as specified in Article 9.

Article 3: National definitions of hazardous wastes

1. Each Party shall, within six months of becoming a Party to this Convention, inform the Secretariat of the Convention of the wastes, other than those listed in Annexes I and II, considered or defined as hazardous under its national legislation and of any requirements concerning transboundary movement procedures applicable to such wastes.

2. Each Party shall subsequently inform the Secretariat of any significant changes to the information it has provided pursuant to paragraph 1.

3. The Secretariat shall forthwith inform all Parties of the information it has received pursuant to paragraphs 1 and 2.

4. Parties shall be responsible for making the information transmitted to them by the Secretariat under paragraph 3 available to their exporters.

Article 4: General obligations

1. (a) Parties exercising their right to prohibit the import of hazardous wastes or other wastes for disposal shall inform the other Parties of their decision pursuant to Article 13.

(b) Parties shall prohibit or shall not permit the export of hazardous wastes and other wastes to the Parties which have prohibited the import of such wastes, when notified pursuant to subparagraph (a) above.

(c) Parties shall prohibit or shall not permit the export of hazardous wastes and other wastes if the State of import does not consent in writing to the specific import, in the case where that State of import has not prohibited the import of such wastes.

2. Each Party shall take the appropriate measures to:

(a) Ensure that the generation of hazardous wastes and other wastes within it is reduced to a minimum, taking into account social, technological and economic aspects;

(b) Ensure the availability of adequate disposal facilities, for the environmentally sound management of hazardous wastes and other wastes, that shall be located, to the extent possible, within it, whatever the place of their disposal;

(c) Ensure that persons involved in the management of hazardous wastes or other wastes within it take such steps as are necessary to prevent pollution due to hazardous wastes and other wastes arising from such management and, if such pollution occurs, to minimize the consequences thereof for human health and the environment;

(d) Ensure that the transboundary movement of hazardous wastes and other wastes is reduced to the minimum consistent with the environmentally sound and efficient management of such wastes, and is conducted in a manner which will protect human health and the environment against the adverse effects which may result from such movement;

(e) Not allow the export of hazardous wastes or other wastes to a State or group of States belonging to an economic and/or political integration organization that are Parties, particularly developing countries, which have prohibited by their legislation all imports, or if it has reason to believe that the wastes in question will not be managed in an environmentally sound manner, according to criteria to be decided on by the Parties at their first meeting;

(f) Require that information about a proposed transboundary movement of hazardous wastes and other wastes be provided to the States concerned, according to Annex V A, to state clearly the effects of the proposed movement on human health and the environment;

(g) Prevent the import of hazardous wastes and other wastes if it has reason to believe that the wastes in question will not be managed in an environmentally sound manner;

(h) Co-operate in activities with other Parties and interested organizations, directly and through the Secretariat, including the dissemination of information on the transboundary movement of hazardous wastes and other wastes, in order to improve the environmentally sound management of such wastes and to achieve the prevention of illegal traffic.

3. The Parties consider that illegal traffic in hazardous wastes or other wastes is criminal.

4. Each Party shall take appropriate legal, administrative and other measures to implement and enforce the provisions of this Convention, including measures to prevent and punish conduct in contravention of the Convention.

5. A Party shall not permit hazardous wastes or other wastes to be exported to a non-Party or to be imported from a non-Party.

6. The Parties agree not to allow the export of hazardous wastes or other wastes for disposal within the area south of 60° South latitude, whether or not such wastes are subject to transboundary movement.

7. Furthermore, each Party shall:

(a) Prohibit all persons under its national jurisdiction from transporting or disposing of hazardous wastes or other wastes unless such persons are authorized or allowed to perform such types of operations;

(b) Require that hazardous wastes and other wastes that are to be the subject of a transboundary movement be packaged, labelled, and transported in conformity with generally accepted and recognized international rules and standards in the field of packaging, labelling, and transport, and that due account is taken of relevant internationally recognized practices;

(c) Require that hazardous wastes and other wastes be accompanied by a movement document from the point at which a transboundary movement commences to the point of disposal.

8. Each Party shall require that hazardous wastes or other wastes, to be exported, are managed in an environmentally sound manner in the State of import or elsewhere. Technical guidelines for the environmentally sound management of wastes subject to this Convention shall be decided by the Parties at their first meeting.

9. Parties shall take the appropriate measures to ensure that the transboundary movement of hazardous wastes and other wastes only be allowed if:

(a) The State of export does not have the technical capacity and the necessary facilities, capacity or suitable disposal sites in order to dispose of the wastes in question in an environmentally sound and efficient manner; or

(b) The wastes in question are required as a raw material for recycling or recovery industries in the State of import; or

(c) The transboundary movement in question is in accordance with other criteria to be decided by the Parties, provided those criteria do not differ from the objectives of this Convention.

10. The obligation under this Convention of States in which hazardous wastes and other wastes are generated to require that those wastes are managed

in an environmentally sound manner may not under any circumstances be transferred to the States of import or transit.

11. Nothing in this Convention shall prevent a Party from imposing additional requirements that are consistent with the provisions of this Convention, and are in accordance with the rules of international law, in order better to protect human health and the environment.

12. Nothing in this Convention shall affect in any way the sovereignty of States over their territorial sea established in accordance with international law, and the sovereign rights and the jurisdiction which States have in their exclusive economic zones and their continental shelves in accordance with international law, and the exercise by ships and aircraft of all States of navigational rights and freedoms as provided for in international law and as reflected in relevant international instruments.

13. Parties shall undertake to review periodically the possibilities for the reduction of the amount and/or the pollution potential of hazardous wastes and other wastes which are exported to other States, in particular to developing countries.

Article 5: Designation of competent authorities and focal point

To facilitate the implementation of this Convention, the Parties shall:

1. Designate or establish one or more competent authorities and one focal point. One competent authority shall be designated to receive the notification in case of a State of transit.

2. Inform the Secretariat, within three months of the date of the entry into force of this Convention for them, which agencies they have designated as their focal point and their competent authorities

3. Inform the Secretariat, within one month of the date of decision, of any changes regarding the designation made by them under paragraph 2 above.

Article 6: Transboundary movement between Parties

1. The State of export shall notify, or shall require the generator or exporter to notify, in writing, through the channel of the competent authority of the State of export, the competent authority of the States concerned of any proposed transboundary movement of hazardous wastes or other wastes. Such notification shall contain the declarations and information specified in Annex V A, written in a language acceptable to the State of import. Only one notification needs to be sent to each State concerned.

2. The State of import shall respond to the notifier in writing, consenting to the movement with or without conditions, denying permission for the movement, or requesting additional information. A copy of the final response of the State of import shall be sent to the competent authorities of the States concerned which are Parties.

3. The State of export shall not allow the generator or exporter to commence the transboundary movement until it has received written confirmation that:

(a) The notifier has received the written consent of the State of import; and

(b) The notifier has received from the State of import confirmation of the existence of a contract between the exporter and the disposer specifying environmentally sound management of the wastes in question.

4. Each State of transit which is a Party shall promptly acknowledge to the notifier receipt of the notification. It may subsequently respond to the notifier in writing, within 60 days, consenting to the movement with or without conditions, denying permission for the movement, or requesting additional information. The State of export shall not allow the transboundary movement to commence until it has received the written consent of the State of transit. However, if at any time a Party decides not to require prior written consent, either generally or under specific conditions, for transit transboundary movements of hazardous wastes or other wastes, or modifies its requirements in this respect, it shall forthwith inform the other Parties of its decision pursuant to Article 13. In this latter case, if no response is received by the State of export within 60 days of the receipt of a given notification by the State of transit, the State of export may allow the export to proceed through the State of transit.

5. In the case of a transboundary movement of wastes where the wastes are legally defined as or considered to be hazardous wastes only:

(a) By the State of export, the requirements of paragraph 9 of this Article that apply to the importer or disposer and the State of import shall apply mutatis mutandis to the exporter and State of export, respectively;

(b) By the State of import, or by the States of import and transit which are Parties, the requirements of paragraphs 1, 3, 4 and 6 of this Article that apply to the exporter and State of export shall apply mutatis mutandis to the importer or disposer and State of import, respectively; or

(c) By any State of transit which is a Party, the provisions of paragraph 4 shall apply to such State.

6. The State of export may, subject to the written consent of the States concerned, allow the generator or the exporter to use a general notification where hazardous wastes or other wastes having the same physical and chemical characteristics are shipped regularly to the same disposer via the same customs office of exit of the State of export via the same customs office of entry of the State of import, and, in the case of transit, via the same customs office of entry and exit of the State or States of transit.

7. The States concerned may make their written consent to the use of the general notification referred to in paragraph 6 subject to the supply of certain information, such as the exact quantities or periodical lists of hazardous wastes or other wastes to be shipped.

8. The general notification and written consent referred to in paragraphs 6 and 7 may cover multiple shipments of hazardous wastes or other wastes during a maximum period of 12 months.

9. The Parties shall require that each person who takes charge of a transboundary movement of hazardous wastes or other wastes sign the movement

document either upon delivery or receipt of the wastes in question. They shall also require that the disposer inform both the exporter and the competent authority of the State of export of receipt by the disposer of the wastes in question and, in due course, of the completion of disposal as specified in the notification. If no such information is received within the State of export, the competent authority of the State of export or the exporter shall so notify the State of import.

10. The notification and response required by this Article shall be transmitted to the competent authority of the Parties concerned or to such governmental authority as may be appropriate in the case of non-Parties.

11. Any transboundary movement of hazardous wastes or other wastes shall be covered by insurance, bond or other guarantee as may be required by the State of import or any State of transit which is a Party.

Article 7: Transboundary movement
from a Party through States which are not Parties

Paragraph 1 of Article 6 of the Convention shall apply mutatis mutandis to transboundary movement of hazardous wastes or other wastes from a Party through a State or States which are not Parties.

Article 8: Duty to re-import

When a transboundary movement of hazardous wastes or other wastes to which the consent of the States concerned has been given, subject to the provisions of this Convention, cannot be completed in accordance with the terms of the contract, the State of export shall ensure that the wastes in question are taken back into the State of export, by the exporter, if alternative arrangements cannot be made for their disposal in an environmentally sound manner, within 90 days from the time that the importing State informed the State of export and the Secretariat, or such other period of time as the States concerned agree. To this end, the State of export and any Party of transit shall not oppose, hinder or prevent the return of those wastes to the State of export.

Article 9: Illegal traffic

1. For the purpose of this Convention, any transboundary movement of hazardous wastes or other wastes:

(a) without notification pursuant to the provisions of this Convention to all States concerned; or

(b) without the consent pursuant to the provisions of this Convention of a State concerned; or

(c) with consent obtained from States concerned through falsification, misrepresentation or fraud; or

(d) that does not conform in a material way with the documents; or

(e) that results in deliberate disposal (e.g. dumping) of hazardous wastes or other wastes in contravention of this Convention and of general principles of international law, shall be deemed to be illegal traffic.

2. In case of a transboundary movement of hazardous wastes or other wastes deemed to be illegal traffic as the result of conduct on the part of the exporter or generator, the State of export shall ensure that the wastes in question are:

(a) taken back by the exporter or the generator or, if necessary, by itself into the State of export, or, if impracticable,

(b) are otherwise disposed of in accordance with the provisions of this Convention, within 30 days from the time the State of export has been informed about the illegal traffic or such other period of time as States concerned may agree. To this end, the Parties concerned shall not oppose, hinder or prevent the return of those wastes to the State of export.

3. In the case of a transboundary movement of hazardous wastes or other wastes deemed to be illegal traffic as the result of conduct on the part of the importer or disposer, the State of import shall ensure that the wastes in question are disposed of in an environmentally sound manner by the importer or disposer or, if necessary, by itself within 30 days from the time the illegal traffic has come to the attention of the State of import or such other period of time as the States concerned may agree. To this end, the Parties concerned shall co-operate, as necessary, in the disposal of the wastes in an environmentally sound manner.

4. In cases where the responsibility for the illegal traffic cannot be assigned either to the exporter or generator or to the importer or disposer, the Parties concerned or other Parties, as appropriate, shall ensure, through co-operation, that the wastes in question are disposed of as soon as possible in an environmentally sound manner either in the State of export or the State of import or elsewhere as appropriate.

5. Each Party shall introduce appropriate national/domestic legislation to prevent and punish illegal traffic. The Parties shall co-operate with a view to achieving the objects of this Article.

Article 10: International co-operation

1. The Parties shall co-operate with each other in order to improve and achieve environmentally sound management of hazardous wastes and other wastes.

2. To this end, the Parties shall:

(a) Upon request, make available information, whether on a bilateral or multilateral basis, with a view to promoting the environmentally sound management of hazardous wastes and other wastes, including harmonization of technical standards and practices for the adequate management of hazardous wastes and other wastes;

(b) Co-operate in monitoring the effects of the management of hazardous wastes on human health and the environment;

(c) Co-operate, subject to their national laws, regulations and policies, in the development and implementation of new environmentally sound low-waste technologies and the improvement of existing technologies with a view to eliminating, as far as practicable, the generation of hazardous wastes and other wastes and achieving more effective and efficient methods of ensuring their management in an environmentally sound manner, including the study of the economic, social and environmental effects of the adoption of such new or improved technologies;

(d) Co-operate actively, subject to their national laws, regulations and policies, in the transfer of technology and management systems related to the environmentally sound management of hazardous wastes and other wastes. They shall also co-operate in developing the technical capacity among Parties, especially those which may need and request technical assistance in this field;

(e) Co-operate in developing appropriate technical guidelines and/or codes of practice.

3. The Parties shall employ appropriate means to co-operate in order to assist developing countries in the implementation of subparagraphs a, b, c and d of paragraph 2 of Article 4.

4. Taking into account the needs of developing countries, co-operation between Parties and the competent international organizations is encouraged to promote, inter alia, public awareness, the development of sound management of hazardous wastes and other wastes and the adoption of new low-waste technologies.

Article 11: Bilateral, multilateral and regional agreements

1. Notwithstanding the provisions of Article 4 paragraph 5, Parties may enter into bilateral, multilateral, or regional agreements or arrangements regarding transboundary movement of hazardous wastes or other wastes with Parties or non-Parties provided that such agreements or arrangements do not derogate from the environmentally sound management of hazardous wastes and other wastes as required by this Convention. These agreements or arrangements shall stipulate provisions which are not less environmentally sound than those provided for by this Convention in particular taking into account the interests of developing countries.

2. Parties shall notify the Secretariat of any bilateral, multilateral or regional agreements or arrangements referred to in paragraph 1 and those which they have entered into prior to the entry into force of this Convention for them, for the purpose of controlling transboundary movements of hazardous wastes and other wastes which take place entirely among the Parties to such agreements. The provisions of this Convention shall not affect transboundary movements which take place pursuant to such agreements provided that such agreements are compatible with the environmentally sound management of hazardous wastes and other wastes as required by this Convention.

Article 12: Consultations on liability

The Parties shall co-operate with a view to adopting, as soon as practicable, a protocol setting out appropriate rules and procedures in the field of liability and compensation for damage resulting from the transboundary movement and disposal of hazardous wastes and other wastes.

Article 13: Transmission of information

1. The Parties shall, whenever it comes to their knowledge, ensure that, in the case of an accident occurring during the transboundary movement of hazardous wastes or other wastes or their disposal, which are likely to present risks to human health and the environment in other States, those States are immediately informed.

2. The Parties shall inform each other, through the Secretariat, of:

(a) Changes regarding the designation of competent authorities and/or focal points, pursuant to Article 5;

(b) Changes in their national definition of hazardous wastes, pursuant to Article 3;

and, as soon as possible,

(c) Decisions made by them not to consent totally or partially to the import of hazardous wastes or other wastes for disposal within the area under their national jurisdiction;

(d) Decisions taken by them to limit or ban the export of hazardous wastes or other wastes;

(e) Any other information required pursuant to paragraph 4 of this Article.

3. The Parties, consistent with national laws and regulations, shall transmit, through the Secretariat, to the Conference of the Parties established under Article 15, before the end of each calendar year, a report on the previous calendar year, containing the following information:

(a) Competent authorities and focal points that have been designated by them pursuant to Article 5;

(b) Information regarding transboundary movements of hazardous wastes or other wastes in which they have been involved, including: (i) The amount of hazardous wastes and other wastes exported, their category, characteristics, destination, any transit country and disposal method as stated on the response to notification; (ii) The amount of hazardous wastes and other wastes imported, their category, characteristics, origin, and disposal methods; (iii) Disposals which did not proceed as intended; (iv) Efforts to achieve a reduction of the amount of hazardous wastes or other wastes subject to transboundary movement;

(c) Information on the measures adopted by them in implementation of this Convention;

(d) Information on available qualified statistics which have been compiled by them on the effects on human health and the environment of the generation, transportation and disposal of hazardous wastes or other wastes;

(e) Information concerning bilateral, multilateral and regional agreements and arrangements entered into pursuant to Article 11 of this Convention;

(f) Information on accidents occurring during the transboundary movement and disposal of hazardous wastes and other wastes and on the measures undertaken to deal with them;

(g) Information on disposal options operated within the area of their national jurisdiction;

(h) Information on measures undertaken for development of technologies for the reduction and/or elimination of production of hazardous wastes and other wastes; and

(i) Such other matters as the Conference of the Parties shall deem relevant.

4. The Parties, consistent with national laws and regulations, shall ensure that copies of each notification concerning any given transboundary movement of hazardous wastes or other wastes, and the response to it, are sent to the Secretariat when a Party considers that its environment may be affected by that transboundary movement has requested that this should be done.

Article 14: Financial aspects

1. The Parties agree that, according to the specific needs of different regions and subregions, regional or sub-regional centres for training and technology transfers regarding the management of hazardous wastes and other wastes and the minimization of their generation should be established. The Parties shall decide on the establishment of appropriate funding mechanisms of a voluntary nature.

2. The Parties shall consider the establishment of a revolving fund to assist on an interim basis in case of emergency situations to minimize damage from accidents arising from transboundary movements of hazardous wastes and other wastes or during the disposal of those wastes.

Article 15: Conference of the Parties

1. A Conference of the Parties is hereby established. The first meeting of the Conference of the Parties shall be convened by the Executive Director of UNEP not later than one year after the entry into force of this Convention. Thereafter, ordinary meetings of the Conference of the Parties shall be held at regular intervals to be determined by the Conference at its first meeting.

2. Extraordinary meetings of the Conference of the Parties shall be held at such other times as may be deemed necessary by the Conference, or at the written request of any Party, provided that, within six months of the request being communicated to them by the Secretariat, it is supported by at least one third of the Parties.

3. The Conference of the Parties shall by consensus agree upon and adopt rules of procedure for itself and for any subsidiary body it may establish, as well as financial rules to determine in particular the financial participation of the Parties under this Convention.

4. The Parties at their first meeting shall consider any additional measures needed to assist them in fulfilling their responsibilities with respect to the pro-

tection and the preservation of the marine environment in the context of this Convention.

5. The Conference of the Parties shall keep under continuous review and evaluation the effective implementation of this Convention, and, in addition, shall:

(a) Promote the harmonization of appropriate policies, strategies and measures for minimizing harm to human health and the environment by hazardous wastes and other wastes;

(b) Consider and adopt, as required, amendments to this Convention and its annexes, taking into consideration, inter alia, available scientific, technical, economic and environmental information;

(c) Consider and undertake any additional action that may be required for the achievement of the purposes of this Convention in the light of experience gained in its operation and in the operation of the agreements and arrangements envisaged in Article 11;

(d) Consider and adopt protocols as required; and

(e) Establish such subsidiary bodies as are deemed necessary for the implementation of this Convention.

6. The United Nations, its specialized agencies, as well as any State not Party to this Convention, may be represented as observers at meetings of the Conference of the Parties. Any other body or agency, whether national or international, governmental or non-governmental, qualified in fields relating to hazardous wastes or other wastes which has informed the Secretariat of its wish to be represented as an observer at a meeting of the Conference of the Parties, may be admitted unless at least one third of the Parties present object. The admission and participation of observers shall be subject to the rules of procedure adopted by the Conference of the Parties.

7. The Conference of the Parties shall undertake three years after the entry into force of this Convention, and at least every six years thereafter, an evaluation of its effectiveness and, if deemed necessary, to consider the adoption of a complete or partial ban of transboundary movements of hazardous wastes and other wastes in light of the latest scientific, environmental, technical and economic information.

Article 16: Secretariat

1. The functions of the Secretariat shall be:

(a) To arrange for and service meetings provided for in Articles 15 and 17;

(b) To prepare and transmit reports based upon information received in accordance with Articles 3, 4, 6, 11 and 13 as well as upon information derived from meetings of subsidiary bodies established under Article 15 as well as upon, as appropriate, information provided by relevant intergovernmental and non-governmental entities;

(c) To prepare reports on its activities carried out in implementation of its functions under this Convention and present them to the Conference of the Parties;

(d) To ensure the necessary coordination with relevant international bodies, and in particular to enter into such administrative and contractual arrangements as may be required for the effective discharge of its function;

(e) To communicate with focal points and competent authorities established by the Parties in accordance with Article 5 of this Convention;

(f) To compile information concerning authorized national sites and facilities of Parties available for the disposal of their hazardous wastes and other wastes and to circulate this information among Parties;

(g) To receive and convey information from and to Parties on:
- sources of technical assistance and training;
- available technical and scientific know-how;
- sources of advice and expertise; and
- availability of resources

with a view to assisting them, upon request, in such areas as:
- the handling of the notification system of this Convention;
- the management of hazardous wastes and other wastes;
- environmentally sound technologies relating to hazardous wastes and other wastes; such as low- and non-waste technology;
- the assessment of disposal capabilities and sites;
- the monitoring of hazardous wastes and other wastes; and
- emergency responses;

(h) To provide Parties, upon request, with information on consultants or consulting firms having the necessary technical competence in the field, which can assist them to examine a notification for a transboundary movement, the concurrence of a shipment of hazardous wastes or other wastes with the relevant notification, and/or the fact that the proposed disposal facilities for hazardous wastes or other wastes are environmentally sound, when they have reason to believe that the wastes in question will not be managed in an environmentally sound manner. Any such examination would not be at the expense of the Secretariat;

(i) To assist Parties upon request in their identification of cases of illegal traffic and to circulate immediately to the Parties concerned any information it has received regarding illegal traffic;

(j) To co-operate with Parties and with relevant and competent international organizations and agencies in the provision of experts and equipment for the purpose of rapid assistance to States in the event of an emergency situation; and

(k) To perform such other functions relevant to the purposes of this Convention as may be determined by the Conference of the Parties.

2. The secretariat functions will be carried out on an interim basis by UNEP until the completion of the first meeting of the Conference of the Parties held pursuant to Article 15.

3. At its first meeting, the Conference of the Parties shall designate the Secretariat from among those existing competent intergovernmental organizations which have signified their willingness to carry out the secretariat func-

tions under this Convention. At this meeting, the Conference of the Parties shall also evaluate the implementation by the interim Secretariat of the functions assigned to it, in particular under paragraph 1 above, and decide upon the structures appropriate for those functions.

Article 17: Amendment of the Convention

1. Any Party may propose amendments to this Convention and any Party to a protocol may propose amendments to that protocol. Such amendments shall take due account, inter alia, of relevant scientific and technical considerations.

2. Amendments to this Convention shall be adopted at a meeting of the Conference of the Parties. Amendments to any protocol shall be adopted at a meeting of the Parties to the protocol in question. The text of any proposed amendment to this Convention or to any protocol, except as may otherwise be provided in such protocol, shall be communicated to the Parties by the Secretariat at least six months before the meeting at which it is proposed for adoption. The Secretariat shall also communicate proposed amendments to the Signatories to this Convention for information.

3. The Parties shall make every effort to reach agreement on any proposed amendment to this Convention by consensus. If all efforts at consensus have been exhausted, and no agreement reached, the amendment shall as a last resort be adopted by a three-fourths majority vote of the Parties present and voting at the meeting, and shall be submitted by the Depositary to all Parties for ratification, approval, formal confirmation or acceptance.

4. The procedure mentioned in paragraph 3 above shall apply to amendments to any protocol, except that a two-thirds majority of the Parties to that protocol present and voting at the meeting shall suffice for their adoption.

5. Instruments of ratification, approval, formal confirmation or acceptance of amendments shall be deposited with the Depositary. Amendments adopted in accordance with paragraphs 3 or 4 above shall enter into force between Parties having accepted them on the ninetieth day after the receipt by the Depositary of their instrument of ratification, approval, formal confirmation or acceptance by at least three-fourths of the Parties who accepted them or by at least two thirds of the Parties to the protocol concerned who accepted them, except as may otherwise be provided in such protocol. The amendments shall enter into force for any other Party on the ninetieth day after that Party deposits its instrument of ratification, approval, formal confirmation or acceptance of the amendments.

6. For the purpose of this Article, "Parties present and voting" means Parties present and casting an affirmative or negative vote.

Article 18: Adoption and amendment of annexes

1. The annexes to this Convention or to any protocol shall form an integral part of this Convention or of such protocol, as the case may be and, unless expressly provided otherwise, a reference to this Convention or its protocols

constitutes at the same time a reference to any annexes thereto. Such annexes shall be restricted to scientific, technical and administrative matters.

2. Except as may be otherwise provided in any protocol with respect to its annexes, the following procedure shall apply to the proposal, adoption and entry into force of additional annexes to this Convention or of annexes to a protocol:

(a) Annexes to this Convention and its protocols shall be proposed and adopted according to the procedure laid down in Article 17, paragraphs 2, 3 and 4;

(b) Any Party that is unable to accept an additional annex to this Convention or an annex to any protocol to which it is party shall so notify the Depositary, in writing, within six months from the date of the communication of the adoption by the Depositary. The Depositary shall without delay notify all Parties of any such notification received. A Party may at any time substitute an acceptance for a previous declaration of objection and the annexes shall thereupon enter into force for that Party;

(c) On the expiry of six months from the date of the circulation of the communication by the Depositary, the annex shall become effective for all Parties to this Convention or to any protocol concerned, which have not submitted a notification in accordance with the provision of subparagraph (b) above.

3. The proposal, adoption and entry into force of amendments to annexes to this Convention or to any protocol shall be subject to the same procedure as for the proposal, adoption and entry into force of annexes to the Convention or annexes to a protocol. Annexes and amendments thereto shall take due account, inter alia, of relevant scientific and technical considerations.

4. If an additional annex or an amendment to an annex involves an amendment to this Convention or to any protocol, the additional annex or amended annex shall not enter into force until such time the amendment to this Convention or to the protocol enters into force.

Article 19: Verification
Any Party which has reason to believe that another Party is acting or has acted in breach of its obligations under this Convention may inform the Secretariat thereof, and in such an event, shall simultaneously and immediately inform, directly or through the Secretariat, the Party against whom the allegations are made. All relevant information should be submitted by the Secretariat to the Parties.

Article 20: Settlement of disputes
1. In case of a dispute between Parties as to the interpretation or application of, or compliance with, this Convention or any protocol thereto, they shall seek a settlement of the dispute through negotiation or any other peaceful means of their own choice.

2. If the Parties concerned cannot settle their dispute through the means

mentioned in the preceding paragraph, the dispute, if the Parties to the dispute agree, shall be submitted to the International Court of Justice or to arbitration under the conditions set out in Annex VI on Arbitration. However, failure to reach common agreement on submission of the dispute to the International Court of Justice or to arbitration shall not absolve the Parties from the responsibility of continuing to seek to resolve it by the means referred to in paragraph 1.

3. When ratifying, accepting, approving, formally confirming or acceding to this Convention, or at any time thereafter, a State or political and/or economic integration organization may declare that it recognizes as compulsory ipso facto and without special agreement, in relation to any Party accepting the same obligation:

(a) submission of the dispute to the International Court of Justice; and/or

(b) arbitration in accordance with the procedures set out in Annex VI.

Such declaration shall be notified in writing to the Secretariat which shall communicate it to the Parties.

Article 21: Signature

This Convention shall be open for signature by States, by Namibia, represented by the United Nations Council for Namibia, and by political and/or economic integration organizations, in Basel on 22 March 1989, at the Federal Department of Foreign Affairs of Switzerland in Berne from 23 March 1989 to 30 June 1989 and at United Nations Headquarters in New York from 1 July 1989 to 22 March 1990.

Article 22: Ratification, acceptance, formal confirmation or approval

1. This Convention shall be subject to ratification, acceptance or approval by States and by Namibia, represented by the United Nations Council for Namibia, and to formal confirmation or approval by political and/or economic integration organizations. Instruments of ratification, acceptance, formal confirmation, or approval shall be deposited with the Depositary.

2. Any organization referred to in paragraph 1 above which becomes a Party to this Convention without any of its member States being a Party shall be bound by all the obligations under the Convention. In the case of such organizations, one or more of whose member States is a Party to the Convention, the organization and its member States shall decide on their respective responsibilities for the performance of their obligations under the Convention. In such cases, the organization and the member States shall not be entitled to exercise rights under the Convention concurrently.

3. In their instruments of formal confirmation or approval, the organizations referred to in paragraph 1 above shall declare the extent of their competence with respect to the matters governed by the Convention. These organizations shall also inform the Depositary, who will inform the Parties of any substantial modification in the extent of their competence.

Article 23: Accession

1. This Convention shall be open for accession by States, by Namibia, represented by the United Nations Council for Namibia, and by political and/or economic integration organizations from the day after the date on which the Convention is closed for signature. The instruments of accession shall be deposited with the Depositary.

2. In their instruments of accession, the organizations referred to in paragraph 1 above shall declare the extent of their competence with respect to the matters governed by the Convention. These organizations shall also inform the Depositary of any substantial modification in the extent of their competence.

3. The provisions of Article 22, paragraph 2, shall apply to political and/or economic integration organizations which accede to this Convention.

Article 24: Right to vote

1. Except as provided for in paragraph 2 below, each Contracting Party to this Convention shall have one vote.

2. Political and/or economic integration organizations, in matters within their competence, in accordance with Article 22, paragraph 3, and Article 23, paragraph 2, shall exercise their right to vote with a number of votes equal to the number of their member States which are Parties to the Convention or the relevant protocol. Such organizations shall not exercise their right to vote if their member States exercise theirs, and vice versa.

Article 25: Entry into force

1. This Convention shall enter into force on the ninetieth day after the date of deposit of the twentieth instrument of ratification, acceptance, formal confirmation, approval or accession.

2. For each State or political and/or economic integration organization which ratifies, accepts, approves or formally confirms this Convention or accedes thereto after the date of the deposit of the twentieth instrument of ratification, acceptance, approval, formal confirmation or accession, it shall enter into force on the ninetieth day after the date of deposit by such State or political and/or economic integration organization of its instrument of ratification, acceptance, approval, formal confirmation or accession.

3. For the purpose of paragraphs 1 and 2 above, any instrument deposited by a political and/or economic integration organization shall not be counted as additional to those deposited by member States of such organization.

Article 26: Reservations and declarations

1. No reservation or exception may be made to this Convention.

2. Paragraph 1 of this Article does not preclude a State or political and/or economic integration organization, when signing, ratifying, accepting, approving, formally confirming or acceding to this Convention, from making declarations or statements, however phrased or named, with a view, inter alia, to the harmonization of its laws and regulations with the provisions of this

Convention, provided that such declarations or statements do not purport to exclude or to modify the legal effects of the provisions of the Convention in their application to that State.

Article 27: Withdrawal

1. At any time after three years from the date on which this Convention has entered into force for a Party, that Party may withdraw from the Convention by giving written notification to the Depositary.

2. Withdrawal shall be effective one year from receipt of notification by the Depositary, or on such later date as may be specified in the notification.

Article 28: Depository

The Secretary-General of the United Nations shall be the Depository of this Convention and of any protocol thereto.

Article 29: Authentic texts

The original Arabic, Chinese, English, French, Russian and Spanish texts of this Convention are equally authentic.

IN WITNESS WHEREOF the undersigned, being duly authorized to that effect, have signed this Convention.

Done at Basel on the 22 day of March 1989.

. . . [Annexes not included]

7.2
United Nations Framework Convention on Climate Change (UNFCCC) (1991)

Encouraged by the success of efforts to address ozone depletion, this treaty was negotiated in a little over two years and opened for signature at the UN Conference on Environment and Development in 1991. The Third Conference of the Parties to the UNFCCC negotiated the Kyoto Protocol.

On the relationship of the climate change and the ozone depleting regimes, see Sebastian Oberthür, "Linkages Between the Montreal and Kyoto Protocols: Enhancing Synergies Between Protecting the Ozone Layer and the Global Climate," International Environmental Agreements *1 (2001): 357–377. On the negotiation of the UNFCCC, see Irving M. Mintzer and J. Amber Leonard, eds.,* Negotiating Climate Change: The Inside Story of the Rio Convention *(Cambridge: Cambridge University Press, 1994); and Mostafa K. Tolba, former executive director of the United Nations Environment Programme,* Global Environmental Diplomacy: Negotiating Environment Agreements for the World, 1973–1992 *(Cambridge, Mass.: MIT, 1998). See also Farhana Yamin and Joanna Depledge,* The International Climate Change Regime: A Guide to Rules, Institutions, and Procedures *(Cambridge: Cambridge University Press, 2004). The UNFCCC has a website at www.unfccc.int.*

The Parties to this Convention,

Acknowledging that change in the Earth's climate and its adverse effects are a common concern of humankind,

Concerned that human activities have been substantially increasing the atmospheric concentrations of greenhouse gases, that these increases enhance the natural greenhouse effect, and that this will result on average in an additional warming of the Earth's surface and atmosphere and may adversely affect natural ecosystems and humankind,

Noting that the largest share of historical and current global emissions of greenhouse gases has originated in developed countries, that per capita emissions in developing countries are still relatively low and that the share of global emissions originating in developing countries will grow to meet their social and development needs,

Aware of the role and importance in terrestrial and marine ecosystems of sinks and reservoirs of greenhouse gases,

Noting that there are many uncertainties in predictions of climate change, particularly with regard to the timing, magnitude and regional patterns thereof,

Acknowledging that the global nature of climate change calls for the widest possible cooperation by all countries and their participation in an effective and appropriate international response, in accordance with their common but differentiated responsibilities and respective capabilities and their social and economic conditions,

Recalling the pertinent provisions of the Declaration of the United Nations Conference on the Human Environment, adopted at Stockholm on 16 June 1972,

Recalling also that States have, in accordance with the Charter of the United Nations and the principles of international law, the sovereign right to exploit their own resources pursuant to their own environmental and developmental policies, and the responsibility to ensure that activities within their jurisdiction or control do not cause damage to the environment of other States or of areas beyond the limits of national jurisdiction,

Reaffirming the principle of sovereignty of States in international cooperation to address climate change,

Recognizing that States should enact effective environmental legislation, that environmental standards, management objectives and priorities should reflect the environmental and developmental context to which they apply, and that standards applied by some countries may be inappropriate and of unwarranted economic and social cost to other countries, in particular developing countries,

Recalling the provisions of General Assembly resolution 44/228 of 22 December 1989 on the United Nations Conference on Environment and Development, and resolutions 43/53 of 6 December 1988, 44/207 of 22 December 1989, 45/212 of 21 December 1990 and 46/169 of 19 December 1991 on protection of global climate for present and future generations of mankind,

Recalling also the provisions of General Assembly resolution 44/206 of 22 December 1989 on the possible adverse effects of sea level rise on islands and coastal areas, particularly low-lying coastal areas and the pertinent provisions of General Assembly resolution 44/172 of 19 December 1989 on the implementation of the Plan of Action to Combat Desertification,

Recalling further the Vienna Convention for the Protection of the Ozone Layer, 1985, and the Montreal Protocol on Substances that Deplete the Ozone Layer, 1987, as adjusted and amended on 29 June 1990,

Noting the Ministerial Declaration of the Second World Climate Conference adopted on 7 November 1990,

Conscious of the valuable analytical work being conducted by many States on climate change and of the important contributions of the World Meteorological Organization, the United Nations Environment Programme and other organs, organizations and bodies of the United Nations system, as well as other international and intergovernmental bodies, to the exchange of results of scientific research and the coordination of research,

Recognizing that steps required to understand and address climate change will be environmentally, socially and economically most effective if they are based on relevant scientific, technical and economic considerations and continually re-evaluated in the light of new findings in these areas,

Recognizing that various actions to address climate change can be justified economically in their own right and can also help in solving other environmental problems,

Recognizing also the need for developed countries to take immediate action in a flexible manner on the basis of clear priorities, as a first step towards comprehensive response strategies at the global, national and, where agreed, regional levels that take into account all greenhouse gases, with due consideration of their relative contributions to the enhancement of the greenhouse effect,

Recognizing further that low-lying and other small island countries, countries with low-lying coastal, arid and semi-arid areas or areas liable to floods, drought and desertification, and developing countries with fragile mountainous ecosystems are particularly vulnerable to the adverse effects of climate change,

Recognizing the special difficulties of those countries, especially developing countries, whose economies are particularly dependent on fossil fuel production, use and exportation, as a consequence of action taken on limiting greenhouse gas emissions,

Affirming that responses to climate change should be coordinated with social and economic development in an integrated manner with a view to avoiding adverse impacts on the latter, taking into full account the legitimate priority needs of developing countries for the achievement of sustained economic growth and the eradication of poverty,

Recognizing that all countries, especially developing countries, need access to resources required to achieve sustainable social and economic development and that, in order for developing countries to progress towards that goal, their energy consumption will need to grow taking into account the possibilities for achieving greater energy efficiency and for controlling greenhouse gas emissions in general, including through the application of new technologies on terms which make such an application economically and socially beneficial,

Determined to protect the climate system for present and future generations,

Have agreed as follows:

Article 1

For the purposes of this Convention:

1. "Adverse effects of climate change" means changes in the physical environment or biota resulting from climate change which have significant deleterious effects on the composition, resilience or productivity of natural and man-

aged ecosystems or on the operation of socio-economic systems or on human health and welfare.

2. "Climate change" means a change of climate which is attributed directly or indirectly to human activity that alters the composition of the global atmosphere and which is in addition to natural climate variability observed over comparable time periods.

3. "Climate system" means the totality of the atmosphere, hydrosphere, biosphere and geosphere and their interactions.

4. "Emissions" means the release of greenhouse gases and/or their precursors into the atmosphere over a specified area and period of time.

5. "Greenhouse gases" means those gaseous constituents of the atmosphere, both natural and anthropogenic, that absorb and re-emit infrared radiation.

6. "Regional economic integration organization" means an organization constituted by sovereign States of a given region which has competence in respect of matters governed by this Convention or its protocols and has been duly authorized, in accordance with its internal procedures, to sign, ratify, accept, approve or accede to the instruments concerned.

7. "Reservoir" means a component or components of the climate system where a greenhouse gas or a precursor of a greenhouse gas is stored.

8. "Sink" means any process, activity or mechanism which removes a greenhouse gas, an aerosol or a precursor of a greenhouse gas from the atmosphere.

9. "Source" means any process or activity which releases a greenhouse gas, an aerosol or a precursor of a greenhouse gas into the atmosphere.

Article 2

The ultimate objective of this Convention and any related legal instruments that the Conference of the Parties may adopt is to achieve, in accordance with the relevant provisions of the Convention, stabilization of greenhouse gas concentrations in the atmosphere at a level that would prevent dangerous anthropogenic interference with the climate system. Such a level should be achieved within a time frame sufficient to allow ecosystems to adapt naturally to climate change, to ensure that food production is not threatened and to enable economic development to proceed in a sustainable manner.

Article 3

In their actions to achieve the objective of the Convention and to implement its provisions, the Parties shall be guided, inter alia, by the following:

1. The Parties should protect the climate system for the benefit of present and future generations of humankind, on the basis of equity and in accordance with their common but differentiated responsibilities and respective capabilities. Accordingly, the developed country Parties should take the lead in combating climate change and the adverse effects thereof.

2. The specific needs and special circumstances of developing country Parties, especially those that are particularly vulnerable to the adverse effects

of climate change, and of those Parties, especially developing country Parties, that would have to bear a disproportionate or abnormal burden under the Convention, should be given full consideration.

3. The Parties should take precautionary measures to anticipate, prevent or minimize the causes of climate change and mitigate its adverse effects. Where there are threats of serious or irreversible damage, lack of full scientific certainty should not be used as a reason for postponing such measures, taking into account that policies and measures to deal with climate change should be cost-effective so as to ensure global benefits at the lowest possible cost. To achieve this, such policies and measures should take into account different socio-economic contexts, be comprehensive, cover all relevant sources, sinks and reservoirs of greenhouse gases and adaptation, and comprise all economic sectors. Efforts to address climate change may be carried out cooperatively by interested Parties.

4. The Parties have a right to, and should, promote sustainable development. Policies and measures to protect the climate system against human-induced change should be appropriate for the specific conditions of each Party and should be integrated with national development programmes, taking into account that economic development is essential for adopting measures to address climate change.

5. The Parties should cooperate to promote a supportive and open international economic system that would lead to sustainable economic growth and development in all Parties, particularly developing country Parties, thus enabling them better to address the problems of climate change. Measures taken to combat climate change, including unilateral ones, should not constitute a means of arbitrary or unjustifiable discrimination or a disguised restriction on international trade.

Article 4

1. All Parties, taking into account their common but differentiated responsibilities and their specific national and regional development priorities, objectives and circumstances, shall:

(a) Develop, periodically update, publish and make available to the Conference of the Parties, in accordance with Article 12, national inventories of anthropogenic emissions by sources and removals by sinks of all greenhouse gases not controlled by the Montreal Protocol, using comparable methodologies to be agreed upon by the Conference of the Parties;

(b) Formulate, implement, publish and regularly update national and, where appropriate, regional programmes containing measures to mitigate climate change by addressing anthropogenic emissions by sources and removals by sinks of all greenhouse gases not controlled by the Montreal Protocol, and measures to facilitate adequate adaptation to climate change;

(c) Promote and cooperate in the development, application and diffusion, including transfer, of technologies, practices and processes that control, reduce or prevent anthropogenic emissions of greenhouse gases not controlled by the

Montreal Protocol in all relevant sectors, including the energy, transport, industry, agriculture, forestry and waste management sectors;

(d) Promote sustainable management, and promote and cooperate in the conservation and enhancement, as appropriate, of sinks and reservoirs of all greenhouse gases not controlled by the Montreal Protocol, including biomass, forests and oceans as well as other terrestrial, coastal and marine ecosystems;

(e) Cooperate in preparing for adaptation to the impacts of climate change; develop and elaborate appropriate and integrated plans for coastal zone management, water resources and agriculture, and for the protection and rehabilitation of areas, particularly in Africa, affected by drought and desertification, as well as floods;

(f) Take climate change considerations into account, to the extent feasible, in their relevant social, economic and environmental policies and actions, and employ appropriate methods, for example impact assessments, formulated and determined nationally, with a view to minimizing adverse effects on the economy, on public health and on the quality of the environment, of projects or measures undertaken by them to mitigate or adapt to climate change;

(g) Promote and cooperate in scientific, technological, technical, socio-economic and other research, systematic observation and development of data archives related to the climate system and intended to further the understanding and to reduce or eliminate the remaining uncertainties regarding the causes, effects, magnitude and timing of climate change and the economic and social consequences of various response strategies;

(h) Promote and cooperate in the full, open and prompt exchange of relevant scientific, technological, technical, socio-economic and legal information related to the climate system and climate change, and to the economic and social consequences of various response strategies;

(i) Promote and cooperate in education, training and public awareness related to climate change and encourage the widest participation in this process, including that of non-governmental organizations; and

(j) Communicate to the Conference of the Parties information related to implementation, in accordance with Article 12.

2. The developed country Parties and other Parties included in annex I commit themselves specifically as provided for in the following:

(a) Each of these Parties shall adopt national policies and take corresponding measures on the mitigation of climate change, by limiting its anthropogenic emissions of greenhouse gases and protecting and enhancing its greenhouse gas sinks and reservoirs. These policies and measures will demonstrate that developed countries are taking the lead in modifying longer-term trends in anthropogenic emissions consistent with the objective of the Convention, recognizing that the return by the end of the present decade to earlier levels of anthropogenic emissions of carbon dioxide and other greenhouse gases not controlled by the Montreal Protocol would contribute to such modification, and taking into account the differences in these Parties' starting points and approaches, economic structures and resource bases, the need to maintain strong and sustainable economic growth, available technologies and other individual circumstances, as well as the need for equitable and appropriate contributions by each of these Parties to the global effort regarding that objective. These Parties may implement such policies and measures jointly with other Parties and may assist other Parties in contributing to the achievement of the objective of the Convention and, in particular, that of this subparagraph;

(b) In order to promote progress to this end, each of these Parties shall communicate, within six months of the entry into force of the Convention for it and periodically thereafter, and in accordance with Article 12, detailed information on its policies and measures referred to in subparagraph (a) above, as well as on its resulting projected anthropogenic emissions by sources and removals by sinks of greenhouse gases not controlled by the Montreal Protocol for the period referred to in subparagraph (a), with the aim of returning individually or jointly to their 1990 levels these anthropogenic emissions of carbon dioxide and other greenhouse gases not controlled by the Montreal Protocol. This information will be reviewed by the Conference of the Parties, at its first session and periodically thereafter, in accordance with Article 7;

(c) Calculations of emissions by sources and removals by sinks of greenhouse gases for the purposes of subparagraph (b) above should take into account the best available scientific knowledge, including of the effective capacity of sinks and the respective contributions of such gases to climate change. The Conference of the Parties shall consider and agree on methodologies for these calculations at its first session and review them regularly thereafter;

(d) The Conference of the Parties shall, at its first session, review the adequacy of subparagraphs (a) and (b) above. Such review shall be carried out in the light of the best available scientific information and assessment on climate change and its impacts, as well as relevant technical, social and economic information. Based on this review, the Conference of the Parties shall take appropriate action, which may include the adoption of amendments to the commitments in subparagraphs (a) and (b) above. The Conference of the Parties, at its first session, shall also take decisions regarding criteria for joint implementation as indicated in subparagraph (a) above. A second review of subparagraphs (a) and (b) shall take place not later than 31 December 1998, and thereafter at regular intervals determined by the Conference of the Parties, until the objective of the Convention is met;

(e) Each of these Parties shall: (i) coordinate as appropriate with other such Parties, relevant economic and administrative instruments developed to achieve the objective of the Convention; and (ii) identify and periodically review its own policies and practices which encourage activities that lead to greater levels of anthropogenic emissions of greenhouse gases not controlled by the Montreal Protocol than would otherwise occur;

(f) The Conference of the Parties shall review, not later than 31 December 1998, available information with a view to taking decisions regarding such amendments to the lists in annexes I and II as may be appropriate, with the approval of the Party concerned;

(g) Any Party not included in Annex I may, in its instrument of ratification, acceptance, approval or accession, or at any time thereafter, notify the Depositary that it intends to be bound by subparagraphs (a) and (b) above. The Depositary shall inform the other signatories and Parties of any such notification.

3. The developed country Parties and other developed Parties included in annex II shall provide new and additional financial resources to meet the agreed full costs incurred by developing country Parties in complying with their obligations under Article 12, paragraph 1. They shall also provide such financial resources, including for the transfer of technology, needed by the developing country Parties to meet the agreed full incremental costs of implementing measures that are covered by paragraph 1 of this Article and that are agreed between a developing country Party and the international entity or entities referred to in Article 11, in accordance with that Article. The implementation of these commitments shall take into account the need for adequacy and predictability in the flow of funds and the importance of appropriate burden sharing among the developed country Parties.

4. The developed country Parties and other developed Parties included in annex II shall also assist the developing country Parties that are particularly vulnerable to the adverse effects of climate change in meeting costs of adaptation to those adverse effects.

5. The developed country Parties and other developed Parties included in annex II shall take all practicable steps to promote, facilitate and finance, as appropriate, the transfer of, or access to, environmentally sound technologies and know-how to other Parties, particularly developing country Parties, to enable them to implement the provisions of the Convention. In this process, the developed country Parties shall support the development and enhancement of endogenous capacities and technologies of developing country Parties. Other Parties and organizations in a position to do so may also assist in facilitating the transfer of such technologies.

6. In the implementation of their commitments under paragraph 2 above, a certain degree of flexibility shall be allowed by the Conference of the Parties to the Parties included in annex I undergoing the process of transition to a market economy, in order to enhance the ability of these Parties to address climate change, including with regard to the historical level of anthropogenic emissions of greenhouse gases not controlled by the Montreal Protocol chosen as a reference.

7. The extent to which developing country Parties will effectively implement their commitments under the Convention will depend on the effective implementation by developed country Parties of their commitments under the Convention related to financial resources and transfer of technology and will take fully into account that economic and social development and poverty eradication are the first and overriding priorities of the developing country Parties.

8. In the implementation of the commitments in this Article, the Parties

shall give full consideration to what actions are necessary under the Convention, including actions related to funding, insurance and the transfer of technology, to meet the specific needs and concerns of developing country Parties arising from the adverse effects of climate change and/or the impact of the implementation of response measures, especially on:

(a) Small island countries;

(b) Countries with low-lying coastal areas;

(c) Countries with arid and semi-arid areas, forested areas and areas liable to forest decay;

(d) Countries with areas prone to natural disasters;

(e) Countries with areas liable to drought and desertification;

(f) Countries with areas of high urban atmospheric pollution;

(g) Countries with areas with fragile ecosystems, including mountainous ecosystems;

(h) Countries whose economies are highly dependent on income generated from the production, processing and export, and/or on consumption of fossil fuels and associated energy-intensive products; and

(i) Land-locked and transit countries.

Further, the Conference of the Parties may take actions, as appropriate, with respect to this paragraph.

9. The Parties shall take full account of the specific needs and special situations of the least developed countries in their actions with regard to funding and transfer of technology.

10. The Parties shall, in accordance with Article 10 take into consideration in the implementation of the commitments of the Convention the situation of Parties, particularly developing country Parties, with economies that are vulnerable to the adverse effects of the implementation of measures to respond to climate change. This applies notably to Parties with economies that are highly dependent on income generated from the production, processing and export, and/or consumption of fossil fuels and associated energy-intensive products and/or the use of fossil fuels for which such Parties have serious difficulties in switching to alternatives.

Article 5

In carrying out their commitments under Article 4, paragraph 1 (g), the Parties shall:

(a) Support and further develop, as appropriate, international and intergovernmental programmes and networks or organizations aimed at defining, conducting, assessing and financing research, data collection and systematic observation, taking into account the need to minimize duplication of effort;

(b) Support international and intergovernmental efforts to strengthen systematic observation and national scientific and technical research capacities and capabilities, particularly in developing countries, and to promote access to, and the exchange of, data and analyses thereof obtained from areas beyond national jurisdiction; and

(c) Take into account the particular concerns and needs of developing countries and cooperate in improving their endogenous capacities and capabilities to participate in the efforts referred to in subparagraphs (a) and (b) above.

Article 6

In carrying out their commitments under Article 4, paragraph 1 (i), the Parties shall:

(a) Promote and facilitate at the national and, as appropriate, subregional and regional levels, and in accordance with national laws and regulations, and within their respective capacities: (i) the development and implementation of educational and public awareness programmes on climate change and its effects; (ii) public access to information on climate change and its effects; (iii) public participation in addressing climate change and its effects and developing adequate responses; and (iv) training of scientific, technical and managerial personnel.

(b) Cooperate in and promote, at the international level, and, where appropriate, using existing bodies: (i) the development and exchange of educational and public awareness material on climate change and its effects; and (ii) the development and implementation of education and training programmes, including the strengthening of national institutions and the exchange or secondment of personnel to train experts in this field, in particular for developing countries.

Article 7

1. A Conference of the Parties is hereby established.

2. The Conference of the Parties, as the supreme body of this Convention, shall keep under regular review the implementation of the Convention and any related legal instruments that the Conference of the Parties may adopt, and shall make, within its mandate, the decisions necessary to promote the effective implementation of the Convention. To this end, it shall:

(a) Periodically examine the obligations of the Parties and the institutional arrangements under the Convention, in the light of the objective of the Convention, the experience gained in its implementation and the evolution of scientific and technological knowledge;

(b) Promote and facilitate the exchange of information on measures adopted by the Parties to address climate change and its effects, taking into account the differing circumstances, responsibilities and capabilities of the Parties and their respective commitments under the Convention;

(c) Facilitate, at the request of two or more Parties, the coordination of measures adopted by them to address climate change and its effects, taking into account the differing circumstances, responsibilities and capabilities of the Parties and their respective commitments under the Convention.

(d) Promote and guide, in accordance with the objective and provisions of the Convention, the development and periodic refinement of comparable methodologies, to be agreed on by the Conference of the Parties, inter alia, for preparing inventories of greenhouse gas emissions by sources and removals by sinks, and for evaluating the effectiveness of measures to limit the emissions and enhance the removals of these gases;

(e) Assess, on the basis of all information made available to it in accordance with the provisions of the Convention, the implementation of the Convention by the Parties, the overall effects of the measures taken pursuant to the Convention, in particular environmental, economic and social effects as well as their cumulative impacts and the extent to which progress towards the objective of the Convention is being achieved;

(f) Consider and adopt regular reports on the implementation of the Convention and ensure their publication;

(g) Make recommendations on any matters necessary for the implementation of the Convention;

(h) Seek to mobilize financial resources in accordance with Article 4, paragraphs 3, 4 and 5, and Article 11;

(i) Establish such subsidiary bodies as are deemed necessary for the implementation of the Convention;

(j) Review reports submitted by its subsidiary bodies and provide guidance to them;

(k) Agree upon and adopt, by consensus, rules of procedure and financial rules for itself and for any subsidiary bodies;

(l) Seek and utilize, where appropriate, the services and cooperation of, and information provided by, competent international organizations and intergovernmental and non-governmental bodies; and

(m) Exercise such other functions as are required for the achievement of the objective of the Convention as well as all other functions assigned to it under the Convention.

3. The Conference of the Parties shall, at its first session, adopt its own rules of procedure as well as those of the subsidiary bodies established by the Convention, which shall include decision-making procedures for matters not already covered by decision-making procedures stipulated in the Convention. Such procedures may include specified majorities required for the adoption of particular decisions.

4. The first session of the Conference of the Parties shall be convened by the interim secretariat referred to in Article 21 and shall take place not later than one year after the date of entry into force of the Convention. Thereafter, ordinary sessions of the Conference of the Parties shall be held every year unless otherwise decided by the Conference of the Parties.

5. Extraordinary sessions of the Conference of the Parties shall be held at such other times as may be deemed necessary by the Conference, or at the written request of any Party, provided that, within six months of the request being communicated to the Parties by the secretariat, it is supported by at least one-third of the Parties.

6. The United Nations, its specialized agencies and the International Atomic Energy Agency, as well as any State member thereof or observers thereto not Party to the Convention, may be represented at sessions of the Conference of

the Parties as observers. Any body or agency, whether national or international, governmental or non-governmental, which is qualified in matters covered by the Convention, and which has informed the secretariat of its wish to be represented at a session of the Conference of the Parties as an observer, may be so admitted unless at least one-third of the Parties present object. The admission and participation of observers shall be subject to the rules of procedure adopted by the Conference of the Parties.

Article 8

1. A secretariat is hereby established.

2. The functions of the secretariat shall be:

(a) To make arrangements for sessions of the Conference of the Parties and its subsidiary bodies established under the Convention and to provide them with services as required;

(b) To compile and transmit reports submitted to it;

(c) To facilitate assistance to the Parties, particularly developing country Parties, on request, in the compilation and communication of information required in accordance with the provisions of the Convention;

(d) To prepare reports on its activities and present them to the Conference of the Parties;

(e) To ensure the necessary coordination with the secretariats of other relevant international bodies;

(f) To enter, under the overall guidance of the Conference of the Parties, into such administrative and contractual arrangements as may be required for the effective discharge of its functions; and

(g) To perform the other secretariat functions specified in the Convention and in any of its protocols and such other functions as may be determined by the Conference of the Parties.

3. The Conference of the Parties, at its first session, shall designate a permanent secretariat and make arrangements for its functioning.

Article 9

1. A subsidiary body for scientific and technological advice is hereby established to provide the Conference of the Parties and, as appropriate, its other subsidiary bodies with timely information and advice on scientific and technological matters relating to the Convention. This body shall be open to participation by all Parties and shall be multidisciplinary. It shall comprise government representatives competent in the relevant field of expertise. It shall report regularly to the Conference of the Parties on all aspects of its work.

2. Under the guidance of the Conference of the Parties, and drawing upon existing competent international bodies, this body shall:

(a) Provide assessments of the state of scientific knowledge relating to climate change and its effects;

(b) Prepare scientific assessments on the effects of measures taken in the implementation of the Convention;

(c) Identify innovative, efficient and state-of-the-art technologies and know-how and advise on the ways and means of promoting development and/or transferring such technologies;

(d) Provide advice on scientific programmes, international cooperation in research and development related to climate change, as well as on ways and means of supporting endogenous capacity-building in developing countries; and

(e) Respond to scientific, technological and methodological questions that the Conference of the Parties and its subsidiary bodies may put to the body.

3. The functions and terms of reference of this body may be further elaborated by the Conference of the Parties.

Article 10

1. A subsidiary body for implementation is hereby established to assist the Conference of the Parties in the assessment and review of the effective implementation of the Convention. This body shall be open to participation by all Parties and comprise government representatives who are experts on matters related to climate change. It shall report regularly to the Conference of the Parties on all aspects of its work.

2. Under the guidance of the Conference of the Parties, this body shall:

(a) Consider the information communicated in accordance with Article 12, paragraph 1, to assess the overall aggregated effect of the steps taken by the Parties in the light of the latest scientific assessments concerning climate change;

(b) Consider the information communicated in accordance with Article 12, paragraph 2, in order to assist the Conference of the Parties in carrying out the reviews required by Article 4, paragraph 2(d); and

(c) Assist the Conference of the Parties, as appropriate, in the preparation and implementation of its decisions.

Article 11

1. A mechanism for the provision of financial resources on a grant or concessional basis, including for the transfer of technology, is hereby defined. It shall function under the guidance of and be accountable to the Conference of the Parties, which shall decide on its policies, programme priorities and eligibility criteria related to this Convention. Its operation shall be entrusted to one or more existing international entities.

2. The financial mechanism shall have an equitable and balanced representation of all Parties within a transparent system of governance.

3. The Conference of the Parties and the entity or entities entrusted with the operation of the financial mechanism shall agree upon arrangements to give effect to the above paragraphs, which shall include the following:

(a) Modalities to ensure that the funded projects to address climate change are in conformity with the policies, programme priorities and eligibility criteria established by the Conference of the Parties;

(b) Modalities by which a particular funding decision may be reconsidered in light of these policies, programme priorities and eligibility criteria;

(c) Provision by the entity or entities of regular reports to the Conference of the Parties on its funding operations, which is consistent with the requirement for accountability set out in paragraph 1 above; and

(d) Determination in a predictable and identifiable manner of the amount of funding necessary and available for the implementation of this Convention and the conditions under which that amount shall be periodically reviewed.

4. The Conference of the Parties shall make arrangements to implement the above mentioned provisions at its first session, reviewing and taking into account the interim arrangements referred to in Article 21, paragraph 3, and shall decide whether these interim arrangements shall be maintained. Within four years thereafter, the Conference of the Parties shall review the financial mechanism and take appropriate measures.

5. The developed country Parties may also provide and developing country Parties avail themselves of, financial resources related to the implementation of the Convention through bilateral, regional and other multilateral channels.

Article 12

1. In accordance with Article 4, paragraph 1, each Party shall communicate to the Conference of the Parties, through the secretariat, the following elements of information:

(a) A national inventory of anthropogenic emissions by sources and removals by sinks of all greenhouse gases not controlled by the Montreal Protocol, to the extent its capacities permit, using comparable methodologies to be promoted and agreed upon by the Conference of the Parties;

(b) A general description of steps taken or envisaged by the Party to implement the Convention; and

(c) Any other information that the Party considers relevant to the achievement of the objective of the Convention and suitable for inclusion in its communication, including, if feasible, material relevant for calculations of global emission trends.

2. Each developed country Party and each other Party included in annex I shall incorporate in its communication the following elements of information:

(a) A detailed description of the policies and measures that it has adopted to implement its commitment under Article 4, paragraphs 2(a) and 2(b); and

(b) A specific estimate of the effects that the policies and measures referred to in subparagraph (a) immediately above will have on anthropogenic emissions by its sources and removals by its sinks of greenhouse gases during the period referred to in Article 4, paragraph 2(a).

3. In addition, each developed country Party and each other developed Party included in annex II shall incorporate details of measures taken in accordance with Article 4, paragraphs 3, 4 and 5.

4. Developing country Parties may, on a voluntary basis, propose projects

for financing, including specific technologies, materials, equipment, techniques or practices that would be needed to implement such projects, along with, if possible, an estimate of all incremental costs, of the reductions of emissions and increments of removals of greenhouse gases, as well as an estimate of the consequent benefits.

5. Each developed country Party and each other Party included in annex I shall make its initial communication within six months of the entry into force of the Convention for that Party. Each Party not so listed shall make its initial communication within three years of the entry into force of the Convention for that Party, or of the availability of financial resources in accordance with Article 4, paragraph 3. Parties that are least developed countries may make their initial communication at their discretion. The frequency of subsequent communications by all Parties shall be determined by the Conference of the Parties, taking into account the differentiated timetable set by this paragraph.

6. Information communicated by Parties under this Article shall be transmitted by the secretariat as soon as possible to the Conference of the Parties and to any subsidiary bodies concerned. If necessary, the procedures for the communication of information may be further considered by the Conference of the Parties.

7. From its first session, the Conference of the Parties shall arrange for the provision to developing country Parties of technical and financial support, on request, in compiling and communicating information under this Article, as well as in identifying the technical and financial needs associated with proposed projects and response measures under Article 4. Such support may be provided by other Parties, by competent international organizations and by the secretariat, as appropriate.

8. Any group of Parties may, subject to guidelines adopted by the Conference of the Parties, and to prior notification to the Conference of the Parties, make a joint communication in fulfilment of their obligations under this Article, provided that such a communication includes information on the fulfilment by each of these Parties of its individual obligations under the Convention.

9. Information received by the secretariat that is designated by a Party as confidential, in accordance with criteria to be established by the Conference of the Parties, shall be aggregated by the secretariat to protect its confidentiality before being made available to any of the bodies involved in the communication and review of information.

10. Subject to paragraph 9 above, and without prejudice to the ability of any Party to make public its communication at any time, the secretariat shall make communications by Parties under this Article publicly available at the time they are submitted to the Conference of the Parties.

Article 13
The Conference of the Parties shall, at its first session, consider the establishment of a multilateral consultative process, available to Parties on their

request, for the resolution of questions regarding the implementation of the Convention.

Article 14

1. In the event of a dispute between any two or more Parties concerning the interpretation or application of the Convention, the Parties concerned shall seek a settlement of the dispute through negotiation or any other peaceful means of their own choice.

2. When ratifying, accepting, approving or acceding to the Convention, or at any time thereafter, a Party which is not a regional economic integration organization may declare in a written instrument submitted to the Depositary that, in respect of any dispute concerning the interpretation or application of the Convention, it recognizes as compulsory ipso facto and without special agreement, in relation to any Party accepting the same obligation:

(a) Submission of the dispute to the International Court of Justice; and/or

(b) Arbitration in accordance with procedures to be adopted by the Conference of the Parties as soon as practicable, in an annex on arbitration.

A Party which is a regional economic integration organization may make a declaration with like effect in relation to arbitration in accordance with the procedures referred to in subparagraph (b) above.

3. A declaration made under paragraph 2 above shall remain in force until it expires in accordance with its terms or until three months after written notice of its revocation has been deposited with the Depositary.

4. A new declaration, a notice of revocation or the expiry of a declaration shall not in any way affect proceedings pending before the International Court of Justice or the arbitral tribunal, unless the parties to the dispute otherwise agree.

5. Subject to the operation of paragraph 2 above, if after twelve months following notification by one Party to another that a dispute exists between them, the Parties concerned have not been able to settle their dispute through the means mentioned in paragraph 1 above, the dispute shall be submitted, at the request of any of the parties to the dispute, to conciliation.

6. A conciliation commission shall be created upon the request of one of the parties to the dispute. The commission shall be composed of an equal number of members appointed by each party concerned and a chairman chosen jointly by the members appointed by each party. The commission shall render a recommendatory award, which the parties shall consider in good faith.

7. Additional procedures relating to conciliation shall be adopted by the Conference of the Parties, as soon as practicable, in an annex on conciliation.

8. The provisions of this Article shall apply to any related legal instrument which the Conference of the Parties may adopt, unless the instrument provides otherwise.

Article 15

1. Any Party may propose amendments to the Convention.

2. Amendments to the Convention shall be adopted at an ordinary session of the Conference of the Parties. The text of any proposed amendment to the Convention shall be communicated to the Parties by the secretariat at least six months before the meeting at which it is proposed for adoption. The secretariat shall also communicate proposed amendments to the signatories to the Convention and, for information, to the Depositary.

3. The Parties shall make every effort to reach agreement on any proposed amendment to the Convention by consensus. If all efforts at consensus have been exhausted, and no agreement reached, the amendment shall as a last resort be adopted by a three-fourths majority vote of the Parties present and voting at the meeting. The adopted amendment shall be communicated by the secretariat to the Depositary, who shall circulate it to all Parties for their acceptance.

4. Instruments of acceptance in respect of an amendment shall be deposited with the Depositary. An amendment adopted in accordance with paragraph 3 above shall enter into force for those Parties having accepted it on the ninetieth day after the date of receipt by the Depositary of an instrument of acceptance by at least three-fourths of the Parties to the Convention.

5. The amendment shall enter into force for any other Party on the ninetieth day after the date on which that Party deposits with the Depositary its instrument of acceptance of the said amendment.

6. For the purposes of this Article, "Parties present and voting" means Parties present and casting an affirmative or negative vote.

Article 16

1. Annexes to the Convention shall form an integral part thereof and, unless otherwise expressly provided, a reference to the Convention constitutes at the same time a reference to any annexes thereto. Without prejudice to the provisions of Article 14, paragraphs 2(b) and 7, such annexes shall be restricted to lists, forms and any other material of a descriptive nature that is of a scientific, technical, procedural or administrative character.

2. Annexes to the Convention shall be proposed and adopted in accordance with the procedure set forth in Article 15, paragraphs 2, 3, and 4.

3. An annex that has been adopted in accordance with paragraph 2 above shall enter into force for all Parties to the Convention six months after the date of the communication by the Depositary to such Parties of the adoption of the annex, except for those Parties that have notified the Depositary, in writing, within that period of their non-acceptance of the annex. The annex shall enter into force for Parties which withdraw their notification of non-acceptance on the ninetieth day after the date on which withdrawal of such notification has been received by the Depositary.

4. The proposal, adoption and entry into force of amendments to annexes to the Convention shall be subject to the same procedure as that for the proposal, adoption and entry into force of annexes to the Convention in accordance with paragraphs 2 and 3 above.

5. If the adoption of an annex or an amendment to an annex involves an

amendment to the Convention, that annex or amendment to an annex shall not enter into force until such time as the amendment to the Convention enters into force.

Article 17

1. The Conference of the Parties may, at any ordinary session, adopt protocols to the Convention.

2. The text of any proposed protocol shall be communicated to the Parties by the secretariat at least six months before such a session.

3. The requirements for the entry into force of any protocol shall be established by that instrument.

4. Only Parties to the Convention may be Parties to a protocol.

5. Decisions under any protocol shall be taken only by the Parties to the protocol concerned.

Article 18

1. Each Party to the Convention shall have one vote, except as provided for in paragraph 2 below.

2. Regional economic integration organizations, in matters within their competence, shall exercise their right to vote with a number of votes equal to the number of their member States that are Parties to the Convention. Such an organization shall not exercise its right to vote if any of its member States exercises its right, and vice versa.

Article 19

The Secretary-General of the United Nations shall be the Depositary of the Convention and of protocols adopted in accordance with Article 17.

Article 20

This Convention shall be open for signature by States Members of the United Nations or of any of its specialized agencies or that are Parties to the Statute of the International Court of Justice and by regional economic integration organizations at Rio de Janeiro, during the United Nations Conference on Environment and Development, and thereafter at United Nations Headquarters in New York from 20 June 1992 to 19 June 1993.

Article 21

1. The secretariat functions referred to in Article 8 will be carried out on an interim basis by the secretariat established by the General Assembly of the United Nations in its resolution 45/212 of 21 December 1990, until the completion of the first session of the Conference of the Parties.

2. The head of the interim secretariat referred to in paragraph 1 above will cooperate closely with the Intergovernmental Panel on Climate Change to ensure that the Panel can respond to the need for objective scientific and technical advice. Other relevant scientific bodies could also be consulted.

3. The Global Environment Facility of the United Nations Development Programme, the United Nations Environment Programme and the International Bank for Reconstruction and Development shall be the international entity entrusted with the operation of the financial mechanism referred to in Article 11 on an interim basis. In this connection, the Global Environment Facility should be appropriately restructured and its membership made universal to enable it to fulfil the requirements of Article 11.

Article 22

1. The Convention shall be subject to ratification, acceptance, approval or accession by States and by regional economic integration organizations. It shall be open for accession from the day after the date on which the Convention is closed for signature. Instruments of ratification, acceptance, approval or accession shall be deposited with the Depositary.

2. Any regional economic integration organization which becomes a Party to the Convention without any of its member States being a Party shall be bound by all the obligations under the Convention. In the case of such organizations, one or more of whose member States is a Party to the Convention, the organization and its member States shall decide on their respective responsibilities for the performance of their obligations under the Convention. In such cases, the organization and the member States shall not be entitled to exercise rights under the Convention concurrently.

3. In their instruments of ratification, acceptance, approval or accession, regional economic integration organizations shall declare the extent of their competence with respect to the matters governed by the Convention. These organizations shall also inform the Depositary, who shall in turn inform the Parties, of any substantial modification in the extent of their competence.

Article 23

1. The Convention shall enter into force on the ninetieth day after the date of deposit of the fiftieth instrument of ratification, acceptance, approval or accession.

2. For each State or regional economic integration organization that ratifies, accepts or approves the Convention or accedes thereto after the deposit of the fiftieth instrument of ratification, acceptance, approval or accession, the Convention shall enter into force on the ninetieth day after the date of deposit by such State or regional economic integration organization of its instrument of ratification, acceptance, approval or accession.

3. For the purposes of paragraphs 1 and 2 above, any instrument deposited by a regional economic integration organization shall not be counted as additional to those deposited by States members of the organization.

Article 24

No reservations may be made to the Convention.

Article 25

1. At any time after three years from the date on which the Convention has entered into force for a Party, that Party may withdraw from the Convention by giving written notification to the Depositary.

2. Any such withdrawal shall take effect upon expiry of one year from the date of receipt by the Depositary of the notification of withdrawal, or on such later date as may be specified in the notification of withdrawal.

3. Any Party that withdraws from the Convention shall be considered as also having withdrawn from any protocol to which it is a Party.

Article 26

The original of this Convention, of which the Arabic, Chinese, English, French, Russian and Spanish texts are equally authentic, shall be deposited with the Secretary-General of the United Nations.

IN WITNESS WHEREOF the undersigned, being duly authorized to that effect, have signed this Convention.

DONE at New York this ninth day of May one thousand nine hundred and ninety-two.

Annex I

Australia, Austria, Belarus,* Belgium, Bulgaria,* Canada, Czechoslovakia,* Denmark, European Community, Estonia,* Finland, France, Germany, Greece, Hungary,* Iceland, Ireland, Italy, Japan, Latvia,* Lithuania,* Luxembourg, Netherlands, New Zealand, Norway, Poland,* Portugal, Romania,* Russian Federation,* Spain, Sweden, Switzerland, Turkey, Ukraine,* United Kingdom of Great Britain and Northern Ireland, United States of America.

Annex II

Australia, Austria, Belgium, Canada, Denmark, European Community, Finland, France, Germany, Greece, Iceland, Ireland, Italy, Japan, Luxembourg, Netherlands, New Zealand, Norway, Portugal, Spain, Sweden, Switzerland, Turkey, United Kingdom of Great Britain and Northern Ireland, United States of America.

---

*Countries that are undergoing the process of transition to a market economy.

Kyoto Protocol to the United Nations Framework Convention on Climate Change (1997)

Particularly since the protocol's entry into force in 2005, considerable focus has been on the three so-called flexibility mechanisms, by which countries can use market mechanisms to help fulfill their protocol commitments to greenhouse gas reductions. The United States has stayed outside the protocol. At an Association of South East Asian Nations (ASEAN) Regional Forum meeting in July 2005 the United States, Australia, China, India, Japan, and the Republic of Korea presented the "Vision Statement for an Asia-Pacific Partnership for Clean Development and Climate," available at www.state.gov/g/oes/rls/fs/ 50335.htm.

On the US approach to climate change, see Joanna Depledge, "Against the Grain: The United States and the Global Climate Change Regime," Pacifica Review *17 (2005): 11–27. There has been increasing interest in the ethical dimension of the climate change issue. On this, see Donald Brown, "The Importance of Expressly Examining Global Warming Policy Issues Through an Ethical Prism,"* Global Environmental Change *13 (2003): 229–234. On the detail of the market mechanisms in the Kyoto Protocol, see David Freestone and Charlotte Streck, eds.,* Legal Aspects of Implementing the Kyoto Protocol Mechanisms: Making Kyoto Work *(Oxford: Oxford University Press, 2005).*

The Parties to this Protocol,

Being Parties to the United Nations Framework Convention on Climate Change, hereinafter referred to as "the Convention,"

In pursuit of the ultimate objective of the Convention as stated in its Article 2,

Recalling the provisions of the Convention,

Being guided by Article 3 of the Convention,

Pursuant to the Berlin Mandate adopted by decision 1/CP.1 of the Conference of the Parties to the Convention at its first session,

Have agreed as follows:

Article 1

For the purposes of this Protocol, the definitions contained in Article 1 of the Convention shall apply. In addition:

1. "Conference of the Parties" means the Conference of the Parties to the Convention.

2. "Convention" means the United Nations Framework Convention on Climate Change, adopted in New York on 9 May 1992.

3. "Intergovernmental Panel on Climate Change" means the Intergovernmental Panel on Climate Change established in 1988 jointly by the World Meteorological Organization and the United Nations Environment Programme.

4. "Montreal Protocol" means the Montreal Protocol on Substances that Deplete the Ozone Layer, adopted in Montreal on 16 September 1987 and as subsequently adjusted and amended.

5. "Parties present and voting" means Parties present and casting an affirmative or negative vote.

6. "Party" means, unless the context otherwise indicates, a Party to this Protocol.

7. "Party included in Annex I" means a Party included in Annex I to the Convention, as may be amended, or a Party which has made a notification under Article 4, paragraph 2 (g), of the Convention.

Article 2

1. Each Party included in Annex I, in achieving its quantified emission limitation and reduction commitments under Article 3, in order to promote sustainable development, shall:

(a) Implement and/or further elaborate policies and measures in accordance with its national circumstances, such as: (i) Enhancement of energy efficiency in relevant sectors of the national economy; (ii) Protection and enhancement of sinks and reservoirs of greenhouse gases not controlled by the Montreal Protocol, taking into account its commitments under relevant international environmental agreements; promotion of sustainable forest management practices, afforestation and reforestation; (iii) Promotion of sustainable forms of agriculture in light of climate change considerations; (iv) Research on, and promotion, development and increased use of, new and renewable forms of energy, of carbon dioxide sequestration technologies and of advanced and innovative environmentally sound technologies; (v) Progressive reduction or phasing out of market imperfections, fiscal incentives, tax and duty exemptions and subsidies in all greenhouse gas emitting sectors that run counter to the objective of the Convention and application of market instruments; (vi) Encouragement of appropriate reforms in relevant sectors aimed at promoting policies and measures which limit or reduce emissions of greenhouse gases not controlled by the Montreal Protocol; (vii) Measures to limit and/or reduce emissions of greenhouse gases not controlled by the Montreal Protocol in the transport sector; (viii) Limitation and/or reduction of methane emissions through recovery and use in waste management, as well as in the production, transport and distribution of energy;

(b) Cooperate with other such Parties to enhance the individual and combined effectiveness of their policies and measures adopted under this Article, pursuant to Article 4, paragraph 2 (e) (i), of the Convention. To this end, these

Parties shall take steps to share their experience and exchange information on such policies and measures, including developing ways of improving their comparability, transparency and effectiveness. The Conference of the Parties serving as the meeting of the Parties to this Protocol shall, at its first session or as soon as practicable thereafter, consider ways to facilitate such cooperation, taking into account all relevant information.

2. The Parties included in Annex I shall pursue limitation or reduction of emissions of greenhouse gases not controlled by the Montreal Protocol from aviation and marine bunker fuels, working through the International Civil Aviation Organization and the International Maritime Organization, respectively.

3. The Parties included in Annex I shall strive to implement policies and measures under this Article in such a way as to minimize adverse effects, including the adverse effects of climate change, effects on international trade, and social, environmental and economic impacts on other Parties, especially developing country Parties and in particular those identified in Article 4, paragraphs 8 and 9, of the Convention, taking into account Article 3 of the Convention. The Conference of the Parties serving as the meeting of the Parties to this Protocol may take further action, as appropriate, to promote the implementation of the provisions of this paragraph.

4. The Conference of the Parties serving as the meeting of the Parties to this Protocol, if it decides that it would be beneficial to coordinate any of the policies and measures in paragraph 1 (a) above, taking into account different national circumstances and potential effects, shall consider ways and means to elaborate the coordination of such policies and measures.

Article 3

1. The Parties included in Annex I shall, individually or jointly, ensure that their aggregate anthropogenic carbon dioxide equivalent emissions of the greenhouse gases listed in Annex A do not exceed their assigned amounts, calculated pursuant to their quantified emission limitation and reduction commitments inscribed in Annex B and in accordance with the provisions of this Article, with a view to reducing their overall emissions of such gases by at least 5 per cent below 1990 levels in the commitment period 2008 to 2012.

2. Each Party included in Annex I shall, by 2005, have made demonstrable progress in achieving its commitments under this Protocol.

3. The net changes in greenhouse gas emissions by sources and removals by sinks resulting from direct human-induced land-use change and forestry activities, limited to afforestation, reforestation and deforestation since 1990, measured as verifiable changes in carbon stocks in each commitment period, shall be used to meet the commitments under this Article of each Party included in Annex I. The greenhouse gas emissions by sources and removals by sinks associated with those activities shall be reported in a transparent and verifiable manner and reviewed in accordance with Articles 7 and 8.

4. Prior to the first session of the Conference of the Parties serving as the

meeting of the Parties to this Protocol, each Party included in Annex I shall provide, for consideration by the Subsidiary Body for Scientific and Technological Advice, data to establish its level of carbon stocks in 1990 and to enable an estimate to be made of its changes in carbon stocks in subsequent years. The Conference of the Parties serving as the meeting of the Parties to this Protocol shall, at its first session or as soon as practicable thereafter, decide upon modalities, rules and guidelines as to how, and which, additional human-induced activities related to changes in greenhouse gas emissions by sources and removals by sinks in the agricultural soils and the land-use change and forestry categories shall be added to, or subtracted from, the assigned amounts for Parties included in Annex I, taking into account uncertainties, transparency in reporting, verifiability, the methodological work of the Intergovernmental Panel on Climate Change, the advice provided by the Subsidiary Body for Scientific and Technological Advice in accordance with Article 5 and the decisions of the Conference of the Parties. Such a decision shall apply in the second and subsequent commitment periods. A Party may choose to apply such a decision on these additional human-induced activities for its first commitment period, provided that these activities have taken place since 1990.

5. The Parties included in Annex I undergoing the process of transition to a market economy whose base year or period was established pursuant to decision 9/CP.2 of the Conference of the Parties at its second session shall use that base year or period for the implementation of their commitments under this Article. Any other Party included in Annex I undergoing the process of transition to a market economy which has not yet submitted its first national communication under Article 12 of the Convention may also notify the Conference of the Parties serving as the meeting of the Parties to this Protocol that it intends to use an historical base year or period other than 1990 for the implementation of its commitments under this Article. The Conference of the Parties serving as the meeting of the Parties to this Protocol shall decide on the acceptance of such notification.

6. Taking into account Article 4, paragraph 6, of the Convention, in the implementation of their commitments under this Protocol other than those under this Article, a certain degree of flexibility shall be allowed by the Conference of the Parties serving as the meeting of the Parties to this Protocol to the Parties included in Annex I undergoing the process of transition to a market economy.

7. In the first quantified emission limitation and reduction commitment period, from 2008 to 2012, the assigned amount for each Party included in Annex I shall be equal to the percentage inscribed for it in Annex B of its aggregate anthropogenic carbon dioxide equivalent emissions of the greenhouse gases listed in Annex A in 1990, or the base year or period determined in accordance with paragraph 5 above, multiplied by five. Those Parties included in Annex I for whom land-use change and forestry constituted a net source of greenhouse gas emissions in 1990 shall include in their 1990 emissions base

year or period the aggregate anthropogenic carbon dioxide equivalent emissions by sources minus removals by sinks in 1990 from land-use change for the purposes of calculating their assigned amount.

8. Any Party included in Annex I may use 1995 as its base year for hydrofluorocarbons, perfluorocarbons and sulphur hexafluoride, for the purposes of the calculation referred to in paragraph 7 above.

9. Commitments for subsequent periods for Parties included in Annex I shall be established in amendments to Annex B to this Protocol, which shall be adopted in accordance with the provisions of Article 21, paragraph 7. The Conference of the Parties serving as the meeting of the Parties to this Protocol shall initiate the consideration of such commitments at least seven years before the end of the first commitment period referred to in paragraph 1 above.

10. Any emission reduction units, or any part of an assigned amount, which a Party acquires from another Party in accordance with the provisions of Article 6 or of Article 17 shall be added to the assigned amount for the acquiring Party.

11. Any emission reduction units, or any part of an assigned amount, which a Party transfers to another Party in accordance with the provisions of Article 6 or of Article 17 shall be subtracted from the assigned amount for the transferring Party.

12. Any certified emission reductions which a Party acquires from another Party in accordance with the provisions of Article 12 shall be added to the assigned amount for the acquiring Party.

13. If the emissions of a Party included in Annex I in a commitment period are less than its assigned amount under this Article, this difference shall, on request of that Party, be added to the assigned amount for that Party for subsequent commitment periods.

14. Each Party included in Annex I shall strive to implement the commitments mentioned in paragraph 1 above in such a way as to minimize adverse social, environmental and economic impacts on developing country Parties, particularly those identified in Article 4, paragraphs 8 and 9, of the Convention. In line with relevant decisions of the Conference of the Parties on the implementation of those paragraphs, the Conference of the Parties serving as the meeting of the Parties to this Protocol shall, at its first session, consider what actions are necessary to minimize the adverse effects of climate change and/or the impacts of response measures on Parties referred to in those paragraphs. Among the issues to be considered shall be the establishment of funding, insurance and transfer of technology.

Article 4

1. Any Parties included in Annex I that have reached an agreement to fulfil their commitments under Article 3 jointly, shall be deemed to have met those commitments provided that their total combined aggregate anthropogenic carbon dioxide equivalent emissions of the greenhouse gases listed in Annex A do not exceed their assigned amounts calculated pursuant to their quantified emis-

sion limitation and reduction commitments inscribed in Annex B and in accordance with the provisions of Article 3. The respective emission level allocated to each of the Parties to the agreement shall be set out in that agreement.

2. The Parties to any such agreement shall notify the secretariat of the terms of the agreement on the date of deposit of their instruments of ratification, acceptance or approval of this Protocol, or accession thereto. The secretariat shall in turn inform the Parties and signatories to the Convention of the terms of the agreement.

3. Any such agreement shall remain in operation for the duration of the commitment period specified in Article 3, paragraph 7.

4. If Parties acting jointly do so in the framework of, and together with, a regional economic integration organization, any alteration in the composition of the organization after adoption of this Protocol shall not affect existing commitments under this Protocol. Any alteration in the composition of the organization shall only apply for the purposes of those commitments under Article 3 that are adopted subsequent to that alteration.

5. In the event of failure by the Parties to such an agreement to achieve their total combined level of emission reductions, each Party to that agreement shall be responsible for its own level of emissions set out in the agreement.

6. If Parties acting jointly do so in the framework of, and together with, a regional economic integration organization which is itself a Party to this Protocol, each member State of that regional economic integration organization individually, and together with the regional economic integration organization acting in accordance with Article 24, shall, in the event of failure to achieve the total combined level of emission reductions, be responsible for its level of emissions as notified in accordance with this Article.

Article 5

1. Each Party included in Annex I shall have in place, no later than one year prior to the start of the first commitment period, a national system for the estimation of anthropogenic emissions by sources and removals by sinks of all greenhouse gases not controlled by the Montreal Protocol. Guidelines for such national systems, which shall incorporate the methodologies specified in paragraph 2 below, shall be decided upon by the Conference of the Parties serving as the meeting of the Parties to this Protocol at its first session.

2. Methodologies for estimating anthropogenic emissions by sources and removals by sinks of all greenhouse gases not controlled by the Montreal Protocol shall be those accepted by the Intergovernmental Panel on Climate Change and agreed upon by the Conference of the Parties at its third session. Where such methodologies are not used, appropriate adjustments shall be applied according to methodologies agreed upon by the Conference of the Parties serving as the meeting of the Parties to this Protocol at its first session. Based on the work of, inter alia, the Intergovernmental Panel on Climate Change and advice provided by the Subsidiary Body for Scientific and Technological Advice, the Conference of the Parties serving as the meeting of

the Parties to this Protocol shall regularly review and, as appropriate, revise such methodologies and adjustments, taking fully into account any relevant decisions by the Conference of the Parties. Any revision to methodologies or adjustments shall be used only for the purposes of ascertaining compliance with commitments under Article 3 in respect of any commitment period adopted subsequent to that revision.

3. The global warming potentials used to calculate the carbon dioxide equivalence of anthropogenic emissions by sources and removals by sinks of greenhouse gases listed in Annex A shall be those accepted by the Intergovernmental Panel on Climate Change and agreed upon by the Conference of the Parties at its third session. Based on the work of, inter alia, the Intergovernmental Panel on Climate Change and advice provided by the Subsidiary Body for Scientific and Technological Advice, the Conference of the Parties serving as the meeting of the Parties to this Protocol shall regularly review and, as appropriate, revise the global warming potential of each such greenhouse gas, taking fully into account any relevant decisions by the Conference of the Parties. Any revision to a global warming potential shall apply only to commitments under Article 3 in respect of any commitment period adopted subsequent to that revision.

Article 6

1. For the purpose of meeting its commitments under Article 3, any Party included in Annex I may transfer to, or acquire from, any other such Party emission reduction units resulting from projects aimed at reducing anthropogenic emissions by sources or enhancing anthropogenic removals by sinks of greenhouse gases in any sector of the economy, provided that:

(a) Any such project has the approval of the Parties involved;

(b) Any such project provides a reduction in emissions by sources, or an enhancement of removals by sinks, that is additional to any that would otherwise occur;

(c) It does not acquire any emission reduction units if it is not in compliance with its obligations under Articles 5 and 7; and

(d) The acquisition of emission reduction units shall be supplemental to domestic actions for the purposes of meeting commitments under Article 3.

2. The Conference of the Parties serving as the meeting of the Parties to this Protocol may, at its first session or as soon as practicable thereafter, further elaborate guidelines for the implementation of this Article, including for verification and reporting.

3. A Party included in Annex I may authorize legal entities to participate, under its responsibility, in actions leading to the generation, transfer or acquisition under this Article of emission reduction units.

4. If a question of implementation by a Party included in Annex I of the requirements referred to in this Article is identified in accordance with the relevant provisions of Article 8, transfers and acquisitions of emission reduction

units may continue to be made after the question has been identified, provided that any such units may not be used by a Party to meet its commitments under Article 3 until any issue of compliance is resolved.

Article 7

1. Each Party included in Annex I shall incorporate in its annual inventory of anthropogenic emissions by sources and removals by sinks of greenhouse gases not controlled by the Montreal Protocol, submitted in accordance with the relevant decisions of the Conference of the Parties, the necessary supplementary information for the purposes of ensuring compliance with Article 3, to be determined in accordance with paragraph 4 below.

2. Each Party included in Annex I shall incorporate in its national communication, submitted under Article 12 of the Convention, the supplementary information necessary to demonstrate compliance with its commitments under this Protocol, to be determined in accordance with paragraph 4 below.

3. Each Party included in Annex I shall submit the information required under paragraph 1 above annually, beginning with the first inventory due under the Convention for the first year of the commitment period after this Protocol has entered into force for that Party. Each such Party shall submit the information required under paragraph 2 above as part of the first national communication due under the Convention after this Protocol has entered into force for it and after the adoption of guidelines as provided for in paragraph 4 below. The frequency of subsequent submission of information required under this Article shall be determined by the Conference of the Parties serving as the meeting of the Parties to this Protocol, taking into account any timetable for the submission of national communications decided upon by the Conference of the Parties.

4. The Conference of the Parties serving as the meeting of the Parties to this Protocol shall adopt at its first session, and review periodically thereafter, guidelines for the preparation of the information required under this Article, taking into account guidelines for the preparation of national communications by Parties included in Annex I adopted by the Conference of the Parties. The Conference of the Parties serving as the meeting of the Parties to this Protocol shall also, prior to the first commitment period, decide upon modalities for the accounting of assigned amounts.

Article 8

1. The information submitted under Article 7 by each Party included in Annex I shall be reviewed by expert review teams pursuant to the relevant decisions of the Conference of the Parties and in accordance with guidelines adopted for this purpose by the Conference of the Parties serving as the meeting of the Parties to this Protocol under paragraph 4 below. The information submitted under Article 7, paragraph 1, by each Party included in Annex I shall be reviewed as part of the annual compilation and accounting of emissions

inventories and assigned amounts. Additionally, the information submitted under Article 7, paragraph 2, by each Party included in Annex I shall be reviewed as part of the review of communications.

2. Expert review teams shall be coordinated by the secretariat and shall be composed of experts selected from those nominated by Parties to the Convention and, as appropriate, by intergovernmental organizations, in accordance with guidance provided for this purpose by the Conference of the Parties.

3. The review process shall provide a thorough and comprehensive technical assessment of all aspects of the implementation by a Party of this Protocol. The expert review teams shall prepare a report to the Conference of the Parties serving as the meeting of the Parties to this Protocol, assessing the implementation of the commitments of the Party and identifying any potential problems in, and factors influencing, the fulfilment of commitments. Such reports shall be circulated by the secretariat to all Parties to the Convention. The secretariat shall list those questions of implementation indicated in such reports for further consideration by the Conference of the Parties serving as the meeting of the Parties to this Protocol.

4. The Conference of the Parties serving as the meeting of the Parties to this Protocol shall adopt at its first session, and review periodically thereafter, guidelines for the review of implementation of this Protocol by expert review teams taking into account the relevant decisions of the Conference of the Parties.

5. The Conference of the Parties serving as the meeting of the Parties to this Protocol shall, with the assistance of the Subsidiary Body for Implementation and, as appropriate, the Subsidiary Body for Scientific and Technological Advice, consider:

(a) The information submitted by Parties under Article 7 and the reports of the expert reviews thereon conducted under this Article; and

(b) Those questions of implementation listed by the secretariat under paragraph 3 above, as well as any questions raised by Parties.

6. Pursuant to its consideration of the information referred to in paragraph 5 above, the Conference of the Parties serving as the meeting of the Parties to this Protocol shall take decisions on any matter required for the implementation of this Protocol.

Article 9

1. The Conference of the Parties serving as the meeting of the Parties to this Protocol shall periodically review this Protocol in the light of the best available scientific information and assessments on climate change and its impacts, as well as relevant technical, social and economic information. Such reviews shall be coordinated with pertinent reviews under the Convention, in particular those required by Article 4, paragraph 2 (d), and Article 7, paragraph 2 (a), of the Convention. Based on these reviews, the Conference of the Parties serving as the meeting of the Parties to this Protocol shall take appropriate action.

2. The first review shall take place at the second session of the Conference of the Parties serving as the meeting of the Parties to this Protocol. Further reviews shall take place at regular intervals and in a timely manner.

Article 10

All Parties, taking into account their common but differentiated responsibilities and their specific national and regional development priorities, objectives and circumstances, without introducing any new commitments for Parties not included in Annex I, but reaffirming existing commitments under Article 4, paragraph 1, of the Convention, and continuing to advance the implementation of these commitments in order to achieve sustainable development, taking into account Article 4, paragraphs 3, 5 and 7, of the Convention, shall:

(a) Formulate, where relevant and to the extent possible, cost-effective national and, where appropriate, regional programmes to improve the quality of local emission factors, activity data and/or models which reflect the socio-economic conditions of each Party for the preparation and periodic updating of national inventories of anthropogenic emissions by sources and removals by sinks of all greenhouse gases not controlled by the Montreal Protocol, using comparable methodologies to be agreed upon by the Conference of the Parties, and consistent with the guidelines for the preparation of national communications adopted by the Conference of the Parties;

(b) Formulate, implement, publish and regularly update national and, where appropriate, regional programmes containing measures to mitigate climate change and measures to facilitate adequate adaptation to climate change: (i) Such programmes would, inter alia, concern the energy, transport and industry sectors as well as agriculture, forestry and waste management. Furthermore, adaptation technologies and methods for improving spatial planning would improve adaptation to climate change; and (ii) Parties included in Annex I shall submit information on action under this Protocol, including national programmes, in accordance with Article 7; and other Parties shall seek to include in their national communications, as appropriate, information on programmes which contain measures that the Party believes contribute to addressing climate change and its adverse impacts, including the abatement of increases in greenhouse gas emissions, and enhancement of and removals by sinks, capacity building and adaptation measures;

(c) Cooperate in the promotion of effective modalities for the development, application and diffusion of, and take all practicable steps to promote, facilitate and finance, as appropriate, the transfer of, or access to, environmentally sound technologies, know-how, practices and processes pertinent to climate change, in particular to developing countries, including the formulation of policies and programmes for the effective transfer of environmentally sound technologies that are publicly owned or in the public domain and the creation of an enabling environment for the private sector, to promote and enhance the transfer of, and access to, environmentally sound technologies;

(d) Cooperate in scientific and technical research and promote the maintenance and the development of systematic observation systems and development of data archives to reduce uncertainties related to the climate system, the adverse impacts of climate change and the economic and social consequences of various response strategies, and promote the development and strengthening of endogenous capacities and capabilities to participate in international and intergovernmental efforts, programmes and networks on research and systematic observation, taking into account Article 5 of the Convention;

(e) Cooperate in and promote at the international level, and, where appropriate, using existing bodies, the development and implementation of education and training programmes, including the strengthening of national capacity building, in particular human and institutional capacities and the exchange or secondment of personnel to train experts in this field, in particular for developing countries, and facilitate at the national level public awareness of, and public access to information on, climate change. Suitable modalities should be developed to implement these activities through the relevant bodies of the Convention, taking into account Article 6 of the Convention;

(f) Include in their national communications information on programmes and activities undertaken pursuant to this Article in accordance with relevant decisions of the Conference of the Parties; and

(g) Give full consideration, in implementing the commitments under this Article, to Article 4, paragraph 8, of the Convention.

Article 11

1. In the implementation of Article 10, Parties shall take into account the provisions of Article 4, paragraphs 4, 5, 7, 8 and 9, of the Convention.

2. In the context of the implementation of Article 4, paragraph 1, of the Convention, in accordance with the provisions of Article 4, paragraph 3, and Article 11 of the Convention, and through the entity or entities entrusted with the operation of the financial mechanism of the Convention, the developed country Parties and other developed Parties included in Annex II to the Convention shall:

(a) Provide new and additional financial resources to meet the agreed full costs incurred by developing country Parties in advancing the implementation of existing commitments under Article 4, paragraph 1 (a), of the Convention that are covered in Article 10, subparagraph (a); and

(b) Also provide such financial resources, including for the transfer of technology, needed by the developing country Parties to meet the agreed full incremental costs of advancing the implementation of existing commitments under Article 4, paragraph 1, of the Convention that are covered by Article 10 and that are agreed between a developing country Party and the international entity or entities referred to in Article 11 of the Convention, in accordance with that Article.

The implementation of these existing commitments shall take into account the need for adequacy and predictability in the flow of funds and the importance of appropriate burden sharing among developed country Parties. The guidance to the entity or entities entrusted with the operation of the financial mechanism of the Convention in relevant decisions of the Conference of the Parties, including those agreed before the adoption of this Protocol, shall apply mutatis mutandis to the provisions of this paragraph.

3. The developed country Parties and other developed Parties in Annex II to the Convention may also provide, and developing country Parties avail themselves of, financial resources for the implementation of Article 10, through bilateral, regional and other multilateral channels.

Article 12

1. A clean development mechanism is hereby defined.

2. The purpose of the clean development mechanism shall be to assist Parties not included in Annex I in achieving sustainable development and in contributing to the ultimate objective of the Convention, and to assist Parties included in Annex I in achieving compliance with their quantified emission limitation and reduction commitments under Article 3.

3. Under the clean development mechanism:

(a) Parties not included in Annex I will benefit from project activities resulting in certified emission reductions; and

(b) Parties included in Annex I may use the certified emission reductions accruing from such project activities to contribute to compliance with part of their quantified emission limitation and reduction commitments under Article 3, as determined by the Conference of the Parties serving as the meeting of the Parties to this Protocol.

4. The clean development mechanism shall be subject to the authority and guidance of the Conference of the Parties serving as the meeting of the Parties to this Protocol and be supervised by an executive board of the clean development mechanism.

5. Emission reductions resulting from each project activity shall be certified by operational entities to be designated by the Conference of the Parties serving as the meeting of the Parties to this Protocol, on the basis of:

(a) Voluntary participation approved by each Party involved;

(b) Real, measurable, and long-term benefits related to the mitigation of climate change; and

(c) Reductions in emissions that are additional to any that would occur in the absence of the certified project activity.

6. The clean development mechanism shall assist in arranging funding of certified project activities as necessary.

7. The Conference of the Parties serving as the meeting of the Parties to this Protocol shall, at its first session, elaborate modalities and procedures with the objective of ensuring transparency, efficiency and accountability through independent auditing and verification of project activities.

8. The Conference of the Parties serving as the meeting of the Parties to this Protocol shall ensure that a share of the proceeds from certified project activities is used to cover administrative expenses as well as to assist developing

country Parties that are particularly vulnerable to the adverse effects of climate change to meet the costs of adaptation.

9. Participation under the clean development mechanism, including in activities mentioned in paragraph 3 (a) above and in the acquisition of certified emission reductions, may involve private and/or public entities, and is to be subject to whatever guidance may be provided by the executive board of the clean development mechanism.

10. Certified emission reductions obtained during the period from the year 2000 up to the beginning of the first commitment period can be used to assist in achieving compliance in the first commitment period.

Article 13

1. The Conference of the Parties, the supreme body of the Convention, shall serve as the meeting of the Parties to this Protocol.

2. Parties to the Convention that are not Parties to this Protocol may participate as observers in the proceedings of any session of the Conference of the Parties serving as the meeting of the Parties to this Protocol. When the Conference of the Parties serves as the meeting of the Parties to this Protocol, decisions under this Protocol shall be taken only by those that are Parties to this Protocol.

3. When the Conference of the Parties serves as the meeting of the Parties to this Protocol, any member of the Bureau of the Conference of the Parties representing a Party to the Convention but, at that time, not a Party to this Protocol, shall be replaced by an additional member to be elected by and from amongst the Parties to this Protocol.

4. The Conference of the Parties serving as the meeting of the Parties to this Protocol shall keep under regular review the implementation of this Protocol and shall make, within its mandate, the decisions necessary to promote its effective implementation. It shall perform the functions assigned to it by this Protocol and shall:

(a) Assess, on the basis of all information made available to it in accordance with the provisions of this Protocol, the implementation of this Protocol by the Parties, the overall effects of the measures taken pursuant to this Protocol, in particular environmental, economic and social effects as well as their cumulative impacts and the extent to which progress towards the objective of the Convention is being achieved;

(b) Periodically examine the obligations of the Parties under this Protocol, giving due consideration to any reviews required by Article 4, paragraph 2 (d), and Article 7, paragraph 2, of the Convention, in the light of the objective of the Convention, the experience gained in its implementation and the evolution of scientific and technological knowledge, and in this respect consider and adopt regular reports on the implementation of this Protocol;

(c) Promote and facilitate the exchange of information on measures adopted by the Parties to address climate change and its effects, taking into account the differing circumstances, responsibilities and capabilities of the Parties and their respective commitments under this Protocol;

(d) Facilitate, at the request of two or more Parties, the coordination of measures adopted by them to address climate change and its effects, taking into account the differing circumstances, responsibilities and capabilities of the Parties and their respective commitments under this Protocol;

(e) Promote and guide, in accordance with the objective of the Convention and the provisions of this Protocol, and taking fully into account the relevant decisions by the Conference of the Parties, the development and periodic refinement of comparable methodologies for the effective implementation of this Protocol, to be agreed on by the Conference of the Parties serving as the meeting of the Parties to this Protocol;

(f) Make recommendations on any matters necessary for the implementation of this Protocol;

(g) Seek to mobilize additional financial resources in accordance with Article 11, paragraph 2;

(h) Establish such subsidiary bodies as are deemed necessary for the implementation of this Protocol;

(i) Seek and utilize, where appropriate, the services and cooperation of, and information provided by, competent international organizations and intergovernmental and non-governmental bodies; and

(j) Exercise such other functions as may be required for the implementation of this Protocol, and consider any assignment resulting from a decision by the Conference of the Parties.

5. The rules of procedure of the Conference of the Parties and financial procedures applied under the Convention shall be applied mutatis mutandis under this Protocol, except as may be otherwise decided by consensus by the Conference of the Parties serving as the meeting of the Parties to this Protocol.

6. The first session of the Conference of the Parties serving as the meeting of the Parties to this Protocol shall be convened by the secretariat in conjunction with the first session of the Conference of the Parties that is scheduled after the date of the entry into force of this Protocol. Subsequent ordinary sessions of the Conference of the Parties serving as the meeting of the Parties to this Protocol shall be held every year and in conjunction with ordinary sessions of the Conference of the Parties, unless otherwise decided by the Conference of the Parties serving as the meeting of the Parties to this Protocol.

7. Extraordinary sessions of the Conference of the Parties serving as the meeting of the Parties to this Protocol shall be held at such other times as may be deemed necessary by the Conference of the Parties serving as the meeting of the Parties to this Protocol, or at the written request of any Party, provided that, within six months of the request being communicated to the Parties by the secretariat, it is supported by at least one third of the Parties.

8. The United Nations, its specialized agencies and the International Atomic Energy Agency, as well as any State member thereof or observers thereto not

party to the Convention, may be represented at sessions of the Conference of the Parties serving as the meeting of the Parties to this Protocol as observers. Any body or agency, whether national or international, governmental or non-governmental, which is qualified in matters covered by this Protocol and which has informed the secretariat of its wish to be represented at a session of the Conference of the Parties serving as the meeting of the Parties to this Protocol as an observer, may be so admitted unless at least one third of the Parties present object. The admission and participation of observers shall be subject to the rules of procedure, as referred to in paragraph 5 above.

Article 14

1. The secretariat established by Article 8 of the Convention shall serve as the secretariat of this Protocol.

2. Article 8, paragraph 2, of the Convention on the functions of the secretariat, and Article 8, paragraph 3, of the Convention on arrangements made for the functioning of the secretariat, shall apply mutatis mutandis to this Protocol. The secretariat shall, in addition, exercise the functions assigned to it under this Protocol.

Article 15

1. The Subsidiary Body for Scientific and Technological Advice and the Subsidiary Body for Implementation established by Articles 9 and 10 of the Convention shall serve as, respectively, the Subsidiary Body for Scientific and Technological Advice and the Subsidiary Body for Implementation of this Protocol. The provisions relating to the functioning of these two bodies under the Convention shall apply mutatis mutandis to this Protocol. Sessions of the meetings of the Subsidiary Body for Scientific and Technological Advice and the Subsidiary Body for Implementation of this Protocol shall be held in conjunction with the meetings of, respectively, the Subsidiary Body for Scientific and Technological Advice and the Subsidiary Body for Implementation of the Convention.

2. Parties to the Convention that are not Parties to this Protocol may participate as observers in the proceedings of any session of the subsidiary bodies. When the subsidiary bodies serve as the subsidiary bodies of this Protocol, decisions under this Protocol shall be taken only by those that are Parties to this Protocol.

3. When the subsidiary bodies established by Articles 9 and 10 of the Convention exercise their functions with regard to matters concerning this Protocol, any member of the Bureaux of those subsidiary bodies representing a Party to the Convention but, at that time, not a party to this Protocol, shall be replaced by an additional member to be elected by and from amongst the Parties to this Protocol.

Article 16

The Conference of the Parties serving as the meeting of the Parties to this

Protocol shall, as soon as practicable, consider the application to this Protocol of, and modify as appropriate, the multilateral consultative process referred to in Article 13 of the Convention, in the light of any relevant decisions that may be taken by the Conference of the Parties. Any multilateral consultative process that may be applied to this Protocol shall operate without prejudice to the procedures and mechanisms established in accordance with Article 18.

Article 17

The Conference of the Parties shall define the relevant principles, modalities, rules and guidelines, in particular for verification, reporting and accountability for emissions trading. The Parties included in Annex B may participate in emissions trading for the purposes of fulfilling their commitments under Article 3. Any such trading shall be supplemental to domestic actions for the purpose of meeting quantified emission limitation and reduction commitments under that Article.

Article 18

The Conference of the Parties serving as the meeting of the Parties to this Protocol shall, at its first session, approve appropriate and effective procedures and mechanisms to determine and to address cases of non-compliance with the provisions of this Protocol, including through the development of an indicative list of consequences, taking into account the cause, type, degree and frequency of non-compliance. Any procedures and mechanisms under this Article entailing binding consequences shall be adopted by means of an amendment to this Protocol.

Article 19

The provisions of Article 14 of the Convention on settlement of disputes shall apply mutatis mutandis to this Protocol.

Article 20

1. Any Party may propose amendments to this Protocol.

2. Amendments to this Protocol shall be adopted at an ordinary session of the Conference of the Parties serving as the meeting of the Parties to this Protocol. The text of any proposed amendment to this Protocol shall be communicated to the Parties by the secretariat at least six months before the meeting at which it is proposed for adoption. The secretariat shall also communicate the text of any proposed amendments to the Parties and signatories to the Convention and, for information, to the Depositary.

3. The Parties shall make every effort to reach agreement on any proposed amendment to this Protocol by consensus. If all efforts at consensus have been exhausted, and no agreement reached, the amendment shall as a last resort be adopted by a three-fourths majority vote of the Parties present and voting at the meeting. The adopted amendment shall be communicated by the secretariat to the Depositary, who shall circulate it to all Parties for their acceptance.

4. Instruments of acceptance in respect of an amendment shall be deposited with the Depositary. An amendment adopted in accordance with paragraph 3 above shall enter into force for those Parties having accepted it on the ninetieth day after the date of receipt by the Depositary of an instrument of acceptance by at least three fourths of the Parties to this Protocol.

5. The amendment shall enter into force for any other Party on the ninetieth day after the date on which that Party deposits with the Depositary its instrument of acceptance of the said amendment.

Article 21

1. Annexes to this Protocol shall form an integral part thereof and, unless otherwise expressly provided, a reference to this Protocol constitutes at the same time a reference to any annexes thereto. Any annexes adopted after the entry into force of this Protocol shall be restricted to lists, forms and any other material of a descriptive nature that is of a scientific, technical, procedural or administrative character.

2. Any Party may make proposals for an annex to this Protocol and may propose amendments to annexes to this Protocol.

3. Annexes to this Protocol and amendments to annexes to this Protocol shall be adopted at an ordinary session of the Conference of the Parties serving as the meeting of the Parties to this Protocol. The text of any proposed annex or amendment to an annex shall be communicated to the Parties by the secretariat at least six months before the meeting at which it is proposed for adoption. The secretariat shall also communicate the text of any proposed annex or amendment to an annex to the Parties and signatories to the Convention and, for information, to the Depositary.

4. The Parties shall make every effort to reach agreement on any proposed annex or amendment to an annex by consensus. If all efforts at consensus have been exhausted, and no agreement reached, the annex or amendment to an annex shall as a last resort be adopted by a three-fourths majority vote of the Parties present and voting at the meeting. The adopted annex or amendment to an annex shall be communicated by the secretariat to the Depositary, who shall circulate it to all Parties for their acceptance.

5. An annex, or amendment to an annex other than Annex A or B, that has been adopted in accordance with paragraphs 3 and 4 above shall enter into force for all Parties to this Protocol six months after the date of the communication by the Depositary to such Parties of the adoption of the annex or adoption of the amendment to the annex, except for those Parties that have notified the Depositary, in writing, within that period of their non-acceptance of the annex or amendment to the annex. The annex or amendment to an annex shall enter into force for Parties which withdraw their notification of non-acceptance on the ninetieth day after the date on which withdrawal of such notification has been received by the Depositary.

6. If the adoption of an annex or an amendment to an annex involves an amendment to this Protocol, that annex or amendment to an annex shall not

enter into force until such time as the amendment to this Protocol enters into force.

7. Amendments to Annexes A and B to this Protocol shall be adopted and enter into force in accordance with the procedure set out in Article 20, provided that any amendment to Annex B shall be adopted only with the written consent of the Party concerned.

Article 22

1. Each Party shall have one vote, except as provided for in paragraph 2 below.

2. Regional economic integration organizations, in matters within their competence, shall exercise their right to vote with a number of votes equal to the number of their member States that are Parties to this Protocol. Such an organization shall not exercise its right to vote if any of its member States exercises its right, and vice versa.

Article 23

The Secretary-General of the United Nations shall be the Depositary of this Protocol.

Article 24

1. This Protocol shall be open for signature and subject to ratification, acceptance or approval by States and regional economic integration organizations which are Parties to the Convention. It shall be open for signature at United Nations Headquarters in New York from 16 March 1998 to 15 March 1999. This Protocol shall be open for accession from the day after the date on which it is closed for signature. Instruments of ratification, acceptance, approval or accession shall be deposited with the Depositary.

2. Any regional economic integration organization which becomes a Party to this Protocol without any of its member States being a Party shall be bound by all the obligations under this Protocol. In the case of such organizations, one or more of whose member States is a Party to this Protocol, the organization and its member States shall decide on their respective responsibilities for the performance of their obligations under this Protocol. In such cases, the organization and the member States shall not be entitled to exercise rights under this Protocol concurrently.

3. In their instruments of ratification, acceptance, approval or accession, regional economic integration organizations shall declare the extent of their competence with respect to the matters governed by this Protocol. These organizations shall also inform the Depositary, who shall in turn inform the Parties, of any substantial modification in the extent of their competence.

Article 25

1. This Protocol shall enter into force on the nineteenth day after the date on which not less than 55 Parties to the Convention, incorporating Parties includ-

ed in Annex I which accounted in total for at least 55 per cent of the total carbon dioxide emissions for 1990 of the Parties included in Annex I, have deposited their instruments of ratification, acceptance, approval or accession.

2. For the purposes of this Article, "the total carbon dioxide emissions for 1990 of the Parties included in Annex I" means the amount communicated on or before the date of adoption of this Protocol by the Parties included in Annex I in their first national communications submitted in accordance with Article 12 of the Convention.

3. For each State or regional economic integration organization that ratifies, accepts or approves this Protocol or accedes thereto after the conditions set out in paragraph 1 above for entry into force have been fulfilled, this Protocol shall enter into force on the ninetieth day following the date of deposit of its instrument of ratification, acceptance, approval or accession.

4. For the purposes of this Article, any instrument deposited by a regional economic integration organization shall not be counted as additional to those deposited by States members of the organization.

Article 26
No reservations may be made to this Protocol.

Article 27
1. At any time after three years from the date on which this Protocol has entered into force for a Party, that Party may withdraw from this Protocol by giving written notification to the Depositary.

2. Any such withdrawal shall take effect upon expiry of one year from the date of receipt by the Depositary of the notification of withdrawal, or on such later date as may be specified in the notification of withdrawal.

3. Any Party that withdraws from the Convention shall be considered as also having withdrawn from this Protocol.

Article 28
The original of this Protocol, of which the Arabic, Chinese, English, French, Russian and Spanish texts are equally authentic, shall be deposited with the Secretary-General of the United Nations.

DONE at Kyoto this eleventh day of December one thousand nine hundred and ninety-seven.

IN WITNESS WHEREOF the undersigned, being duly authorized to that effect, have affixed their signatures to this Protocol on the dates indicated.

Annex A

Greenhouse gases: Carbon dioxide (CO_2), Methane (CH_4), Nitrous oxide (N_2O), Hydrofluorocarbons (HFCs), Perfluorocarbons (PFCs), Sulphur hexafluoride (SF_6),

Sectors/source categories:

Energy—Fuel combustion: Energy industries, Manufacturing industries and construction, Transport, Other sectors, Other

—Fugitive emissions from fuels: Solid fuels, Oil and natural gas, Other

Industrial processes: Mineral products, Chemical industry, Metal production, Other production, Production of halocarbons and sulphur hexafluoride, Consumption of halocarbons and sulphur hexafluoride, Other, Solvent and other product use

Agriculture: Enteric fermentation, Manure management, Rice cultivation, Agricultural soils, Prescribed burning of savannas, Field burning of agricultural residues, Other

Waste: Solid waste disposal on land, Wastewater handling, Waste incineration, Other

Annex B

Party	Quantified emission limitation or reduction commitment (percentage of base year or period)
Australia	108
Austria	92
Belgium	92
Bulgaria*	92
Canada	94
Croatia*	95
Czech Republic*	92
Denmark	92
Estonia*	92
European Community	92
Finland	92
France	92
Germany	92
Greece	92
Hungary*	94
Iceland	110
Ireland	92
Italy	92
Japan	94
Latvia*	92
Liechtenstein	92
Lithuania*	92
Luxembourg	92
Monaco	92
Netherlands	92
New Zealand	100
Norway	101
Poland*	94
Portugal	92
Romania*	92
Russian Federation*	100
Slovakia*	92
Slovenia*	92

(continues)

Party	Quantified emission limitation or reduction commitment (percentage of base year or period)
Spain	92
Sweden	92
Switzerland	92
Ukraine*	100
United Kingdom of Great Britain and Northern Ireland	92
United States of America	93

*Countries that are undergoing the process of transition to a market economy.

7.3
Convention on
Biological Diversity (CBD)
(1992)

With this framework convention, international environmental law shifted from addressing the protection of specific endangered species to protecting biological diversity as a whole. In recognition of the need to reconcile environmental protection with economic imperatives, the convention addresses not only conservation but also the sustainable use of genetic resources and the fair and equitable sharing of the benefits arising from the use of genetic resources. Provisions on intellectual property, access and benefit sharing of genetic resources, and the protection of traditional knowledge have been particularly controversial.

On the growing influence of indigenous peoples' rights on international environmental law, see Jeremy Firestone, Jonathan Lilley, and Isabel Torres de Noronha, "Cultural Diversity, Human Rights, and the Emergence of Indigenous Peoples in International and Comparative Environmental Law," American University International Law Review *20 (March-April 2005): 219–292. The secretariat of the Convention on Biological Diversity has a website at www.biodiv.org. See also Philippe G. Le Prestre, ed.,* Governing Global Biodiversity: The Evolution and Implementation of the Convention on Biological Diversity *(Aldershot, Hants.: Ashgate, 2002).*

The Contracting Parties,

Conscious of the intrinsic value of biological diversity and of the ecological, genetic, social, economic, scientific, educational, cultural, recreational and aesthetic values of biological diversity and its components,

Conscious also of the importance of biological diversity for evolution and for maintaining life sustaining systems of the biosphere,

Affirming that the conservation of biological diversity is a common concern of humankind,

Reaffirming that States have sovereign rights over their own biological resources,

Reaffirming also that States are responsible for conserving their biological diversity and for using their biological resources in a sustainable manner,

Concerned that biological diversity is being significantly reduced by certain human activities,

Aware of the general lack of information and knowledge regarding biological diversity and of the urgent need to develop scientific, technical and institutional capacities to provide the basic understanding upon which to plan and implement appropriate measures,

Noting that it is vital to anticipate, prevent and attack the causes of significant reduction or loss of biological diversity at source,

Noting also that where there is a threat of significant reduction or loss of biological diversity, lack of full scientific certainty should not be used as a reason for postponing measures to avoid or minimize such a threat,

Noting further that the fundamental requirement for the conservation of biological diversity is the in-situ conservation of ecosystems and natural habitats and the maintenance and recovery of viable populations of species in their natural surroundings,

Noting further that ex-situ measures, preferably in the country of origin, also have an important role to play,

Recognizing the close and traditional dependence of many indigenous and local communities embodying traditional lifestyles on biological resources, and the desirability of sharing equitably benefits arising from the use of traditional knowledge, innovations and practices relevant to the conservation of biological diversity and the sustainable use of its components,

Recognizing also the vital role that women play in the conservation and sustainable use of biological diversity and affirming the need for the full participation of women at all levels of policymaking and implementation for biological diversity conservation,

Stressing the importance of, and the need to promote international, regional and global cooperation among States and intergovernmental organizations and the non-governmental sector for the conservation of biological diversity and the sustainable use of its components,

Acknowledging that the provision of new and additional financial resources and appropriate access to relevant technologies can be expected to make a substantial difference in the world's ability to address the loss of biological diversity,

Acknowledging further that special provision is required to meet the needs of developing countries, including the provision of new and additional financial resources and appropriate access to relevant technologies,

Noting in this regard the special conditions of the least developed countries and small island States,

Acknowledging that substantial investments are required to conserve biological diversity and that there is the expectation of a broad range of environmental, economic and social benefits from those investments,

Recognizing that economic and social development and poverty eradication are the first and overriding priorities of developing countries,

Aware that conservation and sustainable use of biological diversity is of critical importance for meeting the food, health and other needs of the growing world population, for which purpose access to and sharing of both genetic resources and technologies are essential,

Noting that, ultimately, the conservation and sustainable use of biological diversity will strengthen friendly relations among States and contribute to peace for humankind,

Desiring to enhance and complement existing international arrangements for the conservation of biological diversity and sustainable use of its components, and

Determined to conserve and sustainably use biological diversity for the benefit of present and future generations,

Have agreed as follows:

Article 1: Objectives

The objectives of this Convention, to be pursued in accordance with its relevant provisions, are the conservation of biological diversity, the sustainable use of its components and the fair and equitable sharing of the benefits arising out of the utilization of genetic resources, including by appropriate access to genetic resources and by appropriate transfer of relevant technologies, taking into account all rights over those resources and to technologies, and by appropriate funding.

Article 2: Use of terms

For the purposes of this Convention:

"Biological diversity" means the variability among living organisms from all sources including, inter alia, terrestrial, marine and other aquatic ecosystems and the ecological complexes of which they are part; this includes diversity within species, between species and of ecosystems.

"Biological resources" includes genetic resources, organisms or parts thereof, populations, or any other biotic component of ecosystems with actual or potential use or value for humanity.

"Biotechnology" means any technological application that uses biological systems, living organisms, or derivatives thereof, to make or modify products or processes for specific use.

"Country of origin of genetic resources" means the country which possesses those genetic resources in in-situ conditions.

"Country providing genetic resources" means the country supplying genetic resources collected from in-situ sources, including populations of both wild and domesticated species, or taken from ex-situ sources, which may or may not have originated in that country.

"Domesticated or cultivated species" means species in which the evolutionary process has been influenced by humans to meet their needs.

"Ecosystem" means a dynamic complex of plant, animal and micro-organism communities and their non-living environment interacting as a functional unit.

"Ex-situ conservation" means the conservation of components of biological diversity outside their natural habitats.

"Genetic material" means any material of plant, animal, microbial or other origin containing functional units of heredity.

"Genetic resources" means genetic material of actual or potential value.

"Habitat" means the place or type of site where an organism or population naturally occurs.

"In-situ conditions" means conditions where genetic resources exist within ecosystems and natural habitats, and, in the case of domesticated or cultivated species, in the surroundings where they have developed their distinctive properties.

"In-situ conservation" means the conservation of ecosystems and natural habitats and the maintenance and recovery of viable populations of species in their natural surroundings and, in the case of domesticated or cultivated species, in the surroundings where they have developed their distinctive properties.

"Protected area" means a geographically defined area which is designated or regulated and managed to achieve specific conservation objectives.

"Regional economic integration organization" means an organization constituted by sovereign States of a given region, to which its member States have transferred competence in respect of matters governed by this Convention and which has been duly authorized, in accordance with its internal procedures, to sign, ratify, accept, approve or accede to it.

"Sustainable use" means the use of components of biological diversity in a way and at a rate that does not lead to the long-term decline of biological diversity, thereby maintaining its potential to meet the needs and aspirations of present and future generations.

"Technology" includes biotechnology.

Article 3: Principle

States have, in accordance with the Charter of the United Nations and the principles of international law, the sovereign right to exploit their own resources pursuant to their own environmental policies, and the responsibility to ensure that activities within their jurisdiction or control do not cause damage to the environment of other States or of areas beyond the limits of national jurisdiction.

Article 4: Jurisdictional scope

Subject to the rights of other States, and except as otherwise expressly provided in this Convention, the provisions of this Convention apply, in relation to each Contracting Party:

(a) In the case of components of biological diversity, in areas within the limits of its national jurisdiction; and

(b) In the case of processes and activities, regardless of where their effects occur, carried out under its jurisdiction or control, within the area of its national jurisdiction or beyond the limits of national jurisdiction.

Article 5: Cooperation

Each Contracting Party shall, as far as possible and as appropriate, cooperate with other Contracting Parties, directly or, where appropriate, through competent international organizations, in respect of areas beyond national jurisdiction and on other matters of mutual interest, for the conservation and sustainable use of biological diversity.

Article 6: General measures for conservation and sustainable use

Each Contracting Party shall, in accordance with its particular conditions and capabilities:

(a) Develop national strategies, plans or programmes for the conservation and sustainable use of biological diversity or adapt for this purpose existing strategies, plans or programmes which shall reflect, inter alia, the measures set out in this Convention relevant to the Contracting Party concerned; and

(b) Integrate, as far as possible and as appropriate, the conservation and sustainable use of biological diversity into relevant sectoral or cross-sectoral plans, programmes and policies.

Article 7: Identification and monitoring

Each Contracting Party shall, as far as possible and as appropriate, in particular for the purposes of Articles 8 to 10:

(a) Identify components of biological diversity important for its conservation and sustainable use having regard to the indicative list of categories set down in Annex I;

(b) Monitor, through sampling and other techniques, the components of biological diversity identified pursuant to subparagraph (a) above, paying particular attention to those requiring urgent conservation measures and those which offer the greatest potential for sustainable use;

(c) Identify processes and categories of activities which have or are likely to have significant adverse impacts on the conservation and sustainable use of biological diversity, and monitor their effects through sampling and other techniques; and

(d) Maintain and organize, by any mechanism data, derived from identification and monitoring activities pursuant to subparagraphs (a), (b) and (c) above.

Article 8: In-situ conservation

Each Contracting Party shall, as far as possible and as appropriate:

(a) Establish a system of protected areas or areas where special measures need to be taken to conserve biological diversity;

(b) Develop, where necessary, guidelines for the selection, establishment and management of protected areas or areas where special measures need to be taken to conserve biological diversity;

(c) Regulate or manage biological resources important for the conservation of biological diversity whether within or outside protected areas, with a view to ensuring their conservation and sustainable use;

(d) Promote the protection of ecosystems, natural habitats and the maintenance of viable populations of species in natural surroundings;

(e) Promote environmentally sound and sustainable development in areas adjacent to protected areas with a view to furthering protection of these areas;

(f) Rehabilitate and restore degraded ecosystems and promote the recovery of threatened species, inter alia, through the development and implementation of plans or other management strategies;

(g) Establish or maintain means to regulate, manage or control the risks associated with the use and release of living modified organisms resulting from biotechnology which are likely to have adverse environmental impacts that could affect the conservation and sustainable use of biological diversity, taking also into account the risks to human health;

(h) Prevent the introduction of, control or eradicate those alien species which threaten ecosystems, habitats or species;

(i) Endeavour to provide the conditions needed for compatibility between present uses and the conservation of biological diversity and the sustainable use of its components;

(j) Subject to its national legislation, respect, preserve and maintain knowledge, innovations and practices of indigenous and local communities embodying traditional lifestyles relevant for the conservation and sustainable use of biological diversity and promote their wider application with the approval and involvement of the holders of such knowledge, innovations and practices and encourage the equitable sharing of the benefits arising from the utilization of such knowledge, innovations and practices;

(k) Develop or maintain necessary legislation and/or other regulatory provisions for the protection of threatened species and populations;

(l) Where a significant adverse effect on biological diversity has been determined pursuant to Article 7, regulate or manage the relevant processes and categories of activities; and

(m) Cooperate in providing financial and other support for in-situ conservation outlined in subparagraphs (a) to (l) above, particularly to developing countries.

Article 9: Ex-situ conservation

Each Contracting Party shall, as far as possible and as appropriate, and predominantly for the purpose of complementing in-situ measures:

(a) Adopt measures for the ex-situ conservation of components of biological diversity, preferably in the country of origin of such components;

(b) Establish and maintain facilities for ex-situ conservation of and research on plants, animals and micro-organisms, preferably in the country of origin of genetic resources;

(c) Adopt measures for the recovery and rehabilitation of threatened species and for their reintroduction into their natural habitats under appropriate conditions;

(d) Regulate and manage collection of biological resources from natural habitats for ex-situ conservation purposes so as not to threaten ecosystems and in-situ populations of species, except where special temporary ex-situ measures are required under subparagraph (c) above; and

(e) Cooperate in providing financial and other support for ex situ conservation outlined in subparagraphs (a) to (d) above and in the establishment and maintenance of ex-situ conservation facilities in developing countries.

Article 10: Sustainable use of components of biological diversity
Each Contracting Party shall, as far as possible and as appropriate:

(a) Integrate consideration of the conservation and sustainable use of biological resources into national decision-making;

(b) Adopt measures relating to the use of biological resources to avoid or minimize adverse impacts on biological diversity;

(c) Protect and encourage customary use of biological resources in accordance with traditional cultural practices that are compatible with conservation or sustainable use requirements;

(d) Support local populations to develop and implement remedial action in degraded areas where biological diversity has been reduced; and

(e) Encourage cooperation between its governmental authorities and its private sector in developing methods for sustainable use of biological resources.

Article 11: Incentive measures
Each Contracting Party shall, as far as possible and as appropriate, adopt economically and socially sound measures that act as incentives for the conservation and sustainable use of components of biological diversity.

Article 12: Research and training
The Contracting Parties, taking into account the special needs of developing countries, shall:

(a) Establish and maintain programmes for scientific and technical education and training in measures for the identification, conservation and sustainable use of biological diversity and its components and provide support for such education and training for the specific needs of developing countries;

(b) Promote and encourage research which contributes to the conservation and sustainable use of biological diversity, particularly in developing countries, inter alia, in accordance with decisions of the Conference of the Parties taken in consequence of recommendations of the Subsidiary Body on Scientific, Technical and Technological Advice; and

(c) In keeping with the provisions of Articles 16, 18 and 20, promote and cooperate in the use of scientific advances in biological diversity research in developing methods for conservation and sustainable use of biological resources.

Article 13: Public education and awareness
The Contracting Parties shall:

(a) Promote and encourage understanding of the importance of, and the measures required for, the conservation of biological diversity, as well as its propagation through media, and the inclusion of these topics in educational programmes; and

(b) Cooperate, as appropriate, with other States and international organizations in developing educational and public awareness programmes, with respect to conservation and sustainable use of biological diversity.

Article 14: Impact Assessment and Minimizing Adverse Impacts

1. Each Contracting Party, as far as possible and as appropriate, shall:

(a) Introduce appropriate procedures requiring environmental impact assessment of its proposed projects that are likely to have significant adverse effects on biological diversity with a view to avoiding or minimizing such effects and, where appropriate, allow for public participation in such procedures;

(b) Introduce appropriate arrangements to ensure that the environmental consequences of its programmes and policies that are likely to have significant adverse impacts on biological diversity are duly taken into account;

(c) Promote, on the basis of reciprocity, notification, exchange of information and consultation on activities under their jurisdiction or control which are likely to significantly affect adversely the biological diversity of other States or areas beyond the limits of national jurisdiction, by encouraging the conclusion of bilateral, regional or multilateral arrangements, as appropriate;

(d) In the case of imminent or grave danger or damage, originating under its jurisdiction or control, to biological diversity within the area under jurisdiction of other States or in areas beyond the limits of national jurisdiction, notify immediately the potentially affected States of such danger or damage, as well as initiate action to prevent or minimize such danger or damage; and

(e) Promote national arrangements for emergency responses to activities or events, whether caused naturally or otherwise, which present a grave and imminent danger to biological diversity and encourage international cooperation to supplement such national efforts and, where appropriate and agreed by the States or regional economic integration organizations concerned, to establish joint contingency plans.

2. The Conference of the Parties shall examine, on the basis of studies to be carried out, the issue of liability and redress, including restoration and compensation, for damage to biological diversity, except where such liability is a purely internal matter.

Article 15: Access to genetic resources

1. Recognizing the sovereign rights of States over their natural resources, the authority to determine access to genetic resources rests with the national governments and is subject to national legislation.

2. Each Contracting Party shall endeavour to create conditions to facilitate access to genetic resources for environmentally sound uses by other

Contracting Parties and not to impose restrictions that run counter to the objectives of this Convention.

3. For the purpose of this Convention, the genetic resources being provided by a Contracting Party, as referred to in this Article and Articles 16 and 19, are only those that are provided by Contracting Parties that are countries of origin of such resources or by the Parties that have acquired the genetic resources in accordance with this Convention.

4. Access, where granted, shall be on mutually agreed terms and subject to the provisions of this Article.

5. Access to genetic resources shall be subject to prior informed consent of the Contracting Party providing such resources, unless otherwise determined by that Party.

6. Each Contracting Party shall endeavour to develop and carry out scientific research based on genetic resources provided by other Contracting Parties with the full participation of, and where possible in, such Contracting Parties.

7. Each Contracting Party shall take legislative, administrative or policy measures, as appropriate, and in accordance with Articles 16 and 19 and, where necessary, through the financial mechanism established by Articles 20 and 21 with the aim of sharing in a fair and equitable way the results of research and development and the benefits arising from the commercial and other utilization of genetic resources with the Contracting Party providing such resources. Such sharing shall be upon mutually agreed terms.

Article 16: Access to and transfer of technology

1. Each Contracting Party, recognizing that technology includes biotechnology, and that both access to and transfer of technology among Contracting Parties are essential elements for the attainment of the objectives of this Convention, undertakes subject to the provisions of this Article to provide and/or facilitate access for and transfer to other Contracting Parties of technologies that are relevant to the conservation and sustainable use of biological diversity or make use of genetic resources and do not cause significant damage to the environment.

2. Access to and transfer of technology referred to in paragraph 1 above to developing countries shall be provided and/or facilitated under fair and most favourable terms, including on concessional and preferential terms where mutually agreed, and, where necessary, in accordance with the financial mechanism established by Articles 20 and 21. In the case of technology subject to patents and other intellectual property rights, such access and transfer shall be provided on terms which recognize and are consistent with the adequate and effective protection of intellectual property rights. The application of this paragraph shall be consistent with paragraphs 3, 4 and 5 below.

3. Each Contracting Party shall take legislative, administrative or policy measures, as appropriate, with the aim that Contracting Parties, in particular those that are developing countries, which provide genetic resources are provided access to and transfer of technology which makes use of those resources,

on mutually agreed terms, including technology protected by patents and other intellectual property rights, where necessary, through the provisions of Articles 20 and 21 and in accordance with international law and consistent with paragraphs 4 and 5 below.

4. Each Contracting Party shall take legislative, administrative or policy measures, as appropriate, with the aim that the private sector facilitates access to, joint development and transfer of technology referred to in paragraph 1 above for the benefit of both governmental institutions and the private sector of developing countries and in this regard shall abide by the obligations included in paragraphs 1, 2 and 3 above.

5. The Contracting Parties, recognizing that patents and other intellectual property rights may have an influence on the implementation of this Convention, shall cooperate in this regard subject to national legislation and international law in order to ensure that such rights are supportive of and do not run counter to its objectives.

Article 17: Exchange of information

1. The Contracting Parties shall facilitate the exchange of information, from all publicly available sources, relevant to the conservation and sustainable use of biological diversity, taking into account the special needs of developing countries.

2. Such exchange of information shall include exchange of results of technical, scientific and socio-economic research, as well as information on training and surveying programmes, specialized knowledge, indigenous and traditional knowledge as such and in combination with the technologies referred to in Article 16, paragraph 1. It shall also, where feasible, include repatriation of information.

Article 18: Technical and scientific cooperation

1. The Contracting Parties shall promote international technical and scientific cooperation in the field of conservation and sustainable use of biological diversity, where necessary, through the appropriate international and national institutions.

2. Each Contracting Party shall promote technical and scientific cooperation with other Contracting Parties, in particular developing countries, in implementing this Convention, inter alia, through the development and implementation of national policies. In promoting such cooperation, special attention should be given to the development and strengthening of national capabilities, by means of human resources development and institution building.

3. The Conference of the Parties, at its first meeting, shall determine how to establish a clearing-house mechanism to promote and facilitate technical and scientific cooperation.

4. The Contracting Parties shall, in accordance with national legislation and policies, encourage and develop methods of cooperation for the development and use of technologies, including indigenous and traditional technologies, in

pursuance of the objectives of this Convention. For this purpose, the Contracting Parties shall also promote cooperation in the training of personnel and exchange of experts.

5. The Contracting Parties shall, subject to mutual agreement, promote the establishment of joint research programmes and joint ventures for the development of technologies relevant to the objectives of this Convention.

Article 19: Handling of biotechnology and distribution of its benefits

1. Each Contracting Party shall take legislative, administrative or policy measures, as appropriate, to provide for the effective participation in biotechnological research activities by those Contracting Parties, especially developing countries, which provide the genetic resources for such research, and where feasible in such Contracting Parties.

2. Each Contracting Party shall take all practicable measures to promote and advance priority access on a fair and equitable basis by Contracting Parties, especially developing countries, to the results and benefits arising from biotechnologies based upon genetic resources provided by those Contracting Parties. Such access shall be on mutually agreed terms.

3. The Parties shall consider the need for and modalities of a protocol setting out appropriate procedures, including, in particular, advance informed agreement, in the field of the safe transfer, handling and use of any living modified organism resulting from biotechnology that may have adverse effect on the conservation and sustainable use of biological diversity.

4. Each Contracting Party shall, directly or by requiring any natural or legal person under its jurisdiction providing the organisms referred to in paragraph 3 above, provide any available information about the use and safety regulations required by that Contracting Party in handling such organisms, as well as any available information on the potential adverse impact of the specific organisms concerned to the Contracting Party into which those organisms are to be introduced.

Article 20: Financial resources

1. Each Contracting Party undertakes to provide, in accordance with its capabilities, financial support and incentives in respect of those national activities which are intended to achieve the objectives of this Convention, in accordance with its national plans, priorities and programmes.

2. The developed country Parties shall provide new and additional financial resources to enable developing country Parties to meet the agreed full incremental costs to them of implementing measures which fulfil the obligations of this Convention and to benefit from its provisions and which costs are agreed between a developing country Party and the institutional structure referred to in Article 21, in accordance with policy, strategy, programme priorities and eligibility criteria and an indicative list of incremental costs established by the Conference of the Parties. Other Parties, including countries undergoing the process of transition to a market economy, may voluntarily assume the obliga-

tions of the developed country Parties. For the purpose of this Article, the Conference of the Parties, shall at its first meeting establish a list of developed country Parties and other Parties which voluntarily assume the obligations of the developed country Parties. The Conference of the Parties shall periodically review and if necessary amend the list. Contributions from other countries and sources on a voluntary basis would also be encouraged. The implementation of these commitments shall take into account the need for adequacy, predictability and timely flow of funds and the importance of burden-sharing among the contributing Parties included in the list.

3. The developed country Parties may also provide, and developing country Parties avail themselves of, financial resources related to the implementation of this Convention through bilateral, regional and other multilateral channels.

4. The extent to which developing country Parties will effectively implement their commitments under this Convention will depend on the effective implementation by developed country Parties of their commitments under this Convention related to financial resources and transfer of technology and will take fully into account the fact that economic and social development and eradication of poverty are the first and overriding priorities of the developing country Parties.

5. The Parties shall take full account of the specific needs and special situation of least developed countries in their actions with regard to funding and transfer of technology.

6. The Contracting Parties shall also take into consideration the special conditions resulting from the dependence on, distribution and location of, biological diversity within developing country Parties, in particular small island States.

7. Consideration shall also be given to the special situation of developing countries, including those that are most environmentally vulnerable, such as those with arid and semi-arid zones, coastal and mountainous areas.

Article 21: Financial mechanism

1. There shall be a mechanism for the provision of financial resources to developing country Parties for purposes of this Convention on a grant or concessional basis the essential elements of which are described in this Article. The mechanism shall function under the authority and guidance of, and be accountable to, the Conference of the Parties for purposes of this Convention. The operations of the mechanism shall be carried out by such institutional structure as may be decided upon by the Conference of the Parties at its first meeting.

For purposes of this Convention, the Conference of the Parties shall determine the policy, strategy, programme priorities and eligibility criteria relating to the access to and utilization of such resources. The contributions shall be such as to take into account the need for predictability, adequacy and timely flow of funds referred to in Article 20 in accordance with the amount of resources needed to be decided periodically by the Conference of the Parties and the importance of burden-sharing among the contributing Parties included in the list referred to in Article 20, paragraph 2. Voluntary contributions may also be made by the developed country Parties and by other countries and sources. The mechanism shall operate within a democratic and transparent system of governance.

2. Pursuant to the objectives of this Convention, the Conference of the Parties shall at its first meeting determine the policy, strategy and programme priorities, as well as detailed criteria and guidelines for eligibility for access to and utilization of the financial resources including monitoring and evaluation on a regular basis of such utilization. The Conference of the Parties shall decide on the arrangements to give effect to paragraph 1 above after consultation with the institutional structure entrusted with the operation of the financial mechanism.

3. The Conference of the Parties shall review the effectiveness of the mechanism established under this Article, including the criteria and guidelines referred to in paragraph 2 above, not less than two years after the entry into force of this Convention and thereafter on a regular basis. Based on such review, it shall take appropriate action to improve the effectiveness of the mechanism if necessary.

4. The Contracting Parties shall consider strengthening existing financial institutions to provide financial resources for the conservation and sustainable use of biological diversity.

Article 22: Relationship with other international conventions

1. The provisions of this Convention shall not affect the rights and obligations of any Contracting Party deriving from any existing international agreement, except where the exercise of those rights and obligations would cause a serious damage or threat to biological diversity.

2. Contracting Parties shall implement this Convention with respect to the marine environment consistently with the rights and obligations of States under the law of the sea.

Article 23: Conference of the Parties

1. A Conference of the Parties is hereby established. The first meeting of the Conference of the Parties shall be convened by the Executive Director of the United Nations Environment Programme not later than one year after the entry into force of this Convention. Thereafter, ordinary meetings of the Conference of the Parties shall be held at regular intervals to be determined by the Conference at its first meeting.

2. Extraordinary meetings of the Conference of the Parties shall be held at such other times as may be deemed necessary by the Conference, or at the written request of any Party, provided that, within six months of the request being communicated to them by the Secretariat, it is supported by at least one third of the Parties.

3. The Conference of the Parties shall by consensus agree upon and adopt

rules of procedure for itself and for any subsidiary body it may establish, as well as financial rules governing the funding of the Secretariat. At each ordinary meeting, it shall adopt a budget for the financial period until the next ordinary meeting.

4. The Conference of the Parties shall keep under review the implementation of this Convention, and, for this purpose, shall:

(a) Establish the form and the intervals for transmitting the information to be submitted in accordance with Article 26 and consider such information as well as reports submitted by any subsidiary body;

(b) Review scientific, technical and technological advice on biological diversity provided in accordance with Article 25;

(c) Consider and adopt, as required, protocols in accordance with Article 28;

(d) Consider and adopt, as required, in accordance with Articles 29 and 30, amendments to this Convention and its annexes;

(e) Consider amendments to any protocol, as well as to any annexes thereto, and, if so decided, recommend their adoption to the parties to the protocol concerned;

(f) Consider and adopt, as required, in accordance with Article 30, additional annexes to this Convention;

(g) Establish such subsidiary bodies, particularly to provide scientific and technical advice, as are deemed necessary for the implementation of this Convention;

(h) Contact, through the Secretariat, the executive bodies of conventions dealing with matters covered by this Convention with a view to establishing appropriate forms of cooperation with them; and

(i) Consider and undertake any additional action that may be required for the achievement of the purposes of this Convention in the light of experience gained in its operation.

5. The United Nations, its specialized agencies and the International Atomic Energy Agency, as well as any State not Party to this Convention, may be represented as observers at meetings of the Conference of the Parties. Any other body or agency, whether governmental or non-governmental, qualified in fields relating to conservation and sustainable use of biological diversity, which has informed the Secretariat of its wish to be represented as an observer at a meeting of the Conference of the Parties, may be admitted unless at least one third of the Parties present object. The admission and participation of observers shall be subject to the rules of procedure adopted by the Conference of the Parties.

Article 24: Secretariat

1. A secretariat is hereby established. Its functions shall be:

(a) To arrange for and service meetings of the Conference of the Parties provided for in Article 23;

(b) To perform the functions assigned to it by any protocol;

(c) To prepare reports on the execution of its functions under this Convention and present them to the Conference of the Parties;

(d) To coordinate with other relevant international bodies and, in particular to enter into such administrative and contractual arrangements as may be required for the effective discharge of its functions; and

(e) To perform such other functions as may be determined by the Conference of the Parties.

2. At its first ordinary meeting, the Conference of the Parties shall designate the secretariat from amongst those existing competent international organizations which have signified their willingness to carry out the secretariat functions under this Convention.

Article 25: Subsidiary body on scientific, technical and technological advice

1. A subsidiary body for the provision of scientific, technical and technological advice is hereby established to provide the Conference of the Parties and, as appropriate, its other subsidiary bodies with timely advice relating to the implementation of this Convention. This body shall be open to participation by all Parties and shall be multidisciplinary. It shall comprise government representatives competent in the relevant field of expertise. It shall report regularly to the Conference of the Parties on all aspects of its work.

2. Under the authority of and in accordance with guidelines laid down by the Conference of the Parties, and upon its request, this body shall:

(a) Provide scientific and technical assessments of the status of biological diversity;

(b) Prepare scientific and technical assessments of the effects of types of measures taken in accordance with the provisions of this Convention;

(c) Identify innovative, efficient and state-of-the-art technologies and know-how relating to the conservation and sustainable use of biological diversity and advise on the ways and means of promoting development and/or transferring such technologies;

(d) Provide advice on scientific programmes and international cooperation in research and development related to conservation and sustainable use of biological diversity; and

(e) Respond to scientific, technical, technological and methodological questions that the Conference of the Parties and its subsidiary bodies may put to the body.

3. The functions, terms of reference, organization and operation of this body may be further elaborated by the Conference of the Parties.

Article 26: Reports

Each Contracting Party shall, at intervals to be determined by the Conference of the Parties, present to the Conference of the Parties, reports on measures which it has taken for the implementation of the provisions of this Convention and their effectiveness in meeting the objectives of this Convention.

Article 27: Settlement of disputes

1. In the event of a dispute between Contracting Parties concerning the interpretation or application of this Convention, the parties concerned shall seek solution by negotiation.

2. If the parties concerned cannot reach agreement by negotiation, they may jointly seek the good offices of, or request mediation by, a third party.

3. When ratifying, accepting, approving or acceding to this Convention, or at any time thereafter, a State or regional economic integration organization may declare in writing to the Depositary that for a dispute not resolved in accordance with paragraph 1 or paragraph 2 above, it accepts one or both of the following means of dispute settlement as compulsory:

   (a) Arbitration in accordance with the procedure laid down in Part 1 of Annex II;

   (b) Submission of the dispute to the International Court of Justice.

4. If the parties to the dispute have not, in accordance with paragraph 3 above, accepted the same or any procedure, the dispute shall be submitted to conciliation in accordance with Part 2 of Annex II unless the parties otherwise agree.

5. The provisions of this Article shall apply with respect to any protocol except as otherwise provided in the protocol concerned.

Article 28: Adoption of protocols

1. The Contracting Parties shall cooperate in the formulation and adoption of protocols to this Convention.

2. Protocols shall be adopted at a meeting of the Conference of the Parties.

3. The text of any proposed protocol shall be communicated to the Contracting Parties by the Secretariat at least six months before such a meeting.

Article 29: Amendment of the Convention or protocols

1. Amendments to this Convention may be proposed by any Contracting Party. Amendments to any protocol may be proposed by any Party to that protocol.

2. Amendments to this Convention shall be adopted at a meeting of the Conference of the Parties. Amendments to any protocol shall be adopted at a meeting of the Parties to the Protocol in question. The text of any proposed amendment to this Convention or to any protocol, except as may otherwise be provided in such protocol, shall be communicated to the Parties to the instrument in question by the secretariat at least six months before the meeting at which it is proposed for adoption. The secretariat shall also communicate proposed amendments to the signatories to this Convention for information.

3. The Parties shall make every effort to reach agreement on any proposed amendment to this Convention or to any protocol by consensus. If all efforts at consensus have been exhausted, and no agreement reached, the amendment shall as a last resort be adopted by a two-third majority vote of the

Parties to the instrument in question present and voting at the meeting, and shall be submitted by the Depositary to all Parties for ratification, acceptance or approval.

4. Ratification, acceptance or approval of amendments shall be notified to the Depositary in writing. Amendments adopted in accordance with paragraph 3 above shall enter into force among Parties having accepted them on the ninetieth day after the deposit of instruments of ratification, acceptance or approval by at least two thirds of the Contracting Parties to this Convention or of the Parties to the protocol concerned, except as may otherwise be provided in such protocol. Thereafter the amendments shall enter into force for any other Party on the ninetieth day after that Party deposits its instrument of ratification, acceptance or approval of the amendments.

5. For the purposes of this Article, "Parties present and voting" means Parties present and casting an affirmative or negative vote.

Article 30: Adoption and amendment of annexes

1. The annexes to this Convention or to any protocol shall form an integral part of the Convention or of such protocol, as the case may be, and, unless expressly provided otherwise, a reference to this Convention or its protocols constitutes at the same time a reference to any annexes thereto. Such annexes shall be restricted to procedural, scientific, technical and administrative matters.

2. Except as may be otherwise provided in any protocol with respect to its annexes, the following procedure shall apply to the proposal, adoption and entry into force of additional annexes to this Convention or of annexes to any protocol:

(a) Annexes to this Convention or to any protocol shall be proposed and adopted according to the procedure laid down in Article 29;

(b) Any Party that is unable to approve an additional annex to this Convention or an annex to any protocol to which it is Party shall so notify the Depositary, in writing, within one year from the date of the communication of the adoption by the Depositary. The Depositary shall without delay notify all Parties of any such notification received. A Party may at any time withdraw a previous declaration of objection and the annexes shall thereupon enter into force for that Party subject to subparagraph (c) below;

(c) On the expiry of one year from the date of the communication of the adoption by the Depositary, the annex shall enter into force for all Parties to this Convention or to any protocol concerned which have not submitted a notification in accordance with the provisions of subparagraph (b) above.

3. The proposal, adoption and entry into force of amendments to annexes to this Convention or to any protocol shall be subject to the same procedure as for the proposal, adoption and entry into force of annexes to the Convention or annexes to any protocol.

4. If an additional annex or an amendment to an annex is related to an amendment to this Convention or to any protocol, the additional annex or

amendment shall not enter into force until such time as the amendment to the Convention or to the protocol concerned enters into force.

Article 31: Right to vote

1. Except as provided for in paragraph 2 below, each Contracting Party to this Convention or to any protocol shall have one vote.

2. Regional economic integration organizations, in matters within their competence, shall exercise their right to vote with a number of votes equal to the number of their member States which are Contracting Parties to this Convention or the relevant protocol. Such organizations shall not exercise their right to vote if their member States exercise theirs, and vice versa.

Article 32: Relationship between this Convention and its protocols

1. A State or a regional economic integration organization may not become a Party to a protocol unless it is, or becomes at the same time, a Contracting Party to this Convention.

2. Decisions under any protocol shall be taken only by the Parties to the protocol concerned. Any Contracting Party that has not ratified, accepted or approved a protocol may participate as an observer in any meeting of the parties to that protocol.

Article 33: Signature

This Convention shall be open for signature at Rio de Janeiro by all States and any regional economic integration organization from 5 June 1992 until 14 June 1992, and at the United Nations Headquarters in New York from 15 June 1992 to 4 June 1993.

Article 34: Ratification, acceptance or approval

1. This Convention and any protocol shall be subject to ratification, acceptance or approval by States and by regional economic integration organizations. Instruments of ratification, acceptance or approval shall be deposited with the Depositary.

2. Any organization referred to in paragraph 1 above which becomes a Contracting Party to this Convention or any protocol without any of its member States being a Contracting Party shall be bound by all the obligations under the Convention or the protocol, as the case may be. In the case of such organizations, one or more of whose member States is a Contracting Party to this Convention or relevant protocol, the organization and its member States shall decide on their respective responsibilities for the performance of their obligations under the Convention or protocol, as the case may be. In such cases, the organization and the member States shall not be entitled to exercise rights under the Convention or relevant protocol concurrently.

3. In their instruments of ratification, acceptance or approval, the organizations referred to in paragraph 1 above shall declare the extent of their competence with respect to the matters governed by the Convention or the relevant

protocol. These organizations shall also inform the Depositary of any relevant modification in the extent of their competence.

Article 35: Accession

1. This Convention and any protocol shall be open for accession by States and by regional economic integration organizations from the date on which the Convention or the protocol concerned is closed for signature. The instruments of accession shall be deposited with the Depositary.

2. In their instruments of accession, the organizations referred to in paragraph 1 above shall declare the extent of their competence with respect to the matters governed by the Convention or the relevant protocol. These organizations shall also inform the Depositary of any relevant modification in the extent of their competence.

3. The provisions of Article 34, paragraph 2, shall apply to regional economic integration organizations which accede to this Convention or any protocol.

Article 36: Entry into force

1. This Convention shall enter into force on the ninetieth day after the date of deposit of the thirtieth instrument of ratification, acceptance, approval or accession.

2. Any protocol shall enter into force on the ninetieth day after the date of deposit of the number of instruments of ratification, acceptance, approval or accession, specified in that protocol, has been deposited.

3. For each Contracting Party which ratifies, accepts or approves this Convention or accedes thereto after the deposit of the thirtieth instrument of ratification, acceptance, approval or accession, it shall enter into force on the ninetieth day after the date of deposit by such Contracting Party of its instrument of ratification, acceptance, approval or accession.

4. Any protocol, except as otherwise provided in such protocol, shall enter into force for a Contracting Party that ratifies, accepts or approves that protocol or accedes thereto after its entry into force pursuant to paragraph 2 above, on the ninetieth day after the date on which that Contracting Party deposits its instrument of ratification, acceptance, approval or accession, or on the date on which this Convention enters into force for that Contracting Party, whichever shall be the later.

5. For the purposes of paragraphs 1 and 2 above, any instrument deposited by a regional economic integration organization shall not be counted as additional to those deposited by member States of such organization.

Article 37: Reservations

No reservations may be made to this Convention.

Article 38: Withdrawals

1. At any time after two years from the date on which this Convention has entered into force for a Contracting Party, that Contracting Party may

withdraw from the Convention by giving written notification to the Depositary.

2. Any such withdrawal shall take place upon expiry of one year after the date of its receipt by the Depositary, or on such later date as may be specified in the notification of the withdrawal.

3. Any Contracting Party which withdraws from this Convention shall be considered as also having withdrawn from any protocol to which it is party.

Article 39: Financial interim arrangements

Provided that it has been fully restructured in accordance with the requirements of Article 21, the Global Environment Facility of the United Nations Development Programme, the United Nations Environment Programme and the International Bank for Reconstruction and Development shall be the institutional structure referred to in Article 21 on an interim basis, for the period between the entry into force of this Convention and the first meeting of the Conference of the Parties or until the Conference of the Parties decides which institutional structure will be designated in accordance with Article 21.

Article 40: Secretariat interim arrangements

The secretariat to be provided by the Executive Director of the United Nations Environment Programme shall be the secretariat referred to in Article 24, paragraph 2, on an interim basis for the period between the entry into force of this Convention and the first meeting of the Conference of the Parties.

Article 41: Depositary

The Secretary-General of the United Nations shall assume the functions of Depositary of this Convention and any protocols.

Article 42: Authentic texts

The original of this Convention, of which the Arabic, Chinese, English, French, Russian and Spanish texts are equally authentic, shall be deposited with the Secretary-General of the United Nations.

IN WITNESS WHEREOF the undersigned, being duly authorized to that effect, have signed this Convention.

DONE at Rio de Janeiro on this fifth day of June, one thousand nine hundred and ninety-two.

Annex 1: Identification and Monitoring

1. Ecosystems and habitats: containing high diversity, large numbers of endemic or threatened species, or wilderness; required by migratory species; of social, economic, cultural or scientific importance; or, which are representative, unique or associated with key evolutionary or other biological processes;

2. Species and communities which are: threatened; wild relatives of domesticated or cultivated species; of medicinal, agricultural or other economic value; or social, scientific or cultural importance; or importance for research into the conservation and sustainable use of biological diversity, such as indicator species; and

3. Described genomes and genes of social, scientific or economic importance.

. . . [Annex II not included]

Cartagena Protocol on Biosafety to the Convention on Biological Diversity (2002)

Genetic and biochemical modification of plants, animals, and microorganisms has been possible since the 1970s, prompting a number of countries to develop laws aimed to ensure the safe transfer, handling, use, and disposal of living modified organisms (LMOs). This protocol seeks to protect biological diversity from potential risks posed by LMOs by addressing biosafety issues arising from the movement of LMOs across international borders.

The protocol has a website at www.biodiv.org/biosafety/default.asp. For an overview of the protocol's negotiation and provisions, see Gareth W. Schweizer, "The Negotiation of the Cartagena Protocol on Biosafety," The Environmental Lawyer *6, no. 2 (2000): 577–602. A key question mark surrounding the implementation of the protocol has been how, in practice, its provisions will relate to the agreements of the World Trade Organization. On this, see Terence P. Stewart and David S. Johanson, "A Nexus of Trade and the Environment: The Relationship Between the Cartagena Protocol on Biosafety and the SPS Agreement of the World Trade Organization,"* Colorado Journal of International Environmental Law and Policy *14 (2003): 1–52.*

The Parties to this Protocol,

Being Parties to the Convention on Biological Diversity, hereinafter referred to as "the Convention,"

Recalling Article 19, paragraphs 3 and 4, and Articles 8 (g) and 17 of the Convention,

Recalling also decision II/5 of 17 November 1995 of the Conference of the

Parties to the Convention to develop a Protocol on biosafety, specifically focusing on transboundary movement of any living modified organism resulting from modern biotechnology that may have adverse effect on the conservation and sustainable use of biological diversity, setting out for consideration, in particular, appropriate procedures for advance informed agreement,

Reaffirming the precautionary approach contained in Principle 15 of the Rio Declaration on Environment and Development,

Aware of the rapid expansion of modern biotechnology and the growing public concern over its potential adverse effects on biological diversity, taking also into account risks to human health,

Recognizing that modern biotechnology has great potential for human well-being if developed and used with adequate safety measures for the environment and human health,

Recognizing also the crucial importance to humankind of centres of origin and centres of genetic diversity,

Taking into account the limited capabilities of many countries, particularly developing countries, to cope with the nature and scale of known and potential risks associated with living modified organisms,

Recognizing that trade and environment agreements should be mutually supportive with a view to achieving sustainable development,

Emphasizing that this Protocol shall not be interpreted as implying a change in the rights and obligations of a Party under any existing international agreements,

Understanding that the above recital is not intended to subordinate this Protocol to other international agreements,

Have agreed as follows:

Article 1: Objective

In accordance with the precautionary approach contained in Principle 15 of the Rio Declaration on Environment and Development, the objective of this Protocol is to contribute to ensuring an adequate level of protection in the field of the safe transfer, handling and use of living modified organisms resulting from modern biotechnology that may have adverse effects on the conservation and sustainable use of biological diversity, taking also into account risks to human health, and specifically focusing on transboundary movements.

Article 2: General provisions

1. Each Party shall take necessary and appropriate legal, administrative and other measures to implement its obligations under this Protocol.

2. The Parties shall ensure that the development, handling, transport, use, transfer and release of any living modified organisms are undertaken in a manner that prevents or reduces the risks to biological diversity, taking also into account risks to human health.

3. Nothing in this Protocol shall affect in any way the sovereignty of States over their territorial sea established in accordance with international law, and

the sovereign rights and the jurisdiction which States have in their exclusive economic zones and their continental shelves in accordance with international law, and the exercise by ships and aircraft of all States of navigational rights and freedoms as provided for in international law and as reflected in relevant international instruments.

4. Nothing in this Protocol shall be interpreted as restricting the right of a Party to take action that is more protective of the conservation and sustainable use of biological diversity than that called for in this Protocol, provided that such action is consistent with the objective and the provisions of this Protocol and is in accordance with that Party's other obligations under international law.

5. The Parties are encouraged to take into account, as appropriate, available expertise, instruments and work undertaken in international forums with competence in the area of risks to human health.

Article 3: Use of terms

For the purposes of this Protocol:

(a) "Conference of the Parties" means the Conference of the Parties to the Convention;

(b) "Contained use" means any operation, undertaken within a facility, installation or other physical structure, which involves living modified organisms that are controlled by specific measures that effectively limit their contact with, and their impact on, the external environment;

(c) "Export" means intentional transboundary movement from one Party to another Party;

(d) "Exporter" means any legal or natural person, under the jurisdiction of the Party of export, who arranges for a living modified organism to be exported;

(e) "Import" means intentional transboundary movement into one Party from another Party;

(f) "Importer" means any legal or natural person, under the jurisdiction of the Party of import, who arranges for a living modified organism to be imported;

(g) "Living modified organism" means any living organism that possesses a novel combination of genetic material obtained through the use of modern biotechnology;

(h) "Living organism" means any biological entity capable of transferring or replicating genetic material, including sterile organisms, viruses and viroids;

(i) "Modern biotechnology" means the application of: a. In vitro nucleic acid techniques, including recombinant deoxyribonucleic acid (DNA) and direct injection of nucleic acid into cells or organelles, or b. Fusion of cells beyond the taxonomic family, that overcome natural physiological reproductive or recombination barriers and that are not techniques used in traditional breeding and selection;

(j) "Regional economic integration organization" means an organization constituted by sovereign States of a given region, to which its member States have transferred competence in respect of matters governed by this Protocol and which has been duly authorized, in accordance with its internal procedures, to sign, ratify, accept, approve or accede to it;

(k) "Transboundary movement" means the movement of a living modified organism from one Party to another Party, save that for the purposes of Articles 17 and 24 transboundary movement extends to movement between Parties and non-Parties.

Article 4: Scope

This Protocol shall apply to the transboundary movement, transit, handling and use of all living modified organisms that may have adverse effects on the conservation and sustainable use of biological diversity, taking also into account risks to human health.

Article 5: Pharmaceuticals

Notwithstanding Article 4 and without prejudice to any right of a Party to subject all living modified organisms to risk assessment prior to the making of decisions on import, this Protocol shall not apply to the transboundary movement of living modified organisms which are pharmaceuticals for humans that are addressed by other relevant international agreements or organisations.

Article 6: Transit and contained use

1. Notwithstanding Article 4 and without prejudice to any right of a Party of transit to regulate the transport of living modified organisms through its territory and make available to the Biosafety Clearing-House, any decision of that Party, subject to Article 2, paragraph 3, regarding the transit through its territory of a specific living modified organism, the provisions of this Protocol with respect to the advance informed agreement procedure shall not apply to living modified organisms in transit.

2. Notwithstanding Article 4 and without prejudice to any right of a Party to subject all living modified organisms to risk assessment prior to decisions on import and to set standards for contained use within its jurisdiction, the provisions of this Protocol with respect to the advance informed agreement procedure shall not apply to the transboundary movement of living modified organisms destined for contained use undertaken in accordance with the standards of the Party of import.

Article 7: Application of the advance informed agreement procedure

1. Subject to Articles 5 and 6, the advance informed agreement procedure in Articles 8 to 10 and 12 shall apply prior to the first intentional transboundary movement of living modified organisms for intentional introduction into the environment of the Party of import.

2. "Intentional introduction into the environment" in paragraph 1 above, does not refer to living modified organisms intended for direct use as food or feed, or for processing.

3. Article 11 shall apply prior to the first transboundary movement of living modified organisms intended for direct use as food or feed, or for processing.

4. The advance informed agreement procedure shall not apply to the intentional transboundary movement of living modified organisms identified in a decision of the Conference of the Parties serving as the meeting of the Parties to this Protocol as being not likely to have adverse effects on the conservation and sustainable use of biological diversity, taking also into account risks to human health.

Article 8: Notification

1. The Party of export shall notify, or require the exporter to ensure notification to, in writing, the competent national authority of the Party of import prior to the intentional transboundary movement of a living modified organism that falls within the scope of Article 7, paragraph 1. The notification shall contain, at a minimum, the information specified in Annex I.

2. The Party of export shall ensure that there is a legal requirement for the accuracy of information provided by the exporter.

Article 9: Acknowledgement of receipt of notification

1. The Party of import shall acknowledge receipt of the notification, in writing, to the notifier within ninety days of its receipt.

2. The acknowledgement shall state:

(a) The date of receipt of the notification;

(b) Whether the notification, prima facie, contains the information referred to in Article 8;

(c) Whether to proceed according to the domestic regulatory framework of the Party of import or according to the procedure specified in Article 10.

3. The domestic regulatory framework referred to in paragraph 2 (c) above, shall be consistent with this Protocol.

4. A failure by the Party of import to acknowledge receipt of a notification shall not imply its consent to an intentional transboundary movement.

Article 10: Decision procedure

1. Decisions taken by the Party of import shall be in accordance with Article 15.

2. The Party of import shall, within the period of time referred to in Article 9, inform the notifier, in writing, whether the intentional transboundary movement may proceed:

(a) Only after the Party of import has given its written consent; or

(b) After no less than ninety days without a subsequent written consent.

3. Within two hundred and seventy days of the date of receipt of notification, the Party of import shall communicate, in writing, to the notifier and to the Biosafety Clearing-House the decision referred to in paragraph 2 (a) above:

(a) Approving the import, with or without conditions, including how the decision will apply to subsequent imports of the same living modified organism;

(b) Prohibiting the import;

(c) Requesting additional relevant information in accordance with its domestic regulatory framework or Annex I; in calculating the time within which the Party of import is to respond, the number of days it has to wait for additional relevant information shall not be taken into account; or

(d) Informing the notifier that the period specified in this paragraph is extended by a defined period of time.

4. Except in a case in which consent is unconditional, a decision under paragraph 3 above, shall set out the reasons on which it is based.

5. A failure by the Party of import to communicate its decision within two hundred and seventy days of the date of receipt of the notification shall not imply its consent to an intentional transboundary movement.

6. Lack of scientific certainty due to insufficient relevant scientific information and knowledge regarding the extent of the potential adverse effects of a living modified organism on the conservation and sustainable use of biological diversity in the Party of import, taking also into account risks to human health, shall not prevent that Party from taking a decision, as appropriate, with regard to the import of the living modified organism in question as referred to in paragraph 3 above, in order to avoid or minimize such potential adverse effects.

7. The Conference of the Parties serving as the meeting of the Parties shall, at its first meeting, decide upon appropriate procedures and mechanisms to facilitate decision-making by Parties of import.

Article 11: Procedure for living modified organisms intended for direct use as food or feed, or for processing

1. A Party that makes a final decision regarding domestic use, including placing on the market, of a living modified organism that may be subject to transboundary movement for direct use as food or feed, or for processing shall, within fifteen days of making that decision, inform the Parties through the Biosafety Clearing-House. This information shall contain, at a minimum, the information specified in Annex II. The Party shall provide a copy of the information, in writing, to the national focal point of each Party that informs the Secretariat in advance that it does not have access to the Biosafety Clearing-House. This provision shall not apply to decisions regarding field trials.

2. The Party making a decision under paragraph 1 above, shall ensure that there is a legal requirement for the accuracy of information provided by the applicant.

3. Any Party may request additional information from the authority identified in paragraph (b) of Annex II.

4. A Party may take a decision on the import of living modified organisms intended for direct use as food or feed, or for processing, under its domestic regulatory framework that is consistent with the objective of this Protocol.

5. Each Party shall make available to the Biosafety Clearing-House copies of any national laws, regulations and guidelines applicable to the import of living modified organisms intended for direct use as food or feed, or for processing, if available.

6. A developing country Party or a Party with an economy in transition may, in the absence of the domestic regulatory framework referred to in paragraph 4 above, and in exercise of its domestic jurisdiction, declare through the Biosafety Clearing-House that its decision prior to the first import of a living modified organism intended for direct use as food or feed, or for processing, on which information has been provided under paragraph 1 above, will be taken according to the following:

(a) A risk assessment undertaken in accordance with Annex III; and

(b) A decision made within a predictable timeframe, not exceeding two hundred and seventy days.

7. Failure by a Party to communicate its decision according to paragraph 6 above, shall not imply its consent or refusal to the import of a living modified organism intended for direct use as food or feed, or for processing, unless otherwise specified by the Party.

8. Lack of scientific certainty due to insufficient relevant scientific information and knowledge regarding the extent of the potential adverse effects of a living modified organism on the conservation and sustainable use of biological diversity in the Party of import, taking also into account risks to human health, shall not prevent that Party from taking a decision, as appropriate, with regard to the import of that living modified organism intended for direct use as food or feed, or for processing, in order to avoid or minimize such potential adverse effects.

9. A Party may indicate its needs for financial and technical assistance and capacity-building with respect to living modified organisms intended for direct use as food or feed, or for processing. Parties shall cooperate to meet these needs in accordance with Articles 22 and 28.

Article 12: Review of decisions

1. A Party of import may, at any time, in light of new scientific information on potential adverse effects on the conservation and sustainable use of biological diversity, taking also into account the risks to human health, review and change a decision regarding an intentional transboundary movement. In such case, the Party shall, within thirty days, inform any notifier that has previously notified movements of the living modified organism referred to in such decision, as well as the Biosafety Clearing-House, and shall set out the reasons for its decision.

2. A Party of export or a notifier may request the Party of import to review a decision it has made in respect of it under Article 10 where the Party of export or the notifier considers that:

(a) A change in circumstances has occurred that may influence the outcome of the risk assessment upon which the decision was based; or

(b) Additional relevant scientific or technical information has become available.

3. The Party of import shall respond in writing to such a request within ninety days and set out the reasons for its decision.

4. The Party of import may, at its discretion, require a risk assessment for subsequent imports.

Article 13: Simplified procedure

1. A Party of import may, provided that adequate measures are applied to ensure the safe intentional transboundary movement of living modified organisms in accordance with the objective of this Protocol, specify in advance to the Biosafety Clearing-House:

(a) Cases in which intentional transboundary movement to it may take place at the same time as the movement is notified to the Party of import; and

(b) Imports of living modified organisms to it to be exempted from the advance informed agreement procedure.

Notifications under subparagraph (a) above, may apply to subsequent similar movements to the same Party.

2. The information relating to an intentional transboundary movement that is to be provided in the notifications referred to in paragraph 1 (a) above, shall be the information specified in Annex I.

Article 14: Bilateral, regional and
multilateral agreements and arrangements

1. Parties may enter into bilateral, regional and multilateral agreements and arrangements regarding intentional transboundary movements of living modified organisms, consistent with the objective of this Protocol and provided that such agreements and arrangements do not result in a lower level of protection than that provided for by the Protocol.

2. The Parties shall inform each other, through the Biosafety Clearing-House, of any such bilateral, regional and multilateral agreements and arrangements that they have entered into before or after the date of entry into force of this Protocol.

3. The provisions of this Protocol shall not affect intentional transboundary movements that take place pursuant to such agreements and arrangements as between the parties to those agreements or arrangements.

4. Any Party may determine that its domestic regulations shall apply with respect to specific imports to it and shall notify the Biosafety Clearing-House of its decision.

Article 15: Risk assessment

1. Risk assessments undertaken pursuant to this Protocol shall be carried out in a scientifically sound manner, in accordance with Annex III and taking into account recognized risk assessment techniques. Such risk assessments shall be based, at a minimum, on information provided in accordance with Article 8

and other available scientific evidence in order to identify and evaluate the possible adverse effects of living modified organisms on the conservation and sustainable use of biological diversity, taking also into account risks to human health.

2. The Party of import shall ensure that risk assessments are carried out for decisions taken under Article 10. It may require the exporter to carry out the risk assessment.

3. The cost of risk assessment shall be borne by the notifier if the Party of import so requires.

Article 16: Risk management

1. The Parties shall, taking into account Article 8 (g) of the Convention, establish and maintain appropriate mechanisms, measures and strategies to regulate, manage and control risks identified in the risk assessment provisions of this Protocol associated with the use, handling and transboundary movement of living modified organisms.

2. Measures based on risk assessment shall be imposed to the extent necessary to prevent adverse effects of the living modified organism on the conservation and sustainable use of biological diversity, taking also into account risks to human health, within the territory of the Party of import.

3. Each Party shall take appropriate measures to prevent unintentional transboundary movements of living modified organisms, including such measures as requiring a risk assessment to be carried out prior to the first release of a living modified organism.

4. Without prejudice to paragraph 2 above, each Party shall endeavour to ensure that any living modified organism, whether imported or locally developed, has undergone an appropriate period of observation that is commensurate with its life-cycle or generation time before it is put to its intended use.

5. Parties shall cooperate with a view to:

(a) Identifying living modified organisms or specific traits of living modified organisms that may have adverse effects on the conservation and sustainable use of biological diversity, taking also into account risks to human health; and

(b) Taking appropriate measures regarding the treatment of such living modified organisms or specific traits.

Article 17: Unintentional transboundary movements and emergency measures

1. Each Party shall take appropriate measures to notify affected or potentially affected States, the Biosafety Clearing-House and, where appropriate, relevant international organizations, when it knows of an occurrence under its jurisdiction resulting in a release that leads, or may lead, to an unintentional transboundary movement of a living modified organism that is likely to have significant adverse effects on the conservation and sustainable use of biological diversity, taking also into account risks to human health in such

States. The notification shall be provided as soon as the Party knows of the above situation.

2. Each Party shall, no later than the date of entry into force of this Protocol for it, make available to the Biosafety Clearing-House the relevant details setting out its point of contact for the purposes of receiving notifications under this Article.

3. Any notification arising from paragraph 1 above, should include:

(a) Available relevant information on the estimated quantities and relevant characteristics and/or traits of the living modified organism;

(b) Information on the circumstances and estimated date of the release, and on the use of the living modified organism in the originating Party;

(c) Any available information about the possible adverse effects on the conservation and sustainable use of biological diversity, taking also into account risks to human health, as well as available information about possible risk management measures;

(d) Any other relevant information; and

(e) A point of contact for further information.

4. In order to minimize any significant adverse effects on the conservation and sustainable use of biological diversity, taking also into account risks to human health, each Party, under whose jurisdiction the release of the living modified organism referred to in paragraph 1 above, occurs, shall immediately consult the affected or potentially affected States to enable them to determine appropriate responses and initiate necessary action, including emergency measures.

Article 18: Handling, transport, packaging and identification

1. In order to avoid adverse effects on the conservation and sustainable use of biological diversity, taking also into account risks to human health, each Party shall take necessary measures to require that living modified organisms that are subject to intentional transboundary movement within the scope of this Protocol are handled, packaged and transported under conditions of safety, taking into consideration relevant international rules and standards.

2. Each Party shall take measures to require that documentation accompanying:

(a) Living modified organisms that are intended for direct use as food or feed, or for processing, clearly identifies that they "may contain" living modified organisms and are not intended for intentional introduction into the environment, as well as a contact point for further information. The Conference of the Parties serving as the meeting of the Parties to this Protocol shall take a decision on the detailed requirements for this purpose, including specification of their identity and any unique identification, no later than two years after the date of entry into force of this Protocol;

(b) Living modified organisms that are destined for contained use clearly identifies them as living modified organisms; and specifies any requirements for the safe handling, storage, transport and use, the contact point for further information, including the name and address of the individual and institution to whom the living modified organisms are consigned; and

(c) Living modified organisms that are intended for intentional introduction into the environment of the Party of import and any other living modified organisms within the scope of the Protocol, clearly identifies them as living modified organisms; specifies the identity and relevant traits and/or characteristics, any requirements for the safe handling, storage, transport and use, the contact point for further information and, as appropriate, the name and address of the importer and exporter; and contains a declaration that the movement is in conformity with the requirements of this Protocol applicable to the exporter.

3. The Conference of the Parties serving as the meeting of the Parties to this Protocol shall consider the need for and modalities of developing standards with regard to identification, handling, packaging and transport practices, in consultation with other relevant international bodies.

Article 19: Competent national authorities and national focal points

1. Each Party shall designate one national focal point to be responsible on its behalf for liaison with the Secretariat. Each Party shall also designate one or more competent national authorities, which shall be responsible for performing the administrative functions required by this Protocol and which shall be authorized to act on its behalf with respect to those functions. A Party may designate a single entity to fulfil the functions of both focal point and competent national authority.

2. Each Party shall, no later than the date of entry into force of this Protocol for it, notify the Secretariat of the names and addresses of its focal point and its competent national authority or authorities. Where a Party designates more than one competent national authority, it shall convey to the Secretariat, with its notification thereof, relevant information on the respective responsibilities of those authorities. Where applicable, such information shall, at a minimum, specify which competent authority is responsible for which type of living modified organism. Each Party shall forthwith notify the Secretariat of any changes in the designation of its national focal point or in the name and address or responsibilities of its competent national authority or authorities.

3. The Secretariat shall forthwith inform the Parties of the notifications it receives under paragraph 2 above, and shall also make such information available through the Biosafety Clearing-House.

Article 20: Information sharing and the Biosafety Clearing-House

1. A Biosafety Clearing-House is hereby established as part of the clearing-house mechanism under Article 18, paragraph 3, of the Convention, in order to:

(a) Facilitate the exchange of scientific, technical, environmental and legal information on, and experience with, living modified organisms; and

(b) Assist Parties to implement the Protocol, taking into account the special needs of developing country Parties, in particular the least developed and small island developing States among them, and countries with economies in transition as well as countries that are centres of origin and centres of genetic diversity.

2. The Biosafety Clearing-House shall serve as a means through which information is made available for the purposes of paragraph 1 above. It shall provide access to information made available by the Parties relevant to the implementation of the Protocol. It shall also provide access, where possible, to other international biosafety information exchange mechanisms.

3. Without prejudice to the protection of confidential information, each Party shall make available to the Biosafety Clearing-House any information required to be made available to the Biosafety Clearing-House under this Protocol, and:

(a) Any existing laws, regulations and guidelines for implementation of the Protocol, as well as information required by the Parties for the advance informed agreement procedure;

(b) Any bilateral, regional and multilateral agreements and arrangements;

(c) Summaries of its risk assessments or environmental reviews of living modified organisms generated by its regulatory process, and carried out in accordance with Article 15, including, where appropriate, relevant information regarding products thereof, namely, processed materials that are of living modified organism origin, containing detectable novel combinations of replicable genetic material obtained through the use of modern biotechnology;

(d) Its final decisions regarding the importation or release of living modified organisms; and

(e) Reports submitted by it pursuant to Article 33, including those on implementation of the advance informed agreement procedure.

4. The modalities of the operation of the Biosafety Clearing-House, including reports on its activities, shall be considered and decided upon by the Conference of the Parties serving as the meeting of the Parties to this Protocol at its first meeting, and kept under review thereafter.

Article 21: Confidential information

1. The Party of import shall permit the notifier to identify information submitted under the procedures of this Protocol or required by the Party of import as part of the advance informed agreement procedure of the Protocol that is to be treated as confidential. Justification shall be given in such cases upon request.

2. The Party of import shall consult the notifier if it decides that information identified by the notifier as confidential does not qualify for such treatment and shall, prior to any disclosure, inform the notifier of its decision, providing reasons on request, as well as an opportunity for consultation and for an internal review of the decision prior to disclosure.

3. Each Party shall protect confidential information received under this Protocol, including any confidential information received in the context of the advance informed agreement procedure of the Protocol. Each Party shall

ensure that it has procedures to protect such information and shall protect the confidentiality of such information in a manner no less favourable than its treatment of confidential information in connection with domestically produced living modified organisms.

4. The Party of import shall not use such information for a commercial purpose, except with the written consent of the notifier.

5. If a notifier withdraws or has withdrawn a notification, the Party of import shall respect the confidentiality of commercial and industrial information, including research and development information as well as information on which the Party and the notifier disagree as to its confidentiality.

6. Without prejudice to paragraph 5 above, the following information shall not be considered confidential:

(a) The name and address of the notifier;

(b) A general description of the living modified organism or organisms;

(c) A summary of the risk assessment of the effects on the conservation and sustainable use of biological diversity, taking also into account risks to human health; and

(d) Any methods and plans for emergency response.

Article 22: Capacity-building

1. The Parties shall cooperate in the development and/or strengthening of human resources and institutional capacities in biosafety, including biotechnology to the extent that it is required for biosafety, for the purpose of the effective implementation of this Protocol, in developing country Parties, in particular the least developed and small island developing States among them, and in Parties with economies in transition, including through existing global, regional, subregional and national institutions and organizations and, as appropriate, through facilitating private sector involvement.

2. For the purposes of implementing paragraph 1 above, in relation to cooperation, the needs of developing country Parties, in particular the least developed and small island developing States among them, for financial resources and access to and transfer of technology and know-how in accordance with the relevant provisions of the Convention, shall be taken fully into account for capacity-building in biosafety. Cooperation in capacity-building shall, subject to the different situation, capabilities and requirements of each Party, include scientific and technical training in the proper and safe management of biotechnology, and in the use of risk assessment and risk management for biosafety, and the enhancement of technological and institutional capacities in biosafety. The needs of Parties with economies in transition shall also be taken fully into account for such capacity-building in biosafety.

Article 23: Public awareness and participation

1. The Parties shall:

(a) Promote and facilitate public awareness, education and participation concerning the safe transfer, handling and use of living modified organisms in relation to the conservation and sustainable use of biological diversity, taking also into account risks to human health. In doing so, the Parties shall cooperate, as appropriate, with other States and international bodies;

(b) Endeavour to ensure that public awareness and education encompass access to information on living modified organisms identified in accordance with this Protocol that may be imported.

2. The Parties shall, in accordance with their respective laws and regulations, consult the public in the decision-making process regarding living modified organisms and shall make the results of such decisions available to the public, while respecting confidential information in accordance with Article 21.

3. Each Party shall endeavour to inform its public about the means of public access to the Biosafety Clearing-House.

Article 24: Non-Parties

1. Transboundary movements of living modified organisms between Parties and non-Parties shall be consistent with the objective of this Protocol. The Parties may enter into bilateral, regional and multilateral agreements and arrangements with non-Parties regarding such transboundary movements.

2. The Parties shall encourage non-Parties to adhere to this Protocol and to contribute appropriate information to the Biosafety Clearing-House on living modified organisms released in, or moved into or out of, areas within their national jurisdictions.

Article 25: Illegal transboundary movements

1. Each Party shall adopt appropriate domestic measures aimed at preventing and, if appropriate, penalizing transboundary movements of living modified organisms carried out in contravention of its domestic measures to implement this Protocol. Such movements shall be deemed illegal transboundary movements.

2. In the case of an illegal transboundary movement, the affected Party may request the Party of origin to dispose, at its own expense, of the living modified organism in question by repatriation or destruction, as appropriate.

3. Each Party shall make available to the Biosafety Clearing-House information concerning cases of illegal transboundary movements pertaining to it.

Article 26: Socio-economic considerations

1. The Parties, in reaching a decision on import under this Protocol or under its domestic measures implementing the Protocol, may take into account, consistent with their international obligations, socio-economic considerations arising from the impact of living modified organisms on the conservation and sustainable use of biological diversity, especially with regard to the value of biological diversity to indigenous and local communities.

2. The Parties are encouraged to cooperate on research and information

exchange on any socio-economic impacts of living modified organisms, especially on indigenous and local communities.

Article 27: Liability and redress

The Conference of the Parties serving as the meeting of the Parties to this Protocol shall, at its first meeting, adopt a process with respect to the appropriate elaboration of international rules and procedures in the field of liability and redress for damage resulting from transboundary movements of living modified organisms, analysing and taking due account of the ongoing processes in international law on these matters, and shall endeavour to complete this process within four years.

Article 28: Financial mechanism and resources

1. In considering financial resources for the implementation of this Protocol, the Parties shall take into account the provisions of Article 20 of the Convention.

2. The financial mechanism established in Article 21 of the Convention shall, through the institutional structure entrusted with its operation, be the financial mechanism for this Protocol.

3. Regarding the capacity-building referred to in Article 22 of this Protocol, the Conference of the Parties serving as the meeting of the Parties to this Protocol, in providing guidance with respect to the financial mechanism referred to in paragraph 2 above, for consideration by the Conference of the Parties, shall take into account the need for financial resources by developing country Parties, in particular the least developed and the small island developing States among them.

4. In the context of paragraph 1 above, the Parties shall also take into account the needs of the developing country Parties, in particular the least developed and the small island developing States among them, and of the Parties with economies in transition, in their efforts to identify and implement their capacity-building requirements for the purposes of the implementation of this Protocol.

5. The guidance to the financial mechanism of the Convention in relevant decisions of the Conference of the Parties, including those agreed before the adoption of this Protocol, shall apply, mutatis mutandis, to the provisions of this Article.

6. The developed country Parties may also provide, and the developing country Parties and the Parties with economies in transition avail themselves of, financial and technological resources for the implementation of the provisions of this Protocol through bilateral, regional and multilateral channels.

Article 29: Conference of the parties
serving as the meeting of the parties to this protocol

1. The Conference of the Parties shall serve as the meeting of the Parties to this Protocol.

2. Parties to the Convention that are not Parties to this Protocol may participate as observers in the proceedings of any meeting of the Conference of the Parties serving as the meeting of the Parties to this Protocol. When the Conference of the Parties serves as the meeting of the Parties to this Protocol, decisions under this Protocol shall be taken only by those that are Parties to it.

3. When the Conference of the Parties serves as the meeting of the Parties to this Protocol, any member of the bureau of the Conference of the Parties representing a Party to the Convention but, at that time, not a Party to this Protocol, shall be substituted by a member to be elected by and from among the Parties to this Protocol.

4. The Conference of the Parties serving as the meeting of the Parties to this Protocol shall keep under regular review the implementation of this Protocol and shall make, within its mandate, the decisions necessary to promote its effective implementation. It shall perform the functions assigned to it by this Protocol and shall:

(a) Make recommendations on any matters necessary for the implementation of this Protocol;

(b) Establish such subsidiary bodies as are deemed necessary for the implementation of this Protocol;

(c) Seek and utilize, where appropriate, the services and cooperation of, and information provided by, competent international organizations and inter-governmental and non-governmental bodies;

(d) Establish the form and the intervals for transmitting the information to be submitted in accordance with Article 33 of this Protocol and consider such information as well as reports submitted by any subsidiary body;

(e) Consider and adopt, as required, amendments to this Protocol and its annexes, as well as any additional annexes to this Protocol, that are deemed necessary for the implementation of this Protocol; and

(f) Exercise such other functions as may be required for the implementation of this Protocol.

5. The rules of procedure of the Conference of the Parties and financial rules of the Convention shall be applied, mutatis mutandis, under this Protocol, except as may be otherwise decided by consensus by the Conference of the Parties serving as the meeting of the Parties to this Protocol.

6. The first meeting of the Conference of the Parties serving as the meeting of the Parties to this Protocol shall be convened by the Secretariat in conjunction with the first meeting of the Conference of the Parties that is scheduled after the date of the entry into force of this Protocol. Subsequent ordinary meetings of the Conference of the Parties serving as the meeting of the Parties to this Protocol shall be held in conjunction with ordinary meetings of the Conference of the Parties, unless otherwise decided by the Conference of the Parties serving as the meeting of the Parties to this Protocol.

7. Extraordinary meetings of the Conference of the Parties serving as the meeting of the Parties to this Protocol shall be held at such other times as may be deemed necessary by the Conference of the Parties serving as the meeting

of the Parties to this Protocol, or at the written request of any Party, provided that, within six months of the request being communicated to the Parties by the Secretariat, it is supported by at least one third of the Parties.

8. The United Nations, its specialized agencies and the International Atomic Energy Agency, as well as any State member thereof or observers thereto not party to the Convention, may be represented as observers at meetings of the Conference of the Parties serving as the meeting of the Parties to this Protocol. Any body or agency, whether national or international, governmental or non-governmental, that is qualified in matters covered by this Protocol and that has informed the Secretariat of its wish to be represented at a meeting of the Conference of the Parties serving as a meeting of the Parties to this Protocol as an observer, may be so admitted, unless at least one third of the Parties present object. Except as otherwise provided in this Article, the admission and participation of observers shall be subject to the rules of procedure, as referred to in paragraph 5 above.

Article 30: Subsidiary bodies

1. Any subsidiary body established by or under the Convention may, upon a decision by the Conference of the Parties serving as the meeting of the Parties to this Protocol, serve the Protocol, in which case the meeting of the Parties shall specify which functions that body shall exercise.

2. Parties to the Convention that are not Parties to this Protocol may participate as observers in the proceedings of any meeting of any such subsidiary bodies. When a subsidiary body of the Convention serves as a subsidiary body to this Protocol, decisions under the Protocol shall be taken only by the Parties to the Protocol.

3. When a subsidiary body of the Convention exercises its functions with regard to matters concerning this Protocol, any member of the bureau of that subsidiary body representing a Party to the Convention but, at that time, not a Party to the Protocol, shall be substituted by a member to be elected by and from among the Parties to the Protocol.

Article 31: Secretariat

1. The Secretariat established by Article 24 of the Convention shall serve as the secretariat to this Protocol.

2. Article 24, paragraph 1, of the Convention on the functions of the Secretariat shall apply, mutatis mutandis, to this Protocol.

3. To the extent that they are distinct, the costs of the secretariat services for this Protocol shall be met by the Parties hereto. The Conference of the Parties serving as the meeting of the Parties to this Protocol shall, at its first meeting, decide on the necessary budgetary arrangements to this end.

Article 32: Relationship with the Convention

Except as otherwise provided in this Protocol, the provisions of the Convention relating to its protocols shall apply to this Protocol.

Article 33: Monitoring and reporting

Each Party shall monitor the implementation of its obligations under this Protocol, and shall, at intervals to be determined by the Conference of the Parties serving as the meeting of the Parties to this Protocol, report to the Conference of the Parties serving as the meeting of the Parties to this Protocol on measures that it has taken to implement the Protocol.

Article 34: Compliance

The Conference of the Parties serving as the meeting of the Parties to this Protocol shall, at its first meeting, consider and approve cooperative procedures and institutional mechanisms to promote compliance with the provisions of this Protocol and to address cases of non-compliance. These procedures and mechanisms shall include provisions to offer advice or assistance, where appropriate. They shall be separate from, and without prejudice to, the dispute settlement procedures and mechanisms established by Article 27 of the Convention.

Article 35: Assessment and review

The Conference of the Parties serving as the meeting of the Parties to this Protocol shall undertake, five years after the entry into force of this Protocol and at least every five years thereafter, an evaluation of the effectiveness of the Protocol, including an assessment of its procedures and annexes.

Article 36: Signature

This Protocol shall be open for signature at the United Nations Office at Nairobi by States and regional economic integration organizations from 15 to 26 May 2000, and at United Nations Headquarters in New York from 5 June 2000 to 4 June 2001.

Article 37: Entry into force

1. This Protocol shall enter into force on the ninetieth day after the date of deposit of the fiftieth instrument of ratification, acceptance, approval or accession by States or regional economic integration organizations that are Parties to the Convention.

2. This Protocol shall enter into force for a State or regional economic integration organization that ratifies, accepts or approves this Protocol or accedes thereto after its entry into force pursuant to paragraph 1 above, on the ninetieth day after the date on which that State or regional economic integration organization deposits its instrument of ratification, acceptance, approval or accession, or on the date on which the Convention enters into force for that State or regional economic integration organization, whichever shall be the later.

3. For the purposes of paragraphs 1 and 2 above, any instrument deposited by a regional economic integration organization shall not be counted as additional to those deposited by member States of such organization.

Article 38: Reservations

No reservations may be made to this Protocol.

Article 39: Withdrawal

1. At any time after two years from the date on which this Protocol has entered into force for a Party, that Party may withdraw from the Protocol by giving written notification to the Depositary.

2. Any such withdrawal shall take place upon expiry of one year after the date of its receipt by the Depositary, or on such later date as may be specified in the notification of the withdrawal.

Article 40: Authentic texts

The original of this Protocol, of which the Arabic, Chinese, English, French, Russian and Spanish texts are equally authentic, shall be deposited with the Secretary-General of the United Nations.

IN WITNESS WHEREOF the undersigned, being duly authorized to that effect, have signed this Protocol.

DONE at Montreal on this twenty-ninth day of January, two thousand.

. . . [Annexes not included]

7.4
Stockholm Convention on Persistent Organic Pollutants (POPs) (2001)

This convention seeks to minimize the human health and environmental damage caused by highly toxic industrial chemicals, by-products of industrial processes, pesticides, and herbicides. Such chemicals tend to persist in the environment for long periods of time and their adverse effects are exacerbated by their tendency to bioaccumulate and to travel large distances by wind and water currents and migratory species. A network of NGOs, the International POPs Elimination Network, played an active role in the negotiation of this convention and continues to work "for the global elimination of persistent organic pollutants, on an expedited yet socially equitable basis."

For commentary on the negotiations and the convention, see Marco A. Olsen, Analysis of the Stockholm Convention on Persistent Organic Pollutants *(Dobbs Ferry, N.Y.: Oceana, 2003). The convention's website is at www.pops.int, and the POPs Elimination Network has a website at www.ipen.ecn.cz. On the attitude of the United States toward the precautionary approach, which is embedded in the convention, see Scott LaFranchi, "Surveying the Precautionary Principle's Ongoing Global Development: The Evolution of an Emergent Environmental Management Tool,"* Boston College Environmental Affairs Law Review *32 (2005): 679–720.*

The Parties to this Convention,

Recognizing that persistent organic pollutants possess toxic properties, resist degradation, bioaccumulate and are transported, through air, water and migratory species, across international boundaries and deposited far from their place of release, where they accumulate in terrestrial and aquatic ecosystems,

Aware of the health concerns, especially in developing countries, resulting from local exposure to persistent organic pollutants, in particular impacts upon women and, through them, upon future generations,

Acknowledging that the Arctic ecosystems and indigenous communities are particularly at risk because of the biomagnification of persistent organic pollutants and that contamination of their traditional foods is a public health issue,

Conscious of the need for global action on persistent organic pollutants,

Mindful of decision 19/13 C of 7 February 1997 of the Governing Council of the United Nations Environment Programme to initiate international action to protect human health and the environment through measures which will reduce and/or eliminate emissions and discharges of persistent organic pollutants,

Recalling the pertinent provisions of the relevant international environmental conventions, especially the Rotterdam Convention on the Prior Informed Consent Procedure for Certain Hazardous Chemicals and Pesticides in International Trade, and the Basel Convention on the Control of Transboundary Movements of Hazardous Wastes and their Disposal including the regional agreements developed within the framework of its Article 11,

Recalling also the pertinent provisions of the Rio Declaration on Environment and Development and Agenda 21,

Acknowledging that precaution underlies the concerns of all the Parties and is embedded within this Convention,

Recognizing that this Convention and other international agreements in the field of trade and the environment are mutually supportive,

Reaffirming that States have, in accordance with the Charter of the United Nations and the principles of international law, the sovereign right to exploit their own resources pursuant to their own environmental and developmental policies, and the responsibility to ensure that activities within their jurisdiction or control do not cause damage to the environment of other States or of areas beyond the limits of national jurisdiction,

Taking into account the circumstances and particular requirements of developing countries, in particular the least developed among them, and countries with economies in transition, especially the need to strengthen their national capabilities for the management of chemicals, including through the transfer of technology, the provision of financial and technical assistance and the promotion of cooperation among the Parties,

Taking full account of the Programme of Action for the Sustainable Development of Small Island Developing States, adopted in Barbados on 6 May 1994,

Noting the respective capabilities of developed and developing countries, as well as the common but differentiated responsibilities of States as set forth in Principle 7 of the Rio Declaration on Environment and Development,

Recognizing the important contribution that the private sector and non-governmental organizations can make to achieving the reduction and/or elimination of emissions and discharges of persistent organic pollutants,

Underlining the importance of manufacturers of persistent organic pollutants taking responsibility for reducing adverse effects caused by their products and for providing information to users, Governments and the public on the hazardous properties of those chemicals,

Conscious of the need to take measures to prevent adverse effects caused by persistent organic pollutants at all stages of their life cycle,

Reaffirming Principle 16 of the Rio Declaration on Environment and Development which states that national authorities should endeavour to promote the internalization of environmental costs and the use of economic instruments, taking into account the approach that the polluter should, in principle, bear the cost of pollution, with due regard to the public interest and without distorting international trade and investment,

Encouraging Parties not having regulatory and assessment schemes for pesticides and industrial chemicals to develop such schemes,

Recognizing the importance of developing and using environmentally sound alternative processes and chemicals,

Determined to protect human health and the environment from the harmful impacts of persistent organic pollutants,

Have agreed as follows:

Article 1: Objective
Mindful of the precautionary approach as set forth in Principle 15 of the Rio Declaration on Environment and Development, the objective of this Convention is to protect human health and the environment from persistent organic pollutants.

Article 2: Definitions
For the purposes of this Convention:

(a) "Party" means a State or regional economic integration organization that has consented to be bound by this Convention and for which the Convention is in force;

(b) "Regional economic integration organization" means an organization constituted by sovereign States of a given region to which its member States have transferred competence in respect of matters governed by this Convention and which has been duly authorized, in accordance with its internal procedures, to sign, ratify, accept, approve or accede to this Convention;

(c) "Parties present and voting" means Parties present and casting an affirmative or negative vote.

Article 3: Measures to reduce or eliminate
releases from intentional production and use
1. Each Party shall:

(a) Prohibit and/or take the legal and administrative measures necessary to eliminate: (i) Its production and use of the chemicals listed in Annex A subject to the provisions of that Annex; and (ii) Its import and export of the chemicals listed in Annex A in accordance with the provisions of paragraph 2; and

(b) Restrict its production and use of the chemicals listed in Annex B in accordance with the provisions of that Annex.

2. Each Party shall take measures to ensure:

(a) That a chemical listed in Annex A or Annex B is imported only: (i) For the purpose of environmentally sound disposal as set forth in paragraph 1

(d) of Article 6; or (ii) For a use or purpose which is permitted for that Party under Annex A or Annex B;

(b) That a chemical listed in Annex A for which any production or use specific exemption is in effect or a chemical listed in Annex B for which any production or use specific exemption or acceptable purpose is in effect, taking into account any relevant provisions in existing international prior informed consent instruments, is exported only: (i) For the purpose of environmentally sound disposal as set forth in paragraph 1 (d) of Article 6; (ii) To a Party which is permitted to use that chemical under Annex A or Annex B; or (iii) To a State not Party to this Convention which has provided an annual certification to the exporting Party. Such certification shall specify the intended use of the chemical and include a statement that, with respect to that chemical, the importing State is committed to: a. Protect human health and the environment by taking the necessary measures to minimize or prevent releases; b. Comply with the provisions of paragraph 1 of Article 6; and c. Comply, where appropriate, with the provisions of paragraph 2 of Part II of Annex B. The certification shall also include any appropriate supporting documentation, such as legislation, regulatory instruments, or administrative or policy guidelines. The exporting Party shall transmit the certification to the Secretariat within sixty days of receipt.

(c) That a chemical listed in Annex A, for which production and use specific exemptions are no longer in effect for any Party, is not exported from it except for the purpose of environmentally sound disposal as set forth in paragraph 1 (d) of Article 6;

(d) For the purposes of this paragraph, the term "State not Party to this Convention" shall include, with respect to a particular chemical, a State or regional economic integration organization that has not agreed to be bound by the Convention with respect to that chemical.

3. Each Party that has one or more regulatory and assessment schemes for new pesticides or new industrial chemicals shall take measures to regulate with the aim of preventing the production and use of new pesticides or new industrial chemicals which, taking into consideration the criteria in paragraph 1 of Annex D, exhibit the characteristics of persistent organic pollutants.

4. Each Party that has one or more regulatory and assessment schemes for pesticides or industrial chemicals shall, where appropriate, take into consideration within these schemes the criteria in paragraph 1 of Annex D when conducting assessments of pesticides or industrial chemicals currently in use.

5. Except as otherwise provided in this Convention, paragraphs 1 and 2 shall not apply to quantities of a chemical to be used for laboratory-scale research or as a reference standard.

6. Any Party that has a specific exemption in accordance with Annex A or a specific exemption or an acceptable purpose in accordance with Annex B shall take appropriate measures to ensure that any production or use under such exemption or purpose is carried out in a manner that prevents or minimizes human exposure and release into the environment. For exempted uses or acceptable purposes that involve intentional release into the environment under

conditions of normal use, such release shall be to the minimum extent necessary, taking into account any applicable standards and guidelines.

Article 4: Register of specific exemptions

1. A Register is hereby established for the purpose of identifying the Parties that have specific exemptions listed in Annex A or Annex B. It shall not identify Parties that make use of the provisions in Annex A or Annex B that may be exercised by all Parties. The Register shall be maintained by the Secretariat and shall be available to the public.

2. The Register shall include:

(a) A list of the types of specific exemptions reproduced from Annex A and Annex B;

(b) A list of the Parties that have a specific exemption listed under Annex A or Annex B; and

(c) A list of the expiry dates for each registered specific exemption.

3. Any State may, on becoming a Party, by means of a notification in writing to the Secretariat, register for one or more types of specific exemptions listed in Annex A or Annex B.

4. Unless an earlier date is indicated in the Register by a Party, or an extension is granted pursuant to paragraph 7, all registrations of specific exemptions shall expire five years after the date of entry into force of this Convention with respect to a particular chemical.

5. At its first meeting, the Conference of the Parties shall decide upon its review process for the entries in the Register.

6. Prior to a review of an entry in the Register, the Party concerned shall submit a report to the Secretariat justifying its continuing need for registration of that exemption. The report shall be circulated by the Secretariat to all Parties. The review of a registration shall be carried out on the basis of all available information. Thereupon, the Conference of the Parties may make such recommendations to the Party concerned as it deems appropriate.

7. The Conference of the Parties may, upon request from the Party concerned, decide to extend the expiry date of a specific exemption for a period of up to five years. In making its decision, the Conference of the Parties shall take due account of the special circumstances of the developing country Parties and Parties with economies in transition.

8. A Party may, at any time, withdraw an entry from the Register for a specific exemption upon written notification to the Secretariat. The withdrawal shall take effect on the date specified in the notification.

9. When there are no longer any Parties registered for a particular type of specific exemption, no new registrations may be made with respect to it.

Article 5: Measures to reduce or
eliminate releases from unintentional production

Each Party shall at a minimum take the following measures to reduce the total releases derived from anthropogenic sources of each of the chemicals listed in

Annex C, with the goal of their continuing minimization and, where feasible, ultimate elimination:

(a) Develop an action plan or, where appropriate, a regional or subregional action plan within two years of the date of entry into force of this Convention for it, and subsequently implement it as part of its implementation plan specified in Article 7, designed to identify, characterize and address the release of the chemicals listed in Annex C and to facilitate implementation of subparagraphs (b) to (e). The action plan shall include the following elements: (i) An evaluation of current and projected releases, including the development and maintenance of source inventories and release estimates, taking into consideration the source categories identified in Annex C; (ii) An evaluation of the efficacy of the laws and policies of the Party relating to the management of such releases; (iii) Strategies to meet the obligations of this paragraph, taking into account the evaluations in (i) and (ii); (iv) Steps to promote education and training with regard to, and awareness of, those strategies; (v) A review every five years of those strategies and of their success in meeting the obligations of this paragraph; such reviews shall be included in reports submitted pursuant to Article 15; (vi) A schedule for implementation of the action plan, including for the strategies and measures identified therein;

(b) Promote the application of available, feasible and practical measures that can expeditiously achieve a realistic and meaningful level of release reduction or source elimination;

(c) Promote the development and, where it deems appropriate, require the use of substitute or modified materials, products and processes to prevent the formation and release of the chemicals listed in Annex C, taking into consideration the general guidance on prevention and release reduction measures in Annex C and guidelines to be adopted by decision of the Conference of the Parties;

(d) Promote and, in accordance with the implementation schedule of its action plan, require the use of best available techniques for new sources within source categories which a Party has identified as warranting such action in its action plan, with a particular initial focus on source categories identified in Part II of Annex C. In any case, the requirement to use best available techniques for new sources in the categories listed in Part II of that Annex shall be phased in as soon as practicable but no later than four years after the entry into force of the Convention for that Party. For the identified categories, Parties shall promote the use of best environmental practices. When applying best available techniques and best environmental practices, Parties should take into consideration the general guidance on prevention and release reduction measures in that Annex and guidelines on best available techniques and best environmental practices to be adopted by decision of the Conference of the Parties;

(e) Promote, in accordance with its action plan, the use of best available techniques and best environmental practices: (i) For existing sources, within the source categories listed in Part II of Annex C and within source categories such as those in Part III of that Annex; and (ii) For new sources, within source categories such as those listed in Part III of Annex C which a Party has not addressed under subparagraph (d).

When applying best available techniques and best environmental practices, Parties should take into consideration the general guidance on prevention and release reduction measures in Annex C and guidelines on best available techniques and best environmental practices to be adopted by decision of the Conference of the Parties;

(f) For the purposes of this paragraph and Annex C: (i) "Best available techniques" means the most effective and advanced stage in the development of activities and their methods of operation which indicate the practical suitability of particular techniques for providing in principle the basis for release limitations designed to prevent and, where that is not practicable, generally to reduce releases of chemicals listed in Part I of Annex C and their impact on the environment as a whole. In this regard: (ii) "Techniques" includes both the technology used and the way in which the installation is designed, built, maintained, operated and decommissioned; (iii) "Available" techniques means those techniques that are accessible to the operator and that are developed on a scale that allows implementation in the relevant industrial sector, under economically and technically viable conditions, taking into consideration the costs and advantages; and (iv) "Best" means most effective in achieving a high general level of protection of the environment as a whole; (v) "Best environmental practices" means the application of the most appropriate combination of environmental control measures and strategies; (vi) "New source" means any source of which the construction or substantial modification is commenced at least one year after the date of: a. Entry into force of this Convention for the Party concerned; or b. Entry into force for the Party concerned of an amendment to Annex C where the source becomes subject to the provisions of this Convention only by virtue of that amendment.

(g) Release limit values or performance standards may be used by a Party to fulfill its commitments for best available techniques under this paragraph.

Article 6: Measures to reduce or eliminate releases from stockpiles and wastes

1. In order to ensure that stockpiles consisting of or containing chemicals listed either in Annex A or Annex B and wastes, including products and articles upon becoming wastes, consisting of, containing or contaminated with a chemical listed in Annex A, B or C, are managed in a manner protective of human health and the environment, each Party shall:

(a) Develop appropriate strategies for identifying: (i) Stockpiles consisting of or containing chemicals listed either in Annex A or Annex B; and (ii) Products and articles in use and wastes consisting of, containing or contaminated with a chemical listed in Annex A, B or C;

(b) Identify, to the extent practicable, stockpiles consisting of or containing chemicals listed either in Annex A or Annex B on the basis of the strategies referred to in subparagraph (a);

(c) Manage stockpiles, as appropriate, in a safe, efficient and environmentally sound manner. Stockpiles of chemicals listed either in Annex A or Annex B, after they are no longer allowed to be used according to any specific exemption specified in Annex A or any specific exemption or acceptable purpose specified in Annex B, except stockpiles which are allowed to be exported according to paragraph 2 of Article 3, shall be deemed to be waste and shall be managed in accordance with subparagraph (d);

(d) Take appropriate measures so that such wastes, including products and articles upon becoming wastes, are: (i) Handled, collected, transported and stored in an environmentally sound manner; (ii) Disposed of in such a way that the persistent organic pollutant content is destroyed or irreversibly transformed so that they do not exhibit the characteristics of persistent organic pollutants or otherwise disposed of in an environmentally sound manner when destruction or irreversible transformation does not represent the environmentally preferable option or the persistent organic pollutant content is low, taking into account international rules, standards, and guidelines, including those that may be developed pursuant to paragraph 2, and relevant global and regional regimes governing the management of hazardous wastes; (iii) Not permitted to be subjected to disposal operations that may lead to recovery, recycling, reclamation, direct reuse or alternative uses of persistent organic pollutants; and (iv) Not transported across international boundaries without taking into account relevant international rules, standards and guidelines;

(e) Endeavour to develop appropriate strategies for identifying sites contaminated by chemicals listed in Annex A, B or C; if remediation of those sites is undertaken it shall be performed in an environmentally sound manner.

2. The Conference of the Parties shall cooperate closely with the appropriate bodies of the Basel Convention on the Control of Transboundary Movements of Hazardous Wastes and their Disposal to, inter alia:

(a) Establish levels of destruction and irreversible transformation necessary to ensure that the characteristics of persistent organic pollutants as specified in paragraph 1 of Annex D are not exhibited;

(b) Determine what they consider to be the methods that constitute environmentally sound disposal referred to above; and

(c) Work to establish, as appropriate, the concentration levels of the chemicals listed in Annexes A, B and C in order to define the low persistent organic pollutant content referred to in paragraph 1 (d) (ii).

Article 7: Implementation plans

1. Each Party shall:

(a) Develop and endeavour to implement a plan for the implementation of its obligations under this Convention;

(b) Transmit its implementation plan to the Conference of the Parties within two years of the date on which this Convention enters into force for it; and

(c) Review and update, as appropriate, its implementation plan on a periodic basis and in a manner to be specified by a decision of the Conference of the Parties.

2. The Parties shall, where appropriate, cooperate directly or through global, regional and subregional organizations, and consult their national stakeholders, including women's groups and groups involved in the health of children, in order to facilitate the development, implementation and updating of their implementation plans.

3. The Parties shall endeavour to utilize and, where necessary, establish the means to integrate national implementation plans for persistent organic pollutants in their sustainable development strategies where appropriate.

Article 8: Listing of chemicals in Annexes A, B and C

1. A Party may submit a proposal to the Secretariat for listing a chemical in Annexes A, B and/or C. The proposal shall contain the information specified in Annex D. In developing a proposal, a Party may be assisted by other Parties and/or by the Secretariat.

2. The Secretariat shall verify whether the proposal contains the information specified in Annex D. If the Secretariat is satisfied that the proposal contains the information so specified, it shall forward the proposal to the Persistent Organic Pollutants Review Committee.

3. The Committee shall examine the proposal and apply the screening criteria specified in Annex D in a flexible and transparent way, taking all information provided into account in an integrative and balanced manner.

4. If the Committee decides that:

(a) It is satisfied that the screening criteria have been fulfilled, it shall, through the Secretariat, make the proposal and the evaluation of the Committee available to all Parties and observers and invite them to submit the information specified in Annex E; or

(b) It is not satisfied that the screening criteria have been fulfilled, it shall, through the Secretariat, inform all Parties and observers and make the proposal and the evaluation of the Committee available to all Parties and the proposal shall be set aside.

5. Any Party may resubmit a proposal to the Committee that has been set aside by the Committee pursuant to paragraph 4. The resubmission may include any concerns of the Party as well as a justification for additional consideration by the Committee. If, following this procedure, the Committee again sets the proposal aside, the Party may challenge the decision of the Committee and the Conference of the Parties shall consider the matter at its next session. The Conference of the Parties may decide, based on the screening criteria in Annex D and taking into account the evaluation of the Committee and any additional information provided by any Party or observer, that the proposal should proceed.

6. Where the Committee has decided that the screening criteria have been fulfilled, or the Conference of the Parties has decided that the proposal should proceed, the Committee shall further review the proposal, taking into account

any relevant additional information received, and shall prepare a draft risk profile in accordance with Annex E. It shall, through the Secretariat, make that draft available to all Parties and observers, collect technical comments from them and, taking those comments into account, complete the risk profile.

7. If, on the basis of the risk profile conducted in accordance with Annex E, the Committee decides:

(a) That the chemical is likely as a result of its long-range environmental transport to lead to significant adverse human health and/or environmental effects such that global action is warranted, the proposal shall proceed. Lack of full scientific certainty shall not prevent the proposal from proceeding. The Committee shall, through the Secretariat, invite information from all Parties and observers relating to the considerations specified in Annex F. It shall then prepare a risk management evaluation that includes an analysis of possible control measures for the chemical in accordance with that Annex; or

(b) That the proposal should not proceed, it shall, through the Secretariat, make the risk profile available to all Parties and observers and set the proposal aside.

8. For any proposal set aside pursuant to paragraph 7 (b), a Party may request the Conference of the Parties to consider instructing the Committee to invite additional information from the proposing Party and other Parties during a period not to exceed one year. After that period and on the basis of any information received, the Committee shall reconsider the proposal pursuant to paragraph 6 with a priority to be decided by the Conference of the Parties. If, following this procedure, the Committee again sets the proposal aside, the Party may challenge the decision of the Committee and the Conference of the Parties shall consider the matter at its next session. The Conference of the Parties may decide, based on the risk profile prepared in accordance with Annex E and taking into account the evaluation of the Committee and any additional information provided by any Party or observer, that the proposal should proceed. If the Conference of the Parties decides that the proposal shall proceed, the Committee shall then prepare the risk management evaluation.

9. The Committee shall, based on the risk profile referred to in paragraph 6 and the risk management evaluation referred to in paragraph 7 (a) or paragraph 8, recommend whether the chemical should be considered by the Conference of the Parties for listing in Annexes A, B and/or C. The Conference of the Parties, taking due account of the recommendations of the Committee, including any scientific uncertainty, shall decide, in a precautionary manner, whether to list the chemical, and specify its related control measures, in Annexes A, B and/or C.

Article 9: Information exchange

1. Each Party shall facilitate or undertake the exchange of information relevant to:

(a) The reduction or elimination of the production, use and release of persistent organic pollutants; and

(b) Alternatives to persistent organic pollutants, including information relating to their risks as well as to their economic and social costs.

2. The Parties shall exchange the information referred to in paragraph 1 directly or through the Secretariat.

3. Each Party shall designate a national focal point for the exchange of such information.

4. The Secretariat shall serve as a clearing-house mechanism for information on persistent organic pollutants, including information provided by Parties, intergovernmental organizations and non-governmental organizations.

5. For the purposes of this Convention, information on health and safety of humans and the environment shall not be regarded as confidential. Parties that exchange other information pursuant to this Convention shall protect any confidential information as mutually agreed.

Article 10: Public information, awareness and education

1. Each Party shall, within its capabilities, promote and facilitate:

(a) Awareness among its policy and decision makers with regard to persistent organic pollutants;

(b) Provision to the public of all available information on persistent organic pollutants, taking into account paragraph 5 of Article 9;

(c) Development and implementation, especially for women, children and the least educated, of educational and public awareness programmes on persistent organic pollutants, as well as on their health and environmental effects and on their alternatives;

(d) Public participation in addressing persistent organic pollutants and their health and environmental effects and in developing adequate responses, including opportunities for providing input at the national level regarding implementation of this Convention;

(e) Training of workers, scientists, educators and technical and managerial personnel;

(f) Development and exchange of educational and public awareness materials at the national and international levels; and

(g) Development and implementation of education and training programmes at the national and international levels.

2. Each Party shall, within its capabilities, ensure that the public has access to the public information referred to in paragraph 1 and that the information is kept up-to-date.

3. Each Party shall, within its capabilities, encourage industry and professional users to promote and facilitate the provision of the information referred to in paragraph 1 at the national level and, as appropriate, subregional, regional and global levels.

4. In providing information on persistent organic pollutants and their alternatives, Parties may use safety data sheets, reports, mass media and other means of communication, and may establish information centres at national and regional levels.

5. Each Party shall give sympathetic consideration to developing mechanisms, such as pollutant release and transfer registers, for the collection and dissemination of information on estimates of the annual quantities of the chemicals listed in Annex A, B or C that are released or disposed of.

Article 11: Research, development and monitoring

1. The Parties shall, within their capabilities, at the national and international levels, encourage and/or undertake appropriate research, development, monitoring and cooperation pertaining to persistent organic pollutants and, where relevant, to their alternatives and to candidate persistent organic pollutants, including on their:

(a) Sources and releases into the environment;

(b) Presence, levels and trends in humans and the environment;

(c) Environmental transport, fate and transformation;

(d) Effects on human health and the environment;

(e) Socio-economic and cultural impacts;

(f) Release reduction and/or elimination; and

(g) Harmonized methodologies for making inventories of generating sources and analytical techniques for the measurement of releases.

2. In undertaking action under paragraph 1, the Parties shall, within their capabilities:

(a) Support and further develop, as appropriate, international programmes, networks and organizations aimed at defining, conducting, assessing and financing research, data collection and monitoring, taking into account the need to minimize duplication of effort;

(b) Support national and international efforts to strengthen national scientific and technical research capabilities, particularly in developing countries and countries with economies in transition, and to promote access to, and the exchange of, data and analyses;

(c) Take into account the concerns and needs, particularly in the field of financial and technical resources, of developing countries and countries with economies in transition and cooperate in improving their capability to participate in the efforts referred to in subparagraphs (a) and (b);

(d) Undertake research work geared towards alleviating the effects of persistent organic pollutants on reproductive health;

(e) Make the results of their research, development and monitoring activities referred to in this paragraph accessible to the public on a timely and regular basis; and

(f) Encourage and/or undertake cooperation with regard to storage and maintenance of information generated from research, development and monitoring.

Article 12: Technical assistance

1. The Parties recognize that rendering of timely and appropriate technical assistance in response to requests from developing country Parties and Parties

with economies in transition is essential to the successful implementation of this Convention.

2. The Parties shall cooperate to provide timely and appropriate technical assistance to developing country Parties and Parties with economies in transition, to assist them, taking into account their particular needs, to develop and strengthen their capacity to implement their obligations under this Convention.

3. In this regard, technical assistance to be provided by developed country Parties, and other Parties in accordance with their capabilities, shall include, as appropriate and as mutually agreed, technical assistance for capacity-building relating to implementation of the obligations under this Convention. Further guidance in this regard shall be provided by the Conference of the Parties.

4. The Parties shall establish, as appropriate, arrangements for the purpose of providing technical assistance and promoting the transfer of technology to developing country Parties and Parties with economies in transition relating to the implementation of this Convention. These arrangements shall include regional and subregional centres for capacity-building and transfer of technology to assist developing country Parties and Parties with economies in transition to fulfil their obligations under this Convention. Further guidance in this regard shall be provided by the Conference of the Parties.

5. The Parties shall, in the context of this Article, take full account of the specific needs and special situation of least developed countries and small island developing states in their actions with regard to technical assistance.

Article 13: Financial resources and mechanisms

1. Each Party undertakes to provide, within its capabilities, financial support and incentives in respect of those national activities that are intended to achieve the objective of this Convention in accordance with its national plans, priorities and programmes.

2. The developed country Parties shall provide new and additional financial resources to enable developing country Parties and Parties with economies in transition to meet the agreed full incremental costs of implementing measures which fulfill their obligations under this Convention as agreed between a recipient Party and an entity participating in the mechanism described in paragraph 6. Other Parties may also on a voluntary basis and in accordance with their capabilities provide such financial resources. Contributions from other sources should also be encouraged. The implementation of these commitments shall take into account the need for adequacy, predictability, the timely flow of funds and the importance of burden sharing among the contributing Parties.

3. Developed country Parties, and other Parties in accordance with their capabilities and in accordance with their national plans, priorities and programmes, may also provide and developing country Parties and Parties with economies in transition avail themselves of financial resources to assist in their implementation of this Convention through other bilateral, regional and multilateral sources or channels.

4. The extent to which the developing country Parties will effectively

implement their commitments under this Convention will depend on the effective implementation by developed country Parties of their commitments under this Convention relating to financial resources, technical assistance and technology transfer. The fact that sustainable economic and social development and eradication of poverty are the first and overriding priorities of the developing country Parties will be taken fully into account, giving due consideration to the need for the protection of human health and the environment.

5. The Parties shall take full account of the specific needs and special situation of the least developed countries and the small island developing states in their actions with regard to funding.

6. A mechanism for the provision of adequate and sustainable financial resources to developing country Parties and Parties with economies in transition on a grant or concessional basis to assist in their implementation of the Convention is hereby defined. The mechanism shall function under the authority, as appropriate, and guidance of, and be accountable to the Conference of the Parties for the purposes of this Convention. Its operation shall be entrusted to one or more entities, including existing international entities, as may be decided upon by the Conference of the Parties. The mechanism may also include other entities providing multilateral, regional and bilateral financial and technical assistance. Contributions to the mechanism shall be additional to other financial transfers to developing country Parties and Parties with economies in transition as reflected in, and in accordance with, paragraph 2.

7. Pursuant to the objectives of this Convention and paragraph 6, the Conference of the Parties shall at its first meeting adopt appropriate guidance to be provided to the mechanism and shall agree with the entity or entities participating in the financial mechanism upon arrangements to give effect thereto. The guidance shall address, inter alia:

(a) The determination of the policy, strategy and programme priorities, as well as clear and detailed criteria and guidelines regarding eligibility for access to and utilization of financial resources including monitoring and evaluation on a regular basis of such utilization;

(b) The provision by the entity or entities of regular reports to the Conference of the Parties on adequacy and sustainability of funding for activities relevant to the implementation of this Convention;

(c) The promotion of multiple-source funding approaches, mechanisms and arrangements;

(d) The modalities for the determination in a predictable and identifiable manner of the amount of funding necessary and available for the implementation of this Convention, keeping in mind that the phasing out of persistent organic pollutants might require sustained funding, and the conditions under which that amount shall be periodically reviewed; and

(e) The modalities for the provision to interested Parties of assistance with needs assessment, information on available sources of funds and on funding patterns in order to facilitate coordination among them.

8. The Conference of the Parties shall review, not later than its second meet-

ing and thereafter on a regular basis, the effectiveness of the mechanism established under this Article, its ability to address the changing needs of the developing country Parties and Parties with economies in transition, the criteria and guidance referred to in paragraph 7, the level of funding as well as the effectiveness of the performance of the institutional entities entrusted to operate the financial mechanism. It shall, based on such review, take appropriate action, if necessary, to improve the effectiveness of the mechanism, including by means of recommendations and guidance on measures to ensure adequate and sustainable funding to meet the needs of the Parties.

Article 14: Interim financial arrangements

The institutional structure of the Global Environment Facility, operated in accordance with the Instrument for the Establishment of the Restructured Global Environment Facility, shall, on an interim basis, be the principal entity entrusted with the operations of the financial mechanism referred to in Article 13, for the period between the date of entry into force of this Convention and the first meeting of the Conference of the Parties, or until such time as the Conference of the Parties decides which institutional structure will be designated in accordance with Article 13. The institutional structure of the Global Environment Facility should fulfill this function through operational measures related specifically to persistent organic pollutants taking into account that new arrangements for this area may be needed.

Article 15: Reporting

1. Each Party shall report to the Conference of the Parties on the measures it has taken to implement the provisions of this Convention and on the effectiveness of such measures in meeting the objectives of the Convention.

2. Each Party shall provide to the Secretariat:

(a) Statistical data on its total quantities of production, import and export of each of the chemicals listed in Annex A and Annex B or a reasonable estimate of such data; and

(b) To the extent practicable, a list of the States from which it has imported each such substance and the States to which it has exported each such substance.

3. Such reporting shall be at periodic intervals and in a format to be decided by the Conference of the Parties at its first meeting.

Article 16: Effectiveness evaluation

1. Commencing four years after the date of entry into force of this Convention, and periodically thereafter at intervals to be decided by the Conference of the Parties, the Conference shall evaluate the effectiveness of this Convention.

2. In order to facilitate such evaluation, the Conference of the Parties shall, at its first meeting, initiate the establishment of arrangements to provide itself with comparable monitoring data on the presence of the chemicals listed in

Annexes A, B and C as well as their regional and global environmental transport. These arrangements:

(a) Should be implemented by the Parties on a regional basis when appropriate, in accordance with their technical and financial capabilities, using existing monitoring programmes and mechanisms to the extent possible and promoting harmonization of approaches;

(b) May be supplemented where necessary, taking into account the differences between regions and their capabilities to implement monitoring activities; and

(c) Shall include reports to the Conference of the Parties on the results of the monitoring activities on a regional and global basis at intervals to be specified by the Conference of the Parties.

3. The evaluation described in paragraph 1 shall be conducted on the basis of available scientific, environmental, technical and economic information, including:

(a) Reports and other monitoring information provided pursuant to paragraph 2;

(b) National reports submitted pursuant to Article 15; and

(c) Non-compliance information provided pursuant to the procedures established under Article 17.

Article 17: Non-compliance

The Conference of the Parties shall, as soon as practicable, develop and approve procedures and institutional mechanisms for determining non-compliance with the provisions of this Convention and for the treatment of Parties found to be in non-compliance.

Article 18: Settlement of disputes

1. Parties shall settle any dispute between them concerning the interpretation or application of this Convention through negotiation or other peaceful means of their own choice.

2. When ratifying, accepting, approving or acceding to the Convention, or at any time thereafter, a Party that is not a regional economic integration organization may declare in a written instrument submitted to the depositary that, with respect to any dispute concerning the interpretation or application of the Convention, it recognizes one or both of the following means of dispute settlement as compulsory in relation to any Party accepting the same obligation:

(a) Arbitration in accordance with procedures to be adopted by the Conference of the Parties in an annex as soon as practicable;

(b) Submission of the dispute to the International Court of Justice.

3. A Party that is a regional economic integration organization may make a declaration with like effect in relation to arbitration in accordance with the procedure referred to in paragraph 2 (a).

4. A declaration made pursuant to paragraph 2 or paragraph 3 shall remain

in force until it expires in accordance with its terms or until three months after written notice of its revocation has been deposited with the depositary.

5. The expiry of a declaration, a notice of revocation or a new declaration shall not in any way affect proceedings pending before an arbitral tribunal or the International Court of Justice unless the parties to the dispute otherwise agree.

6. If the parties to a dispute have not accepted the same or any procedure pursuant to paragraph 2, and if they have not been able to settle their dispute within twelve months following notification by one party to another that a dispute exists between them, the dispute shall be submitted to a conciliation commission at the request of any party to the dispute. The conciliation commission shall render a report with recommendations. Additional procedures relating to the conciliation commission shall be included in an annex to be adopted by the Conference of the Parties no later than at its second meeting.

Article 19: Conference of the Parties

1. A Conference of the Parties is hereby established.

2. The first meeting of the Conference of the Parties shall be convened by the Executive Director of the United Nations Environment Programme no later than one year after the entry into force of this Convention. Thereafter, ordinary meetings of the Conference of the Parties shall be held at regular intervals to be decided by the Conference.

3. Extraordinary meetings of the Conference of the Parties shall be held at such other times as may be deemed necessary by the Conference, or at the written request of any Party provided that it is supported by at least one third of the Parties.

4. The Conference of the Parties shall by consensus agree upon and adopt at its first meeting rules of procedure and financial rules for itself and any subsidiary bodies, as well as financial provisions governing the functioning of the Secretariat.

5. The Conference of the Parties shall keep under continuous review and evaluation the implementation of this Convention. It shall perform the functions assigned to it by the Convention and, to this end, shall:

(a) Establish, further to the requirements of paragraph 6, such subsidiary bodies as it considers necessary for the implementation of the Convention;

(b) Cooperate, where appropriate, with competent international organizations and intergovernmental and non-governmental bodies; and

(c) Regularly review all information made available to the Parties pursuant to Article 15, including consideration of the effectiveness of paragraph 2 (b) (iii) of Article 3;

(d) Consider and undertake any additional action that may be required for the achievement of the objectives of the Convention.

6. The Conference of the Parties shall, at its first meeting, establish a subsidiary body to be called the Persistent Organic Pollutants Review Committee

for the purposes of performing the functions assigned to that Committee by this Convention. In this regard:

(a) The members of the Persistent Organic Pollutants Review Committee shall be appointed by the Conference of the Parties. Membership of the Committee shall consist of government-designated experts in chemical assessment or management. The members of the Committee shall be appointed on the basis of equitable geographical distribution;

(b) The Conference of the Parties shall decide on the terms of reference, organization and operation of the Committee; and

(c) The Committee shall make every effort to adopt its recommendations by consensus. If all efforts at consensus have been exhausted, and no consensus reached, such recommendation shall as a last resort be adopted by a two-thirds majority vote of the members present and voting.

7. The Conference of the Parties shall, at its third meeting, evaluate the continued need for the procedure contained in paragraph 2 (b) of Article 3, including consideration of its effectiveness.

8. The United Nations, its specialized agencies and the International Atomic Energy Agency, as well as any State not Party to this Convention, may be represented at meetings of the Conference of the Parties as observers. Any body or agency, whether national or international, governmental or non-governmental, qualified in matters covered by the Convention, and which has informed the Secretariat of its wish to be represented at a meeting of the Conference of the Parties as an observer may be admitted unless at least one third of the Parties present object. The admission and participation of observers shall be subject to the rules of procedure adopted by the Conference of the Parties.

Article 20: Secretariat

1. A Secretariat is hereby established.

2. The functions of the Secretariat shall be:

(a) To make arrangements for meetings of the Conference of the Parties and its subsidiary bodies and to provide them with services as required;

(b) To facilitate assistance to the Parties, particularly developing country Parties and Parties with economies in transition, on request, in the implementation of this Convention;

(c) To ensure the necessary coordination with the secretariats of other relevant international bodies;

(d) To prepare and make available to the Parties periodic reports based on information received pursuant to Article 15 and other available information;

(e) To enter, under the overall guidance of the Conference of the Parties, into such administrative and contractual arrangements as may be required for the effective discharge of its functions; and

(f) To perform the other secretariat functions specified in this Convention and such other functions as may be determined by the Conference of the Parties.

3. The secretariat functions for this Convention shall be performed by the Executive Director of the United Nations Environment Programme, unless the Conference of the Parties decides, by a three-fourths majority of the Parties present and voting, to entrust the secretariat functions to one or more other international organizations.

Article 21: Amendments to the Convention

1. Amendments to this Convention may be proposed by any Party.

2. Amendments to this Convention shall be adopted at a meeting of the Conference of the Parties. The text of any proposed amendment shall be communicated to the Parties by the Secretariat at least six months before the meeting at which it is proposed for adoption. The Secretariat shall also communicate proposed amendments to the signatories to this Convention and, for information, to the depositary.

3. The Parties shall make every effort to reach agreement on any proposed amendment to this Convention by consensus. If all efforts at consensus have been exhausted, and no agreement reached, the amendment shall as a last resort be adopted by a three-fourths majority vote of the Parties present and voting.

4. The amendment shall be communicated by the depositary to all Parties for ratification, acceptance or approval.

5. Ratification, acceptance or approval of an amendment shall be notified to the depositary in writing. An amendment adopted in accordance with paragraph 3 shall enter into force for the Parties having accepted it on the ninetieth day after the date of deposit of instruments of ratification, acceptance or approval by at least three-fourths of the Parties. Thereafter, the amendment shall enter into force for any other Party on the ninetieth day after the date on which that Party deposits its instrument of ratification, acceptance or approval of the amendment.

Article 22: Adoption and amendment of annexes

1. Annexes to this Convention shall form an integral part thereof and, unless expressly provided otherwise, a reference to this Convention constitutes at the same time a reference to any annexes thereto.

2. Any additional annexes shall be restricted to procedural, scientific, technical or administrative matters.

3. The following procedure shall apply to the proposal, adoption and entry into force of additional annexes to this Convention:

(a) Additional annexes shall be proposed and adopted according to the procedure laid down in paragraphs 1, 2 and 3 of Article 21;

(b) Any Party that is unable to accept an additional annex shall so notify the depositary, in writing, within one year from the date of communication by the depositary of the adoption of the additional annex. The depositary shall without delay notify all Parties of any such notification received. A Party may at any time withdraw a previous notification of non-acceptance in respect of any additional annex, and the annex shall thereupon enter into force for that

Party subject to subparagraph (c); and

(c) On the expiry of one year from the date of the communication by the depositary of the adoption of an additional annex, the annex shall enter into force for all Parties that have not submitted a notification in accordance with the provisions of subparagraph (b).

4. The proposal, adoption and entry into force of amendments to Annex A, B or C shall be subject to the same procedures as for the proposal, adoption and entry into force of additional annexes to this Convention, except that an amendment to Annex A, B or C shall not enter into force with respect to any Party that has made a declaration with respect to amendment to those Annexes in accordance with paragraph 4 of Article 25, in which case any such amendment shall enter into force for such a Party on the ninetieth day after the date of deposit with the depositary of its instrument of ratification, acceptance, approval or accession with respect to such amendment.

5. The following procedure shall apply to the proposal, adoption and entry into force of an amendment to Annex D, E or F:

(a) Amendments shall be proposed according to the procedure in paragraphs 1 and 2 of Article 21;

(b) The Parties shall take decisions on an amendment to Annex D, E or F by consensus; and

(c) A decision to amend Annex D, E or F shall forthwith be communicated to the Parties by the depositary. The amendment shall enter into force for all Parties on a date to be specified in the decision.

6. If an additional annex or an amendment to an annex is related to an amendment to this Convention, the additional annex or amendment shall not enter into force until such time as the amendment to the Convention enters into force.

Article 23: Right to vote

1. Each Party to this Convention shall have one vote, except as provided for in paragraph 2.

2. A regional economic integration organization, on matters within its competence, shall exercise its right to vote with a number of votes equal to the number of its member States that are Parties to this Convention. Such an organization shall not exercise its right to vote if any of its member States exercises its right to vote, and vice versa.

Article 24: Signature

This Convention shall be open for signature at Stockholm by all States and regional economic integration organizations on 23 May 2001, and at the United Nations Headquarters in New York from 24 May 2001 to 22 May 2002.

Article 25: Ratification, acceptance, approval or accession

1. This Convention shall be subject to ratification, acceptance or approval by States and by regional economic integration organizations. It shall be open

for accession by States and by regional economic integration organizations from the day after the date on which the Convention is closed for signature. Instruments of ratification, acceptance, approval or accession shall be deposited with the depositary.

2. Any regional economic integration organization that becomes a Party to this Convention without any of its member States being a Party shall be bound by all the obligations under the Convention. In the case of such organizations, one or more of whose member States is a Party to this Convention, the organization and its member States shall decide on their respective responsibilities for the performance of their obligations under the Convention. In such cases, the organization and the member States shall not be entitled to exercise rights under the Convention concurrently.

3. In its instrument of ratification, acceptance, approval or accession, a regional economic integration organization shall declare the extent of its competence in respect of the matters governed by this Convention. Any such organization shall also inform the depositary, who shall in turn inform the Parties, of any relevant modification in the extent of its competence.

4. In its instrument of ratification, acceptance, approval or accession, any Party may declare that, with respect to it, any amendment to Annex A, B or C shall enter into force only upon the deposit of its instrument of ratification, acceptance, approval or accession with respect thereto.

Article 26: Entry into force

1. This Convention shall enter into force on the ninetieth day after the date of deposit of the fiftieth instrument of ratification, acceptance, approval or accession.

2. For each State or regional economic integration organization that ratifies, accepts or approves this Convention or accedes thereto after the deposit of the fiftieth instrument of ratification, acceptance, approval or accession, the Convention shall enter into force on the ninetieth day after the date of deposit by such State or regional economic integration organization of its instrument of ratification, acceptance, approval or accession.

3. For the purpose of paragraphs 1 and 2, any instrument deposited by a regional economic integration organization shall not be counted as additional to those deposited by member States of that organization.

Article 27: Reservations

No reservations may be made to this Convention.

Article 28: Withdrawal

1. At any time after three years from the date on which this Convention has entered into force for a Party, that Party may withdraw from the Convention by giving written notification to the depositary.

2. Any such withdrawal shall take effect upon the expiry of one year from

the date of receipt by the depositary of the notification of withdrawal, or on such later date as may be specified in the notification of withdrawal.

Article 29: Depositary
The Secretary-General of the United Nations shall be the depositary of this Convention.

Article 30: Authentic texts
The original of this Convention, of which the Arabic, Chinese, English, French, Russian and Spanish texts are equally authentic, shall be deposited with the Secretary-General of the United Nations.

IN WITNESS WHEREOF the undersigned, being duly authorized to that effect, have signed this Convention.

Done at Stockholm on this twenty-second day of May, two thousand and one.

. . . [Annexes not included]

8
The Global Commons

8.1
The Antarctic Treaty (1959)

Seven states claimed sovereignty over sections of the Antarctic continent in the mid-twentieth century: the UK, Australia, New Zealand, Chile, Argentina, France, and Norway. The claims of the UK, Argentina, and Chile overlapped. Some other countries, including the United States and the Soviet Union, had engaged in exploration but had put forward no specific claims. The treaty did not attempt to resolve the competing positions regarding Antarctic territory, but by article 4 "froze" the status quo regarding territorial rights while dedicating the continent to science. The treaty is also significant as a precursor to the establishment of nuclear weapons–free zones. The treaty was supplemented in 1991 by an environmental protocol. In 2004, a secretariat for the Antarctic Treaty System was established in Buenos Aires.

The website of the secretariat is www.ats.org.ar. On Antarctic law and politics, see Christopher C. Joyner, Governing the Frozen Commons *(Columbia: University of South Carolina Press, 1998); and Donald R. Rothwell,* The Polar Regions and the Development of International Law *(Cambridge: Cambridge University Press, 1996). A key journal to consult on political, legal, and scientific issues relating to Antarctica is* Polar Record, *published by the Scott Polar Research Institute in Cambridge, UK.*

The Governments of Argentina, Australia, Belgium, Chile, the French Republic, Japan, New Zealand, Norway, the Union of South Africa, the Union of Soviet Socialist Republics, the United Kingdom of Great Britain and Northern Ireland, and the United States of America,

Recognizing that it is in the interest of all mankind that Antarctica shall continue for ever to be used exclusively for peaceful purposes and shall not become the scene or object of international discord;

Acknowledging the substantial contributions to scientific knowledge resulting from international cooperation in scientific investigation in Antarctica;

Convinced that the establishment of a firm foundation for the continuation and development of such cooperation on the basis of freedom of scientific investigation in Antarctica as applied during the International Geophysical Year accords with the interests of science and the progress of all mankind;

Convinced also that a treaty ensuring the use of Antarctica for peaceful purposes only and the continuance of international harmony in Antarctica will further the purposes and principles embodied in the Charter of the United Nations;

Have agreed as follows:

Article 1

1. Antarctica shall be used for peaceful purposes only. There shall be prohibited, inter alia, any measure of a military nature, such as the establishment of military bases and fortifications, the carrying out of military manoeuvres, as well as the testing of any type of weapons.

2. The present Treaty shall not prevent the use of military personnel or equipment for scientific research or for any other peaceful purpose.

Article 2

Freedom of scientific investigation in Antarctica and cooperation toward that end, as applied during the International Geophysical Year, shall continue, subject to the provisions of the present Treaty.

Article 3

1. In order to promote international cooperation in scientific investigation in Antarctica, as provided for in Article 2 of the present Treaty, the Contracting Parties agree that, to the greatest extent feasible and practicable:

(a) information regarding plans for scientific programs in Antarctica shall be exchanged to permit maximum economy of and efficiency of operations;

(b) scientific personnel shall be exchanged in Antarctica between expeditions and stations;

(c) scientific observations and results from Antarctica shall be exchanged and made freely available.

2. In implementing this Article, every encouragement shall be given to the establishment of cooperative working relations with those Specialized Agencies of the United Nations and other international organizations having a scientific or technical interest in Antarctica.

Article 4

1. Nothing contained in the present Treaty shall be interpreted as:

(a) a renunciation by any Contracting Party of previously asserted rights of or claims to territorial sovereignty in Antarctica;

(b) a renunciation or diminution by any Contracting Party of any basis of claim to territorial sovereignty in Antarctica which it may have whether as a result of its activities or those of its nationals in Antarctica, or otherwise;

(c) prejudicing the position of any Contracting Party as regards its recognition or non-recognition of any other State's rights of or claim or basis of claim to territorial sovereignty in Antarctica.

2. No acts or activities taking place while the present Treaty is in force shall constitute a basis for asserting, supporting or denying a claim to territorial sovereignty in Antarctica or create any rights of sovereignty in Antarctica. No new

claim, or enlargement of an existing claim, to territorial sovereignty in Antarctica shall be asserted while the present Treaty is in force.

Article 5

1. Any nuclear explosions in Antarctica and the disposal there of radioactive waste material shall be prohibited.

2. In the event of the conclusion of international agreements concerning the use of nuclear energy, including nuclear explosions and the disposal of radioactive waste material, to which all of the Contracting Parties whose representatives are entitled to participate in the meetings provided for under Article 9 are parties, the rules established under such agreements shall apply in Antarctica.

Article 6

The provisions of the present Treaty shall apply to the area south of 60° South Latitude, including all ice shelves, but nothing in the present Treaty shall prejudice or in any way affect the rights, or the exercise of the rights, of any State under international law with regard to the high seas within that area.

Article 7

1. In order to promote the objectives and ensure the observance of the provisions of the present Treaty, each Contracting Party whose representatives are entitled to participate in the meetings referred to in Article 9 of the Treaty shall have the right to designate observers to carry out any inspection provided for by the present Article. Observers shall be nationals of the Contracting Parties which designate them. The names of observers shall be communicated to every other Contracting Party having the right to designate observers, and like notice shall be given of the termination of their appointment.

2. Each observer designated in accordance with the provisions of paragraph 1 of this Article shall have complete freedom of access at any time to any or all areas of Antarctica.

3. All areas of Antarctica, including all stations, installations and equipment within those areas, and all ships and aircraft at points of discharging or embarking cargoes or personnel in Antarctica, shall be open at all times to inspection by any observers designated in accordance with paragraph 1 of this Article.

4. Aerial observation may be carried out at any time over any or all areas of Antarctica by any of the Contracting Parties having the right to designate observers.

5. Each Contracting Party shall, at the time when the present Treaty enters into force for it, inform the other Contracting Parties, and thereafter shall give them notice in advance, of

(a) all expeditions to and within Antarctica, on the part of its ships or nationals, and all expeditions to Antarctica organized in or proceeding from its territory;

(b) all stations in Antarctica occupied by its nationals; and

(c) any military personnel or equipment intended to be introduced by it into Antarctica subject to the conditions prescribed in paragraph 2 of Article 1 of the present Treaty.

Article 8

1. In order to facilitate the exercise of their functions under the present Treaty, and without prejudice to the respective positions of the Contracting Parties relating to jurisdiction over all other persons in Antarctica, observers designated under paragraph 1 of Article 7 and scientific personnel exchanged under sub-paragraph 1(b) of Article 3 of the Treaty, and members of the staffs accompanying any such persons, shall be subject only to the jurisdiction of the Contracting Party of which they are nationals in respect of all acts or omissions occurring while they are in Antarctica for the purpose of exercising their functions.

2. Without prejudice to the provisions of paragraph 1 of this Article, and pending the adoption of measures in pursuance of subparagraph 1(e) of Article 9, the Contracting Parties concerned in any case of dispute with regard to the exercise of jurisdiction in Antarctica shall immediately consult together with a view to reaching a mutually acceptable solution.

Article 9

1. Representatives of the Contracting Parties named in the preamble to the present Treaty shall meet at the City of Canberra within two months after the date of entry into force of the Treaty, and thereafter at suitable intervals and places, for the purpose of exchanging information, consulting together on matters of common interest pertaining to Antarctica, and formulating and considering, and recommending to their Governments, measures in furtherance of the principles and objectives of the Treaty, including measures regarding:

(a) use of Antarctica for peaceful purposes only;

(b) facilitation of scientific research in Antarctica;

(c) facilitation of international scientific cooperation in Antarctica;

(d) facilitation of the exercise of the rights of inspection provided for in Article 7 of the Treaty;

(e) questions relating to the exercise of jurisdiction in Antarctica;

(f) preservation and conservation of living resources in Antarctica.

2. Each Contracting Party which has become a party to the present Treaty by accession under Article 13 shall be entitled to appoint representatives to participate in the meetings referred to in paragraph 1 of the present Article, during such times as that Contracting Party demonstrates its interest in Antarctica by conducting substantial scientific research activity there, such as the establishment of a scientific station or the despatch of a scientific expedition.

3. Reports from the observers referred to in Article 7 of the present Treaty shall be transmitted to the representatives of the Contracting Parties participating in the meetings referred to in paragraph 1 of the present Article.

4. The measures referred to in paragraph 1 of this Article shall become effective when approved by all the Contracting Parties whose representatives were entitled to participate in the meetings held to consider those measures.

5. Any or all of the rights established in the present Treaty may be exercised as from the date of entry into force of the Treaty whether or not any measures facilitating the exercise of such rights have been proposed, considered or approved as provided in this Article.

Article 10

Each of the Contracting Parties undertakes to exert appropriate efforts, consistent with the Charter of the United Nations, to the end that no one engages in any activity in Antarctica contrary to the principles or purposes of the present Treaty.

Article 11

1. If any dispute arises between two or more of the Contracting Parties concerning the interpretation or application of the present Treaty, those Contracting Parties shall consult among themselves with a view to having the dispute resolved by negotiation, inquiry, mediation, conciliation, arbitration, judicial settlement or other peaceful means of their own choice.

2. Any dispute of this character not so resolved shall, with the consent, in each case, of all parties to the dispute, be referred to the International Court of Justice for settlement; but failure to reach agreement on reference to the International Court shall not absolve parties to the dispute from the responsibility of continuing to seek to resolve it by any of the various peaceful means referred to in paragraph 1 of this Article.

Article 12

1. (a) The present Treaty may be modified or amended at any time by unanimous agreement of the Contracting Parties whose representatives are entitled to participate in the meetings provided for under Article 9. Any such modification or amendment shall enter into force when the depositary Government has received notice from all such Contracting Parties that they have ratified it.

(b) Such modification or amendment shall thereafter enter into force as to any other Contracting Party when notice of ratification by it has been received by the depositary Government. Any such Contracting Party from which no notice of ratification is received within a period of two years from the date of entry into force of the modification or amendment in accordance with the provision of subparagraph 1(a) of this Article shall be deemed to have withdrawn from the present Treaty on the date of the expiration of such period.

2. (a) If after the expiration of thirty years from the date of entry into force of the present Treaty, any of the Contracting Parties whose representatives are entitled to participate in the meetings provided for under Article 9 so requests by a communication addressed to the depositary Government, a Conference of

all the Contracting Parties shall be held as soon as practicable to review the operation of the Treaty.

(b) Any modification or amendment to the present Treaty which is approved at such a Conference by a majority of the Contracting Parties there represented, including a majority of those whose representatives are entitled to participate in the meetings provided for under Article 9, shall be communicated by the depositary Government to all the Contracting Parties immediately after the termination of the Conference and shall enter into force in accordance with the provisions of paragraph 1 of the present Article.

(c) If any such modification or amendment has not entered into force in accordance with the provisions of subparagraph 1(a) of this Article within a period of two years after the date of its communication to all the Contracting Parties, any Contracting Party may at any time after the expiration of that period give notice to the depositary Government of its withdrawal from the present Treaty; and such withdrawal shall take effect two years after the receipt of the notice by the depositary Government.

Article 13

1. The present Treaty shall be subject to ratification by the signatory States. It shall be open for accession by any State which is a Member of the United Nations, or by any other State which may be invited to accede to the Treaty with the consent of all the Contracting Parties whose representatives are entitled to participate in the meetings provided for under Article 9 of the Treaty.

2. Ratification of or accession to the present Treaty shall be effected by each State in accordance with its constitutional processes.

3. Instruments of ratification and instruments of accession shall be deposited with the Government of the United States of America, hereby designated as the depositary Government.

4. The depositary Government shall inform all signatory and acceding States of the date of each deposit of an instrument of ratification or accession, and the date of entry into force of the Treaty and of any modification or amendment thereto.

5. Upon the deposit of instruments of ratification by all the signatory States, the present Treaty shall enter into force for those States and for States which have deposited instruments of accession. Thereafter the Treaty shall enter into force for any acceding State upon the deposit of its instruments of accession.

6. The present Treaty shall be registered by the depositary Government pursuant to Article 102 of the Charter of the United Nations.

Article 14

The present Treaty, done in the English, French, Russian and Spanish languages, each version being equally authentic, shall be deposited in the archives of the Government of the United States of America, which shall transmit duly certified copies thereof to the Governments of the signatory and acceding States.

8.2
Treaty on Principles Governing the Activities of States in the Exploration and Use of Outer Space, Including the Moon and Other Celestial Bodies (Outer Space Treaty) (1967)

The Outer Space Treaty built on the 1963 Declaration of Legal Principles Governing the Activities of States in the Exploration and Use of Outer Space, which contained a set of principles to guide the exploration and use of outer space, including that it is not to be subject to national appropriation. The treaty provided a foundation for subsequent treaties: the 1968 Agreement on the Rescue of Astronauts, and the Return of Objects Launched into Outer Space; the 1972 Convention on International Liability for Damage Caused by Space Objects; the 1975 Convention on the Registration of Objects Launched into Outer Space; and the 1979 Agreement Governing the Activities of States on the Moon and Other Celestial Bodies (the Moon Agreement). Few states have ratified the Moon Agreement, which explicitly declares the Moon and its natural resources to be the common heritage of mankind.

For discussion of the principle of nonappropriation in outer space and its relationship to the common heritage doctrine, see Lyn M. Fountain, "Creating Momentum in Space: Ending the Paralysis Produced by the 'Common Heritage of Mankind' Doctrine," Connecticut Law Review 35 (2003): 1753–1787. *On current debates regarding the weaponization of space and the possible need for additional space treaties, see the articles in* Arms Control Today, *published by the Arms Control Association and available at www.armscontrol.org. The 1963 Declaration of Legal Principles was adopted by the general assembly as resolution 1962 (XVIII); its text and the texts of all treaties on outer space are available from the website of the UN Office for Outer Space Affairs at www.oosa.unvienna.org. On the factors influencing the evolu-*

tion of space law, see Glenn Harlan Reynolds, "International Space Law in Transformation: Some Observations," Chicago Journal of International Law *6 (2005): 69–81.*

The States Parties to this Treaty,

Inspired by the great prospects opening up before mankind as a result of man's entry into outer space,

Recognizing the common interest of all mankind in the progress of the exploration and use of outer space for peaceful purposes,

Believing that the exploration and use of outer space should be carried on for the benefit of all peoples irrespective of the degree of their economic or scientific development,

Desiring to contribute to broad international co-operation in the scientific as well as the legal aspects of the exploration and use of outer space for peaceful purposes,

Believing that such co-operation will contribute to the development of mutual understanding and to the strengthening of friendly relations between States and peoples,

Recalling resolution 1962 (XVIII), entitled "Declaration of Legal Principles Governing the Activities of States in the Exploration and Use of Outer Space," which was adopted unanimously by the United Nations General Assembly on 13 December 1963,

Recalling resolution 1884 (XVIII), calling upon States to refrain from placing in orbit around the earth any objects carrying nuclear weapons or any other kinds of weapons of mass destruction or from installing such weapons on celestial bodies, which was adopted unanimously by the United Nations General Assembly on 17 October 1963,

Taking account of United Nations General Assembly resolution 110 (II) of 3 November 1947, which condemned propaganda designed or likely to provoke or encourage any threat to the peace, breach of the peace or act of aggression, and considering that the aforementioned resolution is applicable to outer space,

Convinced that a Treaty on Principles Governing the Activities of States in the Exploration and Use of Outer Space, including the Moon and Other Celestial Bodies, will further the purposes and principles of the Charter of the United Nations,

Have agreed on the following:

Article 1

The exploration and use of outer space, including the moon and other celestial bodies, shall be carried out for the benefit and in the interests of all countries, irrespective of their degree of economic or scientific development, and shall be the province of all mankind.

Outer space, including the moon and other celestial bodies, shall be free for exploration and use by all States without discrimination of any kind, on a basis of equality and in accordance with international law, and there shall be free access to all areas of celestial bodies.

There shall be freedom of scientific investigation in outer space, including the moon and other celestial bodies, and States shall facilitate and encourage international co-operation in such investigation.

Article 2

Outer space, including the moon and other celestial bodies, is not subject to national appropriation by claim of sovereignty, by means of use or occupation, or by any other means.

Article 3

States Parties to the Treaty shall carry on activities in the exploration and use of outer space, including the moon and other celestial bodies, in accordance with international law, including the Charter of the United Nations, in the interest of maintaining international peace and security and promoting international co-operation and understanding.

Article 4

States Parties to the Treaty undertake not to place in orbit around the earth any objects carrying nuclear weapons or any other kinds of weapons of mass destruction, install such weapons on celestial bodies, or station such weapons in outer space in any other manner.

The moon and other celestial bodies shall be used by all States Parties to the Treaty exclusively for peaceful purposes. The establishment of military bases, installations and fortifications, the testing of any type of weapons and the conduct of military manoeuvres on celestial bodies shall be forbidden. The use of military personnel for scientific research or for any other peaceful purposes shall not be prohibited. The use of any equipment or facility necessary for peaceful exploration of the moon and other celestial bodies shall also not be prohibited.

Article 5

States Parties to the Treaty shall regard astronauts as envoys of mankind in outer space and shall render to them all possible assistance in the event of accident, distress, or emergency landing on the territory of another State Party or on the high seas. When astronauts make such a landing, they shall be safely and promptly returned to the State of registry of their space vehicle.

In carrying on activities in outer space and on celestial bodies, the astronauts of one State Party shall render all possible assistance to the astronauts of other States Parties.

States Parties to the Treaty shall immediately inform the other States Parties to the Treaty or the Secretary-General of the United Nations of any phenomena they discover in outer space, including the moon and other celestial bodies, which could constitute a danger to the life or health of astronauts.

Article 6

States Parties to the Treaty shall bear international responsibility for national activities in outer space, including the moon and other celestial bodies, whether such activities are carried on by governmental agencies or by non-governmental entities, and for assuring that national activities are carried out in conformity with the provisions set forth in the present Treaty. The activities of non-governmental entities in outer space, including the moon and other celestial bodies, shall require authorization and continuing supervision by the appropriate State Party to the Treaty. When activities are carried on in outer space, including the moon and other celestial bodies, by an international organization, responsibility for compliance with this Treaty shall be borne both by the international organization and by the States Parties to the Treaty participating in such organization.

Article 7

Each State Party to the Treaty that launches or procures the launching of an object into outer space, including the moon and other celestial bodies, and each State Party from whose territory or facility an object is launched, is internationally liable for damage to another State Party to the Treaty or to its natural or juridical persons by such object or its component parts on the Earth, in air or in outer space, including the moon and other celestial bodies.

Article 8

A State Party to the Treaty on whose registry an object launched into outer space is carried shall retain jurisdiction and control over such object, and over any personnel thereof, while in outer space or on a celestial body. Ownership of objects launched into outer space, including objects landed or constructed on a celestial body, and of their component parts, is not affected by their presence in outer space or on a celestial body or by their return to the Earth. Such objects or component parts found beyond the limits of the State Party to the Treaty on whose registry they are carried shall be returned to that State Party, which shall, upon request, furnish identifying data prior to their return.

Article 9

In the exploration and use of outer space, including the moon and other celestial bodies, States Parties to the Treaty shall be guided by the principle of co-operation and mutual assistance and shall conduct all their activities in outer space, including the moon and other celestial bodies, with due regard to the corresponding interests of all other States Parties to the Treaty. States Parties to the Treaty shall pursue studies of outer space, including the moon and other celestial bodies, and conduct exploration of them so as to avoid their harmful contamination and also adverse changes in the environment of the Earth resulting from the introduction of extraterrestrial matter and, where necessary, shall adopt appropriate measures for this purpose. If a State Party to the Treaty has reason to believe that an activity or experiment planned by it or its nationals in outer space, including the moon and other celestial bodies, would cause potentially harmful interference with activities of other States Parties in the peaceful exploration and use of outer space, including the moon and other celestial bodies, it shall undertake appropriate international consultations before proceeding with any such activity or experiment. A State Party to the Treaty which has reason to believe that an activity or experiment planned by another State Party in outer space, including the moon and other celestial bodies, would cause potentially harmful interference with activities in the peaceful exploration and use of outer space, including the moon and other celestial bodies, may request consultation concerning the activity or experiment.

Article 10

In order to promote international co-operation in the exploration and use of outer space, including the moon and other celestial bodies, in conformity with the purposes of this Treaty, the States Parties to the Treaty shall consider on a basis of equality any requests by other States Parties to the Treaty to be afforded an opportunity to observe the flight of space objects launched by those States.

The nature of such an opportunity for observation and the conditions under which it could be afforded shall be determined by agreement between the States concerned.

Article 11

In order to promote international co-operation in the peaceful exploration and use of outer space, States Parties to the Treaty conducting activities in outer space, including the moon and other celestial bodies, agree to inform the Secretary-General of the United Nations as well as the public and the international scientific community, to the greatest extent feasible and practicable, of the nature, conduct, locations and results of such activities. On receiving the said information, the Secretary-General of the United Nations should be prepared to disseminate it immediately and effectively.

Article 12

All stations, installations, equipment and space vehicles on the moon and other celestial bodies shall be open to representatives of other States Parties to the Treaty on a basis of reciprocity. Such representatives shall give reasonable advance notice of a projected visit, in order that appropriate consultations may be held and that maximum precautions may betaken to assure safety and to avoid interference with normal operations in the facility to be visited.

Article 13

The provisions of this Treaty shall apply to the activities of States Parties to the Treaty in the exploration and use of outer space, including the moon and other celestial bodies, whether such activities are carried on by a single State

Party to the Treaty or jointly with other States, including cases where they are carried on within the framework of international intergovernmental organizations.

Any practical questions arising in connection with activities carried on by international intergovernmental organizations in the exploration and use of outer space, including the moon and other celestial bodies, shall be resolved by the States Parties to the Treaty either with the appropriate international organization or with one or more States members of that international organization, which are Parties to this Treaty.

Article 14

1. This Treaty shall be open to all States for signature. Any State which does not sign this Treaty before its entry into force in accordance with paragraph 3 of this article may accede to it at anytime.

2. This Treaty shall be subject to ratification by signatory States. Instruments of ratification and instruments of accession shall be deposited with the Governments of the United Kingdom of Great Britain and Northern Ireland, the Union of Soviet Socialist Republics and the United States of America, which are hereby designated the Depositary Governments.

3. This Treaty shall enter into force upon the deposit of instruments of ratification by five Governments including the Governments designated as Depositary Governments under this Treaty.

4. For States whose instruments of ratification or accession are deposited subsequent to the entry into force of this Treaty, it shall enter into force on the date of the deposit of their instruments of ratification or accession.

5. The Depositary Governments shall promptly inform all signatory and acceding States of the date of each signature, the date of deposit of each instrument of ratification of and accession to this Treaty, the date of its entry into force and other notices.

6. This Treaty shall be registered by the Depositary Governments pursuant to Article 102 of the Charter of the United Nations.

Article 15

Any State Party to the Treaty may propose amendments to this Treaty. Amendments shall enter into force for each State Party to the Treaty accepting the amendments upon their acceptance by a majority of the States Parties to the Treaty and thereafter for each remaining State Party to the Treaty on the date of acceptance by it.

Article 16

Any State Party to the Treaty may give notice of its withdrawal from the Treaty one year after its entry into force by written notification to the Depositary Governments. Such withdrawal shall take effect one year from the date of receipt of this notification.

Article 17

This Treaty, of which the English, Russian, French, Spanish and Chinese texts are equally authentic, shall be deposited in the archives of the Depositary Governments. Duly certified copies of this Treaty shall be transmitted by the Depositary Governments to the Governments of the signatory and acceding States.

IN WITNESS WHEREOF the undersigned, duly authorized, have signed this Treaty.

DONE in triplicate, at the cities of London, Moscow and Washington, the twenty-seventh day of January, one thousand nine hundred and sixty-seven.

8.3
United Nations Convention on the Law of the Sea (LOSC) (1982)

The LOSC, sometimes referred to as a "constitution for the oceans," is the product of a mammoth eight-year negotiating process at the Third United Nations Conference on the Law of the Sea (UNCLOS III). The LOSC largely supersedes the conventions adopted at the First UN Conference on the Law of the Sea in 1958. The convention has two implementing agreements: the 1994 Agreement Relating to the Implementation of Part XI and the 1995 Agreement for the Implementation of the Provisions of the United Nations Convention on the Law of the Sea of 10 December 1982 relating to the Conservation and Management of Straddling Fish Stocks and Highly Migratory Fish Stocks (UN Fish Stocks Agreement).

For an authoritative commentary on the LOSC, see M. H. Nordquist, United Nations Convention on the Law of the Sea 1982: A Commentary *(Dordrecht: M. Nijhoff, 1985–2002). Clyde Sanger has produced a very readable, somewhat journalistic, account of UNCLOS III in* Ordering the Oceans: The Making of the Law of the Sea *(London: Zed, 1986). Annual reports of the UN Secretary-General on developments and issues relating to oceans and the law of the sea are available at www.un.org/Depts/los/general_assembly/general_assembly_reports.htm. The Law of the Sea Tribunal established by the LOSC has a website at www.itlos.org.*

The States Parties to this Convention,

Prompted by the desire to settle, in a spirit of mutual understanding and cooperation, all issues relating to the law of the sea and aware of the historic significance of this Convention as an important contribution to the maintenance of peace, justice and progress for all peoples of the world,

Noting that developments since the United Nations Conferences on the Law of the Sea held at Geneva in 1958 and 1960 have accentuated the need for a new and generally acceptable Convention on the law of the sea,

Conscious that the problems of ocean space are closely interrelated and need to be considered as a whole,

Recognizing the desirability of establishing through this Convention, with due regard for the sovereignty of all States, a legal order for the seas and oceans which will facilitate international communication, and will promote the peaceful uses of the seas and oceans, the equitable and efficient utilization of their resources, the conservation of their living resources, and the study, protection and preservation of the marine environment,

Bearing in mind that the achievement of these goals will contribute to the realization of a just and equitable international economic order which takes into account the interests and needs of mankind as a whole and, in particular, the special interests and needs of developing countries, whether coastal or land-locked,

Desiring by this Convention to develop the principles embodied in resolution 2749 (XXV) of 17 December 1970 in which the General Assembly of the United Nations solemnly declared inter alia that the area of the seabed and ocean floor and the subsoil thereof, beyond the limits of national jurisdiction, as well as its resources, are the common heritage of mankind, the exploration and exploitation of which shall be carried out for the benefit of mankind as a whole, irrespective of the geographical location of States,

Believing that the codification and progressive development of the law of the sea achieved in this Convention will contribute to the strengthening of peace, security, cooperation and friendly relations among all nations in conformity with the principles of justice and equal rights and will promote the economic and social advancement of all peoples of the world, in accordance with the Purposes and Principles of the United Nations as set forth in the Charter,

Affirming that matters not regulated by this Convention continue to be governed by the rules and principles of general international law,

Have agreed as follows:

Part I: Introduction

Article 1: Use of terms and scope

1. For the purposes of this Convention:

(1) "Area" means the seabed and ocean floor and subsoil thereof, beyond the limits of national jurisdiction;

(2) "Authority" means the International Seabed Authority;

(3) "activities in the Area" means all activities of exploration for, and exploitation of, the resources of the Area;

(4) "pollution of the marine environment" means the introduction by man, directly or indirectly, of substances or energy into the marine environment, including estuaries, which results or is likely to result in such deleterious effects as harm to living resources and marine life, hazards to human health, hindrance to marine activities, including fishing and other legitimate uses of the sea, impairment of quality for use of sea water and reduction of amenities;

(5) (a) "dumping" means: (i) any deliberate disposal of wastes or other matter from vessels, aircraft, platforms or other man-made structures at sea; (ii) any deliberate disposal of vessels, aircraft, platforms or other man-made structures at sea;

(b) "dumping" does not include: (i) the disposal of wastes or other matter incidental to, or derived from the normal operations of vessels, aircraft, platforms or other man-made structures at sea and their equipment, other than wastes or other matter transported by or to vessels, aircraft, platforms or other man-made structures at sea, operating for the purpose of disposal of such matter or derived from the treatment of such wastes or other matter on such vessels, aircraft, platforms or structures; (ii) placement of matter for a purpose other than the mere disposal thereof, provided that such placement is not contrary to the aims of this Convention.

2. (1) "States Parties" means States which have consented to be bound by this Convention and for which this Convention is in force.

(2) This Convention applies mutatis mutandis to the entities referred to in article 305, paragraph l(b), (c), (d), (e) and (f), which become Parties to this Convention in accordance with the conditions relevant to each, and to that extent "States Parties" refers to those entities.

Part II:
Territorial Sea and Contiguous Zone

Section 1: General Provisions

Article 2: Legal status of the territorial sea, of the air space over the territorial sea and of its bed and subsoil

1. The sovereignty of a coastal State extends, beyond its land territory and internal waters and, in the case of an archipelagic State, its archipelagic waters, to an adjacent belt of sea, described as the territorial sea.

2. This sovereignty extends to the air space over the territorial sea as well as to its bed and subsoil.

3. The sovereignty over the territorial sea is exercised subject to this Convention and to other rules of international law.

Section 2: Limits of the Territorial Sea

Article 3: Breadth of the territorial sea
Every State has the right to establish the breadth of its territorial sea up to a limit not exceeding 12 nautical miles, measured from baselines determined in accordance with this Convention.

Article 4: Outer limit of the territorial sea
The outer limit of the territorial sea is the line every point of which is at a dis-

tance from the nearest point of the baseline equal to the breadth of the territorial sea.

Article 5: Normal baseline
Except where otherwise provided in this Convention, the normal baseline for measuring the breadth of the territorial sea is the low-water line along the coast as marked on large-scale charts officially recognized by the coastal State.

Article 6: Reefs
In the case of islands situated on atolls or of islands having fringing reefs, the baseline for measuring the breadth of the territorial sea is the seaward low-water line of the reef, as shown by the appropriate symbol on charts officially recognized by the coastal State.

Article 7: Straight baselines
1. In localities where the coastline is deeply indented and cut into, or if there is a fringe of islands along the coast in its immediate vicinity, the method of straight baselines joining appropriate points may be employed in drawing the baseline from which the breadth of the territorial sea is measured.

2. Where because of the presence of a delta and other natural conditions the coastline is highly unstable, the appropriate points may be selected along the furthest seaward extent of the low-water line and, notwithstanding subsequent regression of the low-water line, the straight baselines shall remain effective until changed by the coastal State in accordance with this Convention.

3. The drawing of straight baselines must not depart to any appreciable extent from the general direction of the coast, and the sea areas lying within the lines must be sufficiently closely linked to the land domain to be subject to the regime of internal waters.

4. Straight baselines shall not be drawn to and from low-tide elevations, unless lighthouses or similar installations which are permanently above sea level have been built on them or except in instances where the drawing of baselines to and from such elevations has received general international recognition.

5. Where the method of straight baselines is applicable under paragraph 1, account may be taken, in determining particular baselines, of economic interests peculiar to the region concerned, the reality and the importance of which are clearly evidenced by long usage.

6. The system of straight baselines may not be applied by a State in such a manner as to cut off the territorial sea of another State from the high seas or an exclusive economic zone.

Article 8: Internal waters
1. Except as provided in Part IV, waters on the landward side of the baseline of the territorial sea form part of the internal waters of the State.

2. Where the establishment of a straight baseline in accordance with the method set forth in article 7 has the effect of enclosing as internal waters areas

which had not previously been considered as such, a right of innocent passage as provided in this Convention shall exist in those waters.

Article 9: Mouths of rivers

If a river flows directly into the sea, the baseline shall be a straight line across the mouth of the river between points on the low-water line of its banks.

Article 10: Bays

1. This article relates only to bays the coasts of which belong to a single State.

2. For the purposes of this Convention, a bay is a well-marked indentation whose penetration is in such proportion to the width of its mouth as to contain land-locked waters and constitute more than a mere curvature of the coast. An indentation shall not, however, be regarded as a bay unless its area is as large as, or larger than, that of the semi-circle whose diameter is a line drawn across the mouth of that indentation.

3. For the purpose of measurement, the area of an indentation is that lying between the low-water mark around the shore of the indentation and a line joining the low-water mark of its natural entrance points. Where, because of the presence of islands, an indentation has more than one mouth, the semi-circle shall be drawn on a line as long as the sum total of the lengths of the lines across the different mouths. Islands within an indentation shall be included as if they were part of the water area of the indentation.

4. If the distance between the low-water marks of the natural entrance points of a bay does not exceed 24 nautical miles, a closing line may be drawn between these two low-water marks, and the waters enclosed thereby shall be considered as internal waters.

5. Where the distance between the low-water marks of the natural entrance points of a bay exceeds 24 nautical miles, a straight baseline of 24 nautical miles shall be drawn within the bay in such a manner as to enclose the maximum area of water that is possible with a line of that length.

6. The foregoing provisions do not apply to so-called "historic" bays, or in any case where the system of straight baselines provided for in article 7 is applied.

Article 11: Ports

For the purpose of delimiting the territorial sea, the outermost permanent harbour works which form an integral part of the harbour system are regarded as forming part of the coast. Off-shore installations and artificial islands shall not be considered as permanent harbour works.

Article 12: Roadsteads

Roadsteads which are normally used for the loading, unloading and anchoring of ships, and which would otherwise be situated wholly or partly outside the outer limit of the territorial sea, are included in the territorial sea.

Article 13: Low-tide elevations

1. A low-tide elevation is a naturally formed area of land which is surrounded by and above water at low tide but submerged at high tide. Where a low-tide elevation is situated wholly or partly at a distance not exceeding the breadth of the territorial sea from the mainland or an island, the low-water line on that elevation may be used as the baseline for measuring the breadth of the territorial sea.

2. Where a low-tide elevation is wholly situated at a distance exceeding the breadth of the territorial sea from the mainland or an island, it has no territorial sea of its own.

Article 14: Combination of methods for determining baselines

The coastal State may determine baselines in turn by any of the methods provided for in the foregoing articles to suit different conditions.

Article 15: Delimitation of the territorial sea between States with opposite or adjacent coasts

Where the coasts of two States are opposite or adjacent to each other, neither of the two States is entitled, failing agreement between them to the contrary, to extend its territorial sea beyond the median line every point of which is equidistant from the nearest points on the baselines from which the breadth of the territorial seas of each of the two States is measured. The above provision does not apply, however, where it is necessary by reason of historic title or other special circumstances to delimit the territorial seas of the two States in a way which is at variance therewith.

Article 16: Charts and lists of geographical coordinates

1. The baselines for measuring the breadth of the territorial sea determined in accordance with articles 7, 9 and 10, or the limits derived therefrom, and the lines of delimitation drawn in accordance with articles 12 and 15 shall be shown on charts of a scale or scales adequate for ascertaining their position. Alternatively, a list of geographical coordinates of points, specifying the geodetic datum, may be substituted.

2. The coastal State shall give due publicity to such charts or lists of geographical coordinates and shall deposit a copy of each such chart or list with the Secretary-General of the United Nations.

Section 3: Innocent Passage in the Territorial Sea

Subsection A: Rules Applicable to All Ships

Article 17: Right of innocent passage

Subject to this Convention, ships of all States, whether coastal or land-locked, enjoy the right of innocent passage through the territorial sea.

Article 18: Meaning of passage

1. Passage means navigation through the territorial sea for the purpose of:

(a) traversing that sea without entering internal waters or calling at a roadstead or port facility outside internal waters; or

(b) proceeding to or from internal waters or a call at such roadstead or port facility.

2. Passage shall be continuous and expeditious. However, passage includes stopping and anchoring, but only in so far as the same are incidental to ordinary navigation or are rendered necessary by force majeure or distress or for the purpose of rendering assistance to persons, ships or aircraft in danger or distress.

Article 19: Meaning of innocent passage

1. Passage is innocent so long as it is not prejudicial to the peace, good order or security of the coastal State. Such passage shall take place in conformity with this Convention and with other rules of international law.

2. Passage of a foreign ship shall be considered to be prejudicial to the peace, good order or security of the coastal State if in the territorial sea it engages in any of the following activities:

(a) any threat or use of force against the sovereignty, territorial integrity or political independence of the coastal State, or in any other manner in violation of the principles of international law embodied in the Charter of the United Nations;

(b) any exercise or practice with weapons of any kind;

(c) any act aimed at collecting information to the prejudice of the defence or security of the coastal State;

(d) any act of propaganda aimed at affecting the defence or security of the coastal State;

(e) the launching, landing or taking on board of any aircraft;

(f) the launching, landing or taking on board of any military device;

(g) the loading or unloading of any commodity, currency or person contrary to the customs, fiscal, immigration or sanitary laws and regulations of the coastal State;

(h) any act of wilful and serious pollution contrary to this Convention;

(i) any fishing activities;

(j) the carrying out of research or survey activities;

(k) any act aimed at interfering with any systems of communication or any other facilities or installations of the coastal State;

(l) any other activity not having a direct bearing on passage.

Article 20: Submarines and other underwater vehicles

In the territorial sea, submarines and other underwater vehicles are required to navigate on the surface and to show their flag.

Article 21: Laws and regulations of the coastal State relating to innocent passage

1. The coastal State may adopt laws and regulations, in conformity with the provisions of this Convention and other rules of international law, relating to innocent passage through the territorial sea, in respect of all or any of the following:

(a) the safety of navigation and the regulation of maritime traffic;

(b) the protection of navigational aids and facilities and other facilities or installations;

(c) the protection of cables and pipelines;

(d) the conservation of the living resources of the sea;

(e) the prevention of infringement of the fisheries laws and regulations of the coastal State;

(f) the preservation of the environment of the coastal State and the prevention, reduction and control of pollution thereof;

(g) marine scientific research and hydrographic surveys;

(h) the prevention of infringement of the customs, fiscal, immigration or sanitary laws and regulations of the coastal State.

2. Such laws and regulations shall not apply to the design, construction, manning or equipment of foreign ships unless they are giving effect to generally accepted international rules or standards.

3. The coastal State shall give due publicity to all such laws and regulations.

4. Foreign ships exercising the right of innocent passage through the territorial sea shall comply with all such laws and regulations and all generally accepted international regulations relating to the prevention of collisions at sea.

Article 22: Sea lanes and traffic separation schemes in the territorial sea

1. The coastal State may, where necessary having regard to the safety of navigation, require foreign ships exercising the right of innocent passage through its territorial sea to use such sea lanes and traffic separation schemes as it may designate or prescribe for the regulation of the passage of ships.

2. In particular, tankers, nuclear-powered ships and ships carrying nuclear or other inherently dangerous or noxious substances or materials may be required to confine their passage to such sea lanes.

3. In the designation of sea lanes and the prescription of traffic separation schemes under this article, the coastal State shall take into account:

(a) the recommendations of the competent international organization;

(b) any channels customarily used for international navigation;

(c) the special characteristics of particular ships and channels; and

(d) the density of traffic.

4. The coastal State shall clearly indicate such sea lanes and traffic separation schemes on charts to which due publicity shall be given.

Article 23: Foreign nuclear-powered ships and ships carrying nuclear or other inherently dangerous or noxious substances

Foreign nuclear-powered ships and ships carrying nuclear or other inherently dangerous or noxious substances shall, when exercising the right of innocent passage through the territorial sea, carry documents and observe special precautionary measures established for such ships by international agreements.

Article 24: Duties of the coastal State

1. The coastal State shall not hamper the innocent passage of foreign ships through the territorial sea except in accordance with this Convention. In particular, in the application of this Convention or of any laws or regulations adopted in conformity with this Convention, the coastal State shall not:

(a) impose requirements on foreign ships which have the practical effect of denying or impairing the right of innocent passage; or

(b) discriminate in form or in fact against the ships of any State or against ships carrying cargoes to, from or on behalf of any State.

2. The coastal State shall give appropriate publicity to any danger to navigation, of which it has knowledge, within its territorial sea.

Article 25: Rights of protection of the coastal State

1. The coastal State may take the necessary steps in its territorial sea to prevent passage which is not innocent.

2. In the case of ships proceeding to internal waters or a call at a port facility outside internal waters, the coastal State also has the right to take the necessary steps to prevent any breach of the conditions to which admission of those ships to internal waters or such a call is subject.

3. The coastal State may, without discrimination in form or in fact among foreign ships, suspend temporarily in specified areas of its territorial sea the innocent passage of foreign ships if such suspension is essential for the protection of its security, including weapons exercises. Such suspension shall take effect only after having been duly published.

Article 26: Charges which may be levied upon foreign ships

1. No charge may be levied upon foreign ships by reason only of their passage through the territorial sea.

2. Charges may be levied upon a foreign ship passing through the territorial sea as payment only for specific services rendered to the ship. These charges shall be levied without discrimination.

Subsection B: Rules Applicable to Merchant Ships and Government Ships Operated for Commercial Purposes

Article 27: Criminal jurisdiction on board a foreign ship

1. The criminal jurisdiction of the coastal State should not be exercised on board a foreign ship passing through the territorial sea to arrest any person or

to conduct any investigation in connection with any crime committed on board the ship during its passage, save only in the following cases:

(a) if the consequences of the crime extend to the coastal State;

(b) if the crime is of a kind to disturb the peace of the country or the good order of the territorial sea;

(c) if the assistance of the local authorities has been requested by the master of the ship or by a diplomatic agent or consular officer of the flag State; or

(d) if such measures are necessary for the suppression of illicit traffic in narcotic drugs or psychotropic substances.

2. The above provisions do not affect the right of the coastal State to take any steps authorized by its laws for the purpose of an arrest or investigation on board a foreign ship passing through the territorial sea after leaving internal waters.

3. In the cases provided for in paragraphs 1 and 2, the coastal State shall, if the master so requests, notify a diplomatic agent or consular officer of the flag State before taking any steps, and shall facilitate contact between such agent or officer and the ship's crew. In cases of emergency this notification may be communicated while the measures are being taken.

4. In considering whether or in what manner an arrest should be made, the local authorities shall have due regard to the interests of navigation.

5. Except as provided in Part XII or with respect to violations of laws and regulations adopted in accordance with Part V, the coastal State may not take any steps on board a foreign ship passing through the territorial sea to arrest any person or to conduct any investigation in connection with any crime committed before the ship entered the territorial sea, if the ship, proceeding from a foreign port, is only passing through the territorial sea without entering internal waters.

Article 28: Civil jurisdiction in relation to foreign ships

1. The coastal State should not stop or divert a foreign ship passing through the territorial sea for the purpose of exercising civil jurisdiction in relation to a person on board the ship.

2. The coastal State may not levy execution against or arrest the ship for the purpose of any civil proceedings, save only in respect of obligations or liabilities assumed or incurred by the ship itself in the course or for the purpose of its voyage through the waters of the coastal State.

3. Paragraph 2 is without prejudice to the right of the coastal State, in accordance with its laws, to levy execution against or to arrest, for the purpose of any civil proceedings, a foreign ship lying in the territorial sea, or passing through the territorial sea after leaving internal waters.

Subsection C: Rules Applicable to Warships and Other Government Ships Operated for Non-Commercial Purposes

Article 29: Definition of warships

For the purposes of this Convention, "warship" means a ship belonging to the armed forces of a State bearing the external marks distinguishing such ships of its nationality, under the command of an officer duly commissioned by the government of the State and whose name appears in the appropriate service list or its equivalent, and manned by a crew which is under regular armed forces discipline.

Article 30: Non-compliance by warships
with the laws and regulations of the coastal State

If any warship does not comply with the laws and regulations of the coastal State concerning passage through the territorial sea and disregards any request for compliance therewith which is made to it, the coastal State may require it to leave the territorial sea immediately.

Article 31: Responsibility of the flag State for damage caused by a warship or other government ship operated for non-commercial purposes

The flag State shall bear international responsibility for any loss or damage to the coastal State resulting from the non-compliance by a warship or other government ship operated for non-commercial purposes with the laws and regulations of the coastal State concerning passage through the territorial sea or with the provisions of this Convention or other rules of international law.

Article 32: Immunities of warships and other
government ships operated for non-commercial purposes

With such exceptions as are contained in subsection A and in articles 30 and 31, nothing in this Convention affects the immunities of warships and other government ships operated for non-commercial purposes.

Section 4: Contiguous Zone

Article 33: Contiguous zone

1. In a zone contiguous to its territorial sea, described as the contiguous zone, the coastal State may exercise the control necessary to:

(a) prevent infringement of its customs, fiscal, immigration or sanitary laws and regulations within its territory or territorial sea;

(b) punish infringement of the above laws and regulations committed within its territory or territorial sea.

2. The contiguous zone may not extend beyond 24 nautical miles from the baselines from which the breadth of the territorial sea is measured.

Part III: Straits Used for International Navigation

Section 1: General Provisions

Article 34: Legal status of waters
forming straits used for international navigation

1. The regime of passage through straits used for international navigation

established in this Part shall not in other respects affect the legal status of the waters forming such straits or the exercise by the States bordering the straits of their sovereignty or jurisdiction over such waters and their air space, bed and subsoil.

2. The sovereignty or jurisdiction of the States bordering the straits is exercised subject to this Part and to other rules of international law.

Article 35: Scope of this Part

Nothing in this Part affects:

(a) any areas of internal waters within a strait, except where the establishment of a straight baseline in accordance with the method set forth in article 7 has the effect of enclosing as internal waters areas which had not previously been considered as such;

(b) the legal status of the waters beyond the territorial seas of States bordering straits as exclusive economic zones or high seas; or

(c) the legal regime in straits in which passage is regulated in whole or in part by long-standing international conventions in force specifically relating to such straits.

Article 36: High seas routes or routes through exclusive economic zones through straits used for international navigation

This Part does not apply to a strait used for international navigation if there exists through the strait a route through the high seas or through an exclusive economic zone of similar convenience with respect to navigational and hydrographical characteristics; in such routes, the other relevant Parts of this Convention, including the provisions regarding the freedoms of navigation and overflight, apply.

Section 2: Transit Passage

Article 37: Scope of this section

This section applies to straits which are used for international navigation between one part of the high seas or an exclusive economic zone and another part of the high seas or an exclusive economic zone.

Article 38: Right of transit passage

1. In straits referred to in article 37, all ships and aircraft enjoy the right of transit passage, which shall not be impeded; except that, if the strait is formed by an island of a State bordering the strait and its mainland, transit passage shall not apply if there exists seaward of the island a route through the high seas or through an exclusive economic zone of similar convenience with respect to navigational and hydrographical characteristics.

2. Transit passage means the exercise in accordance with this Part of the freedom of navigation and overflight solely for the purpose of continuous and expeditious transit of the strait between one part of the high seas or an exclu-

sive economic zone and another part of the high seas or an exclusive economic zone. However, the requirement of continuous and expeditious transit does not preclude passage through the strait for the purpose of entering, leaving or returning from a State bordering the strait, subject to the conditions of entry to that State.

3. Any activity which is not an exercise of the right of transit passage through a strait remains subject to the other applicable provisions of this Convention.

Article 39: Duties of ships and aircraft during transit passage

1. Ships and aircraft, while exercising the right of transit passage, shall:

(a) proceed without delay through or over the strait;

(b) refrain from any threat or use of force against the sovereignty, territorial integrity or political independence of States bordering the strait, or in any other manner in violation of the principles of international law embodied in the Charter of the United Nations;

(c) refrain from any activities other than those incident to their normal modes of continuous and expeditious transit unless rendered necessary by force majeure or by distress;

(d) comply with other relevant provisions of this Part.

2. Ships in transit passage shall:

(a) comply with generally accepted international regulations, procedures and practices for safety at sea, including the International Regulations for Preventing Collisions at Sea;

(b) comply with generally accepted international regulations, procedures and practices for the prevention, reduction and control of pollution from ships.

3. Aircraft in transit passage shall:

(a) observe the Rules of the Air established by the International Civil Aviation Organization as they apply to civil aircraft; state aircraft will normally comply with such safety measures and will at all times operate with due regard for the safety of navigation;

(b) at all times monitor the radio frequency assigned by the competent internationally designated air traffic control authority or the appropriate international distress radio frequency.

Article 40: Research and survey activities

During transit passage, foreign ships, including marine scientific research and hydrographic survey ships, may not carry out any research or survey activities without the prior authorization of the States bordering straits.

Article 41: Sea lanes and traffic separation
schemes in straits used for international navigation

1. In conformity with this Part, States bordering straits may designate sea lanes and prescribe traffic separation schemes for navigation in straits where necessary to promote the safe passage of ships.

2. Such States may, when circumstances require, and after giving due publicity thereto, substitute other sea lanes or traffic separation schemes for any sea lanes or traffic separation schemes previously designated or prescribed by them.

3. Such sea lanes and traffic separation schemes shall conform to generally accepted international regulations.

4. Before designating or substituting sea lanes or prescribing or substituting traffic separation schemes, States bordering straits shall refer proposals to the competent international organization with a view to their adoption. The organization may adopt only such sea lanes and traffic separation schemes as may be agreed with the States bordering the straits, after which the States may designate, prescribe or substitute them.

5. In respect of a strait where sea lanes or traffic separation schemes through the waters of two or more States bordering the strait are being proposed, the States concerned shall cooperate in formulating proposals in consultation with the competent international organization.

6. States bordering straits shall clearly indicate all sea lanes and traffic separation schemes designated or prescribed by them on charts to which due publicity shall be given.

7. Ships in transit passage shall respect applicable sea lanes and traffic separation schemes established in accordance with this article.

Article 42: Laws and regulations of States bordering straits relating to transit passage

1. Subject to the provisions of this section, States bordering straits may adopt laws and regulations relating to transit passage through straits, in respect of all or any of the following:

(a) the safety of navigation and the regulation of maritime traffic, as provided in article 41;

(b) the prevention, reduction and control of pollution, by giving effect to applicable international regulations regarding the discharge of oil, oily wastes and other noxious substances in the strait;

(c) with respect to fishing vessels, the prevention of fishing, including the stowage of fishing gear;

(d) the loading or unloading of any commodity, currency or person in contravention of the customs, fiscal, immigration or sanitary laws and regulations of States bordering straits.

2. Such laws and regulations shall not discriminate in form or in fact among foreign ships or in their application have the practical effect of denying, hampering or impairing the right of transit passage as defined in this section.

3. States bordering straits shall give due publicity to all such laws and regulations.

4. Foreign ships exercising the right of transit passage shall comply with such laws and regulations.

5. The flag State of a ship or the State of registry of an aircraft entitled to

sovereign immunity which acts in a manner contrary to such laws and regulations or other provisions of this Part shall bear international responsibility for any loss or damage which results to States bordering straits.

Article 43: Navigational and safety aids and other improvements and the prevention, reduction and control of pollution

User States and States bordering a strait should by agreement cooperate:

(a) in the establishment and maintenance in a strait of necessary navigational and safety aids or other improvements in aid of international navigation; and

(b) for the prevention, reduction and control of pollution from ships.

Article 44: Duties of States bordering straits

States bordering straits shall not hamper transit passage and shall give appropriate publicity to any danger to navigation or overflight within or over the strait of which they have knowledge. There shall be no suspension of transit passage.

Section 3: Innocent Passage

Article 45: Innocent passage

1. The regime of innocent passage, in accordance with Part II, section 3, shall apply in straits used for international navigation:

(a) excluded from the application of the regime of transit passage under article 38, paragraph 1; or

(b) between a part of the high seas or an exclusive economic zone and the territorial sea of a foreign State.

2. There shall be no suspension of innocent passage through such straits.

Part IV: Archipelagic States

Article 46: Use of terms

For the purposes of this Convention:

(a) "archipelagic State" means a State constituted wholly by one or more archipelagos and may include other islands;

(b) "archipelago" means a group of islands, including parts of islands, interconnecting waters and other natural features which are so closely interrelated that such islands, waters and other natural features form an intrinsic geographical, economic and political entity, or which historically have been regarded as such.

Article 47: Archipelagic baselines

1. An archipelagic State may draw straight archipelagic baselines joining

the outermost points of the outermost islands and drying reefs of the archipela-go provided that within such baselines are included the main islands and an area in which the ratio of the area of the water to the area of the land, including atolls, is between 1 to 1 and 9 to 1.

2. The length of such baselines shall not exceed 100 nautical miles, except that up to 3 per cent of the total number of baselines enclosing any archipelago may exceed that length, up to a maximum length of 125 nautical miles.

3. The drawing of such baselines shall not depart to any appreciable extent from the general configuration of the archipelago.

4. Such baselines shall not be drawn to and from low-tide elevations, unless lighthouses or similar installations which are permanently above sea level have been built on them or where a low-tide elevation is situated wholly or partly at a distance not exceeding the breadth of the territorial sea from the nearest island.

5. The system of such baselines shall not be applied by an archipelagic State in such a manner as to cut off from the high seas or the exclusive economic zone the territorial sea of another State.

6. If a part of the archipelagic waters of an archipelagic State lies between two parts of an immediately adjacent neighbouring State, existing rights and all other legitimate interests which the latter State has traditionally exercised in such waters and all rights stipulated by agreement between those States shall continue and be respected.

7. For the purpose of computing the ratio of water to land under paragraph 1, land areas may include waters lying within the fringing reefs of islands and atolls, including that part of a steep-sided oceanic plateau which is enclosed or nearly enclosed by a chain of limestone islands and drying reefs lying on the perimeter of the plateau.

8. The baselines drawn in accordance with this article shall be shown on charts of a scale or scales adequate for ascertaining their position. Alternatively, lists of geographical coordinates of points, specifying the geo-detic datum, may be substituted.

9. The archipelagic State shall give due publicity to such charts or lists of geographical coordinates and shall deposit a copy of each such chart or list with the Secretary-General of the United Nations.

Article 48: Measurement of the breadth of
the territorial sea, the contiguous zone, the
exclusive economic zone and the continental shelf

The breadth of the territorial sea, the contiguous zone, the exclusive economic zone and the continental shelf shall be measured from archipelagic baselines drawn in accordance with article 47.

Article 49: Legal status of archipelagic waters, of the
air space over archipelagic waters and of their bed and subsoil

1. The sovereignty of an archipelagic State extends to the waters enclosed

by the archipelagic baselines drawn in accordance with article 47, described as archipelagic waters, regardless of their depth or distance from the coast.

2. This sovereignty extends to the air space over the archipelagic waters, as well as to their bed and subsoil, and the resources contained therein.

3. This sovereignty is exercised subject to this Part.

4. The regime of archipelagic sea lanes passage established in this Part shall not in other respects affect the status of the archipelagic waters, including the sea lanes, or the exercise by the archipelagic State of its sovereignty over such waters and their air space, bed and subsoil, and the resources contained therein.

Article 50: Delimitation of internal waters

Within its archipelagic waters, the archipelagic State may draw closing lines for the delimitation of internal waters, in accordance with articles 9, 10 and 11.

Article 51: Existing agreements, traditional fishing rights and existing submarine cables

1. Without prejudice to article 49, an archipelagic State shall respect existing agreements with other States and shall recognize traditional fishing rights and other legitimate activities of the immediately adjacent neighbouring States in certain areas falling within archipelagic waters. The terms and conditions for the exercise of such rights and activities, including the nature, the extent and the areas to which they apply, shall, at the request of any of the States concerned, be regulated by bilateral agreements between them. Such rights shall not be transferred to or shared with third States or their nationals.

2. An archipelagic State shall respect existing submarine cables laid by other States and passing through its waters without making a landfall. An archipelagic State shall permit the maintenance and replacement of such cables upon receiving due notice of their location and the intention to repair or replace them.

Article 52: Right of innocent passage

1. Subject to article 53 and without prejudice to article 50, ships of all States enjoy the right of innocent passage through archipelagic waters, in accordance with Part II, section 3.

2. The archipelagic State may, without discrimination in form or in fact among foreign ships, suspend temporarily in specified areas of its archipelagic waters the innocent passage of foreign ships if such suspension is essential for the protection of its security. Such suspension shall take effect only after having been duly published.

Article 53: Right of archipelagic sea lanes passage

1. An archipelagic State may designate sea lanes and air routes thereabove, suitable for the continuous and expeditious passage of foreign ships

and aircraft through or over its archipelagic waters and the adjacent territorial sea.

2. All ships and aircraft enjoy the right of archipelagic sea lanes passage in such sea lanes and air routes.

3. Archipelagic sea lanes passage means the exercise in accordance with this Convention of the rights of navigation and overflight in the normal mode solely for the purpose of continuous, expeditious and unobstructed transit between one part of the high seas or an exclusive economic zone and another part of the high seas or an exclusive economic zone.

4. Such sea lanes and air routes shall traverse the archipelagic waters and the adjacent territorial sea and shall include all normal passage routes used as routes for international navigation or overflight through or over archipelagic waters and, within such routes, so far as ships are concerned, all normal navigational channels, provided that duplication of routes of similar convenience between the same entry and exit points shall not be necessary.

5. Such sea lanes and air routes shall be defined by a series of continuous axis lines from the entry points of passage routes to the exit points. Ships and aircraft in archipelagic sea lanes passage shall not deviate more than 25 nautical miles to either side of such axis lines during passage, provided that such ships and aircraft shall not navigate closer to the coasts than 10 per cent of the distance between the nearest points on islands bordering the sea lane.

6. An archipelagic State which designates sea lanes under this article may also prescribe traffic separation schemes for the safe passage of ships through narrow channels in such sea lanes.

7. An archipelagic State may, when circumstances require, after giving due publicity thereto, substitute other sea lanes or traffic separation schemes for any sea lanes or traffic separation schemes previously designated or prescribed by it.

8. Such sea lanes and traffic separation schemes shall conform to generally accepted international regulations.

9. In designating or substituting sea lanes or prescribing or substituting traffic separation schemes, an archipelagic State shall refer proposals to the competent international organization with a view to their adoption. The organization may adopt only such sea lanes and traffic separation schemes as may be agreed with the archipelagic State, after which the archipelagic State may designate, prescribe or substitute them.

10. The archipelagic State shall clearly indicate the axis of the sea lanes and the traffic separation schemes designated or prescribed by it on charts to which due publicity shall be given.

11. Ships in archipelagic sea lanes passage shall respect applicable sea lanes and traffic separation schemes established in accordance with this article.

12. If an archipelagic State does not designate sea lanes or air routes, the right of archipelagic sea lanes passage may be exercised through the routes normally used for international navigation.

Article 54: Duties of ships and aircraft during their
passage, research and survey activities, duties of the
archipelagic State and laws and regulations of the
archipelagic State relating to archipelagic sea lanes passage.
Articles 39, 40, 42 and 44 apply mutatis mutandis to archipelagic sea lanes
passage.

Part V: Exclusive Economic Zone

Article 55: Specific legal regime of the exclusive economic zone
The exclusive economic zone is an area beyond and adjacent to the territorial
sea, subject to the specific legal regime established in this Part, under which
the rights and jurisdiction of the coastal State and the rights and freedoms of
other States are governed by the relevant provisions of this Convention.

Article 56: Rights, jurisdiction and duties of
the coastal State in the exclusive economic zone
1. In the exclusive economic zone, the coastal State has:
(a) sovereign rights for the purpose of exploring and exploiting, conserving and managing the natural resources, whether living or non-living, of the
waters superjacent to the seabed and of the seabed and its subsoil, and with
regard to other activities for the economic exploitation and exploration of the
zone, such as the production of energy from the water, currents and winds;
(b) jurisdiction as provided for in the relevant provisions of this
Convention with regard to: (i) the establishment and use of artificial islands,
installations, and structures; (ii) marine scientific research; (iii) the protection
and preservation of the marine environment;
(c) other rights and duties provided for in this Convention.
2. In exercising its rights and performing its duties under this Convention in
the exclusive economic zone, the coastal State shall have due regard to the
rights and duties of other States and shall act in a manner compatible with the
provisions of this Convention.
3. The rights set out in this article with respect to the seabed and subsoil
shall be exercised in accordance with Part VI.

Article 57: Breadth of the exclusive economic zone
The exclusive economic zone shall not extend beyond 200 nautical miles from
the baselines from which the breadth of the territorial sea is measured.

Article 58: Rights and duties of other
States in the exclusive economic zone
1. In the exclusive economic zone, all States, whether coastal or land-
locked, enjoy, subject to the relevant provisions of this Convention, the freedoms referred to in article 87 of navigation and overflight and of the laying of

submarine cables and pipelines, and other internationally lawful uses of the sea related to these freedoms, such as those associated with the operation of ships, aircraft and submarine cables and pipelines, and compatible with the other provisions of this Convention.

2. Articles 88 to 115 and other pertinent rules of international law apply to the exclusive economic zone in so far as they are not incompatible with this Part.

3. In exercising their rights and performing their duties under this Convention in the exclusive economic zone, States shall have due regard to the rights and duties of the coastal State and shall comply with the laws and regulations adopted by the coastal State in accordance with the provisions of this Convention and other rules of international law in so far as they are not incompatible with this Part.

Article 59: Basis for the resolution of conflicts regarding the attribution of rights and jurisdiction in the exclusive economic zone

In cases where this Convention does not attribute rights or jurisdiction to the coastal State or to other States within the exclusive economic zone, and a conflict arises between the interests of the coastal State and any other State or States, the conflict should be resolved on the basis of equity and in the light of all the relevant circumstances, taking into account the respective importance of the interests involved to the parties as well as to the international community as a whole.

Article 60: Artificial islands, installations and structures in the exclusive economic zone

1. In the exclusive economic zone, the coastal State shall have the exclusive right to construct and to authorize and regulate the construction, operation and use of:

(a) artificial islands;

(b) installations and structures for the purposes provided for in article 56 and other economic purposes;

(c) installations and structures which may interfere with the exercise of the rights of the coastal State in the zone.

2. The coastal State shall have exclusive jurisdiction over such artificial islands, installations and structures, including jurisdiction with regard to customs, fiscal, health, safety and immigration laws and regulations.

3. Due notice must be given of the construction of such artificial islands, installations or structures, and permanent means for giving warning of their presence must be maintained. Any installations or structures which are abandoned or disused shall be removed to ensure safety of navigation, taking into account any generally accepted international standards established in this regard by the competent international organization. Such removal shall also have due regard to fishing, the protection of the marine environment and the rights and duties of other States. Appropriate publicity shall be given to the

depth, position and dimensions of any installations or structures not entirely removed.

4. The coastal State may, where necessary, establish reasonable safety zones around such artificial islands, installations and structures in which it may take appropriate measures to ensure the safety both of navigation and of the artificial islands, installations and structures.

5. The breadth of the safety zones shall be determined by the coastal State, taking into account applicable international standards. Such zones shall be designed to ensure that they are reasonably related to the nature and function of the artificial islands, installations or structures, and shall not exceed a distance of 500 metres around them, measured from each point of their outer edge, except as authorized by generally accepted international standards or as recommended by the competent international organization. Due notice shall be given of the extent of safety zones.

6. All ships must respect these safety zones and shall comply with generally accepted international standards regarding navigation in the vicinity of artificial islands, installations, structures and safety zones.

7. Artificial islands, installations and structures and the safety zones around them may not be established where interference may be caused to the use of recognized sea lanes essential to international navigation.

8. Artificial islands, installations and structures do not possess the status of islands. They have no territorial sea of their own, and their presence does not affect the delimitation of the territorial sea, the exclusive economic zone or the continental shelf.

Article 61: Conservation of the living resources

1. The coastal State shall determine the allowable catch of the living resources in its exclusive economic zone.

2. The coastal State, taking into account the best scientific evidence available to it, shall ensure through proper conservation and management measures that the maintenance of the living resources in the exclusive economic zone is not endangered by over-exploitation. As appropriate, the coastal State and competent international organizations, whether subregional, regional or global, shall cooperate to this end.

3. Such measures shall also be designed to maintain or restore populations of harvested species at levels which can produce the maximum sustainable yield, as qualified by relevant environmental and economic factors, including the economic needs of coastal fishing communities and the special requirements of developing States, and taking into account fishing patterns, the interdependence of stocks and any generally recommended international minimum standards, whether subregional, regional or global.

4. In taking such measures the coastal State shall take into consideration the effects on species associated with or dependent upon harvested species with a view to maintaining or restoring populations of such associated or

dependent species above levels at which their reproduction may become seriously threatened.

5. Available scientific information, catch and fishing effort statistics, and other data relevant to the conservation of fish stocks shall be contributed and exchanged on a regular basis through competent international organizations, whether subregional, regional or global, where appropriate and with participation by all States concerned, including States whose nationals are allowed to fish in the exclusive economic zone.

Article 62: Utilization of the living resources

1. The coastal State shall promote the objective of optimum utilization of the living resources in the exclusive economic zone without prejudice to article 61.

2. The coastal State shall determine its capacity to harvest the living resources of the exclusive economic zone. Where the coastal State does not have the capacity to harvest the entire allowable catch, it shall, through agreements or other arrangements and pursuant to the terms, conditions, laws and regulations referred to in paragraph 4, give other States access to the surplus of the allowable catch, having particular regard to the provisions of articles 69 and 70, especially in relation to the developing States mentioned therein.

3. In giving access to other States to its exclusive economic zone under this article, the coastal State shall take into account all relevant factors, including, inter alia, the significance of the living resources of the area to the economy of the coastal State concerned and its other national interests, the provisions of articles 69 and 70, the requirements of developing States in the subregion or region in harvesting part of the surplus and the need to minimize economic dislocation in States whose nationals have habitually fished in the zone or which have made substantial efforts in research and identification of stocks.

4. Nationals of other States fishing in the exclusive economic zone shall comply with the conservation measures and with the other terms and conditions established in the laws and regulations of the coastal State. These laws and regulations shall be consistent with this Convention and may relate, inter alia, to the following:

(a) licensing of fishermen, fishing vessels and equipment, including payment of fees and other forms of remuneration, which, in the case of developing coastal States, may consist of adequate compensation in the field of financing, equipment and technology relating to the fishing industry;

(b) determining the species which may be caught, and fixing quotas of catch, whether in relation to particular stocks or groups of stocks or catch per vessel over a period of time or to the catch by nationals of any State during a specified period;

(c) regulating seasons and areas of fishing, the types, sizes and amount of gear, and the types, sizes and number of fishing vessels that may be used;

(d) fixing the age and size of fish and other species that may be caught;

(e) specifying information required of fishing vessels, including catch and effort statistics and vessel position reports;

(f) requiring, under the authorization and control of the coastal State, the conduct of specified fisheries research programmes and regulating the conduct of such research, including the sampling of catches, disposition of samples and reporting of associated scientific data;

(g) the placing of observers or trainees on board such vessels by the coastal State;

(h) the landing of all or any part of the catch by such vessels in the ports of the coastal State;

(i) terms and conditions relating to joint ventures or other cooperative arrangements;

(j) requirements for the training of personnel and the transfer of fisheries technology, including enhancement of the coastal State's capability of undertaking fisheries research;

(k) enforcement procedures.

5. Coastal States shall give due notice of conservation and management laws and regulations.

Article 63: Stocks occurring within the exclusive economic zones of two or more coastal States or both within the exclusive economic zone and in an area beyond and adjacent to it

1. Where the same stock or stocks of associated species occur within the exclusive economic zones of two or more coastal States, these States shall seek, either directly or through appropriate subregional or regional organizations, to agree upon the measures necessary to coordinate and ensure the conservation and development of such stocks without prejudice to the other provisions of this Part.

2. Where the same stock or stocks of associated species occur both within the exclusive economic zone and in an area beyond and adjacent to the zone, the coastal State and the States fishing for such stocks in the adjacent area shall seek, either directly or through appropriate subregional or regional organizations, to agree upon the measures necessary for the conservation of these stocks in the adjacent area.

Article 64: Highly migratory species

1. The coastal State and other States whose nationals fish in the region for the highly migratory species listed in Annex I shall cooperate directly or through appropriate international organizations with a view to ensuring conservation and promoting the objective of optimum utilization of such species throughout the region, both within and beyond the exclusive economic zone. In regions for which no appropriate international organization exists, the coastal State and other States whose nationals harvest these species in the region shall cooperate to establish such an organization and participate in its work.

2. The provisions of paragraph 1 apply in addition to the other provisions of this Part. ·

Article 65: Marine mammals

Nothing in this Part restricts the right of a coastal State or the competence of an international organization, as appropriate, to prohibit, limit or regulate the exploitation of marine mammals more strictly than provided for in this Part. States shall cooperate with a view to the conservation of marine mammals and in the case of cetaceans shall in particular work through the appropriate international organizations for their conservation, management and study.

Article 66: Anadromous stocks

1. States in whose rivers anadromous stocks originate shall have the primary interest in and responsibility for such stocks.

2. The State of origin of anadromous stocks shall ensure their conservation by the establishment of appropriate regulatory measures for fishing in all waters landward of the outer limits of its exclusive economic zone and for fishing provided for in paragraph 3(b). The State of origin may, after consultations with the other States referred to in paragraphs 3 and 4 fishing these stocks, establish total allowable catches for stocks originating in its rivers.

3. (a) Fisheries for anadromous stocks shall be conducted only in waters landward of the outer limits of exclusive economic zones, except in cases where this provision would result in economic dislocation for a State other than the State of origin. With respect to such fishing beyond the outer limits of the exclusive economic zone, States concerned shall maintain consultations with a view to achieving agreement on terms and conditions of such fishing giving due regard to the conservation requirements and the needs of the State of origin in respect of these stocks.

(b) The State of origin shall cooperate in minimizing economic dislocation in such other States fishing these stocks, taking into account the normal catch and the mode of operations of such States, and all the areas in which such fishing has occurred.

(c) States referred to in subparagraph (b), participating by agreement with the State of origin in measures to renew anadromous stocks, particularly by expenditures for that purpose, shall be given special consideration by the State of origin in the harvesting of stocks originating in its rivers.

(d) Enforcement of regulations regarding anadromous stocks beyond the exclusive economic zone shall be by agreement between the State of origin and the other States concerned.

4. In cases where anadromous stocks migrate into or through the waters landward of the outer limits of the exclusive economic zone of a State other than the State of origin, such State shall cooperate with the State of origin with regard to the conservation and management of such stocks.

5. The State of origin of anadromous stocks and other States fishing these

stocks shall make arrangements for the implementation of the provisions of this article, where appropriate, through regional organizations.

Article 67: Catadromous species

1. A coastal State in whose waters catadromous species spend the greater part of their life cycle shall have responsibility for the management of these species and shall ensure the ingress and egress of migrating fish.

2. Harvesting of catadromous species shall be conducted only in waters landward of the outer limits of exclusive economic zones. When conducted in exclusive economic zones, harvesting shall be subject to this article and the other provisions of this Convention concerning fishing in these zones.

3. In cases where catadromous fish migrate through the exclusive economic zone of another State, whether as juvenile or maturing fish, the management, including harvesting, of such fish shall be regulated by agreement between the State mentioned in paragraph 1 and the other State concerned. Such agreement shall ensure the rational management of the species and take into account the responsibilities of the State mentioned in paragraph 1 for the maintenance of these species.

Article 68: Sedentary species

This Part does not apply to sedentary species as defined in article 77, paragraph 4.

Article 69: Right of land-locked States

1. Land-locked States shall have the right to participate, on an equitable basis, in the exploitation of an appropriate part of the surplus of the living resources of the exclusive economic zones of coastal States of the same subregion or region, taking into account the relevant economic and geographical circumstances of all the States concerned and in conformity with the provisions of this article and of articles 61 and 62.

2. The terms and modalities of such participation shall be established by the States concerned through bilateral, subregional or regional agreements taking into account, inter alia:

(a) the need to avoid effects detrimental to fishing communities or fishing industries of the coastal State;

(b) the extent to which the land-locked State, in accordance with the provisions of this article, is participating or is entitled to participate under existing bilateral, subregional or regional agreements in the exploitation of living resources of the exclusive economic zones of other coastal States;

(c) the extent to which other land-locked States and geographically disadvantaged States are participating in the exploitation of the living resources of the exclusive economic zone of the coastal State and the consequent need to avoid a particular burden for any single coastal State or a part of it;

(d) the nutritional needs of the populations of the respective States.

3. When the harvesting capacity of a coastal State approaches a point which would enable it to harvest the entire allowable catch of the living resources in its exclusive economic zone, the coastal State and other States concerned shall cooperate in the establishment of equitable arrangements on a bilateral, subregional or regional basis to allow for participation of developing land-locked States of the same subregion or region in the exploitation of the living resources of the exclusive economic zones of coastal States of the subregion or region, as may be appropriate in the circumstances and on terms satisfactory to all parties. In the implementation of this provision the factors mentioned in paragraph 2 shall also be taken into account.

4. Developed land-locked States shall, under the provisions of this article, be entitled to participate in the exploitation of living resources only in the exclusive economic zones of developed coastal States of the same subregion or region having regard to the extent to which the coastal State, in giving access to other States to the living resources of its exclusive economic zone, has taken into account the need to minimize detrimental effects on fishing communities and economic dislocation in States whose nationals have habitually fished in the zone.

5. The above provisions are without prejudice to arrangements agreed upon in subregions or regions where the coastal States may grant to land-locked States of the same subregion or region equal or preferential rights for the exploitation of the living resources in the exclusive economic zones.

Article 70: Right of geographically disadvantaged States

1. Geographically disadvantaged States shall have the right to participate, on an equitable basis, in the exploitation of an appropriate part of the surplus of the living resources of the exclusive economic zones of coastal States of the same subregion or region, taking into account the relevant economic and geographical circumstances of all the States concerned and in conformity with the provisions of this article and of articles 61 and 62.

2. For the purposes of this Part, "geographically disadvantaged States" means coastal States, including States bordering enclosed or semi-enclosed seas, whose geographical situation makes them dependent upon the exploitation of the living resources of the exclusive economic zones of other States in the subregion or region for adequate supplies of fish for the nutritional purposes of their populations or parts thereof, and coastal States which can claim no exclusive economic zones of their own.

3. The terms and modalities of such participation shall be established by the States concerned through bilateral, subregional or regional agreements taking into account, inter alia:

(a) the need to avoid effects detrimental to fishing communities or fishing industries of the coastal State;

(b) the extent to which the geographically disadvantaged State, in accordance with the provisions of this article, is participating or is entitled to participate under existing bilateral, subregional or regional agreements in the exploitation of living resources of the exclusive economic zones of other coastal States;

(c) the extent to which other geographically disadvantaged States and land-locked States are participating in the exploitation of the living resources of the exclusive economic zone of the coastal State and the consequent need to avoid a particular burden for any single coastal State or a part of it;

(d) the nutritional needs of the populations of the respective States.

4. When the harvesting capacity of a coastal State approaches a point which would enable it to harvest the entire allowable catch of the living resources in its exclusive economic zone, the coastal State and other States concerned shall cooperate in the establishment of equitable arrangements on a bilateral, subregional or regional basis to allow for participation of developing geographically disadvantaged States of the same subregion or region in the exploitation of the living resources of the exclusive economic zones of coastal States of the subregion or region, as may be appropriate in the circumstances and on terms satisfactory to all parties. In the implementation of this provision the factors mentioned in paragraph 3 shall also be taken into account.

5. Developed geographically disadvantaged States shall, under the provisions of this article, be entitled to participate in the exploitation of living resources only in the exclusive economic zones of developed coastal States of the same subregion or region having regard to the extent to which the coastal State, in giving access to other States to the living resources of its exclusive economic zone, has taken into account the need to minimize detrimental effects on fishing communities and economic dislocation in States whose nationals have habitually fished in the zone.

6. The above provisions are without prejudice to arrangements agreed upon in subregions or regions where the coastal States may grant to geographically disadvantaged States of the same subregion or region equal or preferential rights for the exploitation of the living resources in the exclusive economic zones.

Article 71: Non-applicability of articles 69 and 70

The provisions of articles 69 and 70 do not apply in the case of a coastal State whose economy is overwhelmingly dependent on the exploitation of the living resources of its exclusive economic zone.

Article 72: Restrictions on transfer of rights

1. Rights provided under articles 69 and 70 to exploit living resources shall not be directly or indirectly transferred to third States or their nationals by lease or licence, by establishing joint ventures or in any other manner which has the effect of such transfer unless otherwise agreed by the States concerned.

2. The foregoing provision does not preclude the States concerned from obtaining technical or financial assistance from third States or international

organizations in order to facilitate the exercise of the rights pursuant to articles 69 and 70, provided that it does not have the effect referred to in paragraph 1.

Article 73: Enforcement of laws and regulations of the coastal State

1. The coastal State may, in the exercise of its sovereign rights to explore, exploit, conserve and manage the living resources in the exclusive economic zone, take such measures, including boarding, inspection, arrest and judicial proceedings, as may be necessary to ensure compliance with the laws and regulations adopted by it in conformity with this Convention.

2. Arrested vessels and their crews shall be promptly released upon the posting of reasonable bond or other security.

3. Coastal State penalties for violations of fisheries laws and regulations in the exclusive economic zone may not include imprisonment, in the absence of agreements to the contrary by the States concerned, or any other form of corporal punishment.

4. In cases of arrest or detention of foreign vessels the coastal State shall promptly notify the flag State, through appropriate channels, of the action taken and of any penalties subsequently imposed.

Article 74: Delimitation of the exclusive economic zone between States with opposite or adjacent coasts

1. The delimitation of the exclusive economic zone between States with opposite or adjacent coasts shall be effected by agreement on the basis of international law, as referred to in Article 38 of the Statute of the International Court of Justice, in order to achieve an equitable solution.

2. If no agreement can be reached within a reasonable period of time, the States concerned shall resort to the procedures provided for in Part XV.

3. Pending agreement as provided for in paragraph 1, the States concerned, in a spirit of understanding and cooperation, shall make every effort to enter into provisional arrangements of a practical nature and, during this transitional period, not to jeopardize or hamper the reaching of the final agreement. Such arrangements shall be without prejudice to the final delimitation.

4. Where there is an agreement in force between the States concerned, questions relating to the delimitation of the exclusive economic zone shall be determined in accordance with the provisions of that agreement.

Article 75: Charts and lists of geographical coordinates

1. Subject to this Part, the outer limit lines of the exclusive economic zone and the lines of delimitation drawn in accordance with article 74 shall be shown on charts of a scale or scales adequate for ascertaining their position. Where appropriate, lists of geographical coordinates of points, specifying the geodetic datum, may be substituted for such outer limit lines or lines of delimitation.

2. The coastal State shall give due publicity to such charts or lists of geo-

graphical coordinates and shall deposit a copy of each such chart or list with the Secretary-General of the United Nations.

Part VI: Continental Shelf

Article 76: Definition of the continental shelf

1. The continental shelf of a coastal State comprises the seabed and subsoil of the submarine areas that extend beyond its territorial sea throughout the natural prolongation of its land territory to the outer edge of the continental margin, or to a distance of 200 nautical miles from the baselines from which the breadth of the territorial sea is measured where the outer edge of the continental margin does not extend up to that distance.

2. The continental shelf of a coastal State shall not extend beyond the limits provided for in paragraphs 4 to 6.

3. The continental margin comprises the submerged prolongation of the land mass of the coastal State, and consists of the seabed and subsoil of the shelf, the slope and the rise. It does not include the deep ocean floor with its oceanic ridges or the subsoil thereof.

4. (a) For the purposes of this Convention, the coastal State shall establish the outer edge of the continental margin wherever the margin extends beyond 200 nautical miles from the baselines from which the breadth of the territorial sea is measured, by either: (i) a line delineated in accordance with paragraph 7 by reference to the outermost fixed points at each of which the thickness of sedimentary rocks is at least 1 per cent of the shortest distance from such point to the foot of the continental slope; or (ii) a line delineated in accordance with paragraph 7 by reference to fixed points not more than 60 nautical miles from the foot of the continental slope.

(b) In the absence of evidence to the contrary, the foot of the continental slope shall be determined as the point of maximum change in the gradient at its base.

5. The fixed points comprising the line of the outer limits of the continental shelf on the seabed, drawn in accordance with paragraph 4 (a)(i) and (ii), either shall not exceed 350 nautical miles from the baselines from which the breadth of the territorial sea is measured or shall not exceed 100 nautical miles from the 2,500 metre isobath, which is a line connecting the depth of 2,500 metres.

6. Notwithstanding the provisions of paragraph 5, on submarine ridges, the outer limit of the continental shelf shall not exceed 350 nautical miles from the baselines from which the breadth of the territorial sea is measured.

This paragraph does not apply to submarine elevations that are natural components of the continental margin, such as its plateaux, rises, caps, banks and spurs.

7. The coastal State shall delineate the outer limits of its continental shelf, where that shelf extends beyond 200 nautical miles from the baselines from

which the breadth of the territorial sea is measured, by straight lines not exceeding 60 nautical miles in length, connecting fixed points, defined by coordinates of latitude and longitude.

8. Information on the limits of the continental shelf beyond 200 nautical miles from the baselines from which the breadth of the territorial sea is measured shall be submitted by the coastal State to the Commission on the Limits of the Continental Shelf set up under Annex II on the basis of equitable geographical representation. The Commission shall make recommendations to coastal States on matters related to the establishment of the outer limits of their continental shelf. The limits of the shelf established by a coastal State on the basis of these recommendations shall be final and binding.

9. The coastal State shall deposit with the Secretary-General of the United Nations charts and relevant information, including geodetic data, permanently describing the outer limits of its continental shelf. The Secretary-General shall give due publicity thereto.

10. The provisions of this article are without prejudice to the question of delimitation of the continental shelf between States with opposite or adjacent coasts.

Article 77: Rights of the coastal State over the continental shelf

1. The coastal State exercises over the continental shelf sovereign rights for the purpose of exploring it and exploiting its natural resources.

2. The rights referred to in paragraph 1 are exclusive in the sense that if the coastal State does not explore the continental shelf or exploit its natural resources, no one may undertake these activities without the express consent of the coastal State.

3. The rights of the coastal State over the continental shelf do not depend on occupation, effective or notional, or on any express proclamation.

4. The natural resources referred to in this Part consist of the mineral and other non-living resources of the seabed and subsoil together with living organisms belonging to sedentary species, that is to say, organisms which, at the harvestable stage, either are immobile on or under the seabed or are unable to move except in constant physical contact with the seabed or the subsoil.

Article 78: Legal status of the superjacent waters and air space and the rights and freedoms of other States

1. The rights of the coastal State over the continental shelf do not affect the legal status of the superjacent waters or of the air space above those waters.

2. The exercise of the rights of the coastal State over the continental shelf must not infringe or result in any unjustifiable interference with navigation and other rights and freedoms of other States as provided for in this Convention.

Article 79: Submarine cables and pipelines on the continental shelf

1. All States are entitled to lay submarine cables and pipelines on the continental shelf, in accordance with the provisions of this article.

2. Subject to its right to take reasonable measures for the exploration of the continental shelf, the exploitation of its natural resources and the prevention, reduction and control of pollution from pipelines, the coastal State may not impede the laying or maintenance of such cables or pipelines.

3. The delineation of the course for the laying of such pipelines on the continental shelf is subject to the consent of the coastal State.

4. Nothing in this Part affects the right of the coastal State to establish conditions for cables or pipelines entering its territory or territorial sea, or its jurisdiction over cables and pipelines constructed or used in connection with the exploration of its continental shelf or exploitation of its resources or the operations of artificial islands, installations and structures under its jurisdiction.

5. When laying submarine cables or pipelines, States shall have due regard to cables or pipelines already in position. In particular, possibilities of repairing existing cables or pipelines shall not be prejudiced.

Article 80: Artificial islands, installations and structures on the continental shelf
Article 60 applies mutatis mutandis to artificial islands, installations and structures on the continental shelf.

Article 81: Drilling on the continental shelf
The coastal State shall have the exclusive right to authorize and regulate drilling on the continental shelf for all purposes.

Article 82: Payments and contributions with respect to the exploitation of the continental shelf beyond 200 nautical miles
1. The coastal State shall make payments or contributions in kind in respect of the exploitation of the non-living resources of the continental shelf beyond 200 nautical miles from the baselines from which the breadth of the territorial sea is measured.

2. The payments and contributions shall be made annually with respect to all production at a site after the first five years of production at that site. For the sixth year, the rate of payment or contribution shall be 1 per cent of the value or volume of production at the site. The rate shall increase by 1 per cent for each subsequent year until the twelfth year and shall remain at 7 per cent thereafter. Production does not include resources used in connection with exploitation.

3. A developing State which is a net importer of a mineral resource produced from its continental shelf is exempt from making such payments or contributions in respect of that mineral resource.

4. The payments or contributions shall be made through the Authority, which shall distribute them to States Parties to this Convention, on the basis of equitable sharing criteria, taking into account the interests and needs of developing States, particularly the least developed and the land-locked among them.

Article 83: Delimitation of the continental shelf
between States with opposite or adjacent coasts

1. The delimitation of the continental shelf between States with opposite or adjacent coasts shall be effected by agreement on the basis of international law, as referred to in Article 38 of the Statute of the International Court of Justice, in order to achieve an equitable solution.

2. If no agreement can be reached within a reasonable period of time, the States concerned shall resort to the procedures provided for in Part XV.

3. Pending agreement as provided for in paragraph 1, the States concerned, in a spirit of understanding and cooperation, shall make every effort to enter into provisional arrangements of a practical nature and, during this transitional period, not to jeopardize or hamper the reaching of the final agreement. Such arrangements shall be without prejudice to the final delimitation.

4. Where there is an agreement in force between the States concerned, questions relating to the delimitation of the continental shelf shall be determined in accordance with the provisions of that agreement.

Article 84: Charts and lists of geographical coordinates

1. Subject to this Part, the outer limit lines of the continental shelf and the lines of delimitation drawn in accordance with article 83 shall be shown on charts of a scale or scales adequate for ascertaining their position. Where appropriate, lists of geographical coordinates of points, specifying the geodetic datum, may be substituted for such outer limit lines or lines of delimitation.

2. The coastal State shall give due publicity to such charts or lists of geographical coordinates and shall deposit a copy of each such chart or list with the Secretary-General of the United Nations and, in the case of those showing the outer limit lines of the continental shelf, with the Secretary-General of the Authority.

Article 85: Tunnelling

This Part does not prejudice the right of the coastal State to exploit the subsoil by means of tunnelling, irrespective of the depth of water above the subsoil.

Part VII: High Seas

Section 1: General Provisions

Article 86: Application of the provisions of this Part

The provisions of this Part apply to all parts of the sea that are not included in the exclusive economic zone, in the territorial sea or in the internal waters of a State, or in the archipelagic waters of an archipelagic State. This article does not entail any abridgement of the freedoms enjoyed by all States in the exclusive economic zone in accordance with article 58.

Article 87: Freedom of the high seas

1. The high seas are open to all States, whether coastal or land-locked. Freedom of the high seas is exercised under the conditions laid down by this Convention and by other rules of international law. It comprises, inter alia, both for coastal and land-locked States:

    (a) freedom of navigation;

    (b) freedom of overflight;

    (c) freedom to lay submarine cables and pipelines, subject to Part VI;

    (d) freedom to construct artificial islands and other installations permitted under international law, subject to Part VI;

    (e) freedom of fishing, subject to the conditions laid down in section 2;

    (f) freedom of scientific research, subject to Parts VI and XIII.

2. These freedoms shall be exercised by all States with due regard for the interests of other States in their exercise of the freedom of the high seas, and also with due regard for the rights under this Convention with respect to activities in the Area.

Article 88: Reservation of the high seas for peaceful purposes

The high seas shall be reserved for peaceful purposes.

Article 89: Invalidity of claims of sovereignty over the high seas

No State may validly purport to subject any part of the high seas to its sovereignty.

Article 90: Right of navigation

Every State, whether coastal or land-locked, has the right to sail ships flying its flag on the high seas.

Article 91: Nationality of ships

1. Every State shall fix the conditions for the grant of its nationality to ships, for the registration of ships in its territory, and for the right to fly its flag. Ships have the nationality of the State whose flag they are entitled to fly. There must exist a genuine link between the State and the ship.

2. Every State shall issue to ships to which it has granted the right to fly its flag documents to that effect.

Article 92: Status of ships

1. Ships shall sail under the flag of one State only and, save in exceptional cases expressly provided for in international treaties or in this Convention, shall be subject to its exclusive jurisdiction on the high seas. A ship may not change its flag during a voyage or while in a port of call, save in the case of a real transfer of ownership or change of registry.

2. A ship which sails under the flags of two or more States, using them according to convenience, may not claim any of the nationalities in question

with respect to any other State, and may be assimilated to a ship without nationality.

Article 93: Ships flying the flag of the United Nations, its specialized agencies and the International Atomic Energy Agency

The preceding articles do not prejudice the question of ships employed on the official service of the United Nations, its specialized agencies or the International Atomic Energy Agency, flying the flag of the organization.

Article 94: Duties of the flag State

1. Every State shall effectively exercise its jurisdiction and control in administrative, technical and social matters over ships flying its flag.

2. In particular every State shall:

(a) maintain a register of ships containing the names and particulars of ships flying its flag, except those which are excluded from generally accepted international regulations on account of their small size; and

(b) assume jurisdiction under its internal law over each ship flying its flag and its master, officers and crew in respect of administrative, technical and social matters concerning the ship.

3. Every State shall take such measures for ships flying its flag as are necessary to ensure safety at sea with regard, inter alia, to:

(a) the construction, equipment and seaworthiness of ships;

(b) the manning of ships, labour conditions and the training of crews, taking into account the applicable international instruments;

(c) the use of signals, the maintenance of communications and the prevention of collisions.

4. Such measures shall include those necessary to ensure:

(a) that each ship, before registration and thereafter at appropriate intervals, is surveyed by a qualified surveyor of ships, and has on board such charts, nautical publications and navigational equipment and instruments as are appropriate for the safe navigation of the ship;

(b) that each ship is in the charge of a master and officers who possess appropriate qualifications, in particular in seamanship, navigation, communications and marine engineering, and that the crew is appropriate in qualification and numbers for the type, size, machinery and equipment of the ship;

(c) that the master, officers and, to the extent appropriate, the crew are fully conversant with and required to observe the applicable international regulations concerning the safety of life at sea, the prevention of collisions, the prevention, reduction and control of marine pollution, and the maintenance of communications by radio.

5. In taking the measures called for in paragraphs 3 and 4 each State is required to conform to generally accepted international regulations, procedures and practices and to take any steps which may be necessary to secure their observance.

6. A State which has clear grounds to believe that proper jurisdiction and control with respect to a ship have not been exercised may report the facts to the flag State. Upon receiving such a report, the flag State shall investigate the matter and, if appropriate, take any action necessary to remedy the situation.

7. Each State shall cause an inquiry to be held by or before a suitably qualified person or persons into every marine casualty or incident of navigation on the high seas involving a ship flying its flag and causing loss of life or serious injury to nationals of another State or serious damage to ships or installations of another State or to the marine environment. The flag State and the other State shall cooperate in the conduct of any inquiry held by that other State into any such marine casualty or incident of navigation.

Article 95: Immunity of warships on the high seas

Warships on the high seas have complete immunity from the jurisdiction of any State other than the flag State.

Article 96: Immunity of ships used only on government non-commercial service

Ships owned or operated by a State and used only on government non-commercial service shall, on the high seas, have complete immunity from the jurisdiction of any State other than the flag State.

Article 97: Penal jurisdiction in matters of collision or any other incident of navigation

1. In the event of a collision or any other incident of navigation concerning a ship on the high seas, involving the penal or disciplinary responsibility of the master or of any other person in the service of the ship, no penal or disciplinary proceedings may be instituted against such person except before the judicial or administrative authorities either of the flag State or of the State of which such person is a national.

2. In disciplinary matters, the State which has issued a master's certificate or a certificate of competence or licence shall alone be competent, after due legal process, to pronounce the withdrawal of such certificates, even if the holder is not a national of the State which issued them.

3. No arrest or detention of the ship, even as a measure of investigation, shall be ordered by any authorities other than those of the flag State.

Article 98: Duty to render assistance

1. Every State shall require the master of a ship flying its flag, in so far as he can do so without serious danger to the ship, the crew or the passengers:

(a) to render assistance to any person found at sea in danger of being lost;

(b) to proceed with all possible speed to the rescue of persons in distress, if informed of their need of assistance, in so far as such action may reasonably be expected of him;

(c) after a collision, to render assistance to the other ship, its crew and its passengers and, where possible, to inform the other ship of the name of his own ship, its port of registry and the nearest port at which it will call.

2. Every coastal State shall promote the establishment, operation and maintenance of an adequate and effective search and rescue service regarding safety on and over the sea and, where circumstances so require, by way of mutual regional arrangements cooperate with neighbouring States for this purpose.

Article 99: Prohibition of the transport of slaves

Every State shall take effective measures to prevent and punish the transport of slaves in ships authorized to fly its flag and to prevent the unlawful use of its flag for that purpose. Any slave taking refuge on board any ship, whatever its flag, shall ipso facto be free.

Article 100: Duty to cooperate in the repression of piracy

All States shall cooperate to the fullest possible extent in the repression of piracy on the high seas or in any other place outside the jurisdiction of any State.

Article 101: Definition of piracy

Piracy consists of any of the following acts:

(a) any illegal acts of violence or detention, or any act of depredation, committed for private ends by the crew or the passengers of a private ship or a private aircraft, and directed: (i) on the high seas, against another ship or aircraft, or against persons or property on board such ship or aircraft; (ii) against a ship, aircraft, persons or property in a place outside the jurisdiction of any State;

(b) any act of voluntary participation in the operation of a ship or of an aircraft with knowledge of facts making it a pirate ship or aircraft;

(c) any act of inciting or of intentionally facilitating an act described in subparagraph (a) or (b).

Article 102: Piracy by a warship, government ship or government aircraft whose crew has mutinied

The acts of piracy, as defined in article 101, committed by a warship, government ship or government aircraft whose crew has mutinied and taken control of the ship or aircraft are assimilated to acts committed by a private ship or aircraft.

Article 103: Definition of a pirate ship or aircraft

A ship or aircraft is considered a pirate ship or aircraft if it is intended by the persons in dominant control to be used for the purpose of committing one of the acts referred to in article 101. The same applies if the ship or aircraft has been used to commit any such act, so long as it remains under the control of the persons guilty of that act.

Article 104: Retention or loss of the nationality of a pirate ship or aircraft

A ship or aircraft may retain its nationality although it has become a pirate ship or aircraft. The retention or loss of nationality is determined by the law of the State from which such nationality was derived.

Article 105: Seizure of a pirate ship or aircraft

On the high seas, or in any other place outside the jurisdiction of any State, every State may seize a pirate ship or aircraft, or a ship or aircraft taken by piracy and under the control of pirates, and arrest the persons and seize the property on board. The courts of the State which carried out the seizure may decide upon the penalties to be imposed, and may also determine the action to be taken with regard to the ships, aircraft or property, subject to the rights of third parties acting in good faith.

Article 106: Liability for seizure without adequate grounds

Where the seizure of a ship or aircraft on suspicion of piracy has been effected without adequate grounds, the State making the seizure shall be liable to the State the nationality of which is possessed by the ship or aircraft for any loss or damage caused by the seizure.

Article 107: Ships and aircraft which are entitled to seize on account of piracy

A seizure on account of piracy may be carried out only by warships or military aircraft, or other ships or aircraft clearly marked and identifiable as being on government service and authorized to that effect.

Article 108: Illicit traffic in narcotic drugs or psychotropic substances

1. All States shall cooperate in the suppression of illicit traffic in narcotic drugs and psychotropic substances engaged in by ships on the high seas contrary to international conventions.

2. Any State which has reasonable grounds for believing that a ship flying its flag is engaged in illicit traffic in narcotic drugs or psychotropic substances may request the cooperation of other States to suppress such traffic.

Article 109: Unauthorized broadcasting from the high seas

1. All States shall cooperate in the suppression of unauthorized broadcasting from the high seas.

2. For the purposes of this Convention, "unauthorized broadcasting" means the transmission of sound radio or television broadcasts from a ship or installation on the high seas intended for reception by the general public contrary to international regulations, but excluding the transmission of distress calls.

3. Any person engaged in unauthorized broadcasting may be prosecuted before the court of:

(a) the flag State of the ship;

(b) the State of registry of the installation;

(c) the State of which the person is a national;

(d) any State where the transmissions can be received; or

(e) any State where authorized radio communication is suffering interference.

4. On the high seas, a State having jurisdiction in accordance with paragraph 3 may, in conformity with article 110, arrest any person or ship engaged in unauthorized broadcasting and seize the broadcasting apparatus.

Article 110: Right of visit

1. Except where acts of interference derive from powers conferred by treaty, a warship which encounters on the high seas a foreign ship, other than a ship entitled to complete immunity in accordance with articles 95 and 96, is not justified in boarding it unless there is reasonable ground for suspecting that:

(a) the ship is engaged in piracy;

(b) the ship is engaged in the slave trade;

(c) the ship is engaged in unauthorized broadcasting and the flag State of the warship has jurisdiction under article 109;

(d) the ship is without nationality; or

(e) though flying a foreign flag or refusing to show its flag, the ship is, in reality, of the same nationality as the warship.

2. In the cases provided for in paragraph 1, the warship may proceed to verify the ship's right to fly its flag. To this end, it may send a boat under the command of an officer to the suspected ship. If suspicion remains after the documents have been checked, it may proceed to a further examination on board the ship, which must be carried out with all possible consideration.

3. If the suspicions prove to be unfounded, and provided that the ship boarded has not committed any act justifying them, it shall be compensated for any loss or damage that may have been sustained.

4. These provisions apply mutatis mutandis to military aircraft.

5. These provisions also apply to any other duly authorized ships or aircraft clearly marked and identifiable as being on government service.

Article 111: Right of hot pursuit

1. The hot pursuit of a foreign ship may be undertaken when the competent authorities of the coastal State have good reason to believe that the ship has violated the laws and regulations of that State. Such pursuit must be commenced when the foreign ship or one of its boats is within the internal waters, the archipelagic waters, the territorial sea or the contiguous zone of the pursuing State, and may only be continued outside the territorial sea or the contiguous zone if the pursuit has not been interrupted. It is not necessary that, at the time when the foreign ship within the territorial sea or the contiguous zone receives the order to stop, the ship giving the order should likewise be within

the territorial sea or the contiguous zone. If the foreign ship is within a contiguous zone, as defined in article 33, the pursuit may only be undertaken if there has been a violation of the rights for the protection of which the zone was established.

2. The right of hot pursuit shall apply mutatis mutandis to violations in the exclusive economic zone or on the continental shelf, including safety zones around continental shelf installations, of the laws and regulations of the coastal State applicable in accordance with this Convention to the exclusive economic zone or the continental shelf, including such safety zones.

3. The right of hot pursuit ceases as soon as the ship pursued enters the territorial sea of its own State or of a third State.

4. Hot pursuit is not deemed to have begun unless the pursuing ship has satisfied itself by such practicable means as may be available that the ship pursued or one of its boats or other craft working as a team and using the ship pursued as a mother ship is within the limits of the territorial sea, or, as the case may be, within the contiguous zone or the exclusive economic zone or above the continental shelf. The pursuit may only be commenced after a visual or auditory signal to stop has been given at a distance which enables it to be seen or heard by the foreign ship.

5. The right of hot pursuit may be exercised only by warships or military aircraft, or other ships or aircraft clearly marked and identifiable as being on government service and authorized to that effect.

6. Where hot pursuit is effected by an aircraft:

(a) the provisions of paragraphs 1 to 4 shall apply mutatis mutandis;

(b) the aircraft giving the order to stop must itself actively pursue the ship until a ship or another aircraft of the coastal State, summoned by the aircraft, arrives to take over the pursuit, unless the aircraft is itself able to arrest the ship. It does not suffice to justify an arrest outside the territorial sea that the ship was merely sighted by the aircraft as an offender or suspected offender, if it was not both ordered to stop and pursued by the aircraft itself or other aircraft or ships which continue the pursuit without interruption.

7. The release of a ship arrested within the jurisdiction of a State and escorted to a port of that State for the purposes of an inquiry before the competent authorities may not be claimed solely on the ground that the ship, in the course of its voyage, was escorted across a portion of the exclusive economic zone or the high seas, if the circumstances rendered this necessary.

8. Where a ship has been stopped or arrested outside the territorial sea in circumstances which do not justify the exercise of the right of hot pursuit, it shall be compensated for any loss or damage that may have been thereby sustained.

Article 112: Right to lay submarine cables and pipelines

1. All States are entitled to lay submarine cables and pipelines on the bed of the high seas beyond the continental shelf.

2. Article 79, paragraph 5, applies to such cables and pipelines.

Article 113: Breaking or injury of a submarine cable or pipeline

Every State shall adopt the laws and regulations necessary to provide that the breaking or injury by a ship flying its flag or by a person subject to its jurisdiction of a submarine cable beneath the high seas done wilfully or through culpable negligence, in such a manner as to be liable to interrupt or obstruct telegraphic or telephonic communications, and similarly the breaking or injury of a submarine pipeline or high-voltage power cable, shall be a punishable offence. This provision shall apply also to conduct calculated or likely to result in such breaking or injury. However, it shall not apply to any break or injury caused by persons who acted merely with the legitimate object of saving their lives or their ships, after having taken all necessary precautions to avoid such break or injury.

Article 114: Breaking or injury by owners of a submarine cable or pipeline of another submarine cable or pipeline

Every State shall adopt the laws and regulations necessary to provide that, if persons subject to its jurisdiction who are the owners of a submarine cable or pipeline beneath the high seas, in laying or repairing that cable or pipeline, cause a break in or injury to another cable or pipeline, they shall bear the cost of the repairs.

Article 115: Indemnity for loss incurred in avoiding injury to a submarine cable or pipeline

Every State shall adopt the laws and regulations necessary to ensure that the owners of ships who can prove that they have sacrificed an anchor, a net or any other fishing gear, in order to avoid injuring a submarine cable or pipeline, shall be indemnified by the owner of the cable or pipeline, provided that the owner of the ship has taken all reasonable precautionary measures beforehand.

Section 2: Conservation and Management of the Living Resources of the High Seas

Article 116: Right to fish on the high seas

All States have the right for their nationals to engage in fishing on the high seas subject to:

(a) their treaty obligations;

(b) the rights and duties as well as the interests of coastal States provided for, inter alia, in article 63, paragraph 2, and articles 64 to 67; and

(c) the provisions of this section.

Article 117: Duty of States to adopt with respect to their nationals measures for the conservation of the living resources of the high seas

All States have the duty to take, or to cooperate with other States in taking, such measures for their respective nationals as may be necessary for the conservation of the living resources of the high seas.

Article 118: Cooperation of States in the conservation and management of living resources

States shall cooperate with each other in the conservation and management of living resources in the areas of the high seas. States whose nationals exploit identical living resources, or different living resources in the same area, shall enter into negotiations with a view to taking the measures necessary for the conservation of the living resources concerned. They shall, as appropriate, cooperate to establish subregional or regional fisheries organizations to this end.

Article 119: Conservation of the living resources of the high seas

1. In determining the allowable catch and establishing other conservation measures for the living resources in the high seas, States shall:

(a) take measures which are designed, on the best scientific evidence available to the States concerned, to maintain or restore populations of harvested species at levels which can produce the maximum sustainable yield, as qualified by relevant environmental and economic factors, including the special requirements of developing States, and taking into account fishing patterns, the interdependence of stocks and any generally recommended international minimum standards, whether subregional, regional or global;

(b) take into consideration the effects on species associated with or dependent upon harvested species with a view to maintaining or restoring populations of such associated or dependent species above levels at which their reproduction may become seriously threatened.

2. Available scientific information, catch and fishing effort statistics, and other data relevant to the conservation of fish stocks shall be contributed and exchanged on a regular basis through competent international organizations, whether subregional, regional or global, where appropriate and with participation by all States concerned.

3. States concerned shall ensure that conservation measures and their implementation do not discriminate in form or in fact against the fishermen of any State.

Article 120: Marine mammals

Article 65 also applies to the conservation and management of marine mammals in the high seas.

Part VIII: Regime of Islands

Article 121: Regime of islands

1. An island is a naturally formed area of land, surrounded by water, which is above water at high tide.

2. Except as provided for in paragraph 3, the territorial sea, the contiguous zone, the exclusive economic zone and the continental shelf of an island are

determined in accordance with the provisions of this Convention applicable to other land territory.

3. Rocks which cannot sustain human habitation or economic life of their own shall have no exclusive economic zone or continental shelf.

Part IX: Enclosed or Semi-Enclosed Seas

Article 122: Definition
For the purposes of this Convention, "enclosed or semi-enclosed sea" means a gulf, basin or sea surrounded by two or more States and connected to another sea or the ocean by a narrow outlet or consisting entirely or primarily of the territorial seas and exclusive economic zones of two or more coastal States.

Article 123: Cooperation of States bordering enclosed or semi-enclosed seas
States bordering an enclosed or semi-enclosed sea should cooperate with each other in the exercise of their rights and in the performance of their duties under this Convention. To this end they shall endeavour, directly or through an appropriate regional organization:

(a) to coordinate the management, conservation, exploration and exploitation of the living resources of the sea;

(b) to coordinate the implementation of their rights and duties with respect to the protection and preservation of the marine environment;

(c) to coordinate their scientific research policies and undertake where appropriate joint programmes of scientific research in the area;

(d) to invite, as appropriate, other interested States or international organizations to cooperate with them in furtherance of the provisions of this article.

Part X: Right of Access of Land-Locked States To and From the Sea and Freedom of Transit

Article 124: Use of terms
1. For the purposes of this Convention:

(a) "land-locked State" means a State which has no sea-coast;

(b) "transit State" means a State, with or without a sea-coast, situated between a land-locked State and the sea, through whose territory traffic in transit passes;

(c) "traffic in transit" means transit of persons, baggage, goods and means of transport across the territory of one or more transit States, when the passage across such territory, with or without trans-shipment, warehousing, breaking bulk or change in the mode of transport, is only a portion of a complete journey which begins or terminates within the territory of the land-locked State;

(d) "means of transport" means: (i) railway rolling stock, sea, lake and river craft and road vehicles; (ii) where local conditions so require, porters and pack animals.

2. Land-locked States and transit States may, by agreement between them, include as means of transport pipelines and gas lines and means of transport other than those included in paragraph 1.

Article 125: Right of access to and from the sea and freedom of transit

1. Land-locked States shall have the right of access to and from the sea for the purpose of exercising the rights provided for in this Convention including those relating to the freedom of the high seas and the common heritage of mankind. To this end, land-locked States shall enjoy freedom of transit through the territory of transit States by all means of transport.

2. The terms and modalities for exercising freedom of transit shall be agreed between the land-locked States and transit States concerned through bilateral, subregional or regional agreements.

3. Transit States, in the exercise of their full sovereignty over their territory, shall have the right to take all measures necessary to ensure that the rights and facilities provided for in this Part for land-locked States shall in no way infringe their legitimate interests.

Article 126: Exclusion of application of the most-favoured-nation clause

The provisions of this Convention, as well as special agreements relating to the exercise of the right of access to and from the sea, establishing rights and facilities on account of the special geographical position of land-locked States, are excluded from the application of the most-favoured-nation clause.

Article 127: Customs duties, taxes and other charges

1. Traffic in transit shall not be subject to any customs duties, taxes or other charges except charges levied for specific services rendered in connection with such traffic.

2. Means of transport in transit and other facilities provided for and used by land-locked States shall not be subject to taxes or charges higher than those levied for the use of means of transport of the transit State.

Article 128: Free zones and other customs facilities

For the convenience of traffic in transit, free zones or other customs facilities may be provided at the ports of entry and exit in the transit States, by agreement between those States and the land-locked States.

Article 129: Cooperation in the construction and improvement of means of transport

Where there are no means of transport in transit States to give effect to the freedom of transit or where the existing means, including the port installations and equipment, are inadequate in any respect, the transit States and land-locked States concerned may cooperate in constructing or improving them.

Article 130: Measures to avoid or eliminate delays or other difficulties of a technical nature in traffic in transit

1. Transit States shall take all appropriate measures to avoid delays or other difficulties of a technical nature in traffic in transit.

2. Should such delays or difficulties occur, the competent authorities of the transit States and land-locked States concerned shall cooperate towards their expeditious elimination.

Article 131: Equal treatment in maritime ports

Ships flying the flag of land-locked States shall enjoy treatment equal to that accorded to other foreign ships in maritime ports.

Article 132: Grant of greater transit facilities

This Convention does not entail in any way the withdrawal of transit facilities which are greater than those provided for in this Convention and which are agreed between States Parties to this Convention or granted by a State Party. This Convention also does not preclude such grant of greater facilities in the future.

Part XI: The Area

Section 1: General Provisions

Article 133: Use of terms

For the purposes of this Part:

(a) "resources" means all solid, liquid or gaseous mineral resources in situ in the Area at or beneath the seabed, including polymetallic nodules;

(b) resources, when recovered from the Area, are referred to as "minerals."

Article 134: Scope of this Part

1. This Part applies to the Area.

2. Activities in the Area shall be governed by the provisions of this Part.

3. The requirements concerning deposit of, and publicity to be given to, the charts or lists of geographical coordinates showing the limits referred to in article 1, paragraph 1(1), are set forth in Part VI.

4. Nothing in this article affects the establishment of the outer limits of the continental shelf in accordance with Part VI or the validity of agreements relating to delimitation between States with opposite or adjacent coasts.

Article 135: Legal status of the superjacent waters and air space

Neither this Part nor any rights granted or exercised pursuant thereto shall affect the legal status of the waters superjacent to the Area or that of the air space above those waters.

Section 2: Principles Governing the Area

Article 136: Common heritage of mankind
The Area and its resources are the common heritage of mankind.

Article 137: Legal status of the Area and its resources
1. No State shall claim or exercise sovereignty or sovereign rights over any part of the Area or its resources, nor shall any State or natural or juridical person appropriate any part thereof. No such claim or exercise of sovereignty or sovereign rights nor such appropriation shall be recognized.

2. All rights in the resources of the Area are vested in mankind as a whole, on whose behalf the Authority shall act. These resources are not subject to alienation. The minerals recovered from the Area, however, may only be alienated in accordance with this Part and the rules, regulations and procedures of the Authority.

3. No State or natural or juridical person shall claim, acquire or exercise rights with respect to the minerals recovered from the Area except in accordance with this Part. Otherwise, no such claim, acquisition or exercise of such rights shall be recognized.

Article 138: General conduct of States in relation to the Area
The general conduct of States in relation to the Area shall be in accordance with the provisions of this Part, the principles embodied in the Charter of the United Nations and other rules of international law in the interests of maintaining peace and security and promoting international cooperation and mutual understanding.

Article 139: Responsibility to
ensure compliance and liability for damage
1. States Parties shall have the responsibility to ensure that activities in the Area, whether carried out by States Parties, or state enterprises or natural or juridical persons which possess the nationality of States Parties or are effectively controlled by them or their nationals, shall be carried out in conformity with this Part. The same responsibility applies to international organizations for activities in the Area carried out by such organizations.

2. Without prejudice to the rules of international law and Annex III, article 22, damage caused by the failure of a State Party or international organization to carry out its responsibilities under this Part shall entail liability; States Parties or international organizations acting together shall bear joint and several liability. A State Party shall not however be liable for damage caused by any failure to comply with this Part by a person whom it has sponsored under article 153, paragraph 2(b), if the State Party has taken all necessary and appropri-

ate measures to secure effective compliance under article 153, paragraph 4, and Annex III, article 4, paragraph 4.

3. States Parties that are members of international organizations shall take appropriate measures to ensure the implementation of this article with respect to such organizations.

Article 140: Benefit of mankind

1. Activities in the Area shall, as specifically provided for in this Part, be carried out for the benefit of mankind as a whole, irrespective of the geographical location of States, whether coastal or land-locked, and taking into particular consideration the interests and needs of developing States and of peoples who have not attained full independence or other self-governing status recognized by the United Nations in accordance with General Assembly resolution 1514 (XV) and other relevant General Assembly resolutions.

2. The Authority shall provide for the equitable sharing of financial and other economic benefits derived from activities in the Area through any appropriate mechanism, on a non-discriminatory basis, in accordance with article 160, paragraph 2(f)(i).

Article 141: Use of the Area exclusively for peaceful purposes

The Area shall be open to use exclusively for peaceful purposes by all States, whether coastal or land-locked, without discrimination and without prejudice to the other provisions of this Part.

Article 142: Rights and legitimate interests of coastal States

1. Activities in the Area, with respect to resource deposits in the Area which lie across limits of national jurisdiction, shall be conducted with due regard to the rights and legitimate interests of any coastal State across whose jurisdiction such deposits lie.

2. Consultations, including a system of prior notification, shall be maintained with the State concerned, with a view to avoiding infringement of such rights and interests. In cases where activities in the Area may result in the exploitation of resources lying within national jurisdiction, the prior consent of the coastal State concerned shall be required.

3. Neither this Part nor any rights granted or exercised pursuant thereto shall affect the rights of coastal States to take such measures consistent with the relevant provisions of Part XII as may be necessary to prevent, mitigate or eliminate grave and imminent danger to their coastline, or related interests from pollution or threat thereof or from other hazardous occurrences resulting from or caused by any activities in the Area.

Article 143: Marine scientific research

1. Marine scientific research in the Area shall be carried out exclusively for peaceful purposes and for the benefit of mankind as a whole, in accordance with Part XIII.

2. The Authority may carry out marine scientific research concerning the Area and its resources, and may enter into contracts for that purpose. The Authority shall promote and encourage the conduct of marine scientific research in the Area, and shall coordinate and disseminate the results of such research and analysis when available.

3. States Parties may carry out marine scientific research in the Area. States Parties shall promote international cooperation in marine scientific research in the Area by:

(a) participating in international programmes and encouraging cooperation in marine scientific research by personnel of different countries and of the Authority;

(b) ensuring that programmes are developed through the Authority or other international organizations as appropriate for the benefit of developing States and technologically less developed States with a view to: (i) strengthening their research capabilities; (ii) training their personnel and the personnel of the Authority in the techniques and applications of research; (iii) fostering the employment of their qualified personnel in research in the Area;

(c) effectively disseminating the results of research and analysis when available, through the Authority or other international channels when appropriate.

Article 144: Transfer of technology

1. The Authority shall take measures in accordance with this Convention:

(a) to acquire technology and scientific knowledge relating to activities in the Area; and

(b) to promote and encourage the transfer to developing States of such technology and scientific knowledge so that all States Parties benefit therefrom.

2. To this end the Authority and States Parties shall cooperate in promoting the transfer of technology and scientific knowledge relating to activities in the Area so that the Enterprise and all States Parties may benefit therefrom. In particular they shall initiate and promote:

(a) programmes for the transfer of technology to the Enterprise and to developing States with regard to activities in the Area, including, inter alia, facilitating the access of the Enterprise and of developing States to the relevant technology, under fair and reasonable terms and conditions;

(b) measures directed towards the advancement of the technology of the Enterprise and the domestic technology of developing States, particularly by providing opportunities to personnel from the Enterprise and from developing States for training in marine science and technology and for their full participation in activities in the Area.

Article 145: Protection of the marine environment

Necessary measures shall be taken in accordance with this Convention with respect to activities in the Area to ensure effective protection for the marine environment from harmful effects which may arise from such activities. To this end the Authority shall adopt appropriate rules, regulations and procedures for inter alia:

(a) the prevention, reduction and control of pollution and other hazards to the marine environment, including the coastline, and of interference with the ecological balance of the marine environment, particular attention being paid to the need for protection from harmful effects of such activities as drilling, dredging, excavation, disposal of waste, construction and operation or maintenance of installations, pipelines and other devices related to such activities;

(b) the protection and conservation of the natural resources of the Area and the prevention of damage to the flora and fauna of the marine environment.

Article 146: Protection of human life

With respect to activities in the Area, necessary measures shall be taken to ensure effective protection of human life. To this end the Authority shall adopt appropriate rules, regulations and procedures to supplement existing international law as embodied in relevant treaties.

Article 147: Accommodation of activities in the Area and in the marine environment

1. Activities in the Area shall be carried out with reasonable regard for other activities in the marine environment.

2. Installations used for carrying out activities in the Area shall be subject to the following conditions:

(a) such installations shall be erected, emplaced and removed solely in accordance with this Part and subject to the rules, regulations and procedures of the Authority. Due notice must be given of the erection, emplacement and removal of such installations, and permanent means for giving warning of their presence must be maintained;

(b) such installations may not be established where interference may be caused to the use of recognized sea lanes essential to international navigation or in areas of intense fishing activity;

(c) safety zones shall be established around such installations with appropriate markings to ensure the safety of both navigation and the installations. The configuration and location of such safety zones shall not be such as to form a belt impeding the lawful access of shipping to particular maritime zones or navigation along international sea lanes;

(d) such installations shall be used exclusively for peaceful purposes;

(e) such installations do not possess the status of islands. They have no territorial sea of their own, and their presence does not affect the delimitation of the territorial sea, the exclusive economic zone or the continental shelf.

3. Other activities in the marine environment shall be conducted with reasonable regard for activities in the Area.

Article 148: Participation of developing States in activities in the Area

The effective participation of developing States in activities in the Area shall be promoted as specifically provided for in this Part, having due regard to their special interests and needs, and in particular to the special need of the land-locked and geographically disadvantaged among them to overcome obstacles arising from their disadvantaged location, including remoteness from the Area and difficulty of access to and from it.

Article 149: Archaeological and historical objects

All objects of an archaeological and historical nature found in the Area shall be preserved or disposed of for the benefit of mankind as a whole, particular regard being paid to the preferential rights of the State or country of origin, or the State of cultural origin, or the State of historical and archaeological origin.

Section 3: Development of Resources of the Area

Article 150: Policies relating to activities in the Area

Activities in the Area shall, as specifically provided for in this Part, be carried out in such a manner as to foster healthy development of the world economy and balanced growth of international trade, and to promote international cooperation for the over-all development of all countries, especially developing States, and with a view to ensuring:

(a) the development of the resources of the Area;

(b) orderly, safe and rational management of the resources of the Area, including the efficient conduct of activities in the Area and, in accordance with sound principles of conservation, the avoidance of unnecessary waste;

(c) the expansion of opportunities for participation in such activities consistent in particular with articles 144 and 148;

(d) participation in revenues by the Authority and the transfer of technology to the Enterprise and developing States as provided for in this Convention;

(e) increased availability of the minerals derived from the Area as needed in conjunction with minerals derived from other sources, to ensure supplies to consumers of such minerals;

(f) the promotion of just and stable prices remunerative to producers and fair to consumers for minerals derived both from the Area and from other sources, and the promotion of long-term equilibrium between supply and demand;

(g) the enhancement of opportunities for all States Parties, irrespective of their social and economic systems or geographical location, to participate in the development of the resources of the Area and the prevention of monopolization of activities in the Area;

(h) the protection of developing countries from adverse effects on their economies or on their export earnings resulting from a reduction in the price of an affected mineral, or in the volume of exports of that mineral, to the extent that such reduction is caused by activities in the Area, as provided in article 151;

(i) the development of the common heritage for the benefit of mankind as a whole; and

(j) conditions of access to markets for the imports of minerals produced from the resources of the Area and for imports of commodities produced from such minerals shall not be more favourable than the most favourable applied to imports from other sources.

Article 151: Production policies

1. (a) Without prejudice to the objectives set forth in article 150 and for the purpose of implementing subparagraph (h) of that article, the Authority, acting through existing forums or such new arrangements or agreements as may be appropriate, in which all interested parties, including both producers and consumers, participate, shall take measures necessary to promote the growth, efficiency and stability of markets for those commodities produced from the minerals derived from the Area, at prices remunerative to producers and fair to consumers. All States Parties shall cooperate to this end.

(b) The Authority shall have the right to participate in any commodity conference dealing with those commodities and in which all interested parties including both producers and consumers participate. The Authority shall have the right to become a party to any arrangement or agreement resulting from such conferences. Participation of the Authority in any organs established under those arrangements or agreements shall be in respect of production in the Area and in accordance with the relevant rules of those organs.

(c) The Authority shall carry out its obligations under the arrangements or agreements referred to in this paragraph in a manner which assures a uniform and non-discriminatory implementation in respect of all production in the Area of the minerals concerned. In doing so, the Authority shall act in a manner consistent with the terms of existing contracts and approved plans of work of the Enterprise.

2. (a) During the interim period specified in paragraph 3, commercial production shall not be undertaken pursuant to an approved plan of work until the operator has applied for and has been issued a production authorization by the Authority. Such production authorizations may not be applied for or issued more than five years prior to the planned commencement of commercial production under the plan of work unless, having regard to the nature and timing of project development, the rules, regulations and procedures of the Authority prescribe another period.

(b) In the application for the production authorization, the operator shall specify the annual quantity of nickel expected to be recovered under the approved plan of work. The application shall include a schedule of expenditures to be made by the operator after he has received the authorization which are reasonably calculated to allow him to begin commercial production on the date planned.

(c) For the purposes of subparagraphs (a) and (b), the Authority shall establish appropriate performance requirements in accordance with Annex III, article 17.

(d) The Authority shall issue a production authorization for the level of production applied for unless the sum of that level and the levels already authorized exceeds the nickel production ceiling, as calculated pursuant to paragraph 4 in the year of issuance of the authorization, during any year of planned production falling within the interim period.

(e) When issued, the production authorization and approved application shall become a part of the approved plan of work.

(f) If the operator's application for a production authorization is denied pursuant to subparagraph (d), the operator may apply again to the Authority at any time.

3. The interim period shall begin five years prior to 1 January of the year in which the earliest commercial production is planned to commence under an approved plan of work. If the earliest commercial production is delayed beyond the year originally planned, the beginning of the interim period and the production ceiling originally calculated shall be adjusted accordingly. The interim period shall last 25 years or until the end of the Review Conference referred to in article 155 or until the day when such new arrangements or agreements as are referred to in paragraph 1 enter into force, whichever is earliest. The Authority shall resume the power provided in this article for the remainder of the interim period if the said arrangements or agreements should lapse or become ineffective for any reason whatsoever.

4. (a) The production ceiling for any year of the interim period shall be the sum of: (i) the difference between the trend line values for nickel consumption, as calculated pursuant to subparagraph (b), for the year immediately prior to the year of the earliest commercial production and the year immediately prior to the commencement of the interim period; and (ii) sixty per cent of the difference between the trend line values for nickel consumption, as calculated pursuant to subparagraph (b), for the year for which the production authorization is being applied for and the year immediately prior to the year of the earliest commercial production.

(b) For the purposes of subparagraph (a): (i) trend line values used for computing the nickel production ceiling shall be those annual nickel consumption values on a trend line computed during the year in which a production authorization is issued. The trend line shall be derived from a linear regression of the logarithms of actual nickel consumption for the most recent 15-year period for which such data are available, time being the independent variable. This trend line shall be referred to as the original trend line; (ii) if the annual rate of increase of the original trend line is less than 3 per cent, then the trend line used to determine the quantities referred to in subparagraph (a) shall instead be one passing through the original trend line at the value for the first year of the relevant 15-year period, and increasing at 3 per cent annually; provided however that the production ceiling established for any year of the interim period may not in any case exceed the difference between the original trend line value for that year and the original trend line value for the year immediately prior to the commencement of the interim period.

5. The Authority shall reserve to the Enterprise for its initial production a quantity of 38,000 metric tonnes of nickel from the available production ceiling calculated pursuant to paragraph 4.

6. (a) An operator may in any year produce less than or up to 8 per cent more than the level of annual production of minerals from polymetallic nodules specified in his production authorization, provided that the over-all amount of production shall not exceed that specified in the authorization. Any excess over 8 per cent and up to 20 per cent in any year, or any excess in the first and subsequent years following two consecutive years in which excesses occur, shall be negotiated with the Authority, which may require the operator to obtain a supplementary production authorization to cover additional production.

(b) Applications for such supplementary production authorizations shall be considered by the Authority only after all pending applications by operators who have not yet received production authorizations have been acted upon and due account has been taken of other likely applicants. The Authority shall be guided by the principle of not exceeding the total production allowed under the production ceiling in any year of the interim period. It shall not authorize the production under any plan of work of a quantity in excess of 46,500 metric tonnes of nickel per year.

7. The levels of production of other metals such as copper, cobalt and manganese extracted from the polymetallic nodules that are recovered pursuant to a production authorization should not be higher than those which would have been produced had the operator produced the maximum level of nickel from those nodules pursuant to this article. The Authority shall establish rules, regulations and procedures pursuant to Annex III, article 17, to implement this paragraph.

8. Rights and obligations relating to unfair economic practices under relevant multilateral trade agreements shall apply to the exploration for and exploitation of minerals from the Area. In the settlement of disputes arising under this provision, States Parties which are Parties to such multilateral trade agreements shall have recourse to the dispute settlement procedures of such agreements.

9. The Authority shall have the power to limit the level of production of minerals from the Area, other than minerals from polymetallic nodules, under such conditions and applying such methods as may be appropriate by adopting regulations in accordance with article 161, paragraph 8.

10. Upon the recommendation of the Council on the basis of advice from the Economic Planning Commission, the Assembly shall establish a system of compensation or take other measures of economic adjustment assistance including cooperation with specialized agencies and other international organizations to assist developing countries which suffer serious adverse effects on

their export earnings or economies resulting from a reduction in the price of an affected mineral or in the volume of exports of that mineral, to the extent that such reduction is caused by activities in the Area. The Authority on request shall initiate studies on the problems of those States which are likely to be most seriously affected with a view to minimizing their difficulties and assisting them in their economic adjustment.

Article 152: Exercise of powers and functions by the Authority

1. The Authority shall avoid discrimination in the exercise of its powers and functions, including the granting of opportunities for activities in the Area.

2. Nevertheless, special consideration for developing States, including particular consideration for the land-locked and geographically disadvantaged among them, specifically provided for in this Part shall be permitted.

Article 153: System of exploration and exploitation

1. Activities in the Area shall be organized, carried out and controlled by the Authority on behalf of mankind as a whole in accordance with this article as well as other relevant provisions of this Part and the relevant Annexes, and the rules, regulations and procedures of the Authority.

2. Activities in the Area shall be carried out as prescribed in paragraph 3:

(a) by the Enterprise; and

(b) in association with the Authority by States Parties, or state enterprises or natural or juridical persons which possess the nationality of States Parties or are effectively controlled by them or their nationals, when sponsored by such States, or any group of the foregoing which meets the requirements provided in this Part and in Annex III.

3. Activities in the Area shall be carried out in accordance with a formal written plan of work drawn up in accordance with Annex III and approved by the Council after review by the Legal and Technical Commission. In the case of activities in the Area carried out as authorized by the Authority by the entities specified in paragraph 2(b), the plan of work shall, in accordance with Annex III, article 3, be in the form of a contract. Such contracts may provide for joint arrangements in accordance with Annex III, article 11.

4. The Authority shall exercise such control over activities in the Area as is necessary for the purpose of securing compliance with the relevant provisions of this Part and the Annexes relating thereto, and the rules, regulations and procedures of the Authority, and the plans of work approved in accordance with paragraph 3. States Parties shall assist the Authority by taking all measures necessary to ensure such compliance in accordance with article 139.

5. The Authority shall have the right to take at any time any measures provided for under this Part to ensure compliance with its provisions and the exercise of the functions of control and regulation assigned to it thereunder or under any contract. The Authority shall have the right to inspect all installations in the Area used in connection with activities in the Area.

6. A contract under paragraph 3 shall provide for security of tenure.

Accordingly, the contract shall not be revised, suspended or terminated except in accordance with Annex III, articles 18 and 19.

Article 154: Periodic review

Every five years from the entry into force of this Convention, the Assembly shall undertake a general and systematic review of the manner in which the international regime of the Area established in this Convention has operated in practice. In the light of this review the Assembly may take, or recommend that other organs take, measures in accordance with the provisions and procedures of this Part and the Annexes relating thereto which will lead to the improvement of the operation of the regime.

Article 155: The Review Conference

1. Fifteen years from 1 January of the year in which the earliest commercial production commences under an approved plan of work, the Assembly shall convene a conference for the review of those provisions of this Part and the relevant Annexes which govern the system of exploration and exploitation of the resources of the Area. The Review Conference shall consider in detail, in the light of the experience acquired during that period:

(a) whether the provisions of this Part which govern the system of exploration and exploitation of the resources of the Area have achieved their aims in all respects, including whether they have benefited mankind as a whole;

(b) whether, during the 15-year period, reserved areas have been exploited in an effective and balanced manner in comparison with non-reserved areas;

(c) whether the development and use of the Area and its resources have been undertaken in such a manner as to foster healthy development of the world economy and balanced growth of international trade;

(d) whether monopolization of activities in the Area has been prevented;

(e) whether the policies set forth in articles 150 and 151 have been fulfilled; and

(f) whether the system has resulted in the equitable sharing of benefits derived from activities in the Area, taking into particular consideration the interests and needs of the developing States.

2. The Review Conference shall ensure the maintenance of the principle of the common heritage of mankind, the international regime designed to ensure equitable exploitation of the resources of the Area for the benefit of all countries, especially the developing States, and an Authority to organize, conduct and control activities in the Area. It shall also ensure the maintenance of the principles laid down in this Part with regard to the exclusion of claims or exercise of sovereignty over any part of the Area, the rights of States and their general conduct in relation to the Area, and their participation in activities in the Area in conformity with this Convention, the prevention of monopolization of activities in the Area, the use of the Area exclusively for peaceful purposes, economic aspects of activities in the Area, marine scientific research, transfer of technology, protection of the marine environment, protection of human life,

rights of coastal States, the legal status of the waters superjacent to the Area and that of the air space above those waters and accommodation between activities in the Area and other activities in the marine environment.

3. The decision-making procedure applicable at the Review Conference shall be the same as that applicable at the Third United Nations Conference on the Law of the Sea. The Conference shall make every effort to reach agreement on any amendments by way of consensus and there should be no voting on such matters until all efforts at achieving consensus have been exhausted.

4. If, five years after its commencement, the Review Conference has not reached agreement on the system of exploration and exploitation of the resources of the Area, it may decide during the ensuing 12 months, by a three-fourths majority of the States Parties, to adopt and submit to the States Parties for ratification or accession such amendments changing or modifying the system as it determines necessary and appropriate. Such amendments shall enter into force for all States Parties 12 months after the deposit of instruments of ratification or accession by three fourths of the States Parties.

5. Amendments adopted by the Review Conference pursuant to this article shall not affect rights acquired under existing contracts.

. . . [Section 4: The Authority; Section 5: Settlement of Disputes and Advisory Opinions; Part XII: Protection and Preservation of the Marine Environment; Part XIII: Marine Scientific Research; Part XIV: Development and Transfer of Marine Technology not included]

Part XV: Settlement of Disputes

Section 1: General Provisions

Article 279: Obligation to settle disputes by peaceful means
States Parties shall settle any dispute between them concerning the interpretation or application of this Convention by peaceful means in accordance with Article 2, paragraph 3, of the Charter of the United Nations and, to this end, shall seek a solution by the means indicated in Article 33, paragraph 1, of the Charter.

Article 280: Settlement of disputes by any peaceful means chosen by the parties
Nothing in this Part impairs the right of any States Parties to agree at any time to settle a dispute between them concerning the interpretation or application of this Convention by any peaceful means of their own choice.

Article 281: Procedure where no settlement has been reached by the parties
1. If the States Parties which are parties to a dispute concerning the interpretation or application of this Convention have agreed to seek settlement of

the dispute by a peaceful means of their own choice, the procedures provided for in this Part apply only where no settlement has been reached by recourse to such means and the agreement between the parties does not exclude any further procedure.

2. If the parties have also agreed on a time-limit, paragraph 1 applies only upon the expiration of that time-limit.

Article 282: Obligations under general, regional or bilateral agreements

If the States Parties which are parties to a dispute concerning the interpretation or application of this Convention have agreed, through a general, regional or bilateral agreement or otherwise, that such dispute shall, at the request of any party to the dispute, be submitted to a procedure that entails a binding decision, that procedure shall apply in lieu of the procedures provided for in this Part, unless the parties to the dispute otherwise agree.

Article 283: Obligation to exchange views

1. When a dispute arises between States Parties concerning the interpretation or application of this Convention, the parties to the dispute shall proceed expeditiously to an exchange of views regarding its settlement by negotiation or other peaceful means.

2. The parties shall also proceed expeditiously to an exchange of views where a procedure for the settlement of such a dispute has been terminated without a settlement or where a settlement has been reached and the circumstances require consultation regarding the manner of implementing the settlement.

Article 284: Conciliation

1. A State Party which is a party to a dispute concerning the interpretation or application of this Convention may invite the other party or parties to submit the dispute to conciliation in accordance with the procedure under Annex V, section 1, or another conciliation procedure.

2. If the invitation is accepted and if the parties agree upon the conciliation procedure to be applied, any party may submit the dispute to that procedure.

3. If the invitation is not accepted or the parties do not agree upon the procedure, the conciliation proceedings shall be deemed to be terminated.

4. Unless the parties otherwise agree, when a dispute has been submitted to conciliation, the proceedings may be terminated only in accordance with the agreed conciliation procedure.

Article 285: Application of this section to disputes submitted pursuant to Part XI

This section applies to any dispute which pursuant to Part XI, section 5, is to be settled in accordance with procedures provided for in this Part. If an entity other than a State Party is a party to such a dispute, this section applies mutatis mutandis.

Section 2: Compulsory Procedures Entailing Binding Decisions

Article 286: Application of procedures under this section
Subject to section 3, any dispute concerning the interpretation or application of this Convention shall, where no settlement has been reached by recourse to section 1, be submitted at the request of any party to the dispute to the court or tribunal having jurisdiction under this section.

Article 287: Choice of procedure
1. When signing, ratifying or acceding to this Convention or at any time thereafter, a State shall be free to choose, by means of a written declaration, one or more of the following means for the settlement of disputes concerning the interpretation or application of this Convention:

(a) the International Tribunal for the Law of the Sea established in accordance with Annex VI;

(b) the International Court of Justice;

(c) an arbitral tribunal constituted in accordance with Annex VII;

(d) a special arbitral tribunal constituted in accordance with Annex VIII for one or more of the categories of disputes specified therein.

2. A declaration made under paragraph 1 shall not affect or be affected by the obligation of a State Party to accept the jurisdiction of the Seabed Disputes Chamber of the International Tribunal for the Law of the Sea to the extent and in the manner provided for in Part XI, section 5.

3. A State Party, which is a party to a dispute not covered by a declaration in force, shall be deemed to have accepted arbitration in accordance with Annex VII.

4. If the parties to a dispute have accepted the same procedure for the settlement of the dispute, it may be submitted only to that procedure, unless the parties otherwise agree.

5. If the parties to a dispute have not accepted the same procedure for the settlement of the dispute, it may be submitted only to arbitration in accordance with Annex VII, unless the parties otherwise agree.

6. A declaration made under paragraph 1 shall remain in force until three months after notice of revocation has been deposited with the Secretary-General of the United Nations.

7. A new declaration, a notice of revocation or the expiry of a declaration does not in any way affect proceedings pending before a court or tribunal having jurisdiction under this article, unless the parties otherwise agree.

8. Declarations and notices referred to in this article shall be deposited with the Secretary-General of the United Nations, who shall transmit copies thereof to the States Parties.

Article 288: Jurisdiction
1. A court or tribunal referred to in article 287 shall have jurisdiction over any dispute concerning the interpretation or application of this Convention which is submitted to it in accordance with this Part.

2. A court or tribunal referred to in article 287 shall also have jurisdiction over any dispute concerning the interpretation or application of an international agreement related to the purposes of this Convention, which is submitted to it in accordance with the agreement.

3. The Seabed Disputes Chamber of the International Tribunal for the Law of the Sea established in accordance with Annex VI, and any other chamber or arbitral tribunal referred to in Part XI, section 5, shall have jurisdiction in any matter which is submitted to it in accordance therewith.

4. In the event of a dispute as to whether a court or tribunal has jurisdiction, the matter shall be settled by decision of that court or tribunal.

Article 289: Experts

In any dispute involving scientific or technical matters, a court or tribunal exercising jurisdiction under this section may, at the request of a party or proprio motu, select in consultation with the parties no fewer than two scientific or technical experts chosen preferably from the relevant list prepared in accordance with Annex VIII, article 2, to sit with the court or tribunal but without the right to vote.

Article 290: Provisional measures

1. If a dispute has been duly submitted to a court or tribunal which considers that prima facie it has jurisdiction under this Part or Part XI, section 5, the court or tribunal may prescribe any provisional measures which it considers appropriate under the circumstances to preserve the respective rights of the parties to the dispute or to prevent serious harm to the marine environment, pending the final decision.

2. Provisional measures may be modified or revoked as soon as the circumstances justifying them have changed or ceased to exist.

3. Provisional measures may be prescribed, modified or revoked under this article only at the request of a party to the dispute and after the parties have been given an opportunity to be heard.

4. The court or tribunal shall forthwith give notice to the parties to the dispute, and to such other States Parties as it considers appropriate, of the prescription, modification or revocation of provisional measures.

5. Pending the constitution of an arbitral tribunal to which a dispute is being submitted under this section, any court or tribunal agreed upon by the parties or, failing such agreement within two weeks from the date of the request for provisional measures, the International Tribunal for the Law of the Sea or, with respect to activities in the Area, the Seabed Disputes Chamber, may prescribe, modify or revoke provisional measures in accordance with this article if it considers that prima facie the tribunal which is to be constituted would have jurisdiction and that the urgency of the situation so requires. Once constituted, the tribunal to which the dispute has been submitted may modify, revoke or affirm those provisional measures, acting in conformity with paragraphs 1 to 4.

6. The parties to the dispute shall comply promptly with any provisional measures prescribed under this article.

Article 291: Access

1. All the dispute settlement procedures specified in this Part shall be open to States Parties.

2. The dispute settlement procedures specified in this Part shall be open to entities other than States Parties only as specifically provided for in this Convention.

Article 292: Prompt release of vessels and crews

1. Where the authorities of a State Party have detained a vessel flying the flag of another State Party and it is alleged that the detaining State has not complied with the provisions of this Convention for the prompt release of the vessel or its crew upon the posting of a reasonable bond or other financial security, the question of release from detention may be submitted to any court or tribunal agreed upon by the parties or, failing such agreement within 10 days from the time of detention, to a court or tribunal accepted by the detaining State under article 287 or to the International Tribunal for the Law of the Sea, unless the parties otherwise agree.

2. The application for release may be made only by or on behalf of the flag State of the vessel.

3. The court or tribunal shall deal without delay with the application for release and shall deal only with the question of release, without prejudice to the merits of any case before the appropriate domestic forum against the vessel, its owner or its crew. The authorities of the detaining State remain competent to release the vessel or its crew at any time.

4. Upon the posting of the bond or other financial security determined by the court or tribunal, the authorities of the detaining State shall comply promptly with the decision of the court or tribunal concerning the release of the vessel or its crew.

Article 293: Applicable law

1. A court or tribunal having jurisdiction under this section shall apply this Convention and other rules of international law not incompatible with this Convention.

2. Paragraph 1 does not prejudice the power of the court or tribunal having jurisdiction under this section to decide a case ex aequo et bono, if the parties so agree.

Article 294: Preliminary proceedings

1. A court or tribunal provided for in article 287 to which an application is made in respect of a dispute referred to in article 297 shall determine at the request of a party, or may determine proprio motu, whether the claim constitutes an abuse of legal process or whether prima facie it is well founded. If the

court or tribunal determines that the claim constitutes an abuse of legal process or is prima facie unfounded, it shall take no further action in the case.

2. Upon receipt of the application, the court or tribunal shall immediately notify the other party or parties of the application, and shall fix a reasonable time-limit within which they may request it to make a determination in accordance with paragraph 1.

3. Nothing in this article affects the right of any party to a dispute to make preliminary objections in accordance with the applicable rules of procedure.

Article 295: Exhaustion of local remedies

Any dispute between States Parties concerning the interpretation or application of this Convention may be submitted to the procedures provided for in this section only after local remedies have been exhausted where this is required by international law.

Article 296: Finality and binding force of decisions

1. Any decision rendered by a court or tribunal having jurisdiction under this section shall be final and shall be complied with by all the parties to the dispute.

2. Any such decision shall have no binding force except between the parties and in respect of that particular dispute.

Section 3: Limitations and Exceptions to Applicability of Section 2

Article 297: Limitations on applicability of section 2

1. Disputes concerning the interpretation or application of this Convention with regard to the exercise by a coastal State of its sovereign rights or jurisdiction provided for in this Convention shall be subject to the procedures provided for in section 2 in the following cases:

(a) when it is alleged that a coastal State has acted in contravention of the provisions of this Convention in regard to the freedoms and rights of navigation, overflight or the laying of submarine cables and pipelines, or in regard to other internationally lawful uses of the sea specified in article 58;

(b) when it is alleged that a State in exercising the aforementioned freedoms, rights or uses has acted in contravention of this Convention or of laws or regulations adopted by the coastal State in conformity with this Convention and other rules of international law not incompatible with this Convention; or

(c) when it is alleged that a coastal State has acted in contravention of specified international rules and standards for the protection and preservation of the marine environment which are applicable to the coastal State and which have been established by this Convention or through a competent international organization or diplomatic conference in accordance with this Convention.

2. (a) Disputes concerning the interpretation or application of the provisions of this Convention with regard to marine scientific research shall be settled in

accordance with section 2, except that the coastal State shall not be obliged to accept the submission to such settlement of any dispute arising out of: (i) the exercise by the coastal State of a right or discretion in accordance with article 246; or (ii) a decision by the coastal State to order suspension or cessation of a research project in accordance with article 253.

(b) A dispute arising from an allegation by the researching State that with respect to a specific project the coastal State is not exercising its rights under articles 246 and 253 in a manner compatible with this Convention shall be submitted, at the request of either party, to conciliation under Annex V, section 2, provided that the conciliation commission shall not call in question the exercise by the coastal State of its discretion to designate specific areas as referred to in article 246, paragraph 6, or of its discretion to withhold consent in accordance with article 246, paragraph 5.

3. (a) Disputes concerning the interpretation or application of the provisions of this Convention with regard to fisheries shall be settled in accordance with section 2, except that the coastal State shall not be obliged to accept the submission to such settlement of any dispute relating to its sovereign rights with respect to the living resources in the exclusive economic zone or their exercise, including its discretionary powers for determining the allowable catch, its harvesting capacity, the allocation of surpluses to other States and the terms and conditions established in its conservation and management laws and regulations.

(b) Where no settlement has been reached by recourse to section 1 of this Part, a dispute shall be submitted to conciliation under Annex V, section 2, at the request of any party to the dispute, when it is alleged that: (i) a coastal State has manifestly failed to comply with its obligations to ensure through proper conservation and management measures that the maintenance of the living resources in the exclusive economic zone is not seriously endangered; (ii) a coastal State has arbitrarily refused to determine, at the request of another State, the allowable catch and its capacity to harvest living resources with respect to stocks which that other State is interested in fishing; or (iii) a coastal State has arbitrarily refused to allocate to any State, under articles 62, 69 and 70 and under the terms and conditions established by the coastal State consistent with this Convention, the whole or part of the surplus it has declared to exist.

(c) In no case shall the conciliation commission substitute its discretion for that of the coastal State.

(d) The report of the conciliation commission shall be communicated to the appropriate international organizations.

(e) In negotiating agreements pursuant to articles 69 and 70, States Parties, unless they otherwise agree, shall include a clause on measures which they shall take in order to minimize the possibility of a disagreement concerning the interpretation or application of the agreement, and on how they should proceed if a disagreement nevertheless arises.

Article 298: Optional exceptions to applicability of section 2

1. When signing, ratifying or acceding to this Convention or at any time thereafter, a State may, without prejudice to the obligations arising under section 1, declare in writing that it does not accept any one or more of the procedures provided for in section 2 with respect to one or more of the following categories of disputes:

(a) (i) disputes concerning the interpretation or application of articles 15, 74 and 83 relating to sea boundary delimitations, or those involving historic bays or titles, provided that a State having made such a declaration shall, when such a dispute arises subsequent to the entry into force of this Convention and where no agreement within a reasonable period of time is reached in negotiations between the parties, at the request of any party to the dispute, accept submission of the matter to conciliation under Annex V, section 2; and provided further that any dispute that necessarily involves the concurrent consideration of any unsettled dispute concerning sovereignty or other rights over continental or insular land territory shall be excluded from such submission; (ii) after the conciliation commission has presented its report, which shall state the reasons on which it is based, the parties shall negotiate an agreement on the basis of that report; if these negotiations do not result in an agreement, the parties shall, by mutual consent, submit the question to one of the procedures provided for in section 2, unless the parties otherwise agree; (iii) this subparagraph does not apply to any sea boundary dispute finally settled by an arrangement between the parties, or to any such dispute which is to be settled in accordance with a bilateral or multilateral agreement binding upon those parties;

(b) disputes concerning military activities, including military activities by government vessels and aircraft engaged in non-commercial service, and disputes concerning law enforcement activities in regard to the exercise of sovereign rights or jurisdiction excluded from the jurisdiction of a court or tribunal under article 297, paragraph 2 or 3;

(c) disputes in respect of which the Security Council of the United Nations is exercising the functions assigned to it by the Charter of the United Nations, unless the Security Council decides to remove the matter from its agenda or calls upon the parties to settle it by the means provided for in this Convention.

2. A State Party which has made a declaration under paragraph 1 may at any time withdraw it, or agree to submit a dispute excluded by such declaration to any procedure specified in this Convention.

3. A State Party which has made a declaration under paragraph 1 shall not be entitled to submit any dispute falling within the excepted category of disputes to any procedure in this Convention as against another State Party, without the consent of that party.

4. If one of the States Parties has made a declaration under paragraph 1(a), any other State Party may submit any dispute falling within an excepted category against the declarant party to the procedure specified in such declaration.

5. A new declaration, or the withdrawal of a declaration, does not in any way affect proceedings pending before a court or tribunal in accordance with this article, unless the parties otherwise agree.

6. Declarations and notices of withdrawal of declarations under this article shall be deposited with the Secretary-General of the United Nations, who shall transmit copies thereof to the States Parties.

Article 299: Right of the parties to agree upon a procedure

1. A dispute excluded under article 297 or excepted by a declaration made under article 298 from the dispute settlement procedures provided for in section 2 may be submitted to such procedures only by agreement of the parties to the dispute.

2. Nothing in this section impairs the right of the parties to the dispute to agree to some other procedure for the settlement of such dispute or to reach an amicable settlement.

Part XVI: General Provisions

Article 300: Good faith and abuse of rights

States Parties shall fulfil in good faith the obligations assumed under this Convention and shall exercise the rights, jurisdiction and freedoms recognized in this Convention in a manner which would not constitute an abuse of right.

Article 301: Peaceful uses of the seas

In exercising their rights and performing their duties under this Convention, States Parties shall refrain from any threat or use of force against the territorial integrity or political independence of any State, or in any other manner inconsistent with the principles of international law embodied in the Charter of the United Nations.

Article 302: Disclosure of information

Without prejudice to the right of a State Party to resort to the procedures for the settlement of disputes provided for in this Convention, nothing in this Convention shall be deemed to require a State Party, in the fulfilment of its obligations under this Convention, to supply information the disclosure of which is contrary to the essential interests of its security.

Article 303: Archaeological and historical objects found at sea

1. States have the duty to protect objects of an archaeological and historical nature found at sea and shall cooperate for this purpose.

2. In order to control traffic in such objects, the coastal State may, in applying article 33, presume that their removal from the seabed in the zone referred to in that article without its approval would result in an infringement within its territory or territorial sea of the laws and regulations referred to in that article.

3. Nothing in this article affects the rights of identifiable owners, the law of salvage or other rules of admiralty, or laws and practices with respect to cultural exchanges.

4. This article is without prejudice to other international agreements and rules of international law regarding the protection of objects of an archaeological and historical nature.

Article 304: Responsibility and liability for damage

The provisions of this Convention regarding responsibility and liability for damage are without prejudice to the application of existing rules and the development of further rules regarding responsibility and liability under international law.

Part XVII: Final Provisions

Article 305: Signature

1. This Convention shall be open for signature by:

(a) all States;

(b) Namibia, represented by the United Nations Council for Namibia;

(c) all self-governing associated States which have chosen that status in an act of self-determination supervised and approved by the United Nations in accordance with General Assembly resolution 1514 (XV) and which have competence over the matters governed by this Convention, including the competence to enter into treaties in respect of those matters;

(d) all self-governing associated States which, in accordance with their respective instruments of association, have competence over the matters governed by this Convention, including the competence to enter into treaties in respect of those matters;

(e) all territories which enjoy full internal self-government, recognized as such by the United Nations, but have not attained full independence in accordance with General Assembly resolution 1514 (XV) and which have competence over the matters governed by this Convention, including the competence to enter into treaties in respect of those matters;

(f) international organizations, in accordance with Annex IX.

2. This Convention shall remain open for signature until 9 December 1984 at the Ministry of Foreign Affairs of Jamaica and also, from 1 July 1983 until 9 December 1984, at United Nations Headquarters in New York.

Article 306: Ratification and formal confirmation

This Convention is subject to ratification by States and the other entities referred to in article 305, paragraph l(b), (c), (d) and (e), and to formal confirmation, in accordance with Annex IX, by the entities referred to in article 305, paragraph l(f). The instruments of ratification and of formal confirmation shall be deposited with the Secretary-General of the United Nations.

Article 307: Accession

This Convention shall remain open for accession by States and the other enti-ties referred to in article 305. Accession by the entities referred to in article 305, paragraph l(f), shall be in accordance with Annex IX. The instruments of accession shall be deposited with the Secretary-General of the United Nations.

Article 308: Entry into force

1. This Convention shall enter into force 12 months after the date of deposit of the sixtieth instrument of ratification or accession.

2. For each State ratifying or acceding to this Convention after the deposit of the sixtieth instrument of ratification or accession, the Convention shall enter into force on the thirtieth day following the deposit of its instrument of ratification or accession, subject to paragraph 1.

3. The Assembly of the Authority shall meet on the date of entry into force of this Convention and shall elect the Council of the Authority. The first Council shall be constituted in a manner consistent with the purpose of article 161 if the provisions of that article cannot be strictly applied.

4. The rules, regulations and procedures drafted by the Preparatory Commission shall apply provisionally pending their formal adoption by the Authority in accordance with Part XI.

5. The Authority and its organs shall act in accordance with resolution II of the Third United Nations Conference on the Law of the Sea relating to preparatory investment and with decisions of the Preparatory Commission taken pursuant to that resolution.

Article 309: Reservations and exceptions

No reservations or exceptions may be made to this Convention unless express-ly permitted by other articles of this Convention.

Article 310: Declarations and statements

Article 309 does not preclude a State, when signing, ratifying or acceding to this Convention, from making declarations or statements, however phrased or named, with a view, inter alia, to the harmonization of its laws and regulations with the provisions of this Convention, provided that such declarations or statements do not purport to exclude or to modify the legal effect of the provi-sions of this Convention in their application to that State.

Article 311: Relation to other
conventions and international agreements

1. This Convention shall prevail, as between States Parties, over the Geneva Conventions on the Law of the Sea of 29 April 1958.

2. This Convention shall not alter the rights and obligations of States Parties which arise from other agreements compatible with this Convention and which do not affect the enjoyment by other States Parties of their rights or the per-formance of their obligations under this Convention.

3. Two or more States Parties may conclude agreements modifying or suspending the operation of provisions of this Convention, applicable solely to the relations between them, provided that such agreements do not relate to a provision derogation from which is incompatible with the effective execution of the object and purpose of this Convention, and provided further that such agreements shall not affect the application of the basic principles embodied herein, and that the provisions of such agreements do not affect the enjoyment by other States Parties of their rights or the performance of their obligations under this Convention.

4. States Parties intending to conclude an agreement referred to in paragraph 3 shall notify the other States Parties through the depositary of this Convention of their intention to conclude the agreement and of the modification or suspension for which it provides.

5. This article does not affect international agreements expressly permitted or preserved by other articles of this Convention.

6. States Parties agree that there shall be no amendments to the basic principle relating to the common heritage of mankind set forth in article 136 and that they shall not be party to any agreement in derogation thereof.

Article 312: Amendment

1. After the expiry of a period of 10 years from the date of entry into force of this Convention, a State Party may, by written communication addressed to the Secretary-General of the United Nations, propose specific amendments to this Convention, other than those relating to activities in the Area, and request the convening of a conference to consider such proposed amendments. The Secretary-General shall circulate such communication to all States Parties. If, within 12 months from the date of the circulation of the communication, not less than one half of the States Parties reply favourably to the request, the Secretary-General shall convene the conference.

2. The decision-making procedure applicable at the amendment conference shall be the same as that applicable at the Third United Nations Conference on the Law of the Sea unless otherwise decided by the conference. The conference should make every effort to reach agreement on any amendments by way of consensus and there should be no voting on them until all efforts at consensus have been exhausted.

Article 313: Amendment by simplified procedure

1. A State Party may, by written communication addressed to the Secretary-General of the United Nations, propose an amendment to this Convention, other than an amendment relating to activities in the Area, to be adopted by the simplified procedure set forth in this article without convening a conference. The Secretary-General shall circulate the communication to all States Parties.

2. If, within a period of 12 months from the date of the circulation of the communication, a State Party objects to the proposed amendment or to the proposal for its adoption by the simplified procedure, the amendment shall be con-

sidered rejected. The Secretary-General shall immediately notify all States Parties accordingly.

3. If, 12 months from the date of the circulation of the communication, no State Party has objected to the proposed amendment or to the proposal for its adoption by the simplified procedure, the proposed amendment shall be considered adopted. The Secretary-General shall notify all States Parties that the proposed amendment has been adopted.

Article 314: Amendments to the provisions of this Convention relating exclusively to activities in the Area

1. A State Party may, by written communication addressed to the Secretary-General of the Authority, propose an amendment to the provisions of this Convention relating exclusively to activities in the Area, including Annex VI, section 4. The Secretary-General shall circulate such communication to all States Parties. The proposed amendment shall be subject to approval by the Assembly following its approval by the Council. Representatives of States Parties in those organs shall have full powers to consider and approve the proposed amendment. The proposed amendment as approved by the Council and the Assembly shall be considered adopted.

2. Before approving any amendment under paragraph 1, the Council and the Assembly shall ensure that it does not prejudice the system of exploration for and exploitation of the resources of the Area, pending the Review Conference in accordance with article 155.

Article 315: Signature, ratification of, accession to and authentic texts of amendments

1. Once adopted, amendments to this Convention shall be open for signature by States Parties for 12 months from the date of adoption, at United Nations Headquarters in New York, unless otherwise provided in the amendment itself.

2. Articles 306, 307 and 320 apply to all amendments to this Convention.

Article 316: Entry into force of amendments

1. Amendments to this Convention, other than those referred to in paragraph 5, shall enter into force for the States Parties ratifying or acceding to them on the thirtieth day following the deposit of instruments of ratification or accession by two thirds of the States Parties or by 60 States Parties, whichever is greater. Such amendments shall not affect the enjoyment by other States Parties of their rights or the performance of their obligations under this Convention.

2. An amendment may provide that a larger number of ratifications or accessions shall be required for its entry into force than are required by this article.

3. For each State Party ratifying or acceding to an amendment referred to in paragraph 1 after the deposit of the required number of instruments of ratification or accession, the amendment shall enter into force on the thirtieth day following the deposit of its instrument of ratification or accession.

4. A State which becomes a Party to this Convention after the entry into force of an amendment in accordance with paragraph 1 shall, failing an expression of a different intention by that State:

(a) be considered as a Party to this Convention as so amended; and

(b) be considered as a Party to the unamended Convention in relation to any State Party not bound by the amendment.

5. Any amendment relating exclusively to activities in the Area and any amendment to Annex VI shall enter into force for all States Parties one year following the deposit of instruments of ratification or accession by three fourths of the States Parties.

6. A State which becomes a Party to this Convention after the entry into force of amendments in accordance with paragraph 5 shall be considered as a Party to this Convention as so amended.

Article 317: Denunciation

1. A State Party may, by written notification addressed to the Secretary-General of the United Nations, denounce this Convention and may indicate its reasons. Failure to indicate reasons shall not affect the validity of the denunciation. The denunciation shall take effect one year after the date of receipt of the notification, unless the notification specifies a later date.

2. A State shall not be discharged by reason of the denunciation from the financial and contractual obligations which accrued while it was a Party to this Convention, nor shall the denunciation affect any right, obligation or legal situation of that State created through the execution of this Convention prior to its termination for that State.

3. The denunciation shall not in any way affect the duty of any State Party to fulfil any obligation embodied in this Convention to which it would be subject under international law independently of this Convention.

Article 318: Status of Annexes

The Annexes form an integral part of this Convention and, unless expressly provided otherwise, a reference to this Convention or to one of its Parts includes a reference to the Annexes relating thereto.

Article 319: Depositary

1. The Secretary-General of the United Nations shall be the depositary of this Convention and amendments thereto.

2. In addition to his functions as depositary, the Secretary-General shall:

(a) report to all States Parties, the Authority and competent international organizations on issues of a general nature that have arisen with respect to this Convention;

(b) notify the Authority of ratifications and formal confirmations of and accessions to this Convention and amendments thereto, as well as of denunciations of this Convention;

(c) notify States Parties of agreements in accordance with article 311, paragraph 4;

(d) circulate amendments adopted in accordance with this Convention to States Parties for ratification or accession;

(e) convene necessary meetings of States Parties in accordance with this Convention.

3. (a) The Secretary-General shall also transmit to the observers referred to in article 156: (i) reports referred to in paragraph 2(a); (ii) notifications referred to in paragraph 2(b) and (c); and (iii) texts of amendments referred to in paragraph 2(d), for their information.

(b) The Secretary-General shall also invite those observers to participate as observers at meetings of States Parties referred to in paragraph 2(e).

Article 320: Authentic texts

The original of this Convention, of which the Arabic, Chinese, English, French, Russian and Spanish texts are equally authentic, shall, subject to article 305, paragraph 2, be deposited with the Secretary-General of the United Nations.

IN WITNESS WHEREOF, the undersigned Plenipotentiaries, being duly authorized thereto, have signed this Convention.

DONE AT MONTEGO BAY, this tenth day of December, one thousand nine hundred and eighty-two.

. . . [Annex 1: Highly Migratory Species not included]

Annex II: Commission on the Limits of the Continental Shelf

Article 1

In accordance with the provisions of article 76, a Commission on the Limits of the Continental Shelf beyond 200 nautical miles shall be established in conformity with the following articles.

Article 2

1. The Commission shall consist of 21 members who shall be experts in the field of geology, geophysics or hydrography, elected by States Parties to this Convention from among their nationals, having due regard to the need to ensure equitable geographical representation, who shall serve in their personal capacities.

2. The initial election shall be held as soon as possible but in any case within 18 months after the date of entry into force of this Convention. At least three months before the date of each election, the Secretary-General of the United Nations shall address a letter to the States Parties, inviting the submission of nominations, after appropriate regional consultations, within three months. The Secretary-General shall prepare a list in alphabetical order of all persons thus nominated and shall submit it to all the States Parties.

3. Elections of the members of the Commission shall be held at a meeting of States Parties convened by the Secretary-General at United Nations Headquarters. At that meeting, for which two thirds of the States Parties shall constitute a quorum, the persons elected to the Commission shall be those nominees who obtain a two-thirds majority of the votes of the representatives of States Parties present and voting. Not less than three members shall be elected from each geographical region.

4. The members of the Commission shall be elected for a term of five years. They shall be eligible for re-election.

5. The State Party which submitted the nomination of a member of the Commission shall defray the expenses of that member while in performance of Commission duties. The coastal State concerned shall defray the expenses incurred in respect of the advice referred to in article 3, paragraph 1(b), of this Annex. The secretariat of the Commission shall be provided by the Secretary-General of the United Nations.

Article 3

1. The functions of the Commission shall be:

(a) to consider the data and other material submitted by coastal States concerning the outer limits of the continental shelf in areas where those limits extend beyond 200 nautical miles, and to make recommendations in accordance with article 76 and the Statement of Understanding adopted on 29 August 1980 by the Third United Nations Conference on the Law of the Sea;

(b) to provide scientific and technical advice, if requested by the coastal State concerned during the preparation of the data referred to in subparagraph (a).

2. The Commission may cooperate, to the extent considered necessary and useful, with the Intergovernmental Oceanographic Commission of UNESCO, the International Hydrographic Organization and other competent international organizations with a view to exchanging scientific and technical information which might be of assistance in discharging the Commission's responsibilities.

Article 4

Where a coastal State intends to establish, in accordance with article 76, the outer limits of its continental shelf beyond 200 nautical miles, it shall submit particulars of such limits to the Commission along with supporting scientific and technical data as soon as possible but in any case within 10 years of the entry into force of this Convention for that State. The coastal State shall at the same time give the names of any Commission members who have provided it with scientific and technical advice.

Article 5

Unless the Commission decides otherwise, the Commission shall function by way of sub-commissions composed of seven members, appointed in a balanced manner taking into account the specific elements of each submission by a coastal State. Nationals of the coastal State making the submission who are members of the Commission and any Commission member who has assisted a coastal State by providing scientific and technical advice with respect to the delineation shall not be a member of the sub-commission dealing with that submission but has the right to participate as a member in the proceedings of the Commission concerning the said submission. The coastal State which has made a submission to the Commission may send its representatives to participate in the relevant proceedings without the right to vote.

Article 6

1. The sub-commission shall submit its recommendations to the Commission.

2. Approval by the Commission of the recommendations of the sub-commission shall be by a majority of two thirds of Commission members present and voting.

3. The recommendations of the Commission shall be submitted in writing to the coastal State which made the submission and to the Secretary-General of the United Nations.

Article 7

Coastal States shall establish the outer limits of the continental shelf in conformity with the provisions of article 76, paragraph 8, and in accordance with the appropriate national procedures.

Article 8

In the case of disagreement by the coastal State with the recommendations of the Commission, the coastal State shall, within a reasonable time, make a revised or new submission to the Commission.

Article 9

The actions of the Commission shall not prejudice matters relating to delimitation of boundaries between States with opposite or adjacent coasts.

. . . [Annex III: Basic Conditions of Prospecting, Exploration and Exploitation, and Annex IV: Statute of the Enterprise not included]

Annex V: Conciliation

Section 1: Conciliation Procedure Pursuant to Section 1 of Part XV

Article 1: Institution of proceedings

If the parties to a dispute have agreed, in accordance with article 284, to submit it to conciliation under this section, any such party may institute the proceedings by written notification addressed to the other party or parties to the dispute.

Article 2: List of conciliators

A list of conciliators shall be drawn up and maintained by the Secretary-General of the United Nations. Every State Party shall be entitled to nominate four conciliators, each of whom shall be a person enjoying the highest reputation for fairness, competence and integrity. The names of the persons so nominated shall constitute the list. If at any time the conciliators nominated by a State Party in the list so constituted shall be fewer than four, that State Party shall be entitled to make further nominations as necessary. The name of a conciliator shall remain on the list until withdrawn by the State Party which made the nomination, provided that such conciliator shall continue to serve on any conciliation commission to which that conciliator has been appointed until the completion of the proceedings before that commission.

Article 3: Constitution of conciliation commission

The conciliation commission shall, unless the parties otherwise agree, be constituted as follows:

(a) Subject to subparagraph (g), the conciliation commission shall consist of five members.

(b) The party instituting the proceedings shall appoint two conciliators to be chosen preferably from the list referred to in article 2 of this Annex, one of whom may be its national, unless the parties otherwise agree. Such appointments shall be included in the notification referred to in article 1 of this Annex.

(c) The other party to the dispute shall appoint two conciliators in the manner set forth in subparagraph (b) within 21 days of receipt of the notification referred to in article 1 of this Annex. If the appointments are not made within that period, the party instituting the proceedings may, within one week of the expiration of that period, either terminate the proceedings by notification addressed to the other party or request the Secretary-General of the United Nations to make the appointments in accordance with subparagraph (e).

(d) Within 30 days after all four conciliators have been appointed, they shall appoint a fifth conciliator chosen from the list referred to in article 2 of this Annex, who shall be chairman. If the appointment is not made within that period, either party may, within one week of the expiration of that period, request the Secretary-General of the United Nations to make the appointment in accordance with subparagraph (e).

(e) Within 30 days of the receipt of a request under subparagraph (c) or (d), the Secretary-General of the United Nations shall make the necessary appointments from the list referred to in article 2 of this Annex in consultation with the parties to the dispute.

(f) Any vacancy shall be filled in the manner prescribed for the initial appointment.

(g) Two or more parties which determine by agreement that they are in the same interest shall appoint two conciliators jointly. Where two or more parties have separate interests or there is a disagreement as to whether they are of the same interest, they shall appoint conciliators separately.

(h) In disputes involving more than two parties having separate interests, or where there is disagreement as to whether they are of the same interest, the parties shall apply subparagraphs (a) to (f) in so far as possible.

Article 4: Procedure

The conciliation commission shall, unless the parties otherwise agree, determine its own procedure. The commission may, with the consent of the parties to the dispute, invite any State Party to submit to it its views orally or in writing. Decisions of the commission regarding procedural matters, the report and recommendations shall be made by a majority vote of its members.

Article 5: Amicable settlement

The commission may draw the attention of the parties to any measures which might facilitate an amicable settlement of the dispute.

Article 6: Functions of the commission

The commission shall hear the parties, examine their claims and objections, and make proposals to the parties with a view to reaching an amicable settlement.

Article 7: Report

1. The commission shall report within 12 months of its constitution. Its report shall record any agreements reached and, failing agreement, its conclusions on all questions of fact or law relevant to the matter in dispute and such recommendations as the commission may deem appropriate for an amicable settlement. The report shall be deposited with the Secretary-General of the United Nations and shall immediately be transmitted by him to the parties to the dispute.

2. The report of the commission, including its conclusions or recommendations, shall not be binding upon the parties.

Article 8: Termination

The conciliation proceedings are terminated when a settlement has been reached, when the parties have accepted or one party has rejected the recommendations of the report by written notification addressed to the Secretary-General of the United Nations, or when a period of three months has expired from the date of transmission of the report to the parties.

Article 9: Fees and expenses

The fees and expenses of the commission shall be borne by the parties to the dispute.

Article 10: Right of parties to modify procedure

The parties to the dispute may by agreement applicable solely to that dispute modify any provision of this Annex.

Section 2: Compulsory Submission to
Conciliation Procedure Pursuant to Section 3 of Part XV

Article 11: Institution of proceedings

1. Any party to a dispute which, in accordance with Part XV, section 3, may be submitted to conciliation under this section, may institute the proceedings by written notification addressed to the other party or parties to the dispute.

2. Any party to the dispute, notified under paragraph 1, shall be obliged to submit to such proceedings.

Article 12: Failure to reply or to submit to conciliation

The failure of a party or parties to the dispute to reply to notification of institution of proceedings or to submit to such proceedings shall not constitute a bar to the proceedings.

Article 13: Competence

A disagreement as to whether a conciliation commission acting under this section has competence shall be decided by the commission.

Article 14: Application of section 1

Articles 2 to 10 of section 1 of this Annex apply subject to this section.

Annex VI: Statute of the
International Tribunal for the Law of the Sea

Article 1: General provisions

1. The International Tribunal for the Law of the Sea is constituted and shall function in accordance with the provisions of this Convention and this Statute.

2. The seat of the Tribunal shall be in the Free and Hanseatic City of Hamburg in the Federal Republic of Germany.

3. The Tribunal may sit and exercise its functions elsewhere whenever it considers this desirable.

4. A reference of a dispute to the Tribunal shall be governed by the provisions of Parts XI and XV.

Section 1: Organization of the Tribunal

Article 2: Composition

1. The Tribunal shall be composed of a body of 21 independent members, elected from among persons enjoying the highest reputation for fairness and integrity and of recognized competence in the field of the law of the sea.

2. In the Tribunal as a whole the representation of the principal legal systems of the world and equitable geographical distribution shall be assured.

Article 3: Membership

1. No two members of the Tribunal may be nationals of the same State. A person who for the purposes of membership in the Tribunal could be regarded as a national of more than one State shall be deemed to be a national of the one in which he ordinarily exercises civil and political rights.

2. There shall be no fewer than three members from each geographical group as established by the General Assembly of the United Nations.

Article 4: Nominations and elections

1. Each State Party may nominate not more than two persons having the qualifications prescribed in article 2 of this Annex. The members of the Tribunal shall be elected from the list of persons thus nominated.

2. At least three months before the date of the election, the Secretary-General of the United Nations in the case of the first election and the Registrar of the Tribunal in the case of subsequent elections shall address a written invitation to the States Parties to submit their nominations for members of the Tribunal within two months. He shall prepare a list in alphabetical order of all the persons thus nominated, with an indication of the States Parties which have nominated them, and shall submit it to the States Parties before the seventh day of the last month before the date of each election.

3. The first election shall be held within six months of the date of entry into force of this Convention.

4. The members of the Tribunal shall be elected by secret ballot. Elections shall be held at a meeting of the States Parties convened by the Secretary-General of the United Nations in the case of the first election and by a procedure agreed to by the States Parties in the case of subsequent elections. Two thirds of the States Parties shall constitute a quorum at that meeting. The persons elected to the Tribunal shall be those nominees who obtain the largest number of votes and a two-thirds majority of the States Parties present and voting, provided that such majority includes a majority of the States Parties.

Article 5: Term of office

1. The members of the Tribunal shall be elected for nine years and may be re-elected; provided, however, that of the members elected at the first election, the terms of seven members shall expire at the end of three years and the terms of seven more members shall expire at the end of six years.

2. The members of the Tribunal whose terms are to expire at the end of the above-mentioned initial periods of three and six years shall be chosen by lot to be drawn by the Secretary-General of the United Nations immediately after the first election.

3. The members of the Tribunal shall continue to discharge their duties until their places have been filled. Though replaced, they shall finish any proceedings which they may have begun before the date of their replacement.

4. In the case of the resignation of a member of the Tribunal, the letter of resignation shall be addressed to the President of the Tribunal. The place becomes vacant on the receipt of that letter.

Article 6: Vacancies

1. Vacancies shall be filled by the same method as that laid down for the first election, subject to the following provision: the Registrar shall, within one month of the occurrence of the vacancy, proceed to issue the invitations provided for in article 4 of this Annex, and the date of the election shall be fixed by the President of the Tribunal after consultation with the States Parties.

2. A member of the Tribunal elected to replace a member whose term of office has not expired shall hold office for the remainder of his predecessor's term.

Article 7: Incompatible activities

1. No member of the Tribunal may exercise any political or administrative function, or associate actively with or be financially interested in any of the operations of any enterprise concerned with the exploration for or exploitation of the resources of the sea or the seabed or other commercial use of the sea or the seabed.

2. No member of the Tribunal may act as agent, counsel or advocate in any case.

3. Any doubt on these points shall be resolved by decision of the majority of the other members of the Tribunal present.

Article 8: Conditions relating to
participation of members in a particular case

1. No member of the Tribunal may participate in the decision of any case in which he has previously taken part as agent, counsel or advocate for one of the parties, or as a member of a national or international court or tribunal, or in any other capacity.

2. If, for some special reason, a member of the Tribunal considers that he should not take part in the decision of a particular case, he shall so inform the President of the Tribunal.

3. If the President considers that for some special reason one of the members of the Tribunal should not sit in a particular case, he shall give him notice accordingly.

4. Any doubt on these points shall be resolved by decision of the majority of the other members of the Tribunal present.

Article 9: Consequence of ceasing to fulfil required conditions

If, in the unanimous opinion of the other members of the Tribunal, a member has ceased to fulfil the required conditions, the President of the Tribunal shall declare the seat vacant.

Article 10: Privileges and immunities

The members of the Tribunal, when engaged on the business of the Tribunal, shall enjoy diplomatic privileges and immunities.

Article 11: Solemn declaration by members

Every member of the Tribunal shall, before taking up his duties, make a solemn declaration in open session that he will exercise his powers impartially and conscientiously.

Article 12: President, Vice-President and Registrar

1. The Tribunal shall elect its President and Vice-President for three years; they may be re-elected.

2. The Tribunal shall appoint its Registrar and may provide for the appointment of such other officers as may be necessary.

3. The President and the Registrar shall reside at the seat of the Tribunal.

Article 13: Quorum

1. All available members of the Tribunal shall sit; a quorum of 11 elected members shall be required to constitute the Tribunal.

2. Subject to article 17 of this Annex, the Tribunal shall determine which members are available to constitute the Tribunal for the consideration of a particular dispute, having regard to the effective functioning of the chambers as provided for in articles 14 and 15 of this Annex.

3. All disputes and applications submitted to the Tribunal shall be heard and determined by the Tribunal, unless article 14 of this Annex applies, or the parties request that it shall be dealt with in accordance with article 15 of this Annex.

Article 14: Seabed Disputes Chamber

A Seabed Disputes Chamber shall be established in accordance with the provisions of section 4 of this Annex. Its jurisdiction, powers and functions shall be as provided for in Part XI, section 5.

Article 15: Special chambers

1. The Tribunal may form such chambers, composed of three or more of its elected members, as it considers necessary for dealing with particular categories of disputes.

2. The Tribunal shall form a chamber for dealing with a particular dispute submitted to it if the parties so request. The composition of such a chamber shall be determined by the Tribunal with the approval of the parties.

3. With a view to the speedy dispatch of business, the Tribunal shall form annually a chamber composed of five of its elected members which may hear and determine disputes by summary procedure. Two alternative members shall be selected for the purpose of replacing members who are unable to participate in a particular proceeding.

4. Disputes shall be heard and determined by the chambers provided for in this article if the parties so request.

5. A judgment given by any of the chambers provided for in this article and in article 14 of this Annex shall be considered as rendered by the Tribunal.

Article 16: Rules of the Tribunal
The Tribunal shall frame rules for carrying out its functions. In particular it shall lay down rules of procedure.

Article 17: Nationality of members
1. Members of the Tribunal of the nationality of any of the parties to a dispute shall retain their right to participate as members of the Tribunal.

2. If the Tribunal, when hearing a dispute, includes upon the bench a member of the nationality of one of the parties, any other party may choose a person to participate as a member of the Tribunal.

3. If the Tribunal, when hearing a dispute, does not include upon the bench a member of the nationality of the parties, each of those parties may choose a person to participate as a member of the Tribunal.

4. This article applies to the chambers referred to in articles 14 and 15 of this Annex. In such cases, the President, in consultation with the parties, shall request specified members of the Tribunal forming the chamber, as many as necessary, to give place to the members of the Tribunal of the nationality of the parties concerned, and, failing such, or if they are unable to be present, to the members specially chosen by the parties.

5. Should there be several parties in the same interest, they shall, for the purpose of the preceding provisions, be considered as one party only. Any doubt on this point shall be settled by the decision of the Tribunal.

6. Members chosen in accordance with paragraphs 2, 3 and 4 shall fulfil the conditions required by articles 2, 8 and 11 of this Annex. They shall participate in the decision on terms of complete equality with their colleagues.

Article 18: Remuneration of members
1. Each elected member of the Tribunal shall receive an annual allowance and, for each day on which he exercises his functions, a special allowance, provided that in any year the total sum payable to any member as special allowance shall not exceed the amount of the annual allowance.

2. The President shall receive a special annual allowance.

3. The Vice-President shall receive a special allowance for each day on which he acts as President.

4. The members chosen under article 17 of this Annex, other than elected members of the Tribunal, shall receive compensation for each day on which they exercise their functions.

5. The salaries, allowances and compensation shall be determined from time to time at meetings of the States Parties, taking into account the workload of the Tribunal. They may not be decreased during the term of office.

6. The salary of the Registrar shall be determined at meetings of the States Parties, on the proposal of the Tribunal.

7. Regulations adopted at meetings of the States Parties shall determine the conditions under which retirement pensions may be given to members of the Tribunal and to the Registrar, and the conditions under which members of the Tribunal and Registrar shall have their travelling expenses refunded.

8. The salaries, allowances, and compensation shall be free of all taxation.

Article 19: Expenses of the Tribunal

1. The expenses of the Tribunal shall be borne by the States Parties and by the Authority on such terms and in such a manner as shall be decided at meetings of the States Parties.

2. When an entity other than a State Party or the Authority is a party to a case submitted to it, the Tribunal shall fix the amount which that party is to contribute towards the expenses of the Tribunal.

Section 2: Competence

Article 20: Access to the Tribunal

1. The Tribunal shall be open to States Parties.

2. The Tribunal shall be open to entities other than States Parties in any case expressly provided for in Part XI or in any case submitted pursuant to any other agreement conferring jurisdiction on the Tribunal which is accepted by all the parties to that case.

Article 21: Jurisdiction

The jurisdiction of the Tribunal comprises all disputes and all applications submitted to it in accordance with this Convention and all matters specifically provided for in any other agreement which confers jurisdiction on the Tribunal.

Article 22: Reference of disputes subject to other agreements

If all the parties to a treaty or convention already in force and concerning the subject-matter covered by this Convention so agree, any disputes concerning the interpretation or application of such treaty or convention may, in accordance with such agreement, be submitted to the Tribunal.

Article 23: Applicable law

The Tribunal shall decide all disputes and applications in accordance with article 293.

Section 3: Procedure

Article 24: Institution of proceedings

1. Disputes are submitted to the Tribunal, as the case may be, either by noti-

fication of a special agreement or by written application, addressed to the Registrar. In either case, the subject of the dispute and the parties shall be indicated.

2. The Registrar shall forthwith notify the special agreement or the application to all concerned.

3. The Registrar shall also notify all States Parties.

Article 25: Provisional measures

1. In accordance with article 290, the Tribunal and its Seabed Disputes Chamber shall have the power to prescribe provisional measures.

2. If the Tribunal is not in session or a sufficient number of members is not available to constitute a quorum, the provisional measures shall be prescribed by the chamber of summary procedure formed under article 15, paragraph 3, of this Annex. Notwithstanding article 15, paragraph 4, of this Annex, such provisional measures may be adopted at the request of any party to the dispute. They shall be subject to review and revision by the Tribunal.

Article 26: Hearing

1. The hearing shall be under the control of the President or, if he is unable to preside, of the Vice-President. If neither is able to preside, the senior judge present of the Tribunal shall preside.

2. The hearing shall be public, unless the Tribunal decides otherwise or unless the parties demand that the public be not admitted.

Article 27: Conduct of case

The Tribunal shall make orders for the conduct of the case, decide the form and time in which each party must conclude its arguments, and make all arrangements connected with the taking of evidence.

Article 28: Default

When one of the parties does not appear before the Tribunal or fails to defend its case, the other party may request the Tribunal to continue the proceedings and make its decision. Absence of a party or failure of a party to defend its case shall not constitute a bar to the proceedings. Before making its decision, the Tribunal must satisfy itself not only that it has jurisdiction over the dispute, but also that the claim is well founded in fact and law.

Article 29: Majority for decision

1. All questions shall be decided by a majority of the members of the Tribunal who are present.

2. In the event of an equality of votes, the President or the member of the Tribunal who acts in his place shall have a casting vote.

Article 30: Judgment

1. The judgment shall state the reasons on which it is based.

2. It shall contain the names of the members of the Tribunal who have taken part in the decision.

3. If the judgment does not represent in whole or in part the unanimous opinion of the members of the Tribunal, any member shall be entitled to deliver a separate opinion.

4. The judgment shall be signed by the President and by the Registrar. It shall be read in open court, due notice having been given to the parties to the dispute.

Article 31: Request to intervene

1. Should a State Party consider that it has an interest of a legal nature which may be affected by the decision in any dispute, it may submit a request to the Tribunal to be permitted to intervene.

2. It shall be for the Tribunal to decide upon this request.

3. If a request to intervene is granted, the decision of the Tribunal in respect of the dispute shall be binding upon the intervening State Party in so far as it relates to matters in respect of which that State Party intervened.

Article 32: Right to intervene in cases of interpretation or application

1. Whenever the interpretation or application of this Convention is in question, the Registrar shall notify all States Parties forthwith.

2. Whenever pursuant to article 21 or 22 of this Annex the interpretation or application of an international agreement is in question, the Registrar shall notify all the parties to the agreement.

3. Every party referred to in paragraphs 1 and 2 has the right to intervene in the proceedings; if it uses this right, the interpretation given by the judgment will be equally binding upon it.

Article 33: Finality and binding force of decisions

1. The decision of the Tribunal is final and shall be complied with by all the parties to the dispute.

2. The decision shall have no binding force except between the parties in respect of that particular dispute.

3. In the event of dispute as to the meaning or scope of the decision, the Tribunal shall construe it upon the request of any party.

Article 34: Costs

Unless otherwise decided by the Tribunal, each party shall bear its own costs.

Section 4: Seabed Disputes Chamber

Article 35: Composition

1. The Seabed Disputes Chamber referred to in article 14 of this Annex shall be composed of 11 members, selected by a majority of the elected members of the Tribunal from among them.

2. In the selection of the members of the Chamber, the representation of the principal legal systems of the world and equitable geographical distribution shall be assured. The Assembly of the Authority may adopt recommendations of a general nature relating to such representation and distribution.

3. The members of the Chamber shall be selected every three years and may be selected for a second term.

4. The Chamber shall elect its President from among its members, who shall serve for the term for which the Chamber has been selected.

5. If any proceedings are still pending at the end of any three-year period for which the Chamber has been selected, the Chamber shall complete the proceedings in its original composition.

6. If a vacancy occurs in the Chamber, the Tribunal shall select a successor from among its elected members, who shall hold office for the remainder of his predecessor's term.

7. A quorum of seven of the members selected by the Tribunal shall be required to constitute the Chamber.

Article 36: Ad hoc chambers

1. The Seabed Disputes Chamber shall form an ad hoc chamber, composed of three of its members, for dealing with a particular dispute submitted to it in accordance with article 188, paragraph 1(b). The composition of such a chamber shall be determined by the Seabed Disputes Chamber with the approval of the parties.

2. If the parties do not agree on the composition of an ad hoc chamber, each party to the dispute shall appoint one member, and the third member shall be appointed by them in agreement. If they disagree, or if any party fails to make an appointment, the President of the Seabed Disputes Chamber shall promptly make the appointment or appointments from among its members, after consultation with the parties.

3. Members of the ad hoc chamber must not be in the service of, or nationals of, any of the parties to the dispute.

Article 37: Access

The Chamber shall be open to the States Parties, the Authority and the other entities referred to in Part XI, section 5.

Article 38: Applicable law

In addition to the provisions of article 293, the Chamber shall apply:

(a) the rules, regulations and procedures of the Authority adopted in accordance with this Convention; and

(b) the terms of contracts concerning activities in the Area in matters relating to those contracts.

Article 39: Enforcement of decisions of the Chamber

The decisions of the Chamber shall be enforceable in the territories of the

States Parties in the same manner as judgments or orders of the highest court of the State Party in whose territory the enforcement is sought.

Article 40: Applicability of other sections of this Annex

1. The other sections of this Annex which are not incompatible with this section apply to the Chamber.

2. In the exercise of its functions relating to advisory opinions, the Chamber shall be guided by the provisions of this Annex relating to procedure before the Tribunal to the extent to which it recognizes them to be applicable.

Section 5: Amendments

Article 41: Amendments

1. Amendments to this Annex, other than amendments to section 4, may be adopted only in accordance with article 313 or by consensus at a conference convened in accordance with this Convention.

2. Amendments to section 4 may be adopted only in accordance with article 314.

3. The Tribunal may propose such amendments to this Statute as it may consider necessary, by written communications to the States Parties for their consideration in conformity with paragraphs 1 and 2.

Annex VII: Arbitration

Article 1: Institution of proceedings

Subject to the provisions of Part XV, any party to a dispute may submit the dispute to the arbitral procedure provided for in this Annex by written notification addressed to the other party or parties to the dispute. The notification shall be accompanied by a statement of the claim and the grounds on which it is based.

Article 2: List of arbitrators

1. A list of arbitrators shall be drawn up and maintained by the Secretary-General of the United Nations. Every State Party shall be entitled to nominate four arbitrators, each of whom shall be a person experienced in maritime affairs and enjoying the highest reputation for fairness, competence and integrity. The names of the persons so nominated shall constitute the list.

2. If at any time the arbitrators nominated by a State Party in the list so constituted shall be fewer than four, that State Party shall be entitled to make further nominations as necessary.

3. The name of an arbitrator shall remain on the list until withdrawn by the State Party which made the nomination, provided that such arbitrator shall continue to serve on any arbitral tribunal to which that arbitrator has been appointed until the completion of the proceedings before that arbitral tribunal.

Article 3: Constitution of arbitral tribunal

For the purpose of proceedings under this Annex, the arbitral tribunal shall, unless the parties otherwise agree, be constituted as follows:

(a) Subject to subparagraph (g), the arbitral tribunal shall consist of five members.

(b) The party instituting the proceedings shall appoint one member to be chosen preferably from the list referred to in article 2 of this Annex, who may be its national. The appointment shall be included in the notification referred to in article 1 of this Annex.

(c) The other party to the dispute shall, within 30 days of receipt of the notification referred to in article 1 of this Annex, appoint one member to be chosen preferably from the list, who may be its national. If the appointment is not made within that period, the party instituting the proceedings may, within two weeks of the expiration of that period, request that the appointment be made in accordance with subparagraph (e).

(d) The other three members shall be appointed by agreement between the parties. They shall be chosen preferably from the list and shall be nationals of third States unless the parties otherwise agree. The parties to the dispute shall appoint the President of the arbitral tribunal from among those three members. If, within 60 days of receipt of the notification referred to in article 1 of this Annex, the parties are unable to reach agreement on the appointment of one or more of the members of the tribunal to be appointed by agreement, or on the appointment of the President, the remaining appointment or appointments shall be made in accordance with subparagraph (e), at the request of a party to the dispute. Such request shall be made within two weeks of the expiration of the aforementioned 60-day period.

(e) Unless the parties agree that any appointment under subparagraphs (c) and (d) be made by a person or a third State chosen by the parties, the President of the International Tribunal for the Law of the Sea shall make the necessary appointments. If the President is unable to act under this subparagraph or is a national of one of the parties to the dispute, the appointment shall be made by the next senior member of the International Tribunal for the Law of the Sea who is available and is not a national of one of the parties. The appointments referred to in this subparagraph shall be made from the list referred to in article 2 of this Annex within a period of 30 days of the receipt of the request and in consultation with the parties. The members so appointed shall be of different nationalities and may not be in the service of, ordinarily resident in the territory of, or nationals of, any of the parties to the dispute.

(f) Any vacancy shall be filled in the manner prescribed for the initial appointment.

(g) Parties in the same interest shall appoint one member of the tribunal jointly by agreement. Where there are several parties having separate interests or where there is disagreement as to whether they are of the same interest, each of them shall appoint one member of the tribunal. The number of members of the tribunal appointed separately by the parties shall always be smaller by one than the number of members of the tribunal to be appointed jointly by the parties.

(h) In disputes involving more than two parties, the provisions of subparagraphs (a) to (f) shall apply to the maximum extent possible.

Article 4: Functions of arbitral tribunal

An arbitral tribunal constituted under article 3 of this Annex shall function in accordance with this Annex and the other provisions of this Convention.

Article 5: Procedure

Unless the parties to the dispute otherwise agree, the arbitral tribunal shall determine its own procedure, assuring to each party a full opportunity to be heard and to present its case.

Article 6: Duties of parties to a dispute

The parties to the dispute shall facilitate the work of the arbitral tribunal and, in particular, in accordance with their law and using all means at their disposal, shall:

(a) provide it with all relevant documents, facilities and information; and

(b) enable it when necessary to call witnesses or experts and receive their evidence and to visit the localities to which the case relates.

Article 7: Expenses

Unless the arbitral tribunal decides otherwise because of the particular circumstances of the case, the expenses of the tribunal, including the remuneration of its members, shall be borne by the parties to the dispute in equal shares.

Article 8: Required majority for decisions

Decisions of the arbitral tribunal shall be taken by a majority vote of its members. The absence or abstention of less than half of the members shall not constitute a bar to the tribunal reaching a decision. In the event of an equality of votes, the President shall have a casting vote.

Article 9: Default of appearance

If one of the parties to the dispute does not appear before the arbitral tribunal or fails to defend its case, the other party may request the tribunal to continue the proceedings and to make its award. Absence of a party or failure of a party to defend its case shall not constitute a bar to the proceedings. Before making its award, the arbitral tribunal must satisfy itself not only that it has jurisdiction over the dispute but also that the claim is well founded in fact and law.

Article 10: Award

The award of the arbitral tribunal shall be confined to the subject-matter of the dispute and state the reasons on which it is based. It shall contain the names of the members who have participated and the date of the award. Any member of the tribunal may attach a separate or dissenting opinion to the award.

Article 11: Finality of award
The award shall be final and without appeal, unless the parties to the dispute have agreed in advance to an appellate procedure. It shall be complied with by the parties to the dispute.

Article 12: Interpretation or implementation of award
1. Any controversy which may arise between the parties to the dispute as regards the interpretation or manner of implementation of the award may be submitted by either party for decision to the arbitral tribunal which made the award. For this purpose, any vacancy in the tribunal shall be filled in the manner provided for in the original appointments of the members of the tribunal.

2. Any such controversy may be submitted to another court or tribunal under article 287 by agreement of all the parties to the dispute.

Article 13: Application to entities other than States Parties
The provisions of this Annex shall apply mutatis mutandis to any dispute involving entities other than States Parties.

Annex VIII: Special Arbitration

Article 1: Institution of proceedings
Subject to Part XV, any party to a dispute concerning the interpretation or application of the articles of this Convention relating to (1) fisheries, (2) protection and preservation of the marine environment, (3) marine scientific research, or (4) navigation, including pollution from vessels and by dumping, may submit the dispute to the special arbitral procedure provided for in this Annex by written notification addressed to the other party or parties to the dispute. The notification shall be accompanied by a statement of the claim and the grounds on which it is based.

Article 2: Lists of experts
1. A list of experts shall be established and maintained in respect of each of the fields of (1) fisheries, (2) protection and preservation of the marine environment, (3) marine scientific research, and (4) navigation, including pollution from vessels and by dumping.

2. The lists of experts shall be drawn up and maintained, in the field of fisheries by the Food and Agriculture Organization of the United Nations, in the field of protection and preservation of the marine environment by the United Nations Environment Programme, in the field of marine scientific research by the Intergovernmental Oceanographic Commission, in the field of navigation,

including pollution from vessels and by dumping, by the International Maritime Organization, or in each case by the appropriate subsidiary body concerned to which such organization, programme or commission has delegated this function.

3. Every State Party shall be entitled to nominate two experts in each field whose competence in the legal, scientific or technical aspects of such field is established and generally recognized and who enjoy the highest reputation for fairness and integrity. The names of the persons so nominated in each field shall constitute the appropriate list.

4. If at any time the experts nominated by a State Party in the list so constituted shall be fewer than two, that State Party shall be entitled to make further nominations as necessary.

5. The name of an expert shall remain on the list until withdrawn by the State Party which made the nomination, provided that such expert shall continue to serve on any special arbitral tribunal to which that expert has been appointed until the completion of the proceedings before that special arbitral tribunal.

Article 3: Constitution of special arbitral tribunal

For the purpose of proceedings under this Annex, the special arbitral tribunal shall, unless the parties otherwise agree, be constituted as follows:

(a) Subject to subparagraph (g), the special arbitral tribunal shall consist of five members.

(b) The party instituting the proceedings shall appoint two members to be chosen preferably from the appropriate list or lists referred to in article 2 of this Annex relating to the matters in dispute, one of whom may be its national. The appointments shall be included in the notification referred to in article 1 of this Annex.

(c) The other party to the dispute shall, within 30 days of receipt of the notification referred to in article 1 of this Annex, appoint two members to be chosen preferably from the appropriate list or lists relating to the matters in dispute, one of whom may be its national. If the appointments are not made within that period, the party instituting the proceedings may, within two weeks of the expiration of that period, request that the appointments be made in accordance with subparagraph (e).

(d) The parties to the dispute shall by agreement appoint the President of the special arbitral tribunal, chosen preferably from the appropriate list, who shall be a national of a third State, unless the parties otherwise agree. If, within 30 days of receipt of the notification referred to in article 1 of this Annex, the parties are unable to reach agreement on the appointment of the President, the appointment shall be made in accordance with subparagraph (e), at the request of a party to the dispute. Such request shall be made within two weeks of the expiration of the aforementioned 30-day period.

(e) Unless the parties agree that the appointment be made by a person or a third State chosen by the parties, the Secretary-General of the United Nations shall make the necessary appointments within 30 days of receipt of a request under subparagraphs (c) and (d). The appointments referred to in this subparagraph shall be made from the appropriate list or lists of experts referred to in article 2 of this Annex and in consultation with the parties to the dispute and the appropriate international organization. The members so appointed shall be of different nationalities and may not be in the service of, ordinarily resident in the territory of, or nationals of, any of the parties to the dispute.

(f) Any vacancy shall be filled in the manner prescribed for the initial appointment.

(g) Parties in the same interest shall appoint two members of the tribunal jointly by agreement. Where there are several parties having separate interests or where there is disagreement as to whether they are of the same interest, each of them shall appoint one member of the tribunal.

(h) In disputes involving more than two parties, the provisions of subparagraphs (a) to (f) shall apply to the maximum extent possible.

Article 4: General provisions

Annex VII, articles 4 to 13, apply mutatis mutandis to the special arbitration proceedings in accordance with this Annex.

Article 5: Fact finding

1. The parties to a dispute concerning the interpretation or application of the provisions of this Convention relating to (1) fisheries, (2) protection and preservation of the marine environment, (3) marine scientific research, or (4) navigation, including pollution from vessels and by dumping, may at any time agree to request a special arbitral tribunal constituted in accordance with article 3 of this Annex to carry out an inquiry and establish the facts giving rise to the dispute.

2. Unless the parties otherwise agree, the findings of fact of the special arbitral tribunal acting in accordance with paragraph 1, shall be considered as conclusive as between the parties.

3. If all the parties to the dispute so request, the special arbitral tribunal may formulate recommendations which, without having the force of a decision, shall only constitute the basis for a review by the parties of the questions giving rise to the dispute.

4. Subject to paragraph 2, the special arbitral tribunal shall act in accordance with the provisions of this Annex, unless the parties otherwise agree.

. . . [Annex IX: Participation by International Organizations not included]

8.4
Agreement Relating to the Implementation of Part XI of the United Nations Convention on the Law of the Sea of 10 December 1982 (1994)

The LOSC was negotiated as a package, but the departure from market economics in its provisions on deep seabed mining was unpalatable to the United States and some other key industrialized countries. In 1990, the UN Secretary-General initiated "consultations" in an endeavor to ensure universal ratification of the LOSC. On 28 July 1994, the United Nations General Assembly voted 120 to 0 with 7 abstentions (Colombia, Nicaragua, Panama, Peru, the Russian Federation, Thailand, and Venezuela) on this implementing agreement, which effectively amends the convention. The implementing agreement is integral to the convention package that entered into force on 16 November 1994.

On the negotiation of the agreement, see D. H. Anderson, "Further Efforts to Ensure Universal Participation in the United Nations Convention on the Law of the Sea," International and Comparative Law Quarterly *43 (1994): 886–893. On the significance of the agreement for US interests, see Christopher C. Joyner, "The United States and the New Law of the Sea,"* Ocean Development and International Law *27 (1996): 41–58; on its significance for the aspirations of the developing world, see Peter Bautista Payoyo,* Cries of the Sea: World Inequality, Sustainable Development, and the Common Heritage of Humanity *(The Hague: Martinus Nijhoff, 1997).*

The States Parties to this Agreement,

Recognizing the important contribution of the United Nations Convention on the Law of the Sea of 10 December 1982 (hereinafter referred to as "the Convention") to the maintenance of peace, justice and progress for all peoples of the world,

Reaffirming that the seabed and ocean floor and subsoil thereof, beyond the limits of national jurisdiction (hereinafter referred to as "the Area"), as well as the resources of the Area, are the common heritage of mankind,

Mindful of the importance of the Convention for the protection and preservation of the marine environment and of the growing concern for the global environment,

Having considered the report of the Secretary-General of the United Nations on the results of the informal consultations among States held from 1990 to 1994 on outstanding issues relating to Part XI and related provisions of the Convention (hereinafter referred to as "Part XI"),

Noting the political and economic changes, including market-oriented approaches, affecting the implementation of Part XI,

Wishing to facilitate universal participation in the Convention,

Considering that an agreement relating to the implementation of Part XI would best meet that objective,

Have agreed as follows:

Article 1: Implementation of Part XI

1. The States Parties to this Agreement undertake to implement Part XI in accordance with this Agreement.

2. The Annex forms an integral part of this Agreement.

Article 2: Relationship between this Agreement and Part XI

1. The provisions of this Agreement and Part XI shall be interpreted and applied together as a single instrument. In the event of any inconsistency between this Agreement and Part XI, the provisions of this Agreement shall prevail.

2. Articles 309 to 319 of the Convention shall apply to this Agreement as they apply to the Convention.

Article 3: Signature

This Agreement shall remain open for signature at United Nations Headquarters by the States and entities referred to in article 305, paragraph 1(a), (c), (d), (e) and (f), of the Convention for 12 months from the date of its adoption.

Article 4: Consent to be bound

1. After the adoption of this Agreement, any instrument of ratification or formal confirmation of or accession to the Convention shall also represent consent to be bound by this Agreement.

2. No State or entity may establish its consent to be bound by this Agreement unless it has previously established or establishes at the same time its consent to be bound by the Convention.

3. A State or entity referred to in article 3 may express its consent to be bound by this Agreement by:

(a) Signature not subject to ratification, formal confirmation or the procedure set out in article 5;

(b) Signature subject to ratification or formal confirmation, followed by ratification or formal confirmation;

(c) Signature subject to the procedure set out in article 5; or

(d) Accession.

4. Formal confirmation by the entities referred to in article 305, paragraph 1(f), of the Convention shall be in accordance with Annex IX of the Convention.

5. The instruments of ratification, formal confirmation or accession shall be deposited with the Secretary-General of the United Nations.

Article 5: Simplified procedure

1. A State or entity which has deposited before the date of the adoption of this Agreement an instrument of ratification or formal confirmation of or accession to the Convention and which has signed this Agreement in accordance with article 4, paragraph 3(c), shall be considered to have established its consent to be bound by this Agreement 12 months after the date of its adoption, unless that State or entity notifies the depositary in writing before that date that it is not availing itself of the simplified procedure set out in this article.

2. In the event of such notification, consent to be bound by this Agreement shall be established in accordance with article 4, paragraph 3(b).

Article 6: Entry into force

1. This Agreement shall enter into force 30 days after the date on which 40 States have established their consent to be bound in accordance with articles 4 and 5, provided that such States include at least seven of the States referred to in paragraph 1(a) of resolution II of the Third United Nations Conference on the Law of the Sea (hereinafter referred to as "resolution II") and that at least five of those States are developed States. If these conditions for entry into force are fulfilled before 16 November 1994, this Agreement shall enter into force on 16 November 1994.

2. For each State or entity establishing its consent to be bound by this Agreement after the requirements set out in paragraph 1 have been fulfilled, this Agreement shall enter into force on the thirtieth day following the date of establishment of its consent to be bound.

Article 7: Provisional application

1. If on 16 November 1994 this Agreement has not entered into force, it shall be applied provisionally pending its entry into force by:

(a) States which have consented to its adoption in the General Assembly of the United Nations, except any such State which before 16 November 1994 notifies the depositary in writing either that it will not so apply this Agreement or that it will consent to such application only upon subsequent signature or notification in writing;

(b) States and entities which sign this Agreement, except any such State or entity which notifies the depositary in writing at the time of signature that it will not so apply this Agreement.

(c) States and entities which consent to its provisional application by so notifying the depositary in writing;

(d) States which accede to this Agreement.

2. All such States and entities shall apply this Agreement provisionally in accordance with their national or internal laws and regulations, with effect from 16 November 1994 or the date of signature, notification of consent or accession, if later.

3. Provisional application shall terminate upon the date of entry into force of this Agreement. In any event, provisional application shall terminate on 16 November 1998 if at that date the requirement in article 6, paragraph 1, of consent to be bound by this Agreement by at least seven of the States (of which at least five must be developed States) referred to in paragraph 1(a) of resolution II has not been fulfilled.

Article 8: States Parties

1. For the purposes of this Agreement, "States Parties" means States which have consented to be bound by this Agreement and for which this Agreement is in force.

2. This Agreement applies mutatis mutandis to the entities referred to in article 305, paragraph 1(c), (d), (e) and (f), of the Convention which become Parties to this Agreement in accordance with the conditions relevant to each, and to that extent "States Parties" refers to those entities.

Article 9: Depositary

The Secretary-General of the United Nations shall be the depositary of this Agreement.

Article 10: Authentic texts

The original of this Agreement, of which the Arabic, Chinese, English, French, Russian and Spanish texts are equally authentic, shall be deposited with the Secretary-General of the United Nations.

IN WITNESS WHEREOF, the undersigned Plenipotentiaries, being duly authorized thereto, have signed this Agreement.

DONE AT NEW YORK, this twenty-eighth day of July, one thousand nine hundred and ninety-four.

Annex

Section 1: Costs to States Parties and Institutional Arrangements

1. The International Seabed Authority (hereinafter referred to as "the

Authority") is the organization through which States Parties to the Convention shall, in accordance with the regime for the Area established in Part XI and this Agreement, organize and control activities in the Area, particularly with a view to administering the resources of the Area. The powers and functions of the Authority shall be those expressly conferred upon it by the Convention. The Authority shall have such incidental powers, consistent with the Convention, as are implicit in, and necessary for, the exercise of those powers and functions with respect to activities in the Area.

2. In order to minimize costs to States Parties, all organs and subsidiary bodies to be established under the Convention and this Agreement shall be cost-effective. This principle shall also apply to the frequency, duration and scheduling of meetings.

3. The setting up and the functioning of the organs and subsidiary bodies of the Authority shall be based on an evolutionary approach, taking into account the functional needs of the organs and subsidiary bodies concerned in order that they may discharge effectively their respective responsibilities at various stages of the development of activities in the Area.

4. The early functions of the Authority upon entry into force of the Convention shall be carried out by the Assembly, the Council, the Secretariat, the Legal and Technical Commission and the Finance Committee. The functions of the Economic Planning Commission shall be performed by the Legal and Technical Commission until such time as the Council decides otherwise or until the approval of the first plan of work for exploitation.

5. Between the entry into force of the Convention and the approval of the first plan of work for exploitation, the Authority shall concentrate on:

(a) Processing of applications for approval of plans of work for exploration in accordance with Part XI and this Agreement;

(b) Implementation of decisions of the Preparatory Commission for the International Seabed Authority and for the International Tribunal for the Law of the Sea (hereinafter referred to as "the Preparatory Commission") relating to the registered pioneer investors and their certifying States, including their rights and obligations, in accordance with article 308, paragraph 5, of the Convention and resolution II, paragraph 13;

(c) Monitoring of compliance with plans of work for exploration approved in the form of contracts;

(d) Monitoring and review of trends and developments relating to deep seabed mining activities, including regular analysis of world metal market conditions and metal prices, trends and prospects;

(e) Study of the potential impact of mineral production from the Area on the economies of developing land-based producers of those minerals which are likely to be most seriously affected, with a view to minimizing their difficulties and assisting them in their economic adjustment, taking into account the work done in this regard by the Preparatory Commission;

(f) Adoption of rules, regulations and procedures necessary for the conduct of activities in the Area as they progress. Notwithstanding the provisions of Annex III, article 17, paragraph 2(b) and (c), of the Convention, such rules, regulations and procedures shall take into account the terms of this Agreement, the prolonged delay in commercial deep seabed mining and the likely pace of activities in the Area;

(g) Adoption of rules, regulations and procedures incorporating applicable standards for the protection and preservation of the marine environment;

(h) Promotion and encouragement of the conduct of marine scientific research with respect to activities in the Area and the collection and dissemination of the results of such research and analysis, when available, with particular emphasis on research related to the environmental impact of activities in the Area;

(i) Acquisition of scientific knowledge and monitoring of the development of marine technology relevant to activities in the Area, in particular technology relating to the protection and preservation of the marine environment;

(j) Assessment of available data relating to prospecting and exploration;

(k) Timely elaboration of rules, regulations and procedures for exploitation, including those relating to the protection and preservation of the marine environment.

6. (a) An application for approval of a plan of work for exploration shall be considered by the Council following the receipt of a recommendation on the application from the Legal and Technical Commission. The processing of an application for approval of a plan of work for exploration shall be in accordance with the provisions of the Convention, including Annex III thereof, and this Agreement, and subject to the following: (i) A plan of work for exploration submitted on behalf of a State or entity, or any component of such entity, referred to in resolution II, paragraph 1(a)(ii) or (iii), other than a registered pioneer investor, which had already undertaken substantial activities in the Area prior to the entry into force of the Convention, or its successor in interest, shall be considered to have met the financial and technical qualifications necessary for approval of a plan of work if the sponsoring State or States certify that the applicant has expended an amount equivalent to at least US$ 30 million in research and exploration activities and has expended no less than 10 per cent of that amount in the location, survey and evaluation of the area referred to in the plan of work. If the plan of work otherwise satisfies the requirements of the Convention and any rules, regulations and procedures adopted pursuant thereto, it shall be approved by the Council in the form of a contract. The provisions of section 3, paragraph 11, of this Annex shall be interpreted and applied accordingly; (ii) Notwithstanding the provisions of resolution II, paragraph 8(a), a registered pioneer investor may request approval of a plan of work for exploration within 36 months of the entry into force of the Convention. The plan of work for exploration shall consist of documents, reports and other data submitted to the Preparatory Commission both before and after registration and shall be accompanied by a certificate of compliance, consisting of a factual report describing the status of fulfilment of obligations under the pioneer investor regime, issued by the Preparatory Commission in

accordance with resolution II, paragraph 11(a). Such a plan of work shall be considered to be approved. Such an approved plan of work shall be in the form of a contract concluded between the Authority and the registered pioneer investor in accordance with Part XI and this Agreement. The fee of US$ 250,000 paid pursuant to resolution II, paragraph 7(a), shall be deemed to be the fee relating to the exploration phase pursuant to section 8, paragraph 3, of this Annex. Section 3, paragraph 11, of this Annex shall be interpreted and applied accordingly; (iii) In accordance with the principle of non-discrimination, a contract with a State or entity or any component of such entity referred to in subparagraph (a)(i) shall include arrangements which shall be similar to and no less favourable than those agreed with any registered pioneer investor referred to in subparagraph (a)(ii). If any of the States or entities or any components of such entities referred to in subparagraph (a)(i) are granted more favourable arrangements, the Council shall make similar and no less favourable arrangements with regard to the rights and obligations assumed by the registered pioneer investors referred to in subparagraph (a)(ii), provided that such arrangements do not affect or prejudice the interests of the Authority; (iv) A State sponsoring an application for a plan of work pursuant to the provisions of subparagraph (a)(i) or (ii) may be a State Party or a State which is applying this Agreement provisionally in accordance with article 7, or a State which is a member of the Authority on a provisional basis in accordance with paragraph 12; (v) Resolution II, paragraph 8(c), shall be interpreted and applied in accordance with subparagraph (a)(iv).

(b) The approval of a plan of work for exploration shall be in accordance with article 153, paragraph 3, of the Convention.

7. An application for approval of a plan of work shall be accompanied by an assessment of the potential environmental impacts of the proposed activities and by a description of a programme for oceanographic and baseline environmental studies in accordance with the rules, regulations and procedures adopted by the Authority.

8. An application for approval of a plan of work for exploration, subject to paragraph 6(a)(i) or (ii), shall be processed in accordance with the procedures set out in section 3, paragraph 11, of this Annex.

9. A plan of work for exploration shall be approved for a period of 15 years. Upon the expiration of a plan of work for exploration, the contractor shall apply for a plan of work for exploitation unless the contractor has already done so or has obtained an extension for the plan of work for exploration. Contractors may apply for such extensions for periods of not more than five years each. Such extensions shall be approved if the contractor has made efforts in good faith to comply with the requirements of the plan of work but for reasons beyond the contractor's control has been unable to complete the necessary preparatory work for proceeding to the exploitation stage or if the prevailing economic circumstances do not justify proceeding to the exploitation stage.

10. Designation of a reserved area for the Authority in accordance with

Annex III, article 8, of the Convention shall take place in connection with approval of an application for a plan of work for exploration or approval of an application for a plan of work for exploration and exploitation.

11. Notwithstanding the provisions of paragraph 9, an approved plan of work for exploration which is sponsored by at least one State provisionally applying this Agreement shall terminate if such a State ceases to apply this Agreement provisionally and has not become a member on a provisional basis in accordance with paragraph 12 or has not become a State Party.

12. Upon the entry into force of this Agreement, States and entities referred to in article 3 of this Agreement which have been applying it provisionally in accordance with article 7 and for which it is not in force may continue to be members of the Authority on a provisional basis pending its entry into force for such States and entities, in accordance with the following subparagraphs:

(a) If this Agreement enters into force before 16 November 1996, such States and entities shall be entitled to continue to participate as members of the Authority on a provisional basis upon notification to the depositary of the Agreement by such a State or entity of its intention to participate as a member on a provisional basis. Such membership shall terminate either on 16 November 1996 or upon the entry into force of this Agreement and the Convention for such member, whichever is earlier. The Council may, upon the request of the State or entity concerned, extend such membership beyond 16 November 1996 for a further period or periods not exceeding a total of two years provided that the Council is satisfied that the State or entity concerned has been making efforts in good faith to become a party to the Agreement and the Convention;

(b) If this Agreement enters into force after 15 November 1996, such States and entities may request the Council to grant continued membership in the Authority on a provisional basis for a period or periods not extending beyond 16 November 1998. The Council shall grant such membership with effect from the date of the request if it is satisfied that the State or entity has been making efforts in good faith to become a party to the Agreement and the Convention;

(c) States and entities which are members of the Authority on a provisional basis in accordance with subparagraph (a) or (b) shall apply the terms of Part XI and this Agreement in accordance with their national or internal laws, regulations and annual budgetary appropriations and shall have the same rights and obligations as other members, including: (i) The obligation to contribute to the administrative budget of the Authority in accordance with the scale of assessed contributions; (ii) The right to sponsor an application for approval of a plan of work for exploration. In the case of entities whose components are natural or juridical persons possessing the nationality of more than one State, a plan of work for exploration shall not be approved unless all the States whose natural or juridical persons comprise those entities are States Parties or members on a provisional basis;

(d) Notwithstanding the provisions of paragraph 9, an approved plan of work in the form of a contract for exploration which was sponsored pursuant to subparagraph (c)(ii) by a State which was a member on a provisional basis shall terminate if such membership ceases and the State or entity has not become a State Party;

(e) If such a member has failed to make its assessed contributions or otherwise failed to comply with its obligations in accordance with this paragraph, its membership on a provisional basis shall be terminated.

13. The reference in Annex III, article 10, of the Convention to performance which has not been satisfactory shall be interpreted to mean that the contractor has failed to comply with the requirements of an approved plan of work in spite of a written warning or warnings from the Authority to the contractor to comply therewith.

14. The Authority shall have its own budget. Until the end of the year following the year during which this Agreement enters into force, the administrative expenses of the Authority shall be met through the budget of the United Nations. Thereafter, the administrative expenses of the Authority shall be met by assessed contributions of its members, including any members on a provisional basis, in accordance with articles 171, subparagraph (a), and 173 of the Convention and this Agreement, until the Authority has sufficient funds from other sources to meet those expenses. The Authority shall not exercise the power referred to in article 174, paragraph 1, of the Convention to borrow funds to finance its administrative budget.

15. The Authority shall elaborate and adopt, in accordance with article 162, paragraph 2 (o)(ii), of the Convention, rules, regulations and procedures based on the principles contained in sections 2, 5, 6, 7 and 8 of this Annex, as well as any additional rules, regulations and procedures necessary to facilitate the approval of plans of work for exploration or exploitation, in accordance with the following subparagraphs:

(a) The Council may undertake such elaboration any time it deems that all or any of such rules, regulations or procedures are required for the conduct of activities in the Area, or when it determines that commercial exploitation is imminent, or at the request of a State whose national intends to apply for approval of a plan of work for exploitation;

(b) If a request is made by a State referred to in subparagraph (a) the Council shall, in accordance with article 162, paragraph 2(o), of the Convention, complete the adoption of such rules, regulations and procedures within two years of the request;

(c) If the Council has not completed the elaboration of the rules, regulations and procedures relating to exploitation within the prescribed time and an application for approval of a plan of work for exploitation is pending, it shall none the less consider and provisionally approve such plan of work based on the provisions of the Convention and any rules, regulations and procedures that the Council may have adopted provisionally, or on the basis of the norms contained in the Convention and the terms and principles contained in this Annex as well as the principle of non-discrimination among contractors.

16. The draft rules, regulations and procedures and any recommendations relating to the provisions of Part XI, as contained in the reports and recommendations of the Preparatory Commission, shall be taken into account by the Authority in the adoption of rules, regulations and procedures in accordance with Part XI and this Agreement.

17. The relevant provisions of Part XI, section 4, of the Convention shall be interpreted and applied in accordance with this Agreement.

Section 2: The Enterprise

1. The Secretariat of the Authority shall perform the functions of the Enterprise until it begins to operate independently of the Secretariat. The Secretary-General of the Authority shall appoint from within the staff of the Authority an interim Director-General to oversee the performance of these functions by the Secretariat. These functions shall be:

(a) Monitoring and review of trends and developments relating to deep seabed mining activities, including regular analysis of world metal market conditions and metal prices, trends and prospects;

(b) Assessment of the results of the conduct of marine scientific research with respect to activities in the Area, with particular emphasis on research related to the environmental impact of activities in the Area;

(c) Assessment of available data relating to prospecting and exploration, including the criteria for such activities;

(d) Assessment of technological developments relevant to activities in the Area, in particular technology relating to the protection and preservation of the marine environment;

(e) Evaluation of information and data relating to areas reserved for the Authority;

(f) Assessment of approaches to joint-venture operations;

(g) Collection of information on the availability of trained manpower;

(h) Study of managerial policy options for the administration of the Enterprise at different stages of its operations.

2. The Enterprise shall conduct its initial deep seabed mining operations through joint ventures. Upon the approval of a plan of work for exploitation for an entity other than the Enterprise, or upon receipt by the Council of an application for a joint-venture operation with the Enterprise, the Council shall take up the issue of the functioning of the Enterprise independently of the Secretariat of the Authority. If joint-venture operations with the Enterprise accord with sound commercial principles, the Council shall issue a directive pursuant to article 170, paragraph 2, of the Convention providing for such independent functioning.

3. The obligation of States Parties to fund one mine site of the Enterprise as provided for in Annex IV, article 11, paragraph 3, of the Convention shall not apply and States Parties shall be under no obligation to finance any of the operations in any mine site of the Enterprise or under its joint-venture arrangements.

4. The obligations applicable to contractors shall apply to the Enterprise. Notwithstanding the provisions of article 153, paragraph 3, and Annex III, article 3, paragraph 5, of the Convention, a plan of work for the Enterprise upon its approval shall be in the form of a contract concluded between the Authority and the Enterprise.

5. A contractor which has contributed a particular area to the Authority as a reserved area has the right of first refusal to enter into a joint-venture arrangement with the Enterprise for exploration and exploitation of that area. If the Enterprise does not submit an application for a plan of work for activities in respect of such a reserved area within 15 years of the commencement of its functions independent of the Secretariat of the Authority or within 15 years of the date on which that area is reserved for the Authority, whichever is the later, the contractor which contributed the area shall be entitled to apply for a plan of work for that area provided it offers in good faith to include the Enterprise as a joint-venture partner.

6. Article 170, paragraph 4, Annex IV and other provisions of the Convention relating to the Enterprise shall be interpreted and applied in accordance with this section.

Section 3: Decision-Making

1. The general policies of the Authority shall be established by the Assembly in collaboration with the Council.

2. As a general rule, decision-making in the organs of the Authority should be by consensus.

3. If all efforts to reach a decision by consensus have been exhausted, decisions by voting in the Assembly on questions of procedure shall be taken by a majority of members present and voting, and decisions on questions of substance shall be taken by a two-thirds majority of members present and voting, as provided for in article 159, paragraph 8, of the Convention.

4. Decisions of the Assembly on any matter for which the Council also has competence or on any administrative, budgetary or financial matter shall be based on the recommendations of the Council. If the Assembly does not accept the recommendation of the Council on any matter, it shall return the matter to the Council for further consideration. The Council shall reconsider the matter in the light of the views expressed by the Assembly.

5. If all efforts to reach a decision by consensus have been exhausted, decisions by voting in the Council on questions of procedure shall be taken by a majority of members present and voting, and decisions on questions of substance, except where the Convention provides for decisions by consensus in the Council, shall be taken by a two-thirds majority of members present and voting, provided that such decisions are not opposed by a majority in any one of the chambers referred to in paragraph 9. In taking decisions the Council shall seek to promote the interests of all the members of the Authority.

6. The Council may defer the taking of a decision in order to facilitate fur-

ther negotiation whenever it appears that all efforts at achieving consensus on a question have not been exhausted.

7. Decisions by the Assembly or the Council having financial or budgetary implications shall be based on the recommendations of the Finance Committee.

8. The provisions of article 161, paragraph 8(b) and (c), of the Convention shall not apply.

9. (a) Each group of States elected under paragraph 15(a) to (c) shall be treated as a chamber for the purposes of voting in the Council. The developing States elected under paragraph 15(d) and (e) shall be treated as a single chamber for the purposes of voting in the Council.

(b) Before electing the members of the Council, the Assembly shall establish lists of countries fulfilling the criteria for membership in the groups of States in paragraph 15(a) to (d). If a State fulfils the criteria for membership in more than one group, it may only be proposed by one group for election to the Council and it shall represent only that group in voting in the Council.

10. Each group of States in paragraph 15(a) to (d) shall be represented in the Council by those members nominated by that group. Each group shall nominate only as many candidates as the number of seats required to be filled by that group. When the number of potential candidates in each of the groups referred to in paragraph 15(a) to (e) exceeds the number of seats available in each of those respective groups, as a general rule, the principle of rotation shall apply. States members of each of those groups shall determine how this principle shall apply in those groups.

11. (a) The Council shall approve a recommendation by the Legal and Technical Commission for approval of a plan of work unless by a two-thirds majority of its members present and voting, including a majority of members present and voting in each of the chambers of the Council, the Council decides to disapprove a plan of work. If the Council does not take a decision on a recommendation for approval of a plan of work within a prescribed period, the recommendation shall be deemed to have been approved by the Council at the end of that period. The prescribed period shall normally be 60 days unless the Council decides to provide for a longer period. If the Commission recommends the disapproval of a plan of work or does not make a recommendation, the Council may nevertheless approve the plan of work in accordance with its rules of procedure for decision-making on questions of substance.

(b) The provisions of article 162, paragraph 2(j), of the Convention shall not apply.

12. Where a dispute arises relating to the disapproval of a plan of work, such dispute shall be submitted to the dispute settlement procedures set out in the Convention.

13. Decisions by voting in the Legal and Technical Commission shall be by a majority of members present and voting.

14. Part XI, section 4, subsections B and C, of the Convention shall be interpreted and applied in accordance with this section.

15. The Council shall consist of 36 members of the Authority elected by the Assembly in the following order:

(a) Four members from among those States Parties which, during the last five years for which statistics are available, have either consumed more than 2 per cent in value terms of total world consumption or have had net imports of more than 2 per cent in value terms of total world imports of the commodities produced from the categories of minerals to be derived from the Area, provided that the four members shall include one State from the Eastern European region having the largest economy in that region in terms of gross domestic product and the State, on the date of entry into force of the Convention, having the largest economy in terms of gross domestic product, if such States wish to be represented in this group;

(b) Four members from among the eight States Parties which have made the largest investments in preparation for and in the conduct of activities in the Area, either directly or through their nationals;

(c) Four members from among States Parties which, on the basis of production in areas under their jurisdiction, are major net exporters of the categories of minerals to be derived from the Area, including at least two developing States whose exports of such minerals have a substantial bearing upon their economies;

(d) Six members from among developing States Parties, representing special interests. The special interests to be represented shall include those of States with large populations, States which are land-locked or geographically disadvantaged, island States, States which are major importers of the categories of minerals to be derived from the Area, States which are potential producers of such minerals and least developed States;

(e) Eighteen members elected according to the principle of ensuring an equitable geographical distribution of seats in the Council as a whole, provided that each geographical region shall have at least one member elected under this subparagraph. For this purpose, the geographical regions shall be Africa, Asia, Eastern Europe, Latin America and the Caribbean and Western Europe and Others.

16. The provisions of article 161, paragraph 1, of the Convention shall not apply.

Section 4: Review Conference

The provisions relating to the Review Conference in article 155, paragraphs 1, 3 and 4, of the Convention shall not apply. Notwithstanding the provisions of article 314, paragraph 2, of the Convention, the Assembly, on the recommendation of the Council, may undertake at any time a review of the matters referred to in article 155, paragraph 1, of the Convention. Amendments relating to this Agreement and Part XI shall be subject to the procedures contained in articles 314, 315 and 316 of the Convention, provided that the principles, regime and other terms referred to in article 155, paragraph 2, of the Convention shall be maintained and the rights referred to in paragraph 5 of that article shall not be affected.

Section 5: Transfer of Technology

1. In addition to the provisions of article 144 of the Convention, transfer of technology for the purposes of Part XI shall be governed by the following principles:

(a) The Enterprise, and developing States wishing to obtain deep seabed mining technology, shall seek to obtain such technology on fair and reasonable commercial terms and conditions on the open market, or through joint-venture arrangements;

(b) If the Enterprise or developing States are unable to obtain deep seabed mining technology, the Authority may request all or any of the contractors and their respective sponsoring State or States to cooperate with it in facilitating the acquisition of deep seabed mining technology by the Enterprise or its joint venture, or by a developing State or States seeking to acquire such technology on fair and reasonable commercial terms and conditions, consistent with the effective protection of intellectual property rights. States Parties undertake to cooperate fully and effectively with the Authority for this purpose and to ensure that contractors sponsored by them also cooperate fully with the Authority;

(c) As a general rule, States Parties shall promote international technical and scientific cooperation with regard to activities in the Area either between the parties concerned or by developing training, technical assistance and scientific cooperation programmes in marine science and technology and the protection and preservation of the marine environment.

2. The provisions of Annex III, article 5, of the Convention shall not apply.

Section 6: Production Policy

1. The production policy of the Authority shall be based on the following principles:

(a) Development of the resources of the Area shall take place in accordance with sound commercial principles;

(b) The provisions of the General Agreement on Tariffs and Trade, its relevant codes and successor or superseding agreements shall apply with respect to activities in the Area;

(c) In particular, there shall be no subsidization of activities in the Area except as may be permitted under the agreements referred to in subparagraph (b). Subsidization for the purpose of these principles shall be defined in terms of the agreements referred to in subparagraph (b);

(d) There shall be no discrimination between minerals derived from the Area and from other sources. There shall be no preferential access to markets for such minerals or for imports of commodities produced from such minerals, in particular: (i) By the use of tariff or non-tariff barriers; and (ii) Given by States Parties to such minerals or commodities produced by their state enterprises or by natural or juridical persons which possess their nationality or are controlled by them or their nationals;

(e) The plan of work for exploitation approved by the Authority in respect of each mining area shall indicate an anticipated production schedule which shall include the estimated maximum amounts of minerals that would be produced per year under the plan of work;

(f) The following shall apply to the settlement of disputes concerning the provisions of the agreements referred to in subparagraph (b): (i) Where the States Parties concerned are parties to such agreements, they shall have recourse to the dispute settlement procedures of those agreements; (ii) Where one or more of the States Parties concerned are not parties to such agreements, they shall have recourse to the dispute settlement procedures set out in the Convention;

(g) In circumstances where a determination is made under the agreements referred to in subparagraph (b) that a State Party has engaged in subsidization which is prohibited or has resulted in adverse effects on the interests of another State Party and appropriate steps have not been taken by the relevant State Party or States Parties, a State Party may request the Council to take appropriate measures.

2. The principles contained in paragraph 1 shall not affect the rights and obligations under any provision of the agreements referred to in paragraph 1(b), as well as the relevant free trade and customs union agreements, in relations between States Parties which are parties to such agreements.

3. The acceptance by a contractor of subsidies other than those which may be permitted under the agreements referred to in paragraph 1(b) shall constitute a violation of the fundamental terms of the contract forming a plan of work for the carrying out of activities in the Area.

4. Any State Party which has reason to believe that there has been a breach of the requirements of paragraphs 1(b) to (d) or 3 may initiate dispute settlement procedures in conformity with paragraph 1(f) or (g).

5. A State Party may at any time bring to the attention of the Council activities which in its view are inconsistent with the requirements of paragraph 1(b) to (d).

6. The Authority shall develop rules, regulations and procedures which ensure the implementation of the provisions of this section, including relevant rules, regulations and procedures governing the approval of plans of work.

7. The provisions of article 151, paragraphs 1 to 7 and 9, article 162, paragraph 2(q), article 165, paragraph 2(n), and Annex III, article 6, paragraph 5, and article 7, of the Convention shall not apply.

Section 7: Economic Assistance

1. The policy of the Authority of assisting developing countries which suffer serious adverse effects on their export earnings or economies resulting from a reduction in the price of an affected mineral or in the volume of exports of that mineral, to the extent that such reduction is caused by activities in the Area, shall be based on the following principles:

(a) The Authority shall establish an economic assistance fund from a portion of the funds of the Authority which exceeds those necessary to cover the administrative expenses of the Authority. The amount set aside for this purpose shall be determined by the Council from time to time, upon the recommendation of the Finance Committee. Only funds from payments received from contractors, including the Enterprise, and voluntary contributions shall be used for the establishment of the economic assistance fund;

(b) Developing land-based producer States whose economies have been determined to be seriously affected by the production of minerals from the deep seabed shall be assisted from the economic assistance fund of the Authority;

(c) The Authority shall provide assistance from the fund to affected developing land-based producer States, where appropriate, in cooperation with existing global or regional development institutions which have the infrastructure and expertise to carry out such assistance programmes;

(d) The extent and period of such assistance shall be determined on a case-by-case basis. In doing so, due consideration shall be given to the nature and magnitude of the problems encountered by affected developing land-based producer States.

2. Article 151, paragraph 10, of the Convention shall be implemented by means of measures of economic assistance referred to in paragraph 1. Article 160, paragraph 2(l), article 162, paragraph 2(n), article 164, paragraph 2(d), article 171, subparagraph (f), and article 173, paragraph 2(c), of the Convention shall be interpreted accordingly.

Section 8: Financial Terms of Contracts

1. The following principles shall provide the basis for establishing rules, regulations and procedures for financial terms of contracts:

(a) The system of payments to the Authority shall be fair both to the contractor and to the Authority and shall provide adequate means of determining compliance by the contractor with such system;

(b) The rates of payments under the system shall be within the range of those prevailing in respect of land-based mining of the same or similar minerals in order to avoid giving deep seabed miners an artificial competitive advantage or imposing on them a competitive disadvantage;

(c) The system should not be complicated and should not impose major administrative costs on the Authority or on a contractor. Consideration should be given to the adoption of a royalty system or a combination of a royalty and profit-sharing system. If alternative systems are decided upon, the contractor has the right to choose the system applicable to its contract. Any subsequent change in choice between alternative systems, however, shall be made by agreement between the Authority and the contractor;

(d) An annual fixed fee shall be payable from the date of commencement of commercial production. This fee may be credited against other payments due under the system adopted in accordance with subparagraph (c). The amount of the fee shall be established by the Council;

(e) The system of payments may be revised periodically in the light of changing circumstances. Any changes shall be applied in a non-discriminatory manner. Such changes may apply to existing contracts only at the election of the contractor. Any subsequent change in choice between alternative systems shall be made by agreement between the Authority and the contractor;

(f) Disputes concerning the interpretation or application of the rules and regulations based on these principles shall be subject to the dispute settlement procedures set out in the Convention.

2. The provisions of Annex III, article 13, paragraphs 3 to 10, of the Convention shall not apply.

3. With regard to the implementation of Annex III, article 13, paragraph 2, of the Convention, the fee for processing applications for approval of a plan of work limited to one phase, either the exploration phase or the exploitation phase, shall be US$ 250,000.

Section 9: The Finance Committee

1. There is hereby established a Finance Committee. The Committee shall be composed of 15 members with appropriate qualifications relevant to financial matters. States Parties shall nominate candidates of the highest standards of competence and integrity.

2. No two members of the Finance Committee shall be nationals of the same State Party.

3. Members of the Finance Committee shall be elected by the Assembly and due account shall be taken of the need for equitable geographical distribution and the representation of special interests. Each group of States referred to in section 3, paragraph 15(a), (b), (c) and (d), of this Annex shall be represented on the Committee by at least one member. Until the Authority has sufficient funds other than assessed contributions to meet its administrative expenses, the membership of the Committee shall include representatives of the five largest financial contributors to the administrative budget of the Authority. Thereafter, the election of one member from each group shall be on the basis of nomination by the members of the respective group, without prejudice to the possibility of further members being elected from each group.

4. Members of the Finance Committee shall hold office for a term of five years. They shall be eligible for re-election for a further term.

5. In the event of the death, incapacity or resignation of a member of the Finance Committee prior to the expiration of the term of office, the Assembly shall elect for the remainder of the term a member from the same geographical region or group of States.

6. Members of the Finance Committee shall have no financial interest in any activity relating to matters upon which the Committee has the responsibility to make recommendations. They shall not disclose, even after the termination of their functions, any confidential information coming to their knowledge by reason of their duties for the Authority.

7. Decisions by the Assembly and the Council on the following issues shall take into account recommendations of the Finance Committee:

(a) Draft financial rules, regulations and procedures of the organs of the Authority and the financial management and internal financial administration of the Authority;

(b) Assessment of contributions of members to the administrative budget of the Authority in accordance with article 160, paragraph 2(e), of the Convention;

(c) All relevant financial matters, including the proposed annual budget prepared by the Secretary-General of the Authority in accordance with article 172 of the Convention and the financial aspects of the implementation of the programmes of work of the Secretariat;

(d) The administrative budget;

(e) Financial obligations of States Parties arising from the implementation of this Agreement and Part XI as well as the administrative and budgetary implications of proposals and recommendations involving expenditure from the funds of the Authority;

(f) Rules, regulations and procedures on the equitable sharing of financial and other economic benefits derived from activities in the Area and the decisions to be made thereon.

8. Decisions in the Finance Committee on questions of procedure shall be taken by a majority of members present and voting. Decisions on questions of substance shall be taken by consensus.

9. The requirement of article 162, paragraph 2(y), of the Convention to establish a subsidiary organ to deal with financial matters shall be deemed to have been fulfilled by the establishment of the Finance Committee in accordance with this section.

Acronyms

ABM	anti-ballistic missile
BWC	The Convention on the Prohibition of the Development, Production and Stockpiling of Bacteriological (Biological) and Toxin Weapons and on their Destruction
CAT	Convention Against Torture and Other Cruel, Inhuman or Degrading Treatment or Punishment
CEDAW	Convention on the Elimination of all Forms of Discrimination Against Women
CERD	International Convention on the Elimination of All forms of Racial Discrimination
CROC	Convention on the Rights of the Child
CTBT	Comprehensive Nuclear-Test-Ban Treaty
CTC	Counter-Terrorism Committee
CWC	Convention on the Prohibition of the Development, Production, Stockpiling, and Use of Chemical Weapons and on Their Destruction
CROC	Convention on the Rights of the Child
GA	General Assembly
IAEA	International Atomic Energy Agency
ICBL	International Campaign to Ban Landmines
ICC	International Criminal Court
ICCPR	International Covenant on Civil and Political Rights
ICESCR	International Covenant on Economic, Social and Cultural Rights
ICJ	International Court of Justice
ICRC	International Committee of the Red Cross
LMO	living modified organism
LOSC	United Nations Convention on the Law of the Sea
NGO	non-governmental organization
NPT	Treaty on the Non-Proliferation of Nuclear Weapons
NWS	nuclear weapon States
PCIJ	Permanent Court of International Justice
POPs	persistent organic pollutants

PTBT	Treaty Banning Nuclear Weapon Tests in the Atmosphere, in Outer Space and Under Water (Partial Test-Ban Treaty)
UDHR	Universal Declaration of Human Rights
UK	United Kingdom
UN	United Nations
UNCLOS	United Nations Conference on the Law of the Sea
UNFCCC	United Nations Framework Convention on Climate Change
UNMOVIC	United Nations Monitoring, Verification and Inspection Commission
UNSCOM	United Nations Special Commission
US	United States of America
USSR	Union of Soviet Socialist Republics
WHO	World Health Organization
WMD	weapons of mass destruction

Glossary

ab initio: from the beginning. *See* Vienna Convention on the Law of Treaties, art. 79(4).

ad hoc: for a particular purpose or occasion only. *See* Vienna Convention on Diplomatic Relations, art. 27(6); Convention Against Torture and Other Cruel, Inhuman or Degrading Treatment or Punishment, art. 23; International Covenant on Civil and Political Rights, arts. 42(1)(a) and 43; International Convention on the Elimination of All Forms of Racial Discrimination, art. 12(1)(a); Protocol I Additional to the Geneva Conventions, art. 90(3)(a)(ii).

agrément: host state acceptance of the appointment of the head of a diplomatic mission. *See* Vienna Convention on Diplomatic Relations, art. 4.

attaché: a person attached to a foreign legation or embassy. *See* Vienna Convention on Diplomatic Relations, art. 7.

biota: plant and/or animal life of a specific region or period. *See* United Nations Framework Convention on Climate Change, art. 1.

bona fide: genuine; good faith. *See* The Rome Statute of the International Criminal Court, art. 77(2)(b).

cautio judicatum solvi: a plaintiff's security for court costs. *See* Convention Relating to the Status of Refugees, art. 16(2).

de facto: existing in practice whether strictly legal or not. *See* Convention on the Elimination of All Forms of Discrimination Against Women, art. 4(1).

ex aequo et bono: based on what is right and fair rather than on legal rules. *See* Statute of the International Court of Justice, art. 38(2).

force majeure: events entirely outside the party's control; acts of God. *See*

Vienna Convention on Diplomatic Relations, art. 40(4); United Nations Convention on the Law of the Sea, art. 18(2).

in situ: in natural, original position. *See* United Nations Convention on the Law of the Sea, art. 133(a).

inter alia: among other things. *See* Vienna Convention on Diplomatic Relations, arts. 3(1) and 43; Chemical Weapons Convention, arts. 2(8)(a)(2)(ii), 3(1)(d), 8(36), 10(1), 12(2), and 23; Comprehensive Nuclear Test-Ban Treaty, arts. 2(41), 2(43), 4(3), 5(1), 5(2), and (24)(b); Convention on the Prohibition of the Use, Stockpiling, Production and Transfer of Anti-Personnel Mines and on Their Destruction, preamble, arts. 6(3) and 6(7); International Convention for the Suppression of Terrorist Bombings, preamble; The Rome Statute of the International Criminal Court, arts. 7(2)(b), 41(2)(a), 42(7), 64(9), 69(4), 81(3)(c)(i), 93(10)(b)(i), and 97; International Convention for the Suppression of the Financing of Terrorism, art. 18(1); International Covenant on Civil and Political Rights, art. 39(2); International Convention for the Elimination of All Forms of Racial Discrimination, art. 4; Convention on the Elimination of All Forms of Discrimination Against Women, art. 14(2)(d); Convention on the Rights of the Child, arts. 20(3) and 24(2)(c); Protocol I Additional to the Geneva Conventions, arts. 5(1), 5(3), and 43(1); Basel Convention on the Control of Transboundary Movements of Hazardous Wastes and Their Disposal, arts. 10(4), 15(5)(b), 17(1), 18(3), and 26(2); United Nations Framework Convention on Climate Change, arts. 3 and 7(2)(d); Kyoto Protocol to the United Nations Framework Convention on Climate Change, arts. 5(2), 5(3), and 10(b)(i); Convention on Biological Diversity, arts. 2, 6(a), 8(f), 12(b), and 18(2); Stockholm Convention on Persistent Organic Pollutants, arts. 6(2) and 13(7); The Antarctic Treaty, art. 1(1); United Nations Convention on the Law of the Sea, preamble, arts. 62(3), 62(4), 69(2), 70(3), 87(1), 116(b), 144(2)(a), 145, and 310.

ipso facto: by that very fact. *See* Charter of the United Nations, art. 93(1); Statute of the International Court of Justice, art. 36(2); Convention Relating to the Status of Refugees, art. 1(D); Basel Convention on the Control of Transboundary Movements of Hazardous Wastes and Their Disposal, art. 20(3); United Nations Framework Convention on Climate Change, art. 14(2); United Nations Convention on the Law of the Sea, art. 99.

mutatis mutandis: once the necessary changes have been made. *See* Basel Convention on the Control of Transboundary Movements of Hazardous Wastes and Their Disposal, art. 7; Kyoto Protocol to the United Nations Framework Convention on Climate Change, arts. 14(2), 15(1), and 19; Cartagena Protocol on Biosafety to the Convention on Biological Diversity, arts. 28(5), 29(5), and 31(2); United Nations Convention on the Law of the Sea, arts. 54, 80, 110(4), 111(6)(a), and 233.

ne bis in idem: the principle that one should not be tried twice for the same matter. *See* The Rome Statute of the International Criminal Court, art. 20.

nulla poena sine lege: the principle that there should be no punishment without pre-existing law authorizing it. *See* The Rome Statute of the International Criminal Court, art. 23.

nullum crimen sine lege: the principle that there should be no crime without a pre-existing law. *See* The Rome Statute of the International Criminal Court, art. 22.

persona non grata: a person unacceptable to the host country. *See* Vienna Convention on Diplomatic Relations, art. 9(1).

plenipotentiary: a person invested with authority to act for another, especially a diplomat authorized to represent a state. *See* Vienna Convention on Diplomatic Relations, testimonium; Vienna Convention on the Law of Treaties, testimonium; Letter from Mr Webster to Lord Ashburton in the *Caroline* case.

prima facie: at first sight but subject to further information. *See* Cartegena Protocol to the Convention on Biological Diversity, art. 9(2)(b); United Nations Convention on the Law of the Sea, art. 290(1).

procès verbal: authenticated written report of proceedings; the official record of an international conference. *See* Convention on the Prevention and Punishment of the Crime of Genocide, art. 13; Vienna Convention on the Law of Treaties, arts. 79(2)(a) and 79(6).

proprio motu: acting on its own initiative. *See* The Rome Statute of the International Criminal Court, art. 15(1); United Nations Convention on the Law of the Sea, arts. 188(2)(b) and 289.

quorum: minimum number of persons required to be in attendance for a body to conduct valid transactions. *See* Statute of the International Court of Justice, art. 25(3); International Covenant on Civil and Political Rights, art. 30(4); Convention on the Elimination of All Forms of Discrimination Against Women, art. 17(4); Convention on the Rights of the Child, art. 43(5).

ratione personae: by reason of the person. *See* The Rome Statute of the International Criminal Court, art. 24.

ratione temporis: by reason of time. *See* The Rome Statute of the International Criminal Court, art. 11.

signature ad referendum: the signing of a treaty by a representative subject to confirmation by the state. *See* Vienna Convention on the Law of Treaties, arts. 10(b) and 12(2)(b).

Chronology of Treaties, with Status (as of February 2006)

Date Concluded	Treaty	Date of Entry into Force	No. of Parties	US Status	Canada Status	UK Status	Australia Status
26 June 1945	Charter of the United Nations	24 Oct. 1945	191	(s) 26 June 1945 (r) 8 Aug. 1945	(s) 26 June 1945 (r) 9 Nov. 1945	(s) 26 June 1945 (r) 20 Oct. 1945	(s) 26 June 1945 (r) 1 Nov. 1945
9 Dec. 1948	Convention on the Prevention and Punishment of the Crime of Genocide	12 Jan. 1951	138	(s) 11 Dec. 1948 (r) 25 Nov. 1988	(s) 28 Nov. 1949 (r) 3 Sept. 1952	(a) 30 Jan. 1970	(s) 11 Dec. 1948 (r) 8 July 1949
12 Aug. 1949	Geneva Convention Relative to the Treatment of Prisoners of War (Third Geneva Convention)	21 Oct. 1950	192	(s) 12 Aug. 1949 (r) 2 Aug. 1955	(s) 8 Dec. 1949 (r) 14 May 1965	(s) 8 Dec. 1949 (r) 23 Sept. 1957	(s) 4 Jan. 1950 (r) 14 Oct. 1958
12 Aug. 1949	Geneva Convention Relative to the Protection of Civilian Persons in Time of War (Fourth Geneva Convention)	21 Oct. 1950	192	(s) 12 Aug. 1949 (r) 2 Aug. 1955	(s) 8 Dec. 1949 (r) 14 May 1965	(s) 8 Dec. 1949 (r) 23 Sept. 1957	(s) 4 Jan. 1950 (r) 14 Oct. 1958
28 July 1951	Convention Relating to the Status of Refugees	22 Apr. 1954	143	Not party	(a) 4 June 1969	(s) 28 July 1951 (r) 11 Mar. 1954	(a) 22 Jan. 1954
1 Dec. 1959	The Antarctic Treaty	23 June 1961	45	(s) 1 Dec. 1959 (r) 18 Aug. 1960	(a) 4 May 1988	(s) 1 Dec. 1959 (r) 31 May 1960	(s) 1 Dec. 1959 (r) 23 June 1961
18 Apr. 1961	Vienna Convention on Diplomatic Relations	24 Apr. 1964	184	(s) 29 June 1961 (r) 13 Nov. 1972	(s) 5 Feb. 1962 (r) 26 May 1968	(s) 11 Dec. 1961 (r) 1 Sept. 1964	(s) 30 Mar. 1962 (r) 26 Jan. 1968

(continues)

Date Concluded	Treaty	Date of Entry into Force	No. of Parties	US Status	Canada Status	UK Status	Australia Status
21 Dec. 1965	International Convention on the Elimination of All Forms of Racial Discrimination	4 Jan. 1969	170	(s) 28 Sept. 1966 (r) 21 Oct. 1994	(s) 24 Aug. 1966 (r) 14 Oct. 1970	(s) 11 Oct. 1966 (r) 7 Mar. 1969	(s) 13 Oct. 1966 (r) 30 Sept. 1975
16 Dec. 1966	International Covenant on Civil and Political Rights (ICCPR)	23 Mar. 1976 for all except art. 41.; 28 Mar. 1979 for provisions of art. 41	155	(s) 5 Oct. 1977 (r) 8 June 1992	(a) 19 May 1976	(s) 16 Sept. 1968 (r) 20 May 1976	(s) 18 Dec. 1972 (r) 13 Aug. 1980
16 Dec. 1966	International Covenant on Economic, Social and Cultural Rights (ICESC)	3 Jan. 1976	152	(s) 5 Oct. 1977 (r) —	(a) 19 May 1976	(s) 16 Sept. 1968 (r) 20 May 1976	(s) 18 Dec. 1972 (r) 10 Dec. 1975
16 Dec. 1966	(First) Optional Protocol to the International Covenant on Civil and Political Rights	23 Mar. 1976	105	Not party	(a) 19 May 1976	Not party	(a) 25 Sept. 1991
27 Jan. 1967	Treaty on Principles Governing the Activities of States in the Exploration and Use of Outer Space, Including the Moon and Other Celestial Bodies	10 Oct. 1967	98	(s) 27 Jan. 1967 (r) 10 Oct. 1967	(s) 27 Jan. 1967 (r) 10 Oct. 1967	(s) 27 Jan. 1967 (r) 10 Oct. 1967	(s) 27 Jan. 1967 (r) 10 Oct. 1967
31 Jan. 1967	Protocol Relating to the Status of Refugees	4 Oct. 1967	143	(a) 1 Nov. 1968	(a) 4 June 1969	(a) 4 Sept. 1968	(a) 13 Dec. 1973

(continued)

Date Concluded	Treaty	Date of Entry into Force	No. of Parties	US Status	Canada Status	UK Status	Australia Status
1 July 1968	Treaty on the Non-Proliferation of Nuclear Weapons (NPT)	5 Mar. 1970	189	(s) 1 July 1968 (r) 5 Mar. 1970	(s) 23 July 1968 (r) 8 Jan. 1969	(s) 1 July 1968 (r) 27 Nov. 1968	(s) 27 Feb. 1970 (r) 23 Jan. 1973
23 May 1969	Vienna Convention on the Law of Treaties	27 Jan. 1980	105	(s) 24 Apr. 1970 (r) —	(a) 14 Oct. 1970	(s) 20 Apr. 1970 (r) 25 June 1971	(a) 13 June 1974
10 Apr. 1972	Convention on the Prohibition of the Development, Production and Stockpiling of Bacteriological (Biological) and Toxin Weapons and on Their Destruction (BWC)	26 Mar. 1975	152	(s) 10 Apr. 1972 (r) 26 Mar. 1975	(s) 10 Apr. 1972 (r) 18 Sept. 1972	(s) 10 Apr. 1972 (r) 26 Mar. 1975	(s) 10 Apr. 1972 (r) 5 Oct. 1977
26 May 1972	Treaty Between the United States of America and the Union of Soviet Socialist Republics on the Limitation of Anti-Ballistic Missile Systems (ABM)	3 Oct. 1972	2	(s) 26 May 1972 (r) 3 Oct. 1972			
8 June 1977	Protocol Additional to the Geneva Conventions of 12 August 1949 and Relating to the Protection of Victims of International Armed Conflicts	7 Dec. 1978	163	(s) 12 Dec. 1977 (r) —	(s) 12 Dec. 1977 (r) 20 Nov. 1990	(s) 12 Dec. 1977 (r) 28 Jan. 1998	(s) 7 Dec. 1978 (r) 21 June 1991

(continues)

Date Concluded	Treaty	Date of Entry into Force	No. of Parties	US Status	Canada Status	UK Status	Australia Status
8 June 1977	Protocol Additional to the Geneva Conventions of 12 August 1949 and Relating to the Protection of Victims of Non-International Armed Conflicts	7 Dec. 1978	159	(s) 12 Dec. 1977 (r) —	(s) 12 Dec. 1977 (r) 20 Nov. 1990	(s) 12 Dec. 1977 (r) 28 Jan. 1998	(s) 7 Dec. 1978 (r) 21 June 1991
18 Dec. 1979	Convention on the Elimination of All Forms of Discrimination Against Women (CEDAW)	3 Sept. 1981	181	(s) 17 July 1980 (r) —	(s) 17 July 1980 (r) 10 Dec. 1981	(s) 22 July 1981 (r) 7 Apr. 1986	(s) 17 July 1980 (r) 28 July 1983
10 Dec. 1982	United Nations Convention on the Law of the Sea (LOSC)	16 Nov. 1994	149	Not party	(s) 10 Dec. 1982 (r) 7 Nov. 2003	(a) 25 July 1997	(s) 10 Dec. 1982 (r) 5 Oct. 1994
28 July 1984	Agreement Relating to the Implementation of Part XI of the United Nations Convention on the Law of the Sea of 10 December 1982	Provisionally 16 Nov. 1994; definitively 28 July 1996	122	(s) 29 July 1994	(s) 29 July 1994 (r) 7 Nov. 2003	(s) 29 July 1994 (r) 25 July 1997	(s) 29 July 1994 (r) 5 Oct. 1994
10 Dec. 1984	Convention Against Torture and Other Cruel, Inhuman or Degrading Treatment or Punishment (CAT)	26 June 1987	141	(s) 18 Apr. 1988 (r) 21 Oct. 1994	(s) 23 Aug. 1985 (r) 24 June 1987	(s) 15 Mar. 1985 (r) 8 Dec. 1988	(s) 10 Dec. 1985 (r) 8 Aug. 1989

(continues)

Date Concluded	Treaty	Date of Entry into Force	No. of Parties	US Status	Canada Status	UK Status	Australia Status
22 Mar. 1989	Basel Convention on the Control of Transboundary Movements of Hazardous Wastes and Their Disposal	5 May 1992	167	(s) 22 Mar. 1990 (r) —	(s) 22 Mar. 1989 (r) 28 Aug. 1992	(s) 6 Oct. 1989 (r) 7 Feb. 1994	(a) 5 Feb. 1992
20 Nov. 1989	Convention on the Rights of the Child (CROC)	2 Sept. 1990	192	(s) 16 Feb. 1995 (r) —	(s) 28 May 1990 (r) 13 Dec. 1991	(s) 19 Apr. 1990 (r) 16 Dec. 1991	(s) 22 Aug. 1990 (r) 17 Dec. 1990
15 Dec. 1989	Second Optional Protocol to the International Covenant on Civil and Political Rights	11 July 1991	56	Not party	Not party	(s) 31 Mar. 1999 (r) 10 De.c 1999	(a) 2 Oct. 1990
9 May 1992	United Nations Framework Convention on Climate Change (UNFCC)	21 Mar. 1994	189	(s) 12 June 1992 (r) 15 Oct. 1992	(s) 12 June 1992 (r) 4 Dec. 1992	(s) 12 June 1992 (r) 8 Dec. 1993	(s) 4 June 1992 (r) 30 Dec. 1992
5 June 1992	Convention on Biological Diversity (CBD)	29 Dec. 1993	188	(s) 4 June 1993 (r) —	(s) 11 June 1992 (r) 4 Dec. 1992	(s) 12 June 1992 (r) 3 June 1994	(s) 5 June 1992 (r) 18 June 1993
3 Sept. 1992	Convention on the Prohibition of the Development, Production, Stockpiling and Use of Chemical Weapons and on Their Destruction (CWC)	29 Apr. 1997	177	(s) 13 Jan. 1993 (r) 25 Apr. 1997	(s) 13 Jan. 1993 (r) 26 Sept. 1995	(s) 13 Jan. 1993 (r) 13 May 1996	(s) 13 Jan. 1993 (r) 6 May 1994
10 Sept. 1996	Comprehensive Nuclear Test-Ban Treaty (CTBT)	Not yet in force	129	(s) 24 Sept. 1996 (r) —	(s) 24 Sept. 1996 (r) 18 Dec. 1998	(s) 24 Sept. 1996 (r) 6 Apr. 1998	(s) 24 Sept. 1996 (r) 9 July 1998

(continues)

Date Concluded	Treaty	Date of Entry into Force	No. of Parties	US Status	Canada Status	UK Status	Australia Status
18 Sept. 1997	Convention on the Prohibition of the Use, Stockpiling, Production and Transfer of Anti-Personnel Mines and Their Destruction (Ottawa Convention)	1 March 1999	149	Not party	(s) 3 Dec. 1997 (r) 3 Dec. 1997	(s) 3 Dec. 1997 (r) 31 July 1998	(s) 3 Dec. 1997 (r) 14 Jan. 1999
11 Dec. 1997	Kyoto Protocol to the United Nations Framework Convention on Climate Change	16 Feb. 2005	161	(s) 12 Nov. 1998 (r) —	(s) 29 Apr. 1998 (r) 17 Dec. 2002	(s) 29 Apr. 1998 (r) 31 May 2002	(s) 29 Apr. 1998 (r) —
15 Dec. 1997	International Convention for the Suppression of Terrorist Bombings	23 May 2001	145	(s) 12 Dec. 1998 (r) 26 June 2002	(s) 12 Jan. 1998 (r) 3 Apr. 2002	(s) 12 Jan. 1998 (r) 7 Mar. 2001	(a) 9 Aug. 2002
17 July 1998	The Rome Statute of the International Criminal Court	1 July 2002	100	(s) 31 Dec. 2000 (r) —	(s) 18 Dec. 1998 (r) 7 July 2000	(s) 30 Nov. 1998 (r) 4 Oct. 2001	(s) 9 Dec. 1998 (r) 1 July 2002
9 Dec. 1999	International Convention for the Suppression of the Financing of Terrorism	10 Apr. 2002	150	(s) 10 Jan. 2000 (r) 26 June 2002	(s) 10 Feb. 2000 (r) 19 Feb. 2002	(s) 10 Jan. 2000 (r) 7 Mar. 2001	(s) 15 Oct. 2001 (r) 26 Sept. 2002
29 Jan. 2000	Cartagena Protocol on Biosafety to the Convention on Biological Diversity	11 Sept. 2003	132	Not party	(s) 19 Apr. 2001 (r) —	(s) 24 May 2000 (r) 19 Nov. 2003	Not party
22 May 2001	Stockholm Convention on Persistent Organic Pollutants (POPs)	17 May 2004	119	(s) 23 May 2001 (r) —	(s) 23 May 2001 (r) 23 May 2001	(s) 11 Dec. 2001 (r) 17 Jan. 2005	(s) 23 May 2001 (r) 20 May 2004
24 May 2002	Treaty on Strategic Offensive Reductions (SORT)	1 June 2003	2	(s) 24 May 2002 (r) 6 May 2003			

Index

About the Book

Unique in its breadth of coverage, this carefully designed collection presents the key documents of international law at the global level.

The collection encompasses the full spectrum of central issues, with the documents grouped in eight subject areas: foundations, the use of force, arms control, international crime, human rights, humanitarian law, the environment, and the global commons. A short introduction to each document provides context and also points to supplementary documents. With only a few exceptions, each document is presented in its entirety.

Other useful features include a glossary of terms; a chronological list of the treaties in the book, indicating the date the treaty was signed, the date it entered into force, the number of parties to the treaty, and other data; and a complete index.

Shirley V. Scott is associate professor of international relations at the University of New South Wales. She is author of *International Law in World Politics: An Introduction.*